STEP -BY- STEP HOME REPAIR MANUAL

MALLARD PRESS
An imprint of BDD Promotional Book Company, Inc.,
666 Fifth Avenue, New York, N.Y. 10103

Mallard Press and its accompanying design and logo
are trademarks of BDD Promotional Book Company, Inc.

CLB 2654
Copyright © Eaglemoss Publications Ltd 1988, 1989
Published in the United States of America in 1990
by The Mallard Press
Printed and bound in Spain
All rights reserved.
0-792-45440-5

STEP -BY- STEP HOME REPAIR MANUAL

MALLARD
PRESS

CONTENTS

1 POWER TOOLS

2 DECORATING

3 BUILDING

4 CARPENTRY

5 STORAGE

6 PLUMBING

7 ELECTRICS

INTRODUCTION

Each chapter of The Step-by-Step Home Repair Manual includes:
- Guidance in basic skills you'll need to use again and again
- Practical advice on buying materials
- Information about the special tools you're likely to need

The first chapter gives advice on choosing **power tools** and accessories.

Decorating is full of practical guidance on the basics – painting and hanging wallpaper – as well as jobs like fixing tiles and laying floorcoverings. There are lots of tips on how to make light work of preparation, the key to a really good-looking finish.

Building tells you how to look after the structure of your home – from installing insulation and laying floor tiles to repairing damp patches and dealing with rotten woodwork.

Carpentry begins by examining the different types of wood and manmade board which you can buy. It teaches you all the basic skills you need to give you confidence when tackling repair jobs on windows, doors and interior woodwork.

The chapter on **storage** is packed with suggestions on how to exploit wood's versatility as a material for shelves, wardrobes and built-in cabinets.

Plumbing includes everything you need to know to deal with your home's water system, plus ideas on how to repair, modernize and improve your plumbing.

Electrics explains how your home's electrical system works – electricity is not something to tamper with unless you know exactly what you're doing. There are also clear instructions for plenty of jobs which the amateur can tackle safely

1

POWER TOOLS

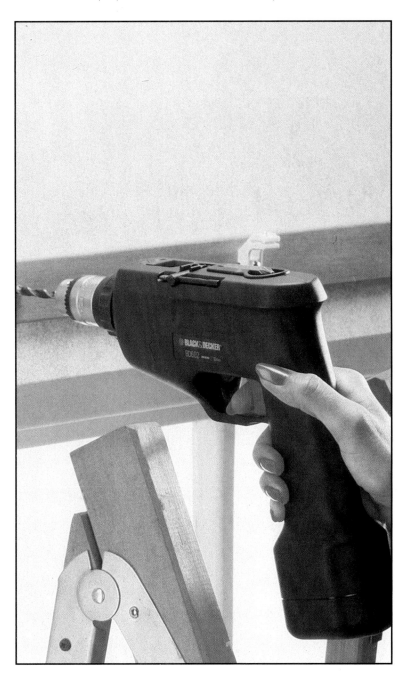

CHOOSING A POWER DRILL

Of all DIY tools, a power drill is probably the most essential – and certainly the most versatile. Modern drills have come a long way from the early low-powered, fixed-speed models, and can be used for all kinds of jobs.

Knowing what you want

Any drill will make small screw holes in wood or brick, but more powerful models are capable of drilling pipe-sized holes through solid masonry, or cutting large holes in metal. To be sure of getting the right drill at the right price, make sure you know:

■ What the manufacturer's technical specifications really mean.
■ Which features you need for the sort of jobs you plan to tackle.

You might also want to consider what accessories are available for your chosen make of drill, and which are likely to prove a good investment. Choosing accessories is covered on pages 13-18.

WHAT THE JARGON MEANS

The manufacturer's specifications commonly include a number of details about a drill's operating performance:

No load speed is the speed at which the drill runs on its own, when not drilling into anything or powering an attachment. It will run slower in use, depending on the job it is doing.

No load impact rate is the speed of the hammer action when a hammer drill runs on its own, without drilling into anything.

Torque is the turning force exerted by the drill. The higher the torque, the tougher the jobs it can tackle, and the less easily it will jam.

Drilling capacity is the maximum diameter of hole which can be drilled. This varies according to the material, but should only matter if you need to drill large holes in masonry or metal.

Power input and output are the amount of power the drill draws in use without overheating, and the amount turned into useful work. Most manufacturers quote the input power of the drill but not the output power, which is usually much less. Generally, output is about 50% of input; more expensive tools tend to have better input/output ratios.

Double insulated means that all electrically live parts are protected; the tool housing itself is an insulating material. Double-prong cords are usually suitable for light-duty tools; grounded triple-prong cords must be used for heavy-duty tools.

ANATOMY OF A DRILL

Before buying a drill, think about what you are going to use it for. The drill shown here has all the features you are ever likely to need for DIY work, but not all of them are essential. If you aren't sure what features you want, cover the points below and you won't go far wrong.

Speed The choices are single, variable, or reversible variable speed. The single-speed drill is useful for basic drilling into materials such as wood and Plexiglass. It can also drill into light metals where there is a starter hole.

A variable-speed drill rotates between 1rpm and its maximum speed. Fixed speeds can be locked in. Variable-speed drills are essential for driving screws.

Power If you want a drill to cover a wide range of jobs, choose the most powerful model available that you can afford.

Capacity A 13mm (½") chuck is more versatile than a 10mm (⅜") one unless you only ever intend to drill small holes.

Maximum hole size depends mainly on what you're drilling. For example, the largest bit that can be used for drilling mild steel is roughly the same size as the chuck jaws; in hard masonry around one and a half times its size; and in soft materials about twice the chuck size. Hole-drilling capacity is also affected by the drill's power output.

Comfort The most powerful, multi-feature drills can be very heavy and are much larger than simple models. If you need to work in tight corners, this can be a handicap.

Handle styles vary. It's best to try out a range of drills in the store to see which sort of grip and balance feels comfortable.

Important features

Some features are important for virtually all DIY jobs including:
- Hammer action, which comes as standard on most 13mm (½") drills. Making holes in concrete is difficult, if not impossible, without it.
- Removable chuck – essential for running many larger accessories (see pages 16-17), which are connected directly to the drill's spindle.
- Low speed setting – essential for running a screwdriving attachment (see page 15); get a reversing model if you want to be able to remove screws too. A low speed setting is also useful for drilling into crumbly materials like plaster, for very hard masonry, and for making large holes in wood.

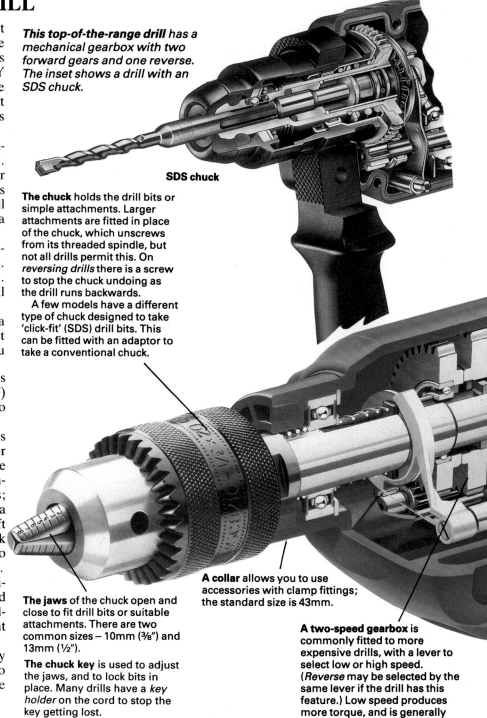

This top-of-the-range drill has a mechanical gearbox with two forward gears and one reverse. The inset shows a drill with an SDS chuck.

SDS chuck

The chuck holds the drill bits or simple attachments. Larger attachments are fitted in place of the chuck, which unscrews from its threaded spindle, but not all drills permit this. On *reversing drills* there is a screw to stop the chuck undoing as the drill runs backwards.

A few models have a different type of chuck designed to take 'click-fit' (SDS) drill bits. This can be fitted with an adaptor to take a conventional chuck.

The jaws of the chuck open and close to fit drill bits or suitable attachments. There are two common sizes – 10mm (⅜") and 13mm (½").

The chuck key is used to adjust the jaws, and to lock bits in place. Many drills have a *key holder* on the cord to stop the key getting lost.

A collar allows you to use accessories with clamp fittings; the standard size is 43mm.

A two-speed gearbox is commonly fitted to more expensive drills, with a lever to select low or high speed. (*Reverse* may be selected by the same lever if the drill has this feature.) Low speed produces more torque, and is generally for materials which are hard to drill.

Trade tip

Better to rent?

❛ It really isn't worth buying a power tool or costly attachment that's only going to be used once or twice. Many shops will rent out all the popular tools (and they're usually heavy-duty models so they'll do the job better too!).

This could even apply to the drill itself; if you only have occasional need for a powerful drill, it may be better to buy a light duty model that's easy to handle, then rent a bigger one when you need it. ❜

Hammer action vibrates the chuck backwards and forwards as well as rotating it – especially useful for smashing particles of masonry, but only when used with special tungsten-carbide tipped bits. Don't use hammer on wood or metal.

There are different systems, including a 'pneumatic' type which cuts down vibration for the user.

Variable torque control is used when screwdriving. If the pre-selected torque is reached, the drill automatically shuts down to prevent overtightening. Anti-jamming devices are similar.

The motor is rated in watts (W). Motor sizes for domestic drills vary from around 350W to 700W. The higher the rating, the more powerful the drill.

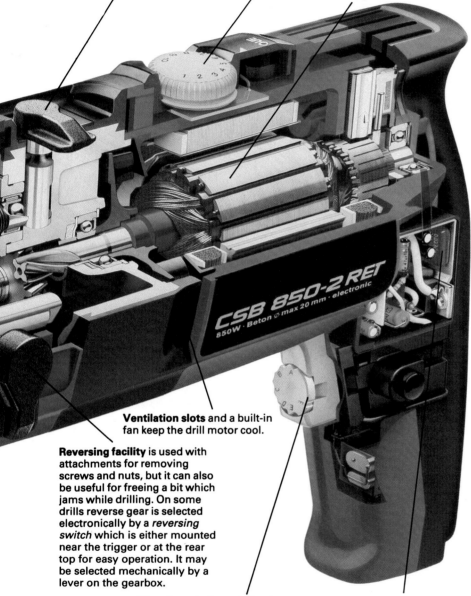

CSB 850-2 RET
850W · Beton ⌀ max 20 mm · electronic

Ventilation slots and a built-in fan keep the drill motor cool.

Reversing facility is used with attachments for removing screws and nuts, but it can also be useful for freeing a bit which jams while drilling. On some drills reverse gear is selected electronically by a *reversing switch* which is either mounted near the trigger or at the rear top for easy operation. It may be selected mechanically by a lever on the gearbox.

The trigger is the on/off switch. On variable speed drills it may be called an *acceleration trigger* because the drill speed is varied according to the amount of pressure applied. This is useful, since it allows you to start drilling slowly then accelerate up to full speed once the drill bit 'bites'.

Some models have an adjustable *speed selector* controlled by a wheel which limits the amount the trigger can be pulled in.

The lock-in switch is pressed in to hold the trigger down – avoiding the need to apply constant finger pressure.

Electronic feedback keeps the drill speed constant, even when the load on it increases.

The alternative to a two-speed gearbox is an **electronic speed selector** which gives you a choice of low or high speeds. It is not as useful, since it produces *less* torque at low speeds rather than more.

CORDLESS DRILLS

Cordless drills are designed for situations where it's difficult or impossible to plug into a wall socket. They don't give the same sort of performance as ordinary models – the maximum speed may be as low as 400rpm, compared with the 2,000–3,000rpm of the conventional type – but they are perfectly adequate for drilling screw holes in wood and masonry, and excellent for low-speed jobs like screwdriving.

For drilling larger holes and working with materials like steel, where greater twisting force (torque) is needed, it's best to have a drill with two gears rather than electronic speed control.

Most cordless drills have a reverse action switch, and the more powerful ones have a hammer action. Because it is relatively easy to overload the motor, a protective cut-out may be fitted. The chuck size is generally not as big as larger conventionally-powered models – 10mm (3/8") is normal.

Power is provided by a rechargeable battery pack which is usually built into the handle. A charger is supplied with the drill to top up the batteries, and some battery packs are removable so that a spare can be used while the first one is being recharged. With other models, the whole drill has to be plugged in to the charger.

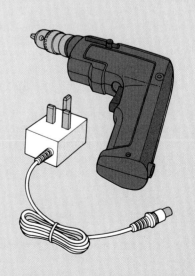

Most cordless drills come with a charger to recharge the built-in batteries.

DRILL SAFETY

General safety: electrical
■ Choose a double-insulated drill with a plastic non-conducting body.
■ Protect the cord from oil, abrasive sharp edges and heat, and keep it out of the way of the bit or attachment in use. Never lift a drill by its cord, and use a special extension cord if it is too short.
■ If possible, keep the drill in a stand or wall bracket rather than letting it lie on the floor or workbench between use.
■ Have the drill serviced regularly.

General safety: physical
Keep small children away whenever you use a drill.
■ Check that the drill is not switched on before plugging it in. It's safest to unplug the drill before changing bits – and always remove the chuck key before plugging it back in.
■ Don't wear loose clothing, and tie back long hair.
■ Wear safety goggles and other protective clothing–especially when drilling masonry or hard materials.

When drilling walls:
■ Locate the position of electric cables and water pipes before you start – they normally run in a straight line, but this isn't always true. The safest way to trace them is with a metal detector.

When working outdoors:
■ Protect the drill and its leads from dampness. A plug-in circuit ground fault receptacle will safeguard against shocks.
■ Wear rubber soled shoes outdoors.

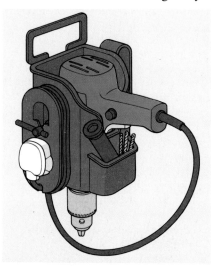

A drill holder keeps a drill ready for instant action, and guards against accidental damage.

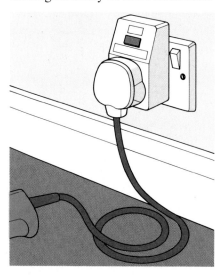

Fit a plug-in ground fault receptacle to guard against shocks if the cord gets damaged.

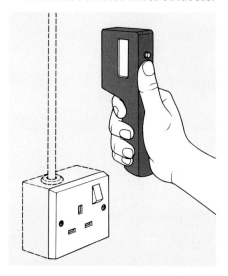

Use a metal detector to check for hidden cables and water pipes before drilling a wall.

■ PROBLEM SOLVER ■

Avoiding breakdowns
The main cause of breakdowns is that the drill has been overstressed by using it on tougher materials than it was designed for. A light-duty DIY hammer drill, for instance, is fine for drilling screw holes in brick or masonry; but if you try to drill a large, deep hole in concrete with it, you could well burn out the motor.

If you think there is a risk of overheating the motor, stop at intervals to let the drill cool off. If you let it run for a short while with no load, the fan will help it to cool – but only if the ventilation slots on the drill's outer casing are free from oil and grime.

Use a slim screwdriver to clean out any accumulated bits that have blocked the ventilation slots – don't let any fall into the casing or it may damage the motor. Don't forget to unplug first.

Stop frequently when drilling tough materials, to give the drill a chance to cool down.

Clean out the ventilation slots at regular intervals to prevent the drill from overheating.

Servicing and repairs
Although spares for common models are sometimes available, it's inadvisable to repair a drill yourself unless you know what you are doing; you could make the drill dangerous, as well as invalidating any service warranty which may be in force.
Instead get the drill serviced by the manufacturer's agents. Most popular makes have regional service centers listed in their instruction leaflets. Otherwise take the drill to a store which stocks that make.

Ask for an estimate before committing yourself; a faulty trigger action (a common reason for failure) is quite cheap to repair. If the motor has burnt out on an expensive drill, it is probably worth having it replaced, but on a simple drill the cost of replacement may not be much less than the price of a brand new one.

CHOOSING DRILL ACCESSORIES

Accessories extend the scope of the average power drill way beyond drilling, transforming it into an all-purpose tool with countless uses around the home.

The range, which is enormous, broadly divides into three groups:
Drill stands and guides make drilling easier or more accurate. They may be custom-built to suit a particular make, but many fit any drill.
Chuck-mounted accessories use the motor as a power source for jobs other than drilling. They have a spindle small enough to use with both 10mm (⅜″) and 13mm (½″) chucks, and fit most drills.
Drill-powered attachments convert the drill into some other type of power tool, which usually entails removing the chuck. They tend to be custom-made for a particular model.

Below and overleaf is a group-by-group accessory guide and the chart on page 18 summarizes their uses and points out any special details.

STANDS AND GUIDES

Controlling a power drill with complete precision takes more practice than many people imagine. Drill stands and guides are designed to hold or align the drill so that accurate work is virtually guaranteed.

Horizontal drill stands (also called *bench stands*) hold the drill on a workbench so that your hands are left free to work. Their main use is with wire brushes, polishing mops or grinding wheels. Some types clamp on the edge of a workbench and swivel through 90° for extra versatility.

Vertical drill stands, sometimes called *drill presses*, are useful if you do a lot of very accurate drilling (for instance in furniture making when drilling dowel joints). The drill is clamped in a sliding cage which moves up and down the stand when a hand lever is pulled; there should also be a depth stop allowing holes of the same depth to be drilled repeatedly. they may be custom-made or universal to fit any drill with a standard collar.

Drilling guides ensure that holes are drilled squarely or to a set depth. Many drills have a depth stop built in (usually as part of the side handle), but a drilling guide helps to keep the drill square on to the work face.

Guides are particularly useful for making holes in boards that are too big to fit under a vertical stand, and for drilling accurate holes into walls.

Clip-on spirit levels fit to any drill with a standard collar and help to ensure that the drill is lined up accurately when drilling vertically or horizontally.

A vertical drill stand makes drilling more accurate.

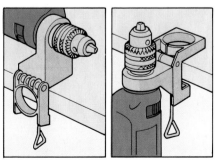

Some horizontal stands can be swivelled through 90°.

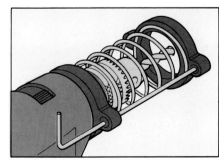

Drill guides keep the drill straight and level.

CHUCK-MOUNTED ACCESSORIES

Smaller drill accessories which fit in the chuck jaws are often excellent value, and make light work of laborious jobs such as sanding, rust-cleaning and polishing.

Accessories normally have a drive spindle small enough to fit both 10mm (3/8″) and 13mm (1/2″) chucks. If you need the larger chuck size for large drills and your existing chuck is removable, you should be able to buy a 13mm replacement.

Standard accessories can't be used with a click-fit SDS chuck, but a converter chuck is available for drills with this feature.

Trade tip

Neat 'n tidy

❛ Keep your drill, drill bits and other accessories neatly together in a **drill holder** (see right). Made of impact-resistant plastic, most types have a built-in carrying handle, and some can be hung on the wall when not in use. ❜

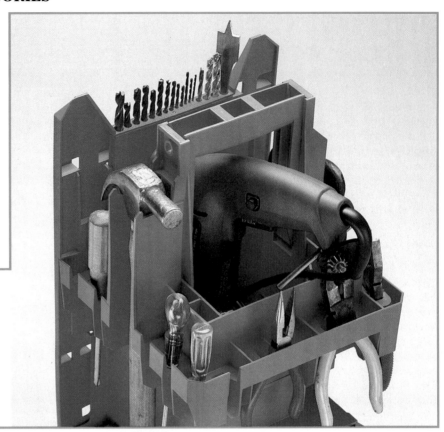

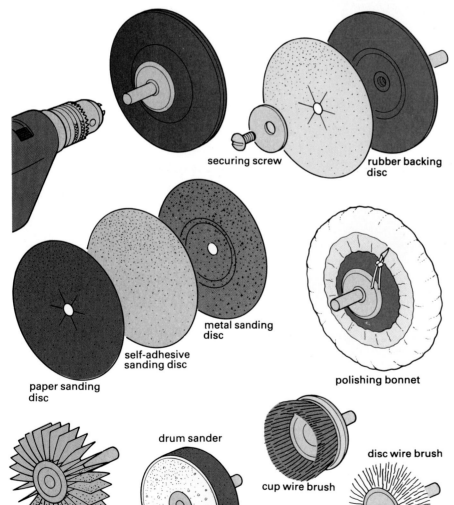

securing screw

rubber backing disc

metal sanding disc

self-adhesive sanding disc

paper sanding disc

polishing bonnet

flapwheel

drum sander

cup wire brush

disc wire brush

A rubber backing pad is used as the base for a number of useful accessories, the most common of which are paper or metal *sanding discs*. Some designs hold the discs with a central screw; others are for use with self-adhesive discs. Sanding discs are good for rough work, but tend to gouge the surface. A more sophisticated version that cuts down on gouging has the backing pad fitted with a universal joint. This allows the disc to remain flat on the work even if the drill is tilted.

Polishing bonnets slip over the backing pad.

Flapwheels are made from strips of abrasive paper (in a choice of grades) mounted on a shaft. They are very good at stripping paint and rust and won't clog in use.

Drum sanders aren't as fierce as disc sanders but are still quite coarse in action. They work best on flat or gently curved surfaces.

Wire brushes come in a variety of shapes and sizes to cover virtually any job. The two main types are *discs*, which brush at right angles to the drill shaft, and *cups*, which brush in line with it. Some discs have their own shank for fitting into the drill chuck; others must be mounted on an *arbor*.

Grinding wheels and stones can be used for sharpening tools or finishing metal. **Rotary rasps** are used for wood shaping.

A drill arbor is a multi-purpose shaft on which you can mount other accessories such as *grinding wheels, disc wire brushes* and *polishing mops*. These accessories are often used in conjunction with a *horizontal drill stand*.

Special cutters include: *Hole saws* for cutting large holes. Different types are used for wood or metal. *Tank cutters* are made for cutting metal only. Both these accessories need a drill with a low-speed setting. *Cone cutters* are used in thin wood or metal. The tapered cutting edge opens out a drilled hole to the size you want.

Screwdriver bits have hexagonal heads which fit in the chuck (the drill must have a low speed setting). They make fast work of jobs using a lot of screws, and with a reverse-action drill they allow you to remove screws too. Sets of bits containing a selection of different screw patterns are available.

You can also get a *magnetic bit adaptor* which fits between the chuck and the screwdriver bit to make changing bits easier.

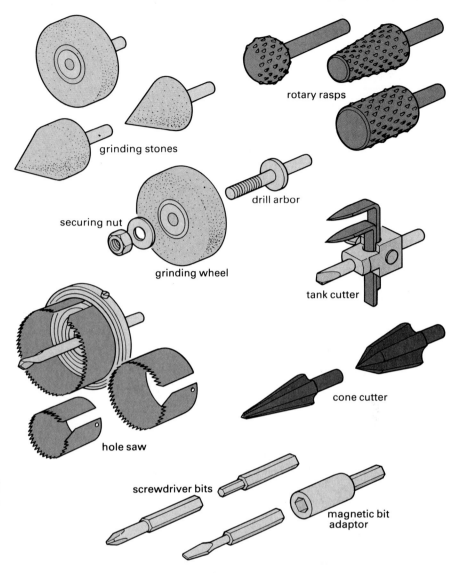

rotary rasps

grinding stones

securing nut

drill arbor

grinding wheel

tank cutter

cone cutter

hole saw

screwdriver bits

magnetic bit adaptor

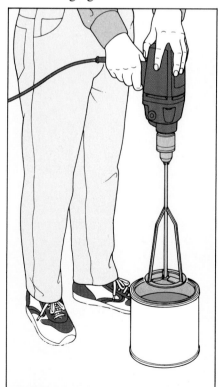

Mix paint or plaster with a powered stirrer.

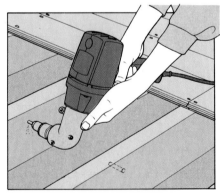

Drill holes at right-angles to the drill with an angle drive.

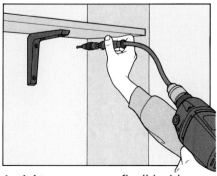

In tight spaces use a flexible drive shaft – but only for light drilling.

Paint stirrers/mixers provide a fast method of thoroughly mixing paint (more robust versions will mix plaster or textured finish paints). However, they aren't always easy to find.

Angle drives make it possible to drill holes at right angles to the drill – useful where room is tight. However, this accessory is expensive unless you anticipate doing a lot of work with it.

Flexible drive shafts allow you to extend the reach of a drill into even tighter spaces: one end fits into the drill chuck, while the other has a miniature chuck.

Flexible drives aren't designed for heavy drilling, but are good for powering small accessories such as polishers. When buying, check the maximum safe speed of the shaft – it may be less than the drill's.

DRILL-POWERED ATTACHMENTS

Think carefully before investing in one of the larger drill attachments. If you don't use power tools very often, they may be a good buy.

However, some attachments – notably power saws and orbital sanders – can, if abused, strain the drill beyond its design limits and shorten the life of the motor. Also, because they are designed as attachments, they are limited by the speed of the drill. This means they may not perform so well as the equivalent self-powered tool which runs at a higher speed.

 Safety wear

Safety equipment must be worn when drilling, grinding or sanding.

■ To protect your eyes wear *safety goggles*.

■ A *dust mask* with replaceable cotton or foam *filters* protects against dust and/ or grit.

 ■ Heavy-duty *leather gloves* must be worn with accessories like saws or grinders.

 ■ Grinding metal produces a lot of sparks, so use a *full-face mask*.

 ■ Wear *ear protectors* when working with noisy tools.

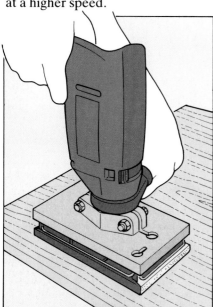

An orbital sander gives a fine finish on large flat areas.

Use a saber saw for freehand sawing and around curves.

A circular saw makes cutting lengths of wood easy.

Saber saws are driven from the drill by an adaptor fitted in place of the chuck. They are custom-made to fit particular models of drill.

Circular saws, like saber saws, have a drive adaptor and are custom-made. Take great care when using one – wear protective gloves.

Orbital sanders have an operating speed much lower than the 10,000rpm of a self-powered sander, so they cannot be considered as effective.

Bench sander/grinders may be chuck- or adaptor-driven and clamp on to the side of the workbench. The sander is used for wood (see below), the grinder for metal. Wear eye protection when using one.

Milling machine/shapers are driven from the chuck. There is wide range of cutting bits available for making slots and grooves or matching up the profile of moldings.

Dovetailers are driven from the chuck and make cutting dovetail joints very easy. The main frame clamps to the wood and the drill-mounted cutter slots into it.

Drill sharpeners are powered from the chuck. They are worth buying if you do a lot of drilling or use expensive, large diameter bits. You can also get chisel/plane sharpeners.

Drill-powered pumps are useful for emptying tanks or fishponds or for mopping up after an accidental flood.

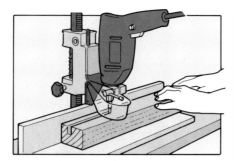

Cutting slots in wood with a milling machine.

A dovetailer helps to make drawer construction easy.

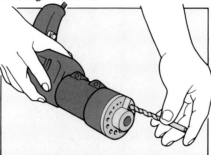

Drill sharpeners will even deal with masonry bits.

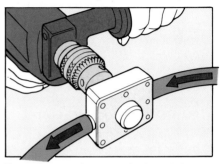

Pumping out large tanks is quick and easy with a drill pump.

Lathes are used to turn wood (right). Some are driven straight from the chuck while on other designs, the chuck is replaced by a drive adaptor.

Although lathe attachments are less efficient than proper self-powered lathes, they are much cheaper.

FITTING ATTACHMENTS

Before fitting any attachment, check the hammer action is off and unplug the drill.
Chuck-mounted accessories Fit the spindle into the chuck jaws and lock with the chuck key. Check that the accessory runs true by hand-rotating the chuck.
Larger attachments Remove the chuck first, supporting the drill carefully. On non-reversing drills the chuck simply unscrews after jarring it with the key as shown; reversing drills have an extra locking screw which **must** be removed first.

Afterwards, fit the spindle adaptor and clamp the tool in place on the collar by tightening the clamping screws – this may require an Allen key.

On an ordinary drill, lock the spindle with an open-ended spanner, then fit the chuck key and tap it sharply in an anticlockwise direction . . .

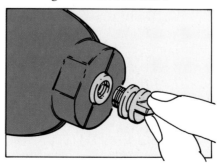

. . . then unscrew the chuck and replace it with the spindle adaptor nut. Slide the attachment on to the collar and tighten the clamping screws.

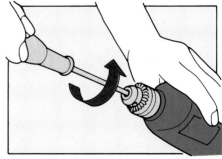

On reversing drills, the chuck is locked by an extra screw. Open the chuck jaws fully to get at it, then remove the chuck in the normal way.

WHAT TO USE A DRILL FOR

JOB	DRILL	BIT TYPE OR ATTACHMENT	DRILL SPEED	HAMMER ACTION	NOTES
DRILLING Small holes in wood (up to 10mm – ⅜″)	Any drill	Twist drill or wood bit	1,800-2,000rpm	Off	
Large holes in wood (over 10mm – ⅜″)	Any drill	Flat bit; hole saw for boards	600-1,500rpm	Off	
Small holes in metal (up to 10mm – ⅜″)	Any drill	High-speed steel (HSS) twist drill	900-1,500rpm	Off	Lubricate with light oil to keep the drill bit cool
Large holes in metal (over 10mm – ⅜″)	Any drill	High-speed steel (HSS) twist drill; hole saw	900-1,000rpm	Off	Lubricate with light oil to keep the drill or hole saw cool
Small holes in plaster or masonry (eg anchors)	Any drill with hammer action	Masonry drill	1,800rpm	On	
Medium holes in plaster and masonry (eg water pipes)	For soft materials, see above; for tough materials, see below	Masonry drill	1,400rpm	On	
Small/medium holes in concrete	Powerful drill with 13mm (½″) chuck and hammer action	Masonry drill	900-1,200rpm	On	
	Electro-pneumatic drill	Masonry drill	900-1,200rpm	On	Best to rent
Large holes in masonry (eg drainpipes)	Heavy duty rotary percussion drill	Masonry drill or core drill	900-1,200rpm	On	Best to rent
Driving screws	Drill with low-speed, acceleration trigger and reversing action	Screwdriving bits or attachment	Lowest speed on drill	Off	A magnetic bit holder is very useful
DECORATING Sanding small areas	Any drill	Sanding discs; flapwheels	Top speed on drill	Off	Sanding discs may gouge the surface
Sanding large areas	Most drills with removable chuck	Orbital sanding attachment	Top speed on drill	Off	Less efficient than an integral machine.
Stripping paint	Any drill	Sanding discs; flapwheels; wire brushes	Top speed on drill	Off	Care needed to avoid damaging the workpiece
Stirring paint	Any drill	Paint stirrer attachment	Top speed on drill	Off	Insert into paint before switching on
De-rusting metal	Any drill	Flapwheels; Wire brushes; sanding discs	Top speed on drill	Off	Wear goggles and dust mask
Grinding metal	Any drill	Grinding wheel	Top speed on drill	Off	Use with care – wear safety equipment
Polishing	Any drill	Polishing bonnet; polishing mop; polishing sponge	Low speed	Off	Avoid hard polishing – it's very easy to go right through the surface finish
WOODWORKING Sawing wood freehand	Drill must be compatible with attachment	Saber saw attachment	Top speed on drill	Off	Less efficient than an integral tool
Sawing wood	Drill must be compatible with attachment	Circular saw attachment	Top speed on drill	Off	Less efficient than an integral tool

Other custom-made woodworking attachments are relatively expensive and in most cases are specially made to fit particular makes of drill. Instructions will vary from make to make.

WORKING WITH POWER TOOLS

An electric drill is an essential part of any DIY toolkit; it provides a versatile power source which can be fitted with a wide range of attachments. But this shouldn't rule out using integral power tools for more specialized tasks. Being designed for the job, they tend to be more powerful, more efficient and easier to handle than their drill attachment equivalents.

The main question to answer before buying an integral power tool is whether you can justify the cost (see panel below). If you are only likely to use it a couple of times a year, you may be better off buying an attachment – and then spending a bit more on a really good quality drill with a powerful motor.

Alternatively, most integral tools can be rented as and when they are needed. This has an advantage in that rented tools are invariably heavy duty models, so there should be no risk of overloading them on domestic jobs – unlike attachments.

ARE THEY WORTH BUYING?

Specialized integral tools make light work of many jobs, but before buying you need to weigh up whether the use they will get justifies their cost.

POWER SANDERS
Orbital sander – a good buy if you do a lot of woodworking or decorating. An attachment is adequate for light work, otherwise rent when needed.
Belt sander – only worth buying if you are an enthusiastic woodworker and will use it a lot, otherwise rent. There is no attachment that does exactly this job.
Power file – a fairly useful tool to have, but few will use it a lot. Not available for rent or as an attachment.

POWER SAWS
Saber saw – worth buying if you expect to do a lot of woodwork, otherwise rent when you need it. Attachments can be used for light duties.
Jigsaw – worth buying if you cut up a lot of logs or heavy lumber otherwise don't bother. Can be hired; there are no similar attachments.
Circular saw – worth buying if you expect to cut up a lot of heavy sheet material, otherwise rent when you need it. Attachments are often rather underpowered.

GENERAL PURPOSE TOOLS
Heat gun stripper – a versatile tool and worth buying. No equivalent attachment.
Glue gun – not essential, but can be useful if you do a lot of repetitive gluing of almost any material. No equivalent attachment.
Electric screwdriver – not really worth the expense unless you do a lot of repetitive screwdriving. A low-speed reversing drill can be used instead.
Angle grinder – won't be needed often, so better to rent than buy.

WOODWORKING TOOLS
Power plane – only real enthusiasts will need one often, so better to rent. No equivalent attachment.
Router – for enthusiasts only. There is no identical attachment but there are plenty of gadgets which you can use to carry out some of its functions.

SANDERS AND SAWS

POWER SANDERS

Orbital sanders

These work best on large flat areas and are better for finishing than for coarse work. They get their name because the abrasive paper is attached to a rubber sole plate which moves with an orbital motion.

Most accept a third of a standard abrasive sheet, although some take half sheets, which means a larger area is sanded in a given time. Check how the paper is changed; it's easier on some machines than others.

The more powerful the motor, the harder you will be able to use the tool. The orbiting speed of the sole plate is also important – faster speeds give a better finish. Most operate at 10,000 orbits per minute, although some are as low as 4,000 or as high as 25,000. Variable speed models are also available; slower speeds can be used with coarse abrasive for initial rough work, followed by faster sanding with finer abrasives.

Sanding produces a lot of fine dust, often simply blown out of an extraction opening. Better models have a dust bag, or connections for a vacuum cleaner.

When using an orbital sander, don't press down too hard – let the weight of the tool do the work, or you may find you interfere with the orbital motion.

Disc sanders

These resemble sanding disc attachments, but rotate with an eccentric motion to avoid scouring a single spot. They can also be used for polishing.

Like orbital sanders, disc sanders produce a lot of fine dust. Dust bags are a common feature, and you may come across special discs with holes that allow the dust to be extracted through them. Disc sanders can also be used for polishing.

Belt sanders

Orbital and disc sanders are far from ideal for jobs like varnishing as they

circular saws

belt sander

orbital sanders

belt sander

disc sander

leave fine scratches which show through the finish. The alternative is to use a belt sander, following the grain of the wood.

Belt sanders have two rollers over which a special 'endless' belt of abrasive paper is fitted. One roller, usually the back, is driven by the motor, while the other is used to tension the belt. A flat rubber or steel plate then presses the belt flat against the piece being worked on.

Again, belt speed is important: the higher the speed, the better the finish. Likewise, the more powerful the motor, the more punishment it will take.

Like orbital sanders, belt sanders are really only suitable for flat surfaces. On the plus side they give a better finish, and remove waste material much more efficiently.

Against this, they are more difficult to use and generally more expensive. Running out of belts can also be a problem, so always have replacements handy.

Power files

A power file is like a narrow belt sander – 6 or 13mm (¼ or ½″) wide – for filing and shaping wood and other materials. The belt is carried on an arm in front of the tool, allowing you to work in confined spaces.

A variable control adjusts the belt speed to suit the job and material. As with a belt sander, you need to keep a supply of sanding belts handy; different types are needed for different materials.

Accessories may include a cranked arm for work on curved surfaces. Dust bags are common.

Sander safety

■ Always switch off at the socket or pull plug out when fitting a new abrasive sheet.
■ Switch on before bringing the abrasive into contact with the workpiece.
■ Unplug when not in use.

POWER SAWS

saber saws

power file

Sanders and saws are more powerful than the equivalent drill attachments and easier to handle. A saber saw and an orbital or disc sander are probly the most versatile for general DIY.

Saber saws

The saber saw is also called either a portable jigsaw or a bayonet saw. It can be thought of as a kind of powered hacksaw. Although it can be used for making straight cuts in wood up to 50 mm (2″) thick, its main purpose is for making curved and short straight cuts in wood, metal and plastic laminates.

It has a slim, narrow, replaceable blade at the front of the tool that is several inches long and which plunges in a reciprocating movement – that is to say, it moves in a continuous up and down motion.

You can buy saber saws in one-, two- or variable-speed versions. Speeds (the number of strokes of the blade per minute) range from 1000 to 3500 spm. The highest spm is best for cutting wood and single-speed models are usually of the 3500 spm variety. Slower speeds are better for cutting plastics and metals.

Variable-speed models allow you to tailor the speed of cutting to suit the job, and to start slowly for greater accuracy. A single-speed (ie high-speed) model will work well if you don't apply as much pressure to the tool. If you tend to work with wood rather than a variety of materials, a single-speed should be all you need.

Useful features on some models include electronic feedback to maintain the cutting speed if the resistance of the piece being worked varies; and a blower to keep sawdust away from your cutting line. A number of models come with swivel bases – this allows you to cut an angle. You can also get accessories to expand the functions of the saw.

Many saber saws also come with a side fence for making long, straight cuts, but this may not be strong enough to hold the blade steady. A better method is to clamp a straight length of wood to the piece being worked on so the edge of the tool's sole-plate can be held against it.

Blades vary according to the material being cut. For the finest cuts you want a blade with the greatest number of teeth to the inch. Thin blades are for fine scroll work; for heavy work the blades will be thick.

The jigsaw is also available again, although not widely. It is useful for cutting especially intricate patterns.

Circular saws

Intended for long, straight cuts in wood, man-made boards, plastic laminates, thin metals, bricks, building blocks and ceramic tiles, the circular saw is a versatile tool, but needs handling with care.

Blades and cutting discs for different materials are made in 125, 150 and 184mm (5, 6 and 7½″) diameters. The larger the blade, the thicker the material that can be cut, and tools made to take large blades have more powerful motors than the smaller versions. (You can of course increase the cutting depths by sawing from both sides.) Blades must be fitted the correct way round, the direction is marked on them.

The blade should have a 360° guard, with a spring loaded lower half that swings out of the way as you begin a cut. Most types have a lever for retracting the guard if you want to begin a cut in the middle of the piece being worked.

A side fence is normally part of a circular saw's standard equipment, but may not be strong or long enough. Overcome this either by fixing a strip of wood to the fence with woodscrews, or by clamping a piece of wood to the workpiece so that the sole plate can be held against it.

⚠ **Power saw safety**

■ Never wear loose-fitting clothing.
■ Always unplug the tool to change saw blades.
■ Keep hands clear of the blade at all times.
■ Release the trigger lock after each cut and switch off at the plug (or unplug) if not making another immediately.
■ Keep cord away from the blade.
■ Keep away from children.
■ Never use outdoors in dampness.

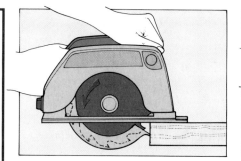

To use a circular saw safely, adjust the depth of cut so that the blade will just cut through the workpiece. Rest the soleplate on the edge of the work.

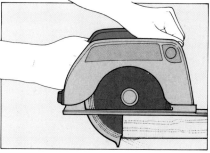

Switch on and allow to reach full speed before you move forward and begin cutting; the guard will be pushed clear. Don't force the saw forward – let it cut its own way.

GENERAL PURPOSE TOOLS

HEAT GUN STRIPPER

The main use of heat guns is for stripping paint and varnish, where they are far less likely to char the wood than a blowtorch. However, they have many other uses too, including thawing frozen pipes, drying glue or damp surfaces, warming plastic pipes to allow them to be bent, and soft soldering.

Basically the gun is like a powerful hair dryer, with heating elements and a fan. Most offer two fixed temperature settings, although it is possible to buy models that provide for variable temperature settings, giving a wide range of heat within a fixed 'high' and 'low'.

Accessories include a range of nozzles that direct the blast of hot air away from anything which might be damaged by the extreme heat. One is fan shaped, for stripping thin moldings and window frames. Another is designed for pipe soldering and heats around the joint.

⚠ Heat gun safety
- Never place your hand in front of the nozzle in use.
- Unplug when not in use.
- Allow the gun to cool before putting away.
- Keep away from children.

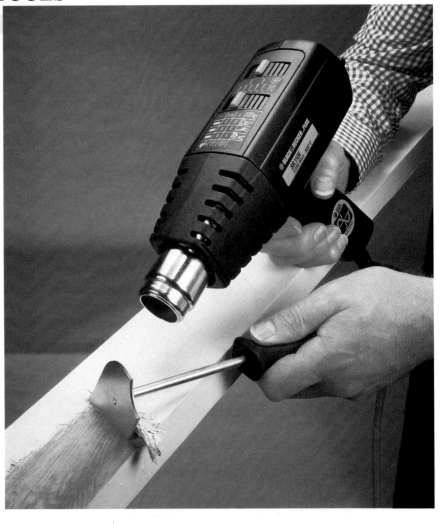

Hot air guns are versatile tools with a wide range of DIY uses, from stripping paint to soldering pipe joints. They come with several different nozzles, allowing them to be adapted to suit the job in hand.

Glue guns come with a range of glue sticks to suit different materials. These are fed in from the back, then melted and forced out of the nozzle as a rapidly drying glue.

⚠ Glue gun safety
- Rest the gun on scrap wood, cardboard or metal when heating up or when not in use.
- Never touch the hot glue.
- Unplug when finished and allow to cool before putting away.
- Keep away from children.

GLUE GUNS

Although sometimes considered a gimmick, a glue gun provides a convenient and effective method of sticking a wide range of materials, including wood, metal and plastic. Shaped like a pistol, the gun contains heating elements that melt a special glue stick fed in from the rear. With some guns, the glue stick is simply pushed in with your thumb, while the more sophisticated versions have a trigger control. The fine nozzle at the front allows the melted glue to be applied just where you want it, even in tight corners.

A major advantage of glue guns is that the glue sets very quickly: parts need only be held together for a short time, and hand pressure is usually enough to ensure a good bond. Some guns also offer a wall-plugging facility, using a special glue, so that holes of any size in brick or concrete can be plugged to accept screws – an ideal solution on old bricks.

ELECTRIC SCREWDRIVER

Cordless rechargeable screwdrivers are designed to save effort on repetitive screwing jobs, though it's questionable whether they are any more effective than conventional spiral ratchet screwdrivers (which cost far less), and they may be too bulky for use in tight corners.

Another drawback is that most models only come with a single screwdriver bit. Although this is double ended to take slotted or cross-head screws, it restricts the tool's uses by limiting you to screws of a certain size.

Most cordless screwdrivers come with a wall mounting bracket and trickle charger so that they are always ready for use. All feature forward and reverse action, allowing screws to be driven in and removed, and most have a spindle lock that allows final tightening by hand. Some models also have variable torque settings to adjust the turning force applied to the screw.

Electric screwdrivers have rechargeable batteries for cordless operation, but may be bulkier and more awkward than a conventional screwdriver.

Angle grinders are powerful, versatile grinding and cutting tools. DIY models are costly and less powerful than industrial versions so you may be better off renting one when you need it.

△ **Angle grinder safety**
Angle grinders are among the most dangerous of all tools.
■ Never wear loose-fitting clothes.
■ Wear a full-face mask, heavy leather gloves and boots.
■ Always start the grinder and allow it to reach full speed before touching it to the work.
■ Always unplug to change discs.
■ Switch off after use, and unplug if not using again immediately.
■ Do not use outside in wet conditions.
■ Keep cord away from disc.
■ Keep away from children.

ANGLE GRINDERS

Angle grinders can be used to cut and grind all types of metal, to remove rust, and – when fitted with the correct type of disc – for cutting brick, stone and concrete. DIY angle grinders come with two basic sizes of grinding or cutting disc: 112mm (4″) and 225mm (9″). The larger size is better for heavy work.

Because of the work they do, the motor should be powerful; on a small machine it is commonly 600W, while on a larger one it may be as much as 1800W. Other points to look for are the ease with which the discs can be changed – some have a spindle lock to prevent the tool rotating while you do this – and whether the side handle position is adjustable. All types should have a guard around the disc which is spring loaded to prevent it contacting the disc.

In addition to being supplied with a cutting disc, the machine should have a rubber backing pad for sanding discs – much like that used with an electric drill. Usually, you have to remove the disc guard to use this.

When grinding, hold the machine with the disc at an angle of about 30° to the work for roughing, or 15° for finishing. Cuts can be made with the disc edge-on to the piece.

WOODWORKING TOOLS

POWER PLANES

A power plane takes the effort out of smoothing rough-sawn wood and sizing wood accurately. It has a rotating cutter which may turn at speeds of anywhere between 14,500 and 19,000 rpm.

The faster the speed, the smoother the finish is likely to be. The power of the motor is also important, since this affects the maximum depth of cut – which can range up to 3.5mm (⅛").

Better power planes also provide chamfering and rabbeting facilities. The maximum depth of these is important; some may offer a rabbet depth of as much as 22 mm (⅞").

When buying, check if spare blades are provided and see whether they can be changed easily. Check, too, how easy it is to adjust the depth of cut, and if the machine has a side fence as standard or as an optional extra.

Ideally, a power plane should

Power planes are capable of high speed finishing and rabbeting.

have two handles so that you can guide it easily, plus a guard to protect the cutters when it is not in use. Some models are provided with a shavings collection bag – useful, as all types produce plenty of waste.

⚠ Planer safety
- Never wear loose-fitting clothing.
- Unplug when removing blades.
- Release the trigger lock at the end of each cut, and switch off at the socket unless making another immediately.
- Retract blade when not in use.
- Keep away from children.

ROUTERS

Routers are simple tools, but have a wide range of uses in specialist woodworking, including cutting decorative chamfers and moldings, and making rabbets, grooves or traditional joints such as dovetails or box joints.

A router is basically an electric motor that slides up and down in guides attached to a baseplate. A specially shaped revolving cutter fitted to the motor spindle then carves out the desired shape as the machine is slid across the wood.

When buying, look for a high power motor and high spindle rpm, since the two combined will prevent the cutter from juddering and produce a cleaner cut. The machine should also be sturdily constructed, with a finely calibrated depth stop so that you can adjust the depth of cut accurately. And check how easily the cutters are changed – on some models it is quite tricky.

To use, begin by setting the depth of cut, then rest the soleplate on the piece being worked and switch on the motor. Press down until the cutter bites into the wood by the desired amount, and slide the machine along the cutting line. Then, when you reach the end of the cut, allow the motor to rise on its springs so that it clears the wood before switching off.

⚠ Router safety
- Never wear loose fitting clothes.
- Always unplug when changing cutters.
- Switch off at the end of each cut, and switch off at the plug if not making another immediately.
- Keep hands clear of the cutter.
- Keep cord away from disc.
- Keep away from children.

Routers can be fitted with a wide range of cutters for creating grooves, rabbets and moldings.

2

DECORATING

TOOLS FOR PREPARATION

Preparing surfaces for decorating is a lot easier if you use the right tools, but there's no sense in buying more than you need.

A basic kit might consist of a stripping knife, filling knife, heat gun stripper, pointing trowel, combination shavehook, sanding block and wire brush. But if your house contains a lot of moldings, you'd be wise to add more scrapers. It's also worth 'doubling up' on some tools if two of you are working at the same time.

As a general rule, buy the best tools you can afford. Providing you look after them (ie clean them after every session), they work out cheaper than 'bargains' which don't last. Quality tools perform better too.

Heat gun strippers (right) make light work of paint stripping.

TOOLS FOR SCRAPING

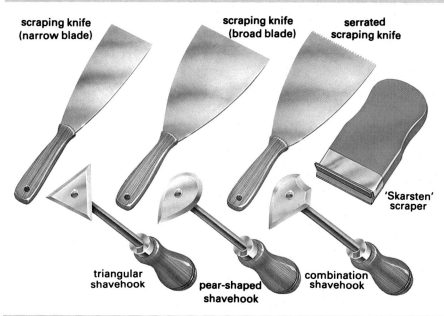

scraping knife (narrow blade)

scraping knife (broad blade)

serrated scraping knife

'Skarsten' scraper

triangular shavehook

pear-shaped shavehook

combination shavehook

Scraping knives are for scraping off wallpaper and large areas of paint. They resemble filling knives, but their broad steel blades are hardened so that they don't flex out of shape.
Serrated scraping knives have a toothed edge for piercing the surface of coated washable papers.
Shavehooks are for scraping paint or other finishes from frames, mouldings and similar awkward areas. Three head patterns are commonly available – *triangular*, *pear-shaped* and *combination*. A combination head is most useful, so long as you have a stripping knife for flat surfaces.
Hook ('Skarsten') scrapers are particularly good for removing thin surface coatings such as flaking varnish; the guarded blade reduces the risk of gouging the underlying surface.

TOOLS FOR FILLING

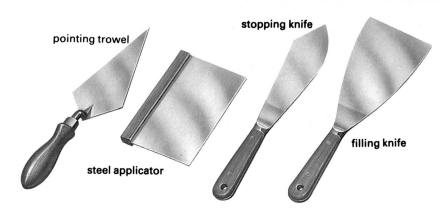

pointing trowel

stopping knife

steel applicator

filling knife

Filling knives look like stripping knives but have a thin, flexible blade. They are only useful as long as the blade remains clean and rust-free.
Stopping knives have shaped blades designed for applying putty and filler to intricately shaped mouldings.
Applicators have a broad flexible steel or plastic blade for 'feathering' layers of filler flush with surrounding surface. They are particularly useful for finishing joints in plasterboard (ie Gypsum Board).
A pointing trowel is invaluable for applying heavier fillers such as sand and cement mortar.

TOOLS FOR APPLYING HEAT

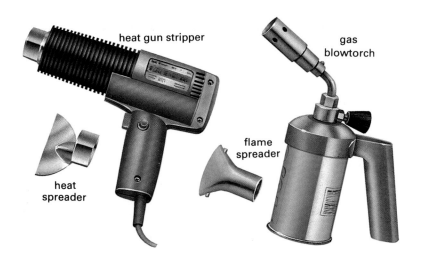

heat gun stripper

gas blowtorch

heat spreader

flame spreader

Electric heat gun strippers are among the handiest of all power tools. As well as stripping paint with only a minimal risk of scorching, they make light work of loosening vinyl tiles and old adhesives. Basic models have a simple heat on/off trigger; more sophisticated versions allow you to vary the air flow too, for greater control. Operating temperature is around 500°C – enough to melt solder.

Gas blowtorches are safer and more reliable than they used to be, and have the advantage of portability.

Both hot-air strippers and blowtorches generally come with fan-shaped nozzle attachments which concentrate the heat for dealing with awkward corners.

TOOLS FOR SANDING

cork sanding block

wire brush

abrasive block

disc sanding attachment

orbital sander

Sanding blocks are sold in wood, cork and resilient foam with an abrasive covering. Wood blocks have a screw-tightened slot for holding the paper. Cork blocks are cheaper, and can be more comfortable to hold. Abrasive blocks tend to clog, and can work out to be expensive on large jobs. They are not suitable for intricate moldings.

A wire brush is useful for cleaning masonry, or scratching a surface prior to repainting. Alternatively, use a *wire brush* drill attachment.

Disc sander drill attachments are cheap and versatile, but too harsh for sanding large surfaces – it's virtually impossible to get an even finish. *Flap wheel* attachments are gentler, and good for sanding mouldings.

Orbital sanders make light work of sanding large surfaces, and are one of the best power tool buys. You can also get orbital sander drill attachments.

ABRASIVES GUIDE		
TYPE OF ABRASIVE	**RANGE AVAILABLE**	**WHERE TO USE**
Sandpaper Traditional type; glass particles bonded to paper backing. *Garnet paper* is similar and lasts longer, but is more expensive.	Grades run from 20 (very coarse), 80 (medium), 150 (fine) to 220+ (very fine).	Wood, manmade boards, filler, light sanding or paintwork.
Aluminum oxide paper Generally green or black. Its high resilience makes it the preferred material for power sanding equipment.	Grades 4½ (extra coarse) to 10/0 (extra fine).	Wood, paintwork, filler, plaster, old decorated surfaces.
Silicon carbide (wet-and-dry) paper Resilient and washable. Gentler action than other types, especially when wet; finest grades are very fine.	Generally graded by grit No. Grit Nos 60-120 are fairly coarse, Nos 150-280 are medium to fine, and Nos 320-500 are fine to extra fine.	Paintwork, (wash to prevent clogging), varnish, bare woodwork, metal (use dry).
Steel wool Often overlooked as a sanding material. Comfortable and convenient for fine finishing.	Generally available in seven grades: 3, 2, 1 (coarse to medium); 0,00 (medium to fine); and 000, 0000 (very fine).	Paint topcoats (prior to repainting), intermediate varnish coats, old polished surfaces.

PREPARING TO REDECORATE

Redecorating an entire room the way you want it is among the most rewarding of all DIY jobs. It's also one of the most cost-effective, because in this case time, not skill, is what you pay a professional for.

The following pages of this chapter take you step by step through every stage of redecorating a room, from removing old finishes and preparing the surfaces, to wallpapering and repainting. But in most rooms in need of a major overhaul, there are things which need doing long before you pick up a scraper or paintbrush. And if you rush straight in, the chances are you'll get held up by problems you hadn't bargained for.

The answer is to treat decorating a room like any other major structural project, working to a sequence and planning it through in advance.

Start at the beginning

The place to start planning for redecoration is not your local paint and paper store, but the room you're about to transform.

Before you go any further, carry out a thorough survey based on the plan overleaf so that you can anticipate the kind of structural and cleaning problems that might otherwise disrupt work later.

Then work out your own room redecoration program, balancing what needs to be done against your own time and resources.

Decorating even a small room calls for a surprising number of tools.
For preparation: Scrapers, stripping compounds, heat gun stripper, fillers, wood putty, filling knife, sandpaper and block, dust sheets.
For painting: Brushes, rollers and trays, brush cleaner.
For papering: Stepladder, shears, carpenter's level, pasting table.

WHAT ORDER TO DO THINGS IN

The following list highlights the major stages in a full redecoration program. Use it to pick out the relevant points and plan your own program.

1 Check for structural problems
- Carry out a thorough survey of room (see opposite).
- Make yourself a checklist of essential repairs.

2 Organize tools and materials
- Choose decorative options.
- Make checklist of materials and tools.
- Buy materials and buy or borrow tools.

3 Clear room and cover up
- Remove as much furniture as possible.
- Mask or remove fitted furniture and wall fixtures (see *Surveying the room* opposite). Cover up floor.

4 Preliminary clean
- Remove foam insulation strips from windows/doors.
- Clean condensation mold off windows.
- Vacuum clean all surfaces.

5 Remove old decorations
- Remove unwanted paneling/cladding.
- Strip old ceiling paint/coverings.
- Strip wallcoverings and woodwork.

6 Carry out modifications
- Unblock or rebuild fireplace.
- Install wiring for wall lights and new sockets.
- Move ceiling light fittings.
- Fit new decorative mouldings.

7 Carry out repairs
- Repair damaged plasterwork and make good.
- Patch damaged wood; sand stripped woodwork.

8 Final cleaning
- Wash down walls and ceilings with detergent.
- Wipe over woodwork with detergent; vacuum floor.

9 Redecorate ceiling

10 Redecorate walls
(but if papering, do paintwork first.)

11 Redecorate paintwork

12 Refit fixtures and refurnish

Trade tip

Covering up

❝ Experts are forever disagreeing about the best way to cover things up – here are my own favorite methods:
□ Use cloth dust sheets in preference to plastic ones on floors – plastic sheets are cheap and easy to lay, but they can get extremely slippery when wet. Anything that's spilt tends to run straight off the surface on to what you're trying to protect.
□ Plastic sheets come into their own when covering soft furnishings. Use them under cloth sheets to provide a waterproof layer.

□ Dust sheets may be rented, but old sheets, curtains or blankets will do just as well.
□ When laying dust sheets, shake them outdoors beforehand and allow plenty of overlap – they always get scuffed up. Shake them outdoors again to remove dust before painting.
□ Tape or tack dust sheets to the baseboards where possible, then mask by hand when you paint the woodwork.
□ Always use masking tape for tricky bits, and don't leave it in place for too long – it will stick fast. ❞

Survey a room (above) before you decorate, so that you can pinpoint problems which might otherwise hold up work.

Cover up thoroughly (left).
A. Tape or pin the edges of dust sheets to the skirtings.
B. Cover small fixtures using plastic bags held on with masking tape.
   Move any remaining furniture to the middle of the room and protect with a double layer of plastic and cloth dust sheets.

SURVEYING THE ROOM

Ceilings Check for leaks (brown staining), and for cracking or loose plasterboard (shown by blistering along the joints).
Texture painted ceilings may hide defective lath and plaster: if possible, check from above.
Check for old distemper or other unstable finishes; if the finish comes off on your fingers, it must be removed completely.

Decorative moldings Check for loose or damaged moldings such as covings, picture rails, baseboards and architraves. Fix or replace before decorating.
Tops of moldings gather hidden dust and dirt; make a note to clean.

Walls Check for dampness, especially around and under windows. Embossed or textured paper may disguise defective plaster; paneling could hide damp walls or poor plaster.
If necessary, arrange for someone to investigate suspect areas.
Remove or mask off fixtures attached to the wall. Pull out old anchors. If plugs are to be reused, mark their positions with matchsticks

Services Let down radiators if possible (see overleaf). Remove lampshades and mask fixtures. Decide whether to remove light fixtures/ sockets or install additional outlets.
Ideally, get an electrician to remove wall lights and isolate supply.

Windows Remove any foam insulation strips. Clean off condensation mold around frames. Sticking windows may need removing and overhauling, disturbing the surrounding walls. Remove all window dressings and tracks/rods.

Doors Sticking doors may need trimming. Remove door handles etc if at all possible.

Fireplace With open fires, have the chimney swept. Cover fire surround unless painting. Decide whether to unblock fireplace or build in new surround.

Furniture Remove as much furniture as possible. Move remaining furniture to middle of room and cover with plastic dust sheets (cotton ones may let through spillages).
Cover or mask built-in furniture which can't be taken down.

Floorcoverings Lift wall-to-wall carpeting if possible (see overleaf). Protect and cover remaining floorcoverings.

Floors Check wooden floors for loose boards and nail or screw down.
Check solid floors for signs of damp: tape a piece of glass over the bare surface and leave for a day – moisture on the underside indicates dampness.

LOWERING A RADIATOR

There's usually enough 'give' in the pipes to lift a light panel radiator off its brackets and lower it to the floor without having to drain the system and disconnect it. Beware, though, of radiators with staining around the pipes or valves; this indicates weeping joints, which may fall apart if you interfere with them. And if the radiator doesn't give easily, don't try to force it.

Refitting is the exact reverse of dismantling. Make sure you open the lockshield valve the exact number of turns it took to close it, and bleed the radiator afterwards.

1 Turn off the heating. Close the radiator on/off valve, then lift off or unscrew the cover of the lockshield valve fitted to the pipe on the other side.

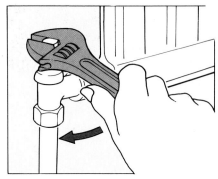

2 Use an adjustable wrench or spanner to close the valve, turning the movable head fully clockwise. Make a note of how many turns it takes to do this.

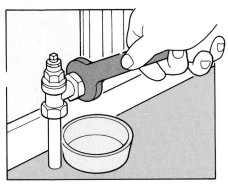

3 Place a receptacle under both valves and use your adjustable wrench to loosen off the connector nuts **one full turn only**. At this stage, water will start to drip.

4 Lift the radiator upwards, using your foot as a lever, until you feel it disengage from its wall brackets. Then lower it gently towards you.

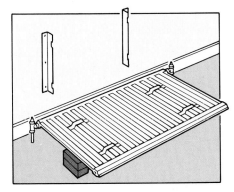

5 Support the radiator at both ends to take the strain off the pipework. Retighten the connector nuts temporarily to stop the water leaking.

REMOVING A CARPET

Foam-backed wall-to-wall carpet is stuck down with double-sided tape, and is difficult to lift successfully without the backing disintegrating.

Protect them instead with layers of first plastic and then cloth dust sheets. Fix the edges of the sheets to the baseboard with masking tape or tacks while painting the walls, then hand-mask when you come to paint the woodwork.

Burlap-backed fitted carpets with a separate underlay are secured by gripper strips around the edge of the room, and by cover strips at doorways. You may also find tacks holding down awkward areas or the whole carpet.

Removing a carpet like this requires a carpet fitter's bolster and knee-kicker, both of which you can rent cheaply.

Once you have freed the carpet, roll it up tightly across the shortest dimension. Either store it in another room, or turn it round so that it is clear of the walls and cover with a dust sheet.

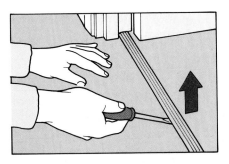

1 At the doorways, prize off cover strips. If there is no carpet on the other side, the strip will fit over the edge and may need to be levered up gently.

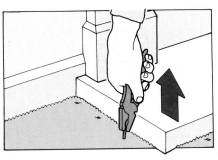

2 Pull out any tacks you can find, using a tack lifter or pliers. When you're fairly sure only the grippers are holding the carpet, start to free it.

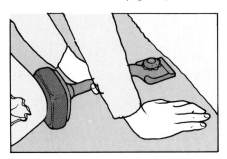

3 Kneel facing the edge and push the teeth of the knee-kicker into the carpet ahead of you. Jolt it forward and pull upwards to free the grippers.

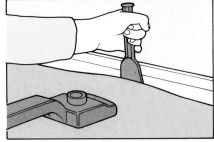

4 If you find it difficult to free the edge, use a bolster to prize it up as you kick. Carry on along the edges until you have freed the whole carpet.

HOW TO STRIP WALLPAPER

Any papered wall that is to be recovered with wallpaper must be stripped first. Many home-owners face the additional problem of stripping painted walls that have been lined with ugly or poorly applied textured papers.

There are two basic methods, depending on the type of paper, so check the panel on the right and make sure you know what you're dealing with before you start.

Soak and strip is the cheapest and still the most effective method for most wallpapers.

Soaking the paper loosens the paste, causing it to peel away – a process which you can speed up by adding a little detergent or wallpaper stripper to the water. Another trick is to score the paper first, helping the water to penetrate the outer surface.

Steam stripping using a rented steam stripper is faster and more effective on heavy and painted-over papers, but it does have some disadvantages (see overleaf), and the rental cost mounts up if you don't tackle the work all at once.

Stripping tools

A decent stripping knife is essential. Spend a little more on one with a rigid blade which won't flex and dig into the plaster; don't be tempted to economize by using a filling knife instead.

There's also a patented scraper with a roller on the base which keeps the blade at the correct angle for stripping. These are useful for fragile surfaces such as plasterboard, where it's easy to slip and gouge the surface.

KNOW YOUR WALLPAPER	
WALLPAPER TYPE	**STRIPPING METHOD**
Uncoated – plain, non-washable paper.	Soak and scrape. Pre-pasted types peel off easily if left to soak. Other types need scraping as well, depending on thickness.
Coated – washable paper coated with thin film of PVC.	Score, soak and strip. Water must be given time to penetrate outer water resistant coating.
Vinyl – plastic washable coating on thin paper backing.	Peel off. Vinyl layer separates easily from backing and can be peeled off in whole lengths. If necessary, strip backing by soaking and scraping.
Plain lining paper – usually latex painted, but may be found under surface paper.	Score, soak and strip. Water must be given time to penetrate behind paint. Paint may have penetrated paper, requiring heavy scraping.
Woodchip – textured lining paper in which wood pulp is sandwiched between heavy backing and light facing paper; usually painted.	Score and steam strip. Try to avoid layers separating. Avoid prolonged steaming if plaster underneath is in poor condition.
Embossed – textured relief paper containing plaster and other additives. Two types: medium (ie Anaglypta) and heavy (ie Supaglypta). May be printed or latex painted.	Score and steam strip. Let steam soften paint coating before attempting to scrape. Older embossed papers are very hard work to remove.

Wallpaper stripping requires plenty of energy, but little in the way of equipment. A wire brush provides a gentle means of scoring the surface of light paper; for heavier ones use a home-made scorer.

washing up bowl

wallpaper stripper

home-made scoring tool

stripping tool with roller

heavy cloth

stripping knife.

wire brush

STRIPPING BY HAND

Stripping wallpaper is a messy business, so cover up the floor even if you've cleared the room. The debris will be sticky and wet, so if you're using cloth dust sheets, place a plastic sheet or an opened-out garbage can liner underneath the area you're working on. (Don't cover the whole floor in plastic sheets – they become slippery and unsafe.)

With so much water around, it's a good idea to turn off the electricity at the fusebox. Don't let the room get warm, or the soaked paper may dry out before you get around to stripping it.

 Trade tip

Avoid a flood

❝ When you're soaking a really stubborn paper, water tends to slosh all over the place instead of soaking into the surface.

A trick I use is to add a small handful of ordinary wallpaper paste to the water first. Not surprisingly this makes it slightly sticky, helping it adhere to the wall instead of running down it and over the floor. ❞

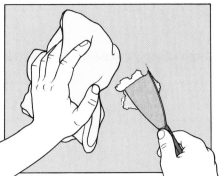

1 Soak the paper thoroughly with a sponge or old floor cloth, leave a couple of minutes, then test to see if it has loosened. If not, you must score it.

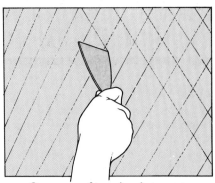

2 One way of scoring is to use the corner of your stripping knife, held as shown to stop it gouging the plaster. Score in a diamond pattern.

3 Alternatively, knock some nails through a block of wood so the heads just show through. Run this lightly across the paper in criss-cross bands.

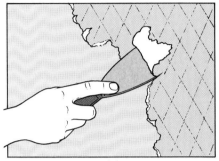

4 Keep the blade angle shallow as you remove the paper, so you don't cut into the wall. Stubborn patches may need an extra soaking before they shift.

STEAM STRIPPING

Nearly all papers that need steam stripping benefit from being scored thoroughly first. The art of using a steam stripper is to work two-handed, holding the plate against the paper just long enough to soften it, then scraping off the debris before it dries out. It takes a while to judge this correctly, so don't overdo the steam to start with or you risk damaging the wall.

On textured papers, wait until the steam has penetrated right through before scraping – stripping a layer at a time is much harder.

Trade tip

Protect the ceiling

❝ Steam strippers are notorious for softening what they're not supposed to, and ceiling lining papers are the most vulnerable – the steam rises and condenses, soaking into the paper and leaving gravity to do the rest.

! stop this happening by taping cheap plastic dust sheets to the part of the ceiling I'm working under (in a small room cover the whole ceiling). ❞

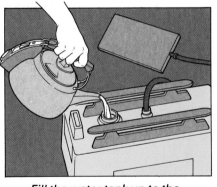

1 Fill the water tank up to the level indicator, then lay down the plate vent side up and switch on. When steam begins to emerge, the machine is ready for use.

2 Hold the plate against the surface for 15 seconds, then check with your knife to see if the steam has penetrated every layer. Repeat if necessary.

3 As the paper gives way, move the plate on to the next sector and push away the debris with your knife. Angle the plate upwards to stop it dripping .

4 Remove stubborn bits after you've cleared the bulk of the paper. Apply the steam in 10-second bursts, scraping down immediately.

PREPARING WALLS AND CEILINGS

Although it's possible to give walls and ceilings a quick facelift if the surface is in good condition, on most redecorating jobs there is no substitute for preparation. Modern paints and wallpapers are a great deal more efficient than they used to be, but if the underlying surface is poor, then no amount of hastily applied finish will disguise it.

At the very least, you should make sure that the surface is clean and dry. But walls and ceilings which have been repaired, stripped, or cleared of attached decorations may need more extensive treatment. For example, after filling all the obvious blemishes, the surface may still be uneven enough to warrant lining with paper before painting or wallpapering. Or it may need sealing prior to finishing.

Assuming that you have already made any necessary repairs, and that the room is cleared ready for action, check the chart below to find out what surfaces need what treatment.

....Shopping List....

General cleaning: bucket or basin, detergent, clean cloths, dust sheets, access equipment.
Filling: filler, filling knife, wire brush, sanding equipment.
Priming/sizing: large wall brush, primer/sealer, plaster stabilizer, sealer, thinned latex paint, sizing or thinned paste.
Lining with paper: papering tools, paste, lining paper (see overleaf).

PREPARATION GUIDE

SURFACE	BEFORE PAINTING . . .	BEFORE WALLPAPERING . . .
Latex paint (sound)	■ Sand down bumps and bits of paint ■ Fill depressions ■ Wash down	■ Fill large holes ■ Sand smooth ■ Coat with sizing
Latex paint (cracked/flaking)	■ Sand back to sound edge ■ Fill depressions with fine surface filler ■ If area is large, hang lining paper	■ Sand back to sound edge ■ Fill large holes ■ Coat with sizing
Latex paint (over lining paper)	■ Check surface is dry ■ Stick down peeling edges ■ Wash *lightly*	■ Strip unless completely sound; otherwise treat as latex
Oil or alkyd paint (sound)	■ Sand with wet and dry paper to key surface for new coat ■ Fill depressions and wash down	■ Fill large holes ■ Sand smooth ■ Coat with sizing
Oil or alkyd paint (cracked/bubbling)	■ Sand back to sound edge ■ Cover depressions with fine surface filler	■ Sand back to sound edge ■ Fill large holes ■ Coat with sizing
New plaster	■ Leave in bare state for at least a month ■ Brush off any deposits ■ Use latex paint *only;* do not decorate again for 6 months	■ Leave for 6 months ■ Coat with sizing
Old plaster	■ Fill holes/cracks ■ Sand smooth ■ Wash off last traces of old decorations ■ Coat repairs and unprepared patches with primer/sealer or stabilizer ■ If heavily patched, hang lining paper	■ Fill large holes ■ Sand smooth and cover filled areas with sizing ■ Ideally, hang lining paper
Bare plasterboard	■ Fill holes/dents ■ If new, 'spot' nail heads with primer ■ Cover cracked joints between boards with joint compound and paper or glass fiber tape ■ Sand smooth ■ Wash lightly	■ Fill holes/dents ■ Sand smooth ■ Coat with sizing
Bare brick	■ Remove dirt/powdery deposits with stiff or wire brush ■ Coat with primer/sealer	

WASHING DOWN

The one step you can't avoid when repainting an existing painted surface is washing down. Even though it's often hardly noticeable, the dirt and grease that accumulates on old paint can discolor the new coat or stop it from drying. In extreme cases it may even cause the finish to lift off or crack.

To clean a wall surface prior to papering or painting, simply wipe it down with a solution of warm water and soap or household ammonia. You don't need to scrub walls clean – the important thing is to clear away any grease on the surface.

On plasterboard, and on heavy lining papers (ie textured, Anaglypta) which have already been painted, take care not to let the washing water soak into the surface. Work on small areas at a time and sponge off frequently.

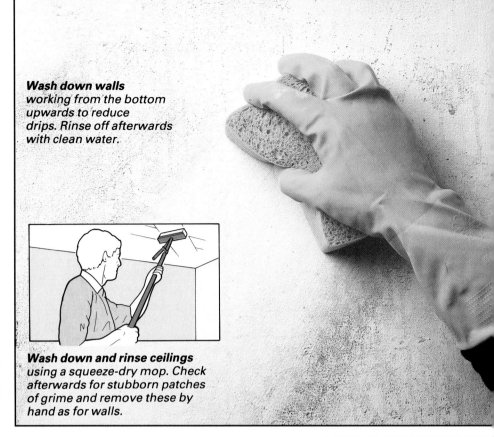

Wash down walls *working from the bottom upwards to reduce drips. Rinse off afterwards with clean water.*

Wash down and rinse ceilings *using a squeeze-dry mop. Check afterwards for stubborn patches of grime and remove these by hand as for walls.*

HANGING LINING PAPER

Hanging lining paper is a simple way to smooth a wall that's been stripped or heavily repaired. Wallpaper manufacturers also recommend it before hanging delicate printed wallpapers and unbacked fabrics. If you are painting over lining paper, hang it vertically like ordinary wallpaper. If it is to be papered over, hang the strips horizontally – called *cross-lining.*

Lining paper comes in various grades. The basic rule is to use liner over rough or damaged walls; and the rougher the walls, the heavier the liner. (You can also get special lining paper designed to cover cinder block.) The heavier the paper you use, the better the finished result will be.

Using lining paper

Lining paper is easier to hang than wallpaper – there's no pattern to worry about, and the paper sticks readily using standard wallpaper paste if it is not pre-pasted.

Sand down any bumps ahead of time, but don't worry about the hollows – these can be filled, along with any other imperfections, once the paper is up. Leave the paper to dry for 24 hours.

Vertical hanging

Treat the paper like ordinary wallpaper. Align the first strip on each wall against a vertical guideline just under a roll's width from the corner, butt the next strip against it

(don't overlap), and so on down the wall as far as you can go.

At corners (which are never square), paper in towards the corner from one side leaving an overlap. Then paper back in from the other side to cover the overlap left by the first strip.

Trim off the excess at the top and bottom of the wall, and at corners, using a sharp knife held against the blade of a stripping knife.

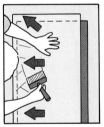

2 *Cut a length of paper 100mm (4") longer than the height of the wall. Paste in a criss-cross pattern out towards the edges to avoid getting paste on the table.*

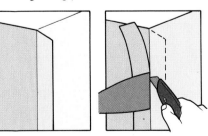

4 *At internal corners, turn the first length around the corner then hang the second over it. Trim off the excess, using a stripping knife as a guide.*

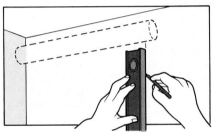

1 *For vertical hanging, use a carpenter's level to draw a line on each wall slightly less than a roll's width from the nearest corner.*

3 *Align the pasted length with the guideline, leaving a 50mm (2") overlap top and bottom. Smooth out with a dry cloth, then trim off the excess.*

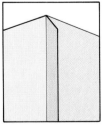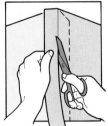

5 *Follow the same sequence for external corners: turn the first length around, hang the length on the return side over it, then trim the overlap.*

PREPARING BARE PLASTER

What you do with bare plaster depends on its age and condition.

New plaster must be left to dry for at least a month. If salt crystals (efflorescence) appear during this time, brush them off.

Old plaster needs to be made good. Coat patches with general purpose primer/sealer; if crumbly, apply plaster stabilizer. Damp plaster may indicate a problem area. If not, leave to dry out before decorating.

Sealing the surface

Dry plaster tends to suck the moisture out of paint or wallpaper paste before these can bond properly. The answer is to apply a sealing coat first – often called *sizing*.

Before painting, seal with primer/sealer or a thinned coat of the paint you are using. Mix latex paint with one quarter of its volume of water. Use *alkali-resisting* primer before applying oil or alkyd paint.

Before papering/lining, apply a coat of sizing or a coat of wallpaper paste. Use a fungicidal paste or sizing to prevent mold growth – especially under vinyl papers.

Seal the surface of bare plaster with primer or paint if painting, sizing if papering. Stabilizing solution will help to bind crumbling old plaster.

Brush off efflorescence on the surface of new plaster. It is caused by salts crystalizing as the plaster dries. Continue at intervals until no more appears.

Cross-lining

Work out beforehand how many widths it takes to cover the wall, allowing an extra 50mm (2″) top and bottom for trimming. Then draw a horizontal guideline right around the room, to align the first strip on each wall.

Fold the strips accordion-fashion after pasting, then unfold them on the wall, smoothing as you go. As they're so narrow, you can run them straight around corners.

1 **To cross-line the walls,** start by drawing a horizontal guideline right around the room, just under a roll's width from where the ceiling and walls meet.

2 As you paste each strip, fold it accordion-fashion into an easily manageable length. Grip it between your fingers and thumbs, keeping the folds intact.

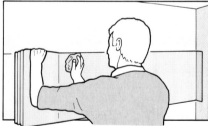

3 Begin in a corner. Align the top edge of the first strip with the guideline, leaving a small overlap. Then unfold along the wall, smoothing as you go.

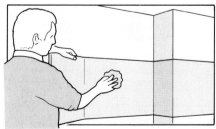

4 The lengths are narrow enough to be continued around corners without falling out of alignment. After completing the wall, trim off top and bottom.

Trade tip

Don't spare the paste!

❝ The underlying surface you create is crucial to the finished wall. The lining paper should adhere to every inch of wall. Make sure the lengths are thoroughly wet before you hang them, or the paper will dry and shrink unevenly, leaving unsightly gaps at the joints. ❞

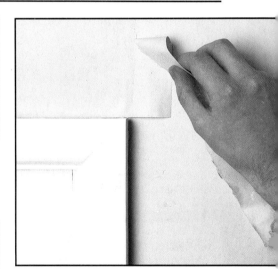

Where narrow strips join, leave an overlap and let the paper dry, then tear off . . .

. . . to leave a barely visible 'feathered' edge which you can then fill to hide it completely.

PREPARING CEILINGS

Although you can generally treat ceilings as you would walls, they have special problems of their own.

If the ceiling has been lined and painted over, it's worth doing your best to keep the lining paper intact. Wash down gently, using as little water as possible, and carry out any minor repairs as shown.

Relining a ceiling is much more difficult. Not only is there the problem of access, but for the lining to be effective you'll probably need to use a heavyweight covering such as Anaglypta (which is more difficult to hang). Papering ceilings is covered on pages 77-80.

Cracks in ceilings may not respond to normal filling treatment if they are caused by movement in the floor above – the filler simply shakes loose. In this case fill with flexible sealant instead, allowing a few days for a skin to form before you paint over it.

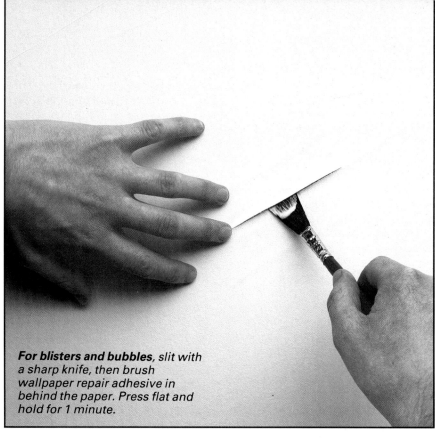

For blisters and bubbles, slit with a sharp knife, then brush wallpaper repair adhesive in behind the paper. Press flat and hold for 1 minute.

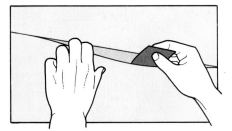

1 *To fix peeling edges in lining paper, start by sanding behind them to remove all traces of dust and old paste. Clean afterwards with a damp cloth.*

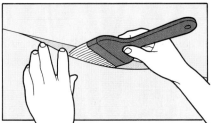

2 *Brush wallpaper repair adhesive behind the edges and press flat. If they curl, secure with sticking putty while the adhesive dries.*

If part of the paper is missing, but the rest is largely sound, cover the area with ready mixed skimming plaster. Smooth level with the surrounding edges.

◣ PROBLEM SOLVER ◢

Dealing with blemishes

On painted surfaces, you may come across blemishes which no amount of washing down will remove. These include:
- Stains such as nicotine.
- Water marks left on a ceiling after a leak.
- Mold patches

Stains must be sealed before repainting, otherwise there's a risk that they will bleed through the new finish. Use spray-on stain blocking compound – a relatively new innovation – or, alternatively, a standard sealer or primer.

Kill mold patches by washing with bleach solution or a brand name product specifically made to remove deposits of mold.

If the blemish has ruined the surface of lining paper, cut out the damaged area and paste on a patch as shown.

Spray indelible stains with aerosol stain blocking compound. Alternatively, paint with primer/ sealer, feathering the edges of the patch.

Treat black mold with a solution of one part bleach to three parts water. Apply with a sponge-type scourer, working it well into the surface of the paint.

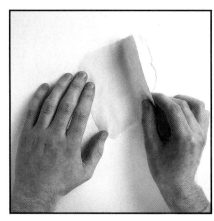

Patch damaged lining paper by tearing a new piece roughly to fit so that it has thin, feathered edges. Paste in place, then cover the edges with filler.

PREPARING WOODWORK AND FIXTURES

As with everything else in decorating, getting a good finish on baseboards, doors and window frames depends on good preparation. On sound surfaces, this may be as simple as giving the paint a quick rub-down and clean. But if there is any damage to the surface, or faults in the original finish, make sure these get dealt with at the same time.

Bare wood should only need a light rub-down with sandpaper to remove any roughness or sharp edges. Fill the end grain and any other blemishes, then apply knotting compound and a coat of primer.

Painted wood in good condition should be lightly rubbed down and then cleaned. Minor imperfections can be filled or sanded as appropriate; prime any spots where you have rubbed through to bare wood.

If the paint surface is very poor, it's often wiser to strip it completely and start again from bare wood (see pages 43-46). Serious damage or rot in the underlying wood must be treated and then replaced with a new section, cut and shaped to fit.

Metal fittings need thorough cleaning, and all traces of corrosion must be removed. Afterwards, coat with primer or a one-coat paint.

.... Shopping List ....

Depending on the job, you may need a wide range of materials for cleaning and preparation:

Cleaners include detergent and turpentine (useful for degreasing metal surfaces or old, dirty paintwork). A supply of clean cloths is essential.

Abrasives include sandpaper or garnet paper for sanding woodwork, and wet and dry or aluminum oxide paper for rubbing down metal. Wet and dry paper used wet gives a finer finish on painted wood, but is messy. Steel wool is a handy alternative for cleaning metal, and gives a smooth finish to bare wood.

Flap wheel and rotary wire brush drill attachments make light work of metal fixtures in need of extensive rubbing down.

Fillers include general purpose acrylic or cellulose filler for larger cracks and dents, plus fine surface filler for dents shallower than 3mm (⅛″) and patches where the grain has become raised.

Fiberglass resin and epoxy fillers

are better for repairing areas subject to heavy wear and tear. They are quick setting and very strong, with a non-absorbent surface which takes a good finish – but they are expensive. Use flexible or aerosol foam filler for joints with adjoining surfaces which are likely to move.

Sealers and primers include *knotting compound* to stop resin oozing out of knots, *general purpose primer* for bare wood, *aluminum primer* for patches which have been heat stripped, and *metal primer* for fittings. Rusty metal is best treated with chemical *rust remover/neutralizer*.

You also need scrapers and filling tools, an electric drill, and woodworking tools if you have any patching to do.

Preparation materials can cover a surprising number of different products: assess the job before you start and lay on supplies of everything needed.

knotting compound • metal primer • general purpose primer • rust remover • flexible filler • turpentine • general purpose filler (ready mixed) • fine surface filler • resin filler (flexible) • resin filler (rigid) • flap wheel attachment • wire brush attachments • scrapers • wet and dry paper • sandpaper

PREPARING WOODWORK

PREPARING SOUND PAINTWORK

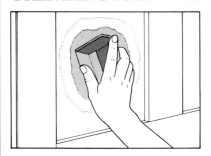

1 Rub down blemishes and runs with medium grade sandpaper and a sanding block, feathering the edges into the surrounding surface. Rub down the whole surface with fine sandpaper or steel wool to 'key' it.

2 After sanding, wash down the surface with a solution of detergent to remove the dust and clean off any grease (which might contaminate the new paint). Pay special attention to awkward areas such as moldings.

MINOR DAMAGE AND GAPS

Splits, dents and cracked joints should be filled and sanded to blend into the surrounding surface. Use whatever filler suits the situation.

Splits and dents can be repaired with general purpose filler – either powder or ready mixed. But for small irregularities, ready mixed fine surface filler bonds more readily and gives a smoother finish.

Vulnerable edges which have received knocks are likely to be knocked again. Use resin or epoxy filler (both of which are stronger than the wood itself) to fill these areas.

Cracked joints are often subject to movement, so use a flexible filler. If the movement is due to looseness rather than shrinkage, strengthen the joint first with screws or nails.

Gaps along adjoining surfaces may also be prone to movement. Pack with pieces of styrofoam or cardboard packing material, then fill with flexible sealant or foam filler. Let sealant form a skin before painting. Foam filler can be shaped once dry.

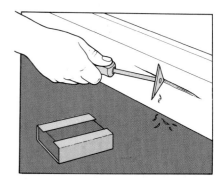

Sand painted surfaces so that the filler can get a grip. Rake out and scrape any loose material from cracks back to a sound edge using the corner of a scraper.

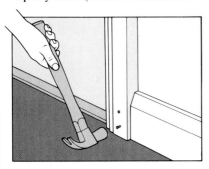

Check whether cracks in joints are due to shrinkage or looseness. Strengthen loose joints with extra screws or nails to prevent further movement.

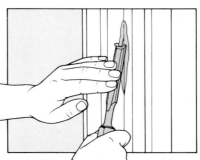

Resin filler must be mixed with hardener and cures quickly. After hardening, shape it with woodworking tools and smooth with wet and dry paper.

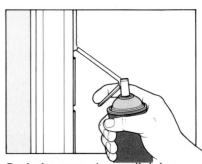

Pack the gaps along adjoining surfaces with pieces of styrofoam or cardboard. Then fill with flexible sealant or aerosol foam filler.

DEFECTIVE PAINTWORK

Where large patches of the existing paintwork are badly blistered or flaking, it's best to strip it back to bare wood and start again. Choose between the three methods below, depending on the situation.

Heat from a heat gun stripper or blowlamp is cheap, efficient and fairly easy. But on a window you risk cracking the glass, and blowlamps can char woodwork.

Abrasives or scrapers are hard work, but convenient for small areas. On moldings, however, it is easy to damage the details – especially if using power tools.

Chemicals are expensive and messy, but they don't damage the wood, and are ideal for fiddly areas and moldings. Make sure any residue is neutralized and cleaned off, or it may affect the paint. For removable items like doors, professional dipping is a possible, but costly, option.

Use a heat gun together with a stripping knife, working it under the blistered paint. Keep a container handy to hold the scrapings.

Powered sanders and drill attachments help when removing paint with abrasives, but avoid using on moldings – these should be tackled by hand.

Scraping on its own works best on curves. Check constantly that the blade doesn't dig in: if it does, alter the angle in case you are catching the grain.

Chemical stripper removes several coats in one go – providing you give it time to penetrate. Clean thoroughly after scraping up the softened residue.

Trade tip

Spot checks

❝ Discoloring and marks on a painted surface suggest that it wasn't prepared properly first time around. Treat them now, or they'll work their way through the new topcoat too.

Knots show up as oily looking rings in the paint. The cure is to sand a small area back to bare wood, and apply knotting compound. Follow with coats of primer and undercoat, then sand to blend into the surface.

Rust marks caused by nail or screw heads also need sanding back. Apply metal primer to seal the head and fill if necessary, then refinish as above. ❞

PREPARING METAL FIXTURES

Most corrosion-free metal fixtures only need degreasing and a very light rubdown. The simplest method is to use fine steel wool dipped in turpentine; for areas which need smoothing as well, rub with wet and dry paper first. Wash down, rinse and dry the fixtures thoroughly before priming.

Dealing with corrosion

Whether the metal is bare or painted, all traces of corrosion must be removed before painting.

Rusty patches on steel or cast iron need a thorough wire brushing to remove loose flakes. Afterwards, either sand them back to bare, sound metal using aluminum oxide paper or a flap wheel, or treat them with chemical rust remover/neutralizer (as used for car repairs).

There are several types of rust remover, but most contain acids and can be dangerous: follow the manufacturer's instructions, and be sure to wear gloves and goggles.

After treatment, wash down and rinse in clean water to remove all traces. Dry, then prime quickly to prevent corrosion recurring.

Metal windows may need rust-treating inside and out – even if you leave the exterior painting until later. Use a separate container to dip the brush in, so you don't contaminate the rest of the fluid.

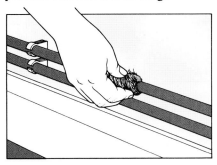

Aluminum, copper and brass need only a light clean using fine steel wool soaked in alcohol or turpentine. Use wet and dry paper to rub down pitted areas.

A rotary wire brush attachment is less tiring than brushing by hand where you're faced with a large area of rusty, flaking steel or cast iron.

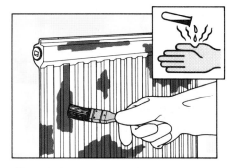

Chemical rust cures often contain strong acids – apply with care using an old brush. Afterwards, wash down and rinse to neutralize the residue, then leave to dry.

▌ PROBLEM SOLVER

Dealing with rot

Any localized patches of rot in the woodwork must be repaired – and the cause investigated – before preparation.

Small patches are usually *wet rot*, which you can deal with yourself: either cut back the affected section to sound wood and join in a new section, or cut out the rot and patch it with a kit containing anti-rot fungicidal pellets.

Call in a specialist surveyor if you suspect *dry rot*, which is much more serious and must be treated professionally.

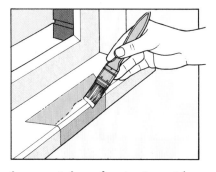

Large patches of wet rot must be sawn or chiseled out, and new wood glued and nailed in their place. Coat the repair with preservative before priming.

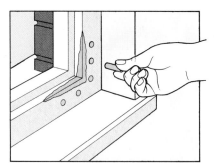

Small areas can be patched with a repair kit. Brush on hardener and apply the resin filler, then insert fungicidal pellets to kill any remaining rot spores.

STRIPPING WOODWORK

Whether you are decorating the house or renovating furniture it's sometimes necessary to give woodwork more than just a light rubdown.

There are several reasons for stripping back to bare wood:
■ If you want to show off the grain, any paint must be removed before staining and/or varnishing it.
■ Thick paint may have obscured the detail of moldings or carving. Stripping should restore the original form, before refinishing.
■ Paint or varnish which was faulty (or which was badly applied) may have peeled and lifted. Removing it will avoid further problems.

How to strip
There are three main ways to remove paint and varnish from wood. In every case, start by removing fittings, handles, catches and so on. The options are:
Heat stripping, using a blowtorch or heat gun to soften and blister the paint so it will scrape off.
Chemical stripping, applying a liquid, gel or paste to the surface, then leaving it to soften the paint or varnish before scraping it off.
Sanding or scraping with hand or power tools. This may be all you need, but must be done in any case after heat or chemical stripping.

The chart overleaf shows the pros and cons of each method. The final choice often depends on the nature of the surface and whether you are applying varnish or paint afterwards. The first thing to know is what you are dealing with.

What finish do you have?
Paint is obvious, but test clear finishes by dabbing an inconspicuous spot – first with turpentine then alcohol – on a clean white cloth and seeing if any comes off.
■ Turpentine removes oiled and waxed finishes. Both are easier to restore than to remove.
■ You will find that alcohol removes French polish, a high-gloss finish traditionally used for pianos and fine furniture. Similar (but cheaper) shellac polish responds to the same treatment.

All these finishes require special treatment (see page 245). Most other clear finishes respond to chemical or heat stripping, with the following exceptions:
■ Two-part plastic coating (a modern finish found mainly on floors and furniture) only responds to heat.
■ Stained wood may be a 'skin-deep' varnish/stain which comes away easily. If the wood has been dyed before varnishing, the colour will be hard to shift and you may have to resort to bleaching the wood.

WORTH STRIPPING?
Thick paint may conceal a surface which is not what you expected. Interior woodwork such as doors may have been patched with filler, and it was once common to improve the surface of furniture by filling the grain with plaster of Paris. If possible, test a concealed patch first to see whether the paint comes off easily, and to get an idea of the condition of the wood underneath.

If you plan to renovate an old piece of furniture, there are several points to note;
■ Before stripping *any* old piece, check that it is not valuable. Sometimes even a rough original finish is more highly valued than a modern, hardwearing version.
■ Beware of stripping veneered furniture. Most methods which remove the finish tend to lift the veneer as well.

STRIPPING PAINT AND VARNISH

METHOD	BEST USED FOR	RELATIVE COST	TOOLS REQUIRED
Blowtorch	Large areas, but not under clear finishes as the wood may scorch. Do not use near glass, as there is a danger of cracking it.	Low. Canisters are fairly cheap and small ones last up to 3 hours (large ones 5 hours).	Paraffin or spare gas canisters for large jobs; selection of scrapers and shave hooks. Nozzles.
Heat gun stripper	Large areas, including simple moldings. Use with care near glass. Needs mains power nearby.	Fairly low. Stripper costs slightly more to run than blowtorch.	Scrapers and shave hook according to work in hand. Extension cable for use outdoors. Nozzles.
Liquid and gel stripper	Carved shapes, such as wooden mouldings and banisters. Furniture.	Fairly high, particularly if you have to neutralize it with white spirit afterwards.	Old paintbrush, tough rubber gloves, selection of scrapers and shave hooks, cloth and solvent.
Paste stripper	Small, intricately shaped areas.	High. Leave paste in place for a long time to avoid a second application.	Old knife or spatula, cloth, rubber gloves, scrapers and shave hooks.
Dipping	Large items, eg doors, which do not require a fine finish. Dipping loosens glued joints and can dry out the wood.	Fairly high – there may be transport charges as well if you don't have a large car or van.	Tools to remove and re-fit doors.
Power sander	Large, flat areas, particularly where there is only a thin coat of paint.	Apart from the cost of the power tools, sandpaper will be the main expense.	Plenty of abrasive paper in a range of grades, face mask.
Scraping	Flat areas, convex curves and simple moldings, particularly if the finish is brittle. Also use after heat or chemical stripping.	Economical, but you may find you can only use scrapers in conjunction with other techniques.	Scrapers and shave hooks, Skarsten scraper (with interchangeable blades for mouldings), goggles.
Hand sanding	Rarely used for stripping, but essential for finishing, particularly if the grain has been raised.	Economical. Tougher aluminum oxide paper lasts longer on large areas but costs more.	Sanding block; plenty of sandpaper in a range of grades.

HEAT STRIPPING

The choice is between a gas blow-torch (or new-style gas-heated gun), and an electric heat gun.

■ Protect the area below with plenty of layers of damp newspaper.

■ With a blowtorch it is important to keep moving, to avoid scorching the wood – hot air guns are less likely to cause this problem.

■ As the paint bubbles under the heat, use a scraper to lift it off. Use shaped shave hooks to remove paint from moldings. The amount of heat you need to apply depends on the age and thickness of the paint.

■ Directional nozzles can be fitted to torches and guns to concentrate the heat into awkward areas.

 Fire hazards

Remember that both the shreds of paint and the protective newspaper are flammable. Keep an eye open for over-heated paint dropping on to the paper. Handle blowtorches with care and only point them at the work.

With a blowtorch play the flame over the paintwork, from side to side. Keep the flame moving over the surface as it starts to bubble, to prevent scorching.

Use a stripping knife to scrape away the softened paint, working with the grain. Make sure the shreds do not fall on you – they may still be hot enough to burn.

With an electric heat gun stripper the technique is much the same. Although scorching is less likely, do not hold it on one spot or the gun may overheat.

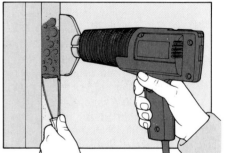

Use a directional nozzle if you have to work near to glass. Turn it round so that it deflects the heat away from the glass to stop it cracking.

CHEMICAL STRIPPING

Chemical strippers are easy to use but must be handled with care. Lay dust sheets in case of spills and cover the area with thick paper to collect the debris.

Types of stripper

First decide whether to use a liquid, gel or paste stripper:

■ Pastes tend to be more efficient, but cost more. Some types must be wrapped to prevent them drying out while they are softening the paint. Several layers of paint should peel away with the wrapping, which saves scraping and damaging the surface.

■ Liquids can only be used where they are unlikely to run off the surface. For vertical surfaces and mouldings, use a gel or paste.

Cleaning solvents

Next check how the surface should be cleaned. Some strippers are water-soluble while others are solvent-based and must be cleaned off with turpentine.

■ Water-soluble strippers are cheaper (you do not need extra solvent) but the water tends to raise the grain of the wood. They are best used for joinery which does not require a fine finish – or where you are intending to bleach the surface, since this process will raise the grain anyway.

■ Solvent-based strippers may need large quantities of turpentine for thorough cleaning, but do not raise the grain of the wood.

■ Water-soluble strippers can be used to strip paint from metal fixtures (but dry iron and steel thoroughly to prevent rust – a hairdryer will help). Solvent-based strippers do not promote rust.

DIP AND STRIP

The easy alternative to painting on a chemical stripper and scraping away the softened finish is to use a commercial dipping service. These are reasonably cheap and effective but there are several limitations:

■ You can only strip movable joinery or items of furniture.

■ The strong chemicals remove the paint easily, but also extract the natural oils, often leaving the wood looking lifeless and dull.

■ The treatment is likely to raise the grain, which then needs sanding smooth.

■ Dipping may also cause glued joints to loosen.

Trade tip

Stripping fixtures

Remove metal fittings and tie together with a piece of string. Dunk in a glass jar of stripper and leave for several minutes. Remove and clean thoroughly.

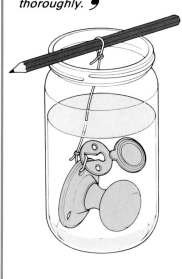

Chemical safety
Be careful how you handle chemical strippers – wear rubber gloves and rinse off splashes immediately. Don't be tempted to decant them into plastic containers while you are working, or you may find the stripper eats through the plastic and leaves you without a bottom to the container.

1 *Apply gel or liquid stripper with an old paintbrush, leaving it for a few minutes to soften the paint. Cover no more than 1sq m (1sq yd) at a time. When the paint bubbles up, use a scraper to lift it off, ensuring surrounding surfaces are well protected.*

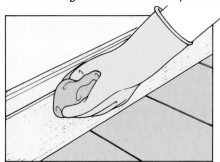

2 *Repeat until all paint has been lifted, then wash down with water or turpentine using a cloth or old paintbrush to neutralize the chemicals.*

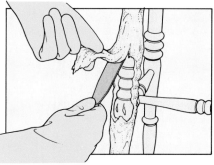

Apply paste stripper with a broad spatula, then wrap if recommended. Leave for several hours before lifting the blanket or scraping off, then neutralize.

SANDING AND SCRAPING

Some sanding or scraping is always needed after using heat or chemicals, and in some circumstances may be enough by itself. The main points to think about are:

■ Always work along the grain.

■ Work in slow stages as it is easy to damage the surface – especially with thin veneer or fine moldings.

■ Wear suitable protective gear – goggles when scraping brittle paint, a face mask when power sanding.

■ When stripping old paintwork, take particular care not to inhale the dust in case it contains lead. Vacuum it up as soon as possible.

Scraping Whatever other method you use it pays to start by using a scraper to remove loose paint or varnish. You may find that as you scrape the flakes, more comes away. Use a flat scraper to finish large areas, shaped ones for moldings.

Sanding With varnish and thin paint a power sander (see below) will strip and finish the surface at the same time, but can only be used on totally smooth, flat surfaces. Most work needs to be finished by hand, with sandpaper or steel wool.

Use a Skarsten scraper along the grain of the wood, with the handle at about 45° to the surface. Shaped blades are available for moldings.

Use a shave hook in a suitable shape for the surface: a combination hook is the most useful, since it has several different profiles.

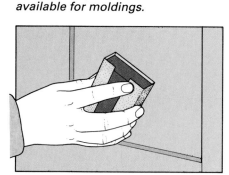

Finish roughened surfaces and smooth away raised grain by hand sanding, particularly in areas where you cannot use a power sander.

Steel wool and water or turpentine can be used to neutralize and smooth in one go. This is good for moldings, where it is impossible to sand evenly.

■ PROBLEM SOLVER

Difficult surfaces

Some surfaces may be damaged by attempting to strip them in the same way as wood:

Aluminum (eg window frames) may react with chemical stripper, so be careful when stripping wooden subframes round metal windows.

Cast iron fireplaces and **steel window frames** are difficult to strip with a blowtorch or hot air blower, since the metal conducts the heat away before the paint has softened. Chemical strippers should be used.

Marble fire surrounds which have been painted over may be indistinguishable from wood. They cannot easily be heat-stripped and although chemicals work well, they destroy the surface polish – plan to have the marble professionally refinished.

Plastics cannot be stripped with either heat or chemicals, which will damage them. Some types of paints chemically combine with plastics so that they are impossible to strip. If the paint is flaking, you can peel it off, but well bonded paint must be painted over.

POWER SANDERS

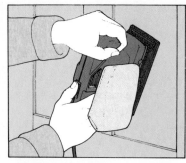

Orbital sanders have a large, flat surface, which moves in a circular, polishing motion – good for fine work. Most have a dust bag.

Disc sanders can be fitted to power drills: always hold at a slight angle as shown, and keep the surface moving along the wood to prevent scouring.

Drum sanders which can be attached to power drills have very limited use along edges and convex curves.

Eccentric sanders are like an integral version of the disc sander, designed to avoid the problem of scouring.

INDOOR PAINT FINISHES 1: WALLS AND CEILINGS

Although emulsion is the most popular choice for walls and ceilings, it is also worth thinking about oil-based eggshell, gloss, and specialized paints for problem areas.

Latex paint

All latex paints are water-based, so they dry quickly by evaporation, with little smell. Most contain ingredients to give a tough surface, but they come in a variety of finishes.

Matte latex is non-reflective and good at hiding lumps and hollows.

Semi-gloss has a soft sheen and is slightly less opaque. There are various qualities, generally the glossier the finish, the more resistant to steamy atmospheres. (Confusingly, the word semi-gloss is also used to describe some oil-based paints – see below). Marks wipe off all latex paints, but semi-gloss is easier to clean.

Latex paint is made in different consistencies, which affects how it is applied.

Liquid paint is usually the least expensive and can be applied with brush or roller, but tends to spatter.

Non-drip paint clings in jelly-like lumps but flows smoothly when applied with a brush or roller.

'Solid' ('roller') paint is even thicker and comes in a tray. It is particularly good for ceilings since spattering is kept to a minimum.

Oil-based semi-gloss

Oil-based semi-gloss (sometimes known as eggshell) is based on an oil solvent rather than water. It takes longer to dry and smells more than latex paint, and requires turpentine or brush cleaner for cleaning tools and mopping up.

Eggshell can normally be applied direct to walls and ceilings, and gives a tough, easy-clean surface with a soft sheen. It can also be used on wood and metal, but may need a primer or undercoat first.

Other options

Problem areas and special finishes may mean choosing an alternative type of paint.

Gloss paints used on walls are hardwearing and damp-resistant but tend to show up faults. Available in both liquid and non-drip form, most glosses are oil-based, but there are water-based types too. All are covered on pages 49–50.

Texture paints are thick, water-based coatings which give a textured or patterned surface. They are good at covering faults and cracks but hard to remove if you fancy a change. There are two types: *ready mixed* texture paint is like a thick latex; *powder* texture paint comes in bags for mixing with water.

Masonry paints contain tough reinforcing additives and can be used on exposed brickwork and utility areas such as cellars and outhouses.

Damp-resistant and cellar paints are another choice for problem areas.

Choosing the right sort of paint *depends both on the look you want and on the type of surface you are covering (see overleaf).*

Trade tip

Color limitations

❢ *Latex paint is sold in a wide range of colors in both liquid and non-drip form. But shades which have to be mixed aren't available in non-drip. 'Solid' paints come in a limited range of colors – brilliant white and a few pastel shades.*

Oil or alkyd paint has a comprehensive color range, but special-purpose paints (like cellar paints) are often limited to a few shades.

Texture paints can be tinted by adding pigment or overpainted with a colored topcoat. ❢

WHICH PAINT TO USE WHERE

TYPE OF SURFACE	SUITABLE PAINTS	APPLICATION NOTES
Old paint	Any topcoat should be suitable if the old paint is sound. Major color changes may need extra coats. Oil-based semi-gloss is good at hiding colors.	Clean with detergent. Sand down old gloss so new paint sticks. Clean off distemper and treat the surface with stabilizing primer.
Lining paper/textured papers	Use matte or semi-gloss latex – the latter looks particularly good over lining paper. Only use oil-based semi-gloss if you prime first.	Latex paint is applied direct with no special treatment. Prime with latex or acrylic primer before coating with oil-based semi-gloss.
Bare plaster/absorbent surfaces	Use any type of matte or semi-gloss, but in all cases prime surface first so it won't absorb moisture from paint too rapidly and cause flaking.	If using matte latex, a first coat of three parts paint to one of water will effectively seal the surface. Use general-purpose primer on very absorbent surfaces.
Walls subject to condensation	Use gloss or semi-gloss – the shiny surface resists moisture. Avoid matte latex which lets moisture penetrate the plaster.	Ensure the wall is thoroughly dry and any mold is treated with diluted bleach or mold killer. Protect from condensation until the paint is dry.
New plaster	Use matte latex *only* as this allows the wall to breathe – essential until the plaster is completely dry.	Seal with a first coat of three parts paint to one of water.
Irregular surfaces	Use matte or semi-gloss – shiny finishes tend to show the faults more. Texture paint can be used to conceal cracks and hollows, but is difficult to remove. Consider using ready mixed skim plaster instead.	Fill and sand before painting unless using texture paint. Heavy patches of new filler may need more coats of paint than the rest of the wall.
Plasterboard	Paint with any type of latex or use oil-based semi-gloss.	Seal with thinned latex or primer before using oil-based semi-gloss.
Bare brick	Paint with latex or exterior masonry paint.	Seal with alkali-resisting primer/sealer.
Powdery/loose plaster	Paint with gloss or semi-gloss after sealing the surface.	Seal with alkali-resisting primer/sealer after brushing off debris.
Cellar walls	If dry, use latex or masonry paint. If slightly prone to damp, waterproofing or 'cellar paint' may help – but not if the water penetration is severe.	Brush down any powdery residues and make good any damaged mortar pointing. Apply special waterproofing paints according to the manufacturer's instructions.

PAINT COVERAGE

The figures below are a guide to the amount of paint needed on a sound, normally absorbent surface. The range given allows for variations between makes, surfaces and techniques, but note these points:
- Very absorbent surfaces and heavy textures may need more.
- A major color change may require extra coats.

- Paint tends to go on thicker when it is warm and dry than when it is cold or damp.
- Non-drip paint may cover less but should require fewer coats.

Don't buy too little paint. If you have to buy a second batch, you may find it difficult to get a good color match — especially if the color is non-standard and has to be mixed specially.

Area covered per gallon of paint

Walls/ceiling	50.16 sq m	60 sq yd
Plasterboard	33.44 sq m	40 sq yd
Texture paint	1.5-2.0 sq m	1½-2 sq yd

Your local store or supplier will be able to give you the best information for your particular needs.

DRYING TIME

The figures below give typical times taken for paint to form a skin which is dry to the touch – and if you are applying another coat, a guide to how long it should be left to harden properly. But note that drying times are affected by the weather and conditions in the room being painted. Warm, dry air speeds up drying; cold, wet conditions slow it. Don't try to speed up the drying time artificially, as this may affect the paint's stability.

	Touch dry	Re-coatable
Latex	2 hrs	4 hrs
Oil	4-6 hrs	16 hrs

INDOOR PAINT FINISHES 2: WOODWORK AND HARDWARE

Interior woodwork and hardware present you with a wide range of different surfaces. Most can be painted quite easily, but some need special paints or preparation. The most common general purpose finish is gloss paint, but semi-gloss can be used for a soft sheen.

Gloss paint

This comes in several formulas, each with advantages and disadvantages. For metal, use only oil-based paints.

Liquid gloss is normally oil-based which delays the drying time and gives it a lingering smell. It dries to a tough shine which some say is still the best looking gloss. Brushes and splashes must be washed with turpentine or brush cleaner.

Non-drip gloss doesn't spatter so easily. It usually has a synthetic base such as polyurethane, and with some types brushes and splashes can be cleaned with a strong solution of detergent and warm water. Non-drip normally covers in one coat but tends not to go so far as liquid gloss and some painters find it harder to get a really good finish without marks.

Acrylic gloss paints are water-based. They dry quickly with very little smell and you can apply a second coat the same day. You can also use them on wood which has been washed or rained on without having to wait for it to dry thoroughly (useful if you are painting outdoors as well). Brushes and splashes clean up with water.

Microporous coatings are gloss finishes for outdoor use which flex and allow wood to 'breathe'. They should not be necessary indoors.

Undercoats are formulated to match the gloss they are used with. They are not always needed, but provide a sound base for the topcoat, and help to mask any base colour.

Eggshell

This paint has a soft sheen, and may be described as an oil-based 'satin'. It is used on walls with no undercoat, but an undercoat may be needed on wood and metal.

Enamel paint

Enamels are mainly used for small jobs as they are rather expensive. They have good covering power because they contain large amounts of fine coloring material.

Rust resistant enamel also contains rust preventing agents. Primer and undercoat are not needed, and many enamels are very quick drying. The solvent varies – check the instructions for cleaning brushes and splashes in case you need a special cleaner. Some solvents may react with certain types of old paint and plastics. If in doubt, check compatibility on a concealed area.

Spray paints for household use are normally a type of enamel. Car touch-up cans are also useful, but check compatibility.

Special purpose paints

Radiator and heat resisting enamels – not essential for heating pipes and so on, but may last longer.

Bath and porcelain enamels for repairing or refinishing fittings.

Primers

Primers needed for various surfaces are listed in the table overleaf.

Different surfaces require a variety of paints.

Lead in paints

Paint for children's rooms and toys must be lead-free. Almost all new paint is – the greatest risk is from existing coats of very old paint. But as some paints may still contain lead, don't use any paint unless it says LEAD-FREE on the can.

WHICH PAINT TO USE WHERE

TYPE OF SURFACE	SUITABLE PAINTS	APPLICATION NOTES
Bare softwood/manmade boards	One or two coats of gloss paint or oil-based semi-gloss after preparation.	Fill, sand, seal knots with knotting. Apply primer, then undercoat, or use a primer/undercoat.
Bare hardwood	Most hardwood looks good varnished rather than painted. If you do choose paint, treat as softwood.	Oily woods like teak may affect the paint's ability to bond. Wipe with turpentine to remove the oil.
Sound old paint	Apply one or two coats of gloss or oil-semi-gloss. Enamel is an option on small items but check compatibility with existing paint.	Wash with detergent or rub down lightly so paint can grip the surface. Use undercoat if changing color radically.
Unsound old paint on wood	One or two coats of gloss or oil-based semi-gloss. Use fine surface filler and undercoat if surface is patchy after preparation.	If mainly sound, sand patches and treat as bare wood. If not, strip and repaint. Use aluminum primer if wood is charred by heat stripping.
Varnished/stained wood	Use gloss paint or oil-based semi-gloss after preparation.	Strip thoroughly with varnish remover. Treat as bare wood.
Aluminum/alloys (eg door hardware/windows)	Paint is unnecessary. Use gloss, or enamel without primer. Rust resistant enamel may be unsuitable.	Rub down lightly with fine steel wool and turpentine. Prime with zinc chromate before applying gloss.
Stainless steel/chrome plate (eg pipes/bathroom fittings)	Paint is unnecessary, but you can use enamel or gloss without primer.	Degrease with turpentine. Do not rub down unless pitted.
Copper and brass (eg pipework)	Paint with gloss, oil-semi-gloss or enamel. No primer/undercoat needed.	Rub down lightly with fine steel wool and turpentine. Wipe clean and dry.
Sound cast iron/steel	Use gloss, eggshell or enamel. Rust resistant enamel is an option in areas where it may get damp.	Degrease with turpentine, wash and dry. Prime at once with zinc phosphate primer.
Rusty cast iron/steel	Use rust resistant enamel without primer. Otherwise use gloss, oil-semi-gloss or enamel after priming.	Remove rust and fill with epoxy putty. Treat at once with zinc phosphate primer.
Galvanized steel (eg older metal window frames)	Use gloss or oil-semi-gloss after priming. Some enamels are unsuitable.	DON'T sand unless rusty. Wash and prime with calcium plumbate (LEAD).
Plastics	Rigid plastic: use enamel or gloss direct – check compatibility. Flexible plastic: don't paint.	Degrease with turpentine. Sand down lightly with wet and dry paper or steel wool to key the surface.
Baths/basins	Use bath enamel/repair paint or have resurfaced professionally.	Rub down with wet and dry paper. May need special undercoat.
Children's furniture/toys	Enamel or gloss – MUST be lead-free. If in doubt, don't use it.	Strip any old paint (especially primer) that might contain lead.
Radiators and hot pipes	Gloss, eggshell, radiator enamel or heat resisting enamel.	Rub down lightly and degrease with turpentine.

CHOOSING PRIMERS AND SEALERS

With few exceptions, most types of bare surface need special treatment before you can apply a topcoat of paint. In most cases, you use a primer, often followed by a suitable undercoat. On problem surfaces you may also need to apply a sealer before priming.

Primers provide a sound base for the decorative finish, and protect the underlying surface from deterioration due to weathering or chemical attack.

By themselves, most primers only offer a limited amount of weather protection to the surface underneath, so for outside work apply undercoat and topcoat as soon as possible. However, two coats of primer alone provide useful protection for the hidden surfaces of any woodwork (such as a window frame) which is fixed against masonry.

Applying a primer is much like using any other type of paint. A brush is normally the best tool – there is no need to use a top quality one – but on large areas a roller is often quicker. Depending on the type of surface, you may need to vary your painting technique.

Sealers may be needed before applying a primer to masonry or woodwork. They are designed either to bind a weak or loose surface, or to prevent chemicals in the surface from working their way through the paint.

Sealers aren't necessary when painting iron and steel, but you may need to apply a rust remover or neutralizer to prevent corrosion from continuing under the paint surface.

Preparation and application

Smooth surfaces should be clean and dry. Prepare by filling and rubbing down the irregularities. Apply one coat of primer, making sure that the surface is well covered, and allow to dry thoroughly. Then rub down lightly to remove any roughness (caused by the surface absorbing moisture), dust or impurities in the finish.

Uneven surfaces such as pitted metal or rough masonry should be brushed down to remove loose particles, and you may need to treat or seal the surface before priming. The irregularities make it difficult to apply any coating evenly, so if necessary use a combination of brushing and stippling techniques – it's important that the entire surface gets covered. There is no need to rub down the primer.

If you have a large area to do, it could be worth hiring a spray gun, while for small areas – metal in particular – an aerosol may be the simplest option.

Specialized primers (below) are designed to deal with the problems posed by painting a variety of different surfaces.

TYPES OF PRIMER AND SEALER

WOOD PRIMERS/ SEALERS

Acrylic primer water-based general purpose wood primer; dries in about 2 hours. Normally white.

Aluminum wood primer oil-based; dries in 16–24 hours. Silver-gray.

Knotting alcohol-based knot sealer; can be overpainted after 1 hour. Pale brown in color.

Sanding sealer Normally alcohol-based; used on bare wood to seal the pores and fibers prior to sanding, or to stop topcoats from bleeding through.

Wood primer oil-based; dries in about 12 hours. White or pink.

WARNING: Although most versions are non-toxic, a few types contain lead. These are not suitable for children's rooms, toys or furnishings.

MASONRY PRIMERS/ SEALERS

Alkali-resisting primer oil-based; for use under oil-based paints on masonry surfaces containing cement/lime, or which are affected by efflorescence. Dry after 16–24 hours. Normally off-white.

Primer sealer oil-based; used for sealing porous or crumbly surfaces – but add thinners if surface is highly absorbent. Dries in 24 hours. Normally off-white in color.

Stabilizing primer Off-white primer used to bind masonry surfaces which have become powdery. Provides a color base for painting.

Stabilizing solution Clear fluid for binding masonry surfaces which have become powdery. Does not color the surface.

Stain blocker Off-white spray sealer for small stains which may bleed through latex painted finish (not suitable under gloss or oil-based semi-gloss). Dries in 10 minutes.

METAL PRIMERS/ RUST TREATMENTS

Calcium plumbate Use on new, untreated galvanized iron, such as traditional metal window frames. CONTAINS LEAD. Not suitable for children's rooms, toys or furnishings. Dries in 16–24 hours.

Etch primer Specialist coating (care needed in use) with excellent bonding to clean metals; used as preparation under metal primer. Dries in 1–4 hours.

Zinc chromate Suitable for most metals, including aluminum, iron and steel; dries in 1–2 hours. Often yellow in color, but may be tinted dark red. Normally sold in large cans only.

Zinc phosphate Buff or light gray non-toxic primer suitable for most metals including aluminum, iron and steel; dries in 2–3 hours. Normally only available in large cans.

Red oxide primer Used on mild steel; dries in 1–2 hours. Dark red.

Red lead primer Used on iron and steel; has excellent corrosion resistance. CONTAINS LEAD. Not suitable for children's rooms, toys or furnishings. Dries in 24 hours.

Rust converter/neutralizer Chemically combines with rust to form a stable compound (usually a black phosphate), works in 15 minutes.

Rust remover Usually a form of acid which dissolves rust on iron and steel in around 15 minutes.

Rust resisting primer Quick-drying primer with rust inhibitors to prevent corrosion. Normally dark brown or black in color.

GENERAL-PURPOSE PRIMERS

Acrylic primer/undercoat White, water-based coating suitable for woodwork, plasterboard and masonry, but not bare metal. (Nail heads in wood or plasterboard should be spot-treated with metal primer.) Dries in half an hour.

Universal (all-purpose) primer Oil-based coating suitable for most materials including metal – though not necessarily as effective as specialized primers. White or off-white. Dries in about 6 hours.

WHAT TO USE WHERE

TYPE OF SURFACE	PREFERRED TREATMENT	OTHER OPTIONS
WOODWORK		
Softwood/manmade boards	Seal knots with knotting and apply wood primer or primer/undercoat.	Aluminium primer (resinous/charred wood); calcium plumbate (around metal frames).
Hardwood	Aluminum wood primer (thin slightly).	Wood primer or acrylic primer/undercoat.
Hardboard	Do not use wood primer – use thinned latex paint or acrylic primer/undercoat.	Aluminium wood primer.
Before varnishing	Seal with a first coat of thinned varnish.	Sanding sealer.
MASONRY		
Bare plaster/absorbent walls	Before latex, seal with a first coat thinned with one quarter water.	General-purpose primer (on very absorbent surfaces) or acrylic primer/undercoat.
Bare brick	Seal with thinned alkali-resisting primer/sealer.	Stabilizing solution.
Powdery/loose plaster	Brush down and seal with alkali-resisting primer/sealer.	Stabilizing primer. Stabilizing solution.
Crumbling render	Brush down and seal with stabilizing solution.	Stabilizing primer.
METALS		
Aluminium/alloys	Zinc chromate. Do not use rust treatments.	Etch primer, general purpose primer.
Sound cast iron/steel	Degrease and dry. Apply zinc phosphate or red oxide primer.	General purpose primer.
Rusty cast iron/steel	Remove/neutralize rust and fill with epoxy putty. Prime at once with zinc phosphate.	Rust resisting primer.
Galvanized steel	Do NOT sand unless rusted. Wash, then prime with calcium plumbate.	General-purpose primer (allow new galvanized steel to dull first).

CHOOSING PAINTING TOOLS

Choosing the right painting tool can make any decorating job simpler and quicker. It also helps to get a good finish, whatever type of paint you want to apply and whatever surface you are decorating.

Painting walls and ceilings

For large areas, a roller is usually quicker and less tiring to use than a brush, and the paint tends to go on thinner and more evenly. Because of this, using a roller gives a good 10% more coverage in most cases.

The drawbacks are that you may get more spatter when using liquid paint, and some people dislike the 'orange peel' texture which can be left by a roller. Also, you still need a small brush or pad to finish off edges and corners, and cleaning up the sleeve afterwards can waste time, cleaner and paint. On small jobs, it's likely to be less trouble to use a brush.

You can use a roller for any type of paint providing you fit the right sort of sleeve (see overleaf). For textured papers or texture paint, use one with a pile which is long enough to cope with bumps and dips without skipping over the surface.

If you prefer to use a brush, pick one at least 100mm (4″) wide – commonly called a *wall brush*. Most people find this the most comfortable size – larger brushes are heavy when loaded with paint and can be hard on the wrists. Alternatively, you can use a large paint pad. In both cases, you still need a smaller brush or pad for edging. When painting masonry, choose a brush designed for the job – rough walls are hard on brushes.

An option which gives very even coverage and a good finish is to use a spray gun. These can be rented, but may work out very expensive unless you have a large area to do. It also takes a long time to mask the areas you don't want painted.

Painting woodwork and fittings

Use brushes or pads as you prefer. Narrow rollers can also be used for large wood panels. Pads allow a more even coverage than brushes, but can be tricky in corners. They are also harder to clean properly – especially when using oil-based paint – so you may prefer to use the disposable type.

A 50mm (2″) brush for large areas plus a 25mm (1″) one for smaller ones will cope with most

jobs – although you may want another, smaller brush for awkward areas. The equivalent pad sizes are normally around 60×50mm (2½×2″) and 100×50mm (4×2″).

Varnishing

Varnish is best applied with brushes, and you need the same sizes as for paint. But it's a good idea to keep a set of brushes just for varnishing – there is always a risk of discoloring the finish if the bristles are not completely clean.

Painting problem areas

Some areas require special tools.
Edging and glazing bars are easier to paint with an angular brush, or edging, sash or crevice pad. A hand-held paint shield helps guard areas you don't want to paint.
Radiators are hard to paint behind – although you only have to worry about the areas you can see. Either move the radiator from the wall (see page 32), or use a radiator brush or roller.
Pipes and railings are difficult to paint evenly. If you have a lot to do, you can use a special pipe roller or sheepskin paint glove.

paint can

edging pad

roller tray

large paint pad

extension handle

roller

sash pad

small plain pad

wall brush

angular brush

BRUSHES

wall brush

paint can

Paint brushes commonly range in width from 12mm (½″) to 150mm (6″). The most useful widths are 25mm (1″) for windows, 50mm (2″) for large areas of woodwork and 100mm (4″) for walls.

Cheap brushes are best for rough work and things like concrete paint (which is hard to clean off) because they can be thrown away. Where finish is important, medium priced brushes work just as well as expensive ones (which take hours of use before they're 'broken in').

Look for a thick filling of fairly long bristles – tapered evenly at the ends and split to aid the paint flow. Brushes for masonry paint have tougher bristles than those for indoor work. All new brushes lose some bristles; flick backwards and forwards across your fingers to tease them out, and don't use a new brush for topcoats immediately.

You can keep paint in the roller tray: rubbing the paintbrush over the ridges allows you to control the amount of paint on the brush.

ROLLERS

standard roller

roller tray

narrow roller

Standard rollers are usually either 190mm (7″) or 225mm (9″) wide, but larger rollers 305mm (12″) and 460mm (18″) wide are also made. You need a roller tray to fit the roller unless using 'solid' roller paint which comes with its own.

Rollers have a metal or plastic frame with a removable sleeve. The sleeve can be made from foam, synthetic fiber, mohair or sheepskin. The pile varies in length. Sheepskin is expensive but holds the most paint. It must not

be used with gloss. Fiber and mohair are cheaper and can be used with gloss. Foam is cheap but spatters badly and gives a poor finish in most cases.

Narrow rollers about 50mm (2″) wide are for large areas of woodwork.

Ceiling rollers have a long handle and a tray to hold the paint. Ordinary rollers can be used by fitting an extension handle. More expensive types have a telescopic handle; simpler ones have a hollow in the handle into which a broom stick can be jammed.

PAINT PADS

pad tray

large paint pad

small plain pad

Paint pads are made from rectangles of mohair or synthetic pile about 6mm (¼″) thick, backed with foam and clipped into a frame in a metal or plastic handle. There are various sizes ranging from about 60×50mm (2½×2″) to 225×100mm (9×4″). In general, the large ones are for walls, the small ones for awkward areas and woodwork.

For the best results, it's important only to load the pile with paint – if paint clogs the foam and hardens, the pile will not brush the surface evenly. Paint pad 'kits' often include a tray with a built-in roller to make loading easier. Some makes feature clip-on replacement pads, others must be discarded complete if worn or clogged.

SPECIAL PURPOSE PAINTING TOOLS

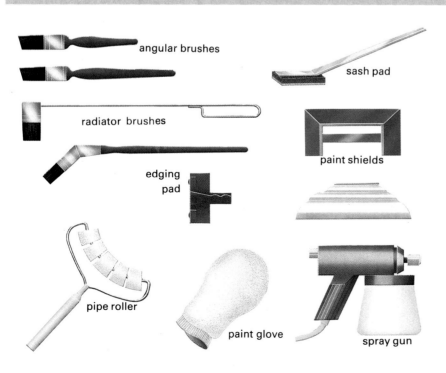

angular brushes

radiator brushes

edging pad

pipe roller

paint glove

sash pad

paint shields

spray gun

Angular brushes have their bristles set to finish at a slant. This makes it easier to run down an edge when painting round windows or where two colors join in a corner.

Edging, sash and crevice pads are for awkward areas and corners. They cover a smaller area than ordinary pads, and edging pads have guide wheels to help them follow a line accurately.

Paint shields are held against a surface you don't want to paint.

Radiator brushes have long handles and an angled head to reach down into the narrow gap behind a radiator.

Pipe rollers or curved rollers are for painting plumbing fittings – they are spring loaded to mold themselves to awkward shapes.

Paint gloves are for very awkward areas like railings.

Sprayers are expensive but can be rented. They make quick work of large areas of paintwork, but you must mask the area thoroughly. Aerosols can be used for small jobs.

PAINTING WALLS AND CEILINGS

Aside from good preparation, there are three rules for achieving a successful finish when painting walls and ceilings.

■ Choose the right tools for the job.

■ Paint in the right order so that you don't smudge previously painted areas, or find yourself having to stop at an inconvenient place.

■ Arrange proper access so that you're always painting from a comfortable position.

Before you start, gather together a supply of newspaper, old rags and plastic garbage bags, plus a cloth for wiping drips. If you're using oil-based gloss or semi-gloss, make sure you have plenty of brush cleaner.

Arranging access

Two stepladders – one about 1.8m (6') high and one about 1.2m (4') – are your most useful pieces of equipment. On ceilings, place a scaffold board between them to create a platform stretching across a comfortable working area. On walls, two of you can use a stepladder each to reach the high spots.

Make sure the top steps are wide enough to take a roller tray. (You can also buy bolt-on roller tray attachments for stepladders.)

Scaffold boards can be rented (ask at the store when you buy paint), but you could consider buying one since they have many other uses.

Position your working platform so that you can paint the walls comfortably between chest and shoulder height. Painting at full stretch is tiring, and makes tools hard to control.

Trade tip
Avoiding mess

❛ ■ Keep paint cans together and make a point of replacing the lids right away.
■ Never leave painting tools, cans or trays on the floor.
■ Discard paint-soaked newspaper and rags immediately into a garbage bag.
■ Keep a damp (or solvent-soaked) rag close by to mop up splashes as soon as they occur.
■ Keep your hands and tools as clean as possible at all times. ❜

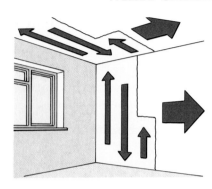

WHAT ORDER TO PAINT IN

■ As a general rule, paint the ceiling first, then the walls. If the room has molding and this is to be the same color as the ceiling, paint it at the same time.

Otherwise, leave it until you've painted the walls.

■ Always start at the window end of a room and paint away from the light; this makes it easier to see where you've just painted. If there is more than one window, choose the largest. On other walls, start on the right if you are right-handed, on the left if you are left-handed.

■ Aim to complete whole walls (or ceilings) in one go – stopping part-way through could leave unsightly drying marks. If there are two of you, work on separate areas and complete them both in the same session.

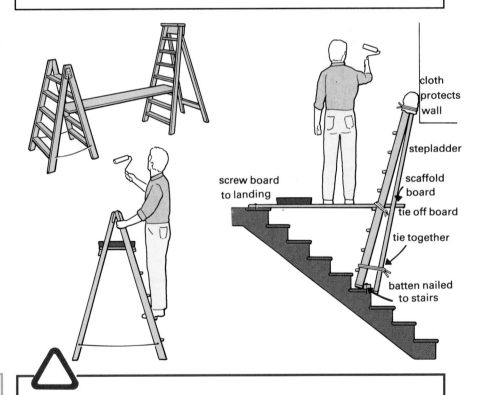

cloth protects wall

stepladder

scaffold board

tie off board

tie together

batten nailed to stairs

screw board to landing

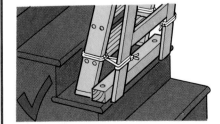

On stairwells you may have to improvise a working platform. For safety, nail a batten to the staircase to hold the larger pair of stepladder legs steady.

Avoid using chairs as supports, as they are rarely strong enough. Strong wooden crates, a portable workbench, or steps laid on their side are good alternatives.

PREPARING THE PAINT

Paint cans can be large and unwieldy. You might consider pouring it off into a smaller can to make it more manageable. Alternatively, you can use a roller tray.

If the paint is old and a skin has formed on the surface, you may be able to 'rescue' it by straining it into the container through a pair of old panty hose. Lift the skin carefully from one side so as not to break it up. However, it's wiser to discard the paint, as partial drying may have changed its consistency.

Unless the tin specifically says otherwise, stir the paint thoroughly using a clean stick.

A smaller can gives you room to dip in a brush without getting paint on the ferrule (the metal part). It's also lighter to carry than a large paint can.

Tie a length of string taut between the handle pivots and use it to scrape off excess paint as you withdraw the brush. You can also use it as a brush rest.

BRUSH TECHNIQUES

Even if you use a roller or paint pad to cover the main area, you still need a brush to fill in around the edges; the ideal size is 50mm (2″).

On a small area, or one containing lots of awkward corners, it's often simpler to use a 75–100mm (3–4″) brush for the whole job.

Some people also find brushes handier for applying resin-based paints, as they are easier to clean than roller and pad equipment.

Always brush away from a wet edge rather than into it so that the paint thins out (called 'feathering'). This stops unsightly lines forming between areas of paint.

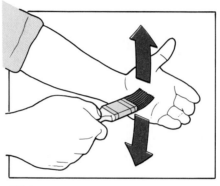

Flick the brush across your hand to 'tease' out any loose bristles. Then load it about a third of the way up to avoid getting paint on the ferrule.

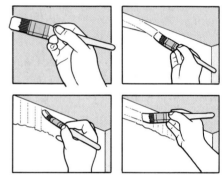

When painting narrow strips, hold the brush between finger and thumb. Cover with loose strokes, draw off at right angles, then smooth with one continuous stroke.

On larger areas, apply the paint in broad vertical bands, gripping the brush as shown. Continue brushing until the bristles show signs of emptying . . .

To paint a clean edge, bend the bristles so that a bead of paint forms. Twist the brush so the bristles thin out and draw the bead along the edge.

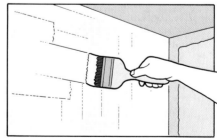

. . . **then, without reloading,** brush across the bands using much gentler stokes to even out the paint. Finish with light vertical strokes to remove the brushmarks.

56

ROLLER PAINTING

Choose your roller according to the surface and type of paint. Use a short pile for smooth surfaces, a long pile if the surface is uneven or textured. Cheap foam rollers are really only suitable for latex, while for gloss or eggshell, a short pile synthetic or mohair roller is the best choice.

When loading a roller, take care not to dip it too far into the tray; roll on the ramp several times to spread the paint and avoid drips.

Trade tip

Which direction?

❝ With latex, it's easiest to work across the wall in bands. Start at the top, working from a platform or stepladder, then remove the platform and do the lower half.

With oil-based paints, it's wiser to work up and down the wall so that drips and roller lines can be rolled out as soon as they occur. ❞

Paint in zig-zag or criss-cross strokes until the roller begins to empty. Then run back across the area with parallel strokes to remove the streaks.

TECHNIQUES FOR CEILINGS

Cover a ceiling in bands about a meter (or yard) wide, working away from the main light source. Keeping the roller just in front of you helps avoid drips.

An extension roller can be used instead of a platform on low ceilings, but is less easy to control. You still need to brush-paint around the edges first.

When brush painting, slip a paper plate or piece of cardboard over the handle to catch drips. Paint small areas at a time, and take care not to overload the brush.

USING PAINT PADS

1 Load the pad from a roller tray or paint pad tray (these have built-in rollers to make loading easier). Try not to get paint on the backing or handle.

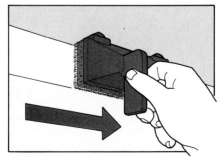

2 Do the edges first, using a small pad or edging pad. Rest the wheels of an edging pad against the wall and run along it in a single continuous stroke.

3 Cover an area of about a square meter (or square yard) working across the surface in short, random strokes. Then go back and sweep over any marks.

CLEANING EQUIPMENT

Even cheap disposable tools must be cleaned thoroughly between sessions: flecks of partly dried paint on bristles and rollers are guaranteed to ruin the finish. With rollers, it's helpful to blot the excess paint in a sheet of newspaper before slipping the sleeve off its frame.

Latex paint can be washed off in the sink using warm water and dishwashing detergent. Work your fingers through the bristles of brushes and the fibers of rollers or pads to shift any paint that's already partly dried. Rinse under cold water until the water runs clear and pat dry between sheets of newspaper.

Water washable semi-glosses and glosses are easier to clean if you work dishwashing detergent into the bristles prior to washing in warm water. Rinse and pat dry.

Oil-based semi-glosses and glosses must be dissolved first using turpentine or brush cleaner. Pour the solvent into a jar and do the brushes first, working the bristles vigorously. Then pour the contents of the jar into a can or paint tray to clean rollers or pads. Afterwards, wash the tools in warm water and dishwashing detergent, rinse in cold water, then pat dry.

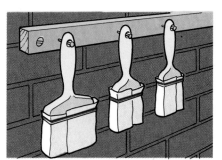

Wrap painting tools in kitchen wrap or plastic bags if you have to take a quick break.

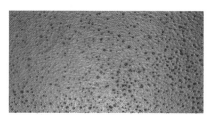

Store brushes with the bristles wrapped in newspaper held on with rubber bands.

Seal rollers in plastic bags – but make sure they're dry first. Store handles separately.

■ PROBLEM SOLVER ■

What went wrong?

With paint faults, prevention is better than cure: most can only be put right by stripping or rubbing down the faulty coat and starting again.

The following precautions will also guard against faults:
- If in doubt about the compatibility of paint surfaces, test on a hidden area first.
- Don't use old paint.
- Make sure previously stored tools are clean and dry.

Staining may be due to contaminated paint, or to substances in the wall becoming 'activated' by solvents in the paint.
To cure: leave to dry, then treat with aerosol stain block or sealer before repainting.

Poor coverage of an underlying color cannot be cured simply by applying the paint more thickly, which leads to drips and runs. Either switch to a 'one coat' topcoat (these contain denser pigments for increased covering power), or apply one thin coat and another when dry.

Blistering is common when painting over lining paper, but most of the bubbles will disappear as the paint dries. Slit any that remain with a trimming knife and slip a little wallpaper repair adhesive behind. Retouch when dry. Blistering of paint surfaces could be due to incompatibility. Cure as for crazing.

Crazing indicates that the topcoat is incompatible with the underlying paint.
To cure: leave to dry, then rub down and apply a coat of primer/sealer.

'Orange peel' is an effect produced by cheap foam rollers. If it's not to your liking, repaint using good quality synthetic pile or lambswool.

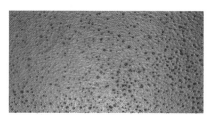

Partially dried runs and drips are easy to miss when painting walls and ceilings. Don't attempt to brush out.
To cure: leave to dry, then rub down and repaint, 'feathering' the edges.

Flaking occurs when the topcoat fails to grip the underlying surface. This could be because the surface hasn't been properly prepared, or (rarely) because the paint itself is faulty.
To cure: rub down when dry and apply a coat of primer/sealer.

Wrinkling is a sign that the underlying paint surface hasn't dried properly. It usually appears within a few minutes.
To cure: stop immediately and wipe off the blistered topcoat with a clean rag. Leave to dry out thoroughly, then rub down and repaint.

PAINTING WOODWORK AND HARDWARE

Assuming you've prepared the surfaces properly, getting a good finish on woodwork and metal is as much about painting in the right order as it is about skill with a brush. The secret is not to rush, and to plan things so that you always work out from an edge which is still wet: brushmarks and ridges are nearly always the result of painting over previously painted areas after these have begun to dry.

Within any one room, aim to paint the movable woodwork – doors and windows – early in the day so that they'll be dry enough to close by nighttime. Paint the rest of the fixtures working from the highest point downwards: this way, any dust that's disturbed will fall on to unpainted areas.

Tools and equipment

Brushes are still the best painting tools for woodwork and metal. Normally, you can get by with just two: a 50mm (2″) brush for flat areas, and a 25mm (1″) brush for moldings and rabbets. For very large areas, a 75mm (3″) brush will do the job quicker but not necessarily better. And a 19–25mm (¾–1″) angular brush is a good buy if you have a lot of windows to paint.

Other requirements will depend on the areas being painted (see overleaf), but may include:
■ Access equipment.
■ A paint can, plus jars for storing and cleaning brushes.

Use masking tape to get a clean edge when painting window frames.

■ Cleaning rags and appropriate solvent for the paint being used.
■ Screwdrivers and other tools for removing door/window hardware.
■ A paint shield and masking tape.
■ Fine and medium sandpapers or steel wool, for rubbing down.

BRUSH TECHNIQUES

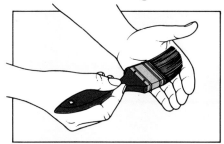

Tease out loose bristles on the flat of your hand. If you spot flecks of old paint, soak in brush restorer or paint stripper and flush clean under cold water.

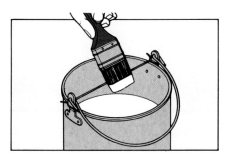

Use a small paint can, and don't dip the bristles more than a third of the way in. Scrape off excess paint – the prime cause of runs – against a piece of string.

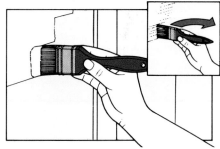

Paint in strips, using long, even strokes running with the grain. Continue until the brush empties, then 'lay off' with reduced pressure and shorter strokes.

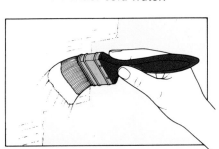

After filling the brush, blend the next strokes with the first by fanning the bristles slightly. Always work to a wet edge, so you don't overpaint partly dried areas.

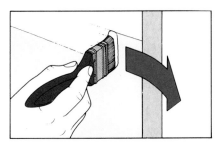

Always paint towards an edge and brush off it, or the paint will 'catch' and run. Where necessary, paint the end grain first using short, dabbing strokes.

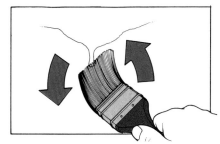

Deal with runs as they appear by working the paint over the surface before it can dry. Where there's a choice, it helps if you start at the top and work down.

PAINTING WINDOWS

Windows must be painted in a strict order (see below), depending on whether they are double-hung or casements. Before you start, remove the stays, catches, locks and any other hardware. If the screws are clogged with old paint, dab on a little paint stripper to clear the slots and then remove the hardware.

Sealing the glass

Carry the paint about 3mm (⅛") on to the panes so that it forms a weather seal between the glass and the frame. There are two ways to ensure you get a clean edge:

Paint the frame direct using an angular brush or a paint shield (see below). Both methods take practice, but are convenient if you are doing a lot of painting.

Mask the frame first using masking tape. This is effective, but costly and time-consuming. Make sure the contact edge of the tape is stuck down throughout its length – not forgetting the 3mm (⅛") for the weather seal – or paint may creep underneath. Remove the tape before the paint dries hard.

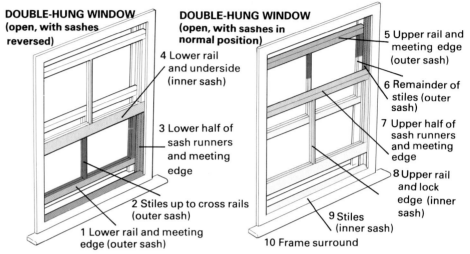

CASEMENT WINDOW
1 Wooden bars and rabbets
4 Meeting stile
3 Hinge stile and edge
5 Frame
2 Upper and lower rails

DOUBLE-HUNG WINDOW (open, with sashes reversed)
4 Lower rail and underside (inner sash)
3 Lower half of sash runners and meeting edge
2 Stiles up to cross rails (outer sash)
1 Lower rail and meeting edge (outer sash)

DOUBLE-HUNG WINDOW (open, with sashes in normal position)
5 Upper rail and meeting edge (outer sash)
6 Remainder of stiles (outer sash)
7 Upper half of sash runners and meeting edge
8 Upper rail and lock edge (inner sash)
9 Stiles (inner sash)
10 Frame surround

Painting order – casement window. Hold the casement open with coathanger wire while you paint it. Drive a small nail into the bottom rail, hook the wire over it, then hook the other end in one of the vacant screw holes in the frame.

Painting order – double-hung window. They must be painted in two sessions, starting with the sashes reversed. Take extra care with the runners – paint them as thinly as you can get away with, and adjust the sashes slightly as soon as the paint is touch-dry to release any stuck areas. After completing the full sequence, touch up any missed areas.

STAIRS, BASEBOARDS AND MOLDINGS

When painting any type of fixed woodwork, the golden rules are:
■ Apply the paint thinly – even if this means you need two coats.
■ Use the right size brushes – a 25mm (1") brush for rabbets, moldings and rounds (ie balusters), and a 50mm (2") brush for the larger areas.

Plan the work so that you aren't rushed and don't have to finish at anything other than a definite edge. Stairs may have to be painted in two sessions: do all the risers and alternate treads in one, then paint the remaining treads in the other.

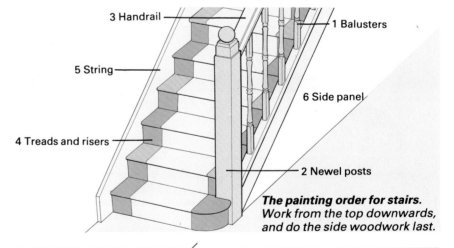

3 Handrail
1 Balusters
5 String
6 Side panel
4 Treads and risers
2 Newel posts

The painting order for stairs. Work from the top downwards, and do the side woodwork last.

Trade tip

Keep it clean

❝ No matter how clean the surfaces are after preparation, dust is bound to settle on them – so wipe everything down again just before you paint it. Some stores sell sticky tack rags precisely for this purpose. Otherwise use a just-damp lint-free cloth – an old linen handkerchief is ideal. ❞

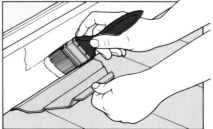

Use a paint shield on baseboards – even where you have rolled back the carpet – otherwise the paint brush will pick up dust from the gap below.

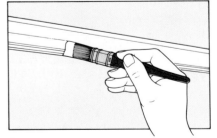

On picture rails and other mouldings, define the edges with a small brush, then switch to a larger brush to cover the remaining area.

PAINTING DOORS AND FRAMES

Like windows, there is a set sequence for painting doors depending on whether they are flush-paneled, glass or full-paneled.

Again, it's advisable to remove as much of the furniture – handles, lock covers, fingerplates – as possible before you start. Wedge the door partway open so that you can get at the edges and avoid being locked in (but keep the handle with you in the room just in case).

As a general rule, on each section work down from the top (so that you catch any drips), and from the center towards the edges. Apply the paint sparingly to avoid runs.

On paneled and glass doors, paint the molding areas in thin coats using a 25mm (1") brush.

Treat a glass door or French window as you would a casement window.

Paint a panel door starting with the panels and mouldings. The door can be left at this point if you need to take a break before completing the rails and stiles.

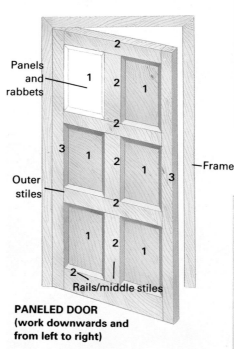

PANELED DOOR
(work downwards and from left to right)

Paint a flush door in one session, working quickly so that the edges stay wet. Keep your strokes long, but light, and don't overbrush.

GLASS DOOR
(work downwards and from left to right)

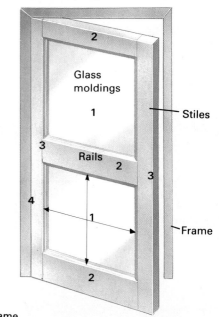

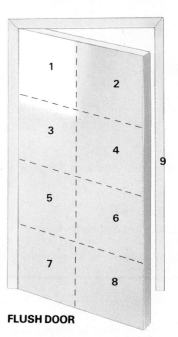

FLUSH DOOR

Trade tip

Painting in two colors

❛ If you are painting a door different colors either side, paint the side on which the door opens first. Then paint the lock edge, the meeting edges of the door stops and the hinge side of the architrave the same colour.

Switch to the second colour and paint the reverse side of the door, followed by the hinge edge, and the architrave up to and including the door stops. ❜

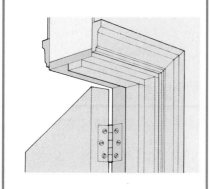

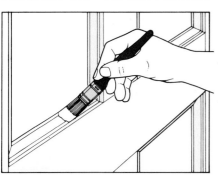

Paint the molded rabbets on a paneled door as if they were separate pieces of wood, using a small brush. This will help to avoid drips on the panels.

Take extra care at the edges: paint with light strokes, angled outwards as shown, so that there is no danger of the paint catching and forming runs.

Trade tip

Undercoat or not?

❛ Think of undercoat as a very thin filler – for disguising pits in the surface, hiding an old color, or building up the 'body' of the paint film so that it looks smooth and hard. Like filler, too, undercoat is made to be sanded before overpainting.

Normally, it's only necessary to undercoat bare wood. But if a painted surface is heavily sanded and patched, undercoat helps draw the patches together. ❜

PAINTING METAL FITTINGS

As long as the surface is properly prepared, there should be no need to apply a layer of undercoat to metal fixtures.

Intricate decorative metalwork is best removed and spray painted.

Radiators should be painted cold, though if you turn them on after about an hour you'll speed the drying process. Work from the center outwards with a 50mm (2″) brush, taking extra care not to catch paint on the sharp edges. Avoid getting paint near the valves.

Pipes should be painted with a 25mm (1″) brush. Apply the paint as thinly as possible, and on vertical sections work down from the top.

Windows must also be painted thinly or they won't fit (the tolerances are closer on metal frames). If the paint build-up is already heavy, it may be better to strip it first using chemical stripper.

When painting, follow the same sequence as for wooden casements.

Using enamel

Painting metal with hard-curing enamel calls for a slightly different technique to gloss or semi-gloss:
- Use the larger of your two brushes wherever possible.
- Apply the paint thinly, using minimal pressure and long, steady strokes.
- Work quickly. On a flat surface, it's easier to pour on the paint straight from the can, then use the brush to spread it evenly.

When using enamel paint, work quickly with long, light strokes and keep the paint coat thin. Use a large brush wherever possible.

1 *Use pieces of cardboard to protect other surfaces when painting around the back of pipes. Apply the paint thinly, to avoid runs.*

2 *Take extra care when painting radiators not to let the paint 'catch' on the sharp edges. Avoid getting paint on the control valves or their connections.*

▌PROBLEM SOLVER

Runs and blemishes

If you discover a run or other blemish after the paint has started to dry, don't attempt to brush it out.

Leave the paint to dry fully, then rub down with fine grade sandpaper and touch in with fresh paint.

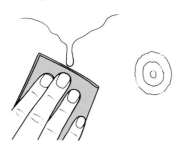

Stuck sashes

If sashes are sticking due to the new paint, you should be able to release them with an old kitchen knife.

Once you've got the sashes moving again, tape a piece of medium grade wet and dry paper over the blade and use this to smooth down the previously stuck edges. Where necessary, touch in any patches that show with a very thin coat of paint.

TOOLS FOR HANGING WALLCOVERINGS

Although most wallpapering tools are quite specialized, you can't really do without them. Measured against the cost of calling in a professional, they are relatively inexpensive, and if you have a full set (see panel) you'll find the job goes a lot more smoothly.

Access equipment

Before considering hand tools, spare a thought for access. A single stepladder should allow you to reach everywhere you need to, but check first. If you are tall, you may find an improvised stool or low folding steps more convenient.

Papering ceilings and stairwells raise special access difficulties. These are discussed in the relevant chapters.

A BASIC TOOLKIT

For measuring and marking:
- Plumbline and chalk

or
- Carpenter's level and straightedge
- Tape measure

For pasting and hanging:
- Pasting table
- Pasting brush
- Plastic buckets (2–3)
- Smoothing brush
- Seam roller

For cutting and trimming:
- Special wallpaper scissors
- Pair of ordinary scissors
- Sharp trimming knife

Wallpapering tools tend to be used one after the other in quick succession, and it's easy to mislay them when the room is covered in trimmings. The answer is to use an apron with a wide front pocket, so that everything stays close to hand.

MARKING AND MEASURING TOOLS

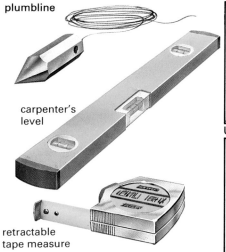

plumbline

carpenter's level

retractable tape measure

Using a plumbline . . .

Using a carpenter's level . . .

A plumbline is the most convenient tool for marking vertical lines on walls (which ensure that drops are hung straight). Consisting of a long, thin cord with a weight attached to the end, you pin it at the top of the wall, rub the cord with chalk, then snap it against the wall to leave a mark once the weight has stopped moving.

Professional plumblines have the weight shaped to a point for accuracy; but for wallpapering, you can easily make your own from a length of thin garden twine and a heavy steel bolt.

Alternatively, use a **carpenter's level and straightedge** and mark the lines in pencil.

A retractable metal tape measure – ideally the 3m (10′) size – is the best tool for measuring long drops.

TOOLS FOR CUTTING AND TRIMMING

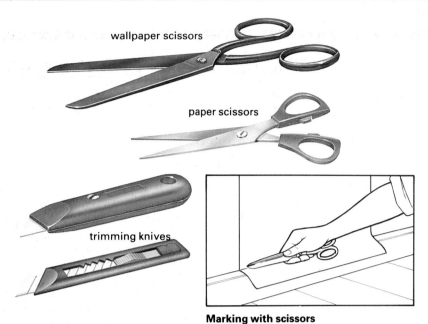

wallpaper scissors

paper scissors

trimming knives

Marking with scissors

Wallpaper scissors (sometimes called *shears*) are absolutely essential, both for cutting drops to size, and for trimming them once they are on the wall. The ideal overall length is 250–300mm (10–12"), which helps give clean, straight cuts.

The backs of wallpaper scissor blades are specially designed for creasing the paper so that you know where to trim. However, in confined spaces and around awkward shapes you may find ordinary **paper scissors** easier to handle. **A sharp trimming knife** should never be used for cutting drops to size, or for trimming – the paste-soaked paper will simply tear. But with vinyl coverings, you'll find one useful for trimming through the overlaps at corners.

There are also a number of cutting gadgets on sale. These may be useful, but if possible you should see how they suit you before buying.

TOOLS FOR PASTING AND HANGING

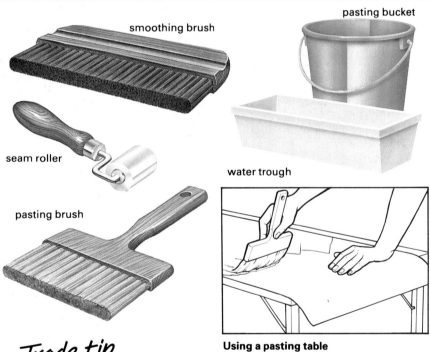

smoothing brush

pasting bucket

seam roller

water trough

pasting brush

Using a pasting table

A pasting table provides the ideal flat surface on which to paste wallpaper, and is a better investment than you might think. (If you're really trying to economize, you could use a flush door or a sheet of manmade board propped on chairs or trestles.)

Specially made pasting tables are made of hardboard with a softwood frame and fold flat for easy storage. Choose one measuring around 2m (6'6") long by about 600mm (2') wide – just wider than a roll of wallpaper. **Plastic buckets** come in handy for mixing paste and cleaning tools. If you have a lot of papering to do, mix the paste in two buckets so that one batch can be left to stand while you use the other. A piece of string tied across the top of the bucket provides an easy way to wipe excess paste off the brush. **Pasting brushes** are available, but an ordinary paintbrush will do just as well – 100mm (4") is the ideal size. **A water trough** is essential for most pre-pasted papers (though with some, you brush water on the drops as if you were pasting). You can buy plastic troughs complete, or a flat-packed cardboard kit which you fold together. **A smoothing brush** is a wide brush with soft, good-quality bristles and no handle, used to smooth out the paper on the wall. You may find a **dry sponge** easier to use with vinyls, and for high quality, hand-printed papers, a special **felt roller** is recommended. **Seam rollers** are for pressing down the joints between drops to ensure the edges don't lift. They are more efficient than using a soft cloth and won't damage the paper.

For most types of paper, use a **wooden seam roller**; for relief wallcoverings, which are easy to crush, use a wide, **foam-covered roller** instead.

Trade tip

The versatile dowel

❛I keep a piece of 12mm (½") diameter wooden dowel, slightly longer than the width of a roll of wallpaper (about 600mm – 2') in with my decorating kit. This has several uses:
- Use it to hold back the rolled end of a drop during pasting.
- Tape it between two chairs and use it to hang drops after pasting and folding.
- When papering a ceiling, use it to hold a concertina-folded drop as you carry it to the ceiling, and to support the drop as you smooth it out. ❜

CHOOSING PAPER AND PASTE

Wallcoverings come in a huge range of designs and materials, which means that for most jobs you'll be spoilt for choice. The various types are described in detail overleaf, but to make choosing easier, start by asking yourself these questions:

When do you plan to start? Some wallcoverings have to be ordered days or weeks in advance; if you want to start hanging straight away, this immediately limits you to designs stocked by the shop.

Is this your first attempt at papering? If it is, you should avoid cheap papers (which tend to stretch), expensive papers (which must be kept free of paste on the right side) and speciality coverings such as flocks and foils (which are difficult to handle).

What is the condition of the wall? Lumps and bumps will show up even more if you choose a very thin wallcovering, or one with a glossy finish or regularly striped pattern. Textured wallcoverings, however, help to disguise uneven walls.

Are the walls irregularly shaped, with awkward obstacles? This makes pattern matching difficult. If possible, choose papers with a random pattern match so that you don't have to spend ages trying to match motifs between lengths.

Are you papering a ceiling? Look out for patterns specially designed for ceilings. These have small or subdued patterns and do not have a 'right way up'.

Is there a lot of direct sunlight on various parts of the room at differ-

ent times of the day? Look out for colorfast papers which won't fade (see symbols box below).

Is the room prone to condensation? Spongy vinyls have a slight insulating effect, helping to reduce condensation. They are also easy to clean, which makes them a good choice for kitchens and bathrooms.

How much wear and tear will the covering have to withstand? In hallways, kitchens and children's rooms, it may be a good idea to use a covering with a wipeable – or even scrubbable – finish (see below).

Clever choice of wallcoverings adds a designer touch to any room.

Strong textures and patterns can also help to disguise marks.

What type of wallcovering are you using? If you are hanging a delicate printed paper you may be advised to put up lining paper first. This involves much more work, so be sure to check the maker's label.

Will you want to redecorate soon? If so, you may want to choose strippable or peelable papers which make redecoration easy.

WALLCOVERING SYMBOLS

Whatever a wallcovering is made of, standardized symbols on the manufacturer's label will give clues to the surface finish and any other special features. These symbols can often be found in wallpaper pattern books as well. The most common symbols are shown on the right, so if you're looking for a specific quality (eg good light fastness) be sure to check before buying.

There may also be special instructions for hanging (and stripping) the wallcovering – either on the label, or in a separate leaflet. Read these before buying any equipment.

～	Wipeable
≈	Washable
≋	Super-washable
▬	Scrubbable
☀ (half)	Moderate light fastness
☀	Good light fastness
Strippable	Strippable
Peelable	Peelable
Pre-pasted	Pre-pasted
Paste-the-wall	Paste-the-wall
→|←	Straight match
→|←	Offset match
50/25 cm	Design repeat Distance offset
Co-ordinated	Co-ordinated fabric available
↑	Direction of hanging
↑↓	Reverse alternate lengths
→|○	Free match

TYPES OF WALLCOVERING

WALLPAPERS

This group covers a wide range of wallcoverings from the cheapest to the most expensive. Different types of paper have their own limitations.

■ Cheaper lightweight papers tend to crease or tear and may stretch.

■ Expensive printed papers are often unwieldy and may be ruined if you get paste on the right side.

Coated papers are wipeable and easy to handle.

Embossed wallpapers have a relief pattern stamped into them. They are recommended for use on bumpy walls, but are easily crushed and may be difficult to stick. (See *Relief wallcoverings* right.)

RELIEF WALLCOVERINGS

This term covers a range of plain white wallcoverings which have a deeply embossed or relief pattern. All help to disguise bumps and other surface defects, and most are designed to be painted.

Woodchip is an economical covering made of wood chippings sandwiched between layers of paper.

Anaglypta is a brand name for a heavy-duty embossed wallpaper, with the pattern stamped on the surface. The range includes copies of original Victorian designs.

Relief vinyls have a deeply embossed pattern and flat paper backing, making them easier to handle.

Blown vinyl relief coverings come in pastel shades as well as white, which don't need painting.

Lincrusta is a top-of-the-range covering made (like linoleum) from oxidized linseed oil and fillers. It comes in rolls or panels, for use below chair rails (dados), in halls and areas receiving heavy wear.

DECORATIVE BORDERS

Decorative borders have become quite common over the last few years. You can use them to contrast or coordinate with a wallcovering, or to decorate a plain painted wall. Some types are pasted like conventional wallpaper; others are pre-pasted for soaking and sticking, or are self-adhesive with a protective, peel-off backing, which makes them easier to stick to vinyls. They are not suitable for use with high relief wallcoverings.

VINYLS

Vinyls divide broadly into *plain* and *textured* types. There are several different methods of manufacture, but look for ones with a *flat back* (paper-backed), as this gives an even, absorbent surface for pasting and makes the covering easy to strip. Many vinyls come pre-pasted; if not, make sure you use a paste containing fungicide.

Plain vinyls may be smooth or have a very slight surface texture. They are easy to hang and are available in a wide range of patterns, often with coordinating fabrics. Some types have a light-reflective finish which gives the wall a soft sheen; not recommended for bumpy surfaces.

Textured vinyls undergo various heat treatments during manufacture to produce a random or regular relief pattern, combined with an embossed color pattern. *Blown vinyl* has a flat back and a puffy texture. *Sculptured vinyl* is a heavier duty version with a deeply textured spongy layer – often imitating wall tiles. It is flat-backed, crush-resistant, and suitable for use on uneven walls.

Textured vinyls are also well suited to condensation-prone rooms, where they provide a waterproof, insulating layer.

SPECIALITY COVERINGS

The wallcoverings in this group are distinguished by their unusual surface, or by the way they're hung.

Polyethylene coverings are available, with a soft feel, almost like felt. They are very light, easy to hang and a good choice for ceilings. You paste the wall, not the covering.

Metal foil coverings have shiny patterns. They are unsuitable for poor surfaces – the shine highlights blemishes. Again, paste the wall.

Paper-backed fabrics include burlap and grasscloth. The thicker types can be unwieldy to hang, and with all types you need to take great care not to get paste on the right side.

Unbacked fabrics are generally expensive and need skill to hang – you have to paste the wall, and use special trimming techniques. They are covered elsewhere.

Flocks have a velvety pile on a paper backing. Vinyl flocks are easier to hang and clean.

WALLPAPER PASTES

Modern wallpaper pastes come in two forms – as a **powder** to mix with cold water, and **ready mixed** in tubs.

Starch-based pastes stay workable the longest and have good adhesion, but they are susceptible to mold growth and are not a good choice where there is damp or condensation.

Cellulose-based pastes give slightly less adhesion, but resist mold growth and are less likely to stain the face of the wallcovering.

PVA-based pastes aren't really pastes but adhesives. They usually come ready mixed in special formulas for hanging speciality coverings such as fabrics.

Some makes use a combination of the above bases. But whatever the base, look for a paste marked **'with fungicide'** if you plan to hang vinyl wallcoverings.

What strength?

Pastes range in strength from 'regular', through 'all purpose', to 'heavy duty'. The labeling varies between brands, so check the instructions or ask your supplier's advice when buying the wallcovering. Generally, the heavier the covering, the stronger the paste, but it's always worth using stronger-than-usual paste on gloss-painted walls and areas subject to heat.

How much?

Coverage for ready-mixed types varies, but should be specified on the tub. With powder types much depends on the absorbency of the covering and the porosity of the wall, but as a rule of thumb 2.5 liters (½ gal) will cover 3-4 rolls.

Other products

Overlap/repair/border adhesive is formulated for sticking paper backing to a vinyl surface. It is usually sold in tubes or tubs.

Sizing is sold in powder form for sealing absorbent surfaces prior to pasting. Unless the surface is very poor, you can make your own sizing by diluting ordinary wallpaper paste to half its normal strength.

Always check the manufacturer's instructions to make sure the paste suits the wallcovering and the surface you are hanging it on.

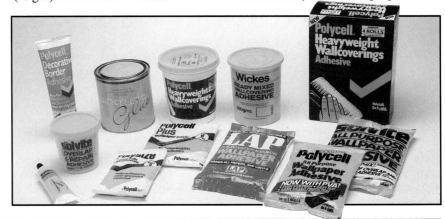

BUYING WALLCOVERINGS

Wallpaper comes in a number of different sized rolls, but the most common is 18in wide and 24ft long. The chart below will help you calculate how much paper you will need to buy to cover the walls as well as the ceiling.

■ Measure the height of the walls.

■ Measure the total distance around the room. Include ordinary doors and windows, but exclude any large areas (eg fitted cupboards) that don't need papering.

■ Read off on the chart the number of rolls needed for the height and distance around the room.

If the room size does not correspond with the sizes given on the chart, or the rolls are a non-standard size, either consult the manufacturer's own coverage chart or use the following method:

■ Measure the height of the wall being papered – the drop length.

■ Where appropriate, round up the drop length to take in an exact number of pattern repeats.

■ Divide the length of the roll by the drop length, to find how many drops you can cut from each roll.

■ Measure around the room to see how many drops you need. Round up to the nearest whole number.

■ Divide the total number of drops by the number of drops per roll, to give the total number of rolls.

Trade tip

Check the color

❝ Although wallpaper colors can vary even within the same batch, there may be quite startling variations between one batch and another.

Avoid the problems this creates by checking that all your rolls are from the same batch – the batch number should be given on the manufacturer's label. It's also worth estimating on the generous side: it's safer to buy a bit extra than go back for more rolls from a different batch. ❞

NUMBER OF ROLLS REQUIRED																	
WALLS																	
Distance around room	32′	36′	40′	44′	48′	52′	56′	60′	62′	66′	70′	76′	80′	84′	86′	90′	92′	96′
Ceiling height																		
8′	8	9	10	11	12	13	14	15	15	16	17	19	20	21	21	22	23	24
9′	9	10	11	12	14	15	16	17	17	18	20	21	22	23	24	25	26	27
CEILINGS																		
Distance around room	32′	36′	40′	44′	48′	52′	56′	60′	62′	66′	70′	76′	80′	84′	86′	90′	92′	96′
	2	3	4	4	5	6	7	8	8	9	10	11	12	13	14	15	16	18

This chart is based on standard wallpaper rolls 24ft long and 18in wide.

HANGING WALLPAPER

Although it's true to say that wallpapering isn't as easy as the professionals make it look, it isn't that difficult either. Much depends on doing things in the right order so that you avoid problems rather than create them. There are also several things you can do to make life easier before you start.

If you're new to wallpapering:
■ Choose a medium sized, regularly shaped room for your first attempt. (More difficult jobs such as papering ceilings and stairwells are covered on pages 77-82.)
■ Choose a vinyl or good-quality medium weight paper that won't stretch during hanging. That way, you are less likely to run into any serious problems on your first attempt at hanging wallpaper.

And even if you consider yourself an 'old hand' at papering:
■ Check the paper manufacturer's label for advice on which paste/adhesive to use and any special preparation or hanging instructions.
■ Make sure you have the essential

tools: pasting table, bucket, pasting brush, plumbline or carpenter's level, papering scissors, tape measure, smoothing brush and seam roller.

Preparing the walls

As with all decorating, there is no substitute for proper preparation.
■ Existing wallcoverings must be stripped, and the wall cleaned down and made good. How much time you spend on this depends on the thickness of the new covering, but generally the more the better – even thick, heavy duty lining papers show up bumps and hollows.
■ If the old covering is a 'peelable' vinyl on a paper backing, check that the back is firmly stuck – if not, strip it.
■ Rub down gloss-painted walls with coarse sandpaper or steel wool to help the paste grip.

Lining paper may be recommended by the paper manufacturer. If not, the choice is yours – lining is more work, but gives superior results. It also makes the wallcovering easier

to hang, which cuts down the risk of blemishes. **Sealing** ('sizing') is essential if the wall is bare plaster, advisable in other cases. Otherwise, the paste soaks too quickly into the wall and the paper bubbles or peels.
■ On old, very porous plaster it's best to use a specially made wallpaper sizing unless you've already sealed the surface with stabilizer.
■ On painted walls, use your chosen wallpaper paste diluted with around three to four parts water.
■ On new plaster, you should delay hanging any wallcoverings until the surface has dried out – which could take up to six months. In the meantime, give the plaster a coat of latex matte thinned with four parts paint to one part water: this will make it easier to live with, and provide a good surface for pasting at a later date.

Fixtures

Anything fixed to the walls with anchors is best removed – the clearer the walls, the easier it is to paper them. Mark the positions of the anchors with matchsticks, then let these poke through the paper as you hang it to mark the holes.

Electrical fixtures don't need to be removed – normally, you can loosen them and paper behind, but turn off the main supply first.

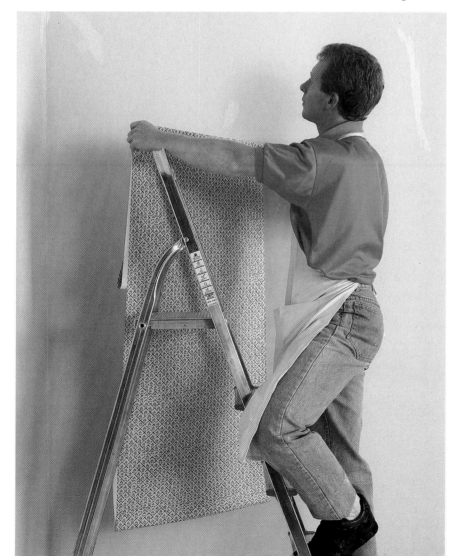

Trade tip

Hide the seam

❛ If there is an uneven line between the wall and ceiling, and you're hanging a covering which contrasts strongly with the color of the ceiling, it's worth putting up a cornice or coving to give yourself a clean line to paper up to. Fill any gaps and paint before starting to paper. ❜

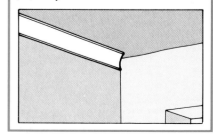

***Easy does it** – hanging the critical first drop (left).*

GETTING STARTED

Before you start cutting or pasting, establish the following points.

Color consistency Unwrap the rolls and check the color under both daylight and artificial light. If there is any variation, plan to keep identically colored rolls together on the same wall – any changes will be less noticeable if they occur at corners.

How the pattern works If the wallpaper has any sort of pattern, make sure you know where to cut and hang it so that it matches between drops. The panel on the right shows the four most common variations; there should also be advice on pattern matching on the manufacturer's label.

Where to start If the paper is plain, or there is no strong motif in the pattern, start somewhere which doesn't call for an exact pattern match (your starting point will also be your finishing point).

Bold patterns look better centered on the most prominent wall in the room (usually the chimney breast or wall opposite the door).

Finally, check that your chosen starting point doesn't leave any awkward, narrow drops.

PLUMBING A LINE

When you've decided roughly where to start, mark exactly where to hang the first drop. Don't rely on anything in the room being true; draw a vertical line with a plumbline or carpenter's level to make sure the paper will be straight.

If you start at a corner (or against a window or closet), mark the line 500mm (20″) away from it. This allows you to hang a full-width drop to one side of the line, then hang and trim the corner drop (which has to be trimmed at the side as well as top and bottom). Work around the room and back to the starting point.

If you start on a prominent wall, find the midpoint, then draw the line exactly half a roll's width from here. Hang the central drop first, against this line, then work around the room from *both* sides towards the least conspicuous corner (often the one nearest the door).

Usually, it's best to start close to a corner, built-in closet or full-length window. But if the pattern is bold, center the first drop on the most prominent wall.

MATCHING THE PATTERN

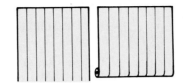

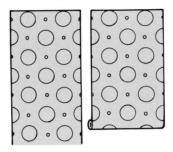

A continuous pattern *won't need matching – you can cut the drops wherever you like.*

With some random patterns, *drops have to be hung in alternate directions so that any repeat in the pattern isn't obvious. This should be specified on the label.*

A straight match pattern *has the same part of the pattern running down each side of the paper. When cutting, simply make sure there is enough overlap top and bottom to align the motifs exactly.*

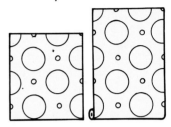

A drop match pattern *has the motifs staggered between drops, which means allowing extra when cutting. The amount of stagger should be specified on the label. If it is large, you may be able to save on paper by cutting alternate drops from different rolls.*

1 *Draw a vertical line to mark your starting point – ie where to hang the first drop. To use a plumbline, pin it against the top of the wall and rub with chalk . . .*

2 *. . . then let the line hang vertically, press it against the foot of the wall with one hand, and snap it with the other to leave a chalk impression.*

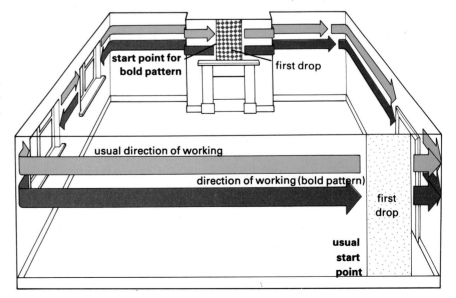

start point for bold pattern

first drop

usual direction of working

direction of working (bold pattern)

first drop

usual start point

CUTTING AND PASTING

For coverings that need pasting, it's up to you whether you cut several drops at a time or cut and paste as you go. If you are working with a partner, it is usually easiest if one person cuts and pastes while the other hangs and trims. And a helper definitely comes in handy when matching and cutting long drops.

Mixing paste

Powder paste usually has to stand for a while before it's ready for use, so mix it before you start measuring and cutting. Follow the instructions carefully (normally you mix the powder to a creamy consistency with a little water, then dilute it) and stir thoroughly.

Pre-pasted paper is soaked a piece at a time to activate the paste. Cut each drop to size, then place the soaking trough directly below where you're going to hang it.

Measuring and cutting

■ On the first drop, measure from the cornice or picture rail to the top edge of the baseboard, and then add 100mm (4″) for trimming top and bottom.

■ On subsequent drops, allow extra for matching the pattern; in other words, check before you cut that the drop has the same number of pattern repeats, plus at least 50mm (2″) trimming allowance top and bottom.

■ Keep any short lengths of wallpaper which are left over to fill in gaps above doors, or above and below windows.

■ Use the edge of the pasting table as a guide when cutting, to make sure you cut straight and at the correct point in the pattern.

■ Always cut before you paste – not when the paper is pasted and folded, as is sometimes recommended when cutting a drop lengthways (this method creases the folds and makes it hard to follow the pattern).

After pasting and folding, be sure to let the paste soak in for the recommended time – if you don't, it will bubble.

1 *Always use long wallpapering scissors for cutting. Use the edges of table to square up the paper, crease along the side edge, then slide along and cut.*

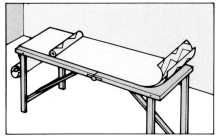

2 *After the first drop, don't forget to allow extra for matching the pattern – plus the usual 100mm (4″) trim allowance – when measuring and cutting.*

PASTING TECHNIQUES

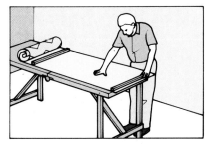

1 *Lay the drop wrong side up with the nearest long edge and the top edge overhanging the table slightly. Leave the rest of the drop loosely rolled.*

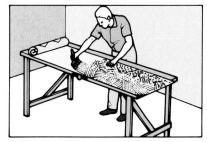

2 *Paste in a criss-cross pattern, from the center towards the overhanging edges. Then slide the paper away from you and paste the far edges.*

3 *Fold the pasted part over on itself and slide it off the table. Paste the rest of the drop in the same way, making sure you don't get paste on the table.*

4 *Having pasted the rest of the drop, fold this part in on itself too. Leave the paste to soak into the drop for the time recommended on the label.*

For pre-pasted paper, *half fill the soaking trough with water. Roll the cut drop loosely from the bottom, right side out, and immerse it in the trough . . .*

. . . ***leave it to soak*** *for the time recommended by the manufacturer. Then simply grasp the drop by the top corners and lift it out on to the wall.*

HANGING AND TRIMMING

Once the paper has been pasted and soaked, the next step is to hang it. Be sure you know which is the top of the paper: with pre-pasted papers, it should be the end which comes out of the trough first; with other types, it will be the end you pasted and folded first.

Always try to hang a complete drop (ie full width, no obstacles) first, so that you get the 'feel' of the paper. And keep a clean, damp cloth ready at hand to wipe the tools you use to smooth down the paper (smoothing brush, seam roller and scissors).

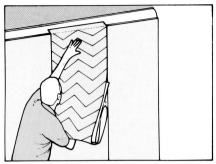

1 Unfold the top half of the first drop and press it gently against the wall, leaving an overlap at the top. Check the pattern starts where you want it.

2 Slide the paper gently to and fro until the side edge aligns exactly with the plumbed line on the wall – but don't forget to maintain the top overlap.

3 Smooth the paper with the brush, working from the middle outwards. With the top half flat, unfold and smooth out the lower half in the same way.

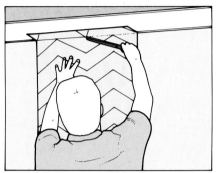

4 To trim top and bottom, gently press the paper into the angle of the ceiling, moulding or skirting with the back of your wallpapering scissors.

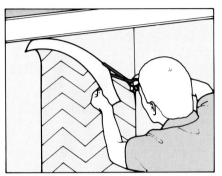

5 Then peel back enough paper to expose the crease that's formed and cut along it with the scissors. Smooth the paper back, then wipe off any excess paste.

Always smooth down the top before unfolding the lower portion of the drop.

6 With the second length pasted, folded and soaked, repeat the process so the next drop butts up to the first length. Check that the pattern matches.

7 After smoothing, marking and trimming the second drop, run the seam roller up and down the length of the seam, to make sure the edges do not lift.

DOORS AND WINDOWS

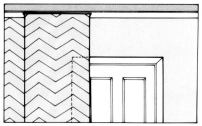

When you come to a door or window align the drop with the previous one and let it flap over the architrave or recess. If there is a lot of waste, hold the paper against the wall and trim off some of the excess so that it doesn't pull away . . .

. . . then cut diagonally into the paper as far as the architrave or recess and smooth down the rest of the flap with the brush. Afterwards, mark and trim along the top and side in the usual way, taking care not to tear the corner.

COPING WITH CORNERS

You can never rely on internal and external corners being square, so the rule is:

■ Cut a drop lengthwise to fit the gap on one side of the corner, plus a little extra.

■ Paste this in position and turn the overlap around the corner.

■ Plumb a new line on the return wall the same distance from the corner as the width of the offcut.

■ Paste the offcut in position to cover the overlap on the first drop.

Using this method, you can be sure that the corner is filled with paper and that the pattern is maintained. The only points to watch are:

■ That the offcut is a reasonable width. If it isn't, use a fresh drop (which, ideally, you should trim lengthwise to hold the pattern).

■ That the corner is reasonably square. If it's badly 'out', you'll need to increase the recommended overlap to take up the variations.

■ That you cut the corner drop accurately. Take your time, and use the edge of the table as a guide.

With vinyl wallcoverings, you may have difficulty getting the overlap to stick – use overlap/repair adhesive to stick the overlap down, or trim away the bulk of it with a sharp knife and metal straight edge.

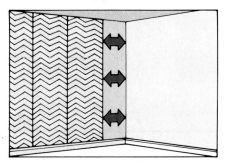

1 At internal corners measure into the corner from the edge of the last drop at several points. Add 25mm (1") to the widest measurement.

2 Cut a measured length to this width, then paste and hang it so that it just overlaps the adjacent wall. If wrinkles appear, clip or notch the edge.

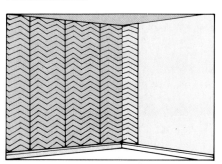

3 Plumb a new vertical the same distance from the corner as the width of the offcut. Hang the offcut so it slightly overlaps the previous strip.

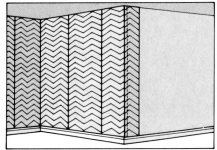

4 Treat external corners in the same way: turn the first part of the drop around the corner, then plumb a new line and hang the offcut to cover the overlap.

When hanging vinyls, you can avoid sticking down the overlap by cutting through both layers of paper, then peeling back and discarding the waste.

PAPERING AWKWARD AREAS

Unfortunately, no room is completely problem-free, and you're likely to have to cope with light switches and radiators as well as larger problems such as arches and window recesses.

SMALL OBSTACLES

Deal with small obstacles such as light switches and radiators as shown below. (Don't use the light switch technique on foil wallcoverings – they conduct electricity, so trim instead.)

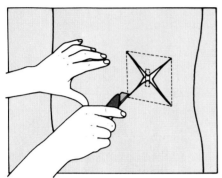

1 **Turn off at the fusebox** before papering around a light switch. Press paper over the edges of the switch so that it creases, and make diagonal cuts to each corner.

To paper behind a radiator, smooth down the drop as far as you can, then make vertical cuts in line with the bracket positions. Smooth the flaps down behind the radiator with any convenient padded tool.

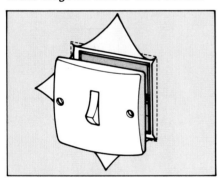

2 **Loosen the switch cover** screws and trim off the flaps of waste paper to leave a 9mm (⅜") margin all round. Smooth down the paper behind the switch cover.

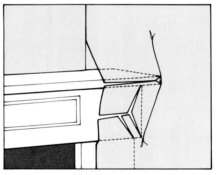

1 **Fireplace and window sills** may have extra angles to cut around. The rule is: clip into the waste part of the paper up to each change in angle . . .

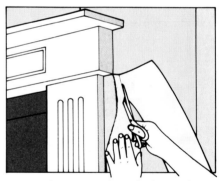

2 . . . then smooth and trim each flap in turn against the obstruction. You may find it easier to use ordinary scissors to make the smaller cuts.

■ PROBLEM SOLVER ■

Creases and wrinkles

These occur when the paper hasn't been smoothed out properly, or because it has been smoothed out working from the outside inwards.

To cure, peel the paper back to the problem area and smooth out again. If the paper has started to dry, apply a little more paste to the wall.

Always double-check that there are no wrinkles – especially along the fold line – before you start trimming the top and bottom edges.

Bubbles

Bubbles indicate that the paper hasn't been sufficiently pasted or that it hasn't soaked for long enough.

If the paper is still wet, lift it away from the wall and smooth it out again – if necessary applying a little extra paste to the wall.

If the paper has partly dried, make a pin-prick in the bubble to release the air and press down. If this doesn't work, make a cross-shaped cut with a sharp trimming knife and squeeze in some repair adhesive.

Bumps

If the wall has been properly prepared, bumps which suddenly appear will be caused by lumps or foreign matter in the paste. Peel back the paper immediately and remove; if necessary, brush a little more paste on the wall.

Blotches

These are simply the result of the paste showing through the paper. They may look awful just after hanging, but should disappear as the paste dries out – which can sometimes take several days.

WINDOW RECESSES

The diagram on the right shows the sequence for papering a recess with reasonably straight sides:

■ Hang a full-length drop at one side (1), overlapping the recess. Cut into the overlap at the soffit and the sill, then try to wrap the paper into the recess.

■ Continue with short drops above the recess, turning them back under the soffit (2,3,4).

■ Hang similar short drops below the sill, maintaining the pattern (5,6,7).

■ Hang a second full-length drop in the same way as the first, aligning it carefully against the last two short drops (8).

■ Fill in the spaces in the corners of the soffit with offcuts, tucking under the surrounding paper (9,10).

■ If the full-length drops aren't wide enough to fit to the back of the recess, hang further narrow width strips (11).

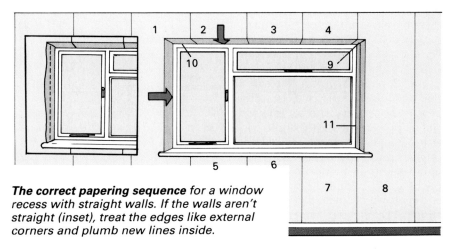

The correct papering sequence for a window recess with straight walls. If the walls aren't straight (inset), treat the edges like external corners and plumb new lines inside.

With uneven walls, treat the edges of the recess as any other external corner – leave a 25mm (1") overlap and plumb a line inside the recess.

Planning the job

To make this sequence work, you must make sure the full-length drops overlap the recess by a sufficient amount, and that you're left with an exact number of widths in between. For this reason, it's probably easier to paper the recess first, before tackling the rest of the room.

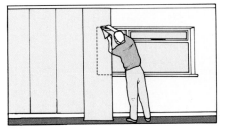

1 Hang the first full-length drop to overlap the recess. Fit at the ceiling, then cut horizontally at the soffit and sill using a sharp blade.

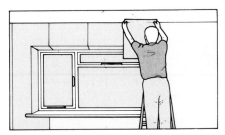

2 Wrap the overlap into the recess and fit the back edge, then fit at the baseboard and sill. Hang short drops above window, wrapping under soffit.

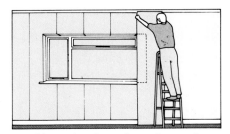

3 Hang the short drops beneath the window, then hang the second full-length drop as in step 1, matching the edge to the short drops as closely as possible.

4 Prepare patches to fill the gaps under the soffit, making them 25mm (1") larger all around with one machined edge matched to adjacent strip. Lift paper around recess, paste patch in position then smooth down.

ARCHES AND ARCHED ALCOVES

On an open archway which is being papered both sides, paper the inside of the arch with the least dominant of the two patterns.

■ Paper the faces of the two walls first, trimming and turning the drops 25mm (1") into the arch; make toothed cuts (called 'clipping') to stop the overlap crinkling.

■ Then paper the inside of the arch with a single long strip, pasted and folded accordion-fashion for easy handling. (If you haven't enough paper left, use two strips with a seam at the crown of the arch.)

In an arched recess paper the face of the wall as above, then plumb a line on the back of the recess. Paper the back of the recess using this line as a guide, taking care to match the pattern both horizontally and vertically with the paper on the face. Trim the paper, wrapping 25mm (1") on to the inside of the arch, and cut notches so it lies flat.

Finally, paper the inside of the arch to cover the overlaps.

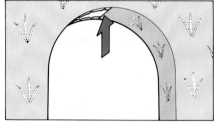

On an open arch, start by papering the walls on either side; trim and turn the overlaps 25mm (1") into the arch, clipping them so that they don't wrinkle. Afterwards, cut a strip of paper to fit the inside and paste in place.

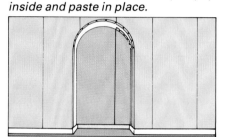

With an arched recess paper the outer wall first. Plumb a line down the back of the recess and paper this, making sure the pattern aligns, then paper the inside.

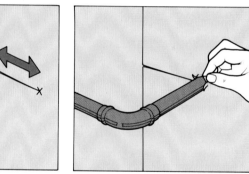

With some patterns it's easier to get a match if you use two strips for the inside of the arch. Arrange for the seam to be at the crown of the arch.

SMALL ROOMS

Lack of working space is one of the main problems in a small room. Set up the pasting table in a nearby room, and use the accordion method (see page 79) for folding the paper so that you can carry it easily. Leave the pasted lengths to soak on a small table outside the room being decorated.

Pipes and shelves may have to be papered around using small patches. Mark any patches directly on to the unpasted roll, leaving a small overlap. Cut and paste them one at a time, to be sure of getting a good pattern match.

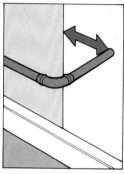

1 *Around pipes, measure the distance from the edge of the paper to the pipe. Cut into the paper and cut a cross at the position of the pipe.*

2 *Then slip the paper round the pipe and smooth down to match the edge of the previous drop. Clip into the paper so it fits around the pipe, then trim.*

▌PROBLEM SOLVER

Disguising seams and overlaps

Making perfect butt seams on a clear, straight wall presents few problems. But when wallpapering awkward areas, you often have to join drops or patches at points other than the manufactured edge of the covering. There are several ways to make such seams less noticeable, depending on the covering:

■ On all types, choose an easily identifiable part of the pattern motif to cut through, so that the match between offcuts is consistent.

■ With heavily textured coverings (such as blown vinyls), overlap the layers with the pattern matching, then cut through both together to make a perfect butt seam.

■ With thin wallcoverings and those which don't tear easily, cut the underlapping layer in a wavy line as this makes the seams less obvious.

■ With good quality papers, coated wallpapers and paper-backed vinyls, tear the underlapping layer to make a 'feathered' join.

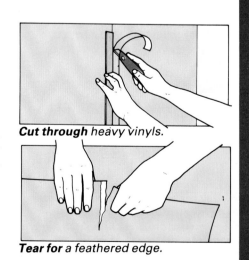

Cut through heavy vinyls.

Tear for a feathered edge.

WALLPAPERING CEILINGS AND STAIRS

Papering a ceiling is not as difficult as you might think, though unless you've got plenty of wallpapering experience it's definitely a job for two people. Compared with walls, there are usually fewer obstructions, and no awkward corners to turn. The only real problem is organizing the equipment to get you up there.

Prepare a ceiling for papering by stripping off old wallcoverings, washing off distemper or chipping off acoustic tiles and glue. If the ceiling was previously decorated with textured paint, either remove it or plaster over it (easier). If it was flat but gloss painted, rub down to provide a good key. Seal or size absorbent surfaces.

Choosing a ceiling paper

If you want a pattern on the ceiling, choose it carefully. Small or random match patterns are easier to align on long strips than large patterns. And in most cases a soft, pale pattern is more appropriate than a bolder one, which could draw the eye to the ceiling and create a slightly oppressive effect.

If the ceiling has a poor finish, choose a textured effect: either a white relief decoration, or a pastel blown vinyl, for example.

Another consideration is the weight of the wallcovering. Remember, the heavier it is, the more your arms are likely to ache at the end of the day.

Special techniques, such as using a broom support, help to make ceiling papering straightforward.

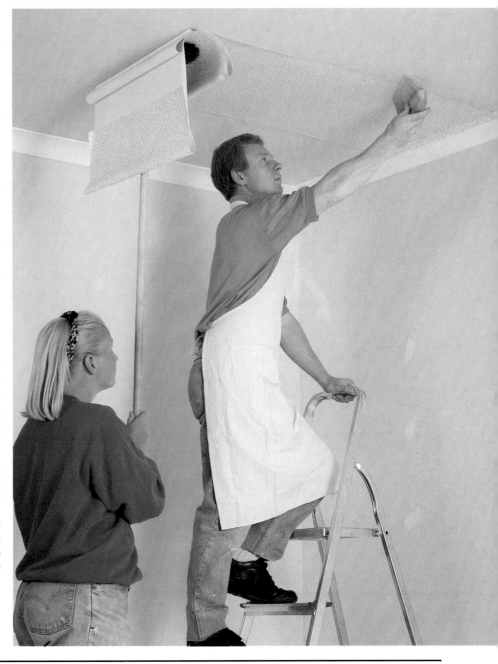

HOW MANY ROLLS?

For standard rolls – 18in wide and 24ft long – and a regularly shaped ceiling area, simply measure the height of the ceiling and the distance around the room and then read off the number of rolls required from the chart on page 68.

If the room is L-shaped, divide it into smaller rectangles. Measure the distance around each of them and read off the rolls required on the chart (page 68). Then add the figures together to find the total number of rolls.

To double check, you should come to the same result by using the method described below for non-standard rolls.

For non-standard rolls, use a calculator to divide the length of a roll by the length of the ceiling area to find how many full strips you can get from each roll. Then divide the width of the area by the width of the roll to find how many strips are needed to cover the area. Finally, divide the total number of strips needed by the number of strips you can get out of one roll, to give the number of rolls. Round up to the nearest whole number.

ACCESS AND SAFETY

The main problem when decorating ceilings is getting yourself to the right level so that you don't have to stretch too far.

The simplest arrangement is to rest a pair of sturdy planks between two stepladders as shown. Scaffold boards, which measure around 38×225mm (1½×9″) are ideal for this – they are available for rent, or you may be able to borrow them from a local supplier.

If you only have one stepladder, support the other ends of the planks on a sturdy pair of kitchen steps, a portable workbench or even a stout table, depending on the height of the ceiling.

In rooms with fairly low ceilings, a pair of sturdy wooden boxes or crates may be just as good. But if you have a whole house to decorate, it may be worth investing in one of the new lightweight aluminum ladders that double as 'hop-ups' and trestles.

Safety points

■ If the boards bow, reduce the span between them or sandwich two together. There's little point in trying to span the entire length of the room: use a soft broom wrapped in a clean cloth to support the paper while you shift the platform from one part to another.
■ Never stretch or try to reach too far to either side of the platform – always get down and move it.

Arrange ladders and scaffold boards so that you can reach the ceiling with the palm of your hand, and your head is just below the level of the ceiling.

Trade tip

Getting up there

❛ As a tall person, I never go on any decorating job without my 'hop-up' – made from glued and nailed offcuts of 12mm (½″) plywood and composition board.

If the ceiling is low I can usually paper it with the 'hop-up' alone, simply by shuffling it along the floor as I go. A shorter person would find the 'hop-up' just as useful for reaching the tops of walls or above built-in closets. ❜

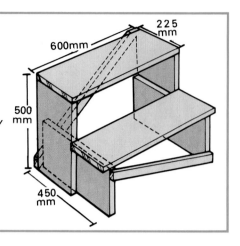

WHERE TO START

When ceilings were papered with overlapping seams, it was usual to start along the main window wall so that the seams didn't catch the light. But if you butt-joint the strips, this no longer applies. Instead, paper across the width of the room – the shorter the strips, the easier they are to hang and the less you have to move the platform.

On an unobstructed ceiling start just under a roll's width from the wall with the fewest obstacles. Hang a full-width strip first, so you can fit and trim the strip along the wall once you have got used to the basic hanging technique.

If there's a large plaster medallion, it's easier to start just beside this and then work outwards.

On a clear ceiling, measure 500mm (20″) out from the wall at each end. Stretch a chalk-covered line between the two points and snap it to give a straight start line.

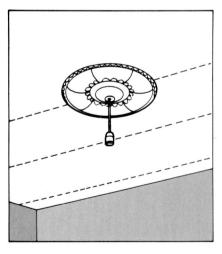

At a ceiling medallion, work out the easiest way for the strips to fall (normally one either side), then measure and mark a starting line accordingly.

CUTTING, PASTING AND HANGING

You measure, cut and paste ceiling strips in the same way as drops for walls, allowing a 50mm (2″) margin for trimming both ends. But gravity, combined with the length of the strips, means you need to fold the strips accordion-fashion before carrying them up to the platform. Don't forget to leave the strips to soak for the recommended time.

You'll find it easiest to set up the platform slightly to one side of the start line. If there are two of you, one person should paste, fold (and if necessary support strips) while the other smooths and trims.

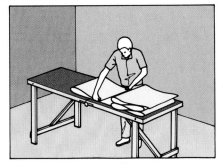

1 After cutting and pasting the first strip, fold accordion-fashion allowing 300–500mm (12–20″) between folds. Fold a further 500mm (20″) at the end.

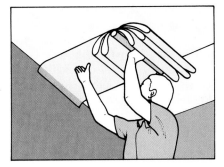

2 Carry the folded strip up to the ceiling, supported on a spare roll or wood dowel. Align with the start line, allow for the overlap, and smooth down.

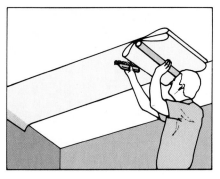

3 Work back down the platform, unfolding and smoothing along the start line. If you need to move the platform, support the remaining folds with a broom.

4 Crease and trim the ends of the first strip, then hang the second. Make sure of a perfect seam as you unfold by smoothing out towards the trimming edge.

5 At a recess – an alcove, for example – make a straight cut down the strip in line with the edge of the corner, then smooth down the flaps and trim.

6 When fitting a strip into a corner, make release cuts by clipping diagonally into the paper. Afterwards, smooth the paper into the corner, then crease and trim in the usual way.

LIGHT FIXTURES

As with a socket or light switch, the neatest way to deal with a light fitting is to paper behind it. Before you do so, **disconnect the power at its main source.** If this leaves you in darkness, remove both lighting circuit fuses (marked '5 amp', or with a white dot), switch the power back on, and then run a side lamp from a nearby power outlet.

When cutting and trimming:
■ Paper up to the ceiling medallion fitting as you mark its position, and press on the wire outlet to indicate the center of the cross.
■ Don't cut the cross back too far: slip the pendant and the medallion gently through it, unscrew or unclip the fixture, then trim back triangular flaps just enough to clear the medallion itself. Finally, refit the cover.

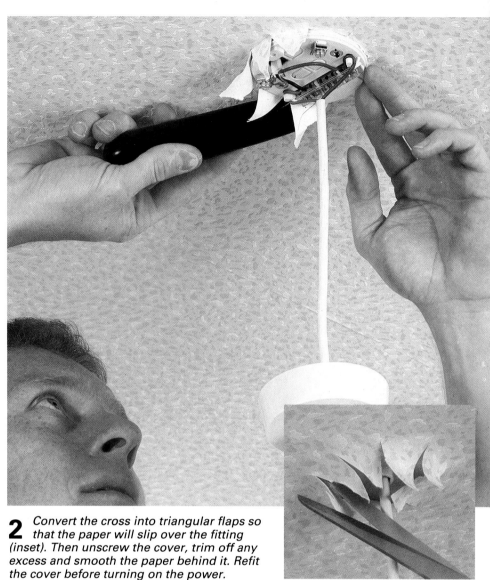

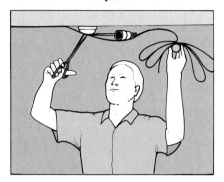

1 When you come to the light fitting, press the strip against it to leave a mark. Cut a cross at this point and slip the lampholder through.

2 Convert the cross into triangular flaps so that the paper will slip over the fitting (inset). Then unscrew the cover, trim off any excess and smooth the paper behind it. Refit the cover before turning on the power.

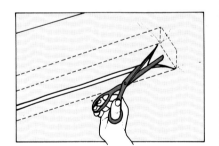

■ PROBLEM SOLVER ▪

Dealing with other obstructions

Decorative plaster medallions may have intricate shaping around the edge, making it difficult to trim the paper neatly.

Start by cutting into the side of the strip and trimming it roughly to shape so that it begins to lie flat. Then make further radial cuts every 25mm (1″) or so into the waste, following the outside edge. Smooth the paper down as you do so, and trim off any remaining excess. (On some styles, there is a lip around the edge which disguises the trimmed ends completely.)

Strip lights, spots and tracks are treated differently according to how they are fixed.

Spot clusters can be papered behind like a pendant light fitting, but with tracks it's usually easier to turn off the power and remove the track altogether prior to papering.

With a fluorescent light tube, or a track that's difficult to remove, make a slit in the paper roughly corresponding to the center of the fixture, then clip out towards the corners. Press the paper down over the light and trim in the normal way to butt up to the fitting.

Slit and clip the paper around a fluorescent fixture or track.

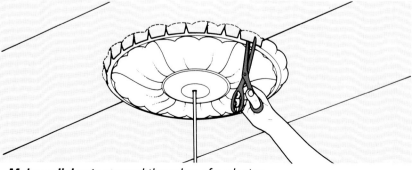

Make radial cuts around the edge of a plaster medallion, then smooth down and trim the excess.

ACCESS FOR STAIRWELLS

There are numerous ways of arranging working platforms on stairwells, depending on the shape of the stairs and what's available.

If you are lucky, the stairs will be straight with a solid head wall above, a few steps from the bottom. But many houses have at least one quarter turn, necessitating a more complex arrangement.

The examples shown here are based around simple ladder/scaffold board set-ups and can be adapted to fit most staircase layouts. However, for a large or double-flight staircase it may be less trouble to rent a scaffold tower (see overleaf).

Whatever the arrangement, check before you start that you can reach everywhere you need to without stretching.

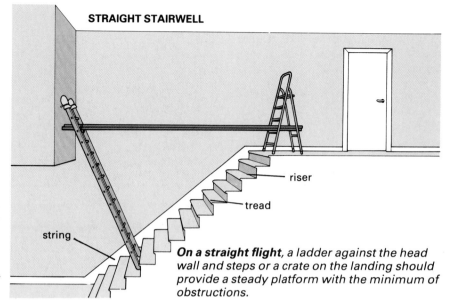

STRAIGHT STAIRWELL

riser

tread

string

On a straight flight, a ladder against the head wall and steps or a crate on the landing should provide a steady platform with the minimum of obstructions.

QUARTER-TURN STAIRCASE

Try to plan the job so that you don't have to lean a ladder support against a newly decorated wall. Where this isn't feasible, wrap the top of the ladder in old cloths to protect the surface.

Avoid resting ladders or scaffold boards on banisters – they are seldom strong enough.

Test other supports for strength before using: a portable workbench and strong crates are all suitable; small tables are suspect. Never use anything mounted on wheels.

Use scaffold boards measuring at least 225×38mm (9×1½"). On spans of more than 1.5m (4½'), sandwich two boards together.

Hold scaffold boards in place by lashing them around nails driven in the ends, or by clamping them with C-clamps.

Stepladders used as supports should be tied securely together. Anchor the foot between strips of wood.

Get your helper to steady the foot of any ladder you are climbing.

Position the foot of a ladder in the angle between a tread and the adjacent riser. Nail a batten to the tread to steady it.

Remove stair carpets if possible. Otherwise, tack cloth dust sheets along the strings and treads, or tape pieces of brown paper to each tread. Don't use plastic sheets.

Trade tip

Steadying influence

❝ If you are using your own scaffold boards, try this tip where they have to cross each other at right angles.

Set the boards up and steady the supports. Then, where boards cross, drill a hole through both and slip in a long bolt, large nail or screw. This braces the boards laterally – the only way they can fall – and helps to strengthen the entire structure. Don't drill rented boards though – use C-clamps instead. ❞

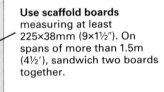

With a deep quarter turn, adapt the basic arrangement to form a cross-over platform. If the quarter landing is wide enough, open out the steps and lash to nails driven into the floorboards. Otherwise, tie the steps together and sandwich the feet between a pair of battens. Pad the top to guard against slipping.

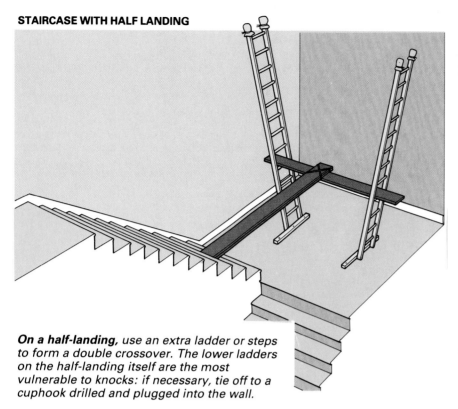

On a half-landing, use an extra ladder or steps to form a double crossover. The lower ladders on the half-landing itself are the most vulnerable to knocks: if necessary, tie off to a cuphook drilled and plugged into the wall.

A rented scaffold tower may be the only way to reach all parts of a large staircase. Miss out one or more metal sections to fit the treads and level with wooden planks.

GETTING STARTED

Prepare the walls in the normal way, stripping off existing wallcoverings and washing down paintwork. Seal bare plaster before hanging a new wallcovering.

If possible, remove stair carpets; if you can't, cover the treads individually with tough brown paper or pieces of dust sheet, taped or pinned in place. Do not use plastic sheeting, which would be dangerously slippery on most stair carpets. And pay particular attention to any protective covering while you are working: bumps and wrinkles are a common cause of accidents.

As a general rule, you should start near the corner of the stairwell which has the longest drop. This will help to keep awkward trimming to a minimum in what is probably the area which is most difficult of all to reach.

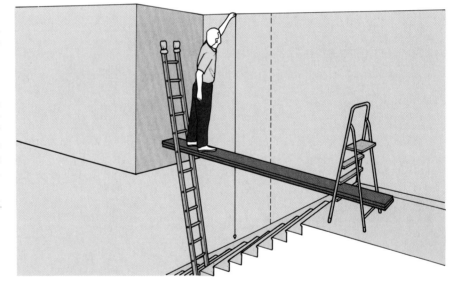

Plumb a line to mark your starting point 500mm (20") from where the floor/ceiling or head wall meets the side wall of the well. Hang the first drop away from the obstruction, to get the feel of the paper.

1 Measure the first drop, allowing for extra for the angle of the strings (baseboards). Cut, then paste generously so the paper doesn't dry out as you work.

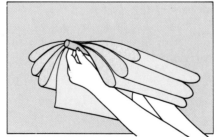

2 Fold the paper accordion-fashion and support it on a spare roll or wooden dowel. Get your helper to hold it while you get up the ladder.

Trade tip

A short soak

❝ When using a wallcovering with a long soaking time on a stairwell, I always reduce the manufacturer's recommended time by five to ten minutes. Soaked paper is more likely to stretch, so by reducing the time, you should avoid some of the problems of matching unevenly stretched drops. ❞

RENOVATING CERAMIC AND QUARRY TILES

Ceramic and quarry tiles are among the most hardwearing of all wall and floor surfaces – but like anything else they may begin to show their age after years of exposure to steam, dirt and accidental knocks. Their most valuable qualities – solidity and permanence – can also be a problem if you don't like the color, or you're in the process of making major alterations to the rest of the room.

Hacking off tiles and starting from scratch is a major job which more often than not involves replastering or rescreeding. Fortunately, there are simpler solutions – whether you just want to give the existing surface a facelift, or blend it subtly into a new decorative scheme.

CLEANING AND RESEALING

Although giving tiles a quick wipe-over is usually enough on a day-to-day basis, they need more vigorous cleaning occasionally to remove grease and stains on the grout.

■ Use a household cleaner recommended for tiles and apply with a nylon (not metal) scouring pad. Rinse afterwards to remove smears, especially on unglazed quarries.

■ Where there is mold on grout, scrub it off with a solution of 1 part bleach to 6 of water. If the grout starts to chip away, however, then renew it (see overleaf).

■ Scrub discolored epoxy grout (eg on countertops) with a nylon scouring pad and bleach.

Resealing

Wherever the tiles meet other surfaces, renewing seals which have become damaged or discolored can work wonders for the appearance of a tiled wall, as well as guarding against dampness.

For the new seal choose from:
Silicone or acrylic sealant, both of which come in a variety of colors. If the seal is to be white, choose acrylic – it doesn't discolor so much. Don't use on gaps over 6mm (¼") as the sealant is likely to sag and look uneven.

Quadrant tiles which are sold in kits containing end and corner pieces. If you can't get an exact match, consider a contrasting colour. Bed in ready-mixed tile adhesive/grout unless the surface is likely to move, in which case use flexible sealant as the adhesive instead.

Sealing strips, which come in both flexible and rigid types in a variety of colours. Many are self-adhesive; if not, use contact adhesive.

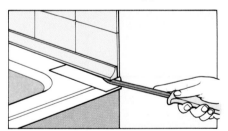

***Prize off** badly fitting quadrant tiles or sealing strip with an old kitchen knife, being careful not to damage the surrounding surfaces. Clean off old adhesive.*

***Old sealant** must be patiently gouged out and scraped off with an old chisel. Afterwards, clean and degrease the surface with a cloth soaked in mineral spirits.*

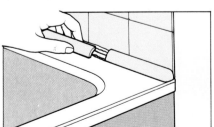

***Bed new quadrant tiles** in tile adhesive or flexible sealant, depending on whether or not there is likely to be movement. Grout between tiles in the normal way.*

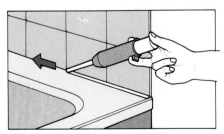

***Apply new sealant** from the tube or in a gun, working away from you. Do each gap in one pass, steadying your arm against the wall so your hand doesn't shake.*

***Flexible sealing strips** are often self-adhesive – unpeel the backing as you stick the strip in place. Miter the corners and fill any gaps with matching sealant.*

RENEWING GROUT

Grout which is simply badly stained or faded can easily be given a complete facelift with paint-on grout coloring.

However, if the grout itself is badly damaged – chipped or flaking away – it's not worth trying to patch it. Instead, rake it out and replace it with new grout. You can buy a special tool for raking out; alternatively use an old wood chisel or a stripping knife.

Afterwards, regrout in the normal way (see page 90). If you're tired of plain white, you can buy powdered grout coloring pigment for adding to the basic mix.

Stained grout which is otherwise sound can simply be painted over with tile grout coloring. Apply with a brush, then wipe away the excess from the tiles with a damp cloth.

Badly chipped or flaking grout must be raked out joint by joint and replaced. You can buy a special tool (above), or use a wood chisel or stripping knife. For a fresh new look, you could consider using powdered grout coloring in the new mix.

REPLACING BROKEN TILES

Cracked and chipped ceramic tiles should be replaced, particularly if they are on a kitchen work surface or back splash. They not only look unsightly, but also harbor germs.

How difficult the job is depends on the thickness of the tiles. Wall tiles normally splinter fairly readily when smashed, allowing the bits to be dug out without disturbing neighboring tiles. On floors and counters, make sure the force of your hammer blows is concentrated on the center of the tile, not the edges. If you don't, there's a possibility that you may crack the surrounding tiles and make matters worse.

Epoxy grout presents a special problem, since it is very hard. The easiest way to release it is by drilling a series of small holes around the edge of the broken tile. Trim off the remains with an old wood chisel once the tile has been removed.

With the old tile out of the way, chip off all traces of the old adhesive. Coat the back of the replacement tile with fresh adhesive and bed in place, applying firm but even pressure and letting any excess squeeze out of the joints. Afterwards, regrout in the normal way.

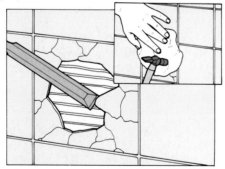

On walls, use a hammer and piece of cloth to smash the broken tile into fragments. Lever out the pieces with an old chisel, starting from the center.

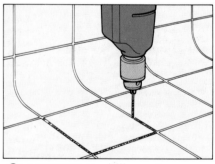

On countertops, drill a series of small holes in the epoxy grout to release it from the broken tile. Afterwards, proceed as for walls.

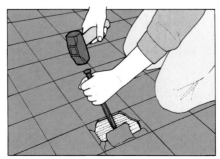

On floors, hack up the broken tile with a hammer and cold chisel, wearing gloves and goggles for protection. Again, work from the center outwards.

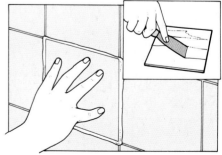

After chipping away the remains of the old adhesive, spread the back of the replacement tile with a generous layer of adhesive and press firmly in place.

FIXING WALL TILES 1: PREPARATION

As any professional will tell you, the secret of successful wall tiling is to plan the job properly. Before you actually buy any tiles, you should be thinking about what sort of surface you'll be tiling on, and how to avoid awkward cuts. If you want to incorporate a design or pattern, it pays to work this out on paper first; mistakes made on the wall can be expensive!

WHAT YOU CAN TILE ON

There are no short cuts to preparing surfaces for tiling: they must be structurally sound, flat, dry, and free of dust and grease – otherwise the tiles won't stay up.

Wallpaper Definitely unsuitable. Strip it and treat the wall as below, depending on what you find.

Paint Start by making sure the wall is flat: remove any bumps on solid walls by bashing them with a hammer, and fill depressions over 3mm (⅛″) deep with general purpose filler. Pull out old wallplugs.

For gloss, rub down any flaky patches back to a sound surface, then rub over the entire area to provide extra grip for the adhesive. Finally, wash down with detergent to remove dust and grease.

For latex matte, it's essential that the paint itself is firmly stuck to the wall (see Tip). Rub down flaky or powdery paint and then seal with tile adhesive primer (available in cans from tile suppliers). Wash down sound paint with detergent.

Plaster Leave new plaster for at least a monthy before tiling. Seal all types of bare plaster with tile adhesive primer.

Plasterboard Fine, providing it is on a proper framework that doesn't allow it to bend. Treat as for paint or plaster, whichever is appropriate.

Old tiles Perfectly suitable so long as they're firmly fixed; remove any that aren't and level with filler. Rub over the surface with coarse silicon carbide paper to 'key' (scratch) the glaze, then wash with ammonia and water. Bear in mind that on old tiles the adhesive will take much longer to dry; you need to leave it at least 72 hours before grouting.

Wood Existing paneling is best removed as you can't guarantee it will remain stable. Hardboard paneling is totally unsuitable. New paneling should be at least 12mm (½″) thick and preferably in either wallboard or an exterior quality grade of ply-wood. Do not use particleboard. It is totally unsuitable and swells when wet.

Panels must be supported every 300mm (12″) so that there is not the slightest chance of them bending. Screw, rather than nail, them to the supporting framework. Paint **all** bare wood with an oil-based primer, preferably a couple of days before tiling, otherwise the adhesive may fail as it dries.

Trade tip

Know the score

❝ Tiles stick perfectly well to latex matte paint, but in my experience the paint itself often stops sticking to the wall – the tile adhesive softens it.

As a precaution against this happening, I always advise people to score the surface criss-cross fashion with the corner of a paint scraper, making the scores about 100mm (4″) apart. This way, the adhesive can penetrate and grip the plaster behind. ❞

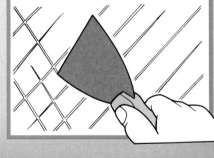

TILE ACCESSORIES

PLASTIC EDGING & SEALING STRIPS

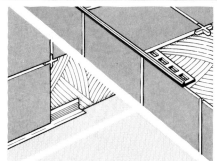

Plastic edging gives a neat finish to corners and edges where the tile edges are unglazed or where you do not have shaped corner tiles for joins.

Sealing strip forms a watertight seal along the joints with countertops, baths and sinks.

Both types are simply bedded in the tile adhesive before fixing the last row of tiles. They are sold in various lengths in a range of colors.

'TRUTILE' TILING GRID

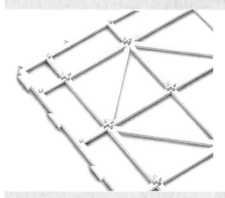

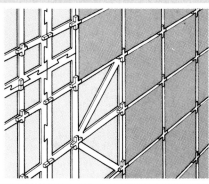

Ingenious system of plastic interlocking grids which are stuck to the wall with tiling adhesive or household glue. Small cross pieces within the grids then allow tiles to be spaced and levelled automatically. Obstructions are easily cut around with scissors or a knife.

Does away with the need for traditional setting out with battens, but can work out expensive on large areas, and only available for certain tile sizes.

FLEXIBLE SEALANT

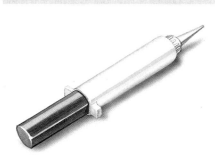

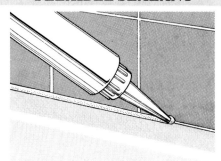

Silicone or acrylic-based sealants used to fill gaps up to 6mm (¼") wide between tiles and counters or plumbing fixtures (sealants slump in wider gaps – use quadrant tiles or sealing strip instead). Also used in place of grout on tiled panels that need to be removed.

Best bought in cartridge form. Several colors are available; white quickly discolors.

WALL TILE ADHESIVE

Most wall tile adhesives are sold ready mixed in a range of different sized litre tubs. The standard type is PVA-based and only semi-water resistant; for walls prone to dampness or condensation (such as showers, bath surrounds) use a water resistant acrylic-based adhesive. Acrylic based adhesives also have better non-slip characteristics and some types can be used to grout the tiles as well; however, they are generally more expensive.

Cement based tile adhesive (more usual for floor tiling), can be used where the unevenness of the surface makes it necessary to apply a bed thickness of more than 3mm (⅛"). It comes in powder form in bags, and is mixed with water in a bucket.

Many tile adhesive ranges include a special surface primer, sold in cans, which reduces the risk of failure.

Your supplier can advise on appropriate quantities for your needs.

WALL TILE GROUT

Standard wall tile grouts come either ready mixed or in powder form. Ready mixed grouts are acrylic based and sold in tubs. Powder grouts are cement based, and come in bags for mixing with water; they are slightly easier to apply.

Both types are reasonably water resistant and can cope quite happily with showers or back splashes. They cannot, however, take prolonged soaking (in a swimming pool, for example), and they are unsuitable for

countertops as they can harbor germs. In such situations, use a two-part epoxy resin grout – sold in a pack consisting of resin and hardener. This is impervious and non-toxic, but more expensive than standard grouts and much harder to apply.

Grouts are now available in a range of colors. Or, you can color powdered grout with pigment additive.

Your supplier can advise on appropriate quantities for your needs.

FIXING WALL TILES 2: BACK SPLASHES

Thanks to modern tools and materials, fixing wall tiles has become one of the most satisfying and rewarding of all decorating jobs. But if you've never done any tiling before – or you have, but it hasn't worked out too well – it's best to start with a small area like a kitchen back splash or bath surround.

After preparing the surface (see page 85), remove obstructions wherever possible. Shaver and power points look better if the tiling fits behind them – isolate the supply and loosen their fixing screws. If necessary, get this done by an electrician before you start.

Tools for the job
The next stage is to get together a set of tiling tools.

Tile cutter For tiles up to around 150×200mm ($6 \times 8''$), buy an inexpensive cutting set consisting of a measuring jig/cutting guide, and a combined cutting wheel/tile snapper; you'll find this easier to use than the old method of scoring and snapping tiles over a pencil.

For larger (and therefore thicker)

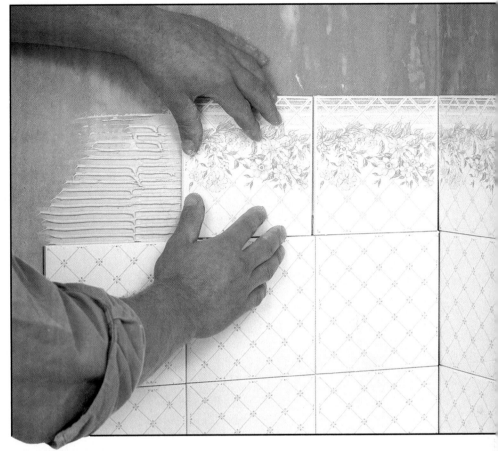

tiles, or if you plan to do any floor tiling, invest in a proper cutting tool; these make light work of even the toughest tiles. Many tile dealers will rent or supply necessary tools.

Tile edge sander An inexpensive tool which smooths the edges of cut tiles and makes all the difference to the finish; the abrasive pads are replaceable.

Adhesive and grout spreaders A notched adhesive spreader is a must: the furrows it creates aid suction, helping the tiles to stick. Sometimes spreaders are supplied with the adhesive, otherwise buy one. Just as important is a rubber bladed grout spreader for spreading and removing excess grout.

Grout joint finisher A cheap plastic tool for rubbing grout joints to a smooth finish. Alternatively, use a piece of 6mm ($\frac{1}{4}''$) wooden dowel (*don't* use your fingers).

A typical set of tiling tools for small-scale jobs: tile cutting guide (A), combined cutter/snapper (B), notched adhesive spreader (C), edge sander (D), four-stage grouting tool (E) and grout spreader (F).

.... Shopping List ....

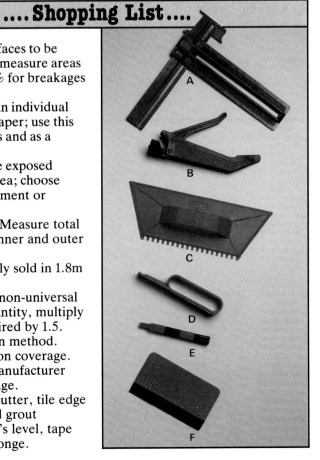

Plain tiles Divide surfaces to be tiled into rectangles, measure areas and combine; add 5% for breakages and waste.

Motif/border tiles Plan individual designs on squared paper; use this to estimate quantities and as a positioning guide.

Edging strip Measure exposed edges around tiled area; choose strip color to complement or contrast with tiling.

Shaped, curved tiles Measure total length required for inner and outer angles.

Sealing strip Normally sold in 1.8m (6') lengths.

Spacers For spacing non-universal tiles; to estimate quantity, multiply number of tiles required by 1.5.

Adhesive Depends on method. Supplier will advise on coverage.

Grout Supplier or manufacturer will advise on coverage.

Tools checklist Tile cutter, tile edge sander, adhesive and grout spreaders, carpenter's level, tape measure, bucket, sponge.

SETTING OUT

For a back splash or bath surround only a few rows high, there's normally no need to bother with traditional supporting laths. However, you *must* have a firm, level surface – such as a countertop or bath edge – to use as a base.

Your aim should be to place the tiles where they look easiest on the eye, and to avoid unsightly cuts. Usually, this means finding the middle of the wall, and then tiling outwards from here so that any gaps at the ends are the same width.

However, narrow gaps look ugly, so you need to decide now whether to start tiling *on* the midpoint, or *to one side* of it. The illustrations on the right show how to do this for three common situations – either by laying out the tiles in a 'dry run', or measuring along the wall in tile widths. (In both cases, don't forget to allow for 2mm (1/16") for the grout if the tiles are square edged.)

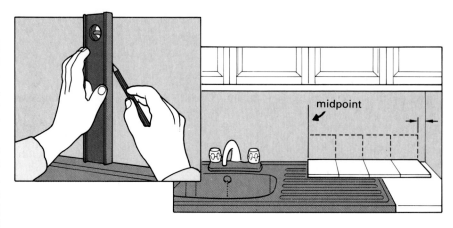

Find the midpoint by measuring the wall, then draw a vertical line using a carpenter's level (above). The line isn't strictly necessary, but it makes it easier to align the tiles when you come to fix them.

Lay out a row of whole tiles in a dry run, starting from one side of the midpoint (above right). If the gap at the end of the wall is too narrow, fix the tiles with the first tile centered over the midpoint instead (right).

FIXING TILES

Spread out the adhesive and fix tiles in 'blocks' of roughly one square metre, working *along* the wall.

If you're using sealing strip at the bottom, or finishing strip at the top, remember to bed this into the adhesive before fixing the adjoining row of tiles (if it won't stay put, tack it in place temporarily with a couple of nails). With sealing strip, you might find you have to apply the adhesive quite thickly to take up the lip at the back.

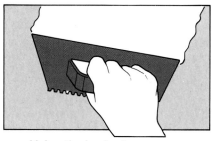

1 Using the back of your spreader, scoop the adhesive out of the tub and press it against the wall to one side of (or on) the midpoint.

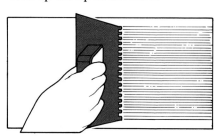

2 Gripping the spreader as shown, spread the adhesive in an even layer 2-3mm (1/16") thick. Apply enough to cover roughly 1 sq m (1 sq yd) of wall.

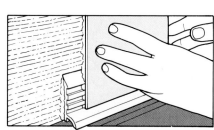

3 If you're using sealing strip, bed this into the adhesive. Then grip the first tile between your fingers and press it gently on to the wall.

4 Having checked the tile sits square to the base or strip, bed spacers into the adhesive top and bottom and position the next tile in the same way.

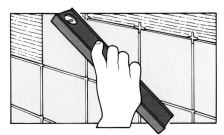

5 Continue spacing and fixing, making sure the tiles engage the spacers. Stop every so often and check with your level that the tiles are sitting flush.

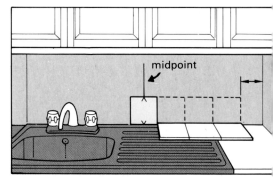

marking the end line

spreading adhesive

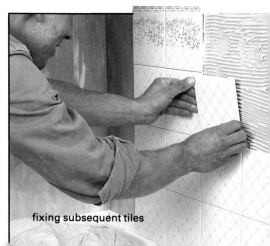

fixing subsequent tiles

For a sink back splash, mark the midpoint as shown on the previous page and then see which layout looks best by marking off in whole tile widths. Don't let the tiles overhang the edge of the sink too far: they won't have sufficient support.

midpoint

Around a bath, plan things so that any cut tiles on the end wall(s) are in the corner, allowing you to finish on whole tiles. (If necessary, let the tiles overhang the bath slightly so the cut tiles aren't too narrow.) Having worked out the layout, draw a vertical line where the whole tiles end to use as a guide when fixing.

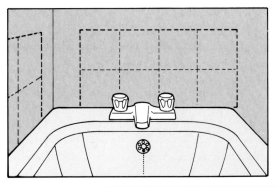

Trade tip

Start level

❛ If you're unlucky, the counter or bath you're tiling above has an upstand or molded edge which makes it impossible to 'sit' the first row of tiles.

In this case, you have to fix up a supporting strip of wood. Nail it to the wall a tile's height above the base, making sure it is level; leave the nail heads protruding, for easy removal.

Tile above the wood in the usual way then, when the tiles have set, remove the strip of wood and fill in the bottom row. ❜

CUTTING TILES

On a back splash or bath surround there should be no need for anything other than straight cuts. Marking and cutting awkward shapes is covered on pages 91-94. Tile cutting guides like the one shown have a built-in marking gauge which you set to the width of the gap prior to cutting. However, this assumes the wall is square – which it often isn't – so double check by measuring the gap top and bottom, allowing for the grout.

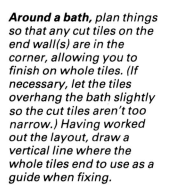

sizing up sealing strips

placing the first tile

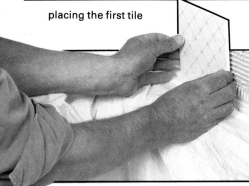

1 Check that the space for a cut tile is square by measuring it top and bottom. If it is, set the guide as shown; if not, transfer the measurements to the tile.

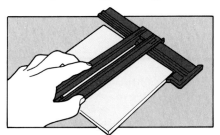

2 For a square cut, simply lay the tile in the guide. For an angled cut, rule a line on the glazed side in felt pen and align it with the slotted cutting guide.

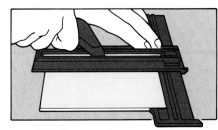

3 Holding the tile and guide steady with one hand, place the cutting tool in the guide and draw it firmly towards you along the slot. Keep the pressure even.

4 To break the tile, hold it as shown and position the snapping jaws of the cutting tool directly over the cutting line; squeeze gently to snap.

5 Without disturbing the adhesive bed, check that the cut piece fits. If it does, support it, then smooth the edge with your tile file.

GROUTING AND FINISHING

Leave the tiles to set for the time recommended by the adhesive manufacturers (normally at least 12 hours) before grouting.

If the grout is in powder form, add it to the specified amount of water in a bucket and mix to a smooth, but fairly stiff, consistency. If it's ready-mixed, stir in the tub and then apply direct to the wall.

Bear in mind that grouting is a messy job, so cover everything else before you start. Time is of the essence, since the grout hardens rapidly and becomes impossible to work into the joints, so make sure you have enough to do the job in one go. And – just as important – don't allow any grout to dry on the surface of the tiles; it's *very* difficult to remove once hard.

When you apply the grout, leave the joint along the adjoining surface clear (or scrape out the grout before it dries). Later, when the grout has set, fill the joint with silicone or acrylic sealant. This provides a flexible seal that won't disturb the tiles if there's any movement.

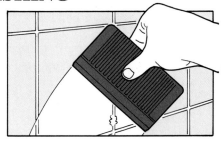

1 Use your adhesive spreader to daub grout over tiles, then quickly work it over the surface and into the joints with the grout spreader.

2 Wipe away the excess with a sponge, washing it out frequently. Take care not to leave any ungrouted 'pin holes' between the joints.

3 When the grout has begun to harden, rub down the joints to smooth them off to an even width. Check for any stray grout still on the tiles.

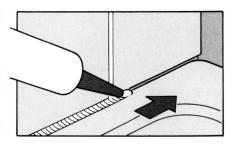

4 Finally, seal any gaps along the adjoining bath edge or countertop with sealant. Remember to push the tube away from you.

PROBLEM SOLVER

Tiles not flush

Check constantly while you are fixing to make sure all the tiles sit flush with one another. If one stands proud of, or below, the surface (and assuming you've prepared the surface properly), the problem is almost certainly that the adhesive bed is uneven at this point.

Remove the tile immediately by prizing it from behind with an old kitchen knife, taking care not to disturb the others. Then scrape off **all** the adhesive from both surfaces, spread a fresh bed, and continue as before.

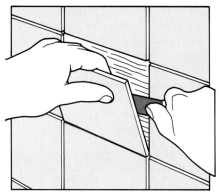

Ease the tile away gently with a kitchen knife to break the suction of the adhesive bed.

Use the kitchen knife to scrape the tile. It's easier to clean down the wall with your spreader.

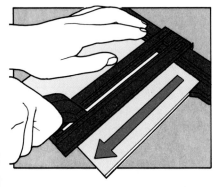

Draw the cutter towards you in a single firm stroke when cutting tiles in a guide.

Cutting problems

If your tiles aren't snapping cleanly when you cut them, it's probably because you are being too hesitant with the cutter. As with glass, you need to score in one firm, even pass so that the cutter's wheel penetrates the glaze to a consistent depth. If you hesitate, press too lightly, or go back over the same line more than once, you'll find yourself left with a jagged edge that no amount of filing or grouting can disguise.

Tiles slumping

If the tiles begin to slump downwards as you build up the rows, it means you've gone too far without arranging proper support. The method shown here relies on starting from a solid, level base and only fixing 4-5 rows in a single session. If you want to fix more, leave the first batch for at least 12 hours before continuing.

Unfortunately, the only cure for slumping is to start again before the adhesive dries.

FIXING WALL TILES 3: LARGE AREAS

Wall-tiling a whole room involves much the same fixing and cutting techniques as those described in the previous section. But this time you are working on a larger scale, which means taking a lot more care over the way you set out the job. Also, unless you're lucky, you'll find yourself having to cut and shape tiles to clear obstructions and awkward corners.

Tools and materials

In addition to the basic tiling tools listed on page 87, you need to make yourself a marking stick (see below). Also, because of the amount of cutting, it's worth renting a professional-style tile cutter.

The best tool for cutting awkward shapes in tiles is a tile saw (if you have a carpenter's coping saw, buy a specially designed blade and use this instead). Sawing is far more efficient than the old 'score and nibble' method, though you must take care to support the tiles properly or they may crack.

If you plan to drill tiles, buy a special spear-shaped bit.

Apart from the usual tiling materials, get in a supply of wood for the support strips – 50×25mm (2×1″) is the ideal size, since it's light and easy to fix.

How the job runs

Setting out is the most crucial stage of tiling a whole room, and the one that many people get wrong.

Normally you'll be tiling to the floor or baseboard, both of which are likely to be too uneven to use as a base. So your first job (shown below) is to draw a horizontal base line which allows every row of tiles to be level.

The next stage is to adjust your base line, depending on what's in the room, to avoid having to make unsightly cuts anywhere between floor and ceiling level.

From here you can judge where to place the setting out strips of wood that support the rows of tiles above and keep them level. Having fixed all the tiles inside the strips of wood, you then remove them and fill in the remaining gaps.

....Shopping List....

Tile materials checklist:
Plain tiles, motif and/or border tiles, shaped, curved tiles (if available for angles), quadrant tiles (for finishing wide gaps), sealing strip (alternative to quadrant tiles), spacers (square-edged tiles only), adhesive and grout.
Other materials:
Wood Buy enough strips to cover the length and height of the walls.
Nails For fixing strips of wood (on a solid wall use masonry nails).
Tool checklist:
Tile cutting equiment, marking stick, tile sander, tile saw, adhesive and grout spreaders, carpenter's level, tape measure, bucket, hammer.

Right: Using a strip of wood to check that the tiles lie flat.

DRAWING A BASE LINE

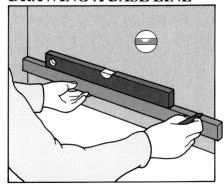

1 Using a wooden strip and carpenter's level, draw a line right around the room just under a tile's width above where the tiles are to finish.

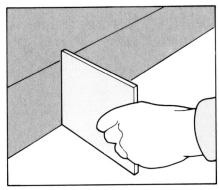

2 Nowhere should the line be more than a tile's width above the finishing point. Check that this is so: if it isn't, draw a new base line lower down.

Trade tip

Make your mark

6 No tiler would be without his marking stick, a tool allowing him to gauge at a glance how many tiles fit between two points. To make one, take a piece of 50 ×25mm (2×1″) wood about 1.5m (4″) long and mark it off in whole tile widths; allow for the group gaps if necessary. 9

SETTING OUT THE ROOM

Setting out allows you to place cut tiles where they'll be least noticeable, and shows where to fix the supporting strips of wood.

Start by using marking stick to measure the tile widths between the base line and any fixtures on the wall. Follow the sequence shown on the right, and mark where the cuts fall. Then adjust the height of the base line to get rid of cuts where you don't want them – for example along a window sill, or the top edge of the bath panel. Try to keep the cuts you *do* have to make even.

When you've done this, redraw the base line right around the room. This shows where to fit the horizontal support battens.

Use the same technique to check from side to side. Mark out each wall so that you avoid cut tiles at external corners and at the sides of windows. Where cuts are required at both ends of a wall, find its midpoint and measure out from here so that both lots are equal.

Finally, mark where the last column of whole tiles finishes on the left hand side of each wall. Plumb lines here, showing where to fix the vertical wooden strips.

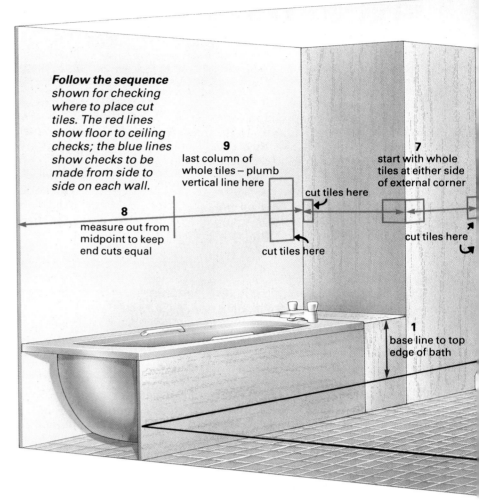

Follow the sequence shown for checking where to place cut tiles. The red lines show floor to ceiling checks; the blue lines show checks to be made from side to side on each wall.

9 last column of whole tiles – plumb vertical line here

7 start with whole tiles at either side of external corner

cut tiles here

cut tiles here

cut tiles here

8 measure out from midpoint to keep end cuts equal

1 base line to top edge of bath

TILING USING WOODEN STRIPS

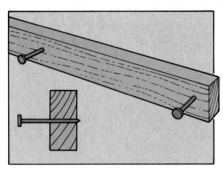

1 *After making your base line (previous page), part-drive nails into the first wooden strip at 300mm (1') intervals; the points should just show through.*

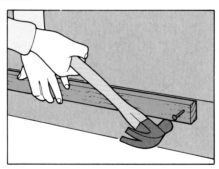

2 *Position the wooden strip level with the base line and drive in the nails until they hold; leave the heads protruding so you can remove the strip later.*

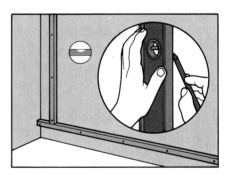

3 *Having evened up the cuts from side to side, draw a vertical line to mark the last column of whole tiles. Fix the side strip of wood against this line.*

4 *Spread about 1 sq m (1 sq yd) of adhesive in the usual way and fix the first tile in the corner of the two strips of wood. Continue, working along the wall.*

5 *After completing the area inside the strips of wood, leave it to set for an hour. Then slide a knife blade along the edges to clear the joints.*

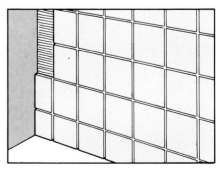

6 *Remove the strips of wood by pulling out the fixing nails with pliers. Measure and cut tiles to fit the gaps, and fix them in place in the usual way.*

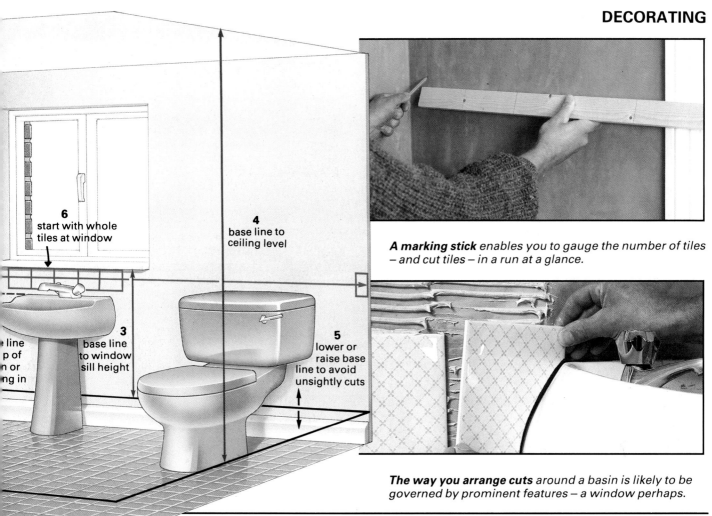

6 start with whole tiles at window

4 base line to ceiling level

3 base line to window sill height

5 lower or raise base line to avoid unsightly cuts

line p of n or ng in

A marking stick enables you to gauge the number of tiles – and cut tiles – in a run at a glance.

The way you arrange cuts around a basin is likely to be governed by prominent features – a window perhaps.

TILING AWKWARD AREAS

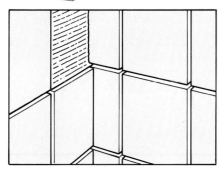

1 At internal corners, you overlap one set of cut edges with another. Work out in advance which way to arrange the overlap so it's least noticeable.

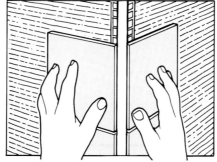

2 External corners can be finished with trim strip. Bed the strip in the adhesive, then simultaneously fix both 'columns' of tiles so you can align them.

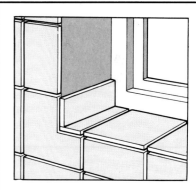

Tile a window recess after the main wall. Arrange for equal size cuts on either side.

3 Alternatively, overlap tiles in the direction that's least noticeable. (Around a bath, tiles on a horizontal surface must overlap those on a vertical one.)

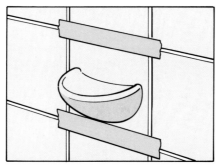

4 Give a heavy insert tile extra support by taping it to the surrounding tiles. Use decorator's masking tape – you'll find it easier to remove later.

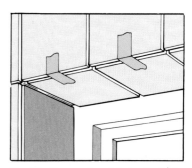

Tackle the underside last of all (the tiles on the wall above should overhang slightly to hide the edges). Tape the tiles for extra support.

Tiling curved areas

Objects like pedestals or waste pipes have large-radius curves that can be difficult to tile around. The answer is to make a pattern for each tile (see Tip), then mark and cut the tiles individually to fit. In most cases, the object will be symmetrical so you can use the patterns twice – once for each side. Do the actual cutting with a tile saw.

When you come to fix the pieces of cut tile, you may find that the adhesive bed has thinned out around the obstruction. Allow for this by adding an extra dab of adhesive, press the tile home, and let the excess squeeze out around the edges. Scrape off immediately.

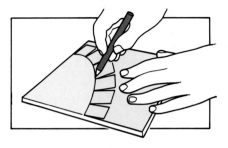

Use a paper pattern to mark the curve on each tile.

Add extra adhesive when you fit the cut piece.

Trade tip

Making a pattern

❛ I find the best way of making patterns is the 'cut and tape' method. Cut some paper into tile size pieces, then cut strips about 12mm (½") wide in the sides. Press the paper 'tiles' against the object so that the strips fan out, describing the line of the curve. Afterwards, stick tape across them to hold the line; tear off the waste. ❜

CUTTING AND SHAPING

A tile saw makes light work of cutting awkward shapes out of tiles, though you need to clamp them securely – use pieces of cloth to protect the surface glaze.

This leaves you with just one problem – marking the tiles to fit. Where possible, use something the same (or nearly the same) size as the object you're tiling around as a pattern (see step 5).

For pipes, don't attempt to cut all the waste out of one tile – it will break. Instead cut the tile level with the center of the pipe, then make equal sized cut-outs in each piece using a pattern.

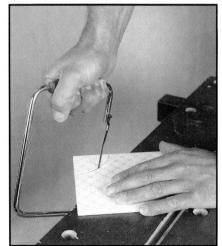

A tile saw cuts awkward shapes quickly and accurately – a lot more efficient than 'nibbling' the tiles with pincers. You may prefer to support a tile as shown.

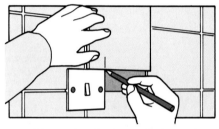

1 To mark a tile for an L shaped cut, start by holding the tile up to one side of the obstruction as shown and mark off against the edge with a felt tip pen.

3 Having clamped the tile securely, cut down each line in turn using your tile saw. Take care not to stray past the corner where the lines join.

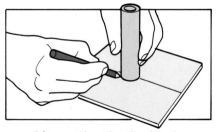

5 After cutting the tile, lay the two pieces together and mark the pipe cut-outs – preferably using a piece of pipe of the same diameter.

2 Now hold the tile against the other side of the obstruction and mark off again. Use your cutting guide to convert the marks into squared cutting lines.

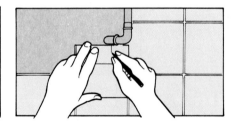

4 Use the same technique around a small pipe. Mark the pipe's position on a tile, then mark the tile for cutting level with the pipe's center line.

6 To drill holes in tiles, use a spade shaped tile bit and switch your drill to a low speed setting. Stick tape over your marks to stop the bit slipping.

LIFTING AND REPAIRING FLOORBOARDS

Floorboards which creak or wobble are both a nuisance and a potential danger. And splinters, bumps or protruding nail heads will shorten the life of any floorcovering laid over the top.

Faults like these can often be put right quite easily using only basic tools, once the offending boards have been exposed. But sometimes during the course of repairs it's necessary to lift and replace boards – a job calling for much more specialized tools and techniques. The same applies if you need to get to the cavity under the floor – for example, to lay pipes or cables.

POSSIBLE FAULTS AND SIMPLE REPAIRS

Nail heads may protrude due to wear or shrinkage of the boards. Hammer level and punch just below the surface. If the boards are to be left exposed, fill the indents with a slightly darker wood filler – it's less noticeable than a light one.

Broken or split boards are dangerous – remove and replace.

Sagging points to problems in the supporting joists. See Problem Solver.

Warped boards can be trimmed to remove high spots using a Surform or power sander. If the warping is bad, it's easier to replace.

Splintering may have developed in an old board. If minor, glue the loose pieces with woodworking adhesive and clamp in position with a weight on a plastic bag to stop it sticking. Otherwise, replace the board.

Loose boards creak at best, and at worst may trip someone up. Punch all existing nails below the surface, then drive in extra nails (cut steel nails or 2″ barbed fasteners) or secure with countersunk screws.

If the creaking persists, try driving a short, thick countersunk screw **between** the boards to jam them together.

Knots are harder and less prone to shrinkage than the wood around them, which often leads to bumps. Level them with a plane or Surform – if you try to sand them, you're likely to remove more of the surrounding wood.

 Watch out for concealed cables or pipes which may be notched into the tops of the joists. They should have been laid in the center of the boards, so always nail about 20mm (¾″) from each side.

Gaps cause drafts. They also look unsightly if left exposed, and can set up ridges in carpet laid over them. Insert wood strips or papier maché (see below) or cover with hardboard before laying carpet.

Trade tip

Stopping squeaks

❝ Squeaking in floorboards is often the result of two boards rubbing together. Where this is the case, lubricate the gap between the boards by putting in talcum powder or powdered graphite and working it down with an old table knife blade – the squeak should soon stop. ❞

Fill large gaps between boards with strips of wood shaped to a slight taper. Coat with glue and hammer into the gap, then plane level after the glue dries.

Fill narrow gaps with papier-maché. Mix up some torn-up newspaper, wallpaper paste and boiling water (you can also add wood stain to match the boards) . . .

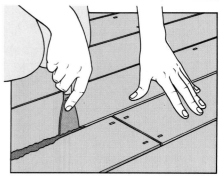

. . . then force the pulp between the boards with a filling knife. Leave the filler slightly proud of the surface, then sand it smooth when hard.

LIFTING INDIVIDUAL BOARDS

Lifting floorboards which have been lifted before isn't generally too difficult: neither end will be trapped, so once you've checked for extra screw fixings you can simply insert a bolster or crowbar into the gaps and lever gently.

Removing a full-length board is a different matter. One or both ends will be trapped under baseboards or partition walls, so before you can lift it you have to saw through it somewhere along its length.

First, check whether the board is square edged or tongued and grooved (T&G): poke a blade between the gaps and see if it slips through easily; if it stops halfway, the board is T&G and you need to saw through the tongues on both sides to release it.

There are two ways of sawing through the board itself:
- Over a joist, using a special curved-bladed floorboard saw or a backsaw.
- Next to a joist, using a saber saw. This is much quicker, but risks harming underfloor cables or pipes. Adjusting the sole plate on the saw to cut at an angle of 30° gives a much neater join. For extra safety, cut over a block of wood as shown below to restrict the blade depth.

For T&G boards, saw a short way down both sides to sever the tongues using a backsaw or floorboard saw. The rest should split away when you start lifting.

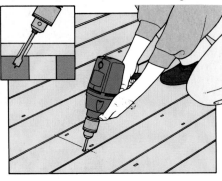

To saw beside a joist, find the edge of the joist with a blade and mark a cutting line across the board. Drill a hole big enough to admit the sawblade . . .

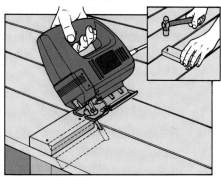

. . . then nail a block of wood parallel with the line. Adjust the saber saw sole plate to 30°, insert the blade, and saw through the block and board together.

To saw over a joist, look for the rows of nails indicating its position and mark a cutting line just inside one of the rows. Cut along the line using short, flat strokes, then if necessary sever the unreachable ends using a woodworking chisel.

1 To lift the severed board, prize up the cut end from one side using a brick chisel. Apply enough force to get the jaws of a claw hammer under the end.

2 Continue levering until you can slide a length of wood under the raised board. Using both hands, force the strip towards the next joist.

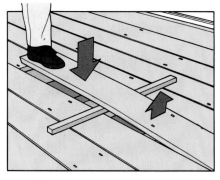

3 When the strip will go no further, put your weight on the cut end to 'spring' the board from the next joist. Repeat this until you reach the end.

FITTING A NEW FLOORBOARD

Floorboards exist in a range of widths and thicnesses, but if you're only patching the odd section there is little point hunting through lumberyards for an exact match. Instead, buy the nearest size you can find and then adapt it to fit:

■ If the board is too wide, plane down the edges to a slight taper.
■ If the board is too thick, mark the joist positions and then cut shallow notches with a chisel.
■ If the board is too thin, fit cardboard or plywood packing over the joists before fixing.

Where you've sawn beside a joist, screw on a strip to support the replacement board before fixing. Screw, rather than nail, the board for future access.

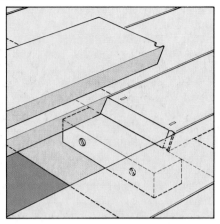

If you've sawn next to a joist, screw a wood strip to the side of the joist to support the new board. Bevel the end of the board if you cut the old section at an angle.

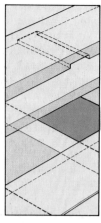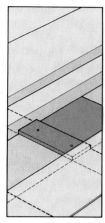

Notch a board which is too thick where it passes over the joists. *Pack underneath* a board which is too thin using slips of cardboard or plywood.

■ PROBLEM SOLVER

Problems with joists

Numerous warped, split or damaged boards – or serious sagging in the floor as a whole – point to faults in the floor joists below. Joist problems are more common on ground floors, where the danger of damp is ever-present. But in any event, it's worth checking on the condition of the joists whenever you have to lift more than one or two boards.

Rot or termites should be immediately obvious, and need prompt treatment. Any signs of dampness, dark staining or general deterioration suggest that the joists are beginning to rot, in which case they can be rescued if caught in time. By far the best course of action is to have an inspection carried out by a preservation specialist.

Sagging in an otherwise sound joist could be due to one of several things:
■ Overloading, either now or at some time in the past.
■ Over-weakening, where the joist has been notched to take pipes and cables.
■ Weakness in the joist itself.

These faults can usually be cured by strengthening the joist with a new section of lumber, or by bracing it against its neighbors with lumber struts. Bear in mind, however, that you may have to remove a considerable number of boards to gain sufficient access for putting in the struts.

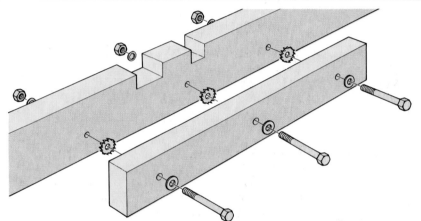

Strengthen a weakened joist by bolting a matching piece of lumber alongside it. The new section should be at least 900mm (3') long to be effective. Bolt at 300mm (12") intervals, using star washers (special connectors) between the sections to lock them together.

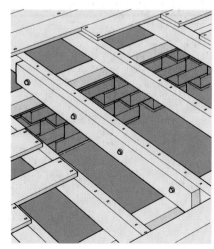

On a ground floor only, you may be able to strengthen a sagging joist by bolting a new section of lumber to it and supporting the ends on the two nearest sleeper walls . . .

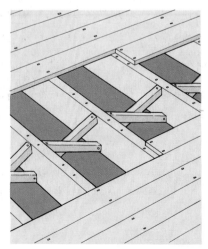

. . . alternatively, for all joists make up struts from lengths of 50×50mm (2×2") lumber. Toenail the struts between the affected joist and its neighbors at 600mm (2') intervals.

RELAYING FLOORBOARDS

Relaying larger areas of floorboards is generally more difficult and disruptive than replacing individual sections. Although it's easy to prize up the boards once the first one is out of the way, you have to make sure the ends are free before you can lift them.

Where the boards are trapped by a baseboard, remove this first: prize it away from its wall fixings with a bolster or crowbar, using a block of wood for leverage. Where boards disappear under a partition wall, you have no choice but to saw them off at the nearest convenient joist.

Replacing boards

With the boards up, pull out the old nails and then repair any boards that are salvageable. Boards with only surface damage can often be re-used the other way up.

Take a sample of board with you when buying replacements. New boards are stocked by lumberyards and building suppliers, but for older properties you may be better off going to an architectural salvage yard for secondhand boards.

Relaying

The main problem when relaying a number of floorboards – especially the square-edged type – is forcing them tightly together so that the gaps are as small as possible. There are two ways of doing this: with a pair of folding wedges (which you can make), or using a *floorboard clamp* (which you can rent).

In both cases it's worth buying a supply of cut steel, screw-type nails, or 2″ brad fasteners. The size of the nail (5d, 7d or 8d) depends on the board size. Use nails at least twice as long as the boards are thick, allowing two per joist. Screw rather than nail down any boards which you might need to lift for access in the future (and if they are T&G, saw off the tongues).

Joints and edges

Aim to relay the boards with as few joints as possible, and vary the lengths so that no two joints are next to each other. Wedge or clamp after every four or five boards.

If you're relaying the whole floor, decide whether or not you need to remove the baseboards; often, they can be left in place and the edge boards slipped underneath.

When you reach the far side of the room, you may have to cut the last board along its length to fit the gap. There's no need to do this neatly, as the cut edge will be concealed by the baseboard.

With T&G boards, start with the groove side towards the wall. At the far side, lock the last three boards together and 'spring' them under the baseboard before fixing.

Trade tip

Shrinking new boards

❛ When buying new floorboards, check that they are thoroughly seasoned or they may warp after fixing. In all cases, leave replacement boards stacked in the room they are going in for at least two days before laying. This will help them acclimatize, and minimize the risk of shrinkage in the future. ❜

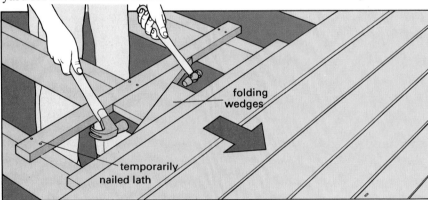

If you use folding wedges to pack the boards, nail a batten temporarily across the joists and place an offcut against the edge of the nearest board. Drive in the wedges from both sides to force the boards tightly together. Repeat every four or five boards.

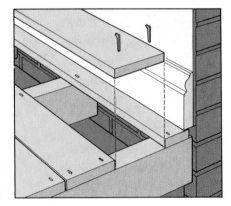

A square-edged end board may have to be sawn along its length and slid underneath the baseboard to hide the cut edge. Do this before nailing the previous board.

If you use a floorboard clamp, start by positioning the tool on a convenient joist and tightening the clamp. Place an offcut against the floorboards being packed, then turn the handle on the clamp to force them tightly together. Take care not to over-clamp.

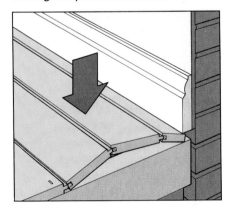

T&G boards should be interlocked and 'sprung' under the baseboard as shown. Again, you may have to cut down the last board to fit the remaining gap.

STRIPPING AND SEALING FLOORBOARDS

In older homes, the original pine floorboards (or, if you are very lucky, oak ones) can be sanded and sealed to give a warm, natural finish that provides the perfect complement to rugs or area carpet. Sanding down and sealing is also among the most economical ways of finishing a floor, although equipment rental and the cost of the sealant can push up the price further than you might expect. Much depends, too, on the condition of the boards: if they are badly damaged or deeply stained already, lining them with hardboard and laying a budget floorcovering such as sheet vinyl or foam-backed carpet is likely to be more sensible.

If you decide to go ahead, make sure you are well prepared. Clear the room completely of furnishings and make sure that any repairs to the boards have been carried out before committing yourself to any expenditure.

■ Punch nails below the surface and fill large gaps.
■ Replace or turn over damaged and stained boards.

The same principles apply to sanding and refinishing other types of wood floor, such as solid wood strip and traditional parquet.

Old floorboards *in almost any condition can be renovated and sealed to give a durable floor surface.*

....Shopping List....

Floor sanding equipment can be rented. Look in the Yellow Pages. You need a *floor sanding machine* to deal with the main area, plus an *edging sander* for finishing the edges and any awkward corners. (If you have an orbital sander this may do instead, but it will take heavy punishment).

The store you rent from may supply *abrasive sheets* to fit both machines on a sale-or-return basis. Ask for a mixture of coarse, medium and fine grades in both cases.
Protective gear is essential for floor sanding, which is a very noisy and messy job. Make sure you have a dust mask, ear protectors, overalls, and goggles.
Sealants may also be sold by the store you rent from, but shop around for a wider selection.

Polyurethane varnish is the usual choice. It is economical, but slow to dry and picks up dust easily; you need at least 3 (and preferably 4) coats. *Two-part plastic coating* is tougher and dries within the hour, but is more unpleasant to apply and can work out costlier, even though you only need 2 coats. An *oleo-resinous sealant* is the best choice if you plan to give the floor a wax polished finish, though this will be hard work to maintain. You could also consider staining or colored varnish (see overleaf).

When buying sealant, be sure to check the recommended coverage per coat. For polyurethane, you need mineral spirits for thinning.

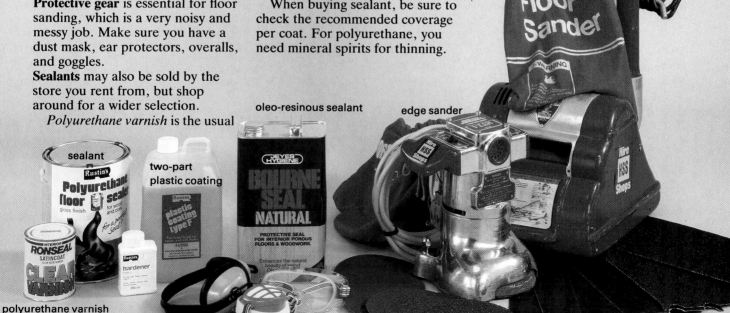

floor sander

oleo-resinous sealant

edge sander

sealant

two-part plastic coating

polyurethane varnish

protective gear

SANDING THE FLOOR

The dust and noise raised by sanding a floor can be considerable, so warn family and neighbors. Immediately before you start:

■ Double-check that the boards are firmly fixed and that there are no sharp nail heads or screws protruding above the surface.

■ Seal up the cracks around doors with parcel tape, and block the gaps underneath with newspaper.

■ Keep any windows open while actually sanding. Close them again after each stage, and vacuum to keep the dust level down.

Follow the sanding sequence shown on the right, checking the abrasive sheets every so often to make sure they're not clogged. With badly marked floors, work diagonally in both directions before working along the grain. Don't change to fine abrasives until all the marks have gone.

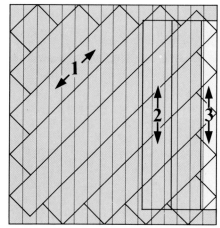

The correct sanding sequence.
Start with the floor sander and work diagonally across the boards using coarse, then medium, abrasives (1). Next, run along the grain of the boards using medium, then fine, abrasives (2). Switch to the edge sander (3): use coarse and medium abrasive to clear the marks; fine to finish.

Trade tip

Using a drum sander

❛ Floor sanders are powerful machines, to be used with care.
■ Always unplug before changing abrasive sheets.
■ Make sure the sheet is taut and firmly locked in place.
■ Never start the machine while the drum is in contact with the ground. Rock the machine back to lift it, then lower gradually when it reaches full speed. Be prepared for it to pull forward.
■ Similarly, rock back to lift the drum before switching off.
■ Empty the dust bag regularly; they have been known to catch fire spontaneously if allowed to become over-full.
■ If the sheet catches on a nail it may shatter with a resounding bang, so be prepared. ❜

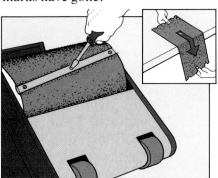

The floor sander sheets are wrapped over the drum, and held by a screw-down bar. Scrape the backing over the edge of a bench to give the sheet a curl before fitting, then pull it taut.

The sander will naturally pull away from you. Use it like a lawn mower and keep the cord over your shoulder so it is out of the way. Avoid 'resting' during a pass, as you risk gouging the boards.

Use the edge sander running in the direction of the grain wherever possible, and keep it flat to avoid score marks. Take care not to scrape the disc against the baseboard.

FINISHING AND SEALING

However you plan to seal the surface, leave the bare boards for as long as possible – and at least a day – to give the dust a chance to settle. (A few squirts into the air with an indoor plant spray will help to speed up the process). Afterwards vacuum the floor thoroughly, along with the baseboard, door and window frames, and any other places where dust might have collected.

Immediately before sealing, wipe over the floor with a cloth soaked in mineral spirit (don't use water, as this raises the wood grain).
Polyurethane varnish should be thinned with mineral spirit on the first coat, see manufacturer's instructions. This allows it to soak into the grain of the wood.

Close all doors and windows. Apply the varnish running with the grain, using a 100mm (4″) brush.

After each coat, sand the surface lightly using fine sandpaper on a block, or a wad of medium grade steel wool. Vacuum again and wipe over with the mineral-spirit-soaked cloth before applying the next coat.
Two-part coatings give off strong fumes, so keep the room well ventilated; put sheets over windows to stop dust entering.

Mix the coating in the container in which it is supplied according to the instructions. Apply with a brush that you won't want to use again – it will be ruined – or use a sponge mop. Sand, if necessary, and vacuum between coats.
Oleo-resinous sealants do not need mixing or thinning. Decant the sealant into a clean can and apply with a large brush.

Trade tip

Adding color

❛ The natural tones of the wood can be altered by staining, or by using colored polyurethane varnish.
■ Apply the stain before sealing: use an alcohol-based stain, and apply it with a cloth pad, not a brush. This gives a more even coverage.
■ If using colored varnish, choose the gloss type. Apply a thinned coat of clear varnish first. This seals the surface so that it will absorb the color evenly, then follow with two or more colored coats. Finish with another clear coat – gloss, matte or semi-gloss according to your preference. ❜

LEVELING A WOODEN FLOOR

Wooden boarded floors, although strong and hardwearing, make a less than ideal surface on which to lay modern floorcoverings such as sheet vinyl, vinyl tiles and foam backed carpet.

Most boarded floors are now at an age where years of lifting and patching have taken their toll, leaving a loose or uneven surface that quickly shows through a thin floorcovering and sets up localized patches of wear. Wooden floors also tend to give under load and shrink in dry weather, either of which can play havoc with tiles laid on top.

The solution is to prepare the floor – and level it at the same time – by nailing down sheets of hardboard or plywood. Although time consuming, this is a relatively simple job that requires only basic carpentry skills. The time taken will be well repaid in terms of extra comfort, and prolonged life for the floorcovering going on top. And on a ground floor, leveling has the added advantage of reducing heat loss through gaps between boards.

Hardboard is ideal for leveling wood floors: it's easy to cut and leaves a flat, smooth surface.

....Shopping List....

The usual material for lining floors is 3mm (⅛″) hardboard, which comes in several sheet sizes. The most useful are 2440×1220mm (8×4′) and 1220×610mm (4×2′). It also comes in two grades. *Standard* grade is perfectly adequate. Standard is rough on one side and smooth on the other. The

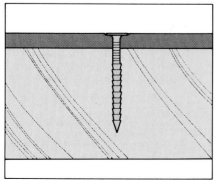

Use ring shank nails on hardboard.

smooth side is tempered, making it moisure resistant. You can also buy hardboard which is smooth (ie tempered) on both sides.

If you plan to lay ceramic tiles, use 9mm (⅜″) or 12mm (½″) plywood instead, depending on the condition of the floor. This is very much more expensive but the cheapest grade will do. It comes in various sheet sizes, most commonly 2440×1220mm (8×4′).

When calculating how many sheets to buy, bear in mind that some material will inevitably go to waste filling the margins around the edge of the floor. This is where smaller sheets are useful. Ideally, draw a quick scale plan of the room (in this case it's easiest to work in feet) and fill in the plan sheet by sheet.

Nails Use *ring shank nails* – 19mm

(¾″) for hardboard, 25mm (1″) for plywood. These have ridged shanks and round heads that grip the sheets securely. A 0.5kg (1lb) bag should be enough for most rooms.

Tools checklist: Crosscut saw, string or garden twine, small piece of chalk, hammer, plane or planer, nail punch, trimming knife, steel rule or carpenter's level.

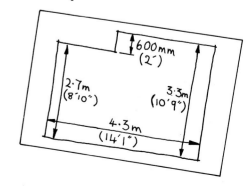

A typical sketched floor plan.

101

PREPARING THE SHEETS

When you get the sheets home, begin by cutting them in half with a crosscut saw. This makes them easier to manoeuver and lay, especially around the edges of the room. If you are using standard hardboard, some say you should condition it before laying. Place the cut sheets on edge and lightly spray the rough sides with clean water. Use about 0.5 liter (¾ pint) of water per board.

Stack the sheets flat in pairs, rough sides together, and leave them for at least 48 hours in the room being boarded. This allows them to acclimatize as they dry, and prevents buckling when you lay them. The drying process continues after laying, causing the sheets to shrink and form a tight, flat skin.

Spray sheets of standard hardboard with water on the rough side. Stack them flat, rough sides together, in the room they are going in and leave for 48 hours.

Trade tip

Match the sheets

❝ When you cut the sheets in half, keep track of which halves go together by numbering each pair on the cut edges. Otherwise, there will be gaps in the joints and they won't line up square. ❞

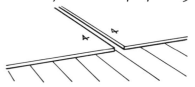

Setting out against chalk lines avoids leaving awkward spaces around the edge of the room. If you need access to underfloor pipes or cables, arrange for narrower strips to be fitted at these points so that you can lift them easily in an emergency.

separate panel for underfloor access

adjust positions of sheets to avoid narrow strip on return wall

chalk line 2

chalk lin

Trade tip

Underfloor access

❝ Mark any boards which might need lifting in the future to get at pipes or cables. Then, when you come to set out the sheets, arrange things so that small panels are laid over these areas.

This allows you to gain access to the floorboards without disrupting the entire surface. ❞

PREPARING THE FLOOR

Check the floor for boards that are loose or curled at the edges, and for protruding nail heads. These faults must be put right before you go ahead. Do not line the floor if there is any suspicion of damp, rot or woodworm in the boards or in the joists below.

Loose boards can be secured with screws, but lift them first to check that there are no pipes or cables notched into the joists below.

Badly damaged boards must be lifted and replaced. If you have difficulty finding lumber as thick as the old boards, fit slips of hardboard or cardboard underneath to make up the difference when you nail down the new boards.

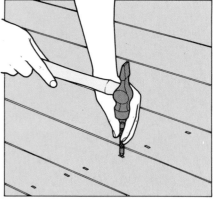

Curling edges are a problem on boards which have shrunk with age. Plane down, or flatten with a belt or orbital sander (wear goggles for protection).

Punch nail heads below the surface, working systematically across the room so that you don't miss any. Secure loose boards with extra nails or screws.

SETTING OUT

Lay the sheets in a staggered pattern, working out from the middle of the room. This breaks up the joints and makes it more economical to fill in the spaces around the edge of the floor.

Mark two lines at right angles across the room as a laying guide. Use a chalked string line for this (it's easier than drawing the lines).

Next, lay out your half sheets in pairs as a dry run to see what spaces are left around the edges. Adjust the sheets to avoid leaving small, fiddly gaps.

1 Pin a length of string at one end of the room, halfway along the wall. Stretch it taut, rub it thoroughly with chalk, and pin it at the opposite end.

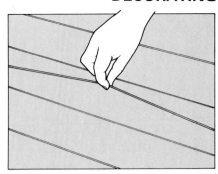

2 Grasp the string between finger and thumb and snap it against the floor to leave an impression in chalk. Snap another line at right angles to it.

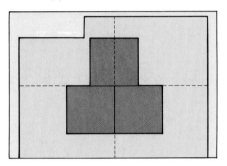

3 Butt the first two sheets against each other where the lines meet. Then lay two more sheets against them, staggered by half their width.

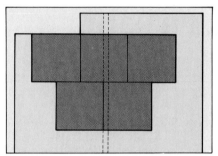

4 Lay out the remaining whole sheets, then adjust their positions to even up the spaces around the edges and avoid awkward cuts.

Trade tip

Which way up?

❛ Opinions differ as to which way up to lay hardboard. I follow the rule that if the floorcovering is going to be stuck down lay it rough side up, otherwise lay it smooth side up. Often, though, flooring and adhesive manufacturers specify which surface best suits their products on the packaging. ❜

Position first sheet between chalk lines

NAILING THE SHEETS

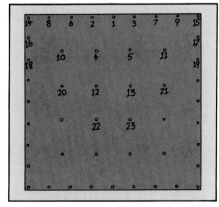

Fix the sheets working clockwise from the middle of the room. Nail hardboard in a pyramid pattern, starting from the middle of one edge, to stop it buckling.

1 Nail sheets 12mm (½") in from the edges, spacing the nails 150mm (6") apart. Space the nails at 225mm (9") intervals over the rest of the sheet.

2 Use pieces of wood cut to length as spacers, but adjust the spacing if you nail through a gap between boards. Make sure no nail heads are left protruding.

DEALING WITH EDGES

The sheets don't have to be an exact fit around the edges of the room, but you'll waste time and material if you try to cut them by eye alone – it's better to scribe the edges first using a block of wood and a pencil.

Scribe sheets to fit straight edges as shown on the right, making use of any offcuts where you can. Deal with corners as shown below: butt the straightest edge against the baseboard, scribe the adjacent edge, then mark off where to trim against neighboring joints.

Trimming sheets

Hardboard Don't bother to saw hardboard to size where you are trimming straight pieces. Score the sheet on the marked side using a trimming knife and steel rule or carpenter's level. Kneel on the main board, grasp the waste on both sides, and snap along the score.

Plywood Normally it's easiest to trim sheets with a crosscut saw though you may find a saber saw more useful for making fiddly cuts around awkward edges. Bear in mind that since the floor will be tiled, there's no need to get an exact fit – 12mm (½") gaps are perfectly acceptable.

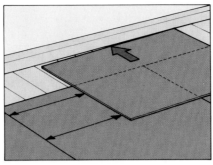

1 To scribe a sheet, center it over the neighboring whole sheets. Keeping the sheet square to the others, slide it forward until it touches the baseboard.

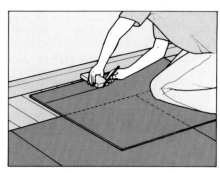

2 Run a block and pencil along the wall edge as shown, marking the profile of the baseboard. Trim the sheet along this line.

3 Lay the sheet back in position and butt the scribed edge against the baseboard. Mark off the waste against the two neighboring sheets and trim.

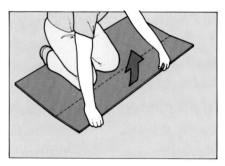

To cut straight edges of hardboard, score with a trimming knife and metal straightedge, then kneel on the main piece of board and snap off the waste.

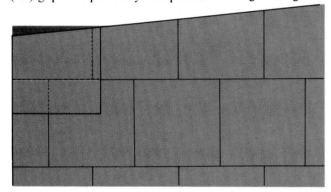

At corners, scribe and trim one wall edge (red area) then mark where to trim the remaining waste (blue lines).

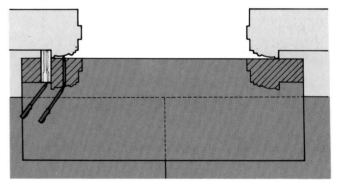

At a doorway, swap the scribing block for a pencil so that you can trace the profiles of the architraves.

▌PROBLEM SOLVER▐

Dealing with doorways
Lining the floor will raise the level (substantially in the case of plywood) so lift any inward opening doors off their hinges before you start. The final level will probably be higher still, depending on what type of floorcovering you plan to lay, so leave trimming the bottoms of the doors until later.

Concrete hearths
Sheets can't be nailed over a concrete fire hearth built into the floor. Instead, glue them down with impact adhesive.

Underfloor ventilation
Although lining the floor cuts out drafts between the floorboards, on a ground floor it can also restrict the circulation of air in the space beneath the joists. This is a major cause of wet and dry rot, particularly in older houses where there may be dampness. Check that all crawlspace ventilation openings are intact and unblocked. If any have been partially covered – for example, by a raised patio – the area immediately in front of the ventilation must be dug out to restore the flow of air.

Check ventilation around the house walls to make sure they are unblocked and in good condition.

LAYING SHEET VINYL FLOORING

Sheet vinyl flooring is ideal wherever you need a hardwearing, waterproof surface that's easy to keep clean and comfortable to walk on. This makes it a good choice not only for kitchens, bathrooms and halls, but for playrooms, dining areas and utility rooms as well.

There's a wide choice of patterns, ranging from plain geometric to simulated quarry tile and woodgrain. Most have some surface texture, and in the case of simulated types this is pronounced enough to give a realistic effect.

Sheet vinyl comes in widths of 2m (about 6'6"), 3m (9'9") and 4m (13'). This means that many rooms can be covered with one sheet – although sometimes it may be easier to join two narrower sheets.

Overleaf is a guide to estimating how much (and what width) to buy, depending on the shape of the room. But you may not find wider sheets in all patterns, so check availability before making a final choice.

.... **Shopping List** ....

There are two main types of vinyl, both of which come in a wide range of styles and patterns:
Rotovinyl consists of a single layer of solid vinyl; only the thicker types are textured. Most unbacked vinyls won't lay flat naturally and must be glued to the floor.
Inlaid vinyl consists of multiple layers, the most important of which is a foam backing that makes it softer and warmer to walk on in bare feet. The surface is usually textured.

Some inlaid vinyl is designed to lay flat naturally and doesn't need gluing. (One exception is under a heavy kitchen appliance, such as an oven, where gluing stops the vinyl dragging if the appliance has to be moved.) Non-'lay flat' types only need to be glued near the edges and along any seams.
Other materials: If the vinyl needs sticking down, check the manufacturer's instructions for suitable adhesives. Most types come with a spreader.

Seam adhesive gives a professional finish to joins between sheets (see page 110).

Adhesive tape is essential for several stages, and you may need metal cover strips for doorways. Use brown wrapping paper or heavy lining paper to make cutting quides (see page 109).
Tools checklist: Trimming knife, soft broom, metal rule or straight edge, blocks of wood. (Extra tools are needed if the floor has to be prepared first – see overleaf.)

Cross-sections of rotovinyl and a typical inlaid vinyl.

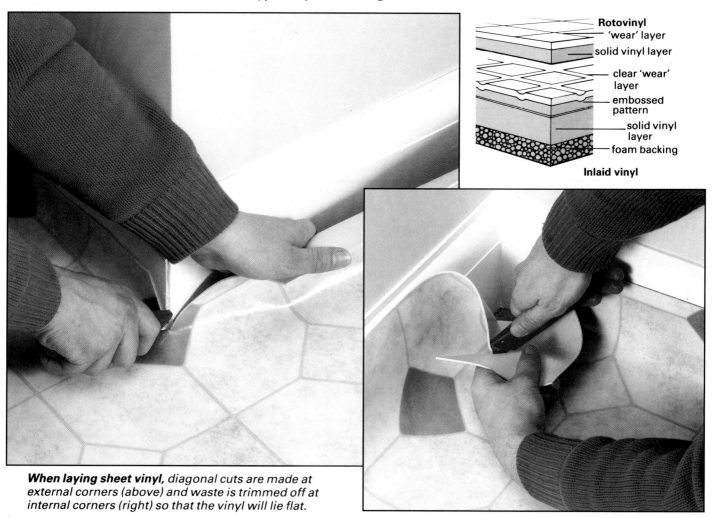

Rotovinyl
— 'wear' layer
— solid vinyl layer

— clear 'wear' layer
— embossed pattern
— solid vinyl layer
— foam backing

Inlaid vinyl

When laying sheet vinyl, *diagonal cuts are made at external corners (above) and waste is trimmed off at internal corners (right) so that the vinyl will lie flat.*

PREPARATION AND PLANNING

The plans given here show what's involved in laying sheet vinyl in three different situations. Start by seeing what needs to be done to the existing floor surface, then work out the best way to lay the sheet.

Preparing the floor

Vinyl must only be laid on a surface which is even, clean and dry. Any bumps or hollows will eventually show through, and damp can damage a cushioned backing as well as being a problem in its own right.

Floorboards Level old pine boarded floors with sheets of hardboard. With new boards or particleboard, make sure nail heads are punched below the surface, fill any gaps with general purpose filler, and vacuum.

Concrete Make sure the floor is not damp. If the surface is smooth but dusty, vacuum and apply a coat of concrete sealer; if it is uneven, level with self-smoothing compound.

Quarry/ceramic tiles Check that the tiles are securely fixed and level the joints with filler.

Old glued floor coverings Lift linoleum or felt backed vinyl; to remove any remaining backing felt, soak with one part household ammonia to three of water and scrape off.

Old vinyl tiles can stay if firmly fixed; otherwise warm with a hot air stripper to soften the adhesive and lift, scraping off all traces of old adhesive. Old thermoplastic tiles discolor vinyl sheet, so either lift them or screed over the top with latex-based self-smoothing compound.

In all cases it's a good idea to remove inward opening doors and trim the undersides.

Planning how much to buy

Measure the maximum width and length of the room – going right into any recesses or door openings – then draw a sketch plan and put in the dimensions. Take the longest and widest measurements and add 200mm (8″) for a trimming allowance on each side. This represents the minimum sheet size needed to fill the room.

Aim to choose a width that allows you to cover the whole area with a single piece. (If the room is seriously out of square, allow extra for trimming or you may get caught out.) Most stockists sell in lengths to the nearest metre or half metre so you may end up with a bit extra.

Where the size or shape of the room makes it impossible to use a single piece, use your plan to work out the best way of fitting in two or more pieces bearing in mind the following points:
■ Seams between sheets tend to lift and curl in time, so place them where they won't receive heavy wear.
■ A seam which runs at right angles to the main light source is less noticeable than one running parallel.
■ It's not normally a good idea to use sheets of different widths on the same floor – they will have been made on a different run and are seldom an exact color match. However, you can save a lot of wastage this way, especially if the second piece is small and not in a prominent place.
■ Allow extra overlap between pieces for matching the pattern. Manufacturers normally specify the size of the pattern repeat.

EXAMPLE 1: A REGULARLY SHAPED ROOM

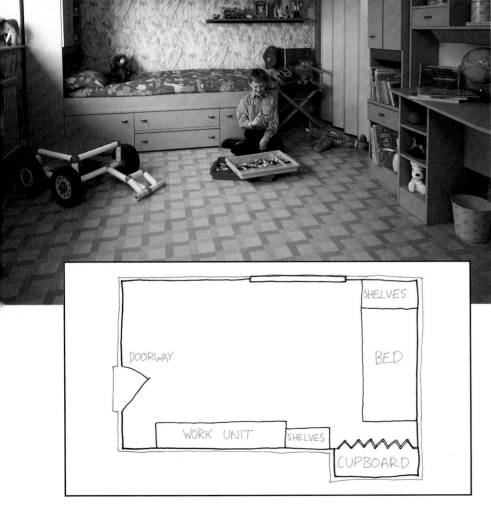

Most rooms are fairly regular in shape with no awkward areas, except perhaps a chimney breast. Providing the maximum width is less than 4m (13′) you should be able to use a single piece.

If you choose a vinyl with an irregular pattern, it won't matter if the walls are slightly out of true. Otherwise, take into account that the pattern must line up with the longest wall or dominant feature (eg a run of kitchen units), or the floor won't look 'right'.

And if the vinyl has a large pattern, like tile squares, it's a good idea to allow extra for trimming so that you can balance the breaks in the pattern between all sides of the room – small slivers of pattern always look like patched mistakes.

A rectangular room with few obstructions (above) can usually be covered in one piece. Check this by drawing a sketch plan (left), not forgetting to allow extra where the sheet has to fit into alcoves and doorways. Lay the vinyl by unrolling it in the room and trimming the sides to fit each wall in turn.

EXAMPLE 2: A 'THROUGH' ROOM

If you want to lay vinyl in two connected areas, such as a kitchen and breakfast room, you have two choices:

■ Lay a single piece trimmed to fit both rooms and the partition between them. This can be tricky – especially if there is a narrow opening or a thick partition – and is only feasible if the maximum width of the area (plus trimming allowance) is less than 4m (13′).

■ Lay two pieces with a seam between the room or in a convenient area of one of them. This is less neat, and it can be hard to match the pattern, but it's much easier to do.

In an L-shaped through room, like the one shown, it's tempting to place the seam across the partition. But a better solution in this case is to lay a single piece over the part receiving the heaviest wear – usually the area between two doorways – then fit a second piece in the corner which gets used the least. A sensible furniture arrangement may help here.

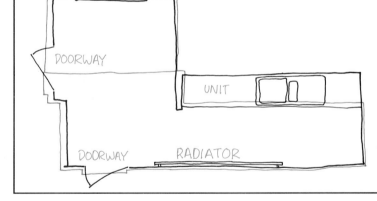

An L-shaped through room
(above) poses the problem of what width to buy and where to place the seams. Try out different layouts on a sketch plan (left).

Here, the most economical way is to cover the area between the doorways with one piece, then fit a second in the relatively unused area by the dining table. If the kitchen were wider, it might be possible to cover both rooms with a single piece.

EXAMPLE 3: AN OBSTACLE-FILLED ROOM

Some rooms are an awkward shape or full of obstacles, such as a small bathroom with a toilet, pedestal basin and towel rail. In these situations, it's very difficult to lay vinyl directly and cut round the various shapes.

A better method is to make a paper pattern of the whole area, showing the obstacles, and use this in order to cut the sheet before you fit it (see page 109). However, don't use this method for a room larger than a couple of yards square, as the pattern is unlikely to be accurate enough. Instead, unfurl the vinyl in the room as best you can, then make separate patterns of the obstacles.

In small rooms full of obstacles, it's easier to cut the vinyl following a paper pattern. Cut on the generous side, then do a final trim with the sheet in position.

LAYING THE VINYL

Unless the supplier has done it for you, start by cutting the sheet roughly to size, allowing about 100mm (4″) trim on all four sides. If you have to work outside, make sure it is dry. Use a trimming knife or kitchen scissors, and check every measurement; pull the waste down and away from the sheet to ensure a clean edge.

Re-roll the sheet across the shorter dimension to take it into the room (large sheets are difficult to handle, so get a helper).

If possible, leave the vinyl rolled loosely in the room for 1–2 days – with the heating on if the weather is cold. This acclimatizes it and makes it easier to handle. Immediately before you start work, reverse-roll the sheet so that the pattern will be face up when it is unrolled.

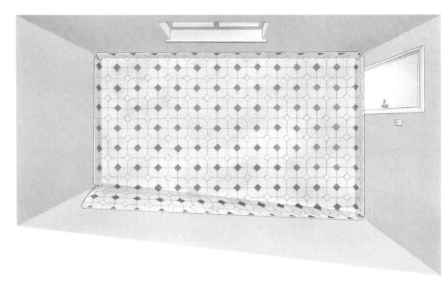

Always try to line up the pattern with the longest wall or most prominent feature. If either of these are out of true, align the pattern so that it runs at right angles to the wall with the most used doorway.

1 Lay the roll at a slight angle to the longest wall or dominant feature. Unroll about 1m (3′) and ease the sheet round so it rides up by about 100mm (4″).

2 Align the pattern, then unroll fully – allowing the edges to overlap the walls and ride over obstructions. Flatten out the air pockets with a soft broom.

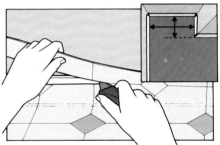

3 Trim off any excess to leave roughly 100mm (4″) overlap all round. At recesses, measure the depth, add a further 100mm (4″), and leave this much overlapping.

SCRIBING AN EDGE

Once you're satisfied that the sheet is lying square to the walls with the pattern in the right alignment, start cutting and trimming to fit. Experts trim all sides freehand like carpet (see *Direct Trimming*) but this is very difficult to get right first time – it's much easier to fit the longest side by scribing the edge.

When cutting, always trim off less than you think you need, then re-trim if necessary – it's difficult to patch an overtrimmed sheet.

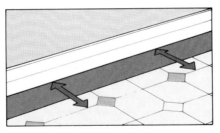

1 Take the edge along the longest wall or dominant feature. Pull the sheet slightly away from the wall, maintaining the alignment of the pattern.

Trade tip

Get it taped

❝ Once you've scribed and trimmed the longest edge to fit, it's a good idea to tape it securely to the wall so that the sheet doesn't 'creep' out of position while you are trimming the rest. ❞

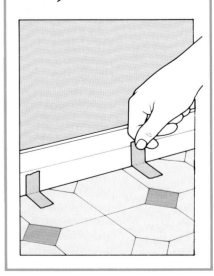

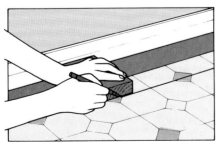

2 Hold a marker pen against a block of wood about 100mm (4″) square. Draw the block along the wall or baseboard so the pen marks the wall's profile on the vinyl.

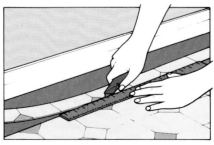

3 Cut along this line with a trimming knife or scissors. Slide the sheet back to the wall so that the cut edge butts up to it and re-trim where necessary.

DIRECT TRIMMING

Start by making release cuts at the corners as shown (right) so that the sheet begins to lie flat.

When you come to the edges, don't forget to compensate for the way the vinyl curves into the angle between the floor and baseboard or wall – it's easy to cut it too short. Practice with an offcut before you start trimming the main sheet.

Until you get used to the 'feel' of the vinyl, you may find the knife blade wanders off-line when trimming long edges. In this case it's safer to use the *Step at a time* technique shown below. Begin at a corner next to the scribed edge, and deal with obstacles as shown below.

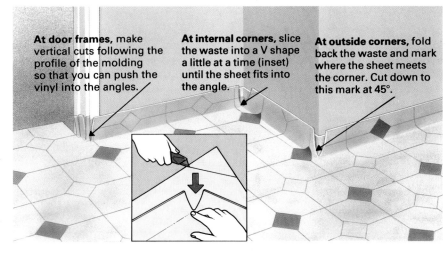

At door frames, make vertical cuts following the profile of the molding so that you can push the vinyl into the angles.

At internal corners, slice the waste into a V shape a little at a time (inset) until the sheet fits into the angle.

At outside corners, fold back the waste and mark where the sheet meets the corner. Cut down to this mark at 45°.

Make release cuts, starting at external corners, so the sheet lies flat.

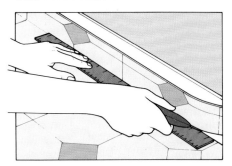

To direct-trim, push the sheet hard into the angle with a metal ruler, adjust the ruler to allow for the curve, then cut along it. Holding the knife with your thumb 'trapped' against the waste helps to control the blade.

Trade tip

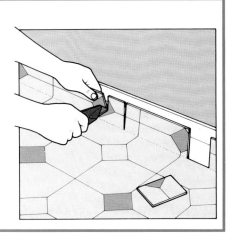

A step at a time

❛ Try this technique when you first start trimming to be sure of getting a straight cut:
■ Cut a rectangular pocket in the waste about 50mm (2″) wide and continue the cuts down to where the wall and floor meet.
■ Cut further pockets along the wall at 300mm (12″) intervals.
■ Fold back the flaps which this creates and check the fit.
■ Run a straight edge along the folds and cut off the flaps. ❜

DEALING WITH OBSTACLES

Use paper patterns to deal with obstacles like a basin or toilet. (In a very small room, tape several sheets of paper together and make a pattern of the entire floor area as shown on page 107.) Use brown wrapping or heavy lining paper; newspaper is too flimsy. Scribing the outline of the obstacle avoids having to cut the pattern to an exact fit – but be sure to scribe back again on to the vinyl or you'll end up trimming it in the wrong place.

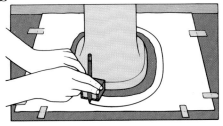

1 Rough-cut the paper to fit around the obstacle leaving a 25mm (1″) gap all around. Then scribe around the obstacle with a wood block and pencil.

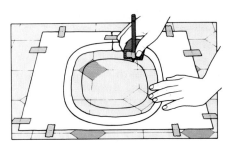

2 Lay the finished pattern in position on the vinyl and tape it down. Now scribe back on to the vinyl from the outline marked on the pattern.

3 Make the cut-outs in the vinyl following the marked lines, then make a straight cut to the edge of the sheet in a place where the seam won't be noticeable.

For a room-sized pattern, rough-cut and tape together enough sheets to fill the floor. After marking the obstacles, mark around the walls too.

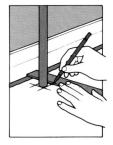

Mark a pipe's position on the pattern by drawing a square around it. Transfer the square to the vinyl, then draw a circle just touching the lines.

SEAMS, EDGES AND FINISHING

Where you need to join sheets, start by scribing and direct-trimming the first sheet to fit. Leave plenty of overlap along the joining edge so that you can match the pattern.

After matching and trimming the join with the second sheet as shown, stick down the edges with a 150mm (6″) band of adhesive (see below) before you trim the rest of the second sheet to fit. This stops it slipping out of position.

At doorways, take care to cut the overlap to the full width of the doorway – not just the width of the door stop in the middle. Finish the seam between the two coverings with an aluminum cover strip.

Gluing and finishing

Unbacked vinyl must be glued all over. Spread the adhesive over half the floor following manufacturer's instructions, lay the trimmed sheet lightly in position, then smooth out towards the edges with a soft broom to remove air bubbles. Repeat for the other part of the floor.

Inlaid vinyl normally only needs sticking down with a 150mm (6″) band of adhesive at seams, but glue it all over where it is laid under heavy appliances. Both jobs can be done with the sheet in position.

Afterwards, smooth down the glued areas with a piece of wood wrapped in a soft cloth.

At doorways, fit a metal cover strip with a ramp to match the thickness of the floorcovering in the adjoining room. Nail or screw the strip in place over the vinyl.

1 *To join two pieces,* fit the first sheet and lay the second on top. Align their patterns, leaving at least 100mm (4″) overlap on the opposite wall.

2 Fold back the second sheet and choose where to make the join (a 'line' in the pattern is ideal). Mark this line and cut along it against a straight edge.

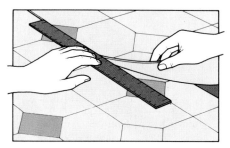

3 Tuck the second sheet under the first sheet. Butt a straight edge against the trimmed edge, fold back this edge, then cut the second sheet.

◼ PROBLEM SOLVER ◼

Tight fits

Trimmed edges sometimes become a tight fit along walls as the sheet begins to settle and flatten. If this happens, mark where the sheet fits perfectly on either side of the problem area, then fold back the sheet and join the marks with a straight line. Re-trim along this line using a straightedge.

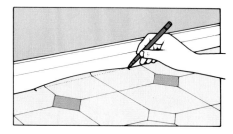

Marking a tightly fitting edge.

Accidental cuts

If the knife slips or you cut in the wrong place, repair the cut with non-stain double sided tape and seaming adhesive – both available from vinyl dealers.

Cut a length of tape and run the sticky side down the cut on the underside of the sheet. Remove the backing from the tape and press down the sheet.

Now run a thin bead of seaming adhesive along the full length of the cut so that it just fills it. The adhesive will bond the edges together so that they are barely noticeable.

Patch cuts with double sided tape and seaming adhesive.

Sheet overtrimmed

When you've fitted the first edge and come to trim the second, you still have room for maneuver if you trim too much: slide the sheet along a bit, mark the first edge again, then re-trim.

If the problem occurs after you have fitted two or more edges and you're left with an unsightly gap, one answer is to pin softwood quarter round molding around the baseboard to disguise it (see below).

Alternatively, patch in a strip using tape and seaming adhesive. Disguise the join in the patch by running it along a line in the pattern.

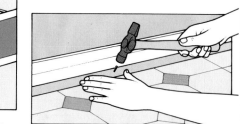

Using quarter round molding.

LAYING CORK FLOOR TILES

Cork tiling is a warm, resilient and very economical floorcovering. The tiles are light and relatively easy to handle, and the pre-sealed types require little finishing work.

Choosing tiles

Most cork tiles are 12" (305mm) square, and are sold in packs of nine to cover 1 sq yd (just under 1 sq m). Although they are available in different grades to suit different levels of wear, the main choice is between *sealed* and *unsealed* – some have a protective coat of acrylic varnish, lacquer or PVC applied in the factory, while others are sanded but left 'raw'. You can also get cork tiles with a self-adhesive backing, in which case they can be treated like self-adhesive vinyl tiles.

Sealed tiles are ready to walk on as soon as they are laid, but the square-edged type must be closely butted together or there is a risk of water seeping down between the joints. Some better quality tiles have lipped edges which interlock to seal the joints.

Unsealed tiles must be sealed before taking any foot traffic. The normal method is to give them at least three coats of polyurethane varnish, allowing each coat to dry thoroughly before applying the next, so it could take several days before the floor is ready for use.

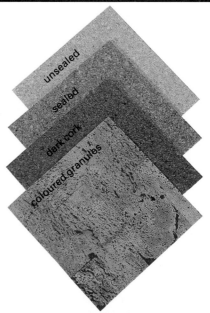

unsealed

sealed

dark cork

coloured granules

Most manufacturers provide charts on their packaging indicating how many tiles you need for a given area allowing for wastage. But to make use of this information, you must first measure the floor.

In a regularly shaped room, simply multiply the length by the width. In a room full of awkward shapes it's safer to draw a sketch plan and divide the area into a number of rectangles; find the area of each one, then add them together to get the total area.

Adhesive choice is critical, and will make all the difference to the durability of the floor. In theory, most water-based PVA flooring adhesives are suitable, but recent research suggests that some brands cause certain types of cork to expand and contract as they dry out, leading to shrinkage and gaps.

The problem is less acute on unsealed tiles, where the adhesive can evaporate more easily, and on vinyl-backed tiles, where it doesn't come into contact with the cork. But always follow manufacturer's recommendations where given.

Coverage depends on the porosity of the subfloor and on the tiles. As a rough guide, 1 litre will cover around 3–4 sq m (4 sq yd) on a concrete screed – more if the floor is lined with hardboard or the tiles have a smooth backing.

Sealant is usually gloss polyurethane varnish, but again you should follow the manufacturer's own recommendations. You need at least three coats, but on a floor taking heavy wear it's worth applying an extra one for good measure.

One litre of polyurethane covers about 16 sq m (19 sq yd) per coat, but allow for the fact that the first coat should be thinned half and half with mineral spirit to help it soak into the cork.

Tools checklist: Adhesive spreader (often supplied), string and chalk, tape measure, try square, trimming knife and spare blades, steel wool, wall brush (for applying sealant).

Trade tip

Matte finish

6 If you want a semi-gloss or matte finish on cork tiles which you plan to seal yourself, apply a couple of gloss coats first – it is much tougher. You can then use your chosen varnish for the top couple of coats to give a more subdued effect. 9

FLOOR PREPARATION

The first step is to prepare the underlying floor surface.

Boarded floors need lining with sheets of hardboard. Arrange the sheets so they don't coincide with the joints between boards and nail at 225mm (9″) centers (150mm (6″) around the edges).

Solid floors must be level, smooth and dry. If the surface is simply dusty, coat with concrete stabilizer. Localized damage can be repaired with concrete floor repair compound.

If the floor is slightly uneven, heavily patched or covered with small lumps and bumps, resurface it with self-leveling compound. But if the level is badly 'out' – over 12mm (½″) say – or there are signs of dampness, have it rescreeded.

Existing floorcoverings may provide a suitable surface – for example, old cork tiles, vinyl tiles or glued-down sheet vinyl can all be overlaid with cork tiles, as long as they are level and

firmly fixed. Ceramic tiles may be more of a problem if the joints are deeply indented (though you could consider filling them). Old quarry tiled floors need treating with caution, as they may have been laid without a vapor barrier underneath. It's safer to lift them and rescreed.

Always check the adhesive manufacturer's instructions – they may recommend priming or sealing a particular surface to make sure of a good bond.

DECIDING WHERE TO START

Few rooms have walls which are exactly square to one another, and even fewer are the right size to take a whole number of tiles. So the standard procedure for laying floor tiles is to start from a point near the center of the floor, and work out towards the edges.

The exact starting point depends on how the gaps fall around the edges. By laying out the tiles in a 'dry run' as shown below, you can adjust it so that the gaps are more or less even right around the room, with no unsightly narrow strips.

Taking a line

If there is a major feature in the room which catches the eye – for example, a run of units – it may be better for the line of the tile joints to run parallel with this, rather than the walls. (Otherwise, the tiles could appear to be askew when in position.)

Arrange for this by making sure that one of the setting-out lines runs parallel to the feature concerned. Then reset the other line at right angles to it.

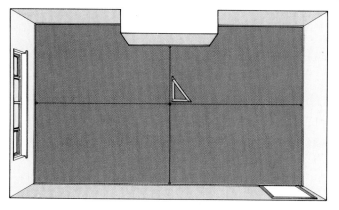

Find the center of the room by measuring and marking the midpoints of the four walls, then stretching string between them. Check with a try square where the lines cross, and adjust one line until you get a right angle.

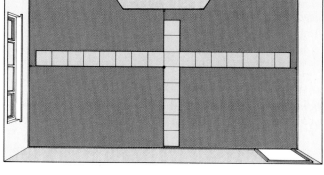

Lay 'dry runs' of tiles out from the center point towards the walls and see what sort of gaps are formed around edges of the room. Ideally, there should be about half a tile's width all around.

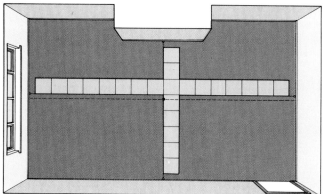

Reposition the center tile(s) if necessary so that the gaps are evened up – for example, position the first tile over the cross instead of in the angle. If none of the positions is satisfactory, try moving one or both of the string lines.

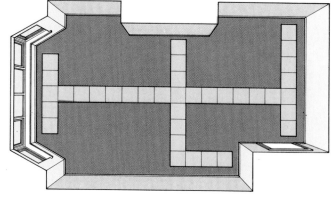

If the room is an awkward shape, lay further dry runs towards each obstacle and check the gaps here. Some awkward cuts will be unavoidable, but try to keep them to unobtrusive areas.

Trade tip

Check the tiles

6 Before you start laying the tiles, check them carefully for grain pattern and color. This is easiest while you have them laid out in a dry run.

Some tiles have very definite markings, with chips of cork aligned in rows. If a grain like this is laid running the same way right across the floor, it makes the tiles less obvious; conversely, alternating the grain direction actually strengthens the tiled effect. Decide which you prefer and lay the tiles accordingly.

At the same time, check for color variation between packs. Unlike wallpaper, cork tiles aren't produced in batch numbers since some colour variation occurs naturally. Even so, you can avoid blocks of lighter or darker tiles by mixing the packs and then laying different tones at random. 9

When laying cork tiles use a recommended adhesive. Spread the adhesive on the subfloor then position the tiles.

LAYING WHOLE TILES

Once you have decided on your starting point, adjust the strings to align with the central tile(s), then cover them with chalk and snap them against the floor to mark two straight guidelines.

Lay the tiles in a pyramid shape, working from the center of the room to the wall furthest from the door. Fill in the corners with whole tiles, then work back towards the door in the same way.

When all the whole tiles are in position, leave the adhesive to set for 24 hours before filling in gaps. This way, there's no danger of them becoming dislodged.

1 Starting from the marked point, use a notched spreader to apply enough adhesive to lay about nine tiles. Work towards the wall furthest from the door.

2 Lay two or three tiles along one line, then start outwards along the intersecting line. Fill in the angle, butting to two edges where possible.

3 Use a clean cloth to wipe off any adhesive which squeezes out of the joints on to the tile surface. Moisten the rag with mineral spirit if necessary.

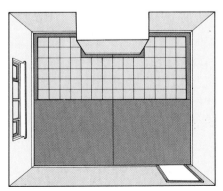

4 Work out from the centre line until half the room is covered. Then repeat for the second half, until all the whole tiles are laid.

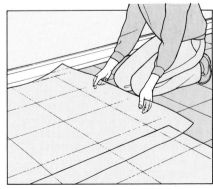

5 If you are using unsealed tiles, protect them by laying sheets of plastic over the surface of the tiles. Leave until the next day before sealing.

FILLING IN THE EDGES

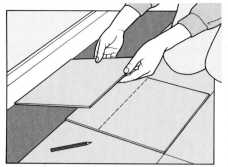 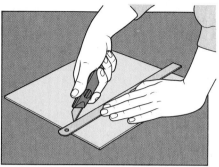 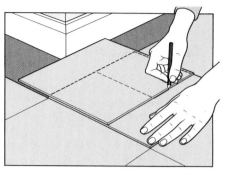

1 Lay the tile to be cut over the last complete tile, aligning the edges exactly. Position an uncut tile on top, so one edge butts against the wall.

2 Using the top tile as a guide, mark a cutting line on the tile to be cut. Then lay the tile on a hard surface and trim along the marked line with a trimming knife.

3 At external angles, use the same technique twice to mark both cutting lines. If you are using unsealed tiles, be careful not to mark beyond the angle.

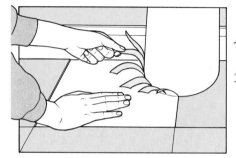 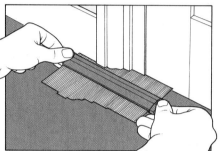 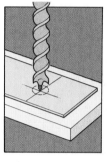 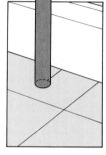

4 For rounded shapes like a basin pedestal, use a paper pattern. Tear back the paper so it fits around the obstacle, then use it to mark the tile.

5 For awkward obstacles, such as the ornate architrave around a doorway, use a profile gauge to trace the exact shape then cut it out a notch at a time.

6 Around pipes, trim the tile to fit the gap, then measure the position of the pipe and cut or drill a suitable hole. Finally, slit the tile and slide in place.

SEALING THE TILES

Unsealed tiles have to be coated to protect the surface from everyday wear and tear. Cork in its natural state is highly absorbent, leaving it vulnerable to grease marks and water penetration (which could cause the tiles to lift).

If there is any unevenness in the surface (there shouldn't be if the floor has been properly prepared), sand down with medium sandpaper. Before you start, vacuum the floor thoroughly, and wipe over to remove all traces of dust (see Tip).

Trade tip

Dealing with dust

❛ To ensure a dust- and grease-free surface before and during sealing, wipe down the tiles with a clean, white lint-free cloth moistened with mineral spirit. Keep the rag just moist enough to pick up the dust without wetting the tiles. The same trick can be used for other wooden surfaces before painting or varnishing – the spirit doesn't raise the grain the way water would. ❜

Apply at least three coats of polyurethane varnish to unsealed tiles. Rub down with a pad of fine steel wool and wipe off the dust after each coat.

LAYING VINYL AND RUBBER TILES

Vinyl floor tiles give a hard wearing, easy-to-clean surface that's ideally suited to splash-prone rooms such as kitchens and bathrooms. And in a room containing lots of awkward corners, they are likely to be considerably easier to lay than a fitted carpet or sheet vinyl; if you do mis-cut, only a single tile gets wasted.

An expensive, but very durable,

alternative to conventional vinyl tiles is synthetic rubber stud flooring – originally developed for airports and other public places. This also comes in tile form, and is laid in virtually the same way.

Decorative possibilities

One of the most appealing things about vinyl tiles is that different colors and styles can be mixed to

create a range of decorative effects – for example, you could combine a pale, plain-coloured tile for the main floor area with a 'border' of darker patterned tiles.

Preparation and planning

To prepare the floor and to decide where to begin, follow the instructions given on page 112 for laying cork tiles.

follow the instructions given on page 112 for laying cork tiles.

.... Shopping List ....

Vinyl tiles vary widely in price, from relatively economical to very expensive. Some are solid vinyl, others have a cushioned layer, and patterns vary from gently flecked, soft geometric and floral to imitations of brick, cork and other surfaces.

Practically speaking the main choice is between *self adhesive* and *plain* tiles. Self-adhesive tiles are less messy to lay, but stick instantly and don't allow much margin for error. For plain tiles, always use the adhesive recommended by the makers – and where appropriate, buy a supply of suitable *solvent* for cleaning.

Most vinyl tiles are around 300mm (12″) square, and are sold in packs of varying sizes. Coverage per pack is always given on the packaging, so simply divide this figure into the floor area (measured in square yards) and round up to the nearest whole pack to find the total number of packs required. Don't forget that if the room is an awkward shape, it's easier to divide it into smaller rectangles, work out their areas, then add the figures together.

Rubber stud tiles are generally 500mm (20″) square and come in packs of 4. They must be laid with a heavy-duty neoprene rubber-based adhesive, which means taking extra care over preparing the subfloor.

Tools and other materials: Tape measure, pencil, string, chalk, trimming knife, metal rule or straightedge, notched adhesive spreader (if not supplied with the adhesive), mineral spirit, a supply of clean rags.

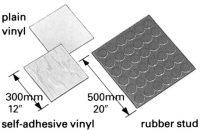

plain vinyl

300mm
12″

self-adhesive vinyl

500mm
20″

rubber stud

Vinyl tiles are available in many styles, appropriate for many different situations. In the kitchen (top) they are a practical choice: this fresh, basketweave pattern is a classic style which will not date easily. Softer patterns (above), with floral motifs, are an appropriate choice in a sun room.
Rubber stud flooring gives a stylish look to this bathroom with a sunken bath.

LAYING THE TILES

Check vinyl tiles carefully before you start. Some designs have patterns with a 'right' and a 'wrong' way, so make sure you know which is which; if necessary, lay out all the whole tiles in a dry run and then stack them in the correct laying sequence.

Self-adhesive tiles are less messy to lay, but the backs of the tiles are *very* sticky and can't be moved around if you position them wrongly. When you start, use the tips of your fingers to hold the tiles just above the floor surface, align the edges with the guide lines, then lower gently into place. Smooth down the tiles with a soft cloth, and keep some mineral spirit handy to wipe adhesive marks off the face of the tiles.

Lay all the whole tiles before cutting the edge tiles. You can do the cutting straight away, since the adhesive acts instantly. When cutting tiles to fit, make all the necessary cuts before you peel off the backing paper.

Do the cutting on a piece of board, using a sharp trimming knife and a steel rule or metal straightedge. Depending on the thickness of the tile, you may not be able to cut it in one go: make repeated passes instead, and keep the straightedge steady.

Plain tiles can be laid in much the same way, but this time spread an area of adhesive large enough to lay four tiles at a time. At the beginning, take care that the adhesive doesn't obscure the guide lines. Wipe off any excess on the face of the tiles immediately.

Lay all the whole tiles, then leave the adhesive to dry for at least 12 hours before fitting the edge tiles. For cut tiles, glue the tiles themselves, not the floor.

Rubber stud tiles are larger than plain vinyl, and the neoprene adhesive is much stickier. So it's advisable only to spread enough adhesive for one tile at a time.

The tiles are designed to create a 'continuous' floor surface, so lay them staggered to hide the joints.

Start tiling where the setting out lines cross. Position the first tile in the angle, then work outwards over the quadrant furthest from the door.

With self-adhesive tiles, peel off the backing and hold the tile just above the floor. Adjust until its position is correct, then press down and smooth.

For plain tiles, spread enough adhesive to lay four tiles at a time. Butt the tiles closely, then wipe off any adhesive which squeezes up through the joints.

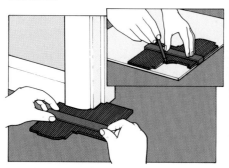

A profile gauge is handy for tricky obstacles: press in place, transfer the shape to the tile, and cut. Then trim the square edge of the tile to fit the gap.

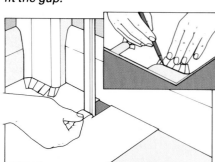

Use sheets of paper the same size as the tiles – or the paper backing on self-adhesive tiles – to make up patterns for large obstacles and pipes.

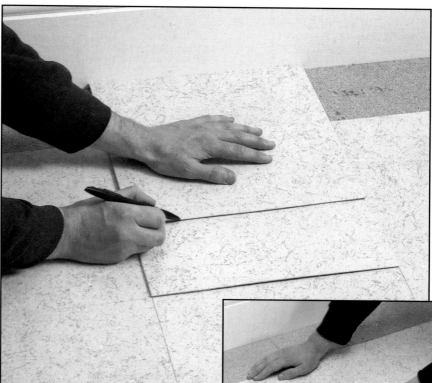

To fit edge tiles, place the tile to be cut on the adjacent, whole tile (inset). Butt a spare tile to the baseboard and use the opposite edge to mark the cutting line.

116

LAYING WOOD MOSAIC FLOORING

The most economical form of hardwood flooring comes as square mosaic panels in a basketweave pattern. These panels are often referred to as 'parquet' or 'woodblock', but they are much thinner and easier to lay than the brick-sized tongued and grooved blocks used on a traditional parquet floor.

The fingers of hardwood making up the panels are generally stuck together with a felt, net or paper backing, though some are strung together with wires which makes cutting slightly trickier. Both methods allow room for expansion and contraction of the wood itself – always the major consideration with a solid wood floor.

Even so, you should ensure the sub-floor is perfectly dry, as well as firm and level. Lift any existing floorcovering and remove all traces of the old adhesive. A concrete floor will probably then need refinishing with self-leveling compound; level a wooden floor with hardboard.

As with other types of wood flooring, you have to leave a small expansion gap around the edges of the room. One way to hide this is to remove the baseboard and notch the door architraves before you start, or you can cover the gap with cork strip or molding (see below).

Warm and welcoming, hardwood mosaic panels (above) provide a long-lasting and naturally resilient floorcovering for relatively little cost.

.... Shopping List....

Wood mosaic panels These are usually sold in packs to cover about 2 square yards, although this varies from dealer to dealer.
Allow a few extra panels in case you cut them badly. Always check the panels are square, by comparing them carefully, turning through 90° to check they are square in both directions.

There are two finishes, sealed and unsealed. When making a choice, bear in mind that the *sealed* panels probably have a better surface than you could apply, and you will save a lot of time because you will not have to apply coats and wait for them to dry before using the room.

With *unsealed* panels, you have to finish them yourself: the varnish will bring out darker and richer tones in the wood.
Adhesive Check the manufacturer's recommendations given with the flooring. You may be able to use a PVA-based general *flooring adhesive*, but many types require a heavier black *bituminous adhesive* to protect the wood from moisture.
Sealant Unsealed panels must have a protective finish, while sealed ones will benefit from an extra coat after laying to stop moisture penetrating the joints.

Polyurethane varnish is the usual choice. Alternatives include quick-drying *two-part lacquer*, which is very hardwearing but considerably more expensive, and *oleo-resinous sealant* which provides a good base for wax polish.

Trim materials The expansion gap around the edge of the room can be filled with *compressible cork strip* (usually stocked by the flooring dealer) or covered with softwood *quarter round* or *scoop molding*. Avoid using cork strip in small rooms, however, as it detracts from the floor's appearance.

Use molding or *aluminum threshold strip* to finish the floor at doorways.

Tools checklist: Pencil, tape measure, string and chalk, trimming knife, backsaw, work bench and hacksaw or pliers (for wired panels), sanding equipment, paintbrush. Extra woodworking tools may be needed for finishing the edges and fitting trim strips.

LAYING THE PANELS

Before you start, double-check that the floor surface is completely smooth. Sand down bumps, punch nail heads below the surface, and vacuum thoroughly.

As with conventional floor tiles, lay the panels in dry runs outwards from the center of the room so that you can start at a point which avoids awkward cuts. (Professionals often start in a corner which is easier for them but trickier for DIY). Note these points when setting out:

■ In a room where the walls are square to each other, the joints between panels should run parallel to them.

■ If the walls are not square, align the joints with the most dominant feature – the longest wall, or a row of units, for example.

■ Allow for a 10mm (3/8") expansion gap (or thereabouts) around the edges of the room.

■ Where cuts are unavoidable, try to confine them to the least obvious parts of the room. Aim to make cuts along the joints between the individual fingers, rather than across the fingers themselves (which is more difficult).

■ If you need underfloor access – to a pipe or cable, for example – ensure the mosaic panel joints coincide with those of the panel in the floor, even if this means more cutting.

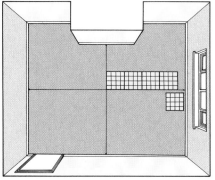

1 Fix string lines at right angles across the center of the floor and lay dry runs of panels to check the fit at the edges. Aim for cuts to coincide with the joints between 'fingers'.

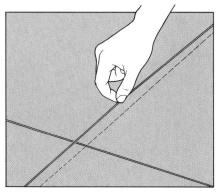

2 When the fit is as good as you can possibly get it, cover the string lines with chalk and snap them to leave guidelines across the floor. Start laying in the quadrant furthest from the door.

4 Spread another panel-sized patch of adhesive, then position the second panel so that it butts tightly against the first. Continue spreading and laying, a panel at a time. Avoid letting adhesive squeeze out of the joints on to the surface of the wood.

3 Starting where the lines cross, spread adhesive over an area slightly larger than a single panel. Position the first panel against the lines.

5 Complete the first quadrant, laying all the whole panels, then work on the other quadrants, finishing at the door. Leave to dry before walking on the panels.

CUTTING PANELS

Cut along the joints between fingers wherever possible. On backed panels, you can simply slice through the backing to separate them. Panels which are wired together along grooves on the underside of the fingers can be severed with tin snips, pincers or a junior hacksaw.

Cutting across the fingers themselves is a little more tricky due to the flexibility of the panels.

■ Begin by marking the cutting line, preferably in pencil.
■ Place the panel on a workbench over an offcut of hardboard. The cutting line should just overhang the edge of the bench.
■ Place a strip of wood on top, as near to the cutting line as you can, and clamp in place.

The panel will now be rigid enough to cut accurately (saw through the hardboard at the same time). Use an electric jigsaw or saber saw, backsaw or coping saw as appropriate.

In awkward areas, it may be easier to separate the panels into single fingers and then trim these individually to fit (but avoid it if you can, since it's difficult to align them). Trim back the backing material to avoid fouling the joints.

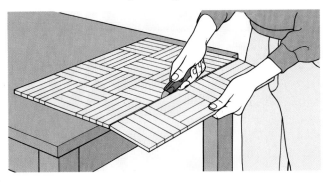

Cut through the backing with a trimming knife to separate individual fingers.

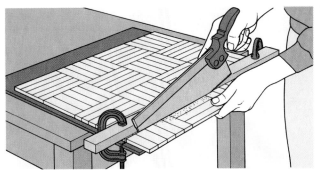

Clamp panels between an offcut of hardboard and a strip of wood to cut across fingers.

FINISHING AROUND THE EDGES

1 To check how much to trim around edge panels, lay the panel to be cut on the last complete panel, then use a spare panel to mark the cutting line.

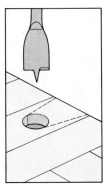

2 At a pipe, mark its position on the panel and drill a hole of a slightly larger diameter. Follow by cutting out a wedge to fit behind the pipe.

3 Around architrave, either cut a paper pattern, or use a profile gauge to copy the shape. Transfer to the panel, then cut to fit.

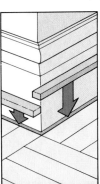

4 Finish edges by pressing cork strip into the expansion gap. Alternatively, cover the gap with softwood molding tacked to the bottom of the baseboard.

5 At doorways, you can fit a tapered molding or hardwood fillet to stop feet catching on the edge of the floor. Or, use an aluminum threshold strip.

SEALING THE FLOOR

After laying and finishing the edges, the final stage is to seal the panels with varnish or lacquer.

Using polyurethane, unsealed panels need at least three coats. Thin the first coat with mineral spirit to help it soak in.

Sand and vacuum thoroughly between coats. You can use fine sandpaper on a sanding block, or even a power sander, but many professionals prefer to use a large wad of medium grade steel wool.

Sealed panels require just a single coat, applied unthinned.

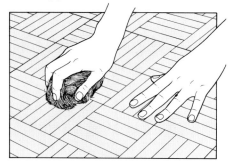

1 *Thin the first coat with 1 part mineral spirit to 10 parts polyurethane. Sand between coats using a wad of medium grade steel wool, then vacuum well.*

2 *As the finish builds up, the rich tones of the wood will start to emerge. Before the final coat, take extra precautions against dust: close any windows, then vacuum the floor and wipe over the surface with a damp cloth.*

■ PROBLEM SOLVER ■

Repairing damaged panels

It's worth keeping a few spare mosaic panels in case of accidental damage – dents from sharp, heavy objects are the most likely cause. In severe cases, you may have to replace an entire panel; it's more likely that the damage is confined to one or two fingers.

■ On backed panels, the fingers can be loosened by scoring around the edges with a trimming knife. With wired panels, you have to sever the wires by tapping sharply along the joints with a bolster or an old wood chisel.

■ Afterwards, prize out the fingers with a claw hammer or old chisel, using an offcut to protect the surrounding surface. Scrape away all traces of the backing and adhesive below.

■ Cut new fingers from a spare panel and check the fit.

With unsealed panels bed the new fingers in place on a fresh layer of adhesive. (If you haven't the correct type, woodworking adhesive should do).

Leave the repair for a couple of days to let the patch acclimatize. If it stands proud, sand level with the surrounding surface, taking care not to remove wood from the other fingers. Finally, sand the entire panel and revarnish.

With sealed panels, check if the replacement fingers stand proud of the surrounding surface. If they do, peel off any backing and sand them on the back to allow them to lie flush when bedded in adhesive. When stuck, sand the top lightly and give one coat of varnish to blend with the surrounding panel.

Sever wired fingers by tapping sharply along the joints with a thin bladed bolster, old wood chisel, or stripping knife. Use a trimming knife on backed panels.

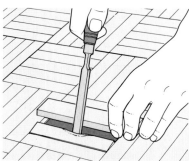

Lever out the damaged fingers with a claw hammer or an old chisel. Afterwards, scrape away all traces of the old adhesive and backing.

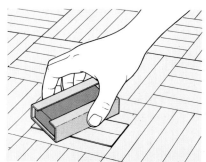

Sand the patched area if necessary, then sand the entire panel so that any color change in the finish occurs between the panel joints.

LAYING WALL-TO-WALL CARPETING

Laying and fitting carpets yourself isn't always a good idea, particularly on large floors or awkwardly shaped areas such as the stairs. Indeed, many suppliers offer free fitting on carpets over a certain value, and professional laying should make sure you get the best wear out of top quality carpets – which have to be stretched tightly so that the pile stands upright.

Even so, there are times when it simply isn't worth calling in the professionals – for example, when laying a cheap foam backed carpet or remnant. You might also want to take carpets with you if you move.

Laying methods

There are three ways to fix carpets.
Foam backed carpets are normally held around the edges of the room with *double-sided carpet tape.*
Canvas backed carpets can be stretched on gripper strips tacked to the floor around the edges of the room. Alternatively, if the subfloor is wooden, the edges can simply be turned over and tacked in place.

Underlay and lining

Foam or felt underlay should always be laid under canvas backed carpets to prolong wear and add a luxurious feel. It is unnecessary under foam backed carpets.
An extra lining (of paper or nylon) is essential for canvas backed carpet laid over floorboards, to prevent dirt from being drawn up from the void beneath the floor. And under foam backed carpets, a lining can help to prevent the backing from sticking to the subfloor.

Preparation

The subfloor must be clean and free from grease, particularly if you are using adhesive or carpet tape. Remove any doors for clearance if necessary (see Problem Solver).
Wooden floors should be level, with no movement in the boards and all nails punched home. If the boards are at all uneven, line the floor with hardboard, as for sheet vinyl.
Solid floors must be level and free from damp. If they are slightly uneven, level with self-leveling compound; if they are crumbling or 'out' by more than 12mm (½"), get them rescreeded.

PLANNING AND MEASURING

Before buying, measure the room.
■ Measure the overall area, taking measurements along and across the room at several points to allow for moderate irregularities. Measure into bays and alcoves where appropriate.
■ Check how square the walls are to one another by measuring the diagonals as well; if they are equal, you should have little trouble deciding how much carpet to order. If one diagonal is considerably longer than the other, allow extra width and length to ensure a good fit.
■ Allow at least 100mm (4") extra all around so you can trim the carpet for an accurate fit.
■ Underlay and lining paper should be laid leaving a 50mm (2") gap all around for double-sided tape, gripper strips or turning and tacking.

Which way around?

Choose a carpet which is wide enough to fit right across the room if possible. If you do have to join widths, plan the job so that seams fall in the areas of least traffic, and make sure that the pile on each piece runs in the same direction.
■ Check the width of the carpet and decide which way to lay it according to the room's proportions. For example, on a floor measuring 2.5×3.8m (8'2"×12'6"), a single piece of 4m (13') carpet could run the length of the room.
■ A woven carpet should ideally be laid so that the direction of the pile runs away from the door (and towards the window if possible). This helps to prevent indentations from footmarks showing as you enter the room.

A patterned, tufted carpet in 80/20 wool/nylon is an ideal choice for a living room. Measure across the room at several points (inset) and check the diagonals as well before ordering.

For fixing buy *double-sided tape, tacks,* or *carpet gripper strip* according to your chosen method, plus a tack hammer for driving in the nails. Note that grippers come part-nailed, so be sure to state whether you're fixing to floorboards or concrete. *A staple gun* is handy for fixing lining or underlay to wood floors.

For joining seams use *double-sided tape* on foam backed carpet, or *woven tape* and *latex adhesive* on canvas backed carpet. *Single-sided carpet tape* is used to join widths of underlay.

For cutting use *scissors* and/or a *trimming knife*, plus a *metal straight edge* and *tape measure*.

Professional tools aren't essential, but make it easier to get a good finish. Aim to rent or improvise the following items, as they are expensive to buy.

A knee-kicker is used to stretch carpet across the room. The head spikes are adjustable to suit the carpet pile.

Position the kicker head near the edge of the carpet, at a slight angle to the run of the gripper strip. Knock the knee pad to force the carpet closer to the wall, then tuck the edge over the gripper.

A carpet layer's hammer has a long slim head for knocking in nails close to baseboard. It can also be held sideways and used for pressing carpet on to grippers.

A carpet layer's bolster is for tucking carpet between gripper strips and the wall. You can use a clean, blunt bricklayer's bolster or wallpaper scraper instead.

Un-nailed grippers are used in the trade where there's a risk of nailing through pipes. These need a special adhesive – ask your supplier.

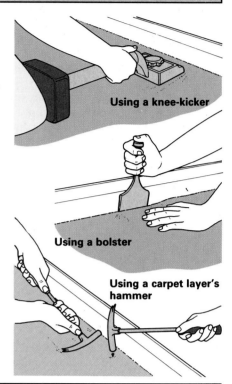

Using a knee-kicker

Using a bolster

Using a carpet layer's hammer

LAYING FOAM-BACKED CARPET

Foam backed carpets are relatively easy to lay – no underlay is used and they don't need stretching.

■ Start by laying the lining if needed. It doesn't have to be fixed, but taping or stapling it in place will stop it shifting around.

■ Check which way the pile runs, and unroll the carpet so it lies the right way round. When it is as flat and smooth as possible, trim to size leaving at least 50mm (2″) lapping up the walls all the way round.

■ Make 'freeing cuts' diagonally into the corners so that the carpet lies as flat as possible.

■ Turn back the edge of the carpet and stick down the tape, leaving the backing paper in place.

■ Start to fit the carpet along one long straight wall. You may be able to butt the edge straight to the wall, but usually it's safer to trim it to fit. Stick the carpet down, unpeeling the tape backing and pulling the carpet tight as you go.

■ With one side held firmly, tread the carpet in place, shuffling across the room to remove wrinkles. Repeat to get the carpet as taut as possible.

■ Trim and fit the opposite edge to the one you fixed, making diagonal cuts to fit it into internal or external corners. Stick it in place.

■ Finally, work up and down the room in the same way and stick the remaining edges.

1 Lay the lining if necessary, stapling or sticking it with double-sided tape. Align the end of the carpet with the wall and unroll. Trim waste to 50mm (2″).

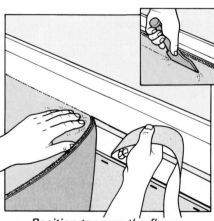

2 Position tape on the floor around the edge of the lining paper. Use a bolster to mark the trim line: ensure the carpet is taut before cutting and sticking.

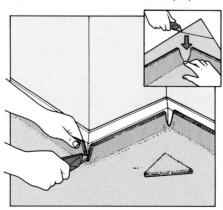

3 Cut across the carpet where it is to fit into internal corners before trimming. At external corners, cut diagonally to the obstruction.

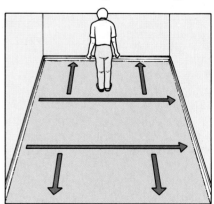

4 Tread the carpet in place across the room, then stick the opposite edge. Finally, work up and down the room and stick the remaining edges in place.

LAYING CANVAS BACKED CARPETS

Canvas backed carpets should be stretched tightly across the room, whether they are turned and tacked or fitted to gripper strips. You can stretch the carpet by shuffling it into place with your feet, but for a professional finish rent a knee-kicker. Proper tensioning makes sure the pile stands as upright as possible, improving its life. Some types of carpet also tend to stretch as they wear in; tensioning should prevent this too.

Lay the lining and underlay first, with a 50mm (2") border. If using grippers, fix them and any threshold strips (see overleaf) next. Watch out for buried pipes and cables.

Before stretching and fitting the carpet, trim it to fit the room allowing about 100mm (4") extra all around. Then, starting from one corner, trim the waste to 20mm (¾") along adjacent edges. Fix these edges for 300mm (1') out from the corner, then stretch the carpet and fit it to the gripper strips along the longer wall. Next stretch it along the shorter wall, out from the same corner. Stretch the carpet across the room towards the corner opposite the starting point, then fit along the remaining walls.

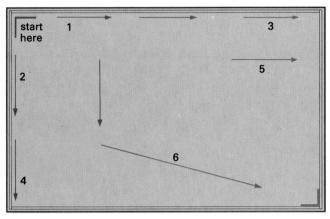

The basic stretching plan is to start from one corner. Fix firmly on both sides of the corner, then stretch and fit along each adjacent wall. Stretch down the longer wall to the opposite corner before fitting the carpet along the remaining walls.

1 Lay the lining and then the underlay, fixing them with staples or tape. Join seams with carpet tape. Nail gripper strips around the room about 5mm (¼") from the wall. At curves, cut short lengths of strip leaving at least two nails for fixing.

2 Unroll the carpet and trim to fit roughly. At the starting corner, trim diagonally across it. Trim the waste to 19mm (¾") and press over the gripper strip.

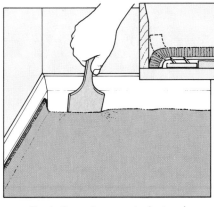

3 Tuck the edge waste between the gripper and baseboard. Stretch the carpet along the first edge, pressing it on to the gripper and tucking in as you go.

4 Work around the room in the order shown above, treading the carpet as flat as possible before stretching it taut and fitting over the grippers.

Trade tip

Working with tufteds

❝If tufted carpets are stored in an unheated place, the backing stiffens up. Leave the carpet in a warm room so that it becomes pliable again – particularly if you plan to lay the carpet in an awkward area. Never fold a tufted carpet, as you will have great difficulty removing the creases.❞

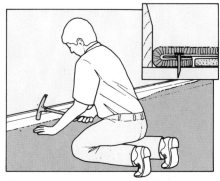

If turning and tacking fit the first corner by turning under about 50mm (2") and tacking it in place every 100mm (4"). Trim away excess fabric across the corner.

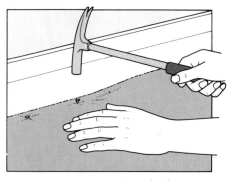

Continue to turn and tack along one edge, stretching it as you go. Repeat for the other edge. Then stretch the carpet across the room, trim, turn and tack.

JOINING WIDTHS

Traditionally, seams between widths of carpet were sewn. Nowadays adhesives and carpet tape are more commonly used. Where possible, join machined edges; otherwise, overlap the two edges to be joined and use one edge as a cutting guide to trim the layer underneath.

With foam backed carpets use the same double-sided tape used to fix the carpet but strengthen the joint with latex adhesive.

With woven backings use woven tape and latex adhesive to make the seam. You should join widths before stretching the carpet to fit.

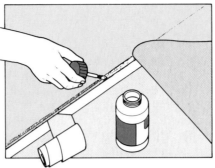

With foam backed carpets position the tape on the floor along the seam line. Apply latex adhesive along the cut edge, peel off the backing and press firmly.

For canvas backed carpet lay woven tape along the seam line, coat it with adhesive, then press the edges in place. Roll the seam afterwards for a good bond.

THRESHOLD STRIPS

Choose a threshold strip *without* spikes for foam backed carpet, *with* spikes for gripper fixing. The type of strip is also governed by what's on the other side of the doorway: where carpets butt up to each other, use a double-sided strip designed to hold carpets on both sides; use a single-sided strip if the carpet finishes here

The threshold strip should be fitted directly under the position of the door when closed. But if there is a hard floorcovering on the other side of the door, the threshold strip must cover its edge.

Position the carpet over the strip, mark the cutting line and trim any waste. Then simply tuck the edge under the cover strip.

To hold foam backed carpets in place, hammer the strip over the edge of the carpet using a piece of wood to protect the metal surface.

Problems with doors

Laying a thick new carpet could involve removing and trimming any inward-opening doors.

■ To remove a door, open it wide and slip magazines underneath to take the weight while you release the hinges.

■ After fitting the carpet, measure down the frame from the lower hinge to the surface of the new carpet, and compare this with the equivalent measurement on the door. Mark the bottom edge for trimming.

■ To trim a small amount – less than 6mm (¼″) or so – simply plane down to the marked line.

■ To trim more, use a crosscut saw and plane smooth, or use a power plane.

■ Check the fit of the door by holding both open and closed. If all is well, place it back on the magazines to align the hinge plates, then refit the screws.

Support the door with magazines while unscrewing the hinges.

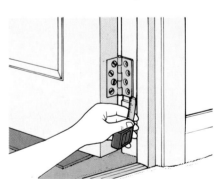

Measure and mark the amount to be trimmed.

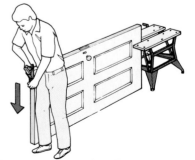

Plane to the marked line.

3

BUILDING

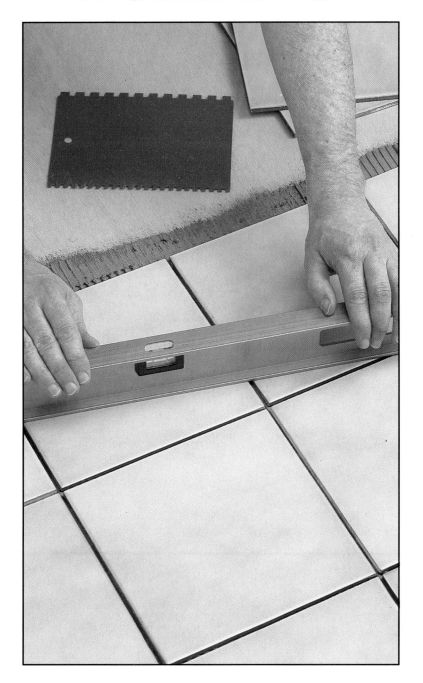

FIXING TO SOLID WALLS

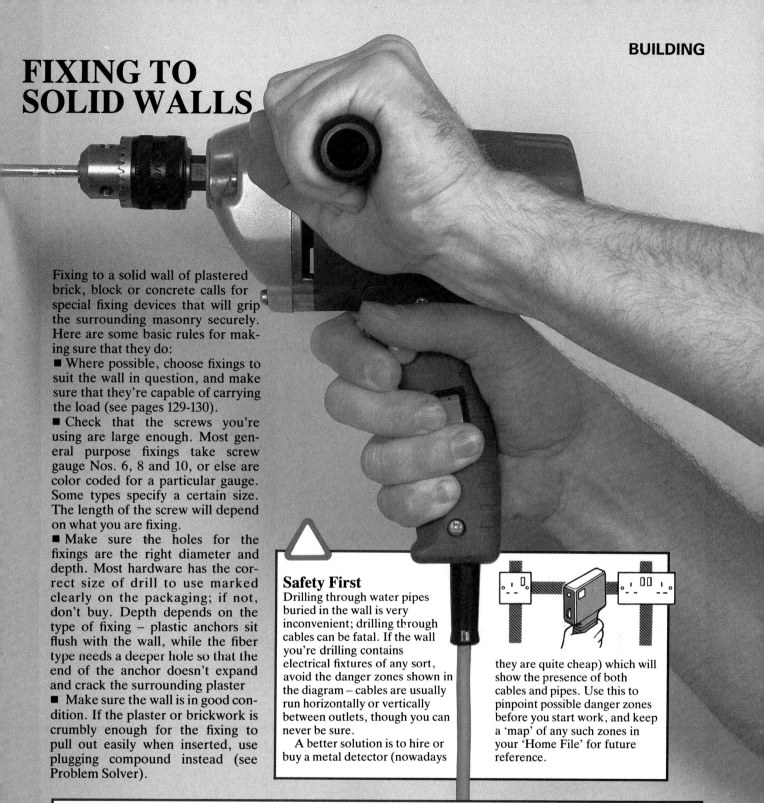

Fixing to a solid wall of plastered brick, block or concrete calls for special fixing devices that will grip the surrounding masonry securely. Here are some basic rules for making sure that they do:

■ Where possible, choose fixings to suit the wall in question, and make sure that they're capable of carrying the load (see pages 129-130).

■ Check that the screws you're using are large enough. Most general purpose fixings take screw gauge Nos. 6, 8 and 10, or else are color coded for a particular gauge. Some types specify a certain size. The length of the screw will depend on what you are fixing.

■ Make sure the holes for the fixings are the right diameter and depth. Most hardware has the correct size of drill to use marked clearly on the packaging; if not, don't buy. Depth depends on the type of fixing – plastic anchors sit flush with the wall, while the fiber type needs a deeper hole so that the end of the anchor doesn't expand and crack the surrounding plaster

■ Make sure the wall is in good condition. If the plaster or brickwork is crumbly enough for the fixing to pull out easily when inserted, use plugging compound instead (see Problem Solver).

Safety First

Drilling through water pipes buried in the wall is very inconvenient; drilling through cables can be fatal. If the wall you're drilling contains electrical fixtures of any sort, avoid the danger zones shown in the diagram – cables are usually run horizontally or vertically between outlets, though you can never be sure.

A better solution is to hire or buy a metal detector (nowadays they are quite cheap) which will show the presence of both cables and pipes. Use this to pinpoint possible danger zones before you start work, and keep a 'map' of any such zones in your 'Home File' for future reference.

BASIC DRILLING TECHNIQUE

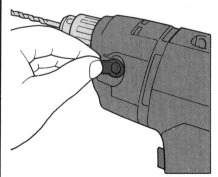

1 *For plaster, set the drill speed to 'low' and the hammer facility (if fitted) to 'off'. If you hit brick or concrete, switch the hammer to 'on'.*

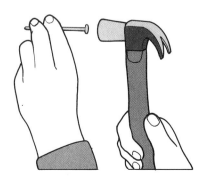

2 *Measure the position of each hole twice to avoid mistakes. Then 'spot' the holes by punching them with an old nail to stop the drill bit from slipping.*

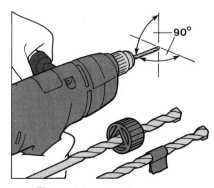

3 *Fit a rubber depth stop or a piece of tape to the drill bit so you know how deep to drill. Check the drill is square to the wall before pulling the trigger.*

AVOIDING MESS

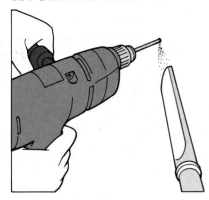

1 One way to reduce the dust thrown up by drilling into a solid wall is to have a helper standing by with a vacuum cleaner – use the dust nozzle.

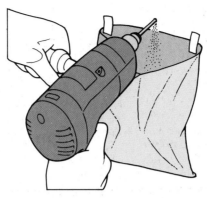

2 Alternatively, tape one side of plastic bag to the wall just below the holes. Let the bag fall open or grasp it in your fingers to catch the debris.

3 When drilling upwards, use an empty yogurt container for the debris: bore a hole in the base, then fit the pot over the drill bit so it rests on the chuck.

PROBLEM SOLVER

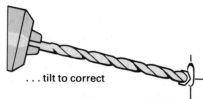

if the drill bit slips . . .   . . . tilt to correct

Missing the point

If the bit slips away from the mark when you start a hole, tilt the drill in the **same direction** as the slip and you should find that it rights itself.

When holes don't align

If you're fitting brackets and one of the holes doesn't line up, try enlarging the bracket hole with a small file rather than re-drilling the wall.

if anchors don't align . . .   . . . try altering bracket

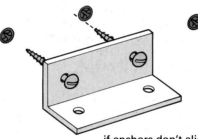

fit anchors to screws where vision is **obscured**

Plugging blind

Where you can't see to line up screws with their anchors, fit the anchors to the ends of the screws instead and juggle the entire assembly into position.

Using plugging compound

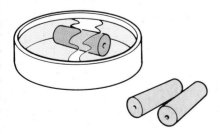

1 Use plugging compound to repair holes in crumbling plaster. Soak an anchor in water for one minute to soften it.

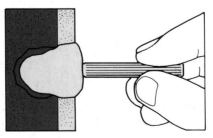

2 Force the softened anchor into the hole with the dowel supplied and smooth off level with the surface of the wall.

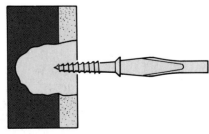

3 Then drive in the fixing screw a third of the way and leave to set for 30 minutes before fixing as normal.

TYPES OF FIXING

Plastic anchors are the most commonly used type of solid wall fixing, and since most anchor sizes each accommodate a range of screw sizes, you should find that with careful selection just two anchor sizes cover you for most jobs around the house.

The exception will be where the screws you're using are very long – say, over 32mm (1¼″) 'in the wall'. In this case, ask yourself if such a deep fixing is really necessary, and if it is, use plastic extruded strip cut to length: otherwise, use shorter screws.

Most of the other fixings shown below have more specialized uses, and many are only available from hardware stores. Expandable wall bolts are quite common, but only as fixings for structural members – joist hangers, wall plates and the like. They are expensive, so buy them when you need them and hire a drill bit of the appropriate size.

Trade tip
Standard kit

❛ I've always found that a pack of standard anchors, a No.12 masonry bit, and No.8 screws in 32mm (1¼″), 38mm (1½″) and 50mm (2″) lengths are fine for 90% of fixing jobs around the house. Remember, the amount the screw thread penetrates the wall should always be the same. ❜

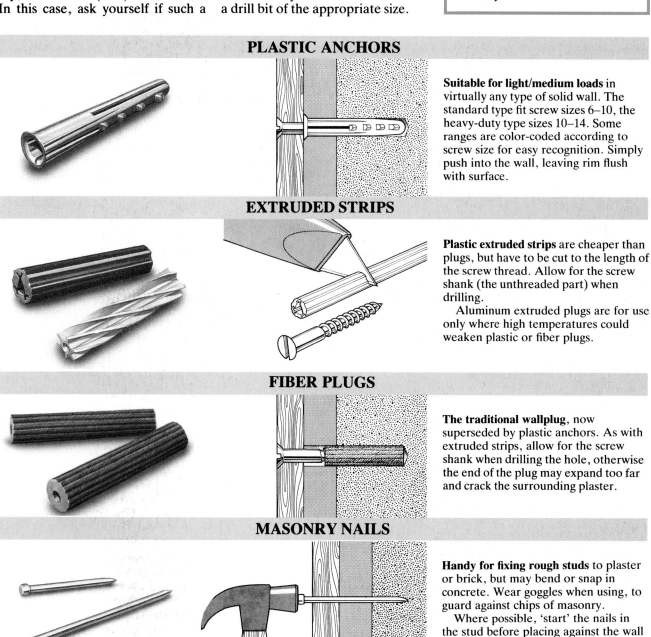

PLASTIC ANCHORS

Suitable for light/medium loads in virtually any type of solid wall. The standard type fit screw sizes 6–10, the heavy-duty type sizes 10–14. Some ranges are color-coded according to screw size for easy recognition. Simply push into the wall, leaving rim flush with surface.

EXTRUDED STRIPS

Plastic extruded strips are cheaper than plugs, but have to be cut to the length of the screw thread. Allow for the screw shank (the unthreaded part) when drilling.

Aluminum extruded plugs are for use only where high temperatures could weaken plastic or fiber plugs.

FIBER PLUGS

The traditional wallplug, now superseded by plastic anchors. As with extruded strips, allow for the screw shank when drilling the hole, otherwise the end of the plug may expand too far and crack the surrounding plaster.

MASONRY NAILS

Handy for fixing rough studs to plaster or brick, but may bend or snap in concrete. Wear goggles when using, to guard against chips of masonry.

Where possible, 'start' the nails in the stud before placing against the wall and angle them for extra grip.

BLOCK FIXINGS

Special anchors that provide extra grip in lightweight cellular blocks.

One type is screwed into hole and fixed in position by tapping in a locking pin down the side. Another has fins which expand as the anchor is driven into the wall.

NAILABLE ANCHORS

Nails with 'built-in' anchors useful where a large number of not-too-strong fixings have to be made, such as on stud frameworks and baseboards. Wall and stud are drilled in one go, then anchor is driven in with a hammer (expanding as it does so). Removable *hammer screw* has a slotted head.

FRAME FIXINGS

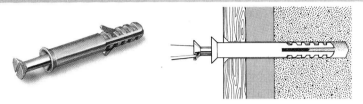

Screw version of nailable anchor invaluable on jobs where alignment of the screw and plug holes may be difficult – for example, when screwing a window frame to the surrounding masonry.

SPECIAL PURPOSE FIXINGS

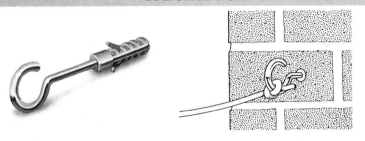

A variety of custom-made steel fixings are sold complete with heavy-duty high-grip anchors, so if you want to fix anything out of the ordinary it's worth asking your hardware dealer. Shown left is a hook fixing for securing a washing line or cable support wire to an outside wall.

EXPANDING WALL ANCHORS

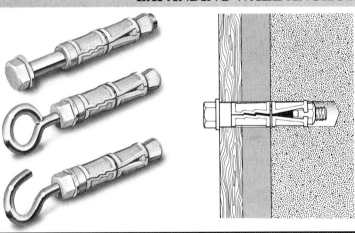

Heavy-duty fixings for securing wooden beams, joist hangers and the like.

On some types the outer metal shell expands as the built-in bolt is driven in. On others, driving the bolt causes the shell to compress and thicken, gripping the wall as it does so. Several types of bolt heads are available, including stud, hook and eye.

Holes for wall anchors must always be drilled in the center of bricks or blocks – *not* in the intervening mortar joints, or the fixings may fail.

MASONRY DRILLS AND BITS

■ It's absolutely essential to use a tungsten carbide tipped masonry bit (below) for drilling solid walls; you can tell one by the spade-shaped insert in the tip.

■ By far the best type of drill for concrete or rendered walls is a hammer drill, which punches as well as bores its way through the small stones in the material. If you don't own one it's worth hiring – but make sure your drill

bits are *'suitable for impact use'*.

■ If your drill has a speed setting, keep it on low unless you feel particular resistance. If it is a variable speed model, start off slowly and increase to medium speed as you go or when you feel extra resistance.

■ Older single speed electric drills will just about cope with blocks and common brick, but operate the drill in bursts to stop the bit blunting.

MASONRY DRILL SIZE CHART

Screw size*	Drill No.	Stan. size	Equiv. metric size
	6	5/32"	4mm
	8	3/16"	4.5mm
	10	7/32"	5.5mm
	12	1/4"	6.5mm
	14	9/32"	7mm
	16	5/16"	8mm
	18	11/32"	9mm
	20	3/8"	10mm

*Screw heads are shown lifesize, and as a guide only. For drilling anchor holes, use the bit size recommended by the manufacturer.

FIXING TO HOLLOW WALLS AND CEILINGS

Fixings for *solid* walls are designed to expand in their holes and get a grip on the surrounding masonry. But in most homes, some of the walls and all the ceilings are hollow, with only a thin plaster or plasterboard skin. This means that there's nothing much for an ordinary wall anchor to get a grip on, and you must use cavity fixings instead.

The right fixing

Although there are many types of cavity fixing, they all work by fitting through a small hole in the surface skin and then expanding behind it so the screw won't pull out. Because each one is suitable for different jobs, and because the surface of a cavity construction is relatively weak, it's even more important to choose the right fixing method.

The first step is to take a look at what you're fixing to. In older houses, *some* of the interior walls are probably cavity constructions. But in modern homes, even exterior walls can have a hollow wooden frame. So if you suspect a wall's hollow, test it to make sure.

Right: Hollow wall fixings like this Rawlplug collapsible metal type bear on the inside surface of the cavity skin – in this case plasterboard.

IDENTIFYING A CAVITY CONSTRUCTION

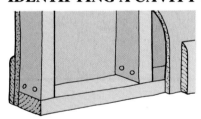

Plasterboard constructions are easily identified because they sound hollow when tapped, except where there are frame studs behind the skin.

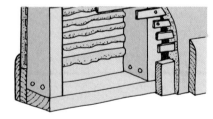

Lath and plaster is much thicker, but may sound hollow if the plaster covering the laths is on the thin side. Drill a small hole to confirm your findings.

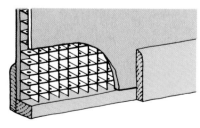

Dry (honeycomb) partition is thinner than other walls (50-63mm). Made of double sheets of 9.5mm (⅜") plasterboard with a cellular core, on wooden frame.

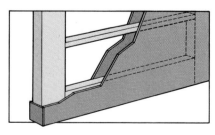

Hollow door Modern interior doors are made from sheets of hardboard or plywood on a wood frame. The cellular core may not sound hollow, so drill to check.

Most cavity walls are based on a framework of substantial vertical strips called *studs*, usually 350-610mm (14-24") apart, which are braced by wooden crosspieces. Ceilings are fixed to the underside of the supporting timbers (*joists*). These are generally spaced 400-610mm (16-24") apart.

In houses built in the past few decades, the framework is usually finished with sheets of 12mm (½") thick plasterboard.

In older houses, lath and plaster was used. With this type of construction, thin strips of wood (the laths) are nailed up at roughly 12mm (½") intervals, then covered with a skin of (often thick) plaster.

Other constructions

There are two other types of cavity construction which you might have to fix to: dry partitioning (used only for walls and not common in ordinary houses), and hollow internal doors.

HOW STRONG?

When you have checked what you are fixing to, think about the weight of what you want to put up. The table on the right shows how to group various items as Heavy, Medium and Light. When deciding how to group something, don't forget to allow for the weight of what's going inside or on top.

Light or Medium fixtures can be put up with the right type of cavity fixing, shown on the following pages. For anything Heavy, do not try to use a cavity fixing. The only really secure way to fix it is to screw directly to the wooden frame as shown below.

WORKING OUT THE LOAD		
HEAVY 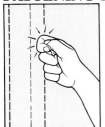	**Walls:** kitchen cabinets, bookshelves, track shelving, radiator, row of coat hooks, curtain tracks and poles, large framed mirrors and pictures.	**Ceilings:** hanging plant holders, heavy light fixtures, pull-cord switches, curtain tracks and poles
MEDIUM 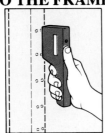	**Walls:** small bathroom cabinet, ornamental shelves, framed pictures, medium sized mirrors, kitchen base units	**Ceilings:** lightweight light fixtures, track lighting tracks, spotlights.
LIGHT	**Walls:** small pictures/prints, message board, clock, small mirror	

FASTENING TO THE FRAME

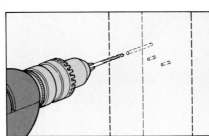

1 Find the studs by tapping at regular intervals to detect a change in the sound, or use a metal detector to trace rows of fixing nails.

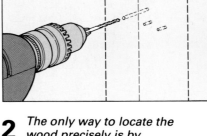

2 The only way to locate the wood precisely is by straddling its position with test holes using a bradawl or thin drill bit.

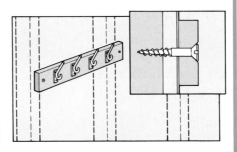

3 Once you have found two studs, you can find others by measuring the gap and then measuring the same distance along. Drill and test to check.

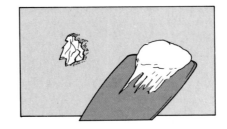

4 Fixing screws should project at least 32mm (1¼") into the wall. If you can't fix to the studs screw a strip of wood to them, then screw to that.

Trade tip

Drilling hollow walls

❛ Most cavity fixings need quite large holes, usually about 9mm (⅜"). Drill at low speed with little pressure and no hammer – be prepared to break through very suddenly. Plaster and plasterboard are quite soft, so if you haven't a masonry bit this size, use an old wood bit instead. This can even give a cleaner hole, though the drill will be spoilt for other jobs. ❜

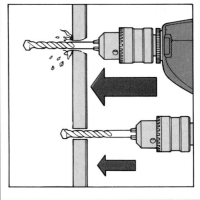

PROBLEM SOLVER

Springing a lath

If the point of the drill pushes a lath away from the plaster instead of going through it, change to a smaller wood bit and try again. If this doesn't get through, try drilling another hole slightly higher or lower.

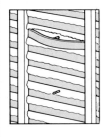 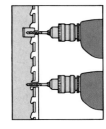

Filling misdrilled holes

The large holes used by cavity wall fixings can be hard to fill if you break through in the wrong place. Mix the filler to a stiff consistency with newspaper to pack out the hole, then smooth over with a final layer of filler when dry.

Fixing to hollow doors

Hardboard hollow doors are sometimes too weak to support a fixing and glued-on fittings may be more secure. If an existing fixing comes out, it will probably split the surface. Try gluing it back in using epoxy adhesive.

TYPES OF CAVITY FIXING

Cavity fixings must be suitable for your wall and the load you are putting up. The table below classes the types of fixings which are suitable for Light or Medium loads and tells you what surfaces they can be used on. If you are in doubt about the weight, choose a fixing from the Medium category.

There are some other points to think about which may affect your decision:

■ If you have to use particular screws with whatever you are putting up, make sure these are suitable for the fixing. Some can only be used with their own built-in screws.

■ If you are buying separate screws, check how far these need to project through into the wall fixing.

■ Note that several types of fixing cannot be used more than once, because if you remove the screw, they fall into the cavity. If you might have to take down the fixture temporarily – for painting, say – use one listed in the table as reusable.

■ A few fixtures are put up by leaving the screw head projecting and then slotting the fixture over it. Very few cavity fixings expand properly unless the screw is tightly home, so be sure to find a suitable one if you have to fix something which uses this method.

PLASTIC WING ANCHOR – LIGHT

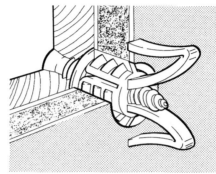

Designed specifically for plasterboard. Requires a 6.5mm hole and accepts standard No. 8 woodscrews. Reusable and inexpensive.

Drill the hole in plasterboard, then tap the plug home and attach the fixture. As you tighten the fixing screw, the legs are forced apart so that they grip the back of the plasterboard.

PLASTIC WEDGE ANCHOR – LIGHT

Two versions available – one for plasterboard walls, and a smaller one for hollow doors. They need 9mm/6.5mm holes and take standard No. 8/No. 6 woodscrews respectively. Reusable and inexpensive.

Fit in the same way as a wing anchor. Tightening the fixing screw causes the sides of the anchor to expand and grip the back of the cavity skin.

PLASTIC PETAL ANCHOR – LIGHT

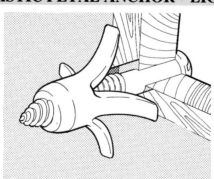

Suits any cavity thickness but is particularly useful for narrow cavities where space for a fixing is limited. Different sizes are available accepting Nos 6, 8 and 10 woodscrews (hole sizes are 6mm, 8mm and 10mm). Very cheap but not reusable.

To fit, drill hole, then attach anchor to fixing screw. When inserted, petals spring back against cavity skin and are drawn into it as screw is tightened.

EXPANDING RUBBER NUT – LIGHT

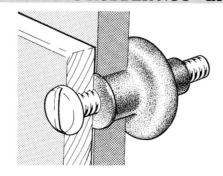

Suitable for various thicknesses of cavity skin, therefore ideal for wood paneling etc. They are also very useful if you're not sure what you are drilling into. Different sizes are available (smallest hole size 8mm). Comes with own fixing bolt (hexagonal or slotted head). Reusable but not cheap.

To use, remove bolt and refit through fixture. Then drill hole, insert fixing and tighten bolt.

HOLLOW DOOR FIXINGS – LIGHT

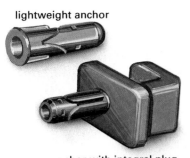

lightweight anchor

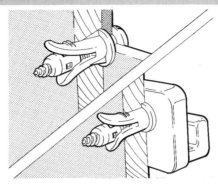

anchor with integral plug

For hollow doors only Special fixings with built-in hooks. Single and double types are available, in a range of colors; double version comes with a drilling guide. Both take 6mm holes.

COLLAPSIBLE FIXING – LIGHT/MEDIUM

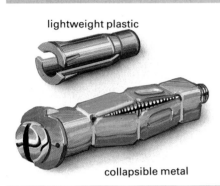

lightweight plastic

collapsible metal

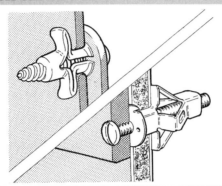

Suitable for different thicknesses of cavity skin, depending on size. Two broad groups – metal and plastic. Plastic types are cheaper, but the cheapest only accept light loads; they accept standard woodscrews (typically Nos 6, 8 and 10). Metal types come with their own machine screws. Hole sizes vary, but are normally 6mm, 8mm or 10mm. Reusable. Fit as for wing anchor.

SELF-HOLDING STRAP TOGGLE – MEDIUM

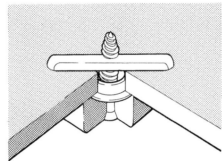

Suitable for different cavity thicknesses up to 50mm (2″). Screw doesn't need full tightening for fixing to hold, so ideal for 'keyhole slot' fixtures. Needs a 10mm hole and No. 8 woodscrews. Reusable, but not cheap. Cavity must be wide enough to allow fixing to open.
  To fit, ease toggle through hole, position collar, then pull strap to engage. Trim strap after inserting fixing screw.

GRAVITY TOGGLE – MEDIUM

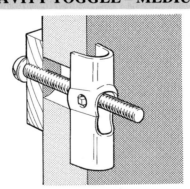

Suitable for different thicknesses of cavity skin, but needs space behind to open. Special type available for ceilings. Robust metal construction, and supplied with own machine screw or hook fixing. Requires large (16mm; ½″) hole. Expensive and not reusable.
  To fit, push right through hole into cavity, allowing backplate to drop. Then pull pack to engage backplate and tighten fixing screw against it.

SPRING TOGGLE – MEDIUM

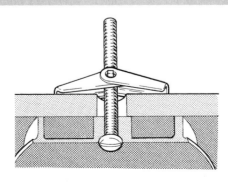

Suitable for different thicknesses of cavity, depending on size chosen, but like gravity toggle needs space behind to open. Particularly suitable for lath and plaster. Robust metal construction, and supplied with own machine screw or hook bolt. Hole size between 11mm and 18mm (⅜″ and ⅝″), depending on size. Expensive and not reusable.

PATCHING HOLES IN PLASTER

The one thing you need when patching holes in plaster is patience. Modern materials have made the job much easier than it used to be, but if you rush, the chances are you'll take twice as long to get a finish that's fit for redecorating.

On small holes and cracks use general purpose filler, building it up in thin layers and allowing each one to dry before applying the next. For the final layer, use fine surface filler

– it is much smoother and takes paint well.

For larger repairs up to around 1 sq m (1 sq yd) you have a choice of using ready-mixed DIY repair and skimming plaster, or mixing your own conventional plaster in a bucket. Each have their advantages and disadvantages (see page 138), but the repairs which are shown here all make use of the ready-mixed type of plaster.

Applying ready mixed skimming plaster.

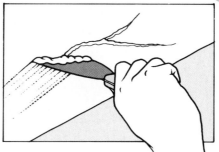

1 For a small crack, give the filler something to grip by enlarging the crack slightly with the corner of your filling knife. Dampen with water afterwards.

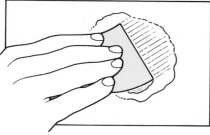

2 Press the filler into the crack, smoothing as you go. Then hold the knife edge-on to the surface of the wall and scrape away the excess.

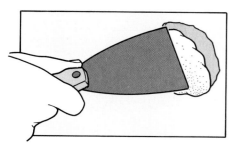

3 For a hole, brush away any loose material and dampen with water. Apply a first layer of filler to a depth of no more than 5mm (¼″) and leave to dry.

4 Build up subsequent layers in the same way until the filler is just below the surface of the wall. Finish by smearing on a layer of fine surface filler.

Trade tip

The spray way

❝ People often fill a hole in plaster roughly, then spend ages sanding it down only to find they have to fill it again. It's far better to get it smooth first time – by using clean tools, and spraying the surface with water as you smooth it using a garden hand spray. It takes a light touch, but with a little bit of practice you soon learn. ❞

MENDING CHIPPED CORNERS

1 Knock some nails into a strip of wood so the tips just show through. Then nail it level with the edge of the corner leaving one side of the chip exposed.

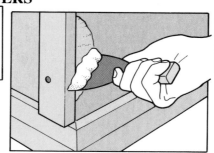

2 Prepare the chipped area as for an ordinary hole, then press in some filler or repair plaster and smooth off against the edge of the wooden strip.

3 When the first side is dry, pull out the nails with pliers and fill the second side. Use the strip of wood as shown to get a clean edge to the repair.

RESURFACING AN UNEVEN WALL

Ready mixed skimming plaster is the perfect material for finishing off a patched repair like the one on the previous page.

However, if there are lots of patches in the same wall, it's worth giving the entire wall another coat after you've finished so that the repairs are completely hidden. The technique is exactly the same in both cases.

Use a large, wide paintbrush to apply the skimming plaster; the better the condition of the bristles, the easier the job is.

1 Apply the plaster with broad upward sweeps of the brush. When you've covered about a square yard, run the brush gently over it to smooth.

Holding the brush like this when smoothing gives you more control.

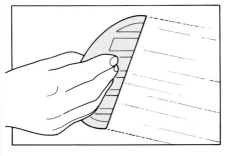

2 Wait until the plaster starts to 'go off' (dry), then use the applicator supplied to smooth out the brushmarks, dipping it frequently in a bowl of water.

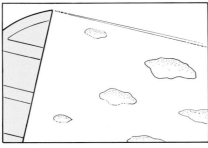

3 Pits like these show that you are 'stretching' the plaster too far; refill them immediately. Don't worry about the ridges – they can be sanded afterwards.

Press the float into the wall as you sweep it across the repair.

PATCHING LARGER HOLES

Holes up to around 1 sq m (1 sq yd) can be patched fairly successfully, but you must make sure the backing is sound. Chip off any loose material (even if this enlarges the hole) using a scraper, an old wood chisel or a brick chisel. If the plaster is crumbly, paint it with stabilizing fluid or PVA adhesive (see page 138).

The best tool for applying the repair plaster is a metal float. Don't spend a fortune on this – a cheap one is perfectly adequate.

1 Prepare the hole by brushing away any loose material, and if necessary paint on some stabilizer (see overleaf). Then chip back the edges.

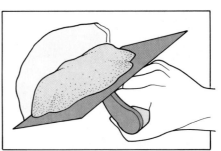

2 Scoop a lump of ready mixed repair plaster on to the back of your float and press it into the hole. Sweep the float upwards to stop it falling out.

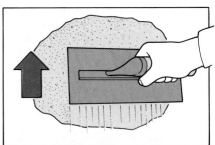

3 When the hole is roughly filled, dip the float in water. Smooth the plaster with gentle sweeps, pressing the blade against the edge of the hole.

MENDING PLASTERBOARD

Use plasterer's scrim tape (from lumberyards) to reinforce a small plasterboard repair.

For larger holes, ask your local lumberyard or home center for an offcut of plasterboard to use as a patch – you don't want to be landed with a whole sheet. Finish the repair with ready mixed skimming plaster as shown opposite. Finding studs in hollow walls is described on page 132.

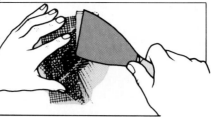

1 For a small repair, stick small pieces of scrim tape crisscross over the hole with PVA adhesive. Fill over the top, feathering away the edges.

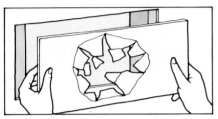

2 For a large hole, use a trimming knife to cut out a rectangular patch in the plasterboard back to the two nearest studs.

3 Cut a new patch to fit from an offcut of plasterboard and nail it to the studs. Plaster over the top using ready mixed skimming plaster or repair plaster.

4 Alternatively, fix string to a piece of plasterboard narrow enough to pass through the hole. Fix it from the back with dabs of filler; then, when this is dry, spread more filler over the top.

— *Trade tip* —

Close to the edge

❝ Here's a trick I use for hiding the edges of a plasterboard repair. Before you cover the patch with plaster, dent the edges with a small hammer or screwdriver blade so that you form a shallow groove all the way around it. This ensures an invisible join when you plaster over the top. ❞

Use a trimming knife to cut out the damaged plasterboard.

PATCHING LATH AND PLASTER

Patching a hole in a lath and plaster partition wall is no problem if the laths are intact: simply fill with repair plaster, then finish off with skimming plaster or fine surface filler. But if the laths are broken, you need to make a more substantial repair as shown right.

Zinc gauze provides the perfect reinforcement; if you can't find it at your local hardware store, try a car accessory shop.

Prepare the hole in the usual way by brushing or chipping away all loose material. If the plaster is crumbly brush on a coat of stabilizer or PVA adhesive.

1 Cut the gauze a little smaller all round than the size of the patch using an old pair of scissors. Wear gloves for protection.

2 Push back the broken laths and press the gauze into the hole so that its edges are just below the surface of the plaster.

3 If possible, secure the patch to any unbroken laths using small nails or staples. Alternatively, glue it in place.

4 Form a depression in the middle of the gauze and cover with repair plaster. Feather away the edges to blend them into the wall.

TYPES OF FILLER

CELLULOSE FILLERS

general purpose fillers

fine surface filler

General purpose cellulose fillers are fine for small holes but don't spread well. In a deep hole, they must be built up in thin layers or they slump.

Ready mixed fillers are more convenient but don't keep well and are too stiff and bulky for some jobs. You can mix powder-type filler to the consistency you want – a definite advantage where you are 'feathering' the edges of a repair to hide them.

Fine surface filler comes ready mixed. It is super-smooth and easy to spread, but must be applied *very* thinly or it won't dry properly. Use it to finish off repairs made with ordinary filler.

READY MIXED DIY PLASTERS

Ready mixed plasters are sold in medium and large size plastic tubs. They are expensive, but their excellent adhesion and long 'open' time (the time they stay workable) makes them perfect for DIY repairs. Also, they are easy to sand down once dry.

Skimming plaster is applied thinly with a large brush, then smoothed using the plastic applicator provided.

Repair plaster is best applied with a metal float, but will fill holes up to 50mm (2″) deep in one coat. Finish afterwards with skimming plaster.

CONVENTIONAL REPAIR PLASTER

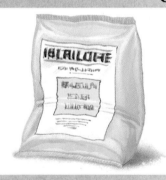

Conventional plaster is sold in various sized bags by hardware stores and home centers. *Bonding* plaster is for filling out the hole; *finishing* (skimming) plaster is for creating the final smooth surface. You can also buy *one coat* plaster which can be used (in layers) for both jobs.

All types are much cheaper than ready mixed plaster, but need conventional plastering skills to apply properly.

FOAM FILLER

Aerosol foam fillers are ideal for filling cracks around skirtings or door architraves, but too costly to use for larger holes.

As the foam is injected via the plastic tube nozzle, it expands and hardens to fill every crevice. It dries hard, but is easily sanded down.

PATCHING ACCESSORIES

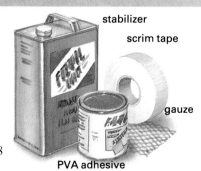

stabilizer

scrim tape

gauze

PVA adhesive

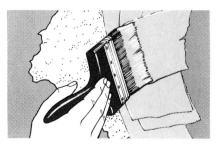

Plaster stabilizing fluid is a brush-on liquid that binds the surface of crumbly old plaster so the filler stays in place.

PVA adhesive does the same job when painted on neat and left to go tacky. It also aids adhesion if you're using conventional plaster.

Scrim tape and zinc gauze add strength to repairs made in plasterboard and lath and plaster respectively.

138

REPAIRING A CONCRETE FLOOR

Solid concrete floors can suffer from several faults, all of which need to be cured before laying a new covering.

General unevenness could be due to the floor not being laid properly in the first place, or to localized wear and tear. It may not be noticeable while the floor is bare, but will show after covering.

If the level is 'out' by less than 12mm (½″) – see *Checking the floor* overleaf – the cure is to resurface the floor using self-smoothing compound. See Problem Solver for how to cope with serious unevenness.

Dampness can be an especially difficult problem in houses where the floor has been laid over bare ground without a vapor barrier. As the concrete becomes more porous with age, moisture rises to the surface and either ruins the floorcovering or works its way up the surrounding walls.

Newer floors can also suffer from dampness if the vapor barrier has been accidentally punctured during the course of earlier building work.

Providing the floor isn't soaking wet (in which case it needs rebuild-

Repairs are essential before laying a new covering.

ing), the cure is to give it a water-proof coating and resurface.

Local damage may be caused by dampness as well as physical damage. Or perhaps the original surface layer has broken down through age, leaving flaking areas and deep pits.

Faults like these always show through soft coverings, and make

hard coverings more difficult to lay. The cure is to patch with repair mortar and resurface.

Dusting is another symptom of old concrete, in which the top surface becomes powdery and starts to break down. If the floor is otherwise smooth, paint with concrete sealer; if uneven, resurface as well.

....Shopping List....

Self-smoothing compound is the standard material for resurfacing a concrete floor. It's sold in 10, 15 and 25kg (11, 33 and 55lb) bags.

Water based compound comes in powder form for mixing with water. It is the easiest to use, but is not strong enough if the floor is being left bare.

Latex based compound is more resilient and resists structural movement. It comes in powder form and is mixed with *latex liquid* which you buy separately.

Acrylic based compound is the strongest, and also the most expensive. It is sold in two-part powder form for mixing with water.

As a rough guide, a 25kg bag of water based compound covers around 6–7 sq m (7–8 sq yd) when laid to the recommended depth of 4–5mm (³⁄₁₆″).

Repair mortar Either use dry-mixed repair mortar, or special *concrete floor repair compound* which comes ready-mixed in 2.5 and 5 liter tubs.

PVA adhesive functions as a primer when you are making patched repairs. Added to repair mortar, it helps it bind to the floor.

Waterproofing compounds for concrete floors are now widely available. The most effective are epoxy resin based (often with bitumen additive), and come in two-part form. Two coats are required; coverage is around 1 sq m (1.2 sq yd) per liter, depending on the smoothness of the surface.

If the floor is being resurfaced (which it must be if laying an adhesive-laid covering), the coating must be *blinded* – sprinkled with sand while tacky so that the compound will stick to it. Special blinding sand is available for this, or use clean sharp sand.

See page 142 for details of finishes for bare concrete.

Tools checklist: Plasterer's steel float, pointing trowel, 2 buckets, strip of wood, carpenter's level, old paintbrush.

CHECKING THE FLOOR

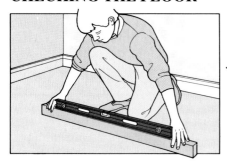

Test for unevenness using a level and wood batten. Try the floor in both directions, and measure the difference between the high and low points.

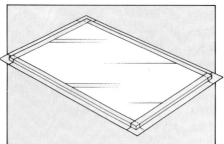

Test for dampness by taping a piece of glass or plastic to the floor. Leave for two days, then inspect: if the underside is cloudy, moisture is present.

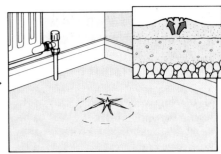

'Swelling' patches suggest localized dampness – possibly the result of a punctured vapor barrier. Look for nearby alterations which might confirm your suspicions.

PATCHING HOLES

1 **For a hole**, brush or vacuum away any dust or loose chips. If filling with mortar, paint on a solution of 1 part PVA adhesive to 3 parts water and leave to dry.

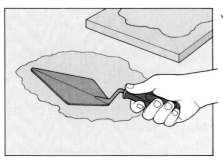

2 Press in some repair compound or mortar and smooth off with a pointing trowel. (For a mortar repair, add a little PVA adhesive to the mixing water.)

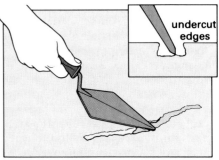

3 **Open out a crack** with the corner of a brick chisel. Brush away the dust. Then patch with repair compound or brush with PVA solution and fill with mortar.

DEALING WITH DAMPNESS

Before waterproofing a damp floor, it's advisable (though not essential) to remove the baseboards and strip any plaster behind to a height of 100mm (4″). This allows you to extend the coating 75-100mm (3-4″) up the walls to the vapor barrier in the wall.

■ Prize the baseboards away from the wall using a claw hammer, brick chisel or crowbar. Use a block of wood to lever against, and to protect the wall surface above.

■ Chop back the plaster using a club hammer and brick chisel. Wear goggles to protect your eyes.

For a localized patch, carefully chop out the concrete using a hammer and brick chisel until you reach the old vapor barrier itself – either a black pitch-like substance or a layer of plastic sheet. Vacuum away the dust and check for holes in the barrier. To repair, coat the area with waterproofing compound, then patch with repair mortar.

If you are resurfacing, lightly sprinkle the surface with sand while the coating is still tacky. This gives the smoothing compound something to grip.

1 Pour the waterproofing compound hardener into the resin following the maker's instructions. Stir until thoroughly mixed.

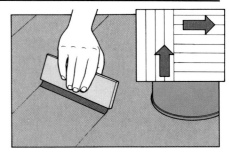

2 Apply the first coat in wide parallel bands using a squeegee. When dry, apply a second coat of waterproofer at right angles to the first.

Self-smoothing compound is thin and flexible enough to need only a light sweep with a steel float. Any bumps and ridges disappear as it dries, leaving a smooth, level surface. Most types are hard within two hours and can be walked on after eight, but leave for a day to dry.

Although the compound is reasonably easy to use, you need to work fast – particularly if you're mixing batches. A bucketful only stays workable for about half an hour, so don't mix more in one go.

Preparation Self-smoothing compound won't stick to concrete that's dirty or greasy, so wash down the surface with detergent. Any old floor adhesive must also be removed; soften with a heat gun stripper and scrape off.

Seal off the edges of the area being resurfaced using strips of wood. This includes doorways and junctions with other surfaces.

Thickness Aim to spread the compound to an average thickness of 5mm (³⁄₁₆″). If this isn't enough to level the floor, apply a second layer once the first is completely dry.

Trade tip

Mixing trick

❝ Mixing is often the trickiest part of using self-smoothing compound: if there are lumps in the mixture when you pour it, you'll never get it to settle.

You need an efficient mixing tool. A lot of people use wood, but this isn't good at breaking up the powder. I prefer an old fish slice, but any similar kitchen implement will do.

Also, be sure to mix in the right sequence. Start with a little of the mixing liquid, add some of the powder and mix to a paste. Then add more liquid, followed by more of the powder, stirring all the time. ❞

Mix the smoothing compound powder in a bucket with the water (or latex fluid, for the latex type). Stir thoroughly to remove the lumps and adjust the mixture until it is the consistency of thick cream.

1 Scrub the floor thoroughly using a mixture of water and detergent, then rinse with cold water. Try not to wet the concrete any more than necessary.

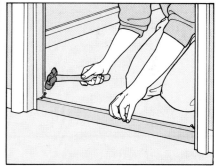

2 Nail strips of wood across doorways and anywhere else you don't want the compound to spread. Screen pipes etc with pieces of cardboard.

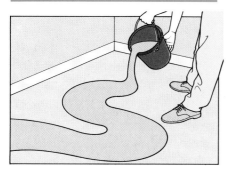

3 Starting furthest from the door, pour the mixture in a 'trail' over the area stirring as you go. Smooth out immediately with a steel float.

4 Check the depth at several points, then smooth again. Use the float in a light, sweeping motion, angling the blade so that just the back edge makes contact.

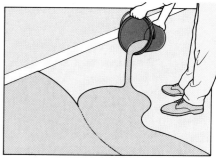

5 As the compound settles, any ridges and bumps disappear. If you need to pour another batch, do so immediately before the first begins to dry.

FINISHES FOR BARE CONCRETE

If the floor being leveled is in a garage or utility room, you may not want to go to the trouble of laying a new covering – self-smoothing compound is smooth enough to be finished direct, although it won't stand up to heavy abuse.

Paint with clear sealer/hardener if you want to leave the concrete bare. This soaks into the floor and gives greater long-term protection than ordinary concrete sealer.

Paint with floor paint for a colored finish. This is only available in a limited range of colors (normally red, green, stone and gray), but is easy to apply by roller and dries to a hardwearing finish. Coverage is in the region of 10 sq m (12 sq yd) per liter (2 qts).

Before applying either finish, make sure the floor is free of dust and wash down with detergent.

A painted finish (right) is ideal for brightening up a garage or playroom/utility room.

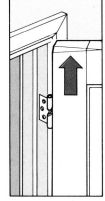

▌ PROBLEM SOLVER ▐

Serious unevenness

If the floor level is 'out' by more than 12mm (½"), don't try to make up the difference using self-smoothing compound alone; above this thickness, it isn't strong enough to take any weight. Instead, build up the low point with screed mortar, then resurface over the top.

■ Start by coating the area to be built up with a solution of 1 part PVA adhesive to 3 parts water. Leave to dry.

■ Make up a fairly dry mortar mix of 1 part cement to 6 of sharp sand, adding a splash of PVA adhesive to the mixing water. Trowel over the area using a steel float.

■ Use a level on a piece of wood to check the level, and add more mortar to pack any low spots. Level high spots by slicing off the mortar with the piece of wood.

■ Leave for a day to dry, then resurface in the usual way.

Use a strip of wood and a level to level repaired patches.

Dealing with doorways

Resurfacing inevitably raises the floor level slightly, which could cause problems at a doorway. However, adding a new floorcovering will raise it further still, so don't forget to take this into account when finding a cure.

If the floor in the next room is lower, fit a metal or hardwood door sill to make up the difference.

If the door jams against the new floor, either trim the base or rehang it on rising butt hinges. These have the effect of lifting the door as it opens, allowing it to clear the floor, while maintaining a snug fit in the frame when the door is closed.

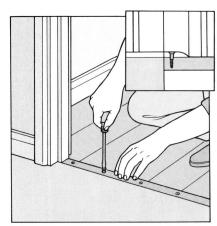

Fit a door sill to make up the slight difference in level at a doorway. Screw down the strip if the adjoining floor is wooden, otherwise use impact adhesive.

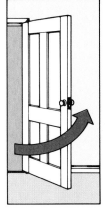

Rehang the door with rising butt hinges if it looks like jamming against the new floor when opened. You may also have to trim a fraction off the top.

LAYING CERAMIC AND QUARRY FLOOR TILES

Of all the readily available coverings for floors, ceramic and quarry tiles are the longest-lived and hardest wearing. Laid properly, a hard-tiled floor should add substantially to the value of your home, and the huge range of styles available leaves plenty of scope for expressing your own personal taste.

Before going ahead, however, it's as well to consider the limitations:

■ Most hard tiles raise the level of the floor substantially, which could involve removing baseboards, trimming doors, and fitting wooden ramps with adjoining floor surfaces.

■ Hard tiles are as good as permanent, so you should think twice before laying them around built-ins – for example, kitchen units; the chances are the units will be the first to go, leaving holes that you may not be able to match.

■ Solid floors are better suited to hard tiling than suspended wooden ones. It is *possible* to tile a wooden floor, but only if it is absolutely free of structural movement, and properly lined with plywood. Remember, too, that you won't have access to utilities running under the floor once the tiles are firmly fixed in place.

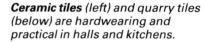

Ceramic tiles (left) and quarry tiles (below) are hardwearing and practical in halls and kitchens.

PRELIMINARY WORK

Aim to get as much preliminary work as possible done before buying the tiles (see overleaf).

■ Baseboards should ideally be removed so that they can be refitted to hide the cut tiles around the edge of the floor. However, this may be more trouble than it's worth if the baseboards are the deep ornate type.

■ Remove as much built-in furniture as you can. Again, ideally, the tiles should run from wall to wall.

■ Line a wooden boarded floor with exterior grade plywood.

■ On a solid floor, check the level: a *thick-bed adhesive* (see overleaf) will accommodate variations of up to about 12mm (½″) but for anything greater, fill hollows then resurface with self-smoothing compound.

■ Remove inward-opening doors ready for trimming later.

■ Nail strips of wood temporarily across doorways to give yourself something to tile against.

Prize off baseboards with a brick chisel or crowbar, using a block of wood to protect the plaster.

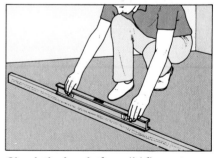

Check the level of a solid floor at various points. If it varies by over 12mm (½″), resurface.

Line a boarded floor with sheets of 12mm (½″) plywood, staggering the joints.

Temporarily nail strips of wood across doors to provide an edge for tiling against.

CHOOSING AND BUYING THE TILES

Home centers and even some department stores stock limited runs of the more popular ranges of ceramic floor tile, but their choice of quarries is generally limited. For the widest selection of all types, visit a tile dealer: most have panels showing the finished effect, which may not be as you imagined.

Floor tiles are normally sold by the square meter or square yard, so make sure you're armed with the room dimensions and add 8–10% extra for wastage depending on how much cutting you anticipate.

Wherever you buy the tiles, the same outlet will also be able to supply the adhesive, grout, and any special tools (see opposite).

Ceramic tiles

Ceramic floor tiles are thicker than wall tiles – most are at least 6mm (1/4″) – but have the same glazed finish. The majority are machine-made; hand-made floor tiles are harder to lay and often expensive.

Many floor tile patterns look identical to wall tiles, so be sure to specify 'floor tiles' when ordering. Others imitate materials such as stone flags, marble or granite. And as well as a choice of color and pattern style, you are likely to come across a variety of surface finishes – for example, matte or gloss, smooth or textured.

Popular square and rectangular sizes are 150×100mm, 150×150mm, 200×150mm and 200×200mm (about 6×4, 6×6, 8×6 and 8×8″). There are also hexagonal and interlocking shapes.

Decorative insets for ceramic floor tiles are often sold as part of a range. But whereas wall insets are usually tile-sized (or multiple tile-sized) motifs, floor insets tend to take the form of much smaller decorative tiles which you interlock with the main tiles or 'build in' at the corner joints.

Quarry tiles

Unglazed quarry tiled floors have enjoyed a revival over the past few years, and their warm, natural tones are well suited to more rustic decorative schemes. Even so, the subtle color ranges, plus the chance to use contrasting ceramic insets, can create exciting effects.

Quarries are sold in the same way as ceramics, and come in similar sizes and shapes, but they are much thicker – from around 10mm (3/8″) to as much as 25mm (1″). They are also never uniform in size, which is part of their appeal.

When choosing quarries, always ask to see a finished panel so that you can gauge the effect.

Adhesives and grout

Ceramic tiles are generally laid using a *thin-bed adhesive*, spread to a thickness of around 3mm (1/8″). This comes ready mixed in tubs of various sizes, or slightly more cheaply in powder form for mixing with water; one type has a latex additive and is designed specially for wooden floors. Coverage is about 2.5litres (1/2 gal) per sq m (1.2sq yd) for ready mixed; 2.75kg (6lb) per sq m for powder.

For thicker ceramic tiles and all quarry tiles, use a *thick-bed adhesive*. This is spread up to 12mm (1/2″) thick, and so is capable of taking up the natural variations in the thickness of the tiles. (Professionals usually lay quarries in a sand and cement screed, but this is a lot harder than it looks and is not recommended for DIY.)

Thick-bed adhesive comes in powder form and looks like cement (on which it is based). Coverage is around 11kg (24lb) per sq m (1.2sq yd), but always order on the generous side.

Grout for floor tiles is generally sold in powder form. There is a range of colours for ceramics, plus more natural looking cement-based types for quarries. Coverage depends on the thickness of the tiles and on how wide you decide to make the joints – ask your supplier's advice.

For quarry tiles, you also need a means of sealing the unglazed surface of the clay. A special silicone sealant will not only protect the tiles, but will also stop the grout from discoloring.

Practical ideas include diagonal tiling in narrow rooms (below) and non-slip finishes (left).

DESIGN CHECKLIST – CERAMICS
- Is the floor in a bathroom, utility room or entrance hall likely to get wet? If so, the tiles should have a non-slip surface.
- Do you prefer a gloss or matte glaze? Floor tiles can have either.
- Have you a basic preference for flat or broken color? Flat colors produce a clean, streamlined effect but you may find it too clinical if used over a large area.
- Is the room long and narrow? In this case, tiling diagonally – ie at 45° to the walls – will give an impression of greater width.

■ Could the floor do with rescreeding? In this case you'd be better getting a professional to lay the tiles the traditional way in a mortar bed.
■ Does the room in question open out on to a small patio or yard? If funds permit, you could consider quarry tiling this too.
■ Do you want to refit the baseboards? Some quarry tile ranges include edging tiles (with special tiles for internal and external corners), but you'll need to allow for these when setting out the tiling (see overleaf).
■ For a high-gloss finish, ask your supplier about special sealants and lacquers.

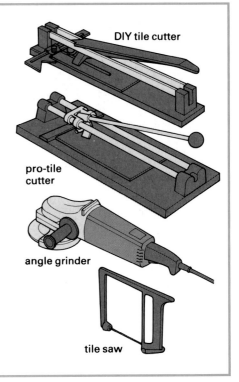

When choosing quarry tiles for a kitchen, a glazed or sealed finish is more practical (left). Larger tiles may help to give a feeling of space (above).

.... Shopping List ....

As well as the tiles and adhesive, you'll need a complete set of tiling tools.

A notched spreader for applying the adhesive; the plasterer's trowel pattern is best for floors.

A tile cutter – see Tip.

A tile file for finishing the edges of cut tiles.

A carpenter's level and wood or metal straightedge for keeping a check on the floor level.

A try square, chalk lines and tape for squaring things up.

Softwood strips for setting out – 50×25mm (2×1") is a useful size. You also need a hammer and nails to fix them.

A bucket and stirring implement (an old slotted spoon is ideal) for mixing the adhesive and grout.

A rubber-covered trowel and sponge for applying grout, plus a wooden dowel for finishing the joints.

Trade tip

Cutting floor tiles

6 Even the thinner floor tiles are much harder to cut than wall tiles, and an ordinary wall tile cutter won't do. Alternatives are:
■ A lightweight floor tile cutter – reasonably cheap to buy, and suitable for most ceramic tiles up to around 6mm (¼") thick.
■ A professional tile cutter – you may be able to rent one from the store where you buy the tiles. This copes easily with ceramic tiles and with thinner quarries.
■ An angle grinder – easily rented – is the best tool for cutting thick quarries, and is useful for 'nibbling' awkward shapes. You also need full protective gear – goggles, gloves and a mask.

If you're not using an angle grinder, a tile saw is the best tool for cutting out small pieces. 9

DIY tile cutter

pro-tile cutter

angle grinder

tile saw

SETTING OUT

As with all floor tiles, the first stage is to set out the tiling so that you avoid awkward cuts and narrow gaps around the edges of the room. The procedure is basically the same for both ceramics and quarries, but differs slightly from that used for other types of floor tile.

Start by snapping chalked string lines to cross at right angles to one another in the center of the room. The first chalk line represents the 'line' of the tile joints as seen from the main doorway: it must run parallel to the dominant visual line in the room – the longest wall, the bath, or a run of kitchen units – otherwise the tiles will appear 'crooked' as you walk into the room.

If you have difficulty deciding on a dominant feature, draw the line from the center – and at right angles to – the main doorway.

After snapping the second line, measure off in whole tiles along the arms of the cross to see what sort of gaps are left at the edges. You can do this by laying out the tiles themselves (not forgetting to allow the correct joint gap – see below), but it's easier to make up a tiling gauge (see Tip).

Ideally, no edge gap should be less than a third of a tile's width. If your measuring reveals otherwise, shift the position of one or both lines so that the gaps are evened up and then try again.

Fixing setting out guides

When you are happy with the positions of the lines, decide in which quadrant to begin tiling, bearing in mind that you'll be starting in one corner and working back towards the door. Use your tiling gauge to mark the positions of the last whole tiles in the quadrant, then join the marks into guidelines using a straightedge.

Next, cut two strips of wood roughly to the length of the guidelines. Nail them along the lines as shown, so that they sit on the 'gap' side, not the 'whole tile' side. Use a carpenter's try square to check that they are at 90°. You are then ready to start laying the tiles.

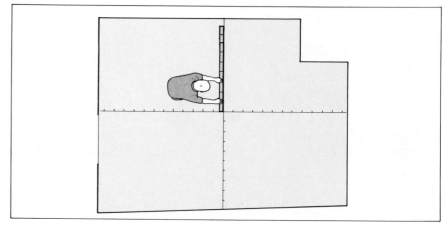

Setting out stage 1: chalk lines across the room to align with the dominant visual feature, then use your tile gauge to find out how the gaps fall at the edges.

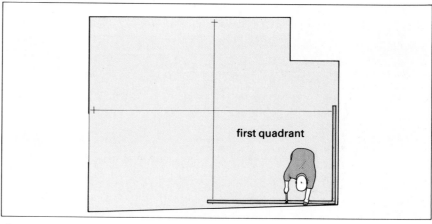

first quadrant

Setting out stage 2: having adjusted the chalk lines as necessary, draw guidelines around the edge of the first quadrant to be tiled and nail wood strips against them.

WHAT JOINT SPACING?

Unlike many wall tiles, floor tiles are always square edged and must be laid with an allowance for the joint spacing. Nor are there any hard and fast rules as to how wide the spacing should be; much depends on the tile, and on the sort of look you want – the wider the joints, the more obviously 'tiled' the finished effect becomes.

As a general rule, for ceramics the spacing should be narrow – between 2 and 4mm (1/16–1/8). For quarries, which don't have straight edges, it must necessarily be wider – approximately 4–10mm (1/8–3/8").

Unless you've seen finished samples of the tiling, it's worth experimenting before you start setting out. When you've decided on the spacing, find something to use as a gauge – a piece of thick cardboard, a thin wall tile or a slip of plywood are all popular choices.

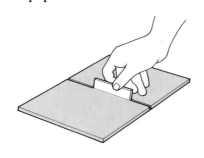

Trade tip

Make a gauge

❝ A tiling gauge makes it easy to measure off whole tile widths with an allowance for the joints.

For ceramics, simply mark off tile widths and joint spacings along a straight strip of wood.

For quarries, where neither the tiles nor the gaps are a consistent width, pick 8–10 tiles at random and lay them out in a row. Adjust the joints until they look more or less even, then mark off. ❞

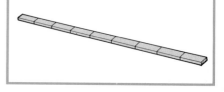

LAYING CERAMICS

The basic laying procedure for ceramics is to start tiling against the setting out strips of wood, then continue laying whole tiles back towards the door. With all the whole tiles laid, leave the adhesive to set for at least 12 hours. Then remove the setting out strips of wood and cut and lay the edge tiles.

Spread the adhesive in batches roughly a yard square. Use the spacing tool to make sure that each tile sits square to its neighbours.

Check regularly that the tiles sit level. In particular, make sure that the tiles on one patch of adhesive are level with those on the next, as this is where problems usually occur. If you find that the level is 'out', lift the tiles immediately and re-trowel the adhesive bed to bring it to the correct thickness.

When it comes to fitting the edge tiles, mark them individually using a whole tile to gauge the profile of the wall. For straight cuts use the tile cutter; see Problem Solver for how to deal with awkward shapes.

When laying the edge tiles, spread the adhesive on the backs of the tiles, and spread it slightly more thickly than you did on the floor.

1 Using a notched spreader, spread a 1yd square layer of adhesive in the corner formed by the wood. Thickness of the bed should be around 3mm (⅛").

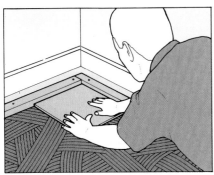

2 Slide the first tile into the corner and press down gently. (Note that if adhesive squeezes up over the edges you are pressing too hard.)

3 Position the next tile, using your spacing gauge to make sure it sits square to the first. Continue in this way until the adhesive area is filled.

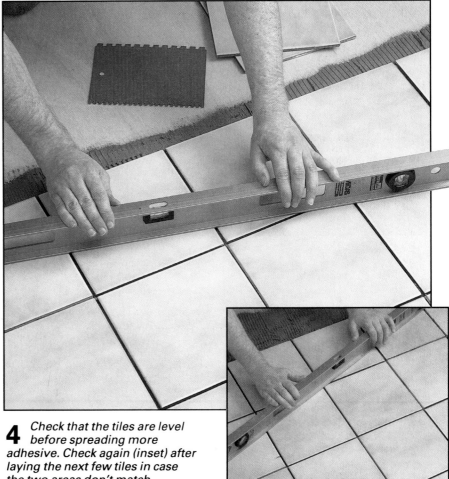

4 Check that the tiles are level before spreading more adhesive. Check again (inset) after laying the next few tiles in case the two areas don't match.

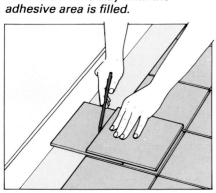

5 Having laid all the whole tiles and allowed the adhesive to dry, mark the edge tiles individually to fit using a whole tile to gauge the wall profile.

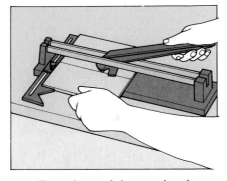

6 To make straight cuts, lay the tile face up in the cutting jig. Score down the marked line, then depress the lever – the tile should snap cleanly.

7 Apply adhesive to the backs of the cut tiles with the notched spreader and position them with the cut edge against the wall. Press gently into place.

LAYING QUARRIES

Quarry tiles stuck with thick-bed adhesive (as opposed to mortar) are laid in virtually the same way as ceramic tiles. The main difference is that the thickness of the adhesive (and the unevenness of some quarries) makes it slightly more difficult to keep everything level.

■ Mix and spread the adhesive in 1yd square batches to a depth of around 10mm (⅜").

■ Set the tiles in place using only very light pressure – don't worry about leveling them.

■ When the patch of adhesive is covered, use a sturdy wood block to press the tiles down level with one another; avoid putting pressure on any one tile in particular.

Repeat this sequence for all the whole tiles, then leave to dry before fitting the edge tiles.

Set quarry tiles in place with very light pressure, spacing the joints as evenly as you can. After covering each spread batch of adhesive, use a stout block of wood to tap the tiles down level with one another.

GROUTING AND FINISHING

Both ceramics and quarries are grouted in the same way as wall tiles – preferably at least 12 hours after fitting the edge tiles.

Mix up the grout in a bucket according to the maker's instructions and stir thoroughly to remove lumps. Use immediately and work fast – it doesn't take long for it to become unworkable. Make sure, too, that you remove the excess grout from the face of the tiles before it dries; quarries in particular are susceptible to staining, since they are unglazed.

Sealing quarry tiles is best done before you grout, to protect the surface from staining, but take your supplier's advice. Apply special silicone sealant according to the manufacturer's instructions.

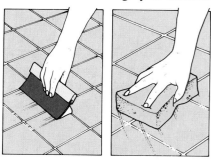

1 *Mix up the grout according to the instructions and spread it over the tiles. Work it into the joints using a rubber-covered trowel, sponge up the excess.*

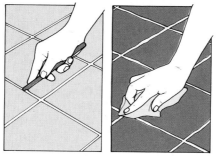

2 *Check that there are no air pockets, then leave the joints until just hard. Finish with a piece of dowel (ceramics) or rub with a coarse cloth (quarries).*

Trade tip

Cleaning off

❝ The best way to clean grout stains off floor tiles is with sawdust. Spread it over the floor and rub with a damp cloth, then just sweep up the residue. ❞

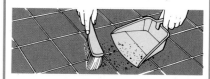

▮ PROBLEM SOLVER

Cutting awkward shapes

Don't be too ambitious when cutting edge tiles to fit tricky shapes such as architraves or pipes – stick to simple, straight cuts (if you try to notch tiles, they'll break), then rely on the grout to fill any gaps.

Ceramics are best cut clamped in a workbench using a tile saw. For quarries, use an angle grinder; work outside, wear full protective gear and take great care – especially to avoid cutting the cord.

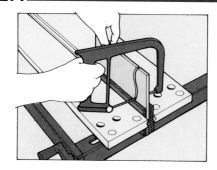

Awkward shapes are best marked by measuring direct. Most ceramic floor tiles can be cut with a tile saw; clamp them in a bench with protective padding.

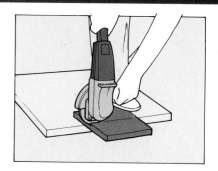

Thick tiles such as quarries are best cut with an angle grinder – wear stout boots and support the tile as shown. Don't put down the grinder until the wheel stops.

REGLAZING WINDOWS AND DOORS

The usual reason for reglazing a window is because of accidental breakage, but there are several other good reasons for renewing existing glass:

■ Low level glazing (below about 750mm – 2′6″) is an accident hazard, especially if there are young children about. It is advisable to reglaze with a shatterproof safety glass.

■ Ordinary glass can be replaced with a practical improvement, such as warmer double-glazed panels, or tougher security glass.

■ Plain or ugly patterned glass can be swapped for a variety of decorative types, ranging from patterned or colored glass to a leaded, stained glass panel.

Before you repair . . .

When glass is broken accidentally, DIY may not be the best option. Check first whether your house contents insurance policy covers fixed glass (ie glazing): if it does, you should be able to claim for a professional repair.

Replacing a small pane is a simple and cheap job.

Trade tip

Temporary security

6 If you can't reglaze a broken window at once, or if the repair isn't completed the same day, you may need to make temporary arrangements.

Where the window is a security risk, use a sheet of plywood cut to fit the frame. Either screw it to the woodwork or drill a hole through the middle and insert a long bolt which can be tightened through a locking bar fitted on the inside.

Simply to keep the weather out, seal a cracked pane with waterproof tape. If the glass is missing or smashed use a sheet of polyethylene taped to the frame on the inside. 9

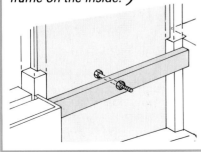

.... Shopping List ....

Glass is made in many different types (see page 151) so check your options carefully. Measure the pane(s) you are glazing and buy glass to fit; the dealer should supply it cut to the dimensions you require.

Putty comes in several forms. *Linseed oil putty* is for wooden frames, *metal casement putty* is for galvanized steel frames, and *general purpose putty* suits either type. *Non-setting putty* is for sealed unit glazing panels. *Brown putty* is for natural hardwood frames.

All types are sold by weight; 1kg (2.2lb) is enough for about 8m (24′) of frame rabbet.

Other materials Check your frame (see page 152) to see what other fixings hold the glass. The main alternatives are *glazing sprigs* (special nails) for wooden frames or patent *clips* for metal frames. On doors and some windows you may need wooden beading instead. If the frame is damaged in any way, make sure you have whatever is needed to repair it. You also need a little general purpose primer.

Protective clothing You need heavy leather gloves, preferably with wrist protection, and safety goggles. Wear long sleeves made from a tough fabric to protect your arms from flying splinters and sturdy shoes in case pieces drop on your foot.

Tools checklist: General tools include a hammer, pincers, paintbrush, dustpan and brush.

Specialized glazing tools are fairly cheap, although it is possible to improvise.

A hacking knife is designed for rough chopping work with a hammer and makes it easy to remove the old putty and chips of glass. An old chisel or stripping knife will do.

A putty knife is specially shaped for applying a neat bead of putty, but you can manage with a filling knife instead.

A glass cutter is needed if you don't buy glass cut to fit. It also helps when removing old glass.

BUYING GLASS

If you are buying plain glass, all you have to worry about is what size and thickness you need; it should be available from stock. Some special glazing materials may need a little more planning to buy, especially as they might have to be made to order.

Local glass dealers stock a surprisingly wide range of glass and will normally order special or unusual types. It's easiest to ask for exactly the sizes you need and get them cut for you. This costs either nothing or very little (usually depending whether you need a special shape or not), so there is little need to cut glass yourself. Glass dealers can also cut shapes and holes (eg for a ventilator fan).

However, having glass cut to size does make it important to measure accurately as you cannot check the glass itself against the frame. Cutting a small sliver off a sheet that is fractionally too large is tricky (see Problem Solver), and if you order the glass too small it will be wasted.

For larger panes it is always worth asking the glass dealer to deliver (local journeys may even be free). Otherwise, if you have a suitable vehicle, have the glass wrapped and then strap it down on a. board to keep it safe in transit. Make sure that it can't slide around.

MEASURING

For accuracy, you must measure right into the *rabbet* – the slot into which the glass is fitted. In some cases it may be easier to remove the old glass first (see page 152), but much depends on how easy it is to secure the window temporarily and whether the glass is in stock.

Measure in millimeters. Check the frame for squareness by measuring the diagonals – they should be more or less identical. Then measure the height and width at three or more points each. Minor variations here (up to about 5mm) don't matter; just take the smallest dimension. Large differences mean the frame is warped.

Where the frame is true, order the glass by quoting its dimensions after deducting 3mm from both the height and width figures to allow a fitting clearance. The exception is if you are buying sealed unit double glazing panels. These need a clearance of about 6mm (¼").

If the frame is very uneven, cut a pattern from paper, cardboard, or even hardboard, depending on which is easiest. Take this with you when you have the glass cut.

Use the same technique if the glass is a complicated shape, but make the pattern from cardboard to make sure it fits exactly. If you want a patterned glass, mark the patterns 'Outside' to ensure that the glass will be cut smooth side out.

see page 152

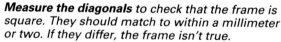

Trade tip

Measuring tips

Avoid using a tape measure for checking the frame – it can all too easily flex and cause inaccuracy. If available, a steel rule is ideal. Otherwise, mark the dimensions on a straight wooden batten and lay this down to measure it with your tape.

■ *When buying glass with a directional pattern, the convention is to quote the height before the width – this ensures that the glass merchant gets the pattern running in the right direction. To replace patterned glass with an identical type, always take a sample with you to check.*

■ *Old glass was sold by weight, not thickness, and also tends to be less even than modern glass. If you are replacing a pane that must match, measure its thickness in millimetres and order the nearest available (if there is no close match buy the glass slightly thicker rather than thinner for safety reasons).*

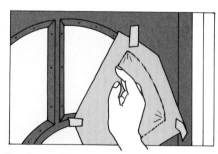

Measure the diagonals *to check that the frame is square. They should match to within a millimeter or two. If they differ, the frame isn't true.*

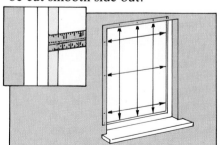

Check the dimensions *at three or more points across the frame's width and height. Take the measurement right into the rabbet in both cases.*

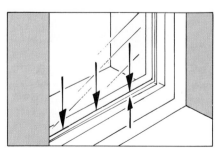

The glass size *should be 3mm smaller than the height and width measurements. If these vary slightly, buy to fit the smallest dimension of the frame.*

For irregular shapes *make a pattern from paper or cardboard. If you have cut this to fit the frame exactly, tell the dealer so he can leave a clearance.*

TYPES OF GLASS

Float glass is the normal form of flat sheet glass and is sold by thickness in millimeters.

■ 3mm glass is only suitable for very small panes.

■ 4mm glass is for panes up to about 1 sq m (11 sq ft).

■ 6mm glass is used for panes over 1 sq m (11 sq ft).

■ 10mm glass is occasionally used in picture windows. For very large panes or low-level glazing, safety glass is preferable.

Toughened (tempered) glass is a fairly low-cost form of safety glass which breaks into harmless chips like a car windscreen. It cannot be cut, so must be ordered and made to size – although standard sizes are often held in stock.

Laminated glass is a more expensive safety glass with a plastic center layer that holds the fragments together in the event of a breakage (making it more secure as well as safer). It comes in thicknesses from 4mm to 8mm and can be cut to the size you require by the dealer from whom you buy it.

Wired glass is 6mm glass with a fine steel wire mesh cast into it. One common type has a 13mm (½") square mesh and a textured face. Wired glass is no stronger than float glass but the mesh stops it shattering. Its main use is in fire doors and windows to stop fire spreading – it is not really a security glazing material.

Patterned glass is embossed on one surface – the other is usually smooth. It provides both decoration and some privacy, depending on the pattern. Clear patterned glass is 4mm or 6mm thick and costs little more than flat glass. It also comes in several colors, and toughened for use in doors and screens.

Colored glass is available in a wide range of shades, but glass dealers are only likely to hold a limited number of popular ones. For the more subtle colors used to replace a leaded window panel, try a specialist in stained glass work.

Solar control glass is tinted or coated to reflect heat without stopping much light. It is costly, but useful on problem windows where direct sun makes the room very hot. It also comes laminated, toughened

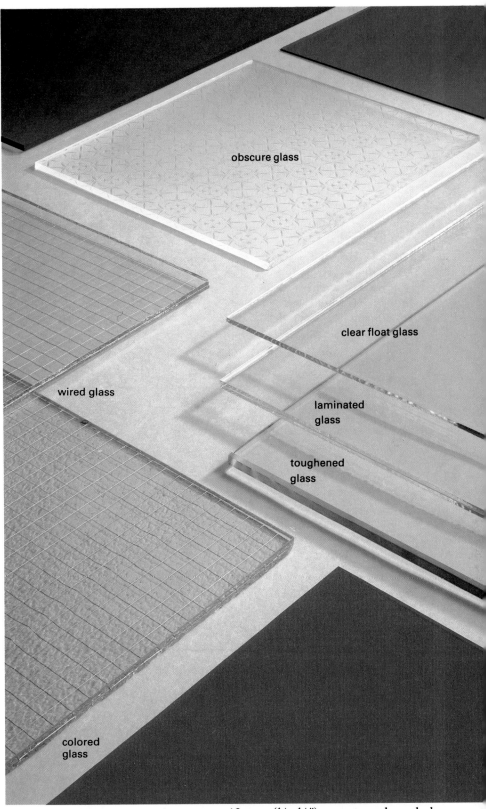

obscure glass

clear float glass

laminated glass

toughened glass

wired glass

colored glass

and double glazed.

Double glazing panels (sealed units) are the type used in modern double glazed windows. They can also be fitted to conventional frames although they tend to be a little less efficient unless the frames seal very well. There are two types; both are expensive and normally to order.

Square edge sealed units consist of two panes spaced between 6 and 12mm (¼–½") apart and sealed around the edge – total thickness is about 15mm (⅝") upwards. Special types of glass can be used and it is best to discuss your exact needs with the dealer.

Stepped sealed units are similar, but used where the rabbet in the window frame is too shallow to take a square edge panel. Only the outer pane fits into the rabbet, the inner one fits through the frame.

REPLACING GLASS

If the window or door is already glazed, the first thing to do is to remove the existing pane and make any necessary repairs. The new pane can then be fitted in its place.

On upper floors, it's far easier if you can take out the whole window or sash and then reglaze it in safety on a workbench. If this is impossible and you are forced to work at a height, make sure you have a sturdy working platform. Bear in mind that you may also need help to lift the new pane into place. Don't attempt to reglaze anything more than a small pane working from a ladder – rent scaffolding and anchor it securely before use.

The job itself depends on the type of window frame and how the glass is fixed. Special types of glass such as sealed units may also need special techniques (see page 154).

How glazing is fixed
Glass is held into the frame in one of four ways:

On wooden frames it is normally bedded in a thin layer of putty and held by flat nails called sprigs. A fillet of putty is applied to seal the glass into the frame.

On sliding sashes, the inner sash may have a groove in the underside of the top rail. The glass fits into this, bedded in putty, but is conventionally puttied on the other three sides.

On galvanized steel frames the glass is bedded in a thin layer of putty and held by spring clips. A fillet of putty is then applied to seal it to the frame.

On aluminum and plastic (uPVC) windows the glazing is normally held in special rubber seals. With this type of window, it is worth contacting the manufacturer or a glazier to find out what is involved in repairing that particular type.

On doors and some wooden windows the glass is bedded in a thin layer of putty but retained by thin strips of wooden beading. These are nailed or screwed to the frame and may be glued up with old paint.

Remove old glass
If broken, this is mainly a matter of carefully breaking away large pieces, then removing whatever fixed it and chopping away remaining slivers. Unbroken panes can sometimes be removed in one piece, which is preferable.

Handling broken glass is the most dangerous part of the job, so wear full protective clothing, keep children and pets away, and use plenty of care.

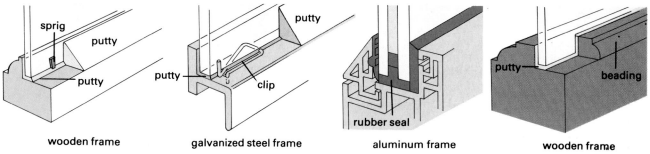

What you may find. There are four common ways to fix glass into the frame, usually depending on the frame material but possibly also on the type of glazing.

1 If the glass is intact, tape across in case of breakage and chop out the putty to release it. Pull out any sprigs or clips, then gently tap the glass free.

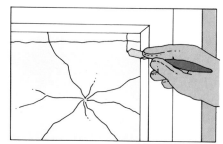

2 Alternatively, score across near the edge with a glass cutter and carefully break large pieces away, working from the top downwards.

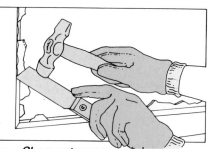

3 Chop out any remaining putty using a hacking knife. Be careful, as it may contain small glass splinters. Prize out any sprigs or clips you find.

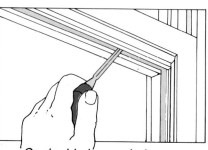

4 On double-hung windows where the glass is held in a groove, clean this out with an old 6mm (¼") chisel, working it in under any glass left in place.

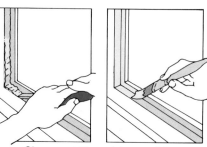

5 Clean out the rabbets with an old chisel. Apply quick-drying primer to protect the bare frame and to stop the oil in the putty being absorbed.

Trade tip

Dangerous rubbish
❛ Dispose of broken glass safely. Small pieces can be dropped in a nearby bottle bank. Otherwise wrap in thick newspaper and take it to a local garbage dump or leave it in a bag or box beside your trash labelled 'Broken Glass'.

Some glass dealers also take it in to be recycled. **❜**

FIXING THE NEW GLASS

Before applying putty to the rabbet, try the glass in place to make sure it fits. The job of fixing the new pane is tackled in a similar way whether the glass is held in putty and sprigs, or whether it is retained by beading.

To putty-in the glass, start by lining the rabbet with a thin layer of putty – the *bedding putty*. The putty should be soft and easily workable without being sticky.

In cold weather, or if it has been allowed to dry out, the putty may be hard and crumbly. If this is the case, knead it in your fingers to warm and soften it; linseed oil putty can be further softened by adding a little oil and working this in the same way. If the putty is too sticky, roll it on wadded newspaper to absorb some of the oil.

Press the glass on to the bedding putty until it is evenly supported, then fit sprigs or clips to retain it. On a double-hung window with a groove in the top rail, slot the top edge of the pane into this first, then lower into the rabbets.

Finish off by applying more putty to the outside to form a weather-proof seal, sloping it off neatly. For ease of working, this putty should be slightly stiffer.

To retain with beading, apply bedding putty in the same way. Prime the new beading and coat the backs of the strips with non-setting putty, then press them into place. Fix by carefully tapping in small nails or pre-drilling the beading and then inserting small brass countersunk woodscrews.

Trade tip

No slip-ups

❛ As soon as the glass is bedded in, tap sprigs into any two edges to hold it in place and prevent it from falling forward. Also, make sure you leave the tools and some sprigs within easy reach – you must not risk letting go of the glass until it is held firmly. ❜

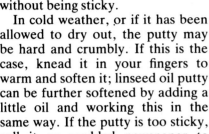

1 Press in a layer of bedding putty by holding a ball in your palm and feeding it through your finger and thumb to fill the rabbet to a depth of 3mm (⅛").

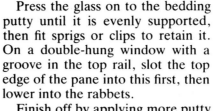

2 Set the glass in place, bottom edge first, and rock it back into the frame. (On sashes with a top groove, set the glass in this first, then lower.)

3 Press the glass home gently, using your hands around the edges only – never the middle – until the putty squeezes out to about 3mm (⅛") thick all round.

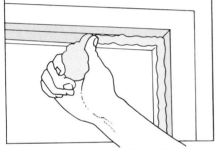

4 Tap in sprigs every 200mm (8") using the back of the hacking knife or a chisel. Slide the tool across the glass as shown to avoid cracking it.

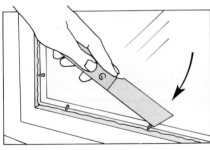

5 On metal frames, fit spring clips at intervals instead of sprigs. The clips hook round the glass and press into holes at convenient points on the frame.

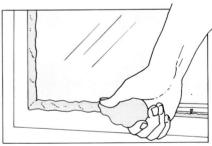

6 Leave the clips or sprigs protruding about 5mm (³⁄₁₆"). Apply more putty to the face of the glass until it completely fills the rabbet.

7 A putty knife is shaped to rest on the woodwork and glass so that you can smooth the putty to a neat 'mitered' finish; dip the blade in water if it sticks.

8 Cut away surplus putty and clean off smears with turpentine. Leave for about three weeks to harden before painting to protect the putty.

Fit glazing beads after coating the back with a thin layer of putty. Press into place and fix with nails or screws, being careful not to crack the glass.

FITTING SEALED UNITS

Sealed unit double glazing panels are fitted much like conventional glass. The main differences are that non-setting putty is used, and that the panels are held with wooden beading on the outside. Because the putty does not set hard, it's also important to use special spacers to keep the glass free of the frame.

Prepare the rabbet as normal and check that the panel fits, remembering that a stepped edge panel must fit through the frame as well as into the rabbet. Then line the rabbet with putty and press in spacers at two points along the bottom. Stand the glass in place and drive in small nails to hold it temporarily. Coat the back of the beading with putty and screw it to the frame to retain the glass.

STEPPED EDGE SEALED UNIT

SQUARE EDGE SEALED UNIT

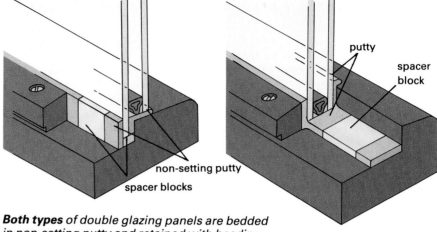

Both types of double glazing panels are bedded in non-setting putty and retained with beading. The spacer blocks are essential to keep the panel standing just free of the frame.

▮ PROBLEM SOLVER ▮

Cutting glass

If you don't get the glass cut by the glass dealer or if the piece which you bought turns out slightly oversized, you may need to cut it yourself. You need a glass cutter, and a flat, padded surface to work on – lay old carpet or layers of newspaper on the worktop.

■ Lay a straightedge along the cut. For a shaped cut, put a paper pattern under the glass. For patterned glass, cut from the flat side. Allow for the distance of the wheel from the face of the cutter.

■ Wet the glass cutter using paraffin or light oil. Holding it like a pencil at about 60°, draw it towards you in a single smooth movement maintaining firm pressure on the glass.

■ Without waiting, lubricate the cut with turpentine then snap it. Either place a thin strip of wood under the glass and press down both sides with even pressure, or tap along the underside of the score with the back of the glass cutter and flex the glass downwards with both hands.

If only a thin strip needs to be removed, you can't snap it in this way. Instead, nibble it away with pliers or the breaker slots on the back of the glass cutter. If the edge is uneven, it can be smoothed with an oilstone or wet and dry paper wrapped over a block – but beware of small, sharp splinters.

Score the cut line using a glass cutter in one smooth movement. Practise on a piece of scrap to see how much pressure is needed for an even mark on the surface.

Lubricate the cut with turpentine, then break over a thin strip of wood using even pressure from both hands on each side of the cut.

Another way to break the glass is to tap along the underside of the cut using the back of the cutter. Then flex the glass downwards using both hands.

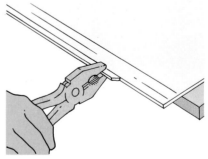

To remove a thin strip, score the cut, then nibble off pieces using a pair of pliers or the breaker slots in the back of many patterns of glass cutter.

SIMPLE DOUBLE GLAZING

Heat loss, condensation and drafts are problems which plague those who live in the northern parts of the country. Modern types of glass, such as 'low E', are beginning to revolutionize the situation. But for the forseeable future, the usual way of coping with the problem is to install double-glazed windows – in very cold areas even triple-glazed windows can be found. (Double glazing almost doubles the insulating value of glass.)

This can be expensive, however, and there is an easy, relatively economical option: do it yourself by fitting what is called secondary double glazing. That is, you install a second pane or set of window panes up against the inside of the existing windows.

Secondary double glazing most often comes in prepackaged assemblage units, which you can cut to fit the size of your particular windows. The glazing material itself will be either glass or plastic.

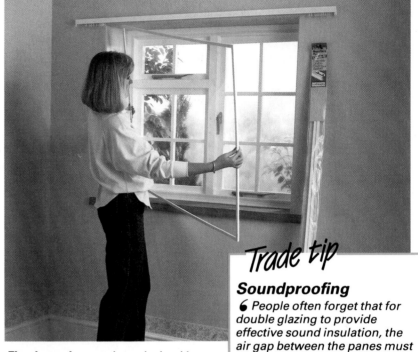

Fixed panel *secondary glazing kits provide an inexpensive and simple means of double glazing.*

TYPES OF SECONDARY GLAZING

Secondary double glazing kits are effectively fixing systems for the new panes, which you buy separately. There are three main types available:
Fixed panel systems aren't really fixed – the glazing panels are designed to be removed for cleaning or ventilation, though not on a regular basis.

Hinged systems work on a similar principle to fixed ones, but have hinges built into the fixing frames which allow the glazing panels to be swung open.
Sliding systems have a track frame which fits to the face of the main window frame or to the sides of the reveal, allowing the glazing panels to be slid open at will.

Trade tip

Soundproofing
❛ People often forget that for double glazing to provide effective sound insulation, the air gap between the panes must be at least 150mm (6″) – as opposed to the 10–20mm (⅜–¾″) needed to keep the heat in. Fitting a secondary system is the only way to provide this. ❜

GLAZING OPTIONS
For the new glazing panels, you have a choice between glass and plastic. Thickness depends on the kit and on what sort of panels you choose, but will be specified on the kit packaging. Some kits can be adapted to take a range of thicknesses – commonly 2–4mm plastic or 4mm glass.
Glass is robust and medium priced, but is unwieldy to handle and too heavy for the lighter types of fixed frame.
Acrylic plastic is light and easy to handle, as well as cheap, but it scratches easily, and needs careful cleaning.
Polycarbonate plastic is the costliest option, but combines the lightness of acrylic with the toughness of glass.

Glass must be cut to size by the dealer. Plastic glazing is sold in various sized sheets by glaziers and home centers, and you can cut it yourself.

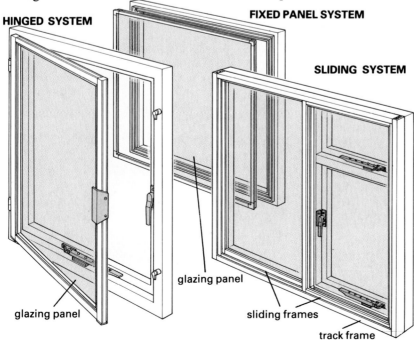

HINGED SYSTEM

FIXED PANEL SYSTEM

SLIDING SYSTEM

glazing panel

glazing panel

sliding frames

track frame

glazing panel

ASSESSING THE OPTIONS

Which type of system you choose to install will depend partly on how much you want to spend, and partly on your windows.

Fixed panels are inexpensive and easy to fit, but inconvenient for windows that get opened frequently – choose an equivalent hinged system instead. Fixed panels are also a potential hazard in the event of a fire, since they could block your escape route, so make sure that at least one opening window in every room has a hinged panel.

On larger windows with both fixed and opening sections, a combination of the two systems is likely to be the best choice.

Sliding systems are costlier and involve more work, but they are much more substantial and often look less obtrusive. It may be worth fitting sliding panels in the most important rooms of the house, and cheaper fixed or hinged panels elsewhere.

Kit compatibility

Not all systems (or kits) fit all windows, and where they do, some look better than others. So once you have a system in mind, note down the following points on the window concerned.

■ Is the frame wood or metal? If it is metal, you could have problems making the panel fixings (see Problem Solver).

■ How wide is the frame? Fixed and hinged panels have to overlap the frame by a certain amount to provide a decent seal.

■ How deep is the frame? If the handle and other hardware protrude too far, you could have difficulty fitting certain types of fixed or hinge panel.

Armed with this information, see what kits you can find locally and check the instruction leaflets. How you measure what you need and buy the glazing depends on the system, so check the notes in the appropriate section.

FITTING FIXED AND HINGED PANELS

With fixed and hinged panels, you measure and buy the glazing before fitting the kit. The diagrams show the options – either fix panels to individual sections, or use a single panel to enclose the entire window.

Refer to the kit instructions to check the thickness of glazing panels required. If you're using plastic, measure on the generous side and then cut the sheets to fit (see page 160) when you get them home. For glass, the exact dimensions are those of the inside of the frame, plus whatever sealing overlap is specified in the kit.

Kits themselves are sold in standard 'height' and 'width' packs, or as complete sets to suit common sizes of window. In all cases, you simply buy the next size up from the actual dimensions of the window, then cut the various parts down.

Fixed panels

There are two common types of fixed panel kit:

Magnetic kits consist of a coated metal strip that goes around the window frame, and a magnetized plastic strip which you cut to fit the edges of the panel. The metal strip is self-adhesive; the magnetic strip is either self-adhesive or clips to the edges of the glazing, depending on the kit.

Clip frame kits use push-on sections of molded plastic channel to frame the panels. The sections normally fit over a rubber sealing gasket and butt-joint at corners, so there is no tricky mitering.

In one kit, the framed panels are then fixed to the window frame with plastic turnbuckle clips. In another, they are a snap-fit into a matching self-adhesive channel which you stick all around the window frame. (In practice aligning the two frames is easy: you simply cut and assemble all the channel sections while they are still clipped together – see steps).

Hinged panels

Some hinged panel kits work on the same principle as the clip-frame fixed type, except that in this case one of the side sections of channel is hinged along its length to allow the panel to swing open. Such kits are ideal for use on large windows, where some lights are fixed and others open.

The hinged section is self-adhesive, enabling you to offer up the panel and position it correctly on the frame. However, because of the extra weight, the fixing then has to be reinforced using the screws supplied with the kit.

Fully hinged panels employ a more complex system of channeling and sealing gaskets to frame the panels. The channel sections are cut to size and joined with special corner pieces in a similar way to sliding panels (see page 158). Hinge pins then slot into the side section and hang from receivers screwed to the window frame.

The panels are sealed against the frame with weather stripping material. Again, you simply cut this to size and slide it into slots in the channel.

Tools checklist: Junior hacksaw, trimming knife, tape measure, drill and bits, screwdrivers (possibly).

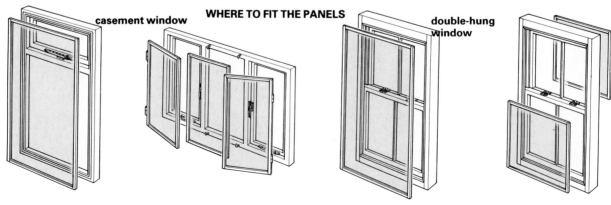

WHERE TO FIT THE PANELS

casement window

double-hung window

single panel fitted to main window frame

fixed and hinged panels fitted to individual sections

single panel fitted to main window frame

fixed panels on inside of inner sash and outside of outer sash to allow for opening

PREPARING THE WINDOW

It isn't worth double glazing a window that's in a poor state of repair, so check for rotten patches, re-putty any loose panes, and repaint if necessary.

Poor weatherproofing can lead to condensation on the insides of the new glazing panels and make the insulation less efficient. Plug gaps between the frame and the wall with flexible sealant or weather stripping material. Other sealing measures depend on the window (see right) and on what weatherproofing products are readily available.

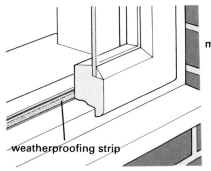

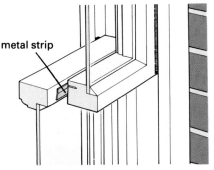

On casement windows, seal the frame with good quality self-adhesive weatherproofing strip. Make sure the surface is clean and dry or it won't stick.

On double-hung windows, seal between the sashes with plastic or metal sprung strip nailed to the outer sash. Seal the sides with stick-on brush pile strips.

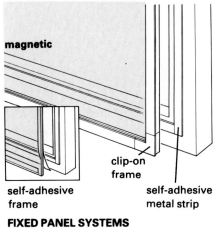

FIXED PANEL SYSTEMS

magnetic — clip-on frame — self-adhesive frame — self-adhesive metal strip

For magnetic fixed systems, draw around the glazing panel in pencil, then use this line as a guide for positioning the self-adhesive metal strip.

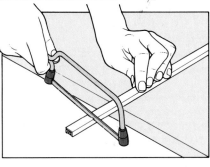

Cut the framing strip for the panel to size, allowing for butt joints at corners. Clip the strip sections around the edges (or stick to the inside) and offer up.

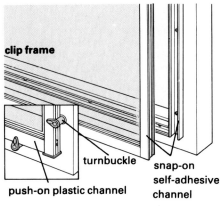

clip frame — turnbuckle — push-on plastic channel — snap-on self-adhesive channel

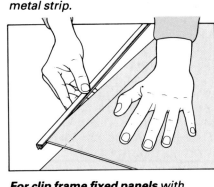

For clip frame fixed panels with channel fixings, measure off against the panel and cut the combined channel sections to size. Slip on around the panel.

Peel off the backing on the inner channel, then hold up the panel and press firmly against the frame. You can then unclip it, leaving the inner channel stuck.

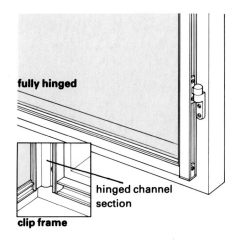

fully hinged — hinged channel section — clip frame

HINGED PANEL SYSTEMS

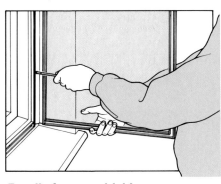

For clip frames with hinges, press the framed panel against the window frame to locate the channels. Open it, support the weight, and screw down the hinge.

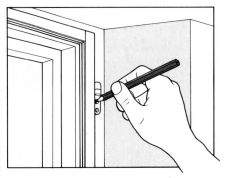

With a fully hinged panel, fit the channels, weatherproofing strips and hinges, then hold up the complete panel and mark the receiver positions on the frame.

FITTING SLIDING PANELS

Like fixed and hinge systems, sliding panel kits are sold in 'height' and 'width' packs or as standard 'window' sets, both of which you cut down to size. The typical kit consists of track sections – in white uPVC, or in white coated or brushed aluminum – plus plastic channel sections to make the sliding frames around each panel. The channels push on over sealing gaskets clipped over the edges of the panels, and are held by screw-on corner pieces.

Depending on the kit, the track sections can be screwed to the face of the window frame or to the sides of the recess. The first is usually easier, but there may not be enough clearance; the second looks neater.

Fitting the tracks
In contrast to fixed and hinged systems, with sliding panels it's safer to fit the track sections to the window **before** you measure up for the glazing. This way, you can be sure the panels fit.

Measure the lengths of the track sections direct from the frame or recess. The sections normally butt together at corners, in which case it's easier to cut and fix the top and bottom tracks, then cut the side tracks to fit. Opposite sides should of course be the same length, or the track frame will be out of square. Also, make sure you don't muddle the different sections up – they aren't normally interchangeable.

Having cut the track sections to length – and on some kits, drilled the screw holes – mark the fixing positions. Then screw to the frame, or into drilled and plugged holes in the reveal.

Use a try square or level to check that the track frame is absolutely square. If it isn't, loosen the screw fixings and pack behind the tracks with pieces of cardboard where necessary.

Fitting the panels
Measure the height and width from the **inside** edges of the track frame to find the total glazing area. Individual panels can be up to 2 sq m (20 sq ft), so two should be enough for most windows. If you need more, it looks better if they are arranged so that the seals between them line up with the frame members between the lights. Typically, to work out the size of each panel:
■ Measure the height and width, then deduct the recommended allowance for fitting the sliding frames.
■ Divide the width measurement by the number of panels.
■ To each width figure, add the recommended allowance to cover the overlap between panels. This gives you the final panel width.

With the panels cut to size, assemble each one as follows:
■ Measure off and cut the channel sections for the sliding frames, allowing for the amount taken up by the corner pieces.
■ Cut and fit the sealing gasket around the edges of the panel. (On some kits this is used to convert between 2mm and 4mm glazing.)
■ Lay the panel on a flat surface and tap on the channel sections. Then fit the corner pieces and tighten their securing screws.

With the panels framed, cut the weatherproofing strip that seals the gap between them and slide it into the appropriate channel sections. Then fit any other bits and pieces, for example glides, or slide assisters, and clip-on handles. The panels can now be slotted into the tracks.

Tools checklist: Hacksaw, trimming knife, tape measure, electric drill and bits, screwdrivers, metal file.

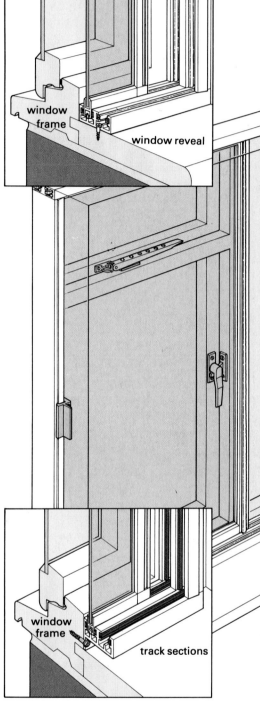

REVEAL-MOUNTED SLIDING PANELS

window frame
window reveal
window frame
track sections

FACE-FIXING SLIDING PANELS

DOUBLE-HUNG WINDOWS
Vertical sliding panel kits are available for these windows, which tend to be taller than they are wide (use one on a narrow hinged window as well). The system relies on special sprung tracks, which grip the panel frames and stop them sliding under gravity. The frame sections where the panels meet are designed to interlock, forming a weatherproof seal.

The kits are intended for use with plastic glazing panels. They are suitable for windows measuring up to 2.4×1.2m (8×4').

CRITICAL GLAZING MEASUREMENTS

Measure the inside dimensions of the track frame from inside the channels. Then deduct the recommended allowances for the sliding frames (A) and (maybe) add the overlap between panels (B).

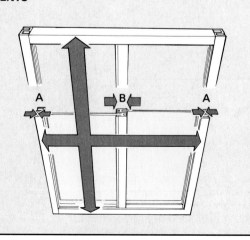

A | B | A

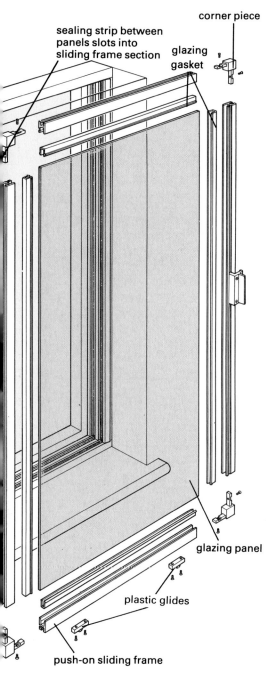

sealing strip between panels slots into sliding frame section

glazing gasket

corner piece

glazing panel

plastic glides

push-on sliding frame

glazing panel frame

glazing panel with seals

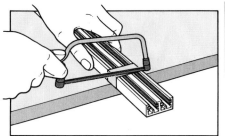

1 Cut the track sections to size with a hacksaw, wrapping tape around the cutting lines to make sure cuts are square. File off any burrs, then remove tape.

2 Hold a level against the track sections when marking the fixing holes on the frame or reveal. Drill and insert anchors for screws where necessary.

3 Check that the track frame is square. If necessary, correct any misalignment by loosening the screws and packing behind the track with cardboard.

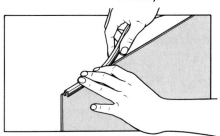

4 Cut the glazing gasket with a trimming knife and clip over the panel edges. It mustn't overlap at the corners or you won't get the channel on.

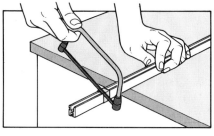

5 Cut the sliding frame sections to size, deducting the recommended amount from the panel dimensions to allow for the corner pieces.

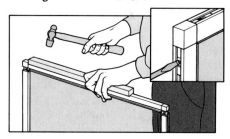

6 Tap the channel sections over the gasket, using a wood block to protect them. Fit the corner pieces (inset) and tighten their screws to lock the frame.

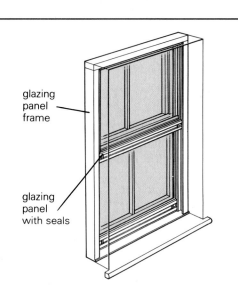

After fitting weatherproofing strip to seal between the panels, lift each panel up into the top track, engage the runners, then lower on to the bottom track.

CUTTING PLASTIC GLAZING PANELS

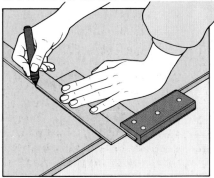

1 Leaving the protective cover sheet on, lay the panel on a flat, stable surface. Measure off the cutting lines, and mark using a try square and felt-tip pen.

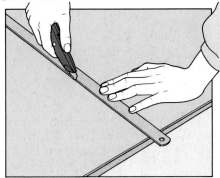

2 Using a metal straight edge and trimming knife with laminate cutting blade, score repeatedly through each line until you're half way through.

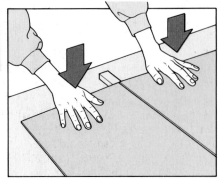

3 Place a strip of wood under the scored line and apply gentle pressure until the sheet snaps. Afterwards, sand rough edges using coarse paper on a block.

■ PROBLEM SOLVER

Metal framed windows

Metal framed windows – or wooden ones with very thin frames – may present problems with certain types of kit. It could be that the frame is too narrow to take the panel fixings, or that the window handle protrudes too far for you to fit panels against the frame at all.

One way out may be to use a sliding panel system mounted in the window recess. The alternative is to make up a simple butt-jointed softwood sub-frame and screw this in front of the frame as shown.

In many cases you should be able to fix the sub-frame to the recess. If you have to fix to a metal window, use self-tapping screws.

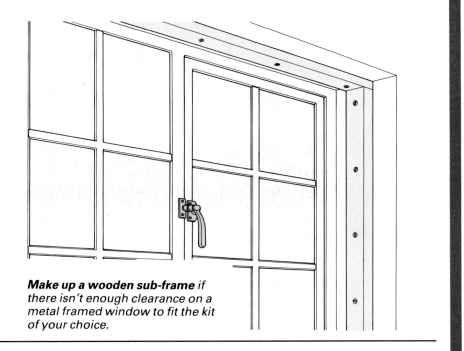

Make up a wooden sub-frame if there isn't enough clearance on a metal framed window to fit the kit of your choice.

Curing condensation

If you find that condensation builds up on the inside of the new panels, try curing it with moisture-absorbing crystals – available from most glazing kit suppliers. Simply place the box of crystals in the cavity between the two panels.

After a couple of months the crystals will stop working, but they can be rejuvenated by drying them out in a warm closet or oven.

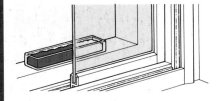

Drilling lintels

Concrete and metal lintels above window recesses can be difficult to drill and fix anchors – if the kit demands it, it's almost worth drilling a test hole to check.

For concrete, you must have a hammer-action drill and a sharp, fairly new masonry bit. Even so, be prepared for the job to take some time – and pause frequently to let the bit cool down.

If you strike metal, you'll find you make no progress at all; poke the hole with a nail to check, then swap for an ordinary high speed steel twist bit.

When drilling a tiled recess, don't forget to start the holes with a spearpoint bit and use tape to stop it from slipping.

Drilling a concrete lintel takes time under the best of circumstances, and won't be possible at all unless your drill has a hammer action.

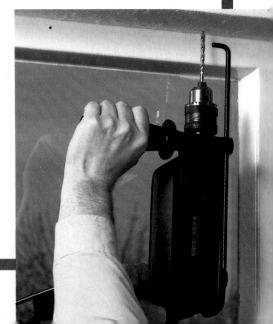

INSULATING PIPES AND TANKS

Insulating cold water supply pipes and storage tanks is a vital precaution against winter freeze-ups. But on hot pipes and the hot water cylinder, insulation can play another, equally important role – by keeping valuable heat sealed in and cutting down on fuel bills.

What to insulate

■ Although it would be unusual, you may have a water storage tank in the roof space, probably in addition to the one you already have in the basement. Top priority must go to insulating this, particularly if insulating material has already been laid between the joists. Such insulation lowers the temperature in the roof space, increasing its vulnerability to frost.

Don't overlook heating pipes, and pipes which conduct water up to attic bedrooms.

■ Next on the list are pipes passing through a cellar, garage, utility room or any room not connected to the heating system. These may survive frost quite happily while the rest of the house is fully heated (ironically, the escaping heat protects

Trade tip

Is your house safe?

❝ Even if your pipes and tanks are already insulated, it pays not to be too complacent. Older insulation materials aren't particularly robust, and in time they have a habit of disintegrating or slipping off (especially in areas where repairs have been carried out).

It's also possible that whoever installed the insulation skimped on the job. Sadly, I've had plenty of customers over the years who thought they were safe from freeze-ups – but weren't. ❞

them). Yet it only takes one severe frost while the family is away to create complete havoc.

■ Check enclosed pipes. If these run along cold walls, the surround will insulate them from warmth inside the house but not from cold outside.

■ Finally, check the hot water system. Hot pipes which pass through rooms can be left, as the heat they give out won't be wasted. But the hot water cylinder and any pipes inside cabinets are prime candidates for insulation – you can save around 75% of heat this way.

The instructions overleaf give suitable insulating materials for each location, so check before you buy. In some places you may be able to use up any materials left over from insulating the attic.

Insulate vulnerable pipework (below) using flexible foam sleeve insulation.

INSULATING PIPES

Covering your water pipes with insulation doesn't only protect them from freezing up in cold weather. It can also keep your hot water hotter (saving both money and energy), and keep pipes from freezers or air conditioners colder and therefore more efficient.

Types of pipe insulation

Although regulations governing types of insulation vary over the country, they are strict and designed to prevent fire and the spread of fire.

Pipe insulation generally falls into three categories: fiber glass, foam rubber and foam polyethylene. These come in either rigid tubes or sleeves, and most types are self-adhesive (although some types must

be secured with tape or wire). They are available in a range of different sizes to suit pipes of different dimensions.

There are also various types of pipe wrap. Felt sleeve is becoming rare nowadays.

Foam sleeves are the easiest to fit. To estimate how much to buy, measure each pipe end to end (this covers wastage at joints) and total the figures. Round up to the nearest multiple of the sleeve length.

For hot water pipes use either a rigid sleeve or pipe wrap. The latter is wound like a spiral, overlapping slightly at each turn. Pipes should then be covered with aluminum foil.

Tools checklist: Sharp knife, miter box, tape measure, pliers.

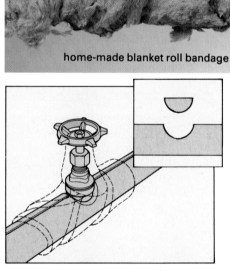

rigid foam sleeve

traditional felt sleeve

home-made blanket roll bandage

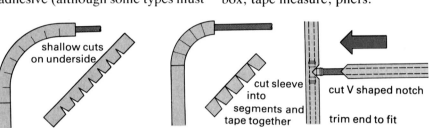

Trim foam sleeve as shown to deal with elbows, bends and T-junctions.

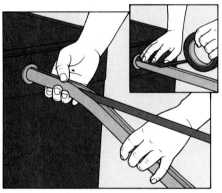

1 To fit foam sleeve insulation, prize the lengths apart and slip them over the pipe. On the non-molded type, cover the split lengthwise with tape.

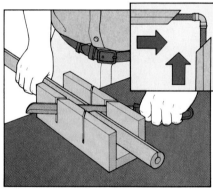

2 Tape lengths together where they butt-join. At corners, it's neater to miter the ends in a miter box – use a sharp kitchen knife to cut the sleeve.

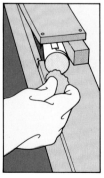

3 Cut notches in the sleeve to clear stopcocks and other fittings (see also Problem Solver). Where necessary, add an extra layer of pipe-wrap.

ENCLOSED PIPES

Insulate enclosed pipes with **loose fill** insulation, which comes in bags of various sizes. Mineral wool loose fill is easier to handle than the granule type, but wear gloves – the fibers irritate the skin.

Open up the cover at places which give good access to the entire pipe run, then push in the loose fill. Use an opened out wire coathanger for this part of the job, and channel the material through a home-made cardboard tube. Distribute it evenly over the pipes until they are completely covered.

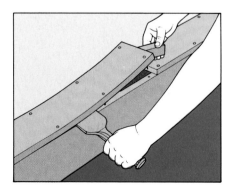

Unscrew the cover at convenient points, or prize it open using a sharp brick chisel or old wood chisel. Prop the loosened end with a block of wood.

Force the loose fill into the space through a home-made tube of cardboard. Use a stick to push it through, then spread it evenly with an opened-out coathanger.

semi-rigid foam sleeve

plastic-backed pipe-wrap

Pipe insulation (left) comes in several different types.

Using pipe-wrap

Pipe-wrap (also called *bandage*) comes in rolls in a variety of materials, including felt, mineral wool and glass fiber. Some makes have a plastic or metal foil backing; others are self-adhesive, which makes fitting easier. Rolls are typically 50mm or 75mm (2–3") wide and 5m (16'5") or 10m (33') long. Make sure you compare like with like when checking prices.

Pipe-wrap is simply rolled around the pipes, overlapping on each turn. It is particularly useful on runs full of bends or joints, and for insulating stopcocks and valves.

Coverage is around half a yard of pipe per yard of roll, but treat this as a rough guide and err on the generous side – your supplier should be prepared to take back unused rolls if they're unopened.

Clean the pipes with a damp cloth before fitting self-adhesive pipe-wrap. For other types, cut lengths of wire to secure the ends.

Blanket roll left over from the attic can be used instead of pipe-wrap providing it is at least 50mm (2") thick. Cut the roll into 75mm (3") 'slices' using a panel saw. Then fix the home-made bandage in place with twists of wire or plastic tape.

Tools checklist: Trimming knife, panel saw (for blanket roll).

Other materials: Stiff wire or suitable adhesive tape (see Tip).

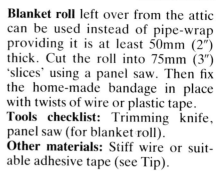

Trade tip

Tape tip

❝ At a pinch, you can use virtually any type of self-adhesive tape to secure foam sleeve, pipe-wrap and polystyrene slabs – but some types are better than others.

Some insulation manufacturers include purpose-made fiberglass reinforced or PVC tape as part of their ranges. A good alternative is 50mm (2") plastic package tape, sold by stationers. Don't use insulating tape, as it tends to lose its adhesion. ❞

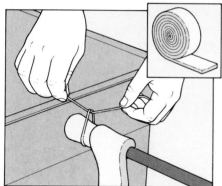

1 *To fit pipe-wrap, start with a double turn and secure with a twist of garden tie-wire. Wind it around the pipe in a spiral, overlapping ⅓ of its width.*

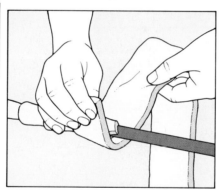

2 *Allow a double overlap where lengths join. Secure the non-adhesive type with wire or tape – but not too tightly, or you'll reduce its effectiveness.*

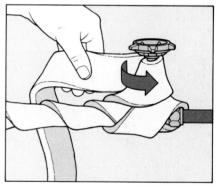

3 *Wrap stopcocks and valves in an 'X' pattern so that the body of the fitting is completely covered, leaving only the handle exposed.*

INSULATING THE HOT CYLINDER

Insulating jackets, consisting of quilted plastic sections filled with mineral or fiberglass wool, are available to fit all common sizes of cylinder. The sections are linked via a wire collar fitted around the topmost pipe, and held in place with elastic or adjustable straps. You'll find it easier to assemble the jacket if you fit the straps first.

If there is another tank fitted, arrange for it to coincide with a joint between sections and leave the cap exposed. The same applies to a cylinder thermostat.

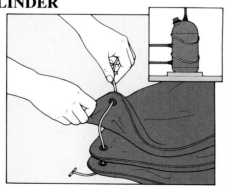

1 *Fit the jacket's straps loosely around the cylinder, a quarter of the way from the top and bottom. Then thread the jacket sections through the wire collar.*

2 *Fit the collar around the top pipe and drape the sections over the cylinder. Tuck the sections under the straps, one by one closing any gaps as you go.*

INSULATING TANKS

If you have the choice, insulate tanks **after** the pipework so that the vulnerable connections are doubly protected. Leave the area below a tank free of insulation to take advantage of rising heat.

Tank insulation kits consist of specially tailored slabs of polystyrene foam, plus tape or straps to secure them. They are made to fit all common sizes of plastic tank, but are unsuitable for round tanks and may not match older, galvanized steel types. Kits are not the cheapest solution, but they are easy to fit.

Slip-over insulating jackets similar to hot water cylinder jackets are available for round tanks.

For either of the above options, be sure to measure the tank dimensions before you buy.

Polystyrene slabs used for attic insulation are easily cut to fit square-sided tanks. The slabs should be at least 25mm (1″) thick. Fix with cocktail sticks and tape.

Left-over blanket roll or batts (minimum 75mm [3″] thick) can also be used, but they are less robust than slabs and trickier to fit. Secure the pieces with string, and tape over

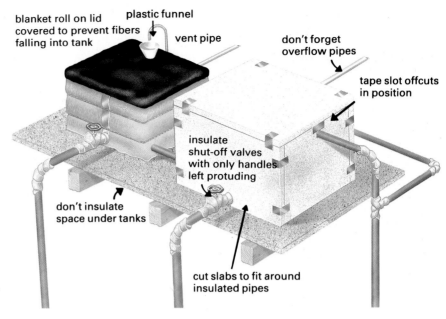

blanket roll on lid covered to prevent fibers falling into tank

plastic funnel

vent pipe

don't forget overflow pipes

tape slot offcuts in position

insulate shut-off valves with only handles left protuding

don't insulate space under tanks

cut slabs to fit around insulated pipes

any vertical joints. Cut another piece to fit on top of the lid and wrap them both in a bin liner.

Where the tank is without a lid, make one from an offcut of 12mm (½″) particleboard or 9mm (⅜″) plywood. Cut slots to clear pipes, then drill out the waste wood.

Other materials: Suitable adhesive

A properly insulated cold storage tank/central heating expansion tank set-up showing polystyrene slab and blanket roll insulation.

tape (see previous page), string or twine, cocktail sticks, funnel.

Tools checklist: Sharp kitchen knife, tape measure, felt-tip pen.

1 *Cut foam slabs* to fit around the sides of the tank using a sharp kitchen knife. Cut slots to clear any pipes, but save the offcuts for taping back on.

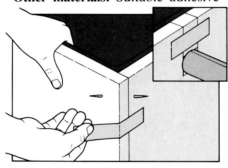

2 Fix the slabs together at the corners with cocktail sticks and reinforce with PVC tape. Then tape back the offcuts where slots were cut for pipes.

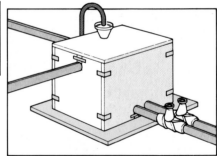

3 Cut a fifth slab for the lid and secure to the sides with tape. Where there is an overhead vent pipe, drive a cheap plastic funnel through the slab.

▌PROBLEM SOLVER▐

Awkward areas

There are likely to be places where space is too restricted to fit conventional insulation. In particular, watch out for outside faucets and the holes where their supply pipes pass through walls. There may be a similar problem at the eaves, where overflows pass to the outside.

Pack these gaps with expanding foam filler, available in aerosol form. Although not cheap, it provides better weather protection than loose fill and is easier to handle.

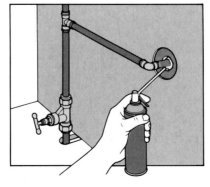

Squirt foam filler into the gaps where supply or overflow pipes pass through outside walls.

Cover outside faucet pipes in a 'sleeve' of foam. This can be sanded smooth when dry.

LAYING INSULATION IN YOUR ATTIC

Keeping your house warm can be expensive at the best of times, but inadequate insulation sends heating costs literally through the roof.

An uninsulated loft lets through 25% of the heat below. And even a layer 50mm (2″) thick loses more than 10%, which makes it well worth increasing the amount of insulation in your attic. Apart from the extra comfort it will create, the saving on fuel bills can cover the cost of the insulation within just a few years.

If your attic isn't used as a living space, the easiest place to insulate is between the ceiling joists, using one of the materials shown below. Any part of the attic used as a living area must be insulated at rafter level to retain heat rising from the rooms below. This is covered elsewhere.

Flat roofs are more difficult to insulate – see Problem Solver for possible solutions.

Insulation slabs are easy to handle and can be cut to fit any joist spacing.

TYPES OF INSULATION MATERIAL

Insulation mats are made from mineral wool or fiber glass. It comes in continuous rolls and as slabs. The rolls are called *batts*; the flat mats or slabs are *blankets*.

Batts (in various lengths) are commonly available in thicknesses ranging from 50mm (2″) to 150mm (6″) and in standard widths to fit the usual 400mm (16″) joist spacing. Wider 1200mm (48″) rolls can be cut into three pieces with a crosscut saw to fit 400mm (16″) joists or two to fit the less common 600mm (24″) spacing. A few brands have an integral vapor barrier to keep out moisture; the 150mm thick rolls sometimes have a separate top layer that can be offset to cover the tops of the joists. *Blankets* are 50mm (2″) thick and have to be cut in three for 400mm joists or two for 600mm.
Loose fill consists of mineral wool fibers or vermiculite granules and is sold in bags. A bag of mineral wool fiber covers roughly 1 sq m (11 sq ft)

to a depth of 50mm (2″). A bag of vermiculite covers 2.25 sq m (24 sq ft) to the same depth, but must be laid thicker to provide the same degree of insulation.
Polystyrene comes in sheets up to 2400×1200mm (8×4′) in size, to a thickness of 100mm (4″).

An alternative to DIY is to employ a contractor to 'blow' cellulose or mineral fiber into the attic. This is very efficient but expensive.

With loose fill or blanket insulation special **eaves vents** and **soffit vents** are available to prevent condensation in the attic.

Mineral wool batt

Fiberglass batt

Eaves vents

Polystyrene sheeting

Mineral wool blanket

Fibre loose fill

Granule loose fill

Soffit vents

Hatch kit

CHOOSING THE RIGHT MATERIAL

Measure the depth of the joists and the spaces between them, checking to see if they are evenly spaced. They may not be suitable for standard width batts, or could be too shallow for some types of loose fill.

If you want to use loose fill and your attic is very drafty, it's better to use the mineral fiber type as vermiculite granules can drift.

The chart below shows the options for different joist spacings and any existing insulation thickness. The depths for each type of material are the minimum recommended and give a rough indication of their relative efficiency. You can put in a thicker layer, but it is unlikely to be as cost-effective.

To calculate how many batts or blankets you need, multiply the joist length by the number of spaces to be filled. Divide this by the length of each blanket or batt section.

For loose fill, multiply together the overall dimensions of the attic in meters for the total area in square meters. The coverage for loose fills given on page 165 includes the area taken up by the joists.

INSULATION OPTIONS

| Joist layout | Suitable insulation | Minimum extra insulation needed if existing insulation thickness is: | | |
		None	Under 30mm (1¼")	Around 50mm (2")
Regular gaps: approx 400mm (16")	Batt: standard width or 1200mm cut in three	100mm (4")	100mm (4")	50mm (2")
	Blanket cut in three	100mm (4")	100mm (4")	50mm (2")
	Fiber loose fill	90mm (3½")	70mm (2¾")	50mm (2")
	Granule loose fill	155mm (6")	not suitable	100mm (4")
	'Blown' fibre	85–110mm (3½–4½")	not suitable	not suitable
Regular gaps: approx 600mm (24")	Batt: 1200mm cut in two	100mm (4")	100mm (4")	50mm (2")
	Blanket cut in two	100mm (4")	100mm (4")	50mm (2")
	Fiber loose fill	90mm (3½")	70mm (2¾")	50mm (2")
	Granule loose fill	155mm (6")	not suitable	100mm (4")
	'Blown' fiber	85–110mm (3½–4½")	not suitable	not suitable
Irregular gaps and awkward corners	Blanket cut to fit	100mm (4")	100mm (4")	50mm (2")
	Fiber loose fill	90mm (3½")	70mm (2¾")	50mm (2")
	Granule loose fill	155mm (6")	not suitable	100mm (4")
	'Blown' fiber	85–110mm (3½–4½")	not suitable	not suitable

PREPARING TO LAY INSULATION

Make sure there is enough light to work in and if necessary set up a temporary light source. Clear the attic and take up any flooring inspecting the joists beneath for rot or termites. Step only on the joists and use a board to kneel on.

Fix any wires that run over the ceiling to the joists above the insulation level – this stops them overheating. Wiring that passes through joists must be removed and refixed over the top. If you find any old rubber sheathed wiring, this is due for replacement.

Pipes running between the joists can be left covered with insulation. Other pipes and any cold water tanks must be individually insulated as shown in the following section.

It's important to be sure that there is constant air circulation through the attic above the insulation. This prevents condensation forming and causing damage to the insulation and roof timbers. Vents can be fitted between the rafters at joist level to ensure the ventilation gaps in the eaves remain unblocked. A vapor barrier of polyethylene sheeting or foil backed-paper fixed between the joists stops water vapor entering the attic.

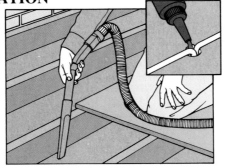

Clean thoroughly between the joists with a soft brush or vacuum cleaner. Seal any gaps where pipes and wires enter with mastic or filler.

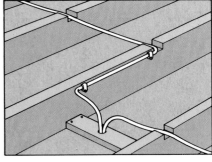

Staple wires to the joists above the level of the insulation. If you are boarding over joists, chisel shallow notches in tops to accept the wires.

Check that there are gaps or holes along the eaves. If there isn't enough air getting in, drill holes or install ventilation grilles in the soffit.

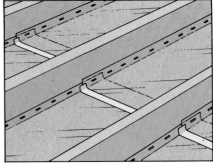

Lay a vapor barrier between the joists, leaving 25mm (1") flaps at each side. Overlap the sections, tape joins and staple or tape to the joists.

PLANNING PAYS

The insulation value of attic insulating materials is expressed as an R value (as in double glazing). The effectiveness of the different kinds of material varies quite considerable. Fiber glass batt, for example, is almost R3.5pi (per inch); rigid fiber glass boards (useful for very small, confined spaces) can rate as high as R7pi.

It is always advisable to shop around before purchasing. Generally, the cost of materials reflects their effectiveness, and you must balance the expense of instaling the insulation against the expected reduction in your fuel bills. In general, it's best to use very expensive materials only in the smallest spaces where outlay can be controlled.

Your local utility or government standards office can give you valuable advice on the best material for you.

Protection
Some mineral or glass wool fibers can irritate the skin and lungs so wear a face mask and gloves when handling insulation made from either of these materials.

LAYING INSULATION

Take the materials up into the attic in their packages – batts expand to up to four times their original size when unwrapped and if you're cutting to size, it's easier to do so before you remove the wrapping.

Batts are designed to fit snugly between standard spaced joists so only trim them to fit the odd non-standard spacing.

If you're not using a kit to insulate the attic hatch cover, cut a piece of the material to size and tie loosely on to the cover. Tape or staple a sheet of polyethylene or heavy plastic over the material to prevent stray fibers escaping into the house.

 *Trade tip*

Getting into the eaves

❝ If you can't get right into the eaves because of the slope of the roof, unroll a convenient length of batt and push the end gently into the eaves with a broom. Be careful not to push it is so far that it blocks off the air holes. ❞

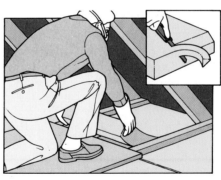

1 *Start laying insulation at the eaves, leaving a 50mm (2") air gap or fitting vents. With blankets trim the ends at an angle to help the airflow.*

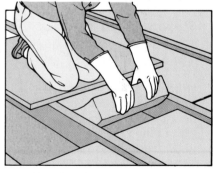

2 *Unroll or fit the material gently without compressing it. Fit tightly up against the joists and butt the pieces up to each other where they meet.*

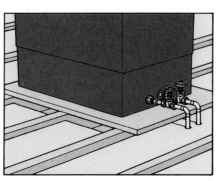

3 *Cut the batt or blanket to fit snugly around any obstacles or pipes using heavy scissors or a kitchen knife. Leave the space under a cold water tank free.*

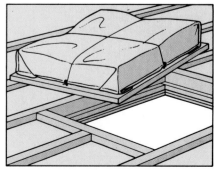

4 *Hammer some nails into the sides of the hatch cover, leaving them 25mm (1") proud. Cover the insulation with polyethylene and tie with string.*

PUTTING IN LOOSE FILL

Cover over any cold pipes that run close to the ceiling with pieces of cardboard or thick paper to stop the loose fill from flowing underneath them. This lets heat from the room below keep the pipes warm.

Do not lay loose fill under any cold water tanks for the same reason. Fit boards between the joists to block off this area.

The simplest way to insulate the hatch cover is to use a slab kit or 100mm (4") thick polystyrene sheeting.

1 Fix eaves vents or pieces of board near the ends of the joists to avoid blocking the ventilation gap. Block off the areas under cold tanks.

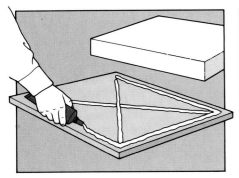

2 Cut a piece of polystyrene sheet to size and glue it on to the inside of the hatch cover. Use adhesive designed for polystyrene ceiling tiles.

3 Spread or pour the loose fill evenly between the joists, except under cold tanks. Gently separate and fluff up mineral wool fiber.

4 Level off the loose fill at the top of the joists. Use a garden rake for wool fibers and a piece of shaped board for vermiculite granules.

PROBLEM SOLVER

Dealing with flat roofs

There are three ways to insulate a flat roof:

Option 1: Internal insulation is only possible if you are prepared to remove the fascia boards and expose the gaps between the joists. This allows you to slide sheets of polystyrene or mineral wool slabs into the roof space. However, it may be easier to have fiber material blown in by a contractor. This is more expensive but could save you time and trouble.

Option 2: A new roof can be laid using special weatherproof insulation slabs bonded to the existing roof with mastic. These are pre-felted, but must be finished with a wood edging.

Option 3: Ceiling insulation is a last resort if access to the fascia or roof is very difficult. For a minimum of insulation, you can stick polystyrene tiles to the ceiling with tile adhesive. But if the ceiling is high enough, it's possible to line it with polystyrene sheeting (plus a polyethylene vapor barrier) and cover it with a false ceiling.

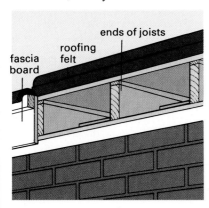

Removing the fascia boards gives access to the spaces between the joists, so they can be filled from the outside with polystyrene sheets or mineral wool blankets.

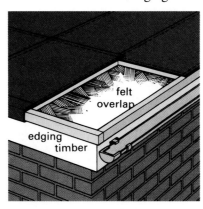

Prefelted roof slabs have flaps which overlap to make a weatherproof roof surface, but require a wooden framework to finish the edges.

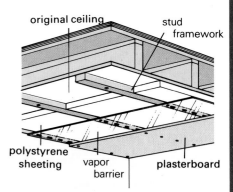

A false ceiling on a wooden framework can be built to conceal a layer of polystyrene insulation so long as it still leaves 2.3m (7' 6") headroom.

IDENTIFYING AND CURING CONDENSATION

Condensation is the scourge of modern homes, and like weeds in the garden it can be frustratingly difficult to get rid of. In a well-designed and sensibly run home there is no reason why it should occur at all, but that's little consolation if you are a condensation sufferer. A more realistic approach is to understand why condensation happens, then set about eliminating the causes one by one.

What is condensation?

Air always contains a certain amount of moisture in the form of water vapor. Like a bath sponge, there's a limit to the amount it can carry, and when it can hold no more it is said to have reached *saturation point*. Unlike a sponge, however, the saturation point of air varies according to its temperature – warm air can hold more moisture than cool air.

When air at saturation point is suddenly cooled – for example, by coming into contact with a cold window pane on a chilly day – its ability to hold moisture as water vapor is immediately reduced. At this point, the excess vapor *condenses* into minute water droplets and the process of condensation begins.

The droplets appear first as a fine film that mists up the glass and causes other cold, smooth surfaces to feel damp. But as more moisture is deposited, the droplets combine into the trickles of water that leave tell-tale pools on window sills and the like.

Condensation takes place whenever warm, damp air is cooled suddenly, reducing its capacity to carry moisture as water vapor.

THE CONSEQUENCES OF CONDENSATION

Surfaces which are continually damp can be a nuisance – even unpleasant – to live with. And owners of condensation-prone homes need no reminding of the damage which continued trickles of water can do to wallcoverings and soft furnishings. But condensation can have more serious consequences too:

Mold growth is the most common, particularly around window frames. Air-borne fungal spores searching for water to help them germinate find an ideal breeding ground on the damp surfaces of a condensation-prone room.

Materials which retain moisture, such as wallpaper or the edges of window frames, are particularly at risk. So are other areas where poor ventilation – itself a prime cause of condensation – keeps the air moisture content high.

Structural decay is less common, but much more serious. Surface condensation can penetrate the cracks in painted woodwork, creating perfect conditions for rot to develop. In walls, the same process causes plaster to break down and crumble.

There is also *interstitial condensation* – condensation which takes place naturally within the structure. In a properly designed and ventilated home, this should quickly be dispersed. But if the condensation is excessive, or is allowed to become trapped, any porous materials – especially timber – soon begin to decay.

INDENTIFYING THE CAUSES

Somewhat surprisingly, we are ourselves a major source of moisture in the air. Our breath is moist and our sweat evaporates; one person 'produces' half a pint of water during eight hours of sleep, and as much as two and a half pints during an active day.

Our domestic activities create even more moisture. Cooking, washing up, bathing, washing and drying clothes and so on produces up to between 15 and 20 pints of water a day, and every pint of fuel burnt in a flueless oil or paraffin heater gives off roughly another pint of water vapor.

We expect the air in the house to 'soak up' this liquid for us. Condensation becomes a problem when it can't, for one or more of the reasons given here.

THE CONSEQUENCES OF CONDENSATION

POOR VENTILATION

The normal way in which moist air is removed from the house is by ventilation. Sometimes this is intentional – for example, when we open windows or switch on an extractor fan. But in the average home there's a fair degree of unintentional ventilation too, as moisture-laden air escapes through old chimney flues and other gaps.

Unfortunately, the quest for warmer homes and reduced heating bills has led to houses becoming much more air-tight than they used to be. Flues are blocked off, windows are double glazed, doors are weatherproofed and floors, walls and ceilings are insulated. Such measures increase comfort but reduce ventilation, increasing the condensation risk.

Poor ventilation is not only a problem within the house; it can affect the structure too, and in particular the roof space. When an attic floor or flat roof is insulated, the air in the space above remains cold. This causes any warm, moist air which finds its way into the space to 'lose' its moisture as condensation. The condensation in turn soaks the insulation, rendering it less effective and encouraging rot.

It is now realized that efficient ventilation of roof spaces by means of special eaves vents and ridge ventilators is essential, and you will see these features on all new houses. However, many older homes don't even benefit from 'accidental' ventilation – especially if the eaves have been packed with attic insulation – and may be beginning to suffer serious problems as a result.

Possible solutions

Top priority must go towards providing a controllable means of getting rid of excess moist air.

■ In kitchens and bathrooms, an extractor fan is usually the answer. This expels the unwanted air quickly, minimizing heat losses, and has the added benefit of dispersing unwanted smells too. In severe cases, you could consider wiring the fan to a *humidity detector* so that operation is automatic.

■ Elsewhere, the simplest solutions are to fit window- and door-mounted slot ventilators, or extra wall-mounted ventilation grilles. But first make sure that any existing grilles are unblocked, and that rooms with secondary double glazing have at least one openable window for emergency ventilation.

■ Unused chimney flues must be vented top and bottom, which serves as a useful back-up to other ventilation measures. If a flue is left blocked, condensation inside can result in damp patches on chimney breast walls.

■ In the roof space, check that there is a vapor barrier of polyethylene or building paper below the attic insulation. Make sure the insulation isn't carried right to the eaves, and fit eaves vents if necessary away from pipes and cisterns.

DEHUMIDIFICATION

Where ventilation problems can't be solved by other means, it may be worth investing in an *electric dehumidifier*. These remove moisture from the air and produce heat as a by-product (although they are most effective where heat and humidity are the main problem, rather than low temperatures).

Portable dehumidifiers can be intrusively noisy to run. *Whole-house* versions are mounted in the roof space and operate through a system of ducts. They are comparitively expensive, but quieter and more efficient.

Check the house room by room for condensation problems. The symbols above show the most common trouble spots and indicate the probable cause – see main text for details.

POOR INSULATION

Wall, floor and ceiling surfaces – not to mention window glass – all become cold as external temperatures fall, even if the interior is adequately warm. This results in condensation as soon as warm, moisture-laden air within the room comes into contact with them.

A poorly insulated home is left wide open to condensation – particularly in areas where natural air circulation is restricted – for example, the corners of rooms, or behind furniture (especially where this is built-in against a cold outside wall). But even where the structure is basically well insulated, condensation may still occur at 'cold bridges' with the outside – for example, window and door recesses and lintels.

Possible solutions

Over and above normal insulating measures – including double glazing – you may need to take additional steps to keep walls warm. One possibility is to redecorate with heat-retaining materials (see overleaf). Very severe cases may call for *cavity wall insulation,* which must be professionally installed by a qualified contractor using approved materials.

INADEQUATE HEATING

Improving insulation must go hand in hand with providing adequate heating; even a well insulated room will eventually become cold enough for condensation to occur, even though the rate of heat loss has been reduced. This applies particularly to rooms which are traditionally heated only for part of the day, such as bedrooms.

Possible solutions

In centrally heated homes, which includes almost all homes nowadays, the solution is to maintain a constant level of heat. By avoiding intermittent heating, room temperatures can be maintained at a sufficient level to stop condensation occurring. This needn't mean an increase in fuel bills – often it is more wasteful to keep warming up a building from cold every time the heating is switched on.

Some homes may not have a central heating system – summer vacation cottages or country homes which rely on a fireplace to heat through the whole house, for instance. In such homes, it is sensible to provide a local heat source for use in every room when the house is occupied. A small electric heater with a thermostatic control is both lightweight and effective.

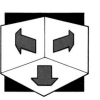

ABSORBENT SURFACES

Condensation is naturally retained for longer by absorbent surfaces and materials than by smooth ones. Not only does this make them harder to clean; it also encourages mold.

Remember this when choosing decorations and furnishings. Vinyl wallcoverings and sheet vinyl, vinyl tiled or sealed cork flooring are good choices for these rooms. For painted surfaces, consider using *alcohol-based primer sealer* (see overleaf). This absorbs excess water vapor until it can evaporate harmlessly, so preventing run-off.

BAD HABITS

You can make a personal contribution towards reducing condensation by a simple change of habits.

■ Keep doors to steamy rooms closed so that moist air can be expelled through proper ventilation instead of finding its way into other (colder) parts of the house.

■ Dry clothes in the open air wherever possible, or invest in a tumble drier. Where you have to dry them indoors, make special ventilation arrangements.
■ Make sure bathrooms and shower rooms are warm before you use them.
■ Keep bedrooms ventilated at night. If it's too cold to have a window open, leave the door ajar.

SIMPLE CURES

Apply anti-condensation paint using ordinary brush or roller techniques. It can be left as a finish in its own right or overpainted when dry.

DECORATIVE IDEAS

When redecorating rooms such as kitchens or bathrooms which have a condensation problem due to cold walls, choose materials which help to prevent condensation.

Alcohol-based primer sealer dries to a white, finely textured finish which resists the formation of condensation and also inhibits mold growth. Once dry it can be overpainted with paint to blend in with your color scheme; the anti-condensation properties are unaffected.

Insulating wallcoverings also help to prevent condensation on cold walls. Two options are to apply an expanded polystyrene or polyethylene lining, or to use a blown vinyl wallcovering. Both contain minute air bubbles which help to retain heat.

WINDOW VENTS

A window vent fitted in a fixed pane is a simple way to allow fresh air to ventilate a room. Wind-driven designs are dependent on there being some airflow outside. There are also static types with an outer wind shield which should permit a constant exchange of air with the minimum of drafts. For areas of heavy condensation you could even install a powered extractor fan.

All such vents are fitted by bolting them together through a hole in the glass. Don't try to cut this yourself – get a glass dealer to supply a pane of glass with a hole cut in it, and reglaze the window.

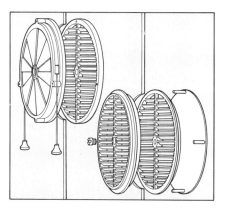

Vents come in two parts which bolt together through the hole. There are various designs, but the main choice is between a revolving or static type.

Trade tip

Soak it up

6 *For minor condensation on windows, self-adhesive foam strip will absorb the water run-off. Don't use it where the window is constantly wet as it must get a chance to dry out.* 9

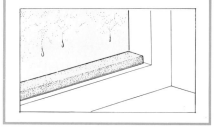

EAVES VENTS

Eaves vents are cheap plastic barriers which hold the attic insulation a short distance away from the roof covering to provide vital air circulation. Fitting is simple – just tuck the bottom flap under the edge of the insulation material to retain it in place.

If the construction of the roof leads you to suspect that air flow through the eaves is insufficient, you can fit *soffit vents* – plastic grilles to trim holes cut in the soffit board. This must be done from the outside, using a ladder or scaffolding, so try to combine it with other oudoor repairs requiring similar access arrangements.

Fit eaves vents where none are present, or when insulating from scratch. These keep the cold roof space well ventilated, minimizing the risk of condensation.

IDENTIFYING DAMPNESS PROBLEMS

Dampness is one one of the most common and potentially serious problems facing housing in temperate climates. Left to its own devices, continual dampness can ruin decorations and cause the structure to deteriorate rapidly. But worse still, it can create the ideal conditions for wet and dry rot – associated problems which cost homeowners millions of dollars each year to put right.

What is dampness?

For a building, suffering from dampness is not the same thing as simply getting wet.

All houses are constantly in contact with moisture in the ground and air, and they frequently get pelted with rain. But if they are properly designed and structurally sound, ground water will be stopped from penetrating, rainwater will run off, and any moisture which does get in should evaporate quickly. At the same time, areas which could suffer if they got wet – the plaster and concealed woodwork for instance – should be well protected.

Dampness occurs when structural defects cause one or more of these built-in safeguards to break down. Moisture gets in and, instead of disappearing, becomes trapped in the house structure. Once inside, it remains where it is or finds its way into more vulnerable areas – by which time the damage has been done.

For this reason alone, preventing dampness is a lot more sensible than trying to cure it once it has taken hold. You can do a lot by giving your home an immediate 'dampness survey' to check out the most vulnerable areas.

TYPES OF DAMPNESS

Builders and damproofing specialists classify dampness by the way in which it is caused. In many cases the symptoms – mold, ruined decorations, rotten woodwork – are the same, but where dampness is concerned you can't possibly hope to put things right unless you identify the cause first.

Rising dampness occurs when the house structure sucks moisture out of the ground. Old houses without a damp-proof course (DPC) and a built-in vapor barrier are especially vulnerable, and brick walls also tend to become more porous with age. But rising dampness can affect newer houses, too, if there are defects in the built-in damp-proofing measures.

Penetrating dampness, the most common kind, occurs when water penetrates and becomes trapped in the house structure. All houses are vulnerable, but older ones particularly so since they are likely to have more structural defects which allow water to get in unhindered.

Dampness caused by leaks from water pipes and the seals around plumbing fittings can pass by unnoticed, but it is very common. All houses are vulnerable.

Hygroscopic dampness occurs when the house absorbs moisture from the atmosphere. It is rarer than the other types, but may be present at the same time as them. Older houses are particularly vulnerable.

Condensation is where water vapor in the air turns to water as it contacts a cooler surface. Although not the same as structural dampness, it can produce the same symptoms, and may be confused with it. Dealing with condensation is covered in separate sections.

The poor condition of the brickwork shown below was caused by a combination of hygroscopic salts, frost attack, rising dampness and leaking rainwater pipes.

FINDING THE CAUSE: OUTSIDE

Under the right conditions, virtually any structural defect can lead to dampness. But some areas of a house are more vulnerable than others and a few are notorious trouble spots.

When matching symptoms inside the house to faults outside, bear in mind that dampness often shows up some way away from the defect which caused it. In walls and ceilings, the moisture tends to 'creep' along structural joints or gaps, then emerge at a weak point – such as a patch of repaired plaster.

Chimneys are another recognized trouble spot.
■ Cracked mortar around the chimney stacks allows water to soak into the stack, causing rapid deterioration.
■ Damaged flashings where the chimney meets the roof covering lead to penetrating dampness in the chimney breast. In time, this may spread to top-floor level.
■ Uncapped chimneys, if left unused, can raise the level of moisture throughout the entire chimney breast. Often this results in small patches of hygroscopic dampness on walls.

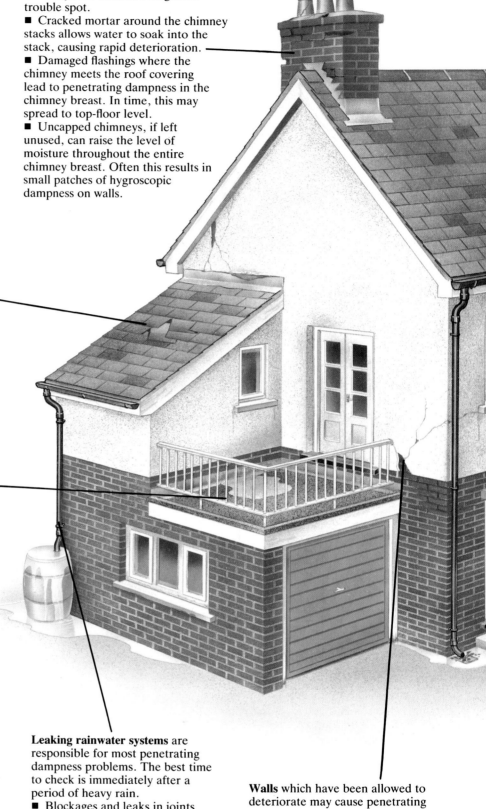

Pitched roofs are surprisingly resistant to penetrating dampness, but that doesn't mean you can ignore them.
■ Slipped slates or tiles may let in rain, and this water penetration often shows up as cracking in top floor ceilings. If there is a layer of felt under the roof covering, this may channel the water away from the hole – possibly as far as the walls.

Flat roofs are a common trouble spot. When water penetrates a flat roof, it gathers above the ceiling below, or runs with the fall to the edges. As well as leaks in the roof covering itself, check for:
■ Damaged flashings where the roof meets the walls. These can cause damp patches lower down inside the house.
■ Cracked or missing stone cappings on parapet walls, which lead to similar problems. Brick-capped parapets should have a DPC.

Trade tip

DPC or not?

❝ If your house was built after 1900, you can be pretty sure it has a damp-proof course – either engineering bricks, slate, or bitumen felt. Before this date, there's a chance it may not.

Over the last 20 years, many DPC-less houses have had a damp-proof course added, usually by chemical injection, but sometimes by fitting ceramic respirators or electro-osmotic equipment. Unfortunately, none of these methods has a 100 per cent success rate – much depends on how efficiently the DPC was installed – so even if your house has been 'damp-proofed', you can't rule out the possiblilty of some rising dampness. ❞

Leaking rainwater systems are responsible for most penetrating dampness problems. The best time to check is immediately after a period of heavy rain.
■ Blockages and leaks in joints should be obvious. On plastic guttering, check, too, that the run isn't bowing and causing overspill at the edges.
■ Check cast-iron drainpipes for rusting, especially around the backs.

Walls which have been allowed to deteriorate may cause penetrating dampness.
■ Check that the pointing is intact.
■ Watch for missing, cracked or *spalled* (deeply pitted) bricks.
■ Check that rendering hasn't cracked or 'blown' by tapping to see if it sounds hollow.
■ On cavity walls, make sure that earlier alterations haven't allowed the cavity to become blocked or 'bridged'. Debris left from replacing a window, and badly sealed waste pipes are two common problems.

Leaking overflows may not be obvious, since they usually drip intermittently to start with. Look for tell-tale green moss patches on the area of wall immediately below.

Windows are a common cause of penetrating dampness.
- Check that the putty around the panes is intact.
- Check stone or concrete sills for signs of cracking.
- Look under each sill and check that the drip groove is clear and intact (some sills have a protruding drip bead). The groove stops rainwater hugging the underside of the sill and running into the wall below; if it is clogged with old paint, there may be penetrating dampness inside the house, below the window.
- Check the seals around the frames; these are particularly vulnerable if made with fillets of mortar rather than caulking.

DPC faults lead to rising dampness. If you can see the DPC, check for cracks caused by subsidence and any other obvious signs of damage. If you can't see the DPC, take it as being at the same height as the lowest doorstep and check right around the house up to this level.
- Earth or other debris piled up against the walls can 'bridge' the DPC. So, too, can an incorrectly laid path or patio.
- Paths and patios laid less than 150mm (6″) below DPC level may cause rainwater 'splashback' on the walls. The effects of this inside the house are likely to be most noticeable in winter.
- Rendering may bridge the DPC if it is continued as far as ground level. (In older houses there may be a rendered plinth hiding a DPC consisting of several courses of engineering bricks. This is acceptable.)
- Adjoining walls will bridge the DPC unless they have one too. Garden walls without a DPC need a vertical DPC where they join a house wall.

Vents protect the ground floor structure from rising dampness by helping moisture under the house to evaporate. Check that they aren't blocked. There may be ventilation grilles higher up the house as well, to ventilate the wall cavity.

Poor surface drainage mainly affects older houses where the DPC is either missing or defective. Its effects inside the house are likely to be seasonal.

Trade tip

Make a sketch

❝ When checking the outside of the house, do what the professionals do and make a sketch plan of each elevation – front, back and sides. As well as noting any obvious faults, don't forget areas that look suspect but which you can't inspect closely – they may need further investigation. ❞

FINDING THE CAUSE: INSIDE

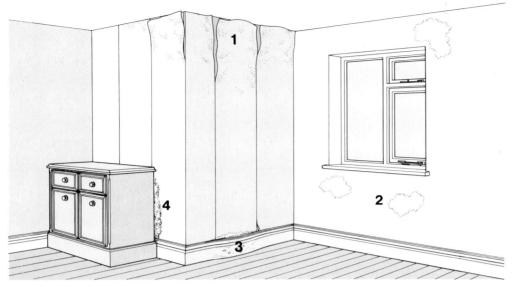

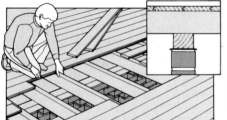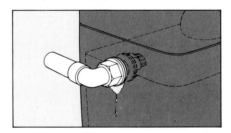

The classic symptoms of dampness include: (1) stained or peeling wallpaper, (2) salt deposits (efflorescence) on painted or bare plastered walls, (3) swollen or blistered painted woodwork, (4) black mold in badly ventilated areas or behind furniture.

As with the outside of the house, when checking the inside it helps if you make a rough sketch plan of each room and note potential trouble spots.

In some places the symptoms of dampness may be obvious (see above) – as may the cause once you know where to look. But it's areas where the dampness lies unseen that frequently cause the most problems. In particular, be sure to check:

■ Behind large cupboards or wardrobes – move them away from the wall if possible.

■ Where pipes are enclosed – remove panels wherever convenient and shine in a torch to inspect.

■ Beneath wooden floors – lift a few boards and shine in a torch; often a musty damp smell is immediately obvious.

■ Around plumbing fittings and (in the attic) storage tanks – remove the bath panel to check the all-important seal around the bath rim.

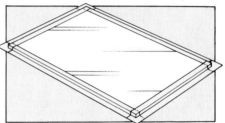

Check for a damp solid floor by taping down a piece of glass and leaving it for a few days. If the glass mists up after this time, there's dampness present.

Lift floorboards to check a wooden ground floor. The 'sleeper' walls supporting the joists should have DPCs above them – but these are often missing in older houses.

Faulty seals around bathroom fittings are a common source of dampness – often only revealed when enough water has collected to bring down the ceiling below!

Overflow pipe connections may have lain untested for years – only to leak undetected as soon as a ballvalve fault occurs. Check tanks for leaks too.

USING A DAMPNESS DETECTOR

If your house is old or prone to dampness problems, a dampness detector could prove a good investment. The latest battery powered models cost no more than a cheap electric drill, and come with a comprehensive instruction booklet.

The detector has a pair of sharp prongs which you insert into different surfaces – walls, woodwork and so on – during the course of making your dampness checks. The dial on the meter then registers whether the moisture level in the surface is safe, in need of some attention,

or a problem that needs urgent action.

When using a dampness detector:
■ Make sure the prongs penetrate any decorative coverings, or you won't get a true reading.
■ Hygroscopic salts in a wall may produce an 'Urgent action' reading, even though the wall may appear dry. But since these salts may cause dampness themselves in the future, they need attention before too long.

When using a dampness detector on a wall make sure the prongs are pushed well in.

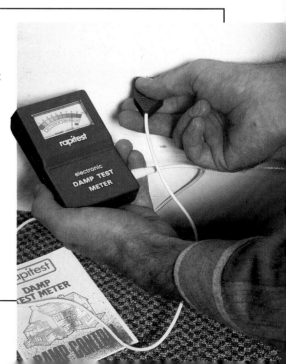

REPAIRING DAMP PATCHES IN WALLS

Damp patches on walls are unsightly and unhealthy, so it makes sense to repair them as soon as possible. But first, and most important, you need to pinpoint and cure what is actually causing the damp.

Penetrating dampness

If the patches are *penetrating dampness,* resulting from a leak or an outside structural fault, they should begin to recede as soon as the fault is repaired. You can speed the drying out process by clearing away all nearby furniture and other fixtures, and then stripping the decorations back to dry plaster.

After a week or so, check the condition of the plaster.

If the plaster is sound, you should be able to do a 'cosmetic' patching job once it has dried fully – see *Curing mild dampness* overleaf. Salt deposits (efflorescence) may appear in the meantime, but this is normal; if possible, leave them until they stop spreading.

If the plaster is ruined – either because the dampness has turned it soft and crumbly, or because it has 'blown' (parted) from the wall, it will need to be chopped back to sound material and replaced (see *Patching damp-soaked plaster* overleaf). The same applies to a patch of **hygroscopic dampness**, where the plaster has become laden with water-attracting salts (usually the result of a previous problem).

Rising dampness

Where the damp patches are caused by rising dampness, it's often less easy to cure the dampness at source. Some faults will be obvious, such as bridging of the damp-proof course. Others may be less so, but should still be traceable – for example, a localized damp patch in a cavity wall suggests that the DPC has been punctured at or around this point.

The real problems tend to occur in older houses where the brickwork has become porous with age and the DPC (if there is one) has ceased to be fully effective. This often results in damp patches all over a wall, usually coinciding with weak points in the brickwork. A badly installed chemical DPC will produce similar symptoms.

Faced by rising damp patches, you have two choices.

Have a new DPC installed. In this case all the affected walls must be stripped and replastered – preferably from floor to ceiling. Depending on the severity of the problem, a damp-proof 'skin' may have to be added between the brickwork and the new plaster.

All this is expensive and highly disruptive, but it should cure the problem once and for all.

Patch up the dampness as and when it occurs, as you would for penetrating dampness. This is not a long-term answer – no matter how well you do the job, the dampness will return in time. But if the dampness isn't too extensive, it's a less disruptive solution than full-scale replastering.

Most of the special compounds used for interior damp-proofing are chlorinated rubber- or solvent-based, and give off strong fumes. Unlike dust, wearing a face mask is no protection – so **never** apply any waterproofing compound in a confined or unventilated space. Open all windows, and stop at the first sign of dizziness. Don't smoke or allow naked flames near the working area.

Make sure, too, that you have a supply of the appropriate cleaner or solvent close to hand. If the waterproofer gets on your skin, wipe off with a rag soaked in the cleaner and wash immediately.

CURING MILD DAMPNESS

Begin by stripping off all traces of old decorations. If the wall is painted, and the paint has bubbled or flaked, scrape it back to a sound surface with a paint scraper and then sand to 'feather' the edges.

If possible, remove any moldings – baseboards, architraves – around the affected area. You won't be able to seal the wall completely if they are left in place, and they may have been affected by the dampness in any case.

The area of wall behind the moldings may have to be made good, in which case see *Patching damp-soaked plaster*.

see *Patching damp-soaked plaster*.

Trade tip

Stir it up

❛ Interior waterproofer separates far more readily than ordinary paint, and won't be effective unless thoroughly stirred. If you use a stick, work it right down to the bottom of the can and keep stirring until the waterproofer is completely uniform in color.

Alternatively, you can use a paint stirring attachment for an electric drill. ❜

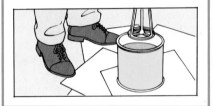

Surface preparation

Brush off any traces of dust and efflorescence. If there are signs of black mold, wash down the wall with a solution of one part bleach to four of water (or use a commercial fungicide) and leave to dry.

Apply the waterproofer, following the manufacturer's recommendations on coating and drying times. Two coats are normally sufficient, but leave up to 24 hours between them otherwise the second coat may cause the first to blister. Coverage is in the region of 5-6 sq m (6-7 sq yd) per liter per coat.

After treatment, touch in any 'missed' areas where the old surface still shows through. The wall can be repainted or papered as desired.

Tools and materials: Interior waterproofer, decorating preparation tools, old wall-size paintbrush, brush cleaner (for removing spills).

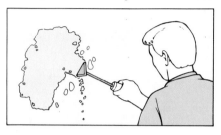

1 Scrape old flaking paint back to a sound edge using a paint scraper. Sand the edges of the stripped patch so that they don't show through.

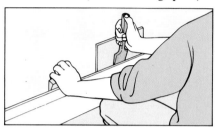

2 Prize off nearby moldings with a brick chisel, using a block of wood as a lever. Check the back of the moldings for rot and replace if necessary.

3 Having prepared the surface, apply waterproofer with broad sweeps, working on a square metre (or yard) at a time. Make sure you don't miss any patches.

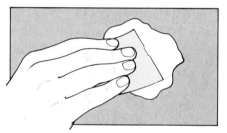

4 After recoating, fill any hollows and smooth over old paint edges with fine surface filler. Sand down, but avoid puncturing the coating.

USING DAMP-PROOF FOIL

This is applied in much the same way as a foil wallcovering – ie by pasting the wall, not the covering itself – and is ideal for use in confined spaces.

Prepare as for interior waterproofer, brushing off all signs of efflorescence and killing any mold patches. Some kits also recommend that the wall is prepared first with a brushed-on coat of the special adhesive.

Cut the strips with scissors to avoid tearing, allowing the usual overlap for trimming. Plumb a line on the wall, then 'paste' with the adhesive.

Hang the first strip against the line and trim in the normal way. On subsequent strips, overlap the joints by around 12mm (½") and brush in more of the adhesive to seal them. Finally, smooth down with a damp cloth.

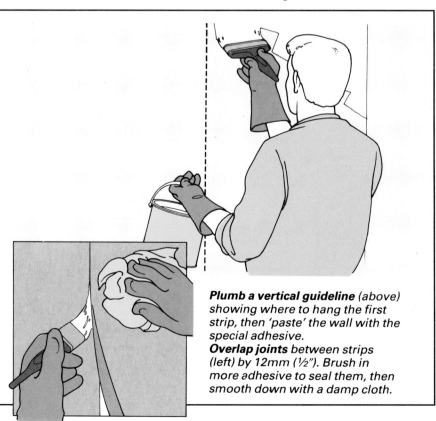

Plumb a vertical guideline *(above) showing where to hang the first strip, then 'paste' the wall with the special adhesive.*
Overlap joints *between strips (left) by 12mm (½"). Brush in more adhesive to seal them, then smooth down with a damp cloth.*

PATCHING DAMP-SOAKED PLASTER

If the plaster is soft and crumbly or has 'blown' from the wall and sounds hollow when you tap it, you have no choice but to hack it out and repair the patch.

Obviously, the smaller the patch the easier this will be. But there is no point in creating several small patches close together, or leaving some unsound plaster on the wall because the patch looks like getting too large. Generally, the larger and more complete the repair, the greater the chances of success.

Getting prepared

Even a small repair of this type is very messy, so prepare the room as if you were decorating and make sure everything is set up in advance. Bear in mind that the repair may take up to a weekend to complete.

When removing the old plaster, lay dust sheets to catch the debris and close all doors – there may be a lot of dust. Protect yourself, as always when using a brick chisel, with safety spectacles or goggles and a mask.

What to use

Having removed the old plaster, you patch the brickwork with repair mortar and apply a waterproof coating prior to making good. This can either be a thick, black brush-on liquid mastic (cheaper and easier to apply) or a clear moisture-curing resin (costly, but more effective if applied in sufficient coats).

When it comes to filling the hole, use a heavyweight bonding plaster – ordinary repair or ready mixed plasters will quickly absorb any dampness left in the surrounding wall. You can, however, use ready mixed skimming plaster to finish off the repair.

Materials: Dry mixed repair mortar, heavyweight bonding plaster liquid mastic or moisture-curing resin, ready mixed skimming plaster, sharp sand, solvent for waterproofer.

Tools checklist: Club hammer, brick chisel, steel float, bucket, mixing stick, old piece of board, old paintbrush, wire brush, safety spectacles, goggles, face mask.

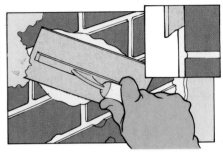

1 *Chop out the area of damaged plaster using a brick chisel and club hammer. Try to 'undercut' the edges of the patch so that the new plaster can get a grip.*

2 *Brush away dust from the brickwork, dampen down, then patch with repair mortar to fill any deep holes and leave a reasonably flat surface.*

3 *When the mortar has dried, apply the first coat of liquid mastic. Work it well in but take care not to splash the surrounding plaster.*

4 *Recoat as directed. As the final coat dries, sprinkle with clean, sharp sand so that the surface is 'keyed' for the bonding plaster.*

5 *Turn out the mixed bonding plaster on to an old board and apply with a steel float. Level off with the surrounding wall using a wooden straightedge.*

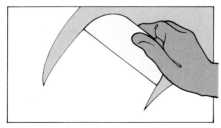

6 *The bonding plaster should be just below the surrounding surface. This allows you to finish with a skim of ready mixed plaster and sand smooth.*

MOISTURE-CURING RESINS

In serious cases, use a moisture-curing resin compound in preference to brush-on liquid mastic. This comes in one- or two-part form; mix in an old container following the manufacturer's instructions. Like interior waterproofer, the compound gives off strong fumes; make sure the area is well ventilated and avoid breathing the fumes in.

Three to four coats are normally required. Work the first well into the mortar-patched brickwork, then apply subsequent coats as the ones before become just touch-dry. Sprinkle the final coat with sharp sand while still tacky.

You can speed the drying process by warming the patch gently with a heater or hair dryer; **don't** use a naked flame.

Moisture-curing resin can be applied directly to the brickwork – as here – but where there are large holes, patch them with mortar first.

EXTERIOR DAMP-PROOFING

If you suspect that the dampness inside the house is caused by porous brickwork on the outside, it makes sense to coat the brickwork with clear silicone-based water repellent at the same time as carrying out any other repairs. On old walls, this is a wise precaution anyway, since even occasional rain splashing can 'reactivate' dampness left inside the masonry and cause efflorescence. Silicone water repellent also helps to prevent badly weathered bricks from deteriorating any further.

Before you start, check the condition of the mortar joints and brickwork following the diagram on the right. Any faults must be put right before the wall is treated.

Applying the repellent

Do this during a dry spell, and at least two days after any rain. To be effective you need to coat the entire wall – which may mean using access equipment. Coverage is around 3–4 sq m (4-5 sq yd) per quart per coat, and one coat is sufficient on all but the most absorbent surfaces.

Tools and materials: Silicone water repellent, soft brush, ladders (maybe). For repairs: dry mixed repair mortar, spare bricks (preferably to match wall), club hammer, brick chisel, pointing trowel.

Scratch the mortar joints with an old penknife. Areas which crumble must be raked out and repointed using 1:3 dry mixed repair mortar.

Wash off green algae using a fungicide for exterior masonry. Let the wall dry completely before treating.

Fill small holes with 1:3 dry mixed repair mortar.

Chop out damaged bricks with a brick chisel and replace.

Check the wall for faults before starting.
Apply the repellent using a wall brush or soft hand broom. Work it well into the brickwork and leave it to dry thoroughly.

▌PROBLEM SOLVER▐

Dampness around sockets

Chaneling electrical cables through walls can weaken the plasterwork's resistance to dampness, causing damp patches to appear on or around power sockets – a potentially very dangerous situation.

In this case, turn off the power at the mains before you do anything else.

Unscrew the socket faceplate and disconnect the circuit cables. Then unscrew and prize away the backing box from the wall, and check the cut-out for any tell-tale signs of moisture.

If the dampness follows the line of one of the cables, gently ease this away from the wall too, chipping off the plaster or filler covering it as you go.

Curing the problem If the plaster appears sound and the damage is limited, simply coat the socket cut-out and cable channel with waterproofer.

But if the damp extends into the surrounding plaster, repair the entire area as if it were a single patch. Afterwards, re-run the cable along the surface of the wall using plastic mini-trunking and convert the socket to a surface mounted type with plastic backing box.

Dampness from floors

Dampness caused by punctured or missing vapor barrier sheeting in a solid floor often continues up the wall. Parts of the floor which have been chaneled for pipes or cables are particularly suspect.

In this case, repair the wall and floor together. Hack away a margin of screed along the affected wall and continue your damp-proofing treatment down as far as the vapor barrier.

If there is no vapor barrier, apply a waterproofing treatment to the floor surface and carry the wall treatment on to this.

Dampness around sockets can often be cured simply by coating the cut-out and cable channel with waterproofer . . .

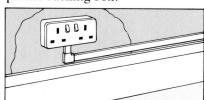

. . . but in severe cases, repair the entire area as if it were a large damp patch and refit the cable and socket on the surface.

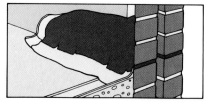

Where damp from a solid floor has passed into the walls, extend the damp-proofing treatment down below the level of the screed.

REPAIRING ROTTEN WOODWORK

Rot is the most common problem affecting woodwork in damp climates – and left to its own devices, the structural decay it causes can have expensive consequences. Softwood is more susceptible than hardwood, but either can be affected.

What is rot?
Wood rot is caused by fungal spores circulating in the air which settle on the wood and use any dampness present to germinate. The fungus then decomposes the wood fibers to obtain food, and eventually destroys the wood completely.

There are two main types of rot fungus – *wet rot* and *dry rot* – and it's vital to know the difference before carrying out any repairs.
Wet rot is the more common of the two, and only affects wood which is actually damp.

Once wet rot has taken hold, it can be repaired by patching in new wood or using a rot cure system. At the same time the surrounding area must be treated with preservative, and steps taken to make sure the timber doesn't become damp again.
Dry rot is far more serious: although the fungus requires damp,

warm conditions to germinate, once established it can spread like wildfire through dry, perfectly sound timber – and even through masonry. Also, unlike wet rot, it doesn't die when the affected wood is removed; the entire area must be treated.

If you have even the slightest suspicion of dry rot (see below), it's worth arranging a damp survey through a preservation specialist. Treating dry rot is nearly always a professional job, and it doesn't pay to take chances – especially where structural wood is at risk.

WET AND DRY ROT – THE TELL-TALE SIGNS
The symptoms of rot are easily spotted and you can test the extent of the damage by using a bradawl or the point of a knife. Sound wood will resist the point; on decayed wood it will go in easily.

Deciding whether the problem is caused by wet rot or dry rot may be more difficult: use the following checklist as a guide.

Wet *or* dry rot
■ Affected areas easily penetrated.
■ Affected areas produce a different sound when tapped.
■ Outward warping on paneling, baseboards etc (on its own, this also can be due to natural shrinkage).
■ Deep cracks across the grain (most common with dry rot but can appear with wet rot).

Wet rot only
■ Wood feels wet and spongy.
■ Paint is lifting from discolored patches of wood, possibly with white or gray fungal strands below.

Dry rot only
■ White, yellowish or rust red fungal growth evident on surface of wood and nearby masonry.
■ Wood dry and brittle, often discolored light brown.
■ Characteristic deep cracks, with the wood split into 'cubes'.

Other fungal problems
You may find black spots (due to damp mold) or blue-gray marks (due to a fungus called *sapstain*) on the surface of otherwise sound timber. Neither presents any

Wet rot (above) is more common but less serious than *dry rot* (right), which under the right conditions can spread rapidly through walls and sound wood.

danger to the wood, though mold could warn of impending dampness.

Where appearance is important, treat with a decorating fungicide (though this may not remove deep sapstain marks completely).

KEEPING ROT AT BAY

Prevention is always better than cure, so save yourself expensive and complicated repair work by doing an annual check on wood which is exposed to dampness. Late summer is a good time for this: dry weather often causes joints to shrink and paint to crack; and if there is a problem, the weather should be good enough to allow you to fix it before the rainy spell starts.

Windows and doors should be checked to see that the paint, putty and joints are in good condition. Make good any damage and refinish to stop water penetrating the wood.

Fascia boards and other exposed roof wood need regular repainting. Leaky gutters may cause local rot.

Fences, etc should be brushed down to remove mold, moss and lichen. Apply preservative every 2-5 years. If the wood has been creosoted, renew this every 2-5 years.

WINDOWS: THE TROUBLE SPOTS

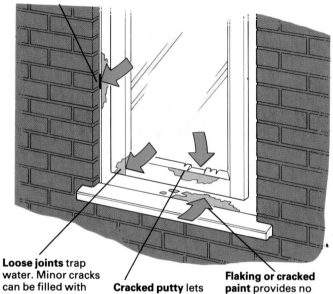

Gaps around frames allow moisture to reach unprotected wood. Seal with frame sealant.

Loose joints trap water. Minor cracks can be filled with flexible filler before repainting or varnishing.

Cracked putty lets water penetrate. Rake out and renew.

Flaking or cracked paint provides no defence against moisture. Rub down and repaint.

DOORS: THE TROUBLE SPOTS

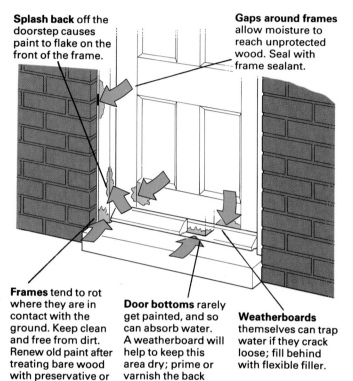

Splash back off the doorstep causes paint to flake on the front of the frame.

Gaps around frames allow moisture to reach unprotected wood. Seal with frame sealant.

Frames tend to rot where they are in contact with the ground. Keep clean and free from dirt. Renew old paint after treating bare wood with preservative or rot killer.

Door bottoms rarely get painted, and so can absorb water. A weatherboard will help to keep this area dry; prime or varnish the back before fitting.

Weatherboards themselves can trap water if they crack loose; fill behind with flexible filler.

PRESERVATIVE TREATMENTS

Preservative treatments are a sensible precaution for any wood which is particularly at risk from rot, whether on a repair or a new project.

Pre-treated wood

Treated wood is rather more expensive than ordinary wood (around 15-20%), but worth using for outdoor work and wherever wood is in contact with the ground. There are various processes for applying the preservative under pressure to ensure deep penetration and trade names vary. Your lumberyard will advise. Cut ends and holes must be given a further coat of preservative fluid.

Preservative fluid

To prevent rot from starting in new or existing sound wood, apply wood preservative. This is made in a range of colors, including clear for use under paintwork. Some makers provide different formulations for use on hardwood items like doors and window frames, and for sheds and garden furniture.

On existing wood, remove any dirt or mold and treat with fungicide or a solution of one part bleach to six of water. Allow to dry thoroughly.

Sand new surfaced wood with fine grade sandpaper to help the preservative soak in.

Either brush on liberally, applying two or three coats, or soak the wood for better penetration. Fence posts need soaking for at least an hour to the depth they will be sunk.

Rot killer fluid

Where wet rot has caused decay, an application of rot killer helps to ensure that it does not recur. After cutting away the damaged wood, brush or spray three coats of the rot killer fluid on to the surface of both the existing wood and any patches. If it is possible to dip the parts in the fluid for ten minutes, this provides even better protection.

The fluid can also be used on new wood as a preservative, in which case two coats are sufficient. If wood is in contact with the ground, it should be soaked in the fluid for between an hour and one day.

Treated wood can be given any type of surface finish once it has dried.

Preservative pellets

These are part of a rot cure system, but can also be used on sound wood to prevent rot. Insert them at 50mm (2″) intervals in high-risk areas, and cover with resin-based filler (see opposite).

USING A ROT CURE SYSTEM

Rot cure systems consist of chemicals designed to stop the rot and preserve the existing wood, plus resin-based filler to make good the damage. The result should be at least as strong as the existing wood.

A big advantage of rot cure systems is that they can cope with complicated frames where replacing the wood would be difficult, if not impossible. But while they are excellent for patching, you cannot expect them to replace structural wood – for example, if the whole corner of a window has rotted.

Making the repair
Start by removing all the decayed wood, although it is not necessary to go right back to sound wood.

1 *Pull or cut away decayed wood fibers (see left) to leave a reasonably firm surface. Strip back any paint or varnish and allow damp patches to dry out.*

Then brush on a wood hardening solution which binds the remaining loose fibers. One type incorporates a preservative treatment to prevent further decay; with other systems this is done separately (see below).

The damaged area is then built up with quick-setting filler. Once this is hardened, it can be shaped and painted just like wood.

Preserving the wood
Systems which don't include preservative treatment at an earlier stage then incorporate a further process, which consists of drilling small holes around the affected area and inserting pellets of solid preservative. Then cap with wood filler and finish off.

2 *Brush on the clear hardening fluid, applying several coats to make sure it penetrates the area fully. Cover to protect from the rain and leave to dry.*

3 *Mix the resin filler and apply with a filling knife. To reinforce deep holes, drive screws into the wood below leaving the heads projecting.*

4 *When set, use a shaper plane or file to carve the filler to shape. Sand smooth, then prime and repaint to match the surrounding wood.*

With another system, *you finish off the treatment by drilling holes for preservative pellets at 50mm (2") intervals into the sound wood around the repair.*

Insert the pellets *and push them well below the surface. (Be sure to wear rubber gloves when handling them as they contain strong fungicide.)*

Cap the holes *with small amounts of the resin filler and sand smooth when dry. The pellets are only activated if the wood becomes moist again.*

PATCHING WOODWORK

Patching the damaged area with new wood is rather harder than using a rot cure system, but it is the only solution where:

■ The wood is varnished or stained.
■ You are repairing a frame which has been weakened by decay.

The repairs shown below are typical. In all cases, use wood which matches the original in both its appearance and dimensions. If you are dealing with a shaped part of a window or door frame, see if you can buy a matching molded section to cut down the amount of reshaping required.

Treat the existing wood and any new patches with preservative to prevent further decay. Refinish the area as soon as possible.

1 **To repair the foot of a door frame,** saw through it about 75mm (3") above the decayed area. Make the cut square across the wood and sloped downwards at 45°.

2 Prize the cut section away from the wall – it may be held by nails or screws. If you find it is set into the sill, saw off square across the bottom.

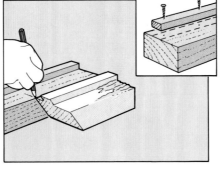

3 Cut a patch from matching wood using the old piece as a pattern. If you can't match the section exactly, join two pieces to make up the right shape.

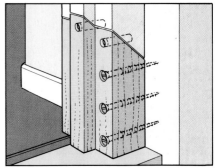

4 Treat with preservative and screw to drilled and anchored holes. Reinforce the sloping joint with screws or dowels, then fill any gaps.

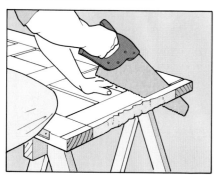

1 **To repair the base** of a door or opening window frame, remove it from its hinges. Saw along a line parallel to the bottom and above the rotted area.

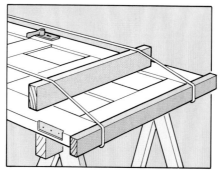

2 Cut the new section slightly oversize and treat both parts with preservative. When dry, apply waterproof woodworking adhesive and clamp together.

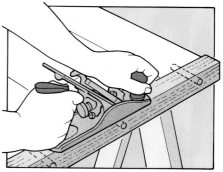

3 Reinforce by inserting glued dowels through both parts (or screws, providing they are well recessed into the wood). Plane to the exact size and rehang.

BUILDING A STUD PARTITION WALL

Constructing a wood-framed *stud partition* wall is generally the easiest way to divide one room into two semi-permanently. Unlike a solid block wall, it is light enough not to need extensive loadbearing support; it is also fairly easy to remove should your space requirements change again at a later date.

From a DIY point of view, the great advantages of stud partitions are that they require no great skill to build, and use cheap, readily available materials. The simplest method (shown here) is to use taper-edge plasterboard and simply fill the joints before decoration; an alternative is to use square-edged sheets and give the whole wall a thin surface skim of plaster.

ANATOMY OF A STUD PARTITION

Top plate – a single length of wood screwed to ceiling joists and used to locate tops of studs.

Studs – vertical lengths of wood nailed between the top and sole plates at both ends and at 400mm (16") intervals.

Cladding – plasterboard or similar sheet material nailed to each side of the framework. Using standard sheet sizes, the edges of panels should fall neatly over the centers of studs spaced at 400mm (16").

400mm (16")

Joints. The V-shaped notches formed by taper-edged plasterboard can be covered with paper tape and special joint filler.

Firestops – horizontal lengths of wood nailed between the studs to brace the frame and provide support for the edges of the cladding panels.

Sole plate – a single length of wood nailed or screwed to floor to locate bottoms of studs.

1220mm (4')

....Shopping List....

Plan the layout and constructional details of the partition (see overleaf), then measure and draw a sketch of the wall showing all the frame members and their relevant dimensions. List the materials on the drawing, then work out the quantities.

Wood for the framework is cheap *rough softwood* rather than surfaced. Minimum size is 75×50mm (3×2"), but for a substantial partition that may have to take wall-hung shelves, cupboards or a washbasin, increase this to 100×50mm (4×2").

Cladding You can clad the frame with virtually any sheet material, but *plasterboard* is generally the easiest to fix and finish. It is also one of the cheapest.

For simple filled joints, use 12.5mm thick *taper-edged* board. This is commonly available in ceiling-height 2440×1220mm (8×4') sheets, though half sheets and smaller sizes may be available for dealing with small gaps.

Moldings You'll need softwood baseboard molding to finish the bottom of the wall on both sides,

plus lining boards and architrave moldings to finish any openings you have to make (see overleaf). Try to match existing moldings where possible.

Finish the joints at the ceiling with stick-on plastic or plaster *coving*, which will be sold with the appropriate adhesive.

Other materials
■ Galvanized dry wall nails for fixing the cladding, and 100mm (4") round wire nails for the frame.
■ 100mm (4") frame fixings or 100mm (4") No.10 countersunk woodscrews (plus suitable anchors) for securing the top and sole plates and the end studs.
■ Plasterboard *paper tape* and *joint filler* for covering the joints between boards. (At the same time it's worth buying the special *applicator* and *jointing sponge* sold with them.)

Tools checklist: hammer, drill and bits, screwdrivers, bradawl, level, plumbline, filling knife, trimming knife, tape measure, crosscut saw, chisel and tenon saw (possibly).

taper-edged plasterboard

joint filler

rough softwood

paper tape

dry wall nails

jointing sponge

PLANNING THE PARTITION

You don't normally need local permission to build a stud partition wall, but there are certain restrictions on how the job is done. For this reason, make sure you consider all of the following points before starting.

■ Will the new rooms formed by the partition both be big enough? Don't forget to allow for the thickness of the wall itself when working out their areas, and make sure the partitioned space is usable. You may have to include a right angle turn in the new wall to be sure.

■ Both new rooms must have some natural light, unless one or the other is a bathroom or toilet. If possible, position the wall to allow for this. Otherwise, you'll have to provide a glazed door or window (see below) so that light can pass from one room to another.

■ Proper ventilation is essential. In a bathroom or toilet without windows, you can satisfy the statutory regulations by fitting an automatic extractor fan. In any other 'habitable' room some regulations require that the area of openable window in each room must be equal to at least 5% of the room's total floor area. Also, at least part of the opening section must be more than 1.75m (5'8") from the floor. This could mean changing an existing fixed window to one that can be opened or has a vent.

■ How will you get into the new rooms? Whatever the walls are made of, it's much easier to build a doorway into the new partition (see below) than to cut an opening in an existing wall.

■ Where the floor is wooden, can you gain access to the joists? And are the upstairs ceiling joists accessible too? If the answer is no in either case, you may be restricted on where you can position the new wall (see below).

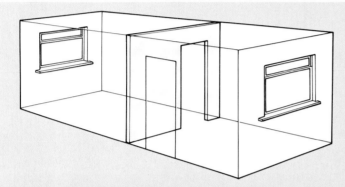

Ideally, the partition should leave more or less equal amounts of natural light and openable window in both the new rooms.

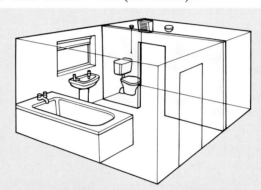

The rules are relaxed, however, in a bathroom: if there is no natural light or ventilation in the new room, fit an automatic extractor fan.

Adding a room 1: a semi-partition with open arch (left) makes it possible to create a self-contained washing/dressing room within a fairly small bedroom without either appearing cramped.

Adding a room 2: partitioning a double windowed room (above) solves the problem of where to put a new arrival in the family. The old room is easily restored if needs change at a later date.

CONSTRUCTIONAL DETAILS

Ideally, a stud partition wall built over a suspended wooden floor should run at right angles to the joists to spread the load.

If it must run parallel to the joists, you have a choice: either sit it directly over a joist (which may be easier – see Tip), or lift the surrounding floorboards and fix nailing blocks across the existing joists as shown right. The nailing blocks should be the same size – and spaced at the same intervals – as the joists themselves. Fix them using metal *joist-to-joist hangers*.

Use the same method where the top plate of the new wall falls between two joists, but space the trimmers at 600mm (2') centers.

Making openings

Door and window openings should be made to suit standard 'off the shelf materials, so choose your door or window first.

There are two methods for framing the opening. One is to fit studs on each side and nail the lintel (header) or window sill between them after cutting housings with a saw and chisel. The other method – costlier but easier – is to support the cross-pieces on shorter *Jack studs* nailed to the full-height studs. In both cases, wide windows need short *cripple studs* above the lintel and below the sill.

Line the openings with 25mm (1") thick softwood, wide enough to conceal the edges of the cladding.

When measuring for a door, space the studs at the door width plus an allowance for the thickness of the lining and an extra clearance of 6mm (¼") to allow for hinging.

When measuring for a window, space the studs to fit the frame plus an allowance for the thickness of the lining. The window is nailed directly to the lined opening.

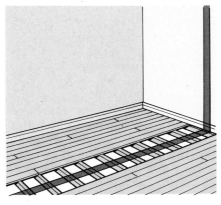

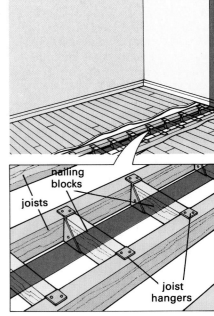

No reinforcement is normally needed if the wall runs at right angles to the floor joists. Where the wall runs parallel, fit nailing blocks between the joists using metal hangers (inset). Use a similar arrangement where the line of the wall falls between two ceiling joists.

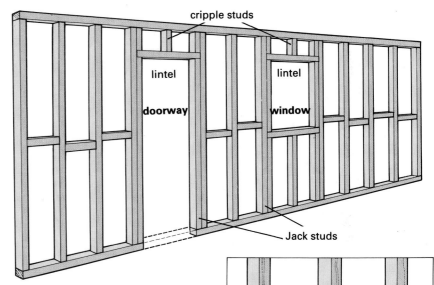

Openings for doors and windows can either be created using Jack studs (above) or by cutting housings for the lintels in the existing studs (inset). With a doorway, the sole plate is cut away after the framework has been nailed together.

Trade tip

Reinforce or not?

6 *One of the trickiest questions facing a builder is whether or not to reinforce a floor joist if a stud wall has to go directly on top of it.*

*By and large, if the wall is normal height, uses a light frame, and won't have anything heavy fixed to it **and** the joist itself measures at least 100×50mm (4×2"), there should be no need to reinforce. But if the wall is likely to be heavier, or the joist is lighter, you'd be advised to err on the safe side.*

Providing reinforcement means coach-bolting a new joist of the same size to the existing one. It should be supported at each end in the same way. 9

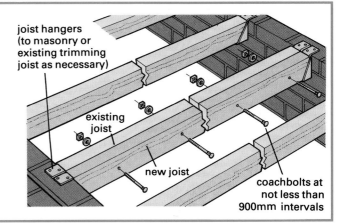

BUILDING THE FRAMEWORK

Start by doing any strengthening work necessary on the floor and ceiling joists. You shouldn't have to lift every floorboard to fit nailing blocks, but there is bound to be some disruption and you should clear the room as far as possible.

Afterwards, mark the nailing block positions on the floor and ceiling, and replace the boards. Make sure the floorboards are firmly fixed and reasonably level along the full length of the new wall.

If you don't need to fit nailing blocks to a wooden floor, just lift a few boards to find the joist positions, then establish where the ceiling joists are by knocking with your fist until you hear a dull sound, then poking with a bradawl.

Setting out
Measure and mark the positions of the top and sole plates and end studs on the floor, wall and ceiling. Use a level or plumbline to mark the verticals, so you can be sure the top plate will sit directly above the sole plate.

This is also the time to decide what to do about any baseboards or other moldings fixed to the adjoining walls (see Problem Solver).

Frame assembly
Assembly of the frame starts with the sole plate, which can be nailed to a wooden floor or screwed to a concrete one. Follow by screwing on the top plate and end studs, then nail on the studs and firestops.

In general, studs should be spaced equally at 400–450mm (16–18″) intervals (and to suit the positions of any openings) with firestops fixed in a line 1200mm (4′) from the floor. However you should work out the actual positions so that the edges of each plasterboard sheet fall over the center of a frame member. Most likely, this will mean fixing an extra stud or two to support part of a sheet. In a high ceilinged room, you may also have fit an extra row of firestops.

Mark the stud positions on the sole plate. Then measure each stud individually and cut them slightly oversize, so they can be wedged in place while you nail them.

Trade tip

Make a gauge
❝ Cut a piece of frame lumber to use as a gauge for spacing the studs and for bracing the top and bottom of each stud when end nailing. ❞

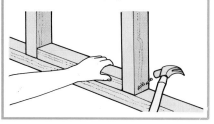

1 Having cleared the room and removed any floorcoverings, inspect the floor. If it is wood, lift a few boards to check the joist positions and spacing.

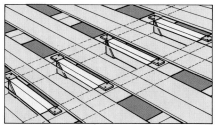

2 If the wall has to run between joists, lift boards at intervals across the room so that you can fix nailing blocks across the joists using metal hangers.

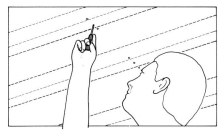

3 Probe the ceiling with a bradawl to locate the joists above and mark their positions. If necessary, fit nailing blocks as for the floor joists.

4 Taking into account the positions of the floor and ceiling joists, mark out the position of the partition on the floor, walls and ceiling.

5 Having removed any moldings, cut the sole plate to size and nail or screw it to the floor, except in doorways. (Over a joist fix at 400mm (16′) centers.

6 Cut the top plate to size and prop in place as shown. Check it is aligned with the marks on the wall and ceiling, then drill and screw to the ceiling joists.

7 Cut the end studs to fit exactly between the two plates, drill clearance holes, then drill and plug the wall. Screw the end studs in position.

8 Cut intermediate studs about 3mm (⅛″) oversize so they're a tight fit between the plates. Wedge in place, check they sit plumb, then end-nail both ends.

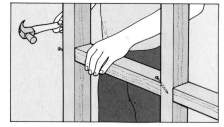

9 Cut and fit the firestops. Nail through the next stud into one end, then end-nail the other end to the previous stud to fix the firestops in line.

OPENINGS AND CORNERS

Assemble the frames for openings as you build the wall, either by housing the lintels in the studs or by fitting Jack studs.

If you have to turn a corner, simply butt the separate sole and top plates against each other, then fit three studs at each turn.

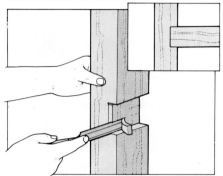

Cut housings for a lintel, then pare out the waste with a broad woodworking chisel. Don't notch the studs by more than half their thickness.

At a doorway, check that the opening framework is secure and make additional fixings where necessary. Then carefully saw off the unwanted section of sole plate.

At a corner, use three studs as shown to provide adequate support for the cladding panels on each side of the angles and to strengthen the structure.

■ PROBLEM SOLVER ■

Dealing with moldings

There are three ways to deal with baseboards and other such obstructions on adjoining walls.

The simplest method is to cut the stud into sections to fit above (and below) the molding and to fit a short section of stud over the molding itself where this is possible. The disadvantage is that you may find it difficult to achieve a neat joint between the existing and new sections of molding.

Another method is to notch the studs around the moldings, if they have a reasonably simple profile and don't protrude far. The same disadvantage applies.

The third method is to remove sections of molding so that the studs, and ideally the cladding, fit against the wall. You may be able to do this in situ, as shown, or you may have to prize off the whole length, then refit it after you have constructed the wall. This way you can miter the cut ends for a neat finish.

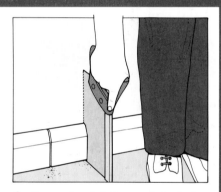

Scribe and notch the end studs to fit around a narrow baseboard. On a heavier baseboard, cut out a section using a tenon saw.

Running services

If you need to fit sockets or plumbing fittings on the new wall, run the pipes and cables while you're building the frame so that they can be hidden in the cavity.

Cables and supply pipes can simply be fed through suitably sized holes bored in the centers of the studs. For a basin waste pipe, cut 60mm (2¼") deep notches in the studs, and cut housings for lengths of 50×25mm (2×1") wood to cover the notches once the pipe is in place. (Don't do this unless you are using 100×50mm – 4×2" – studs).

Make up mountings for socket backing boxes, basin brackets and so on from offcuts of frame wood and plywood. There's no hard and fast rule on how to fix them, though if the mountings are to take any weight they should be screwed to the studs.

Run any pipes and cables within the framework, and fit backing panels for socket outlets (below). Do not run a basin waste through the studs unless they are the 100×50mm (4×2") size.

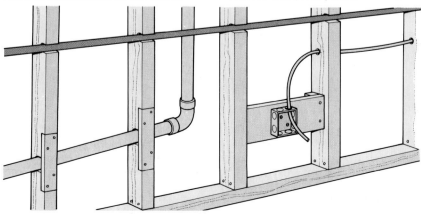

CLADDING THE FRAME

In most houses, full-size sheets of plasterboard nailed on end using a footlifter (see right, and Tip) can go straight on the frame without cutting. There will be a small gap at the bottom, to be concealed with baseboard later.

If the ceiling is lower than the height of a full sheet, simply cut the sheets to size leaving a 25mm (1″) gap for lifting. Where the ceiling is high, however, you may find it easier to nail the sheets lengthways. In this case, nail the upper row first, ensuring the edges are supported on a row of firestops.

In all cases, it's also worth checking that you won't be left with awkward gaps to fill around openings and at the end of the wall. Sheets are easily cut down, but they must be supported by frame members on all sides: you may have to nail on extra firestops to ensure this.

Cutting and fixing

The easiest way to make straight cuts in plasterboard is to score a line with a trimming knife, snap the board over a wooden straightedge, then cut through the paper on the other side. If you need to make shaped cuts, mark out both sides and score with a trimming knife, then cut the board using an old crosscut saw.

Nail the sheets using dry wall nails – spaced at 100mm (4″) around the edges, 150mm (6″) elsewhere. The heads must go below the surface.

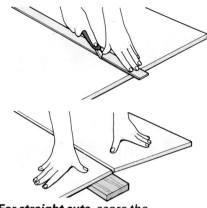

For straight cuts, score the plasterboard with a trimming knife and snap over a wooden straightedge. Then turn over and cut through the other side.

Trade tip

Easy fixing

❛ When fixing plasterboard sheets vertically to the frame, the sheets need to be lifted so that they butt tightly against the ceiling before driving in the nails. The easiest way to do this is with a home-made footlifter, cut from a block of stud wood as shown right.

Where you're fixing sheets horizontally, nail the upper row first and nail a strip of wood temporarily to the frame to use as a supporting ledge. When you nail the second row, stagger the sheets so that the vertical joints aren't continuous. ❜

FINISHING THE WALL

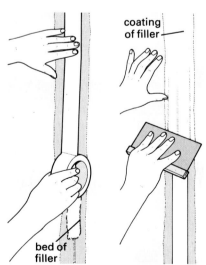

Cover taper joints with strips of paper tape bedded in filler. Press well down and spread more filler over the top. Then feather the edges with a plastic applicator and buff with a jointing sponge.

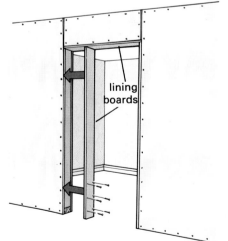

Line openings with boards cut to finish flush with the edges of the plasterboard. Nail them to the lintel and the studs. If you are not fitting architraves to conceal the joint, fill gaps flush with the boards.

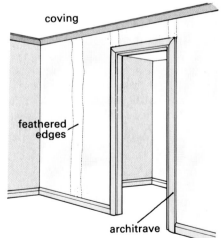

Finish the top of the wall with stick-on plastic or plaster coving, mitered at the corners.
Cover the gap at the bottom – and finish any openings – with softwood baseboard and architrave moldings, nailed to the frame.

4

CARPENTRY

THE RIGHT WOOD FOR THE JOB

Whatever sort of carpentry work you're doing – whether it's putting up shelves, enclosing pipework, or repairing a window – the job starts with choosing suitable lengths of wood, which in one form or another, is among the most basic of all DIY materials.

This section is about softwood, the least expensive, most common and easily worked form of solid wood. Hardwood is much costlier and has far more specialist uses. Man-made boards such as plywood, particleboard and hardboard, are covered on pages 197-200.

What is softwood?

The term softwood does not refer to the wood's hardness but to the way it grows – softwood covers any lumber from trees with needles and cones. These are generally quick-growing, with pronounced rings at seasonal intervals – they grow much faster in summer.

When the tree has been felled and stripped of its bark it is converted into usable lumber. The usual method is *plain sawing*, where slices are cut right across the trunk. This exposes the growth rings to produce a sharply angled grain (which increases the chance of warping), while the ends of any branches appear as knots. A costlier method called *quarter sawing* results in a more even grain.

Before use, the wood is dried in the open air or in a kiln. This removes much of the moisture, although a fair amount (around 20%) is left, and in fact the moisture content varies according to the humidity of the surrounding air.

Below Plain sawing (left) is more economical, but quarter sawing (right) produces better lumber.

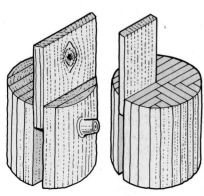

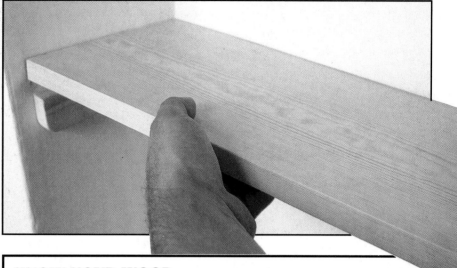

KNOW YOUR WOOD

Pine A common name for several types of lumber. May be Ponderosa red, Eastern or Western white, Jack or Lodgepole. You may also find spruce (also called deal). Grain is coarse and the wood is often knotty. Spruce is lighter than redwood, but both darken with age.

Fir May be called Douglas fir, Balsam, Subalpine fir, or Pacific Silver. Stronger than pine (but prone to split) and, as the trees are larger, is straight grained and knot-free. Useful for structural work, window frames and interior carpentry.

Parana pine Used for interior work, such as stairs. Parana pine is available in large boards with an even texture and is often free of blemishes such as knots – but can be prone to warping or splitting as it dries out. Pale color with darker spots along grain.

Cedar (Western red, Northern white, or Alaska). Contains natural preservative oils so is widely used for exterior work. The oils attack steel fixtures so use brass or plated instead. Knot-free with a close, straight grain, it resists warping well and withstands heat (allowing it to be used near radiators). Has a warm, reddish brown color, but does not take varnish well – use a cedar preservative.

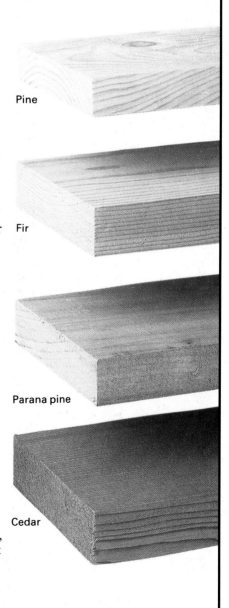

Pine

Fir

Parana pine

Cedar

LUMBER SIZES

Softwood logs are cut into a range of standard dimensions from strips and boards to timbers. Most lumberyards stock a wide range of sizes.

Lumber is supplied in two forms. *Rough lumber* is cheaper, and is used for rough or concealed work

Rough lumber *is closer to its quoted (nominal) size than surfaced, because some wood is lost during machining.*

rough

surfaced

where appearance isn't important. *Surfaced or dressed lumber* is for finished work that is to be painted, stained or varnished. Most surfaced lumber is smoothed on all four sides (called PAR, for 'Planed All Round') although you may occasionally find only two or three finished surfaces.

Lumber sizes can be confusing. They are always referred to as standard measurements but, in fact, the actual dimensions are somewhat smaller. This is because some wood is lost during sawing and even more during the planing process when the lumber is surfaced (dressed). In other words, what you know as 2 by 4s, 2 x 6s, or 4 x 4s can be anywhere between 1/16" and 1/2" smaller on all sides.

Note For ease of reference, wood sizes in this chapter will normally be referred to in feet and inches.

BUYING LUMBER

The best buys depend on what you are after and how much you want. Large lumberyards stock, or can obtain, a wide selection if you need unusual sizes or a specific type of wood. A large lumberyard is also your best bet if you need lumber machined to size, though most small yards do offer a cutting service. For small pieces, a small yard may be a better choice since most carry a stock of short offcuts.

On the other hand, if all you want is a few lengths of wood then the nearest lumberyard or perhaps hardware store will probably both have what you need at more or less the same price. Also, superstores often sell bundles of common sizes (for example, twenty 6 ft lengths of 1"×1") which may work out cheaper if you want a large quantity. There are no rules as to how many there may be in a bundle – it varies from supplier to supplier.

Prices are generally calculated on the *total volume* of lumber, so a given length of 2×4 costs roughly twice as much as the same length of 2×2 and four times as much as 2×1. Small sections can cost proportionately more in view of the wastage and extra work involved, and non-standard sizes carry a price premium.

Value for money is harder to assess. If the appearance or strength of the wood is important, it may be worth paying extra to be able to pick sound lengths.

Trade tip

Bargain buys

❝ Where appearance isn't important I often use secondhand softwood – old floorboards, joists, rafters and so on – which is readily obtainable from demolition sites or salvage merchants. Not only is it cheaper than new – it's also thoroughly seasoned, and may even be better quality.

However, almost all secondhand wood has holes in it, and many pieces contain old screws and nails (or even just dirt) which will damage cutting tools. Also, make absolutely sure that there is no evidence of termites or rot attack. ❞

Natural lumber logs are converted into usable lumber at the sawmill. After sawing into planks which are left to season, the rough-sawn lumber may be planed smooth.

STANDARD SOFTWOOD SIZES

BOARDS

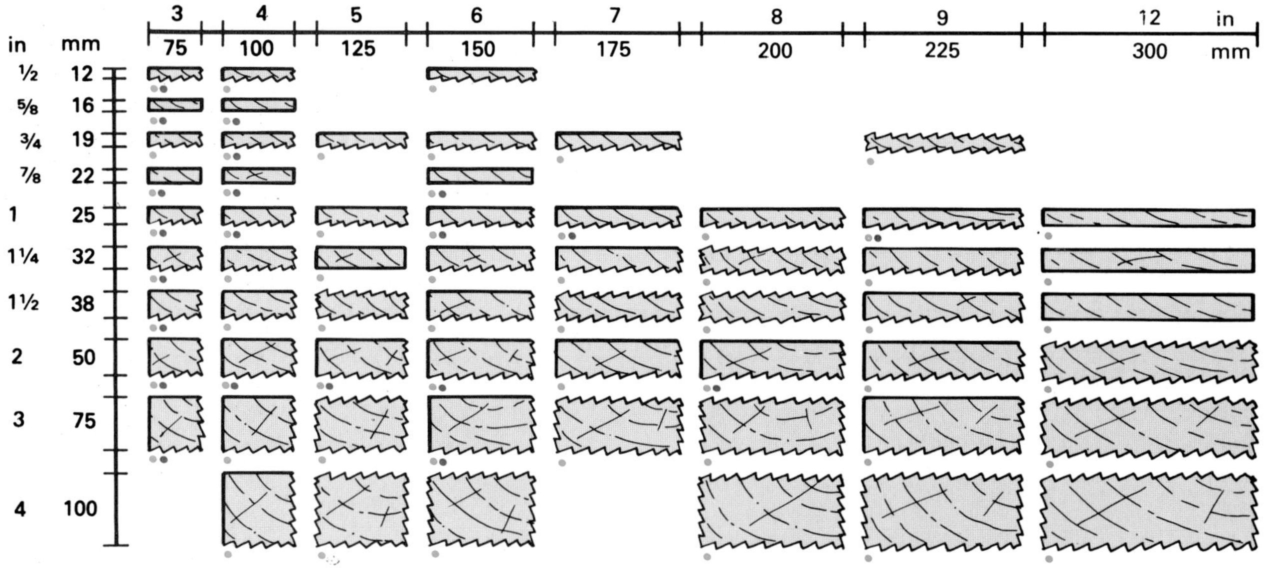

in	mm
3	75
4	100
5	125
6	150
7	175
8	200
9	225
12	300

in	mm
½	12
⅝	16
¾	19
⅞	22
1	25
1¼	32
1½	38
2	50
3	75
4	100

STUDS AND FRAMING

in	mm
½	12
⅝	16
¾	19
1	25
1¼	32
1½	38
2	50

in	mm
½	12
⅝	16
¾	19
⅞	22
1	25
1¼	32
1½	38
2	50

These tables give you a fairly good idea of the ranges of softwood sizes available. Almost all lumberyards either carry these as stock sizes, or can cut them to suit your requirements.

All sizes are *nominal* (see *Lumber sizes*, page 194). Smaller sizes are sometimes sold, and these are covered separately under *Wooden moldings*, page 201. Wide softwood boards made of strips bonded together are covered under *Choosing manmade boards*, page 197.

Common uses

2 × 1″ Shelf cleat, wardrobe frame, slatted shelf
1 × 1″ Lightweight shelf cleat, for enclosing pipework etc.
2 × 4″ Stud partition wall,
2 × 2″ – 4 × 4″ Table legs
¾ × 3″ – 1½ × 4″ Table frame
¾ × ¾″ – 1½ × 1½″ Coffee table legs
¾ × 1¼″ – ¾ × 3″ Coffee table frame
¾ × 3″ – ¾ × 6″ Plinth
¾ × 4″ – 1 × 12″ Shelf

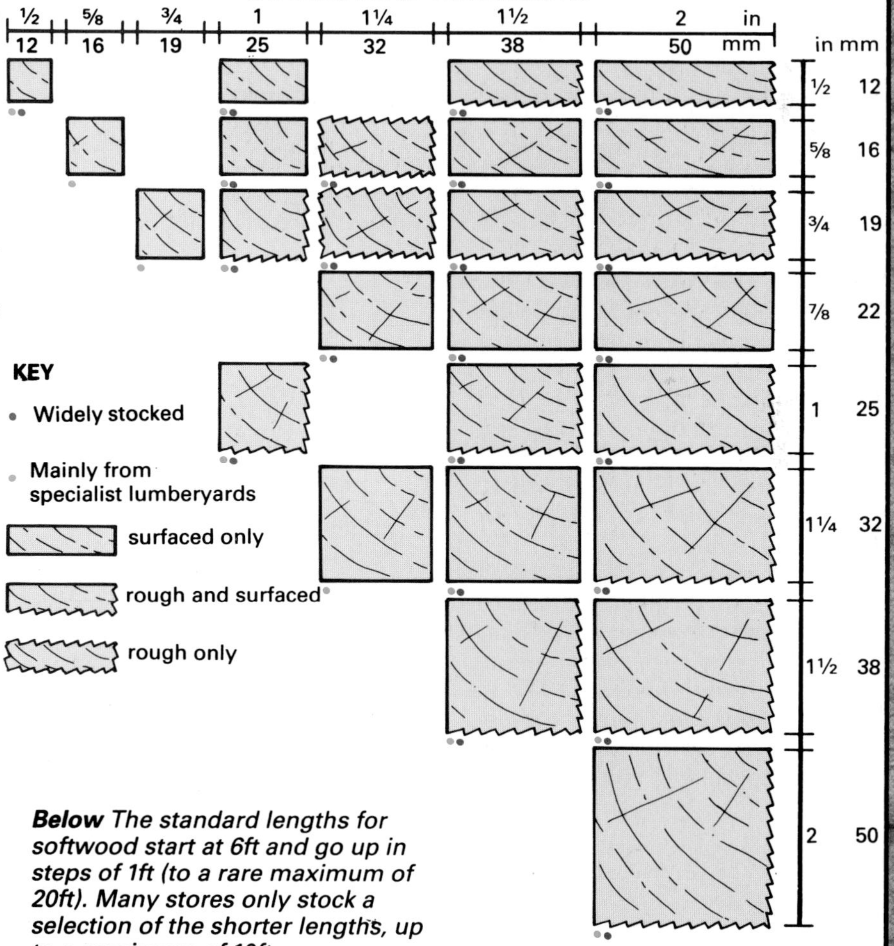

KEY

- Widely stocked
- Mainly from specialist lumberyards

☐ surfaced only

☐ rough and surfaced

☐ rough only

Below The standard lengths for softwood start at 6ft and go up in steps of 1ft (to a rare maximum of 20ft). Many stores only stock a selection of the shorter lengths, up to a maximum of 10ft.

ft	6	7	8	9	10	11	12	13	14
m	1.8	2.1	2.4	2.7	3.0	3.3	3.6	3.9	4.1

Lumber faults

Lumber is a natural material, and varies in quality, but its condition also depends on how well it is stored. As wastage can be costly, it is worth finding a supplier who will let you check for any of the faults described below.

Knots There are two types of knots, both harder than the wood around them.

Tight knots are the result of cutting through the ends of growing branches. They can be a decorative feature and shouldn't affect the strength of the wood too much. However, they need to be sealed with *knotting* before painting because they can ooze sap which stains the paint.

Loose knots are old branches which have a dark ring of bark around them. They are weak points, prone to fall out.

Splitting Also called *checks*, splits can occur in the drying process. Normally you have to saw the wood short of the split before it can be used.

Compression splits are cracks across the grain caused by damage when the tree is felled. Affected lumber is weakened.

Fungal staining Pine is sometimes stained blue-gray by fungus. This does not affect its strength but is unsightly when varnished and resists paint.

Wane The remains of the bark are sometimes left on the edge of the board. This may be intentional, as for rustic fencing, but where it is accidental it has to be planed off before the wood is used, adding to the wastage.

Warping This depends how the lumber was cut, dried and stored and may not be apparent when you buy. See below for details on how to avoid later problems.

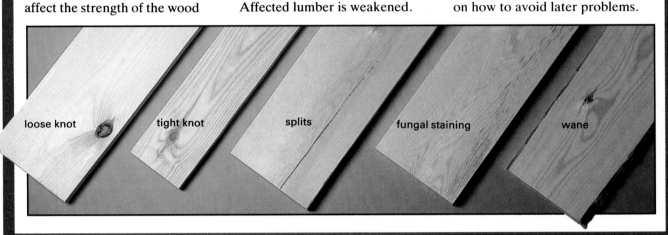

loose knot   tight knot   splits   fungal staining   wane

CARE AND PREPARATION

Lumber which has been stored in the open or an unheated shed contains 15-20% moisture. If the wood is then brought into a normally heated home it loses around half of this, and as a result shrinks slightly. Such shrinkage is most noticeable through the thickness of the growth rings.

Lumber which has the growth rings at a pronounced angle tends to bow more severely as it dries. Lumber which has growth rings running squarely throughout its thickness shrinks the same amount, but is less likely to warp, so it's worth looking out for – especially if you are buying wide planks.

Below Look for lumber with straight growth rings (bottom) – it's much less likely to warp.

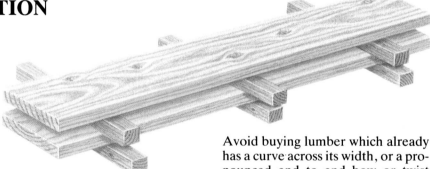

Store wide boards as shown to help air circulate and avoid warping.

Avoid lumber which bows sideways (above), from end to end (below) . . .

. . . or has a pronounced twist (below); these cannot be cured.

Avoid buying lumber which already has a curve across its width, or a pronounced end to end bow or twist (sight along it to check). Such defects are almost impossible to cure, and they are unlikely to improve as the wood dries out.

Storing lumber

Wood that is too damp for the room in which it is going to be used will always tend to shrink or warp, no matter how securely it is fixed or how accurately it is cut.

Ideally, keep it in the house for two or three weeks before use to allow it to acclimatize. Stack the lumber flat with scrap pieces between to allow air to circulate.

Don't on any account store lumber in damp conditions, even for a short time, as this encourages it to absorb moisture and accentuates shrinkage problems when the wood starts to dry out again.

CHOOSING MANMADE BOARDS

Solid wood, versatile as it is, has several disadvantages:
- It's expensive.
- It contains faults such as knots.
- Its width is limited by the thickness of the tree.
- It's prone to warping and splits.
- Softwood rots when it is exposed to damp – unless specially treated.

These are some of the reasons why man-made boards were developed. They are all made from wood, so they have many of its properties. But the disadvantages can be controlled by the manufacturing process.
- They can be made in large sheets with an even thickness and no flaws.
- They can be made damp resistant.
- They can be cheaper than the equivalent-sized lumber.
- They can have a variety of surfaces, some needing no finishing.

The chart below summarizes the main characteristics and uses of different boards. Overleaf are more detailed descriptions of each type.

Modern manmade boards come in all shapes and sizes. This tongued and grooved particleboard flooring is specially designed for attics.

WHICH BOARD TO USE AT A GLANCE

BOARD	USES	STRENGTH	DURABILITY	CUTTING/JOINING	FINISHING
PLYWOOD **Price range** Medium price to expensive depending on grade.	Most constructional jobs from furniture to building material depending on size and type of board.	Good both along and across board, but can warp. Strength depends on number of veneers or plies.	Excellent moisture resistance if the right grade (ie Marine).	Cuts cleanly. Holds screws and nails well, even close to the edge. Easy to glue.	Varnish or prime and paint. May have decorative surface or special veneer.
LUMBER-CORE COMPOSITION BOARD (hardboard) **Price range** Varies	Cabinets, doors, worktops, table tops, wide shelves, general furniture.	Good along board, fair across it. Resists warping but may split in dry, heated rooms.	Unsuitable for exterior applications or in very damp conditions.	Ensure core runs *along* the piece. Takes screws, nails and glue well except in end grain.	May have decorative surface. Varnish or prime and paint. Exposed core needs veneer tape.
PARTICLEBOARD (chipboard) **Price range** mostly cheap, but special types more costly.	Cheap material for flooring, cladding, rough framework, furniture making.	Stiffness poor, but good resistance to warping. Strength depends on density of core material.	Fair moisture resistance if exterior grade, otherwise poor.	Hard on tools; tends to crumble. Glues well; edge joints weak.	Fill and prime before painting. Edges may need veneer tape to conceal core.
FACED & COATED PARTICLEBOARDS **Price range** Medium, but range of sizes means little waste.	Shelving, built-in furniture, cabinet doors, general DIY constructions.	Not quite so strong as plain particleboard – and not available in stronger grades.	Unsuitable for damp conditions. Core will disintegrate if it gets damp.	Surface may split when cut. Use special hardware or dowels and glue to conceal joints.	Finish cut edges with matching veneer/plastic edging. Varnish veneered boards.
HARDBOARD **Price range** Cheap unless special purpose type.	Lightweight cladding and paneling, including curves. Leveling wooden floors.	Poor stiffness and can warp. Standard hardboard may expand and buckle when exposed to damp.	Poor resistance to moisture – use oil tempered board in damp conditions.	Support while cutting. Holds fixings poorly – glue, nail or screw to frame.	May be white painted or have decorative coating. Prime and paint unless prefinished.
FIBERBOARD **Price range** Medium, but ease of working keeps costs down.	Furniture making, built in cabinets, most things that can be made in wood.	Uniform strength – fair in both directions. Resists warping well.	Unsuitable for exterior use. Absorbs moisture fairly readily.	Use any woodworking technique. Holds screws and nails well; easy to glue.	Varnish or prime and paint. Very little preparation needed – no sanding or surface filling.
BONDED SOFTWOOD **Price range** Varies from inexpensive to very expensive.	Wide shelving, cabinets, tabletops where natural wood look is required.	Good in both directions, but can warp. Slightly more stable than solid wood.	As solid wood. Unsuitable for exterior use.	As solid wood. Holds screws and nails well; easy to glue.	Varnish or stain (primer and paint hide decorative grain of the material).

PLYWOOD

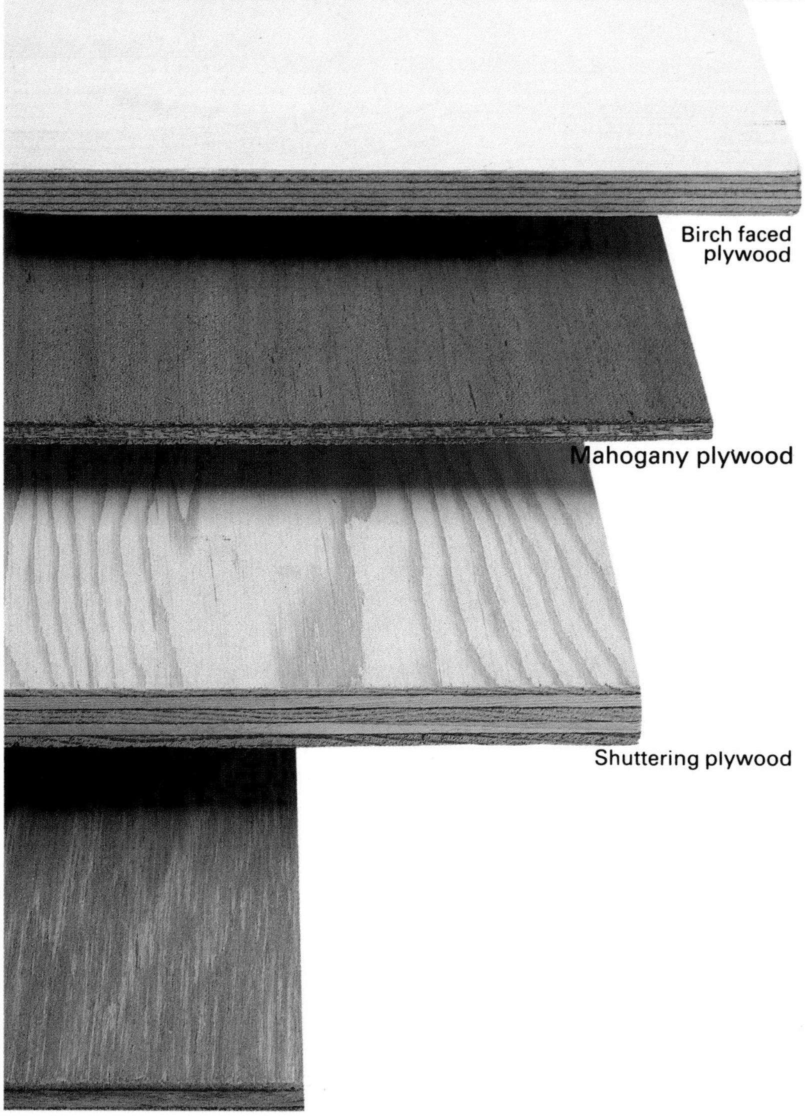

Plywood is made from several layers *(plies)* of thin sheets of wood. Each ply is laid with its grain in the opposite direction to the ones on either side. This reinforces the board.

The number of plies vary for a given thickness – in general the more plies there are, the stronger and better quality the plywood. The type of wood used also varies, and more expensive plywoods have decorative facings such as birch or oak.

Plywood resists splitting and can be nailed or glued close to the edges. It is much stronger than solid wood.

The durability of the plywood depends partly on the wood used and partly on the glue used in its manufacture. If ordinary plywood comes into contact with water for any length of time, the individual plies separate and the wood starts to rot.

'Exterior' denotes that plywood panels have been manufactured with a special waterproof glue. They will withstand long exposure to the elements and the bonding will not split. The top ply itself, if constantly exposed to normal amounts of water, pollution and sunlight, will break down. Coating it in some way – by staining or painting it – will inhibit this. If it will be subjected to constant exposure, you should use pressure-treated plywood.

Laminated plywood is faced with patterned plastic and is used as a decorative paneling. Some versions are also suitable for worktops – they are stronger than particleboard, and need not be so thick and heavy.

Birch faced plywood

Mahogany plywood

Shuttering plywood

Redwood plywood

LUMBER-CORE COMPOSITION BOARD (BLOCKBOARD)

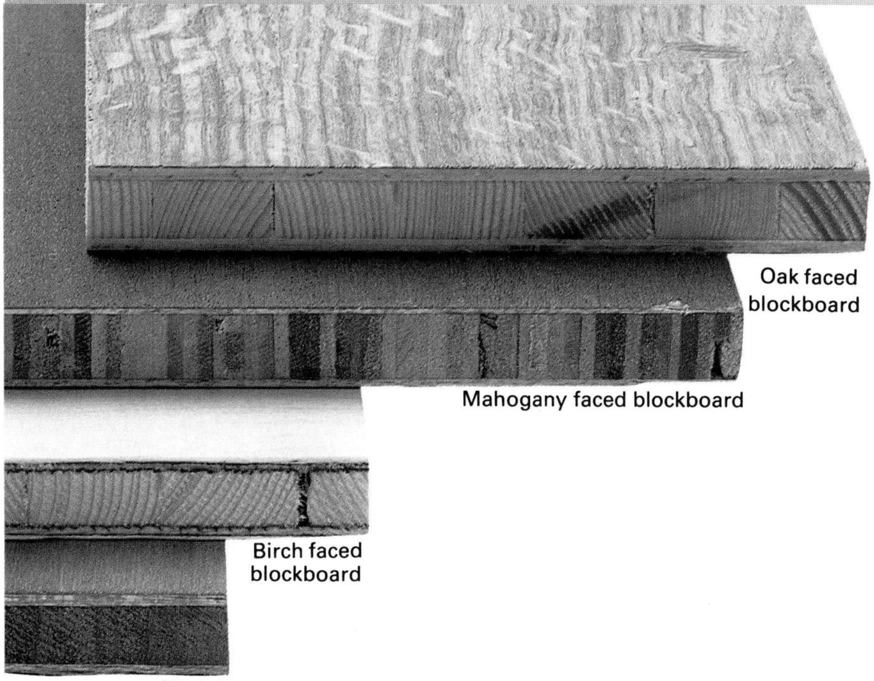

Lumber-core composition board is made from strips of wood laid parallel to one another and glued between continuous sheets of thick veneer. The strips are normally about 25mm (1″) wide, and are arranged so that their grains run in opposite directions to minimize warping. Some boards have narrower strips; others have wider, stud-sized strips.

There is at least one veneer on each side, and sometimes two – the grain of the first veneer running across the strips. The outer veneer forms the facing of the board and can be a decorative wood like oak, teak or mahogany.

Boards normally need edging as the core is visible and there may be gaps and flaws on show.

Oak faced blockboard

Mahogany faced blockboard

Birch faced blockboard

Teak blockboard

PARTICLEBOARD (CHIPBOARD)

Particleboard is made from small fragments of softwood, such as the scraps left over when logs are cut into usable sizes. The fragments are chopped and bonded with resin to form solid sheets.

A phenomenon called 'out-gassing' occurs when conditions of heat together with dampness cause the resin used in the bonding process to give off a formaldehyde smell. If you store the panels for a time in a protected place away from the house (in a garage or shed, for example), a lot of the smell should disappear. Alternatively, seal and paint the panels before you use them indoors.

As well as containing a lot of glue, particleboard sometimes also contains tiny bits of metal which can blunt tools. For this reason, it's worth using tungsten-carbide tipped tools.

Particleboard is available in a variety of different grades, to suit different purposes.

Oriented-strand board (OSB) is made from wood strands which are compressed and resin-bonded. Because it is less expensive, OSB is often used instead of plywood. It can be used for subflooring as well as roofs.

Waferboard is, as its name suggests, manufactured from wafer-like bits of wood. Like oriented-strand board (OSB), it is bonded with phenolic resin and is used for much the same purposes.

Because it is 'good' on both sides, waferboard can be used for shelves or even paneling.

Standard particleboard

Roofing particleboard (pre-asphalted)

Flooring grade particleboard

Exterior particleboard

COATED PARTICLEBOARDS & COUNTERTOPS

Post-formed countertop

'Mahogany' veneered particleboard

Plastic laminated particleboard

Particleboard is often given a decorative facing for furniture making. The commonest finishes are mid-brown 'mahogany' type wood veneer, and white Formica.

Faced and coated boards are made in a wider range of sheet sizes than standard particleboard, including 'planks' of various lengths in widths upwards from 150mm (6″). These have facings on four sides, and sometimes the ends too.

Shelving lengths of plastic laminated particleboard are made in finished sizes, edged all around and may be given a decorative profile. Cut edges normally need covering with a strip of the facing material where the particleboard core is exposed.

Kitchen counters are mostly made from thick particleboard with a scratch-resistant plastic coating. The front edge is usually rounded (postformed), giving a seamless surface which is easier to keep clean than square-edged counters covered with separate laminate.

199

HARDBOARD

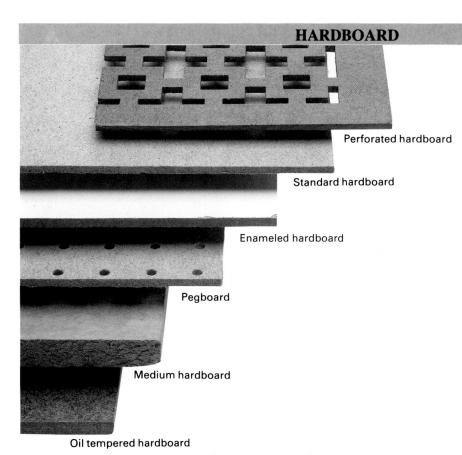

Perforated hardboard

Standard hardboard

Enameled hardboard

Pegboard

Medium hardboard

Oil tempered hardboard

Hardboard is compressed wood pulp. **Standard hardboard** has a smooth, hard finish on one side and a 'woven' texture on the other.

Double-faced hardboard (relatively rare) has a smooth finish both sides. **Enameled hardboard** is finished on the smooth side with paint, which may be embossed with imitation 'tiles' or 'planks'.

Standard hardboard absorbs water and may warp or buckle in use. Avoid this by *tempering* – wetting the back and drying in the room it's to be used in. Sheets can be bent over a former, or by soaking and bending for tighter curves. **Oil tempered hardboard** contains oil to make it water resistant. It is commonly used for leveling wooden floors. **Perforated hardboard** is stamped with holes in a regular pattern and may be smooth both sides. There are patterned boards for partitioning and enclosing.

Pegboard has small holes at 20 or 25mm (1") intervals, and is used for noticeboards and utility racks. **Faced hardboards** have a plastic coating. Commonly used as wallboards. **Medium hardboard** (Sundeala, softboard, fiberboard) is thicker and softer; used for pinboards/insulation.

FIBERBOARD

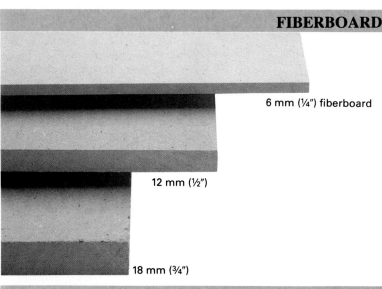

6 mm (¼") fiberboard

12 mm (½")

18 mm (¾")

This smooth, stable material is formed by bonding fine cane or wood fibers together. As the fibers run in all directions, there is no grain and the material is equally strong in every direction.

Although fiberboard is brittle and lacks structural strength, it has one important use. When the fibers are being condensed, many tiny air pockets are formed within the finished board. This makes it excellent for soundproofing and insulation.

However, the fibers are fairly absorbent, so the material must be protected from water; and it cannot be used in exposed situations.

BONDED SOFTWOOD & HARDWOOD

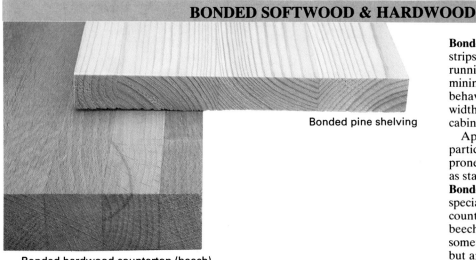

Bonded pine shelving

Bonded hardwood countertop (beech)

Bonded softwood boards consist of strips glued side by side with the grain running in oppostie directions to minimize warping. They look and behave like solid wood, but come in widths suitable for deep shelves, cabinets and tables.

Apart from looks they have no particular advantages. They are less prone to warp than solid wood, but not as stable as other boards. **Bonded hardwoods** are a luxury, specialist material for use as countertops. Woods used include beech and maple. Boards are sometimes available in standard sizes, but are usually only made to measure.

WOODEN MOLDINGS

Moldings are made by running strips of wood through shaped cutters. Their main uses are:
■ As general purpose trims and decoration in woodwork.
■ As decorative features for interior design.
■ As the stock materials for a wide range of joinery and furniture.

The cheapest moldings are made from pine, but if this is stained or varnished rather than painted, it may show unattractive knots and blemishes. Better quality moldings are made from redwood (which has a more regular grain), cedar, or hardwoods such as mahogany.

Most modern moldings are fairly plain, but copies of older, ornate designs can be found. Lumberyards stock the common moldings and some keep a selection of decorative patterns.

For the more unusual feature and constructional moldings, you will probably need to visit several lumberyards – some specialize in period designs, which is useful if you need to match an existing door frame, say. There are also specialists who will machine a hard-to-match shape (an expensive option).

Many moldings are cut from redwood or cedar which is even grained and free from blemishes.

Trade tip

Size it up

❝ Molding sizes often confuse people. Like ordinary softwood, they are quoted as a nominal or standard size based on the wood from which the molding was cut; because of the wastage in machining, the actual size of the molding is normally quite a lot smaller. The exception to this rule is doweling, which is usually very close to the stated diameter. ❞

GENERAL PURPOSE MOLDINGS

Quarter rounds are shaped like a quarter of a circle and are commonly used to trim the joint between two panels which meet at a right angle.
Half round moldings are for trimming joints or the edge of a board. The smallest are a full half circle, but larger sizes have a flatter curve.
Cover moldings are used for similar purposes, but are more decorative. They are also available prefinished and with *embossed* decoration.
Dowels (also called *rounds*) are full circles, used for things like legs, pegs and rails.
External angles are 'L' shaped and normally fit over the edge and face of a board. They come in various sizes and with different length 'arms' on each side. There are square, rounded and molded patterns. There is a whole group of external angle moldings called 'cap moldings'.
Internal angles are also 'L' shaped, with the finished face on the inside of the L. They are used to trim the joint between two panels at a right angle.
Scoop moldings are used for the same purpose. They have one square corner and one scooped out in a curve.

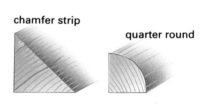

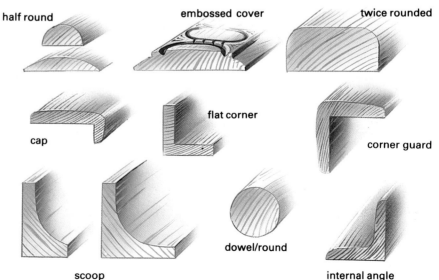

FEATURE MOLDINGS

Feature moldings are used throughout houses as decorative features. All types come in a wide range of patterns (many with traditional names). Some of the most common of each type are illustrated.

Baseboards trim the joint between the wall and the floor, and also protect the plaster. It's common for the baseboard to match the architraves.

Architraves are the moldings which 'frame' a door or window.

Cornices cover the joint between the wall and the ceiling, though wood cornices are less common than plaster or plastic. They are also used to trim the tops of dressers and wardrobes.

Picture rails have a grooved top into which *molding hooks* fit for hanging pictures.

Dado rails (chair rails) are fixed part-way up the wall – usually at about waist height – for protection and to provide a visual break.

Panel moldings are used to frame areas on a flat wall. They can also be used to decorate the front of a plain, flush door by simulating panels (ready cut kits are available for this). *Rabbeted* panel moldings have a grooved edge so they can be used to frame a thin panel.

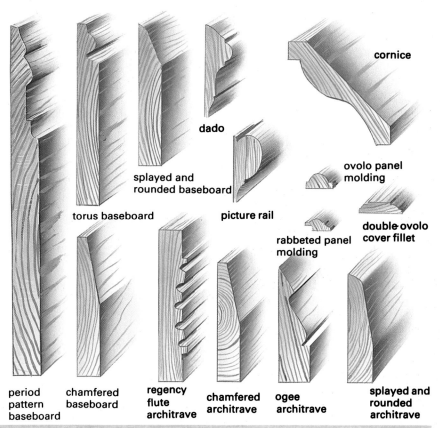

dado

splayed and rounded baseboard

torus baseboard

picture rail

cornice

ovolo panel molding

rabbeted panel molding

double ovolo cover fillet

period pattern baseboard

chamfered baseboard

regency flute architrave

chamfered architrave

ogee architrave

splayed and rounded architrave

CONSTRUCTIONAL MOLDINGS

Softwood moldings are used for the specially shaped members which make up things like window frames, staircases and doors. These are useful for repairs as well as new constructions, but check that the design and dimensions are identical to the original.

Window moldings are available to make all parts of the frame, including:
Rails (in different sections for top and bottom). Sliding sashes have special moldings for the two *meeting rails* in the center.
Stiles, the sides of the window.
Glazing bars where the window is split into smaller panes. *Greenhouse bar* is heavier, and is used for greenhouses and conservatories.
Beading for retaining the glass or the sliding sashes.
Window apron and *window sill* to trim the bottom of the frame.

Door moldings are made for all parts but those in comon use are:
Weatherboard (weatherbar) to keep the train away from the base of the door.
Transom (drip molding) to keep the rain off the upper part of the frame and top of the door.
Sill (sometimes spelled 'cill' in catalogues) to form a threshold.

Stair moldings include:
Handrails in different patterns for wall mounting or use on a balustrade.
Nosings to form the rounded front edge of a tread.

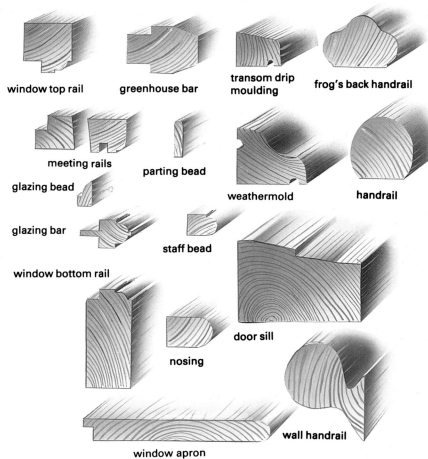

window top rail

greenhouse bar

transom drip moulding

frog's back handrail

meeting rails

glazing bead

parting bead

glazing bar

weathermold

handrail

staff bead

window bottom rail

nosing

door sill

wall handrail

window apron

CUTTING LUMBER AND BOARDS

A secure work surface and a means of clamping the job to it are essential for all kinds of carpentry, as well as a host of other DIY jobs. But since few people have the luxury of a purpose-built workshop, most workbench arrangements have to be more or less temporary.

A portable folding workbench is by far the most popular option, as it is relatively cheap, takes up little space, and has the added benefit of built-in clamps. Even if you have a more permanent workbench set up in a shed or garage, a portable bench is still invaluable for jobs that need to be done on the spot.

Trestles and a top are another way to provide a versatile, low-cost bench, with the useful advantage that the work surface can be as big as you want to make it. Clamping can be a problem, however.

A permanent workbench (folding or free-standing) in a shed, garage or workroom gives you the advantage of a large, sturdy worktop with lots of handy accessories. If you have the space, there is no substitute for really serious carpentry.

A workbench provides a sturdy working platform and a way to clamp things which need to be sawn or planed.

PORTABLE FOLDING WORKBENCHES

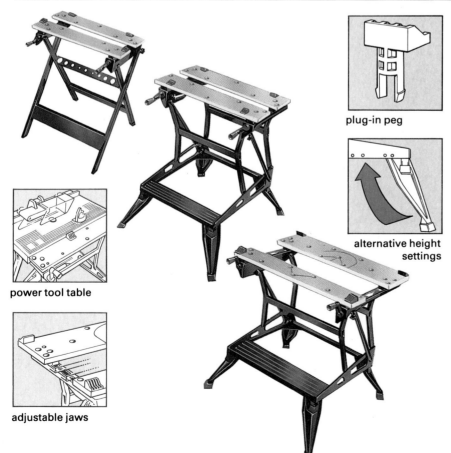

power tool table

adjustable jaws

plug-in peg

alternative height settings

Folding workbenches have become virtually indispensible to do-it-yourselfers and professionals alike. There are several different models, all of which pack flat and have a two-part top that can be screwed in and out like vise jaws. The inner edges of the top are so shaped that rounded and tapering objects can be clamped as easily as square ones.

More sophisticated models have *alternative height settings*. Use the lower setting for sawing and related jobs, and the higher setting for fine work such as planing and chiseling. Larger workbenches also have a wider jaw opening facility, allowing a greater variety of objects to be clamped in the top.

Various accessories include:

Plug-in pegs – standard accessories which allow the worktop to be used as a clamp for objects which are too big to fit the vise jaws.

Extension arms – optional extras fitted into the worktop so that it will clamp objects too large to fit on top.

A power tool table – an optional extra which clips on to the top and accepts a variety of tools such as saws and routers, turning them into more stable fixed machinery.

CUTTING LUMBER BY HAND

Even if you have a power saw, hand sawing is likely to be quicker for small jobs and possibly more accurate, too.

Use a backsaw for fine, accurate cutting of small pieces of wood up to a maximum size of about 100 × 50 mm (4 × 2″).

A tenon saw also comes in handy for small widths of plastic-coated board, where its fine teeth help to minimize surface splintering (see *Cutting Boards* pages 206-207).

Use a crosscut saw where speed is more important than accuracy, and for cutting larger pieces of lumber.

Whichever saw you use, it's essential to support the wood firmly. For small pieces you'll find it easier to work at table or worktop height, preferably with the wood supported in a bench hook or a vise (in which case protect the surface of the wood with offcuts).

For larger lumber and when using a crosscut saw, use a folding workbench, trestle or old chair to support the wood just above knee height and steady it with your own weight.

Posture is all-important when using a crosscut saw. Choose a position that lets you saw comfortably at an angle of roughly 45° – if you're off-balance or pinched up, the cut won't be straight.

STARTING THE CUT

Start the cut off in the right place and there's a good chance it will stay there. You'll find it a big help to hold the saw with your index finger pointing along the side of the handle in line with the blade to steady it.

If you push the saw down to start, the forward angle of the teeth makes them skip on the edge of the wood before cutting into it, and it's hard to get a proper start. The trick is to form a small nick in the edge first by drawing the saw backwards towards you so that the shallow angle of the teeth rides smoothly over the wood.

Remember to start the cut on the waste side of the cutting line, to allow for the thickness of the saw kerf. In practice the kerf should just brush the line – something which you can easily check as you draw the saw back to make the initial nick in the edge.

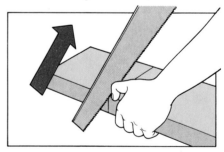

1 *Line up the near end of the saw blade against the top joint of your thumb so that it's fractionally to the waste side of the cutting line.*

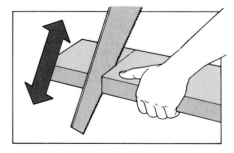

2 *Draw the blade towards you, letting its weight carve a nick in the edge of the wood. Then push forward gently so that the teeth can bite.*

USING A CROSSCUT SAW

■ Never force a crosscut saw – the blade will flex and bind in the cut. Hold it at about 45° to the wood and use a slightly curving stroke, as this helps to prevent the blade from sticking.

■ Cut with light pressure on the forward stroke only. Saw from the shoulder, working up to long strokes of the saw, rather than short bites. It's difficult to bring a crosscut saw back on line, so make sure it doesn't wander from the initial nick. Watch the cutting line on the top of the wood, checking that the kerf stays just clear of the mark, and at the same time keep an eye on the edge to make sure the cut stays square.

■ When sawing down the length of a piece of wood, you may find the cut starts to close up, pinching the blade in the process. If this happens, keep it open by driving in a small wedge.

1 As the teeth begin to bite, exert gentle pressure on the forward stroke only. Move your arm from the shoulder and look straight down the blade.

2 Near the end, lower the cutting angle and shorten your strokes. Support the offcut with your free hand so it doesn't tear as the saw breaks through.

Trade tip
Stop it sticking

❝ If the saw binds in the cut for no obvious reason, it may be because of moisture in the wood. You'll find the blade cuts much more easily if you lubricate it by rubbing with a piece of candle. ❞

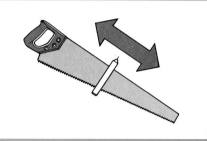

USING A BACKSAW

The backsaw's stiff back makes it easier to keep on line, but you still need to keep a constant check for squareness along the edge or the cut won't be straight.

The sawing position is flatter, but otherwise the same – cut with light pressure on the forward stroke only, working from the shoulder, and gradually increase the length of your strokes.

If there is a long offcut, don't forget to support it to prevent splintering at the end of the cut.

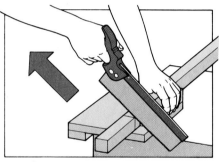

1 Start a backsaw cut at an angle of around 45°, then gradually lower the blade until it cuts horizontally. Keep checking that the cut is square.

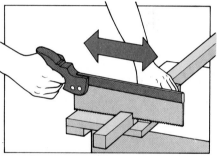

2 As you reach the end, shorten your strokes to reduce the chance of splintering. If you use a bench hook, saw into its base to finish the cut cleanly.

Trade tip

Trimming a short end

❝ You can't easily saw less than 5mm (2") off the end of a piece of wood – and you shouldn't need to if you've marked up accurately!

But if the worst does happen, you'll find it easier to clamp on overlapping pieces of scrap wood, then saw through them all together. The scrap wood holds the saw on line and stops the short end splitting away. ❞

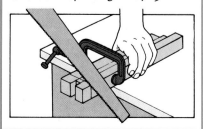

Trade tip

Get a grip on it

❝ Holding the wood firmly is half the battle, and a home-made bench hook is one of the most useful holding tools you can own – particularly for dealing with small pieces. I use one even if I'm working on a portable workbench – it's quicker than the bench's built-in vice, and it's a positive advantage to be able to cut into it.

Make your own bench hook from a piece of stout ply or particleboard about 300mm (12") square and two lengths of 50 × 25mm (2 × 1") wood glued and screwed together as shown. To use it, lock one side against the edge of the bench and press the wood firmly against the back stop to hold it in place. ❞

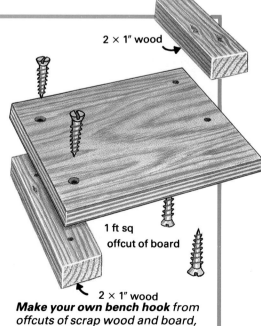

2 × 1" wood

1 ft sq offcut of board

2 × 1" wood

Make your own bench hook from offcuts of scrap wood and board, nailed and glued together.

CUTTING BOARDS

Although there are several types of power driven saw for cutting boards, this section features only the saber saw – the safest and easiest to use. It will cut both straight lines and curves in a wide variety of different types of board. If you don't own a saber saw, you can use a crosscut saw instead.

Whatever the saw, the key to cutting a large board is to support it securely. It's no good propping it both ends and sawing across the middle – this causes the saw blade to pinch as the board begins to sag, and risks the two halves snapping as you near the end. The trick is to imagine the board is already in two pieces and prop it so that each half is individually supported from the beginning.

A portable folding workbench makes a useful trestle for one side; for the other, try two kitchen chairs with lengths of wood stretched between them. Aim to support the board at just above knee height so you can steady it with your weight.

Trade tip

Means of support

❛ Supporting large boards is easy in a fully equipped workshop, but a lot more difficult at home. Here are some ways to improvise your own supports, assuming you can use a portable workbench for one side of the board. ❜

USING A SABER SAW

A saber saw cuts on the up-stroke, so if your board is only finished on one side (like a work-top), cut from underneath. Otherwise, cut where any splintering will show least. To minimize splintering, run masking tape along the cutting line and saw through this.

To keep straight cuts on line, use a guide fence. Some saber saws have a metal fence for following a nearby edge, but for a more accurate guide clamp or nail a straight piece of wood to the board.

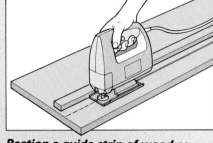

Postion a guide strip of wood so that the blade follows the cutting line as you slide the edge of the sole plate along it. Check its position before you start to cut.

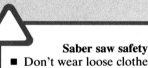

Saber saw safety
- Don't wear loose clothes that could get tangled in the blade.
- Loop the cord over your shoulder to keep it safely away from the cut.
- Don't use a blunt blade.
- Unplug before changing blades.
- Begin a cut slowly and gently, so the blade doesn't buck back.
- Give the saw blade time to stop moving before you put it down.

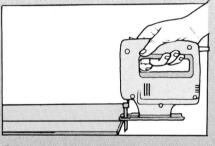

Start the saw and advance the moving blade to the line, resting the sole plate on the edge of the board. Don't force or twist the blade – it will break.

USING A CROSSCUT SAW

Hold the board firmly with your weight on your knee and one hand. Keep your eye over the cutting line, and start the cut as for solid wood (see page 205).

A crosscut saw will splinter the underside of the board. So with faced boards, such as Formica, mark the line on the face that shows, then score along it with a trimming knife to stop the surface chipping. Saw with the blade as flat as possible to reduce the amount it tears the surface.

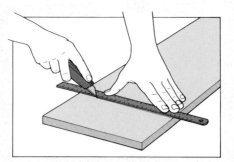

Score the cutting line with a trimming knife and straight edge to help prevent the surface veneer or plastic coating from chipping off.

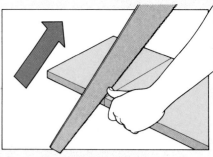

Start the cut as you would for solid wood – draw the blade back gently, steadying it with your thumb, to form a small nick in the edge.

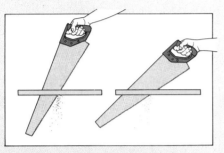

For rough work, you can saw faster at 45°. But keep the saw as flat as possible if you want to avoid splintering the underside of the board.

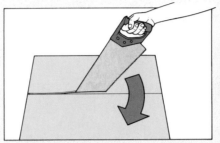

If you run off line, twist the blade slightly as you saw to bring it back on course. Correct the fault gradually, though, or it will leave an unsightly notch.

Trade tip
Stop it flapping

6 Very thin boards such as plywood or hardboard sheets often tend to whip up and down with each saw stroke, making it difficult to saw them cleanly.

I stop a board like this from flexing by laying two lengths of wood across my supports, one just to each side of the cutting line. 9

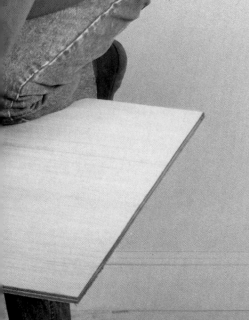

PROBLEM SOLVER

Cutting corners

The way you deal with a corner depends on whether you're using a crosscut saw or a saber saw, and also on the shape of the corner.
External corners Where possible, saw past the corner in both directions so that you get a clean cut. Attempting to stop exactly on the spot usually means ending short and splintering the last little bit.
Internal corners You can't cut past the corner, so take care and stop short if necessary. Any splintering is likely to be on the waste part, so you can trim it off later.
With a saber saw, slow down and watch carefully as you approach the corner. With a crosscut saw, change the angle so you cut vertically into it.

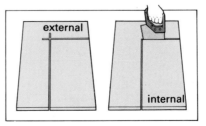

Internal and external corners need to be finished carefully.

Cutting holes

For these, you need a saber saw or a hand saw with a thin blade (such as a padsaw or keyhole saw).

There are two ways to start the cut. The easiest (and only way with a hand saw) is to drill one or more large holes somewhere in the waste area. Insert the blade through the board before you switch on, then cut in the ordinary way.
The alternative if you don't have a large drill bit is to make a *pocket cut*. Stand the saber saw on the end of its soleplate inside the area with the blade not touching the surface. Switch on, and gently angle the blade down to contact the board. It should gradually cut its own way through – but be prepared for it to buck if it touches suddenly.

Start a pocket cut by standing the saber saw soleplate on its end.

THREE ESSENTIAL SAWS

BACKSAW

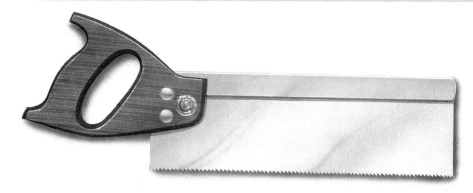

A **backsaw** is designed for making accurate cuts in small pieces of wood. The blade is short – from about 25 to 50mm (1 to 2″). It has fine teeth and when making angled cuts that must be precise it is often used with a miter box.

A **tenon or dovetail saw** is a slightly smaller version of the backsaw. Its teeth are finer than the backsaw and it is used for joints requiring maximum precision, such as the dovetail joint.
Typical ppi range: 12-14

CROSSCUT SAW

A **crosscut saw** has a long flexible blade ranging from around 500 mm (20″) to 660 mm (26″) in length, with fairly coarse teeth along the cutting edge. The length of the blade should match your sawing stroke, but the longer the blade, the less easy it is to control. Unlike a backsaw there is no stiffening back, allowing the blade to cut right through a wide board.

The crosscut saw is similar in appearance to the ripsaw. Technically, the crosscut saw is for cutting *across* the wood grain; the ripsaw for cutting *with* the grain ('ripping'). You will find the crosscut saw is suitable for most woodcutting jobs.
Typical ppi range: 8-12

SABER SAWS (PORTABLE JIGSAWS)

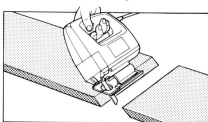

***Some models** have a guide fence.*

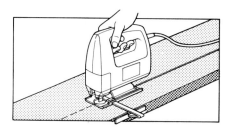

***The sole plate** can be angled at 45°.*

***Scrolling saber saw** blade control.*

A **saber saw** has a narrow blade which works up and down and cuts on the up stroke. They are excellent tools for sawing sheet materials and can also be used to cut smaller pieces of wood.

The simplest type has a single speed and cuts wood up to around 50mm (2″) thick. (With a suitable blade, it also cuts sheet metal up to around 3mm (⅛″) thick.) It can be used freehand for curved or straight cuts, but many models have a guide fence and circle guide for straight lines and regular curves.

The *sole plate* which contacts the surface of the wood normally pivots to an angle of 45° for miter cutting and retracts to allow you to cut right up to an obstacle.

More sophisticated models may incorporate *variable speed* – for different materials and tight curves – and *orbital action*, in which the blade swings back and forth as well as going up and down. Both result in an easier, cleaner cut.

Scrolling saber saws have a hand knob which controls the blade plunger. This allows you to rotate the blade to cut in any direction regardless of the position of the body. As a result you can cut awkward shapes more accurately.
Typical ppi range (for wood): 8-12

MEASURING WOOD TO FIT

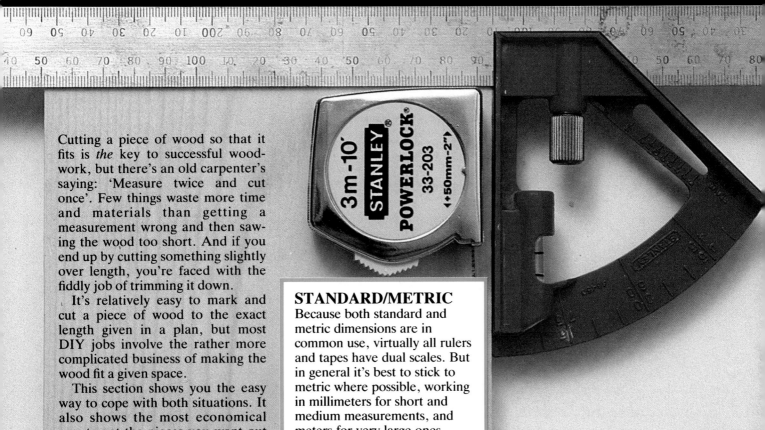

Cutting a piece of wood so that it fits is *the* key to successful wood-work, but there's an old carpenter's saying: 'Measure twice and cut once'. Few things waste more time and materials than getting a measurement wrong and then saw-ing the wood too short. And if you end up by cutting something slightly over length, you're faced with the fiddly job of trimming it down.

It's relatively easy to mark and cut a piece of wood to the exact length given in a plan, but most DIY jobs involve the rather more complicated business of making the wood fit a given space.

This section shows you the easy way to cope with both situations. It also shows the most economical way to get the pieces you want out of standard timber sizes.

STANDARD/METRIC
Because both standard and metric dimensions are in common use, virtually all rulers and tapes have dual scales. But in general it's best to stick to metric where possible, working in millimeters for short and medium measurements, and meters for very large ones.

MEASURING
Short distances are easy to measure accurately. A tape measure is simple to use up to a comfortable arm span – a metre or so – because you can pull it taut with both hands.

Rulers are even easier to handle and are more accurate for short measurements. You can also use the edge of a ruler to draw a straight line on the material. Use a metal ruler for marking with a knife.

If you have to measure something which extends beyond your arm span, or beyond the length of the tape, always double check – it's all too easy to introduce errors.

If you have a helper, they can ensure that the tape is taut. Otherwise you will have to fix the end while you take the measurement. If you are working single handed, the locking button on the tape is useful to stop it springing back if you let it go accidentally. Masking tape is also handy for securing the tape measure temporarily in awkward situations.

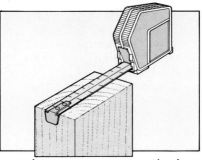

1 A tape measure can only give an accurate reading if it is pulled tight. Don't let it sag, bow or twist, or your measurement will be too long.

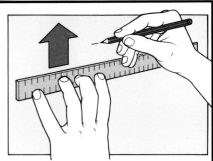

2 Rule a line more accurately by positioning a pencil on the starting point first. Hold the pencil firm, then bring the edge of the ruler up to contact it.

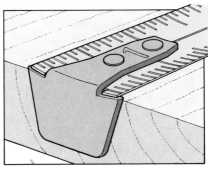

3 If you can't hold the end of the tape, secure it with the hook provided. This automatically aligns the end of the tape with what you are measuring.

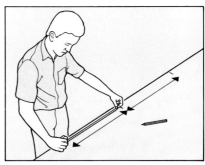

4 To measure something longer than the tape itself, it's best to lock it at a manageable length, then work along in steps, marking at each stage.

MEASURING INTERNAL DISTANCES

There are many situations where you need to know the exact distance between two fixed sides, for example when putting up shelves in an alcove.

You can do this with a tape measure up to a comfortable arm span, but beyond this it gets difficult to keep the tape taut. So a good alternative is to use a pair of extending rods – just lengths of wood, each cut to between two-thirds and three-quarters the opening's width.

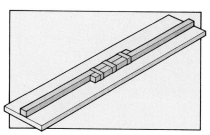

To use a tape measure accurately beyond your reach, get a helper to pull it taut. Add the width of the case to the measurement on the tape.

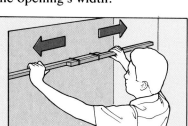

1 Use extending rods by sliding them out until both ends touch the sides. This makes it easy to see whether the width of the opening varies.

2 Tape the rods together securely to retain the dimensions of the opening, then use them to transfer the measurement to your wood.

Direct measuring

❝ Where you just want a piece of wood to fit a given space, in many cases I find that taking the measurement and transferring it to the wood makes the job more complicated and less accurate. Unless you are dealing with very large pieces it's often better to use the wood as its own ruler.

For example, if I want a piece of wood the same length as the depth of a counter, I lay the wood itself across the surface and strike off the exact measurement. ❞

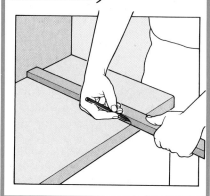

CHOOSING THE RIGHT SIZE

If you refer to the lumber size chart on page 195, and the sheet sizes for manmade boards on pages 198-200, you will see that there's a limited number of standard lengths and widths available.

You may be able to get your supplier to cut the material for you, but if this isn't possible or too expensive you'll need to choose standard sizes from which to cut your own.

Length If you're buying standard lengths of lumber, pick the ones which allow you to cut the pieces you need with the minimum wastage. For example, if you want a large number of lengths of wood measuring 3ft 8in, don't buy bundles 6ft long; 8ft, the next commonly available length, allows you to cut two pieces from a single strip with hardly any wood left over.

Width mainly applies to manmade boards, where you can cut several pieces out of a sheet. For example, if you want strips 7in wide, it's more economical to cut two from a 15in wide board than one from a 9in board.

If you want a large number of odd-sized pieces, see if you can get them all out of a bigger sheet of the same material.

lumber

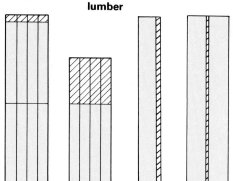

Think carefully about the length and number of pieces of wood you need for a job. Often, what seems the most obvious standard size leaves a lot of wastage, and you need to switch to a larger one.

boards

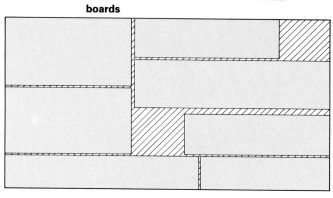

The safest way to see how many pieces you can get out of a standard sheet of board is to draw them all to scale, cut them out, and shuffle them around on a plan. On coated boards you can slot pieces in crosswise; but if there is a grain they should all run the same way.

GETTING A SQUARE END

Before you can transfer the measurement you want on to your material, you need a starting point to measure it from. Normally, this will be one end of the length of lumber or board. But unless the end is cut straight and square you will never get a true measurement.

The first rule of accuracy is never to trust something until you have checked it. In particular, sold lumber is unlikely to be supplied with ends which are square *and* in good condition. And even though manmade boards are usually machined true, the ends may have been knocked or damaged, so you should still check them first.

Inspect the end for damage, including splits or unsightly discoloration in the case of solid wood. Then use a try square to check that the end is cut squarely across its length *and* through its thickness.

Unless this is the case, it is best to use the try square to mark a new, dead square end a little way along the wood.

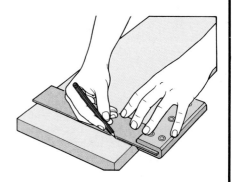

Use the try square to mark a line across the surface of the lumber. Turn the wood over and starting from the same point, square another line down the edge.

MEASURING TO LENGTH

Measure the right distance along from your square end and make a clear but thin mark on the material. Square across to mark the cutting line.

If you have to cut a number of short pieces from a single length of wood, *don't* try measuring them all in one go before cutting them: the result won't be accurate because a small amount of wood is wasted in the width of the saw cut.

It's better to measure, cut, then measure and cut again, even if this takes longer. There are shortcuts you can use if you want several pieces the same size.

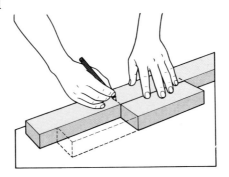

If you want to cut a number of pieces of the same length from one longer piece, cut the first and use it as a guide to mark the rest. For maximum accuracy use the same guide to mark all the pieces.

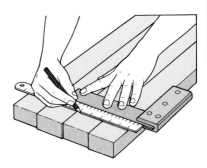

To cut a number of pieces down to the same length, it's best to measure them all at once. Align the ends with a square, tape or clamp them together, then measure the correct length and square a line right across.

DEALING WITH ANGLES

The most common angle you're likely to encounter in woodwork apart from the right angle is the 45 degree miter, used for things like picture frames and architrave moldings. Miter boxes can be used to cut thin sections of wood directly, but to mark out a miter on a larger piece of wood, you need a combination or miter square.

You may also find odd angles like the slope of a stair rail or ceiling in the attic, say.

If you have to cut something to match, it's sometimes possible to mark it directly but otherwise you need a pattern. There is a special tool for this called a T bevel or bevel gauge – basically a try square with a movable lockable blade.

Trade tip

Angle guides

❝ A bevel or gauge is such a specialized tool that it really isn't worth buying one for a single job. Make your own angle guide from two thin strips of wood fixed together at the correct angle, or by cutting a piece of cardboard to the right shape. ❞

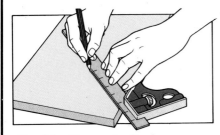

Combination and miter squares are tools that let you rule a 45 degree cutting line across a wider surface than you can fit inside a miter box.

You can swivel the blade of a bevel gauge to reproduce any angle, and lock it in position. You can then use it to transfer the angle to your piece of wood.

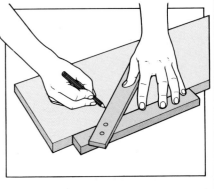

DEALING WITH AWKWARD SHAPES

Although most DIY woodwork involves simply cutting pieces to length from standard sized material, there are times when things aren't quite so straightforward because the wood or board you're using has to be trimmed to a complicated shape.

A case in point is where you want a board to fit snugly against a surface which is irregular or uneven, or where there's an awkward projection. The technique for doing this is called *scribing to fit*.

Use a similar technique where you need to mark along the edge of the material, rather than across it – either to trim a board down by an even amount, or because you want to fit something parallel to the edge.

There may also be times when you have to mark a piece of wood with a curve, or some other irregular shape. Jobs like this require special tools, though luckily you can make some of them yourself.

A profile gauge is the ideal tool for marking awkward shapes such as a door frame molding.

SCRIBING THE EDGE

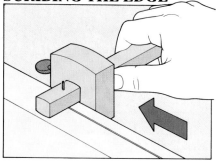

1 A marking gauge is used to mark a line running at a true parallel to the edge or end of a board. Set it to the width you want and run it gently along.

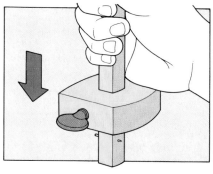

2 To make fine adjustments to a marking gauge, don't use the adjusting screw but knock the end gently on a solid surface to jar it along a fraction.

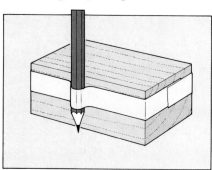

1 A scribing block traces an irregular line along the edge of a board. Improvise your own by taping a pencil to a small block of wood as shown.

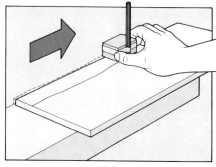

2 To mark the edge of a board, butt it up against the irregular surface, then run the scribing block along the board so that it transfers the outline.

Trade tip

Using patterns
❛ Faced by a really tricky job, like marking a piece of board to fit in an alcove, it's best to make up a pattern and use this.

Start by cutting a piece of card roughly to size, leaving a gap all round. Tape on thin overlapping strips, building up the shape until the pattern fits exactly. **❜**

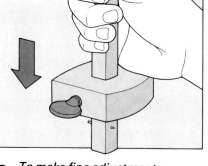

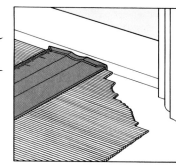

Use a profile gauge to take the pattern of more complex shapes. Press against the object so that the needles mimic the shape, then transfer to your material.

212

DRILLING HOLES IN WOOD

As materials go, wood is soft and fairly easy to drill. But making clean, accurate holes in exactly the right spot isn't always so simple – it needs care, and the right tools.

The normal choice for drilling is a power drill, which in most cases is quick, accurate and takes very little effort. But drilling by hand has certain advantages too:

■ You don't need a power source (though cordless drills get round this problem too).

■ You can work slowly – and therefore often more accurately.

■ Hand drills are smaller and lighter, making them easier to use in awkward corners; they are also less likely to snap thin drill bits.

Whichever method you choose, you also need bits of various shapes and sizes. Some wood bits are designed specifically for power or hand drills and aren't interchangeable, while larger bits (particularly those for hand drilling) are also fairly expensive. Most people find it best to collect a set of general purpose bits in small and medium sizes and then add to them as the need arises. The full range of drilling tools and bits is described on pages 215-216.

BASIC DRILLING TECHNIQUES

Whatever the hole, make sure you use the right bit and the correct technique:

Small holes (up to 6mm – 1/4") are mainly for screws – either straight-through shank clearance holes, or pilot holes for the thread. Accurate positioning is important, but depth is rarely critical since in softwood and most man-made boards the screw cuts its own way in.

Holes like these are normally drilled with twist bits or wood bits, but for small pilot holes it's often easier to use a bradawl, a gimlet or a push drill.

Medium sized holes (6 to 19mm – 1/4 to 3/4") are mainly for dowels, bolts, pipes and metal fittings. They must be positioned accurately, and often have to be drilled to an accurate diameter and depth (see overleaf for details of drilling dowel holes). Use a wood bit, flat bit or auger bit, depending on the size and accuracy required.

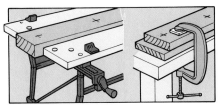

1 Unless the wood's own weight holds it steady, always clamp the work securely. Make sure there is no risk of drilling through into something important.

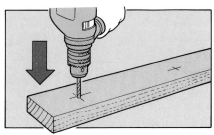

3 Position the bit over the marked point and apply steady pressure, keeping it square to the work. Don't force the bit as this, too, can make it wander.

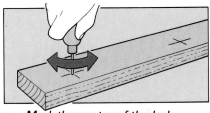

2 Mark the center of the hole with a punch, bradawl or even a nail. This ensures the drill bit goes where you want it, and stops it from wandering off line.

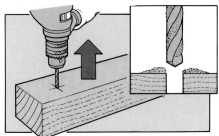

When drilling deep holes, back off periodically to make sure the bit isn't clogged with wood dust. A clogged bit will quickly overheat and go blunt.

Trade tip

Avoid splinters

❝ To stop the underside of a piece of wood from splintering as you drill through it:

■ Clamp a piece of scrap wood firmly to the back and drill through into this.

■ With a flat bit or auger bit, use a double-drilling technique: stop as soon as the center point breaks through the wood, then turn the work over and drill back through the other side. ❞

For greater accuracy, use a try square to align the drill. For perfect accuracy and steadiness – particularly when driling a series of holes – use a drill stand.

DRILLING LARGE HOLES

Large holes – 19mm (¾") to 75mm (3") – are used for a variety of purposes, including housings for cylinder locks, recesses for concealed hinges, and cut-outs for pull handles. Almost always, they must be drilled to an exact size and position and should be finished very cleanly.

Most of the time you'll need a large flat bit or a hole saw, though hinge recesses are cut with a special hinge boring bit (*end mill*) made to suit a normal 35mm diameter hinge boss.

Such bits are tricky to use in a hand-held drill, though a drill stand makes things simpler. Some types of end mill have a raised rim to limit the depth of cut; if yours doesn't, take extra care not to drill too far, or use a drill depth stop.

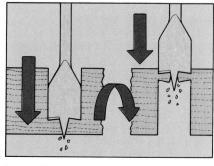

Large flat bits can only be used on fairly thick wood. They are almost certain to tear it if you drill right through, so use the double-drilling technique.

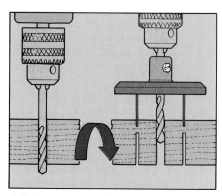

A hole saw cuts thin material very cleanly, but will overheat if forced. On thicker materials, bore through with the centre bit, then use the saw from both sides.

To use a hinge boring bit with a hand-held drill (see left), start by rocking the bit gently from side to side. Continue until you reach the right depth.

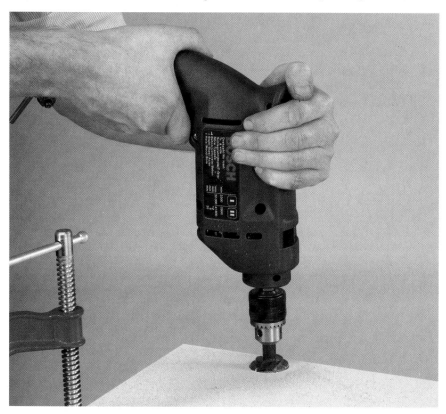

ALIGNING HOLES FOR DOWEL JOINTS

Dowel holes must be drilled cleanly to the right depth and diameter. It's also important that the holes in each part line up perfectly.

Jointing dowels are often sold with matching dowel bits – your best guarantee that the holes are the right size. If your drill hasn't a built-in depth stop, fit one to the bit (or use tape) to gauge the depth.

You can align the holes by carefully measuring and marking both parts, but a safer way is to use a cheap set of *dowel center points* – again, sold to suit various dowel sizes. If you have a lot of joints to make, an inexpensive *doweling jig* could be a worthwhile investment. A vertical drill stand also helps to make sure holes are straight.

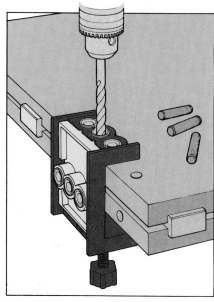

A dowelling jig ensures that both sets of holes get drilled straight and that they align with each other. The jig simply clamps in position on the work.

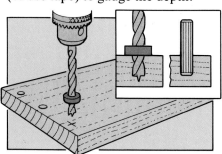

1 Use a dowel bit to make the holes in the first part, taking care to keep the drill square to the wood. Fit a depth stop to check on the depth.

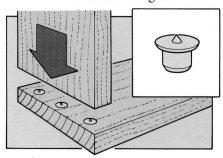

2 Insert dowel center points in the holes you have drilled and press the two parts together to mark the hole centers on the second part ready for drilling.

DRILLING BY HAND

Hand drilling is slower than using a power tool, but gives you far more control. For small holes up to about 10mm (⅜″), use a *hand drill* with a twist bit or wood bit; larger holes must be drilled with a *brace*.

If you have a hand drill as well as a power drill, you'll find that on jobs requiring a number of holes of two different sizes it's easier to use both tools together than to keep swapping bits.

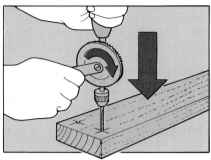

Guide a hand drill and apply pressure with the end handle while you turn the crank. The slow speed makes it simple to keep the bit in alignment.

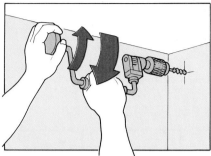

A ratchet brace can be used in a confined space by setting the rachet mechanism and cranking the handle repeatedly through part of a full swing.

DRILLING TOOLS

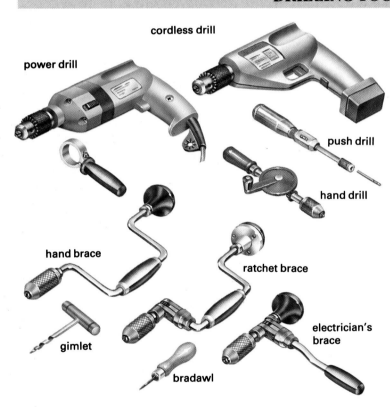

power drill
cordless drill
push drill
hand drill
hand brace
ratchet brace
gimlet
electrician's brace
bradawl

Power drills used for woodworking don't need a hammer action, but it's worth having a two speed model with variable speed control for large or accurate holes. *Cordless drills* come into their own for carpentry, and on many jobs can be used instead of a hand drill.

Hand drills are convenient, lightweight tools for working away from a power source or in confined spaces. On better models the crank wheel generally drives twin gears for more even power. There are various handle designs.

Braces are traditional woodworking tools measured by the size of their sweep (the diameter of a full turn of the handle). The larger the sweep, the greater the power, but the harder the tool is to use in a restricted space. The *electrician's brace* is a specialized tool for drilling holes between joists and similarly restricted areas.

  Most braces have a ratchet action, enabling them to be used in confined spaces by cranking the handle. Plain braces are about two thirds the price of ratchet models.

Bradawls are for boring small screw pilot holes in softwood.

Gimlets (*hand augers*) come in a range of sizes from 3 to 6mm (⅛ to ¼″) for boring small holes.

Push drills to fit *spiral ratchet screwdrivers* can be used instead of a bradawl or gimlet.

DRILLING AIDS

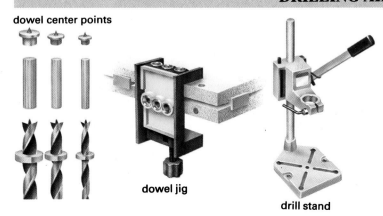

dowel center points
dowel jig
drill stand

Dowel center points are made in various sizes to suit corresponding dowel and dowel bit sizes.

Dowelling jigs consist of a series of guides for positioning dowel holes accurately and drilling them straight. There are various patterns, all designed to clamp to the edge of the work.

Depth stops, on the bit or fitted to the drill itself, enable you to drill to pre-set depths.

Drill stands for power drills help to ensure alignment and depth – especially when drilling large, accurate holes or a series of identically sized holes in different parts. Some stands are made to suit particular drills, but there are universal models, too.

BITS FOR POWER OR HAND DRILLS

twist bit
wood bit
countersinks

Twist bits have a blunt point and long spiral flutes. They are available in *high speed steel* for drilling wood and metal, or carbon steel for drilling wood only.

Twist bits are commonly sold in sets. A typical metric set contains bits from 1 to 6.5mm in 0.5mm steps, the standard equivalent being 1⁄16 to 1⁄4″ in 64ths of an inch. Bits over 6mm (1⁄4″) are usually expensive. When power drilling, use a fast drill speed.

Wood bits resemble twist bits but have a central spur and angled cutting edges for more accurate, cleaner holes. *Dowel bits* are similar, but are accurately matched to various sizes of jointing dowel. When power drilling, use a fast drill speed.

Countersinks are used to make the angled recesses for countersunk screw heads. Not all types are interchangeable. Use at a moderate speed.

SPECIAL BITS FOR POWER TOOLS

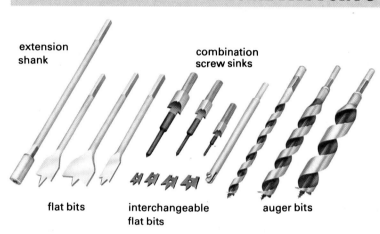

extension shank
combination screw sinks
flat bits
interchangeable flat bits
auger bits

plug cutters
hinge boring bit
hole saw

Flat bits are for rapid drilling of medium-sized holes in wood and must be used at a fast drill speed (at least 1,000 rpm). Sizes normally range from 6 to 38mm (1⁄4 to 1½″) in 3mm (1⁄8″) steps, but as well as separate bits you may also find sets of interchangeable cutters to fit a universal shank. *Extension shanks* are available to fit some types of flat bit for drilling very deep holes.

Combination screwsinks, for drilling screw holes, have stepped cutters that form a pilot, clearance and countersink all in one go. They are exactly matched to particular screw sizes and are unlikely to be worth buying unless you have to fit a large number of identical screws.

Combination auger bits are dual-purpose bits for power drills and hand braces (but not hand drills), the wide spiral and single cutter making them very accurate for large, deep holes. Sizes range from 8 to 32mm (5⁄16 to 1¼″). Use a slow drill speed.

Hole saws have a central pilot bit surrounded by a ring of saw teeth. They are designed for large holes in thin materials and won't work at all at thicknesses over around 38mm (1½″).

Sizes range from 15 to 75mm (5⁄8 to 3″), and you can also buy combination sets with a series of interchangeable blades. Use a fast drill speed, but take care not to force the blade.

Plug cutters remove a plug (core) of scrap wood which can then be glued into a hole in the work itself to conceal a deeply recessed screw head.

Hinge boring bits (*end mills*) are specialized tools for boring the large (35mm; 1½″) recesses needed to fit modern-style concealed cabinet hinges.

SPECIAL BITS FOR BRACES

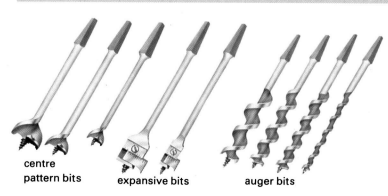

centre pattern bits
expansive bits
auger bits

Center pattern bits drill shallow holes cleanly and quickly. Sizes range from 9 to 38mm (3⁄8 to 1½″).

Expansive bits are similar to centre pattern bits, but have movable cutters with an adjusting screw which allows the cutting diameter to be changed. They are more expensive, but a small bit adjusts from 12–25mm (½–1″), a large one from 22–75mm (7⁄8–3″).

Auger bits are more accurate for deep holes. The central lead screw is surrounded by cutters which give a clean finish, and the shank has long spiral flutes that help to center the bit and channel waste out of the hole. There are various patterns, each with different designs of spiral and cutters. Sizes range from 6 to 38mm (1⁄4 to 1½″).

CHISELS AND CHISELING

Chisels are among the most versatile of all woodworking tools, and on some jobs – such as fitting a hinge or door lock – you can't do without one. Yet simple as they are, they need handling with skill and care for best results.

In general carpentry, chisels are mainly used for *paring* (trimming) excess wood from a piece of lumber. and for cutting *housings* (recesses) or *mortises* (enclosed holes) for joints and fittings. But chisels are also the main tools for carving wood, and in this area there are many special blade shapes for making particular kinds of cut.

Safety first

A sharp chisel can cause serious injury, so always follow these simple safety precautions before using one:
■ Make sure the work is clamped or held securely to keep it under control.
■ Keep your hands and fingers behind the cutting edge at all times.
■ Keep the chisel as sharp as possible – blunt chisels encourage you to apply too much force and increase the likelihood of something slipping.
■ Keep a blade guard on the chisel when it is not in use.

CUTTING A HOUSING

The term housing covers the slots, notches and recesses found in all areas of woodworking.

Housing joints are used in frames for furniture and built-in units, usually with *through housings* in which the wood is notched across its entire width. Although part of the notch can be made by cutting across the wood with a saw, you still need a chisel to remove the waste.

A chisel is even more important for cutting *stopped housings*, which range from the shallow recesses enclosing a hinge plate to the deeper slots used to support shelf boards or stair treads.

Cut the sides of a housing first (left). On shallow housings such as hinge recesses, you can do this with a trimming knife. Or press in the chisel (flat side outwards) to the correct depth right around the outline.

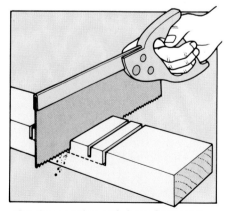

On deeper through housings, cut the sides with a backsaw. On wide housings, make a further series of saw cuts across the center of the waste.

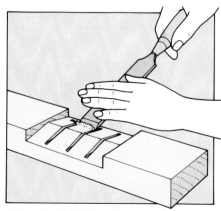

Use the chisel to chop out the waste. Don't attempt to trim to the bottom of the housing first time; take it in easy stages and leave some waste . . .

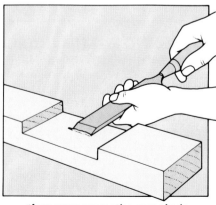

. . . then pare away the remainder using your fingers and palm to guide the blade. Again, cut in thin slices to stop the chisel digging into the grain.

CUTTING A MORTISE

Before cutting a mortise, mark it out accurately. It's much easier to finish the sides of the mortise squarely if you make it the same width as the chisel. But where this isn't possible, use a narrower chisel and trim the sides afterwards.

Proper *mortise chisels* have extra-strong blades and handles so that they can be struck with a mallet. But if, as is likely, you have to use an ordinary *chisel* with a mallet, don't give it anything other than light taps or you risk snapping the blade. Drill out the waste instead, and then use the chisel to square up the sides.

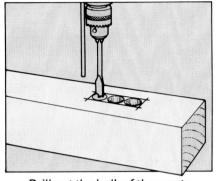

1 *Drill out the bulk of the waste by making a series of holes using a bit the width of the mortise. Gauge the depth with a stop, or tape the bit.*

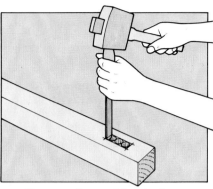

2 *Use a mallet to drive in the chisel at one end of the mortise with the bevel inwards; don't drive it too far, though, or the blade may jam.*

3 *Lever the chisel forward and work along the slot to remove the waste, starting with shallow cuts and then going progressively deeper . . .*

. . . until you reach the correct depth. At this point, reverse the blade and pare away the back of the mortise, ensuring your final cuts are square to the edge.

Trade tip
Gauging the depth

❛ Keep a check on how deep you're going by wrapping a piece of masking tape around the chisel blade. ❜

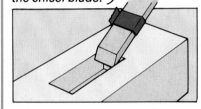

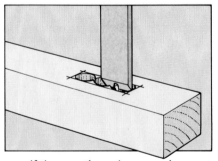

4 *If the mortise edges need trimming, use the widest bladed chisel possible to pare away thin slices. Take care to keep the sides parallel.*

TRIMMING WITH A CHISEL

Chisels can be used to trim and shape the ends of a piece of wood by paring across the grain. But before you start, make sure the wood is held firmly and put a piece of scrap wood underneath (thick plywood is ideal).

You shouldn't need to use a mallet. If the wood is difficult to cut, either you are trying to remove too thick a slice in one go, or the chisel needs sharpening.

For rounded cuts – concave or convex – use a gouge (a chisel with a curved blade) in a similar way.

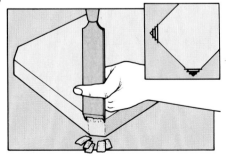

To cut a chamfer, *pare vertically in a series of thin slices. Use your weight to push the chisel through the wood, guiding the blade with your fingertips.*

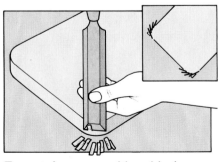

To round a corner *with a chisel, chamfer as much as you can. Then work round the rest in a series of small slices, starting on the edge and working towards the end.*

SHARPENING A CHISEL

Sharp chisels cut more accurately and take less effort, so it's worth keeping them in good condition.

A chisel blade is sharpened to a double angle. The first angle, called the *grinding bevel*, is produced on a grindstone or coarse oilstone. The second, *honing* angle is the actual cutting edge and is produced on a fine oilstone.

Chisels need honing fairly often to keep the cutting edge in trim, but grinding is normally only necessary where the edge has been accidentally chipped, or has thickened up due to frequent sharpening.

Trade tip

Checking the edge

❝ To test whether a chisel is sharp, try the edge against your fingernail. A properly honed blade won't slip. ❞

A new chisel may be sharpened to a grinding angle only, leaving you to hone the final edge before use. Old, blunt chisels may need to be reground first to restore them to use.

Honing the edge

Use a fine oilstone and clamp it firmly (preferably in its box) so that you can use both hands to guide the chisel. Wet the stone with a little oil (olive oil is ideal) to reduce friction. Then, keeping the chisel at the correct angle, rub it back and forth with light pressure.

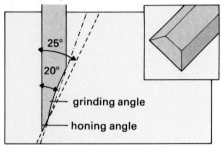

For paring work, the grinding angle should be 20° and the honing angle 25° . . .

Grinding the edge

Grinding can be done on a grindstone (electric or hand-powered), or by hand on the coarse side of an oilstone – which is much slower.

Grinding wheels can be dangerous, if you don't take proper precautions. Powered wheels should have an eyeshield to guard against the shower of sparks and abrasive particles which are thrown off. Drill and hand-powered wheels may not have these, in which case you must wear goggles or a face mask. Don't wear loose clothing in case this gets caught in the wheel.

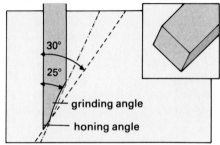

. . . but for mortising this may be too weak – increase the angles to 25° and 30° or 35°.

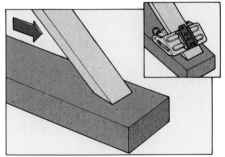

1 If you hone the blade by hand, take care not to rock it or the sharpening angle will be curved. A honing guide helps to keep the angle consistent.

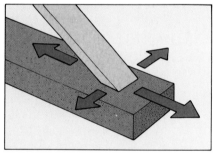

2 Move the chisel across the stone occasionally to stop it from wearing a hollow. When sharpening a narrow blade, use an area near the edge of the stone.

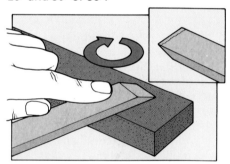

3 Honing produces a slight burr. Flatten the back of the chisel by rubbing it lightly over the stone, then remove the remaining burr on a piece of scrap wood.

Grind a chisel with the wheel revolving towards you and the blade on the rest at the correct angle. Work the blade from side to side to keep the wear even.

A grinding attachment (right) for an electric drill has special clamps to ensure that the blade is held at the right angle.

USING PLANES AND RASPS

Planes are the traditional tools for trimming, smoothing and shaping wood. Use one whenever you need to reduce a piece of wood by an amount which is too thin to cut with a saw, or you want to smooth a rough surface rapidly. Although powered sanders make light work of many finishing tasks, they are no substitute for a plane when it comes to jobs like hanging doors and scribing wood to fit uneven walls.

Modern technology has made the hand plane much easier to use. A plane is only efficient when really sharp, but sharpening aids and planes with replaceable blades mean there's no longer any excuse for blunt tools. And with the advent of power planes, most of the hard work has disappeared, too.

Other tools
It's also worth considering one of the many types of Surform or wood rasp. These don't need sharpening, and cope with a much wider range of materials – although the surface they leave often lacks the smoothness of a planed one.

There are other planes designed for cutting rabbets, grooves and moldings, but these are expensive, specialized tools and only worth buying if you do woodwork on a regular basis. A power router will do many of the same jobs more cheaply and simply.

Trade tip

The main planes
❢ If you only buy one tool for general-purpose work, choose a smoothing plane with a sole about 225–250mm (9–10") long and a blade about 50mm (2") wide. This will cope with a wide range of work on wood and most manmade boards. If you don't already possess the tools for sharpening planes, a replaceable blade model is a sensible buy.

A worthwhile addition to even a basic toolkit is a block plane, for trimming end grain and plastic laminates. ❢

WHAT TO USE WHERE
Use a smoothing plane for surfacing pieces of wood and a block plane for fine trimming or work on end grain. If you have a longer jointer plane, use it for smoothing work on large pieces as it helps to keep the surface flat. Fix the wood securely.

Before starting, take a few seconds to check the plane and make sure it is set properly (see page 222). Then inspect the wood.

Don't plane secondhand wood, which may contain nails that will wreck the blade. On old painted wood, strip the surface first or use a Surform planer instead.

Check which way the grain runs, as this will avoid problems when you start to plane. Wherever possible, plane with the grain – not against it, which may cause the blade to dig in. Where the grain runs in different directions ('curly grain'), hold the plane at a slight angle to stop it digging in.

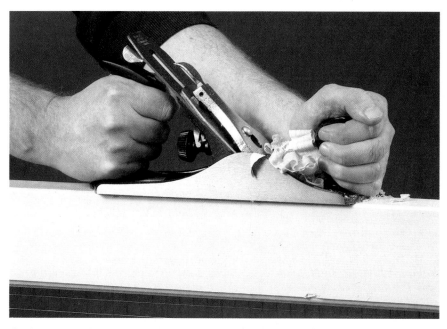

At the start of the cut, *apply pressure to the front of the plane. Aim to run right along the wood with even pressure, easing the weight onto the back of the plane as you reach the end so that it runs off smoothly.*

On end grain, *avoid splintering the corners by planing from one side and then the other towards the middle. Alternatively, plane off the vulnerable corner first.*

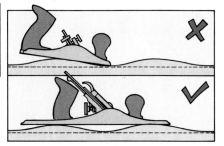

On large boards, *use the longest plane available. A short one tends to ride up and down the hollows instead of knocking down any high spots first.*

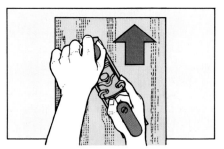

On wide boards, *end grain or 'curly grain', it may be easier to hold the plane at a slight angle so the blade slices across the wood instead of digging in.*

USING A POWER PLANE

Power planes demand very little effort and can be used for almost anything you would tackle with a hand tool, including rabbeting. The drawbacks are that they are larger than hand planes – making them difficult to use where space is re-stricted – and they produce a lot of small shavings.

Some models can be mounted upside down in a workbench so that you pass the wood over the plane. This makes things much easier when trimming the surface of strips of wood, but check that your power plane is designed to be operated in this way and be sure to take proper safety precautions.

 Mind the cutters
It's essential to take some simple precautions: the spinning cutters will rapidly slice through anything they touch and they go on revolving for some time after you switch off.

Always unplug the plane before adjusting it, and when the tool is not in use. Some models have an automatic guard over the cutters; on those which do not, take care not to touch the cutters or allow them to contact anything until they have stopped revolving.

When working with the plane mounted upside down, always feed the wood through with a push stick.

Start the plane and let it reach full speed before allowing the cutters to touch the wood. Push the wood forward with light pressure to avoid gouging.

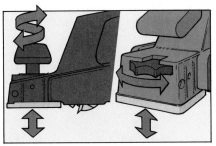

Set the depth of cut required. Some models have a separate adjuster – on others you slacken the front knob and move the front of the sole plate up or down.

For chamfering the edge of a board, some models have a guide groove. Do not hold the body with your fingers underneath so that you risk contacting the cutters.

USING A SURFORM OR RASP

Surform planes/files come in a range of sizes and shapes, allowing them to cope with most of the jobs you might otherwise tackle with a plane. They can also be used on a variety of materials – not just wood – which makes them ideal for use on old painted wood containing nails or filler (both of which could dam-age a plane).

The blades on these tools are designed to be replaced as soon as they become blunt. Some models accept different blades, according to the material being planed.

In general, you use a Surform exactly as you would a plane, ex-cept that the direction of the grain is not as critical. A Surform can even be used to plane across the grain, but the cutting action depends on how you angle the tool relative to the direction of the cut. Similarly, you can use a rasp in any direction.

Use a long Surform plane for jobs like leveling floorboards and planing old wood.

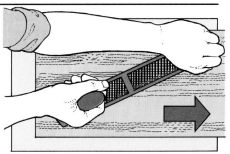

The cutting action depends on how you angle the tool relative to the direction of cut.

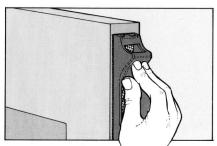

A Surform block plane can be used one-handed for jobs like easing a sticking door or window.

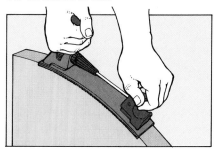

Flexible rasps can be adjusted so that they produce an evenly curved surface.

SHARPENING AND SETTING

Easy, efficient cutting depends on the plane having a sharp blade which is set correctly. On replaceable blade planes, you simply unscrew or unclip the blade and slot in a new one; traditional plane blades need sharpening on an oilstone.

Sharpening blades

Sharpening a plane blade is very similar to sharpening a chisel (see instructions on page 219). If the blade has a separate *cap iron* screwed to it, you should remove this before you sharpen the chisel.

Rub the blade on a fine oilstone moistened with a light machine oil, keeping the angle to a more or less constant 30°; a *honing guide* makes this part of the job much easier. Then, if you're planing a lot of wide boards, use the old carpenter's trick of rounding off the corners very slightly to stop them digging in (you can also get replacement blades made this way). Complete the sharpening process by rubbing the back of the blade on the stone to keep it flat and remove any burr.

Have the blade reground to an angle of 35° whenever the bevel produced by sharpening becomes larger than about 1.5mm (¹⁄₁₆″), or if the edge of the blade becomes nicked too deeply to remove on the oilstone. Re-sharpen as above.

Setting the cap iron

A cap iron is designed to curl away the shavings as they are cut, so if fitted it must be set in the right position relative to the blade. The actual distance varies from plane to plane, and also depends on what you are doing, but is normally in the range of 0.5–1.5mm (¹⁄₆₄–¹⁄₁₆″).

Setting the blade

Sight down the sole to check the position of the blade – it should be just visible as a very thin line. Use the adjusting screw to advance or retract the blade as necessary.

If one side is higher than the other use the sideways adjusting lever to level it.

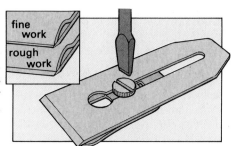

If a cap iron is fitted it is held by a retaining screw which fits into a slot. This is used to alter the position of the cap iron depending on the work you are doing.

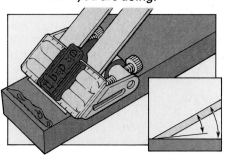

The blade should be ground to an angle of 35° and then honed on an oilstone to 30°. Use a honing guide to ensure the sharpening angle is correct.

GENERAL PURPOSE PLANES

Modern planes are almost always metal with some plastic parts, although old planes had wooden or composite bodies.

Block planes are for one or two-handed use on end grain and general trimming. They have a plain blade with no cap iron, set at a low angle of about 20° to the base. A special version made for trimming plastics has the blade set at 12°.

Jointer planes are for smoothing large boards, mainly along the grain; the blades are fitted with separate cap irons. There are several types divided in order of size: *smoothing* planes range from 200-250mm (8-10″), *jack* planes range from 350-375mm (14-15″), and *fore or try* planes from from 450-550mm (18-22″). Special versions are also made with a *corrugated base* for use on resinous wood.

Rabbet planes are made in various sizes and have cutters which extend the full width of the body so they can be used for planing a rabbet into the ege of a piece of wood. Some models incorporate an optional guide fence to keep them parallel to the work.

Replaceable blade planes are made in both jointer plane and block plane versions. Short, disposable blades are held in the body by a special retaining clamp; when they become blunt, simply undo the clamp and replace the whole blade. The block plane version has an additional advantage in that the blade can be fitted at the front, enabling you to plane right into corners. The jointer plane version can be fitted with a guide fence for cutting rabbets.

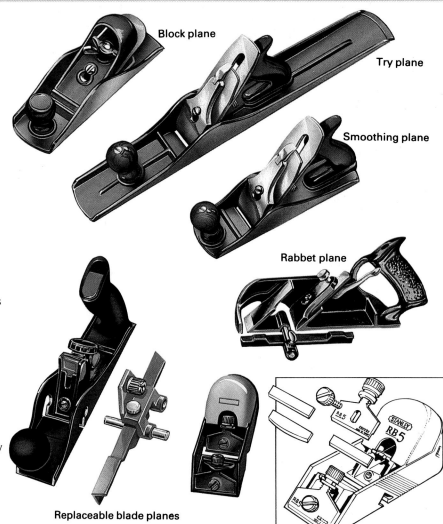

Replaceable blade planes

JOINT SYSTEMS FOR BOARDS AND FRAMES

There are many ways to join two boards or two pieces of wood without having to cut joints into them. All the hardware shown here is capable of making a strong joint and needs no more than a few holes drilled. Many are available for DIY use while some are widely employed in manufactured self-assembly furniture.

Before choosing any joint system, think about:

■ Appearance. Most systems are visible from one side or the other; often this doesn't matter, but sometimes it is critical.

■ Neatness. Some systems project inside the furniture. This is important where it obstructs the fitting of drawers or restricts the amount of storage space.

■ Ease of use. A few joints require the use of special drills or other assembly tools.

■ Price. However cheap an individual fixture may be, a furnishing system might use dozens of them.

■ Security. Is the joint ever likely to need dismantling? If so, choose a knock-down fitting. Where a joint is intended to be permanent, a continuous glue line (possibly reinforced by screws) is stronger than knock-down fittings.

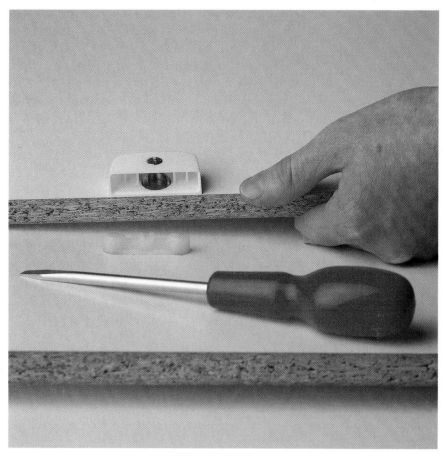

Joint fittings *come in many varieties and are designed to give speedy, reliable joints – especially with man-made boards.*

PLASTIC BLOCK JOINTS

Plastic block joints are inexpensive fixtures which are common for both DIY use and on bought furniture. They are visible on the inside of the casing and because they project up to 20mm (¾") are unsuitable for some applications, such as when drawers are to be fitted. They come in white, brown and beige; choose the colour to suit the material.

One piece blocks have two sets of holes drilled at right angles. They are fixed with screws and are designed for joints which do not need to be undone.

Two piece blocks come in pairs. One part is screwed to each side of the joint and a locking bolt is used to draw them together; use them where the assembly may need to be dismantled. The fitting is quite large but a miniature version is available.

Miniature blocks are plastic anchors which screw into a hole drilled in one part. A screw is then inserted to join the other part.

one piece joint block

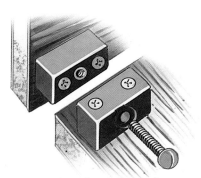

two piece joint block

miniature joint block

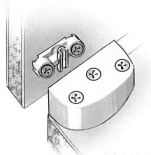

two piece joint block

CAM FITTINGS

Cam fittings are a form of knockdown joint which come in two parts that can be locked together or unlocked by twisting one part of the fitting. As this makes assembly a matter of seconds they are popular on 'flat pack' self-assembly furniture, where a large variety of different fittings in plastic or metal are used.

A few types are also available for DIY use. They have no advantage for furniture which does not need to be dismantled, and disadvantages include a fairly high cost, plus the need for specialised tools to make holes to fit them into the cabinet parts.

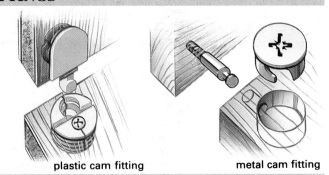

plastic cam fitting   metal cam fitting

SCREW FITTINGS

Use screws for a cheap, permanent fixing. For maximum strength, the joint can be glued as well. Screws do not project on the inside of the cabinet, and by using plastic covers, the heads can be concealed fairly well.

Some screws are designed with special threads for better grip in man-made boards. Many have crosshead slots and can be power driven. Plastic covers can be fitted into the cross of a screw; two piece covers fit on slotted screws. **Connector screws** for man-made boards are much larger in diameter and have a coarse thread which bites into the sides of a pre-drilled hole. The head sinks flush and is unobtrusive, but can be fitted with a plastic cap. The hole must be accurately drilled with the aid of a simple jig and depth stop

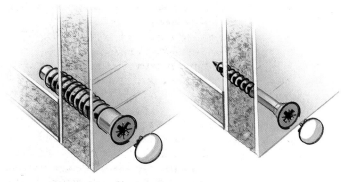

chipboard connector   screw for manmade board

METAL BRACKETS

Metal brackets are cheap fixtures for use with screws. Their appearance means that they are best used where they will not be on show. As well as making corner joints they are good for joining worktops to frames or casings.
Corner brackets join and strengthen the corners of a cabinet and have a central hole which can be used for hanging it. There are several types, commonly made from plated steel. *Angle plates* are flat and are fixed to the back edge. *Corner plates* have turned-over flanges for fixing to the inner faces of the cabinet. Plastic versions are available with clip-on covers to conceal the fixing.
Right angle brackets made of mild steel or plated steel come in various lengths. *Shrinkage plates* are similar but have slotted screwholes designed to allow for a small amount of shrinkage and expansion in the wood.
Interlocking plates are mainly for frame constructions. They come in two halves which are screwed to both parts and then pressed together to make a firm joint.

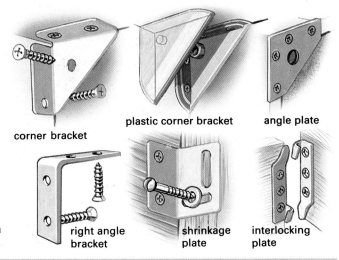

corner bracket   plastic corner bracket   angle plate

right angle bracket   shrinkage plate   interlocking plate

BOLT FITTINGS

Bolts are mainly used for frame construction. Unlike screws, they are designed for joints which have to be dismantled.
Hanger bolts have one end with a machine screw thread, and one end with a woodscrew which can be screwed into the wood after locking two nuts together on the thread. The joint is then made with a *wing nut* or an ordinary nut.
Tee nuts are hammered or pressed into the surface over a predrilled hole so a bolt can be screwed into it.
Screws and cross dowels are mainly for frames. The cross dowel is inserted into a hole in one part, and a screw fitted through the other part screws into it. The screws have socket (Allen) heads and decorative collars are fitted to trim the holes.
Socket head nuts can be used with the above system in conjunction with plain threaded rods (*studding*).
Cabinet connecting screws are used to link two boards back to back – for joining cabinets through their sides.
Countertop connectors (panel connectors) are used to join two panels end to end, particularly countertops.

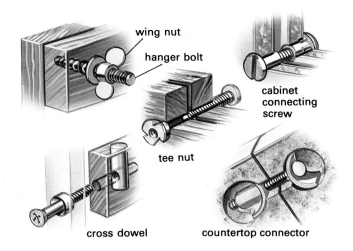

wing nut   hanger bolt   cabinet connecting screw

tee nut

cross dowel   countertop connector

FIXING WOOD WITH NAILS

It's wrong to think of nails as being a 'second-best' way to fix things together. Properly used, they make a quick, strong and permanent joint – in fact, the loadbearing timber-work of the average house is put together using nothing else. Nails also find many applications in quality furniture, and for lots of DIY jobs there is no sensible substitute.

For any job you need to know:
■ Which type of nail to use (you may also have to think about its finish, or what it's made of).
■ What size of nail to use.
■ What quantity to buy.

Types of nails

The chart on page 227 shows all the main types of nail and lists their uses. Each different shape is designed to drive easily and grips well in the materials it is intended for.

Most nails are made from steel wire or stamped out of sheet steel. As a result, they bend quite easily and rust in damp conditions. Some types have a rust-resistant galvanized (zinc) coating, and a few have special or decorative finishes.

Sizes

Nails are made in a range of sizes to cope with different thicknesses of materials. When buying, you only need to specify the length in millimeters or inches; unlike screws, a nail's thickness is fixed by its length.

Drive nails squarely (right) using the full length of the hammer.

BUYING NAILS

Nails are sold in several ways, depending on their type, where you shop, and on whether you want a large or small quantity:
Pre-packs are nails sold in small boxes, tubes or bubble packs. They are a convenient way to buy small nails, and many of the more specialised types are only sold in this form. However, buying larger nails in pre-packs can be expensive unless you only need a few. The packs may be made up by weight (30, 40 or 50gm – 1⅛, 1½ or 1¾oz), or sometimes by number.
Loose Larger nails are commonly sold loose by hardware stores,

lumberyards and some other suppliers. Loose nails are usually bought by the pound (ie by weight). They are normally described in penny sizes (with the letter 'd' after them).

If you want to buy less than a full pound of nails (but more than you are likely to get in a pre-pack), many suppliers will allow you to buy smaller quantities of smaller size nails.
Bulk packs are some stores' equivalent of buying nails loose. Standard quantities (often in ¼lb, 1lb or 4lb) of large nails can be good value.

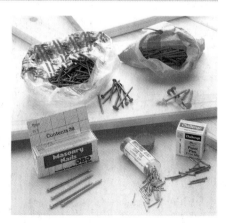

Large nails are usually sold loose, but small or specialised nails come in pre-packs.

NAILING WOOD

Successful nailing is a matter of applying the right basic techniques. shown here, and using the correct nails (see chart opposite).

Where there are special nails for the materials you are fixing, use them. If there is a choice, as in general woodwork, there are some basic rules to follow:

■ Don't use nails unless the joint is designed to be permanent.

■ Where the appearance doesn't matter, large heads give a better grip. If you don't want the nails to show, use ones with heads which can be driven flush.

■ Where the nail may be pulled out or the material is weak, ring shank nails grip better than ordinary ones.

Trade tip

Get the right length

6 When the two things you are joining are nearly the same thickness, choose a nail that will go right through the thinner one, and half to three-quarters through the other.

When joining something thin to something thicker, always nail through the thinner material. The length of the nail should be 2½ to 3 times the thickness of the thinner material.

When driving nails into the end grain of solid wood or boards, use the longer measurements in both cases. 9

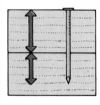

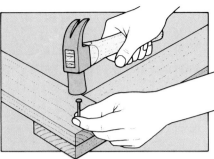

1 To start a nail, grip it firmly and give it a few light, short taps with the hammer until it grips the wood by itself. Make sure it goes in straight.

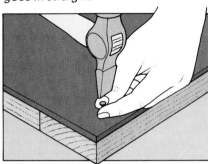

2 A cross peen hammer's wedge shaped head makes it easier to start small nails which are so short that there's a risk of hitting your fingers.

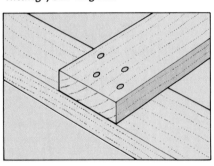

4 Where you are securing a joint with several nails, stagger them along the grain. This reduces splitting and makes a stronger joint.

Trade tip

Holding small nails

6 A good way to start small nails is to push them through a piece of corrugated cardboard. Rip the card away before you drive them fully home. 9

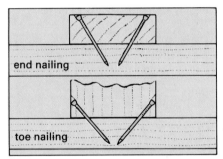

3 Drive in oval and rectangular nails so the longest dimension runs along the grain of the wood. This helps to avoid splits and makes a stronger joint.

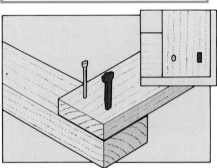

end nailing

toe nailing

5 For extra strength, drive the nails at an angle as shown. End nailing and toe nailing both prevent nails from coming loose or being pulled out easily.

■PROBLEM SOLVER

Avoiding splits and dents

Accidental splits can be minimized by using these methods:

■ Blunt the nail by tapping the point with a hammer. It then punches its way through the wood instead of wedging it apart.

■ Start the hole with a bradawl and then use a hammer.

■ When nailing close to the end, leave the wood overlength and saw it off after nailing.

To avoid dents in the surface, stop a fraction short and use a punch to drive the nail the rest of the way home.

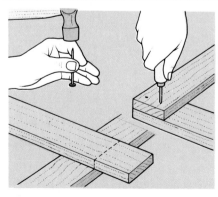

To prevent splits, blunt the nail or start the hole with a bradawl. You may be able to avoid nailing near the end of the wood by leaving surplus to cut off later.

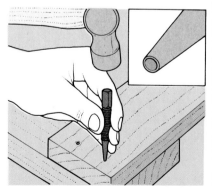

Drive the nail fully home using a nail punch to avoid dents. To conceal the head, punch it right below the surface and cover the hole with filler.

TYPES OF NAILS

NAILS FOR GENERAL WOODWORKING

TYPE	USES	SIZES
Common round nail	 rough carpentary work, eg making wall and roof frames; shuttering concrete	25-150mm (1-6")
Box nail	 finished carpentry, eg door frames; thin, dry wood, especially if nailed close to the edge, eg boxes	30-100mm (1¼-4")
Finishing nail	 carpentry; cabinetry or paneling; secret nailing of tongue and groove boards	25-150mm (1-6")
Brad	 similar to finishing nail; also used for furniture making; glued joints; fixing moldings	12-75mm (½-3")
Molding pin (veneer pin)	 similar to brad, but used for finer work (again, see also finishing nail)	12-25mm (½-1")
Hardboard nail	 specially made for fixing hardboard or plywood panels to frames (ie furring or studs)	12-25mm (½-1")
Sheathing and Drywall nail	 fixing man-made boards. Annular threads give additional holding power	19-75mm (¾-3")
Cut clasp nail	 rough carpentry; also for fixing to blockwork walls. Available with decorative heads	38-100mm (1½-4")
Cut flooring nail	 especially used for fixing floorboards to joists because they are unlikely to split the wood	50-65mm (2-2½")

NAILS FOR SPECIAL PURPOSES

TYPE	USES	SIZES
Clout nail	 fixing roofing felt, building paper, slates. Not much penetration, but good grip	12-75mm (1½-3")
Dry wall nail	 fixing plasterboard and insulation board to frames. Available plain or ribbed to prevent popping out	38mm (1½")
Masonry nail (furring stud)	 fixing furring (studs) to brickwork and concrete floors and walls	12-100mm (½-4")
Corrugated staple	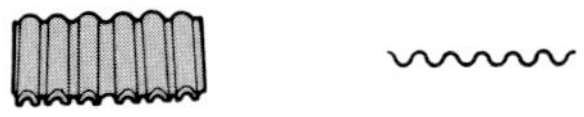 making corner joints in wooden frameworks; used to connect 'flats' (thin sheets of wood)	12-25mm (½-1") deep, widths vary
Galvanized roof nail (drive screw)	 fixing corrugated sheet roofing to rafters. Have special threads to make sure of a good grip	65-100mm (2½-4")
Wire slate nail	 fixing slates to wooden roof framework	32-65mm (1¼-2½")
Glazing sprig	 fixing glass to window frames. Lie flush so that they can be painted and concealed	12 or 16mm (½ or ⅝")
Netting staple	 specially designed for fixing fence wires or netting to wooden posts	12-50mm (½-2")
Insulated staple	 fixing electric cables or telephone connection wiring to woodwork (eg baseboards)	12-25mm (½-1")
Escutcheon pin	 fixing metal fixtures to furniture and used generally in fine carpentry work	16-19mm (⅝-¾")
Tack	 fixing webbing or fabric to frames (ie underlying upholstery framework); laying carpet	6-25mm (¼-1")
Gimp pin	 like fine tacks, for fixing special trims like gimp and braid	9-25mm (⅜-1")
Upholstery tack (chair nail)	 used as decorative trimming in upholstery. Available in chrome, brass or black wrought-iron finish	12-19mm (½-¾")
Wire staple	use with a special, custom-made gun for fixing sheet materials and fabric	6-15mm (¼-⁹⁄₁₆")
Nailplate (lumber connector)	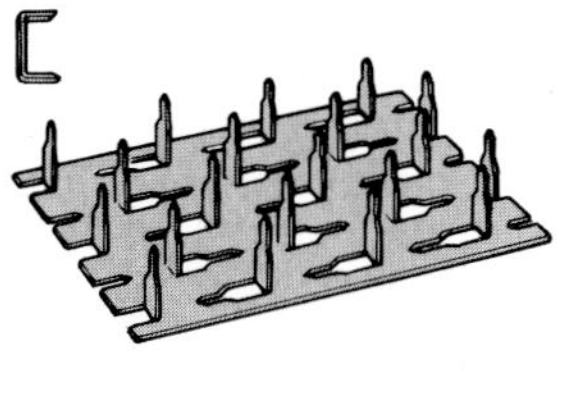 multi-grip fastening to use with roof trusses and other heavy frames requiring strong, firm hold	various rectangular sizes

Note: Nails and other fasteners may be given different names in different geographical areas.

TOOLS FOR NAILING

HAMMERS

Woodworking hammers are divided into two main types, and both come in various weights.

Claw hammers have a head with one round face for driving nails and a claw for pulling them out. They are for general use in carpentry, especially heavy work. The weight ranges from 450gm (16oz) to 675gm (24oz); a 450gm (16oz) hammer is a good general purpose tool. Handles are commonly wood, but may be metal or fiberglass for extra durability.

Tack hammers for carpet laying and upholstery are like miniature claw hammers, weighing about 175gm (6oz); the heads are often magnetised which makes it much easier to drive in very small nails.

Cross peen hammers (also called *Warrington* hammers) have a head with one round face for driving nails and a tapered wedge face which makes it easier to start them. They are lighter than claw hammers, ranging from 110gm (4oz) to 450gm (16oz) and are mainly used for furniture making and light hammering. Smaller cross peen hammers weighing 110gm (4oz) or less are often called *Pin hammers* and are used for very light work.

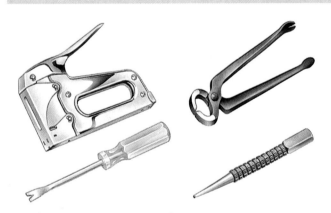

It's well worth buying a good quality hammer. Cheap ones may be prone to various faults including loose heads, poorly hardened striking faces, badly formed claws and weak handles. All of these can affect the hammer's safety as well as its comfort in use.

OTHER NAILING TOOLS

Staple guns are an alternative to using a hammer and nails or tacks, if you have to fix a lot of sheet material. They can be loaded with staples of varying lengths to suit the job.

Pincers are the best tool for removing nails on which a claw hammer cannot get a grip, but are not suitable for very large nails. Some types have a tack lifter blade built into the handle.

Tack lifters are for removing small nails with large heads – particularly tacks. They are not suitable for heavy work and cannot grip nails with small heads.

Nail punches are used with nails which are made for driving in flush or below the surface, such as finishing nails. There are various sizes given in terms of tip widths. The hollow pointed type is best for small nails; it prevents the tip slipping off the head.

PROBLEM SOLVER

Removing nails
Always remove bent or wrongly angled nails rather than trying to correct them. Use a claw hammer or pincers, and protect the wood from damage with a scrap of plywood or thick pad of cardboard. For tacks and similar nails, use a tack lifter.

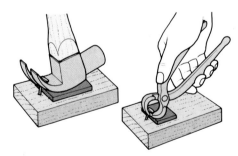

Extract nails with a claw hammer, pincers or a tack lifter. Protect the wood with scrap wood or card.

Loose hammer heads
Loose heads on hammers with wooden handles should be fixed as soon as possible. You can make a temporary repair with a metal wedge, but it's safer to buy a replacement handle of the same size – plus some metal wedges to secure it – from a specialist tool shop.

Remove the old handle by drilling out enough of the wood inside the head to loosen it.

To fit the new handle, make two or three saw cuts in the end and push on the head. Saw off any protruding waste, then drive the wedges into the cuts.

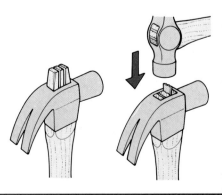

Drive in metal wedges (right) to secure a new hammer handle.

MAKING JOINTS WITH SCREWS

A properly made screwed joint looks neat and is unlikely to fail. Faults usually arise because the screws are the wrong size or type (see overleaf) or have not been fitted correctly.

Screw sizes

Screws come in various lengths, given in millimeters or inches, and in a range of thicknesses which are given gauge numbers from 0 to 24. The higher the number, the thicker the screw. No.4 to No.12 are the most common. Other countries use metric measurements and this is likely to become the case here.

Materials

Steel screws are for general purposes. They are cheap and fairly strong, but rust rapidly outdoors or in damp air, and react with some hardwoods, like oak, causing stains.
Brass screws are decorative and rust resistant, but relatively weak.
Stainless steel screws are less commonly available. They are strong and almost completely rust-proof.
Aluminum screws are less common. They are rust resistant, but weak.
Bright zinc coating is a pale silver color, and is widely used for particleboard screws. The plating resists rust unless damaged.
Black iron screws are painted (japanned) or chemically blacked to make them rust resistant. If damaged they rust easily. Their main use is outdoors and for black iron fittings.
Chrome screws have a shiny plating and resist tarnishing, although the plating may eventually fail. Often used in bathrooms.

SCREW HEAD AND SLOT SHAPES

There are three main shapes:
Countersunk heads sink flush into a recess in the wood or fitting. A deeply recessed head can be concealed with filler.
Roundhead screws project from the surface – mainly for things too thin to countersink.
Raised head screws have a shallow dome with a countersink below, mainly used for putting metal in place.

All head shapes can have different shapes of slot:
Slotted heads vary widely in size with screw gauge so need a wide range of screwdrivers.
Cross head screws only need four screwdrivers to fit all sizes, and tolerate slight misalignment when driving, but are hard to clean if they get clogged with paint. There are three different patterns. *Pozidriv* and *Supadriv* have four small points between the arms of the cross and use the same screwdriver. *Phillips* screws (mainly used on machines) don't have the extra points and need a different screwdriver.

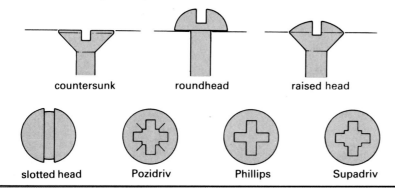

countersunk   roundhead   raised head

slotted head   Pozidriv   Phillips   Supadriv

Buying screws

DIY stores sell packs of various sizes. You can also buy screws loose in multiples of ten from hardware stores, or in boxes of 500 or 200 (popular sizes), 100 or 50 (less popular sizes). Large packs are often the most economical way to buy common sizes – if there are some left over, they can be used for another job. Small pre-packs are usually the most expensive.

Trade tip

Get what you want

❛ To make sure you're given exactly what you want when buying, remember to check all these points:
Quantity
Length
Gauge
Head pattern
Material
Type
For example:
Twenty 1½" No.8 slotted head countersunk brass woodscrews. ❜

TYPES OF SCREWS

WOODSCREWS

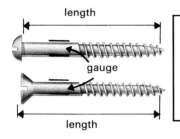

COMMON SIZES				
No.4 (2.7mm)	No.6 (3.5mm)	No.8 (4.2mm)	No.10 (4.9mm)	No.12 (5.6mm)
12mm (½")	12mm (½")	19mm (¾")	25mm (1")	50mm (2")
16mm (⅝")	16mm (⅝")	25mm (1")	32mm (1¼")	63mm (2½")
19mm (¾")	19mm (¾")	32mm (1¼")	38mm (1½")	75mm (3")
	25mm (1")	38mm (1½")	50mm (2")	
	32mm (1¼")	50mm (2")	63mm (2½")	
	38mm (1½")	63mm (2½")	75mm (3")	

Woodscrews have a long, tapering tip and are threaded for about two-thirds of their length. The remaining portion under the head is a plain, unthreaded *shank*. The thread is a single spiral which gets a good grip in the grain of most lumber and some boards, but not always in particleboard. Woodscrews come in many materials and sizes.

PARTICLEBOARD SCREWS

COMMON SIZES				
No.4 (2.7mm)	No.6 (3.5mm)	No.8 (4.2mm)	No.10 (4.9mm)	No.12 (5.6mm)
9mm (⅜")	12mm (½")	19mm (¾")	25mm (1")	50mm (2")
12mm (½")	16mm (⅝")	25mm (1")	32mm (1¼")	63mm (2½")
16mm (⅝")	19mm (¾")	32mm (1¼")	38mm (1½")	50mm (2")
19mm (¾")	25mm (1")	38mm (1½")	50mm (2")	
	32mm (1¼")	50mm (2")	63mm (2½")	
	38mm (1½")	63mm (2½")	75mm (3")	

Particleboard screws are mainly for joining things to particleboard, but can also be used in solid wood, where they help to get a better grip if you have to fix into the end grain. They do not taper as much as woodscrews, the thread is cut deeper and runs the full length of the screw. Particleboard screws come in a wide range of sizes and are usually made of zinc-coated or ordinary steel.

SPECIAL PURPOSE SCREWS

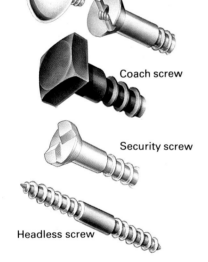

Mirror screws with head covers

Coach screw

Security screw

Headless screw

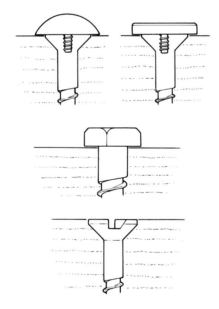

Mirror screws are countersunk woodscrews with a threaded hole in the centre of the head. They have screw-on decorative covers, which hide the head after the screws have been inserted.

Coach screws are like very large woodscrews with a square head designed to be driven with a wrench. They are for heavy constructions – like timber frames and garden furniture – and are sold by diameter, rather than gauge number. Common sizes range from 6mm (¼") to 12mm (½") and lengths up to 150mm (6"). Made of steel, which may be galvanized.

Security screws have a 'one-way' slot in the head so they can be done up but not removed. Ordinary screws can be made into security screws by filing the slots or burring them after insertion.

Headless screws are for joining two pieces of wood invisibly – eg fixing wood knobs. They have a thread at each end so they screw into both parts together.

SCREW ACCESSORIES

Inset screw cup

Screw cup washer

Screw covers

Screw cap

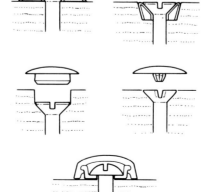

Screw cups give a decorative finish and help the screw grip better without damaging the wood. They are only used with countersunk and raised head screws. There are two sorts: *cup washers* (surface screw cups), normally in brass or chrome, and *insert screw cups*, normally in brass, which plug into a recess in the wood.

Screw caps, made of white or brown plastic, plug into the slot of a crosshead screw or a recess drilled into the wood over the head.

Screw covers, made of white or brown plastic, are in two parts. One goes under the head of a screw and the other clips over it to hide the head.

MAKING SCREW HOLES

Only one size of hole in a given material allows any particular size of screw to turn easily and get the best grip from its threads. This hole is called a *pilot hole*, and should be slightly shorter than the screw.

Woodscrews have an unthreaded shank which must be free to turn easily, so this part must have a wider *clearance hole*. If it doesn't, the screw will be hard to drive and you risk damaging it. Some screws may not have a plain shank, but still need a clearance hole in the part you are fixing so it will be pulled up tight. The chart on the right shows what hole sizes to drill.

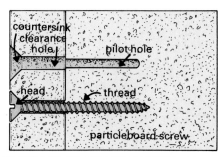

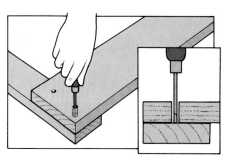

SCREW AND DRILL SIZES

Screw gauge	Clearance	Pilot (softwood)		Pilot (board/hardwood)	
		Woodscrew	Particleboard	Woodscrew	Particleboard
No 4 (2.7mm)	3mm (⅛")	bradawl	1mm (³⁄₆₄")	1.5mm (¹⁄₁₆")	2mm (¹⁄₁₆")
No 6 (3.5mm)	4mm (⁵⁄₃₂")	1.5mm (¹⁄₁₆")	1.5mm (¹⁄₁₆")	2mm (¹⁄₁₆")	2.5mm (³⁄₃₂")
No 8 (4.2mm)	4.5mm (³⁄₁₆")	2mm (¹⁄₁₆")	2mm (¹⁄₁₆")	2.5mm (³⁄₃₂")	3mm (⅛")
No 10 (4.9mm)	5mm (⁷⁄₃₂")	2mm (¹⁄₁₆")	2.5mm (³⁄₃₂")	2.5mm (⅛")	3mm (⅛")
No 12 (5.6mm)	6mm (¼")	2.5mm (³⁄₃₂")	2.5mm (³⁄₃₂")	3mm (⅛")	3.5mm (⅛")

DRILLING AND FIXING

The holes drilled in each part must align and must be the right depth.

■ If you are fixing a pre-drilled fitting, mark the position of the screw holes using a bradawl. Then drill a pilot hole in the thing you are fixing it to, and open out to a clearance size if necessary.

■ If the part you are fixing is not pre-drilled, start by drilling clearance holes in it so you can mark through them, or clamp the parts together and drill the pilot holes through both. Enlarge the holes in the first part to clearance size.

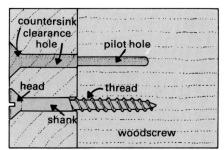

1 *Mark the holes with a bradawl – this stops the drill bit wandering off line. With small screws in softwood, a bradawl hole is all you need.*

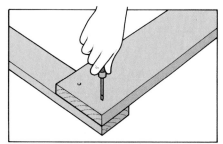

2 *If you are fitting something which is not predrilled, either drill clearance holes first and mark through them on to the other part so you can drill it...*

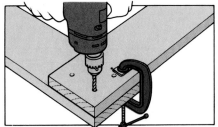

...or clamp the two together and drill pilot holes followed by clearance holes. This ensures that the screws align perfectly through both parts.

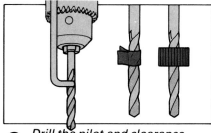

3 *Drill the pilot and clearance holes with the right sized bit. Use a depth stop or put tape on the bit so you stop just short of the length of the screw.*

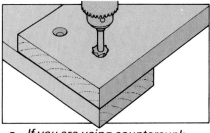

4 *If you are using countersunk screws, finish off with a countersunk bit to the size of the head. Don't let the bit 'chatter' causing a ragged hole.*

Trade tip

Trouble-free fixing

❛ ■ If you are fixing two pieces of wood together, use a screw twice as long as the thickness of the first piece of wood.

■ If you are fitting something very thick, avoid using over-long screws by 'counterboring' part of the clearance hole. Use a drill bit just larger than the head of the screw.

■ Don't put screws near the edge of a piece of wood – it may split. If you have to screw into end grain,

use particleboard screws.
■ If you are fitting lots of screws in a line, 'stagger' them to avoid splitting the wood.
■ Make screws easier to drive and remove by rubbing them on a candle to lubricate the threads.
■ To avoid breaking a brass screw, drive a steel screw in first to open out the hole.
■ Don't change bits unnecessarily – it's less work and less likely to cause mistakes. Do all the pilot holes, then the clearance holes, then the countersinking. ❜

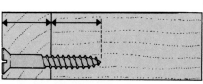

Pick the right length of screw.

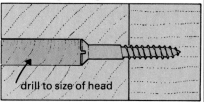

drill to size of head

Counterbore thick pieces of wood.

TOOLS FOR MAKING SCREW JOINTS

BRADAWL

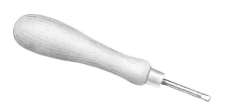

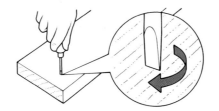

A bradawl has a slim, short blade like a screwdriver, sharpened to a knife edge. It is used for starting small screws in softwood or marking the hole before drilling. Hold it so the blade crosses the grain of the wood, then press and twist it into the surface.

DRILL BITS

Push drill bit

Twist drill set

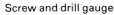

Screw and drill gauge

Twist drills fit an electric or hand drill. A typical 10-piece set contains drills from 1.5-6.5mm or 1/16-1/4" and should cope with all normal screws. They are made in High Speed Steel (HSS) for use in wood or metal, or carbon steel which is for wood only and blunts easily. Blunt drills cut badly and overheat, causing even more blunting. Drill sharpeners are available, but few people bother for small, cheap bits.
Screw and drill gauges help you pick the drill size to match the screw.
Push drill bits fit a spiral ratchet screwdriver for small holes and rough work in softwood. The pointed cutter twists its way gradually into the wood.

COUNTERSINKS

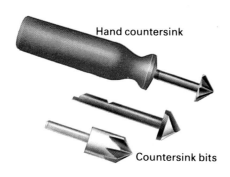

Hand countersink

Countersink bits

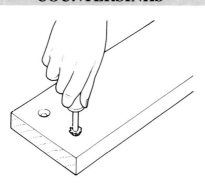

Countersink bits for drills are made in High Speed Steel for metal as well as wood, or in carbon steel, for wood only. It's worth having an HSS one for recutting recesses in metal fittings.

Countersinking with a drill is the least work, but using another tool saves swapping bits. Countersink bits are also made for push drills, while **hand countersinks** have a bit with a stubby handle which you twist back and forth. Both are only suitable for wood.

SCREWDRIVERS

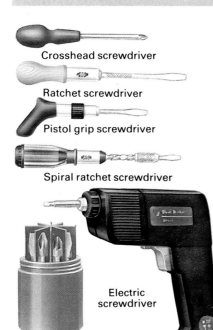

Crosshead screwdriver

Ratchet screwdriver

Pistol grip screwdriver

Spiral ratchet screwdriver

Electric screwdriver

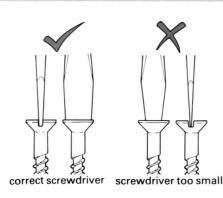

correct screwdriver   screwdriver too small

 Pozidriv screwdriver   Phillips screwdriver

Flat blade screwdrivers for slotted head screws come in many sizes and must fit the screw head accurately.
Crosshead screwdriver sizes vary less. A No.2 Pozidriv driver fits most woodworking screws but not Phillips screws (Phillips drivers work with Pozidriv but don't fit so well).

Both kinds may have rigid plastic or wooden handles. You can also get a range of 'easy action' screwdrivers.
Ratchet screwdrivers have a 'one-way' action which drives or undoes without changing grip or locks rigidly. Some have interchangeable bits. 'Pistol grip' handles apply more pressure.
Spiral ratchet screwdrivers have a push action handle to exert more force than by twisting. They have interchangeable bits and can be locked rigid.
Electric screwdrivers have rechargeable power packs and interchangeable bits, while **electric drills** can be fitted with screwdriver bits if they have a low speed and have a reverse action.

MAKING GLUED JOINTS

Modern woodworking adhesives give a bond which is often much stronger than the materials they are fixing. And as a result, many of the traditional ways of joining wood have been superseded by methods which rely on the strength of the glue alone.

One of the main advantages of using adhesive is that you can often make joints which are virtually invisible. But glued joints are also permanent, quick to make, and can be used where there is no room for screws or nails.

Possible drawbacks

Adhesives have disadvantages, too, so when deciding how to fix something, bear in mind the following:
■ Most adhesives don't give you an 'instant' joint; they may need to be held in position, then left anywhere from an hour to a day to gain full strength.
■ Don't expect butt joints to be very strong, especially when gluing end grain. Although the adhesive is unlikely to fail, the wood fibers themselves may well pull away.
■ Be careful which adhesive you choose when gluing anything subject to changes in temperature and humidity.
■ Don't glue any joint you might need to dismantle.

Many adhesives set slowly to give you time to work – so the joint must be held until it bonds.

THE RIGHT ADHESIVE FOR THE JOB

IF YOU'RE GLUING	CHOOSE
Indoor woodwork (dry conditions)	PVA adhesive or waterproof resin adhesive
Indoor woodwork (damp conditions)	Waterproof PVA adhesive or waterproof resin adhesive
Outdoor woodwork	Waterproof PVA adhesive or waterproof resin adhesive
Plastic laminates on to wood	Contact adhesive
Loose joints	PVA adhesive, or waterproof resin adhesive if large gaps need filling
Wallboards to walls	Styrene-butadiene
Laying wooden flooring	Styrene-butadiene

See full adhesives guide overleaf for product details.

Trade tip

Stick with it

6 Many general purpose repair adhesives will stick wood quite well, including epoxy resins, 'super' glues, and multi-purpose clear adhesives. All these can be useful in an emergency – and epoxy resin is excellent for gluing metal and plastic fittings to wood.

In general, though, repair adhesives tend to work out a lot more expensive than adhesives designed for the job. And even though some of them might in theory give a stronger bond, this is probably stronger than you actually need. 9

ADHESIVES FOR WOODWORK

PVA ADHESIVES

Apply PVA adhesive *from the bottle or tube. On large areas, you can spread it more evenly using a brush or spreader. Clean the tools with water.*

PVA adhesive is often sold under the name 'Woodworking adhesive', and is a good choice for all kinds of indoor woodwork. However, the standard type is not recommended for anything which might get damp, as moisture can cause the bond to fail. There is a special formulation called *Waterproof* PVA adhesive for situations like this.

Both types are sold in squeeze bottles, tubs and tins of various sizes. PVA adhesive tends to 'go off' if stored for a long time, so buying more than you're likely to use in the near future may not be worthwhile.

WATERPROOF RESIN ADHESIVES

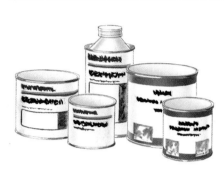

Mix resin adhesive *in a plastic or glass container, not a metal one. Spread it with an old brush or notched spreader and clean the tools as quickly as possible.*

Waterproof resin adhesives normally come in small tins similar to paint tins. They all need to be mixed before use. Some types come in dry powder form for mixing with water. Others are in two parts, one of which may be a liquid hardener.

Resin adhesives give a very strong waterproof bond, so are excellent for work which will be used outdoors or in damp conditions. They fill gaps better than PVA adhesive, and can be used where maximum strength is important.

CONTACT ADHESIVES

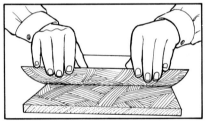

Spread contact adhesive *on both surfaces using a spreader. Allow to dry, then bring the two parts together. Most bond instantly, so take care when positioning.*

Contact ('impact') adhesive is used for bonding sheet materials to boards. The adhesive is spread on both surfaces and allowed to dry before bonding; most then bond instantly, but *thixotropic* (gel) types allow some repositioning. Many formulations are inflammable and give off a toxic vapor until dried; they also need special solvent/cleaner. Non-toxic versions are available.

Contact adhesives are sold in various sized tins, and also in tubes for very small quantities. Most come with a spreader, although some non-toxic types are spread with a foam pad instead.

GLUE GUNS

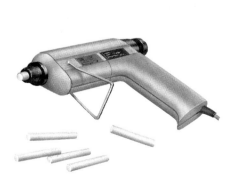

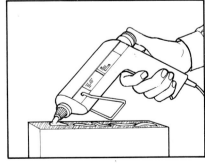

Glue from a gun *can be used as soon as the gun is hot enough for the glue to flow evenly. Bring the parts together as soon as you can and hold for a few moments.*

Glue guns use special sticks of solid adhesive which melt when heated. The molten adhesive is then forced out of the nozzle either by pressing the other end of the stick (on cheaper models) or by pulling a trigger. There are different adhesive sticks to suit wood and other materials, and because they harden on cooling, all types give a strong bond very rapidly. This often eliminates the need for clamps, because the joint can simply pressed together and held until it bonds.

The main drawback is price – guns are fairly expensive and the adhesive sticks themselves may cost more than liquid and powder types. You also need a power source within reach of the job.

HOW TO MAKE GLUED JOINTS

There are three basic ways to stick wood using adhesives.

Glue only. This is a perfectly adequate way to join pieces of wood, providing you can hold the parts firmly enough to stop them from moving before the glue dries.

Normally, the best way to do this is with clamps; but cutting conventional woodworking joints in the parts also helps to secure them and increases the gluing area to.

Glue and pin. After spreading the adhesive, the parts are secured using finishing or casing nails. These contribute a certain amount to the strength of the joint, but their main function is to hold the assembly firmly until the glue has set.

Glue and dowel. This is a simple method for increasing the joint area and adding strength. It is frequently used to join veneered particleboard, where it enables you to glue to the core of the wood, rather than the surface veneer (which is weakly bonded to the particleboard and may be too shiny to take glue well).

Glued joints need to be clamped or otherwise held in place until the adhesive has hardened.

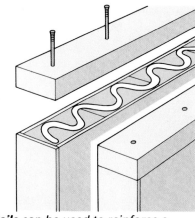

Nails can be used to reinforce a joint and hold it while the adhesive sets.

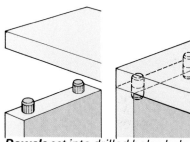

Dowels set into drilled holes help to strengthen glued joints, especially in man-made boards.

1 Lightly sand the area to be glued and dust it off. This cleans the surface and provides a 'key' for the glue to bond on to. Remove any old glue or paint.

2 Apply the adhesive to one surface only, except in the case of contact adhesives. For maximum strength, it should form a thin, even glue line.

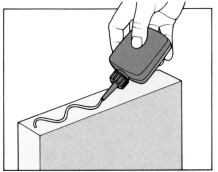

3 If you are gluing end grain, seal it first with a thin coat of glue and allow this to dry. Then spread another layer and make the joint.

PROBLEM SOLVER

Gluing difficult surfaces

Oily woods, eg teak are best glued as soon as possible after sawing or sanding. If the oil content of the wood is left to rise to the surface, it may affect the bond.

Preservative-treated woods need to have their joining surfaces sanded down immediately before gluing. If you are applying preservative, allow it to dry first for several days before using glue.

Loose joints are best filled using resin adhesive, which has better gap-filling properties than PVA types.

Otherwise, avoid filling gaps with adhesive if at all possible.

Damp conditions can swell wood and ruin a glued joint. If there is a chance your work will be exposed to damp, let the wood acclimatize to the conditions for about a week before gluing and be sure to use a waterproof glue.

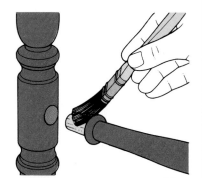

Worn joints are common on old furniture. Resin adhesives can help fill gaps here.

HOLDING THE JOINT TOGETHER

GENERAL PURPOSE CLAMPS

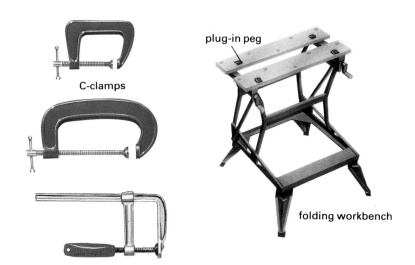

C-clamps

plug-in peg

folding workbench

quick-acting clamp

C-clamps can be used for clamping many different kinds of joints. They come in a range of sizes, measured by their maximum jaw opening, and you can get specially deep versions for holding work which is a long way from the edge. Some C-clamps have soft pads on their jaws.

Folding workbenches have a pair of clamping jaws which can be used to hold a joint (although the bench will be out of action until the glue has hardened). The design of the jaws allows them to grip material up to around 100mm (4") thick and to cope with tapering shapes.

Larger objects, such as frames, can be gripped using plug-in pegs and extension arms which fit into holes in the worktop.

CLAMPS FOR SPECIAL PURPOSES

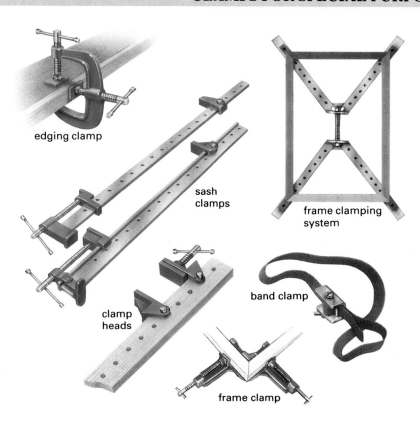

edging clamp

sash clamps

frame clamping system

clamp heads

band clamp

frame clamp

Edging clamps are for holding edging strips in place and may be worth buying if you use a lot of material which needs finishing in this way. (For a one-off job you can usually improvise with adhesive tape or string bindings, protecting the edges with cardboard.)

Frame clamps are worth using if you make pictures frames or anything with similar corner joints. There are cheaper plastic or metal *frame clamping systems* or you can improvise with string and adhesive tape.

Band clamps are for holding large jobs, such as frames, and can be used even on irregular shapes. The webbing is tightened using a wrench or screwdriver and has a ratchet release.

Sash clamps are the best way to hold large objects, such as doors or table tops. They are expensive to buy (particularly as you often need to use them in pairs), but can be rented.

Clamp heads, consisting of end stops plus screw clamps for applying pressure, are a cheaper alternative to sash clamps. The heads are designed to fit into holes drilled in wood, allowing you to make up a sash clamp to any length required.

IMPROVISED CLAMPS

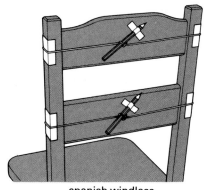

spanish windlass

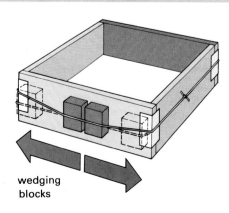

wedging blocks

String can be used to improvise all sorts of clamps – particularly for frames and edgings. Use strong string of a type which doesn't stretch too much, and always protect the surface using cardboard or scraps of wood.

The two most effective ways to pull the string tight are by twisting it with a piece of stick (a 'Spanish windlass'), or by using pairs of blocks to give a wedging action. In both cases, you may need to use tape to hold the tightening devices in position.

SIMPLE JOINTS FOR SOLID WOOD

Making things from solid wood means that you need to join a number of small pieces together. Traditional woodworking used many different forms of joint which were often complicated by the need for them to have a strength which did not depend on the rather weak glues then available. Some joints were also intended to give a decorative appearance to the finished job.

Although modern glues and joint systems have made it easy to join two pieces of wood together strongly, there are still many occasions when it's essential to cut a joint. In some cases this is for added strength; sometimes it makes a neater finished job.

The illustrations below show the most useful joints for things like built-in furniture and household carpentry – together with examples of where to use them.

ANGLED JOINTS

Butt joints are simple to make but depend entirely on the strength of their fixings. They can be glued or reinforced with nails or screws. When paneling is applied to a butt jointed frame it helps to lock and strengthen the joint.
Common uses: Frames for paneling.

Miter joints are a form of decorative butt joint in which no end grain is visible. The miter is normally cut at 45°, but different angles can be used for non-square frames.
Common uses: Picture frames, decorative moldings.

Lap joints are used when two pieces meet at right angles on the wide face. They give a flush surface, while interlocking for strength, and can be used for corners, T or cross shapes.
Common uses: Frames for paneling or in view.

A dado joint is used when two pieces meet at right angles on their narrow face. A stopped joint is used when one piece of wood is narrower than the other.
Common uses: Shelving, steps.

Open mortise and tenon joints are used for corners when more strength is needed, and for a decorative appearance.
Common uses: Furniture frames.

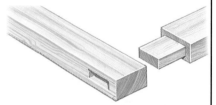

Mortise and tenon joints are the traditional corner joint for sturdy frames. Fairly complicated to make, they are neat and strong.
Common uses: Door, window, table and bed frames.

BOX JOINTS

Dovetail joints interlock strongly and resist being pulled apart. The version shown is machine cut.
Common uses: Drawer sides.

Comb joints are simpler to cut but less strong.
Common uses: Boxes.

LENGTHENING JOINTS

Scarf joints are designed to give maximum strength. Each half can be made with three saw cuts, but these require accurate marking.
Common uses: Repairs to door frames, lengthening rails.

WIDENING JOINTS

Edged glued joints are very strong, but rely on the wood being planed true. The joint can be reinforced with dowels or corrugated fasteners.
Common uses: Worktops, tables.

Tongued and grooved joints can be made using special pre-cut wood.

TECHNIQUES FOR MAKING JOINTS

The techniques shown here are for making the most common and useful forms of joint. The other joints, which are shown on the previous page, are all based on those covered in detail here and can be made by adapting the techniques described below.

Tools needed

As with most woodwork, accurate marking and measuring is the key. As a minimum you need a straight-edge, ruler and try square. A marking gauge is also useful, although it is possible to manage without one.

Most joints are cut with a tenon saw and cleaned up with a chisel, which must be kept sharp. The simpler joints can be cut with a saw alone. For halving joints, finishing them with a chisel is likely to be more accurate, while a chisel is essential for making mortise and tenon joints.

MAKING BUTT JOINTS

Butt joints are the simplest of all to make, but because the two parts don't interlock in any way, they rely on the fixings (glue, nails or screws) for strength. It's also important to cut the wood accurately so that the contact patch is made as large as possible.

Miter joints and scarf joints are made in much the same way, except that the ends are cut at an angle. And similar techniques apply when making edge to edge joints to widen a piece of timber. These are effectively just a long butt joint, but it is essential to plane the wood true and clamp the joint while the adhesive is drying.

Trade tip

Headless nailing

❝For a quick and easy concealed joint, drive nails into one part then cut their heads off with wire cutting pliers. Hammer the second part on to the points this produces. ❞

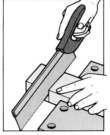

1 Cut the parts to length after marking the cutting lines with a try square to make sure the ends are true. Take care to saw on the right side of the line.

2 Nails make quick and easy fixings. Screws can be used instead, but tend not to grip well since they are driven into end grain.

3 A plain glued butt joint is satisfactory for unstressed areas, where the joint can be held firm until it sets. Nail through for extra strength.

4 For a concealed joint use dowels and glue. The holes in each side must be drilled accurately using a dowel jig or dowel center pins.

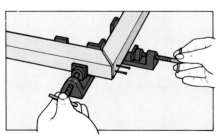

Make a miter joint by cutting the ends at 45° using a miter box. For strength it helps to clamp the joint in a frame clamp, glue and nail or dowel.

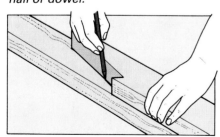

Make a scarf joint by marking one part carefully and sawing to shape. Use this to mark and cut the second, then glue and screw them together.

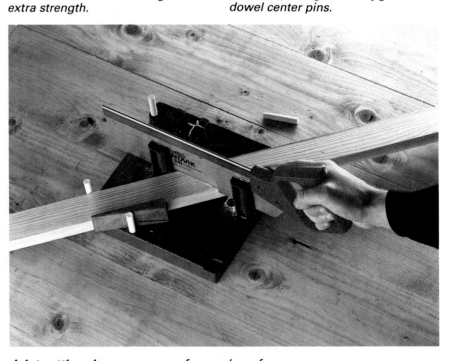

Joint cutting clamps are one of a number of useful aids. They help to guide the saw at the correct angle, and can be adapted to suit a range of joints. They can also be used to hold the pieces together during assembly.

MAKING A LAP JOINT

Lap joints are the most basic form of cut joint, used wherever two frame members meet or cross without gaining thickness.

There are two types of lap joint; the end lap and the cross lap joint. The technique varies slightly depending on which one you are making since it is possible to cut a lap joint on the end of a piece of wood by using two saw cuts. A wood joint in the middle of a piece must be cut with a chisel; dado joints are cut in very much the same way.

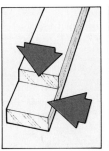
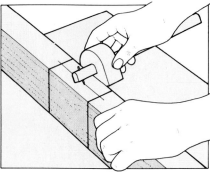

An end lap joint can be made with two saw cuts. A cross lap joint must be chiseled out after sawing down each side to the right depth.

1 Mark each piece to indicate where the other crosses it. Draw the lines with a square, exactly the same width apart as the width of the wood.

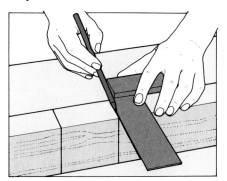

2 Align the square accurately against each side of the wood and continue the lines which you marked across the top all the way down both sides.

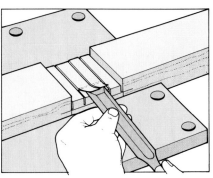

3 On each piece, mark a line halfway through its thickness. The easy way is to use a marking gauge (see Tip) but you can measure and then rule it.

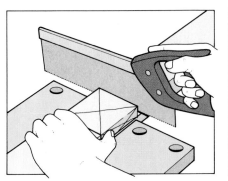

4 Check which part is to be cut away, then saw squarely along the cross lines on each side of the joint down as far as the halfway mark.

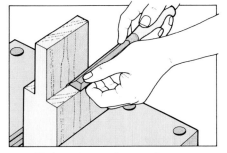

5 Pare out the waste with a chisel working down in shallow steps. On wide joints, a few extra saw cuts in the middle make this easier.

Trade tip

Lapping with a marking gauge

❝Set a marking gauge to half the thickness of the wood this way:
■ Set it to what you think looks right and mark in from both sides to check.
■ If the two marks don't meet or if they overlap, the gauge needs adjusting.
■ To make small adjustments, tap the end of the gauge on the worktop to jar it along.
■ Recheck until the two marks align perfectly. ❞

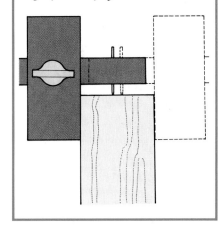

MORTISE AND TENON JOINTS

Mortise and tenon joints rely on accurate marking out. A few basic rules can be applied when doing so.
■ Put the mortise in the vertical part and put the tenon in the horizontal.
■ Make the tenon about one-third the thickness of the wood.
■ Adjust the size of the mortise and tenon to suit the sizes of drill bit and chisel you have available.
■ Where the tenon runs right through the mortised part, the joint will be neater if you make the tenon overlength and trim it off after the joint has been made.

1 Make a tenon by sawing across the two shoulders, then sawing down from the ends. Clean up with a chisel for a neat, accurate joint.

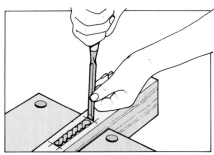

2 Cut the mortise by drilling out most of the waste with a drill bit of the same width, then cut out the rest by chopping down with a chisel.

Joint doesn't fit

Although care in marking and cutting should produce a perfect fitting joint, a mistake can easily leave the joint loose and badly fitting.

The best solution is to make a new piece, but when you can't, you need to ensure that the joint fits together as well as possible, concealing any gaps later if need be.

Where the gaps are small, one solution is to use a resin-based woodworking glue. Whereas a general purpose type such as

PVA tends to run out of the joint, resin glues are far better at filling gaps.

If you are driving in nails or screws, make sure these don't pull the parts out of alignment by trying to close up the gap. If necessary, pack any cracks out with slips of wood to prevent this.

Fill remaining gaps with a general purpose filler if painting, or a wood-colored stopping if the joints are going to be on view.

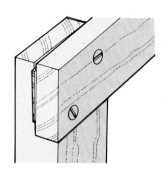

When joints are badly cut ensure that nailing or screwing them together does not pull them out of line. Pack out if necessary to avoid this.

TOOLS FOR MAKING JOINTS

Miter boxes are used with backsaws and tenon saws and are an aid to cutting wood squarely or at a 45° angle. They may be made of wood or plastic, and some have metal inserts. Most boxes are not capable of taking wood over about 50mm (2″) wide; if you buy a wider box you will need a very long saw to use it properly.

It is essential to treat a miter box with care – once the slots become worn and inaccurate it is useless.

Miter blocks are like an open version of the miter box. While they have only one set of slots, making them less accurate, they can take wood of a greater width.

Joint cutting guides are like multi-angle miter boxes. They come with a range of attachments and instructions showing how to set them up for a range of different joints.

Frame clamps are designed to hold a corner joint steady while glueing or nailing it together.

Frame clamping systems hold four or more corners together at once. Particularly useful for picture frames, some types are sturdy enough to make them also suitable for heavier constructions.

Doweling jigs come in various forms. All are designed to do the same job, ensuring that two pieces of wood can be drilled so that the holes in them align perfectly. Most clamp on to the edge of the wood, and may have different guides to fit various sizes of dowel bit.

Dovetailing jigs are drill attachments used for making dovetail or comb joints in thin boards – especially for making drawers and boxes. The wood is clamped in the jig which has a series of parallel guides. A special cutter is then pushed into each guide slot in turn to make one half of the joint – a straight cutter makes a comb joint, and an angled one makes a dovetail. This is then repeated for the other piece of wood.

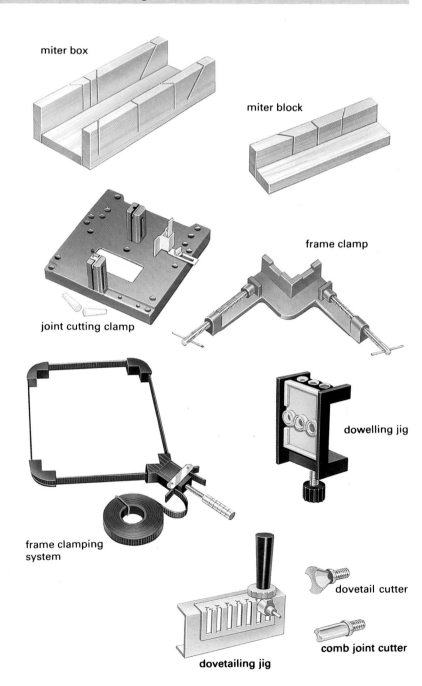

miter box

miter block

frame clamp

joint cutting clamp

dowelling jig

frame clamping system

dovetail cutter

comb joint cutter

dovetailing jig

CLEAR FINISHES FOR INTERIOR WOODWORK

As the final stage in renovating or making wooden furniture and fittings, wood finishing is among the most satisfying of all DIY jobs. The products available for bringing out or enhancing the natural beauty of wood can be numbered in their hundreds, but most fall into one or other of the following groups.

Colourings for modifying the wood's natural colour.

Fillers for disguising blemishes.

Traditional finishes, such as oils and shellac-based polishes.

Varnishes, based on natural oil or synthetic polyurethane resins.

Modern lacquers, which give a much tougher finish than varnishes.

There are also various factory finishes for modern furniture, including cellulose lacquer and polyester or plastic coatings. These need special equipment to apply and are not discussed here.

When choosing a clear wood finish, you need to take into account not only the finished effect, but also the type of wood and the amount of wear and tear it can be expected to receive. The materials described in this section are suitable both for new wood, and for old wood that has been stripped for refinishing. But remember that no clear finish will hide surface imperfections entirely – either repair these first, or choose paint instead.

Clear finishes can bring out or enhance the natural beauty of wood, as well as protecting the surface.

WOOD COLORINGS

Bleaches have to be used if you want to lighten wood, or dye it to a shade which is paler than its natural color.

Two-part bleaches come in a pack with two bottles of solution. The first, which is alkaline, may darken the wood slightly when applied; the second is then added to start the chemical reaction which bleaches the wood.

Oxalic acid (available from specialist retailers) can also be used to lighten wood, but is less effective than two-part bleaches and highly poisonous. The acid must be neutralized by washing the wood with denatured alcohol before further finishing can take place.

If you plan to polish wood which has been bleached, use *white French polish* (see overleaf).

Dyes and stains are used to color wood before finishing. Until a few years ago, the terms 'wood dye' and 'wood stain' were interchangeable, but confusingly some manufacturers now produce *exterior wood stains* – colored surface coatings which simply obscure the grain. A true wood dye or stain penetrates deep into the wood, and when dry must be sealed with some other form of clear finish.

Solvent-based dyes are penetrating, quick drying and do not raise the grain. Some contain translucent pigments which stop them fading, and different colors from the same range can be mixed to produce the shade you want. The disadvantage of solvent dyes is that they dry very quickly, making it difficult to maintain a 'wet edge' and sometimes leading to a rather blotchy effect.

Water and alcohol-based dyes are easier to apply, but tend to raise the grain of the wood and are not as colorfast as solvent-based dyes. They are only available from specialist wood finish retailers.

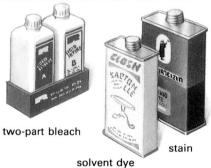

two-part bleach

solvent dye

stain

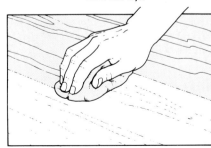

Apply wood dye with a cloth

CRACK AND GRAIN FILLERS

Wood filler or 'stopping' is used to fill cracks in the wood, or cover marks such as screw and nail heads. Some types come in tins or tubes as a ready to use *stiff paste*; others are in *two parts*, with a hardener which is mixed with the stopping immediately before application. Various shades are available, but the filler always stays visible under a clear finish since it breaks up the natural grain lines.

Plastic wood actually contains real wood flour, but tends to shrink more than other stoppers. Apply a little at a time, to allow for drying and shrinkage.

Grain fillers are specifically for filling the grain of wood to make it easier to apply a high gloss finish.

Woods such as oak and teak have an open grained texture that quickly soaks up any finish. And while this is fine for oils or waxes, without grain filler a thinner varnish or lacquer needs multiple coats – with a lot of rubbing down in between – before the surface

is smooth enough to produce a satisfactory gloss.

Traditionally plaster of Paris was used, then wiped over with linseed oil to make the plaster transparent. This is incompatible with modern finishes, so use *ready-mixed paste grain filler* instead.

In some cases, you may be able to use wood dye to color the grain filler so that staining and filling can be carried out in one operation.

paste stopping

ready-mixed grain filler

Trade tip

Color matching
❝ Manufacturers claim that fillers take up wood dyes, but they are likely to do so in a different way to surrounding wood. The solution is to stain the wood first, then stain the filler to match this color as closely as possible. ❞

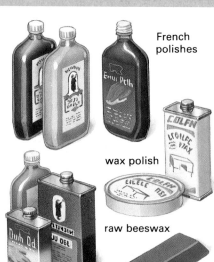

Apply filler with a putty knife or filling knife.

TRADITIONAL CLEAR FINISHES

Oiling is the easiest of all clear finishing processes – you simply rub the oil into the wood. The traditional oil used in Europe is *linseed oil*, derived from the flax plant. This takes about three days to dry in its raw form, so many people prefer to use *boiled linseed oil* which dries in about 18 hours.

Teak oil is specially formulated for teak, normally with extra resins for a tougher finish. *Danish oil* contains oil from the Chinese tung tree, and gives a lustrous finish with less sheen than teak oil or linseed oil.

Waxing is probably the oldest method of treating wood: *beeswax* – the original ingredient – has been known and used for thousands of years. You can make your own wax polish by dissolving blocks of beeswax in an equal quantity of pure turpentine: heat it very gently in a bowl over a saucepan of water to speed up the process.

Many commercial wax polishes are also available, often including *carnauba wax* (from a Brazilian palm) to make the beeswax less sticky.

French polish was invented by a French cabinet maker nearly 200 years ago. It gives a deep, lustrous gloss, but is nothing like as durable as modern varnishes and is particularly susceptible to heat and alcohol. It also takes real skill to apply.

French polish is based on *shellac* – a substance derived from the lac insect which lives on trees in India and the Far East. There are various grades.

White French polish should be used on bleached and pale wood. *Button polish* is golden brown, and is often used in antique restoration. It takes its

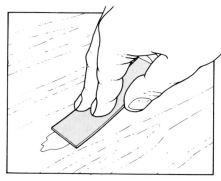

French polishes

wax polish

raw beeswax

wood oils

name from the shellac used to make it, which is in thin discs, like buttons. *Garnet polish* is a darker form of French polish, for use on mahogany and other dark colored woods.

When applying French polish with a cloth in the traditional way, you also need linseed oil to lubricate it, and mineral spirits for 'rubbing off' to a high gloss – the tricky part.

Shellac varnish contains similar ingredients to French polish, and can be applied by brush, rather than by rubbing. *Sanding sealer* is also based on shellac, and can be used to seal the surface before applying most types of finish. (*Knotting*, too, is based on shellac, but is not generally necessary under clear finishes.)

Oiled finish

Waxed finish

French polish

MODERN VARNISHES

Varnish is a tough brush-on finish which is easier to apply than many traditional types, hence its popularity for tables and natural wood carpentry.

Traditional varnishes were based on natural oil resins and tended to be very brittle. Most modern types contain more durable synthetic resins, and offer a choice of high gloss, satin or matte finishes. *Solvent-based polyurethane* varnish (which has to be cleaned off the brush with turpentine) is usually glossier than *water-based* varnish (which contains alkyds). Some types are also available in aerosols, for intricate shapes like wicker chairs and louvre doors.

The quality of polyurethane varnishes varies; the better ones contain a high proportion of solids – the part which is left when the solvents evaporate. Unfortunately, it is difficult to assess this by eye, since some brands have thickeners added, or are formulated as gel rather than liquid.

Varnish stains are varnishes which have been colored with dyes or translucent pigments (or a mixture of both) so that color and finish can be applied in one go. This is the best way of coloring wood where the existing varnish has not been stripped off. It is also recommended for coloring pine, which doesn't take wood dyes very well because of the difference in absorption rate beteen the heart and sap wood.

Unlike wood dyes, varnish stain deepens in color the more coats you apply. If you reach the color you want before the coat is thick enough, switch to clear varnish instead.

Colored transparent finishes are similar to varnish stains, but instead of being wood colored they come in a range of bright primary and other attractive colors. They color wood in the same way as paint, but because the pigments are translucent, the grain of the wood can still be seen. They look particularly good on woods with a strong grain, such as pine and ash.

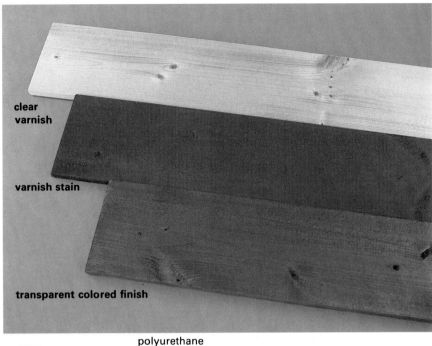

clear varnish

varnish stain

transparent colored finish

polyurethane

traditional oil-based varnish

water-based resin varnish

transparent colored finish

─ *Trade tip* ─

Thinning it out

❝When using polyurethane varnish on bare wood, it is usually advisable to thin the first coat so that it soaks in quickly and seals the grain.

Solvent-based polyurethanes are thinned with turpentine. The amount depends on the quality of the varnish, and could be anything from 10% to 30% – check the manufacturer's instructions. Thinner varnishes obviously need less thinning.

Afterwards, the sealed wood can be finished with further coats of full strength varnish, or wax polished for a more natural finish. ❞

WOOD LACQUERS

Two-part lacquers (properly called *catalyzed cold cure lacquers*) represent the greatest advance in wood finishes. They contain resins and plastics which are activated by mixing in a hardener just before application. Special formulations are available for floors.

Very quick-drying, lacquers are paler in color than white French polish but can be polished to a similar – though much tougher – finish. The naturally glossy surface can also be rubbed down with steel wool and wax polished for a more natural matte or satin effect.

Special thinners are needed for cleaning brushes and spills, so make sure you get some when you buy.

Mix lacquer in a china or glass bowl.

Once the surface of the wood has been prepared, you need only a minimum of tools to apply clear finishes.

Filling knives or **putty knives** are used to apply wood fillers, stoppers and plastic wood. You may need finer tools for working them into small cracks.

Lint-free rags are used to apply many traditional finishes, including dyes, grain filler, oil, wax, and French polish; it's also possible to apply varnish this way.

Old cotton or linen handkerchiefs and sheets are ideal, as are old cotton shirts. You also need some absorbent unmedicated cotton to absorb the polish and to form the rag into a polishing pad.

Steel wool (medium and fine grade) is most convenient for rubbing down and for applying wax polish over hard finishes such as polyurethane varnish

Brushes for applying varnish should be top quality natural bristle, and free from loose hairs and dust. Keep them separate from those used for painting, as it's almost impossible to remove paint sediment entirely. You will need a selection of different widths.

For applying shellac, use broad, (preferably bear hair) artists brushes, which are finer and give a better finish.

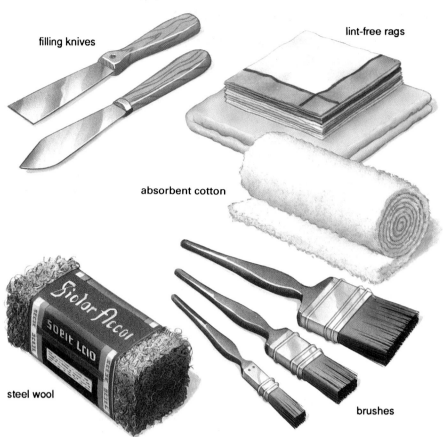

filling knives

lint-free rags

absorbent cotton

steel wool

brushes

CHOOSING A FINISH				
FINISH	**EFFECT**	**BEST USED FOR**	**APPLICATION**	**MAINTENANCE**
Oiling	Dark, rich, very slightly lustrous finish	Draining boards, kitchen counters, tables subject to wear and tear	Easily done with a cloth	Re-oil every couple of months
Waxing	Soft satin sheen	Popular for stripped pine furniture but susceptible to heat, water and alcohol	Fairly easy: the more elbow grease, the higher the sheen	Dust and buff regularly; re-wax every couple of months
French polish and shellac	Produces a very high gloss if traditionally applied; may be finished with wax for a softer look	Traditionally used for fine furniture. Particularly susceptible to heat and alcohol	Traditional French polishing requires practice; easier option is to brush on and wax polish	Dust and polish regularly; if the surface becomes dull or damaged, apply a home-made 'reviver'
Polyurethane varnish	Gloss, satin or matte finish; tends to add a tinge of orange to the wood	Primarily for areas taking heavy wear (including floors) and those which might otherwise be painted – doors, baseboards, stairs, window frames	Easy to apply, but care must be taken for a good finish	Dust regularly and wipe down with a damp cloth when necessary; wax polish if preferred
Two-part lacquer	Very clear finish; polish for a high gloss or apply wax for a satin finish	Table tops, work surfaces, floors; home-made furniture	Work in a well ventilated room. Easy to apply	Wipe down with a damp cloth, or apply wax polish every few weeks

APPLYING SYNTHETIC WOOD FINISHES

As well as being easy to apply, modern synthetic finishes give bare wood a tough protective coating that brings out the grain and enhances its natural color. 'Traditional' finishes still have their place, but tend to be less hardwearing and may need a fair degree of skill and practice to apply successfully.

Choosing a finish

Polyurethane varnishes come in matte, satin and high gloss finishes. Even with a gloss varnish, it takes careful preparation to get a mirror-like surface. Use a *grain filler* to fill the natural pores in the wood, and wood *filler* or *stopper* to repair larger cracks and damage.

Two-part lacquers (plastic coatings) dry very rapidly and can be applied thicker than polyurethane, but you still have to get the surface as smooth as possible for best results. They naturally give a high gloss but can be buffed to a matte sheen.

Colored finishes can be achieved by dyeing the wood under a clear varnish, or by using a colored varnish. Polyurethane varnish comes in several 'natural' wood colors and strong tints. Wood dyes come in an even wider range of shades and can be used under polyurethane or two-part lacquers. Where you are going lighter than the original color bleach the wood first.

Preparing the surface

The ideal surface is sanded new wood, but even this may need sealing and filling. On old wood, the

Varnish and stain to bring out the grain of the wood.

amount of preparation needed depends on any existing finish, as well as on the type of finish you plan to apply.

■ Previously varnished surfaces which are in good condition just need a light rub down with sandpaper. Any peeling or cracked varnish should be totally stripped.

■ Waxed and oiled finishes – and all traces of wax polish which have been applied to wood or over varnish – must also be removed (see below).

■ If the original finish was French

polish, think twice before removing it. It may be easier to refinish.

Tools and equipment

Lint-free rags are used for applying stain, and rubbing in grain filler.

Brushes for varnishing should never be used for anything else – it's almost impossible to remove all traces of old paint. Choose good quality bristle brushes, and work them through your fingers or brush them over bare brickwork, to tease out loose hairs, before starting.

REMOVE OIL AND WAX

Modern varnishes and lacquers must only be applied to surfaces which are free from dirt, grease, oil and wax.

Wax can be removed with wire wool and turpentine, whether applied directly to the wood or used as a polish over varnish.

Oil can also be removed in this way, but the job is more difficult because the oil soaks deep into the wood.

French polish and other shellac finishes can be dissolved and cleaned off with mineral spirits or chemical strippers.

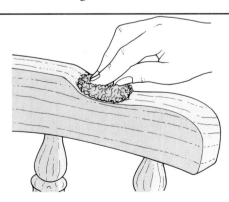

1 To remove all traces of wax or oil, use grade 00 steel wool dipped in turpentine. Rub along the grain, so that you do not scratch the surface.

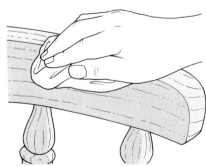

2 Before the turpentine evaporates, wipe the surface with a clean, dry rag. Avoid handling the wood after wiping as even clean hands are greasy.

FILLING AND COLORING

There are several ways to improve the appearance of wood before applying varnish or lacquer. It is important to carry out each process in the right order, so work out which you want to use according to the item you are working on, the type of wood, and the finish required.

You can often omit some stages. For example, dyeing and staining won't be necessary if you use a colored varnish – but you may want to bleach the wood, and you still need to fill it.

Bleaching must always be done first, since the process usually raises the grain of the wood and leaves it in need of further sanding. Use bleach to lighten the color of dark wood, or before using a pale wood dye to alter the shade *and* lighten the color.

Grain filling – which helps to produce the smooth surface required for a glossy finish – is the next stage. (You may be able to dye and fill the grain at the same time.)

Dyeing or staining to change the color of the wood is the next job to do.

Wood filling or stopping should always be done after dyeing – it makes it easier to match the filler to the wood color.

Trade tip

Keep it clean

❝ Once you have finished preparing the wood, keep the room as clean as possible. Any dust particles which settle on the varnish while it is drying will ruin the finish, leaving spots which must be sanded off.

When working on items which have been stripped, don't rest them on old newspapers; marks from the printing ink can easily get transferred to the surface. Use old wallpaper instead. ❞

USING WOOD BLEACH

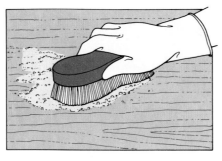

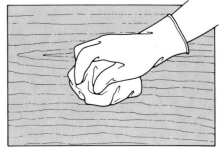

1 Tip the first solution into a clean, empty jam jar. Apply liberally with an old paint brush, and leave for 10 minutes. This tends to darken the wood.

2 Apply the second solution and leave it for several hours or overnight. If a scum appears, remove it with a scrubbing brush and clean water.

3 Finally, rinse with a solution of 50% white vinegar and 50% water. This will raise the grain, so sand smooth before dyeing or finishing the wood.

FILLING THE GRAIN

Even the most carefully planed and sanded wood is full of minute cracks and pores which follow the grain. Some woods show this more than others – mahogany being a prime example – but in all cases the grain should be filled if you want a really fine, glossy finish.

- Sand the surface with very fine sandpaper.
- Thin the grain filler to a thin paste with turpentine.
- Apply with a coarse rag, rubbing it in across the grain.
- Wipe off excess filler across the grain, using a clean rag.
- Leave overnight to harden.

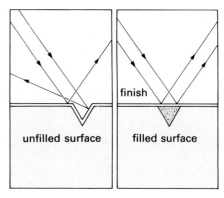

Trade tip

Colored filler

❝ If you plan to dye or stain the wood as well as filling the grain, save work by using alcohol-based dye to color the grain filler. Simply mix the filler to a paste using the dye instead of turpentine. ❞

Improve the surface (above) by smoothing with grain filler before applying a gloss finish. Apply with a coarse cloth across the grain.

Minute cracks and pores in the grain of unfilled wood (right) deflect the light in different directions, dulling the surface. Using grain filler makes the surface more reflective and therefore glossier.

unfilled surface

finish

filled surface

DYEING WOOD

There are several ways to change the color of the wood to imitate more expensive wood, to disguise mismatched panels and repairs or simply to add color.

If you want a darker color you can apply a wood dye or a colored varnish direct. Colored varnish is often harder to apply evenly, but can be used over old varnish. It is also easier to remove in the future.

If you want a lighter color you have to bleach the wood, then use a dye or colored varnish. Remember that even clear varnish will yellow the wood when applied, and continue to darken with age.

Whatever type of dye or stain you choose, start by testing the effect on a piece of wood as similar as possible to the work in hand, or in an inconspicuous spot such as the back of a door or drawer front.

■ Use a cloth rather than a brush to apply wood dye; a brush tends to give an uneven finish, particularly where it first contacts the surface.

■ If you are not happy with the color of the first test, try a second coat, or mix the dye with other colors from the same range to get the shade you want.

■ New pine often has very uneven absorbency, so more dye will soak into the wood in some places, giving a darker color. To prevent this, seal with thinned clear varnish.

■ On end grain, the dye will soak in more, giving a darker color. To prevent this, seal the end grain first with thinned varnish.

■ Glue which has squeezed out of the joints will not take the color. Scrape or sand back to bare wood.

Use a cloth to apply dye more evenly. Tip the dye into a saucer, so that you can judge how much the cloth soaks up each time you charge it. If you apply the dye with a brush more dye will soak into the wood when you first touch it with the bristles.

Seal end grain and uneven surfaces by using a thinned coat of the finish. This stops the dye being absorbed more by some areas than by others.

Glue will not take dye, so smears on the surface or where it has oozed out of the joints must be removed. Scrape with a blade or sand with fine sandpaper.

FILLING BLEMISHES

Cracks and gaps which are not due to the natural grain of the wood need extra attention. The choice is between using a paste filler, plastic wood, or a two-part wood filler. The main problem is getting the filler the same color as the wood you are filling – most manufacturers make a limited range of colors, which are unlikely to give a really good match.

■ Dye or stain the wood first, to the color required.

■ Choose a filler which is paler than the color you require if you can't get an exact match.

■ Some fillers can be blended with wood dye for a better color, but test this first in case the dye stops the filler hardening properly.

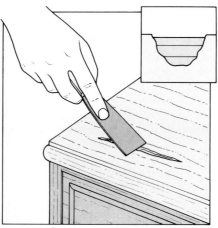

1 When filling deep cracks, apply filler a little at a time, leaving it to harden (and shrink) according to the manufacturer's instructions.

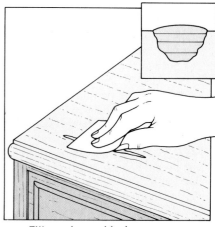

2 Fill cracks and holes very slightly above the surface of the wood, then use a fine grade sandpaper to sand the surface smooth.

APPLYING VARNISH

Most manufacturers recommend thinning the first coat with one part turpentine to 10 of varnish. Then apply at least two full-strength coats of varnish – more if it will be subjected to heavy wear.

■ Gloss polyurethane is usually tougher than matte or satin. For maximum protection without a gloss finish, build up gloss undercoats and apply a matte or satin topcoat.

■ The first coat may be easier to apply with a cloth.

■ Don't overload the brush. Dip it in the varnish and touch the ends of the bristles against the side of the tin – don't scrape them across the lip as this tends to form bubbles.

■ Minute bubbles may appear in the first coat due to air trapped in the pores of the wood. Thinning the first coat and using a cloth should prevent this; otherwise rub down well before applying the next coat.

■ Allow the varnish to dry hard before sanding and recoating – this could take anything from 2 hours to 12 hours, depending on the type of varnish, and the conditions.

Colored varnish

Apply this with extra care – if it is uneven, the color will appear patchy. The more coats you apply, the darker the effect. If you get the color you want before applying enough coats for protection, finish off with clear varnish.

If the color you want to use is not available in the right finish (matte, satin or gloss), use the appropriate clear varnish for the topcoat.

1 Work on an area about 500mm (20") square at a time. Apply the varnish along the grain first, drawing the brush backwards and forwards. If using two-part lacquer, remember that it dries rapidly – work quickly and do not over-brush.

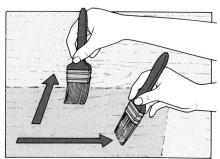

2 Using lighter pressure, brush at right angles across the grain. Then finish off along the grain as lightly as possible using the tip of the brush.

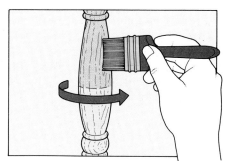

3 When varnishing moldings, work only along the grain or you may find you get a lot of drips. On turnings such as stair spindles work around the pattern.

USING TWO-PART LACQUER

Two-part lacquers (plastic coatings) are applied much like varnishes but harden by chemical reaction instead of drying. This happens very rapidly and gives off strong fumes, so there are several points to watch:

■ Make sure you have a supply of the special cleaner to suit (ordinary brush cleaner will not work). If you buy a kit, this should include a small amount of brush cleaner but it may not be enough to clean the brush more than once.

■ Always provide good ventilation as the fumes are much stronger than those of ordinary varnish.

■ Mix the lacquer and hardener in an old glass or china container (not metal or plastic). Never mix more than you need for each application.

■ Apply the finish liberally using a paintbrush – do not over-brush.

■ A second coat can be applied as soon as the first is dry (after 1–1½ hours).

■ There is no need to rub down between coats unless there are obvious imperfections.

■ Build up three coats, then rub down with fine wet and dry paper until you get a matte surface; shiny patches indicate hollows, and a further coat will be necessary for a smooth finish.

■ Finish the surface with steel wool and wax or burnishing cream (see Tip).

Trade tip

Finishing touches

❛ **To give a sheen** to a high gloss finish, use fine steel wool and solid wax polish or liquid brass polish. Dip the steel wool in the polish and work it gently along the grain. The wax acts as a lubricant, to help the steel wool run smoothly over the surface.
For a high gloss finish (on two-part lacquered surfaces in particular) use a burnishing cream. This is often included in a two-part lacquer kit, otherwise use car body refinishing cream (eg T-Cut). Rub down the surface with fine sandpaper, then polish using a soft rag (such as cotton stockinette). ❜

REPAIRING WOODEN MOLDINGS

Wooden moldings are used all around the house – for baseboards, architraves around doors and windows, and sometimes for picture or dado (chair) rails. As well as providing a decorative feature, they have the important practical function of protecting the plasterwork from damage. This makes them prone to knocks and chips, while other problems include loose fixings, splits, warps and even rot.

Where a molding is basically sound and the damage is minor, patching is the simplest option; most repairs involve little more than using the right filler, plus a few basic carpentry tools.

However, where a molding is badly damaged or so scruffy that repair would involve extensive work, replacement may be simpler. Several factors affect your decision:
■ Is a similar molding easily available? If not, replacement could be difficult and expensive.

Common moldings are sold by many hardware stores, while a larger range is stocked by lumberyards or specialist molding dealers (try under 'carpentry' in Yellow Pages). But older houses often have elaborately carved moldings which may no longer be made, although they can sometimes be replaced by making up from several sections of

replacement moldings or by modifying a similar molding to match (see Problem Solver).

In the last resort, you can have a molding made up specially, but this may be expensive.
■ How much redecoration do you intend to do? If the plaster is in poor condition, removing a molding could loosen it so much that extensive patching is required.
■ If the damage is caused by rot, this may indicate a serious problem, either now or in the past. Replacement of the affected wood is usually essential, but where you suspect dry rot or active dampness, have this checked out first.

SIMPLE REPAIRS

Odd dents and chips, splits, or loose fixings are normally easy to repair. Where filling is needed, there are basically three choices:
■ Use general purpose interior filler for repairs where the molding is firmly fixed and is unlikely to receive heavy knocks.
■ Use a resin wood filler if the patch is in a position where it may receive further knocks.
■ Use a flexible filler if the patch is at all subject to movement – such as where baseboards and architraves are fixed to partition walls.

If a large piece is missing, use a wooden block to replace it and then finish off with filler to match the contours. This is stronger and cheaper than using filler for the whole repair.

Finally, prime the patch and either paint to conceal it, or refinish the whole section.

Loose fixings often cause cracks or splits. Refix with nails, screws or frame fixings, depending on what there is to fix to behind the molding.

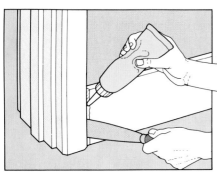

Repair cracks at joints with flexible filler if there is any sign of movement. Ordinary filler is fine for splits along the grain of the wood.

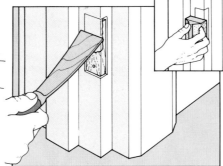

Fill large gaps by pinning a wooden offcut into the hole slightly below the surface. Finish off with filler and sand when dry to match the molding.

Trade tip

Getting to grips

❛ Dents are best repaired with resin filler.

Scrape off the paint first. Then, if the hole is large, hammer some fine nails into the dent so that the filler has something to grip. Sand level with the surface when dry. ❜

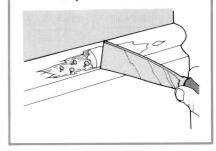

REPLACING MOLDINGS

Where a molding is seriously damaged or badly battered and a matching section is available, replacement is a sensible option.

Before you begin, however, check what's involved. In particular, see if it is necessary to remove a full length of molding, or if the damage is limited to a section of the run. Replacing a section is cheaper, but it must be cut neatly (using a backsaw and miter block) if the repair is not to show. It is also vital that the replacement is an exact match in every detail.

It is sometimes difficult to know whether a replacement is available without removing the original to use as a pattern (see Problem Solver). If you need to do this, try not to damage the old piece too much; if replacement proves impossible, you then have the option of replacing it and patching it up.

REMOVING BASEBOARDS

Baseboards are fitted in several different ways (see below). In some cases, it won't be obvious what you are dealing with until you begin to remove a section from the wall. Be careful not to damage the plaster; put a small piece of offcut wood between the wall and any tool used.

■ To remove a whole run of baseboard, lever it from the wall with a brick chisel then prize it away with the claw of a hammer.

■ To remove a shorter section of baseboard, prize it away from the wall with a brick chisel until it can be wedged out enough to be sawn at both ends with a backsaw; use a miter block for an accurate cut.

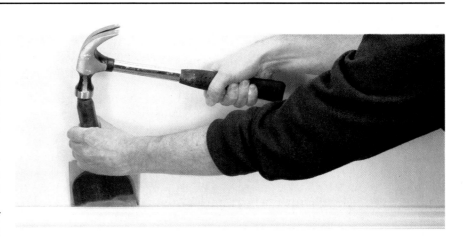

To remove a run of baseboard, start at one end and place a brick chisel at the top edge where it meets the wall. Hammer the chisel in gently, then prize the board away with a hammer. Continue along the run until free.

HOW BASEBOARDS ARE ATTACHED

On a masonry wall, baseboards are often nailed to short lengths of wood called 'grounds' nailed to the wall below the plaster. If damaged, these must be replaced to pack out the baseboard by the right amount.

Another way of fixing to masonry was by nailing into wooden plugs wedged into the mortar joints. When the baseboard is removed the wooden plugs often come away as well; use alternative fixings.

On a wood-frame wall the baseboard is simply nailed through the plasterboard or lath and plaster cladding so that the nails go into the sole plate and the wooden studs fixed at regular intervals behind.

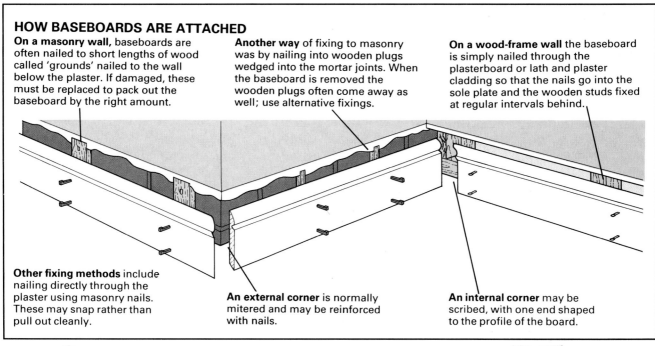

Other fixing methods include nailing directly through the plaster using masonry nails. These may snap rather than pull out cleanly.

An external corner is normally mitered and may be reinforced with nails.

An internal corner may be scribed, with one end shaped to the profile of the board.

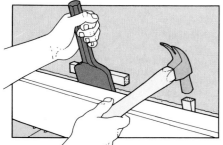

1 *To remove a section* of baseboard prize it away from the wall. Gently hammer in wedges to hold the damaged section away from the wall.

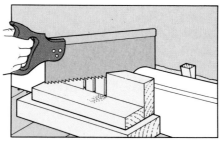

2 Rule a line to show the cutting point, then place a miter block against the board to guide the start of the cut. Raise it on packing if necessary.

3 Continue the cut to the bottom of the board, following the vertical pencil line to help keep the cut straight. Repeat for the other end of the section.

REMOVING ARCHITRAVES

Architraves around door and window frames are normally either nailed to the wooden lining of the opening or to the frame itself. In both cases they can simply be prized away by levering under the edge, using an offcut to gain purchase.

However, before removing a run of architrave, it's usually advisable to score down the edges with a trimming knife to release any overlapping decorations – otherwise you may find they tear away with it.

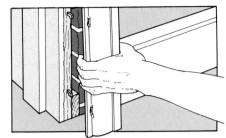

1 To remove an architrave, gently hammer a brick chisel or old wood chisel under its edge. Start at one end and work from the wall side, not the frame.

2 Work along until the whole architrave can be levered free. Avoid denting the wood of the door frame, and pull out any nails which remain.

REMOVING PICTURE RAILS AND DADOS

Most picture rails and dados are simply nailed to the wall and mitered at the corners. If you don't need to remove a whole run, cut the ends to a miter as you saw out the damaged piece. (It is usually possible to do this without having to prize the molding away from the wall as you would for a baseboard.)

The nailed fixings make rails easy to remove, but prizing them free often causes minor damage to the plasterwork. Repair any holes with filler before replacing the rail, which doesn't have to be fixed the same way – or in the same place.

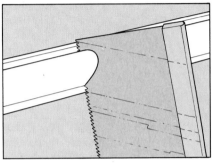

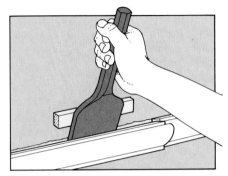

1 Saw across the rail with a backsaw where you are only removing a short section – a miter block helps to start the cut. Avoid sawing into the wall as you finish.

2 Lever off the molding with a brick chisel using a block of wood to protect the plaster. The old nails may snap rather than pull out – remove them later.

▐ PROBLEM SOLVER

Matching moldings

Modern moldings have simple profiles which are easy to match, and in many cases you just need a note of the dimensions. But when buying a replacement for more complicated shapes, take a pattern or a piece of the original molding along to ensure an exact match. The simplest way to make a pattern is to use a profile gauge to copy the shape.

Moldings in older houses are often much more elaborate and may be difficult to match. This applies particularly to baseboard, which may be very deep with a complicated shape at the top. If no exact match is available, the options are:
■ Moldings can be specially machined – at a price. Some lumberyards offer this service, otherwise try a specialist carpentry workshop.
■ Deep baseboard can sometimes be matched by building up several sections of standard moldings.
■ You may be able to plane or sand a similar piece to the required profile.

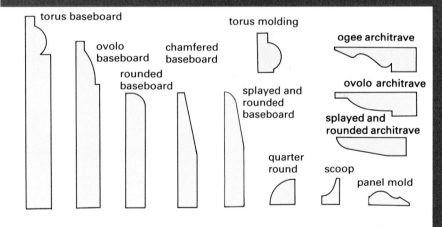

Standard moldings *cover an extensive range. Common, widely available shapes are shown here; for more elaborate ones you may need to go to a specialist.*

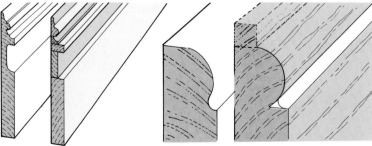

Deep baseboard profiles *can be built up by putting together a number of standard moldings, although this will not produce an exact match.*

Sandpaper or a plane *can be used to smooth rounded profiles. You may also be able to improve the contours by using filler, then sanding to shape.*

FITTING NEW BASEBOARD

To replace either a whole run or short section of baseboard, the new piece must be cut to the right length and its ends must be shaped to fit the existing board.

■ Mitered ends are used on external corners and also where you have cut out a short section. Take care to mark the overall length of the board from the outside of the miter and ensure that the miter slopes the right way.

■ Scribed ends, shaped to fit over the existing board, are needed at most internal corners.

Accuracy in measurement is very important to obtain a tight fit. If the piece you removed is in reasonable condition, you may be able to use it as a pattern to mark the replacement; simply allow a fraction extra on the length for the thickness of the saw cut. Otherwise, either measure the gap or lay the new baseboard against it and strike off the measurements directly.

It is better to cut the board slightly too large as it is easier to trim it down than to fill a gap.

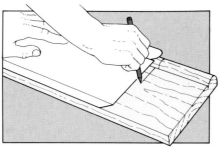

1 Transfer the dimensions of the gap to be filled on to the new board – by striking off directly, measuring, or using the removed piece as a guide.

2 Miter an end by marking a cutting line across the board and using a miter block and backsaw to start the cut. Remove the block to saw right across.

3 To scribe an end, cut a piece of old baseboard and hold it tightly down the cutting line. Draw the outline on the back and cut to shape with a coping saw.

4 Check the fit of the new board in the gap – if tight, plane or sand it down. Refix with nails, or use wallplugs and screws for a more secure fixing.

REPLACING ARCHITRAVES

Use a backsaw to cut the replacement molding to the right length. Although the corners of architraves must be mitered like a picture frame, they may not be exactly square so you cannot always do this in a miter box.

Check the exact length, either by using the old molding as a pattern or by copying the dimensions of the gap. If the corners are a true 45°, use a miter box to guide the cut. Otherwise, mark an accurate cutting line and saw along them freehand.

Nail the new length to the lining using finishing nails or oval wire nails and patch with filler.

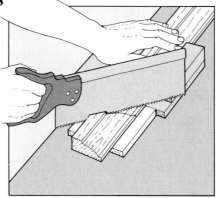

1 Measure and mark carefully. Cut mitered ends in a box if they are true – otherwise, mark the cutting line and use the backsaw freehand.

2 Nail through the replacement close to the edge so that the nails go into the thickness of the wood lining the opening – not into the wall plaster.

REPLACING PICTURE RAILS AND DADOS

Rails can be refixed with masonry nails if the plaster is sound. Where the plaster is weak, or where a picture rail is to carry heavy pictures, screws and wallplugs or frame fixings are more secure.

Measure the length accurately, and cut any miters using a miter box and backsaw. Cut too long rather than too short and trim to an exact fit – gaps are difficult to conceal.

If you are replacing a short section, glue the ends at the joint and insert one or two nails to strengthen it. Finish off with filler then sand to conceal.

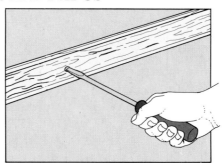

1 Cut a matching section and check that it fits. Fix with masonry nails or screws and plugs at 750–900mm (2'6"–3') intervals. Plug holes with filler.

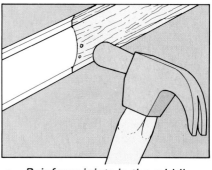

2 Reinforce joints in the middle of a run by gluing and nailing the ends together. Then use filler to patch any gaps, and sand smooth to hide the repair.

REPAIRING DOUBLE-HUNG WINDOWS

Sliding double-hung windows were standard fittings in the majority of Victorian houses, but went out of favor early in the 20th century. This is partly because their construction is more complicated than hinged casements, with a large number of parts. As a result of their age,

many original double-hung windows now need regular repairs to keep them in good working order.

Common faults (apart from rot damage) center around sticking sashes and broken sash cords. Cures for rot and minor sticking are covered on pages 181-184 and 257-258; other

repairs are described here.

Modern improvements and changing tastes have seen a return to the old style of window in some recently built homes. However, these have a completely different form of mechanism requiring much less maintenance.

DOUBLE-HUNG WINDOW CONSTRUCTION

Conventional double-hung windows have two sliding frames (the *sashes*), balanced by heavy *weights* on each side. These weights are concealed in deep side frames (sometimes called a *cased* frame) and are attached to *cords* which pass over *pulleys* at the top. (Occasionally, chains are used instead of cords.)

In most windows a thin strip of wood down the center of the case keeps the weights separate and stops them jamming, but this is not always present. There is also a removable cover which gives

access to the weight pockets.

The two sashes slide in separate grooves. The outer sash is trapped by the outside lining of the frame on one side and is retained on the other by a thin strip called a *parting bead* which is fitted into a grooved channel in the frame. The inner sash slides between the parting bead and an inner molding called the *staff bead* or *stop bead* nailed to the frame.

Modern double-hung windows have a completely different

construction. In place of the deep cases, the side member is solid. Depending on the design, either the frame or the sash have channels up each side in which there are *spring mechanisms* held inside thin tubes. These take the place of weights to balance the weight of the sashes. In some designs the sashes themselves are retained by beading as in a conventional window; in others, they are retained by catches which clip on to the spring mechanisms and can be released quickly.

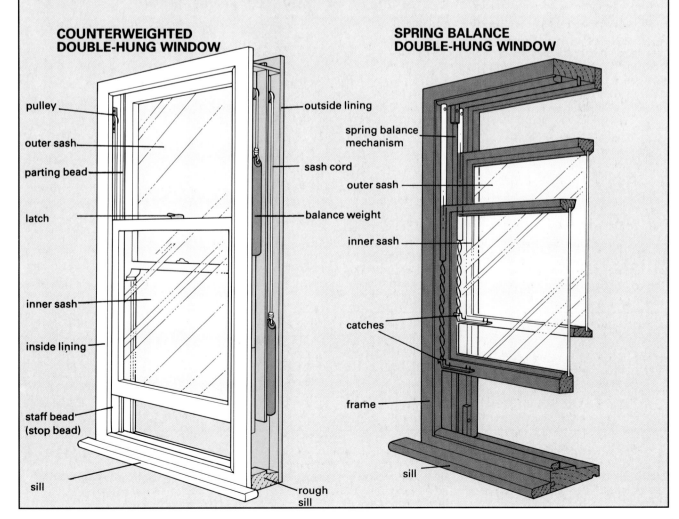

COUNTERWEIGHTED DOUBLE-HUNG WINDOW

pulley — outer sash — parting bead — latch — inner sash — inside lining — staff bead (stop bead) — sill — outside lining — sash cord — balance weight — rough sill

SPRING BALANCE DOUBLE-HUNG WINDOW

spring balance mechanism — outer sash — inner sash — catches — frame — sill

REMOVING A SASH

To take out a sash, the beading must be prized away. If you are careful, it is possible to do this without seriously damaging the paint finish or denting the wood. But if any of the strips of beading do get damaged, buy a replacement section. Staff bead and parting bead are standard moldings and should be readily available, although you may find that new ones are rather heavier looking than the originals.

■ Insert a broad chisel or stiff stripping knife between the window frame and one of the staff beads, somewhere near the middle. Tap with a mallet and prize gently until it bows away from the frame. The nails should then be clearly visible.

■ Carry on prizing close to each nail, as there is less risk of snapping the wood. With luck, the bead will then bow enough to free it from the miters at each end.

■ Where the bead is too tightly fitted, allow it to spring back and then pull the nail heads through the molding – after which it should be easy to slip out.

When both staff beads have been removed, the inner sash should lift away from the frame. At this stage it will still be suspended on the intact cord(s), so if you don't plan to renew the cords, carefully support the sash on a pair of steps or other suitable stand. Otherwise, release each cord by prizing out any fixing nails – or by cutting it. Don't allow the cord to fly back due to the weight on the other end: jam it in the pulley (see Tip).

To remove the outer sash, prize out the parting bead on one side, starting at one end; it will be held in its groove by very few nails. You should then be able to lift out the outer sash in the same way.

Trade tip

Trap the cord

❝ Where possible, stop the cord running back into the weight pocket; it will save work later. One way to do this is to tie a knot in it or jam a wooden wedge into the pulley to stop it turning. An alternative is to take a couple of turns round a scrap of wood – or even a screwdriver as shown. ❞

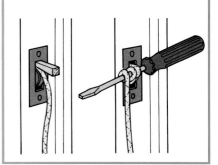

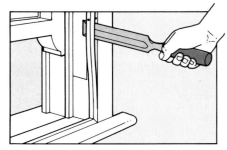

1 Prize the center of the staff bead so that it bows away from the frame. When the fixing pins are visible through the gap, prize near each one.

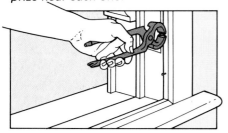

2 If the molding cannot be freed easily by prizing, allow it to spring back then pull out the nails by their exposed heads to free it.

3 Lift out the sash. Any intact cords will still be attached, so if you don't want to replace them, support the sash to one side. Otherwise, remove the cords, making sure the ends do not fall through the pulley.

4 To remove the outer sash, prize the parting bead out of its groove at one side. This may not be nailed at all, but at most there will only be two or three.

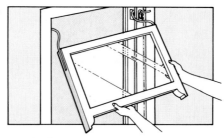

5 It should be possible to lift away the outer sash without disturbing the other bead. Deal with its cords in the same way as for the inner sash.

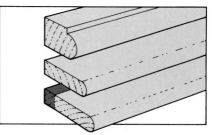

If any of the beads are damaged buy a replacement molding, standard sections are available. If the parting bead is too wide plane the back edge.

RENEWING A SASH CORD

Replace a broken or worn cord with a new length. It is often better to replace all the cords at once – if one has broken, it's likely that the others are well worn.

Sash cord is specially woven to resist stretching or wearing. The modern type is made from synthetic fiber and can be prevented from fraying by melting the end over a match. You also need some 25mm (1") *galvanized nails* to fix it.

At the bottom of the channel in which the window slides is a small cover which gives access to the weight pocket. This may be held by a screw, which must be removed (it can be tricky to locate if it is covered in old paint). Prize out the cover using an old chisel and lift the weight out of the frame.

If the old cord still runs over the pulley, tie a length of string to its end and use it to pull the string through; it will be used to thread the new cord. Otherwise, you need a slim weight which can be tied to one end of the string and which will fit over the pulley – examples are a large bent nail or a length of old bath chain. Pass this over the pulley and let it pull the string down until you can catch it through the weight pocket.

Take the old sash cord and cut a new piece to the same length or a little longer. Tie the cord to the end of the string and pull it through. Thread the end through the hole in the weight and tie it off, copying the old knot.

Nail the other end of the cord into the groove in the sash using a single nail. Make sure that the nail is further down the sash than the distance between the center of the pulley and the top of the window frame. Tap the nails in with great care, as it is very easy to shatter the glass.

With both cords fitted, try sliding the sash up and down:
■ If it will not go to the bottom of the frame, the cord is too short.
■ If the weight hits the bottom of the pocket when the sash is at the top, the cord is too long.
■ If the sash jams before it reaches the top, the nail is too far up.

Adjust the cord if necessary, then insert two or three more fixing nails below the first one.

Tap the pocket cover back into place and tighten the screw if one was fitted. Fit each sash in turn and refix the retaining beads. In most cases, new 25mm (1") finishing nails can be inserted in the old holes and tapped back in. If a beading was damaged, cut a new piece and nail it in place. Fill over the nails before re-decorating.

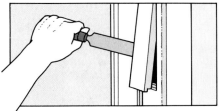

1 Prize off the cover of the weight pocket. Often this is simply wedged in place, but there is sometimes a screw concealed under the old paintwork.

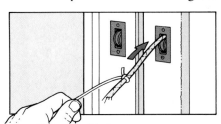

2 If the cord is in place, tie a length of stout string to it and then lift away the weight so that the string is pulled over the pulley.

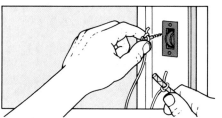

3 If the cord has snapped, pull the string over the pulley using a weight tied to the end. This weight must be slim enough to pass over the pulley.

4 Pull the new cord through and tie it to the weight. (If there are different weights, ensure you don't muddle them up at this stage).

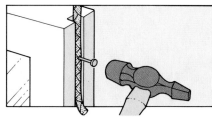

5 Nail the other end to the sash using a single nail. It must be fitted at least the distance shown from the top of the sash.

Trade tip

New pulleys

❝ Old pulleys may have rusted or have developed sharp spots on the rims. They are simply held by two screws and are easy to renew. ❞

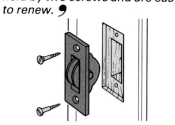

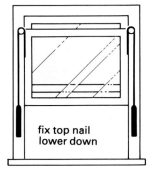 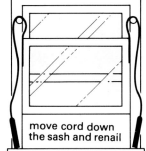 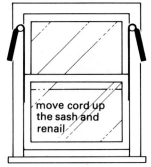

fix top nail lower down

move cord up the sash and renail

move cord down the sash and renail

6 Try the sash back in place temporarily and test the action to ensure that the cord is the right length. Pull out the single fixing nail and adjust its position to correct any of the faults shown.

7 Finish nailing the cords, then refit the pocket cover. To retain the sash, refit the beads and nail them; use the old nail holes where possible.

SPRING SASH REPAIRS

Modern double-hung windows with spring balance mechanisms are much easier to repair than the traditional type. The most common fault is that the spring loses its tension, but this is easy to adjust using the special tool provided by the manufacturer (or failing that, a stiff piece of bent wire). If the sash sticks at one point, the most likely cause is that the spiral needs oiling.

To tension a spring, lift the sash as far as it will go and support it with a length of wood. Hook the adjusting tool into the exposed end of the spiral mechanism and pull it down to free it from the catch.

Pull the mechanism down about 150mm (6″) without allowing it to untwist and lose the spring's tension. Turn the tool two or three times counter-clockwise to add tension, then hook it back in place.

Remove the prop and test the action – if the sash continues to drop, add a turn until it just stays in position.

To oil the spiral mechanism, unhook the mechanism as above, but this time allow it to untwist. Wipe down with an oily rag, then push it back up and wind to add tension.

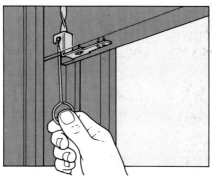

1 With the sashes raised to their full extent and propped in place, unhook the spiral mechanism using the adjusting tool.

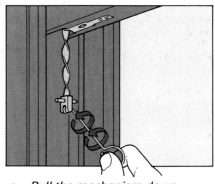

2 Pull the mechanism down about 150mm (6″) without allowing it to untwist. Add tension by turning counter-clockwise two or three turns.

3 Refit and test. The sash should just stay in place against spring tension – if not, repeat the process adding a turn at a time.

Oil the spring mechanism by allowing the spiral to untwist fully, then wiping down with an oiled rag. Twist it back up, then tension using the adjuster.

◤ PROBLEM SOLVER ◢

Curing rattling sashes

Double-hung windows rattle because the sliding sashes are loose in their grooves – a problem which affects the inner sash more than the outer. The most common causes are that the staff bead is fixed too far out, or the parting bead is too thin.

To cure a loose inner sash, remove and refix the staff beads. If the parting bead is worn, replace this first.

If an outer sash is loose and the parting bead is not worn, the only solution is to pack out the sides of the sash frame. A simple way to do this is to line it with strips of *iron-on plastic edging strip*. This is thin enough to take up the wear gradually and provides an ideal wearing surface.

Further cures are to fit cam-type or screw-type *latches* (whether or not window locks are also fitted). These tend to draw the two sashes tightly together at the meeting edge. If there is a gap here, fit a brush or spring strip draft excluder.

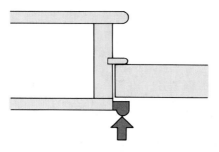

Refix the staff bead closer to the frame to stop the inner sash from rattling. Check the state of the parting bead first, though, and renew it if worn.

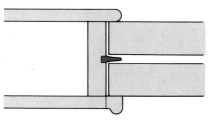

Replace the parting bead if the outer sash is loose. If this does not cure the problem, iron-on plastic strips will take up the wear on the frame.

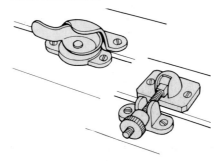

Cam-type and screw-type latches are both designed to draw the two sashes firmly together. Don't rely on them for security – fit bolts or locks as well.

Fit brush strip or spring strip draft excluder to the bottom rail of the outer sash. This will improve the draftproofing and cut down any rattling.

CURING STICKING WINDOWS

There are three main reasons why wooden windows stick:

Swollen wood caused by damp is normally a seasonal problem which only appears in wet weather. Treat by allowing the wood to dry out and preventing further damp penetration. The frame may also need to be trimmed down and repainted.

Paint build-up – often the result of poor preparation when the frames were last painted – is a problem which affects double-hung windows in particular. Treat by removing excess paint and refinishing. In bad cases where the window is stuck shut, extra care is needed to free it.

Dropped frames due to loose joints are the most serious problem. The frames must be repaired and strengthened, then trimmed if necessary and refinished. If a window frame is seriously weakened by rot damage, it may need extensive repairs – or even replacement.

Sticking double-hung windows may also be caused by a broken sash cord, covered on pages 253-256.

DOUBLE-HUNG WINDOW

paint build-up can make tracks tight

loose joints can cause bottom of sash to 'spread'

slight sticking on edge is probably due to damp or paint build-up

paint build-up can cause edge to stick

jamming here if frame has dropped

CASEMENT WINDOW

Diagnose the problem depending on the type of window being mended and where sticking occurs.

CURING SEASONAL SWELLING

When casement windows stick at the onset of damp weather, it's a sign that the wood is swelling as it absorbs moisture. Double-hung windows are less likely to be affected as they work with larger clearances.

A small amount of swelling is virtually inevitable because all timber expands and contracts as the weather gets warmer or cooler. So on a new window, it could simply be that the moving parts are too close a fit – a problem aggravated by redecorating during the summer months (see overleaf).

In many cases, however, swelling shows that moisture is getting into the wood – either because the paint isn't doing its job properly, or because water is seeping in through loose joints and cracked putty. If damp penetration like this is left untreated, there is a risk of wet rot developing.

The cure is to wait for a period of dry weather or arrange a temporary screen over the window so it can dry out. You may have to plane it to ease the sticking, then fill any gaps and repaint to prevent the problem from recurring.

1 *When the wood has dried out, you may need to plane the frame a little to let it shut properly. Use a Surform, which won't be damaged by old paint.*

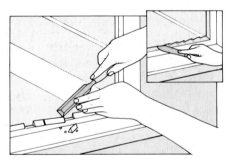

2 *Fill any gaps or cracks between the frame members with a flexible wood filler. If the wood putty is cracking, chip it out and replace.*

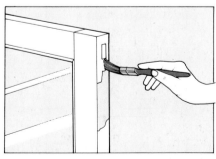

3 *Sand down any areas of thin or flaking paint. Repaint bare wood using primer, undercoat and topcoat, but avoid applying any of these too thickly.*

Trade tip

Easing the way

❛ On double-hung windows, slight sticking is often caused by friction between the sides of the sashes and the beading which holds them in the frame. In many cases this can be cured simply by rubbing a wax candle down all the surfaces in contact with one another. ❜

257

CURING PAINT BUILD-UP

Test the window to find out where the sticking is occuring (see Tip). If there is only a minor problem you may be able to cure it without refinishing the paintwork.

On hinged casements, thick paint normally causes localized sticking, often visible as scuff marks at a few points down the edge. This is easy to treat.

Similarly, double-hung windows which jam at odd points when raised are easily freed. But sashes which are stuck fast because they have been incorrectly painted pose greater problems. There is even a chance you may damage the sash beads while freeing them, though these can be replaced with specially-made moldings from a lumberyard.

Trade tip

Where does it stick?

❝ To test for tight spots, slip a piece of stiff paper into the joint and close the window. Slide the paper down and mark any points where it sticks. ❞

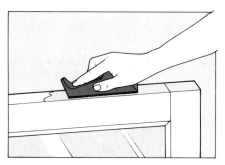

On casement windows, *sand or plane down the area which is sticking. If you go back to bare wood, prime, then apply thin coats of undercoat and topcoat.*

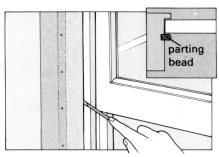

2 *Free a stuck outer sash by prizing out the parting bead set into a groove in the frame. Use a screwdriver or chisel and work it in under one end.*

1 **On double-hung windows,** *free a stuck inner sash by levering off the stop beads. Use a chisel and try to prize each bead free in one piece.*

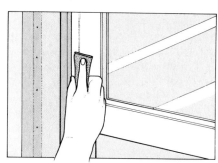

3 *Sand or scrape off excess paint. Refit the sashes and replace the beads in the order they came off. Pin in place, punch in the heads, and fill.*

REPAIRING A LOOSE FRAME

Loose joints often allow a frame to drop out of square, causing it to bind or jam. Where possible, it is better to remake the original joint; but if this is too badly damaged, use angle plates instead.

Hinged windows are simple to unscrew and can be repaired more easily once out of the frame. Double-hung windows can be removed (see above) to remake the joints, but when fitting angle plates it may be easier to leave the sashes in place.

In all cases, be very careful how you go about the job as it is easy to crack the glass.

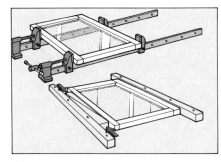

After removal, *a frame can be pulled square with sash clamps. Alternatively lay it on a board or wood floor between two nailed down strips of wood.*

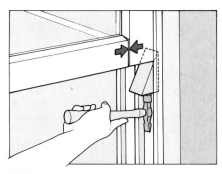

With a double-hung window, *it is sometimes preferable to leave the sashes in the frame and knock in wedges to force the corners of the sash frames back together.*

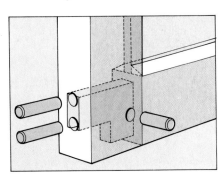

Reinforce a mortise and tenon *joint by drilling into it as shown then inserting glued dowels. Sand smooth and refinish any exposed wood.*

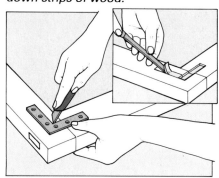

To fit angle plates, *lay them on the surface and cut round the outline using a trimming knife. Chisel out a shallow recess, slightly deeper than the plate . . .*

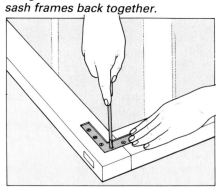

. . . then screw the plates *in place and fill flush with the surface using a resin wood filler. Fill any cracks with the same material, then repaint.*

HANGING A NEW DOOR

There's more to hanging a door than just fitting hinges. Hanging a new door in a new frame shouldn't be too difficult, particularly if you are installing the frame yourself: choose the door first and then build the frame around it. By contrast, hanging a new door in an old frame generally means tailoring the door to fit – and possibly repairing the frame, too.

Both situations involve a wide range of carpentry techniques. The first step is to trim the door so it fits the opening exactly, using a saw and a plane. Chiseling the hinge recesses and fitting the hinges comes next. Finally, you need to fit a lock or latch and any other door hardware.

The secret of success is to work gradually, rather than attempt to get a perfect fit first time. Even the experts often take several goes to make a door fit snugly, as well as opening and shutting smoothly.

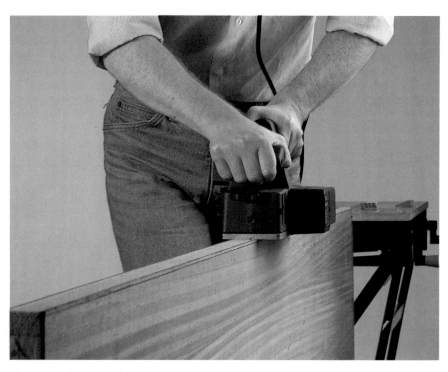

A power plane or sharp smoothing plane is essential if a door needs to be trimmed to fit the existing frame.

....Shopping List....

New doors come in a wide range of styles:
Panel doors have a heavy frame made from solid wood set with four or more thin panels of wood or plywood. Interior quality doors are thinner and cheaper than exterior ones.
Flush doors have smooth sides made from veneered plywood or hardboard. Interior doors have a hollow core filled with a lightweight honeycomb, and solid wood around the edges as reinforcement for the hinges and locks. Exterior doors often have a solid core.
Pressed hardboard interior doors are a form of flush door with an embossed surface resembling a panel door, although they are much lighter and cheaper.

All doors come in a range of standard sizes. The most common for exterior doors are:
- 2134×914mm (7'×3')
- 2032×838mm (6'8"×2'9")
- 2032×813mm (6'8"×2'8")
- 1981×838mm (6'6"×2'9")
- 1981×762mm (6'6"×2'6")

Interior doors are generally 1981mm (6'6") high and 838, 813,

762, 686 or 610mm (2'9", 2'8", 2'6", 2'3" or 2') wide.

Hinges can be either 75mm (3") or 100mm (4") butt hinges, depending on the size and weight of the door. Use pressed steel hinges for an interior door or flush exterior door, cast iron for a panel door which is to be painted, and brass for varnished doors. Buy screws to suit.

If you are replacing an old door, it helps to use the same size hinges (although new ones may not be a perfect match). If the new door is heavier, it may need larger hinges.
Door hardware includes a lock or latch, plus any other security fittings. In the case of a front door, you may also need a knocker or letter plate.
Finish is either varnish or primer, undercoat and paint, depending on the quality of the wood which the door is made from, and the style you choose.

Tools checklist: Crosscut saw or ripsaw, plane, chisels, screwdriver, trimming knife, drill and bits, finishing tools.

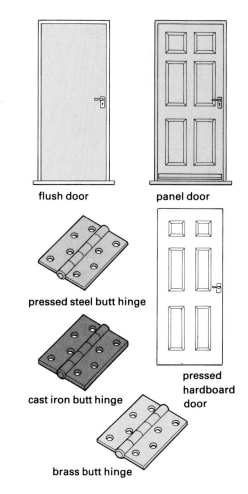

flush door   panel door

pressed steel butt hinge

cast iron butt hinge

pressed hardboard door

brass butt hinge

TRIMMING A DOOR TO FIT

Buy the door to fit the opening as closely as possible – either the exact size, or a little larger to allow for trimming down. If no standard sizes come close, you have a choice:

■ Buy the next size up (if there is a larger one) and cut it down to suit. The disadvantage is that this may involve removing so much wood that the door is seriously weakened. You can safely remove about 20mm (¾") from a panel door and about 10mm (⅜") from a flush door.

■ Buy a size too small and glue strips of wood on the sides and top to bring it up to size. This is only possible if you are painting the door and can conceal the joins.

■ Have a new door made to measure by a door specialist or carpentry workshop. This is the best solution; although expensive, it may not be unduly costly.

After trimming, the door should fit into the opening leaving a small gap all round – if it is too tight it will catch on the frame as it opens and shuts. Exterior doors also tend to expand and contract as the seasons change, so need a little more clearance to allow for this.

The normal clearance is around 3mm (⅛") down the sides and 6mm (¼") at the bottom, but it is best to work slowly and keep trying the door in the frame itself until the fit feels right. You can always trim more off if the door is too tight, but you can't easily restore it if too much has been trimmed off so always err on the cautious side.

If the door is more than a few millimeters too big, aim to take off an equal amount from both sides. On a panel door this keeps the panels in proportion; on a flush door it avoids weakening one side more than the other.

Where an old door was a good fit, use this as a guide to the dimensions. If you are fitting a door for the first time or the old one was a poor fit, measure the door against the frame.

1 If a panel door has 'horns' (extensions of the frame), mark across these square with the top and bottom rails and then cut them off flush.

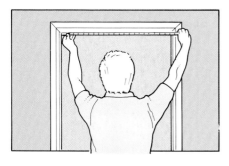

2 Measure the inside of the frame and transfer its dimensions to the door. You may be able to mark the door directly by standing it in the opening.

3 If the door has to be trimmed by a large amount, use a crosscut saw or power saw to cut most of the waste wood away. Make sure you keep well clear of the cutting line to allow for final trimming with a plane.

4 Using a plane, trim the door gradually to size. The height is least critical, so trim the ends first. Stand the door against the frame to check.

5 Trim the sides of the door a little at a time. Test it in the frame until it stands in place, leaving about a 3mm (⅛") gap all down one side.

Trade tip

Easier opening

❛ For a snug-fitting door that doesn't bind on the frame, it helps to plane the lock side to a slight bevel as shown. This counteracts the natural tendency of the inner corner to jam as it swings outwards. ❜

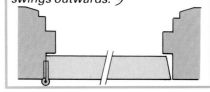

FITTING THE HINGES

Interior doors are hung using two hinges; heavy exterior doors are best hung on three. If there are no hinge recesses already cut in the frame, the top hinge goes about 150mm (6″) down, the bottom hinge goes about 225mm (9″) up, and a third goes midway between them. Where hinge recesses already exist, put the hinges in the same positions, but inspect the old recesses first in case you need to patch them (see Problem Solver).

On a flush door, check whether there are reinforcing blocks for the hinges and locks. Their positions will be marked on the outside.

Fit the hinges to the door first, then attach them to the frame making sure you leave a small clearance at the bottom of the door. The easiest way to do this is by standing the door on a thin piece of scrap plywood or other material.

You may find it easier to fit the lock or latch to the door before hanging it. But if you do so, bear in mind that it will be harder to give the door a final trim if it does not fit perfectly. In any case, don't fit the handles or the lock body (in the case of a rim lock), as these are easily damaged; attach those parts after the door is in the frame, then fit the striking plate to align exactly with the lock.

1 Mark the hinge positions by standing the door in the frame and copying the old recesses. If you are fitting to a new frame without existing recesses to copy, fix the hinge positions by measuring the door itself.

2 Hold each hinge against the edge of the door with the knuckle just projecting as shown. Cut round the hinge with a sharp knife to the depth of one leaf.

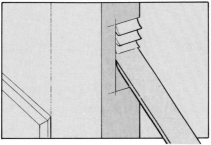

3 Chisel out the wood within the cut, taking care not to splinter it. Test the hinge in place until it just sits flush with the wood of the door.

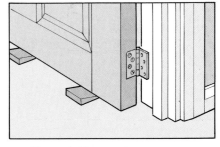

4 Fix each hinge using only one screw until you have tested the fit. Stand the door in the frame, propped up so that it just clears the floor.

5 Check the hinge positions on the frame. If you are making new recesses, mark the positions then cut round a spare hinge before chiseling the frame.

6 When the hinges align, insert one screw in each and test the swing of the door. Adjust as necessary (see Problem Solver), then add the remaining screws.

Trade tip

Out of sight

6 The bottom of an outside door is hard to reach and normally doesn't get painted, making it vulnerable to damp. To give long-term protection, one alternative is to give it two coats of primer and then at least one of topcoat before hanging, or brush on wood preservative – allowing plenty of time for it to dry before hanging the door. 9

Adjusting the hinges

It's not easy to cut the hinge recesses dead right first time around.

If the recesses are too shallow, the door will be too far from the frame, causing binding on the lock side. Chisel a fraction more wood out of one or both sets of recesses to move the door over.

If the recesses are too deep, the door will resist closing fully and tend to spring open; it is said to be 'hinge-bound'. Cure this by packing behind the hinge with slips of cardboard – pieces cut from a breakfast cereal box are ideal. (Contrary to opinion, this isn't botching – even professionals need to do it sometimes.)

Check also that the problem isn't simply due to a screw not being driven fully home.

If the hinges are misaligned, the door will be hard to move and the hinges may squeak. Cure this by setting each hinge parallel to the edge of the door and cutting sections out of the recesses, as necessary, to fit the hinges in new positions.

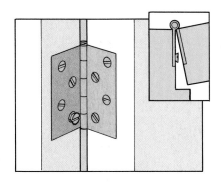

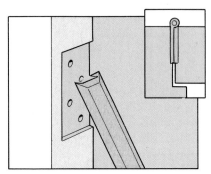

With any hinge problem check first that the hinge itself is not faulty and that the screw heads are not protruding, stopping the door closing properly.

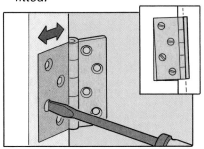

Recut shallow recesses to cure a door which binds on the lock side. Don't try trimming the edge of the door until the hinges are correctly fitted.

Cure hinge-bound doors by packing out the hinges with slips of cardboard. Add extra slips one by one until the leaf of the hinge is flush with the woodwork.

Misaligned hinges can cause all sorts of problems. Recut the recess parallel with the edge, refit the hinge, and test using a different screw hole.

Drill out damaged screw holes and pack with glued slips of wood or short lengths of dowel. Allow to dry before drilling new screw holes.

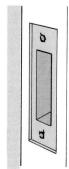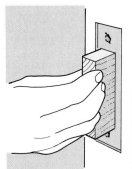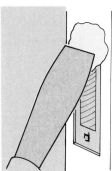

Fill large holes with glued blocks of wood. Small gaps can be plugged with resin filler to help strengthen the repair, then sanded smooth.

Patching the frame

Where possible, you should try to fit the new hinges and locks in the same position as the old ones. But this may mean that damaged existing recesses need to be patched before hanging the new door.

Hinge recesses often need to be repaired because the old screw holes are damaged or slightly offset from the new ones, making it hard to redrill the holes. You may also find that the hinges are a slightly different size, leaving unwanted gaps at the ends or down the sides.

Lock recesses may be a slightly different size, leaving part of the hole to patch. And if the new door has to have a lock in a different place, you need to finish the old hole flush.

General-purpose filler can be used, but is prone to cracks if there is any movement at all in the frame. It's better to use blocks of scrap wood wherever possible, then fill any remaining cracks with resin filler for extra strength.

CHOOSING HINGES

Hinges have countless uses in woodwork, from hanging house doors, cabinet doors and gates, to building folding tables and fitting flaps in furniture. Such a variety of applications has led to an equally varied number of hinge types – an additional complication being that many hinges come in a range of sizes and materials.

In practice, choosing hinges is seldom too difficult, since most DIY stores only stock a small range of popular types – for example, butt hinges for doors, strap hinges for gates and concealed cabinet hinges for kitchen furniture. But if you're keen on woodwork, you'll find that some hardware stores stock a wide selection of specialist and decorative hinges.

Parts of a hinge: *most forms of hinge are broadly similar in construction.*

finial — knuckle

pin

recessed hinge · leaf (flap) · decorative hinge · lift-off hinge

DOOR HINGES

Butt hinges are the normal type of door hinge, and come in different sizes, referred to by the length of the knuckle; 75mm and 100mm (3″ and 4″) hinges are commonly used for house doors – smaller ones are used on furniture and larger ones on very heavy doors. They are usually sold in pairs or sets of three ('1½ pairs').

Butt hinges are made in different materials. *Pressed steel* hinges are for fairly lightweight interior doors and must be painted to resist rusting. *Cast iron* hinges have thicker leaves to suit heavier interior or exterior doors; they, too, must be painted. *Brass* hinges don't need painting and are used to decorate varnished doors.

Rising butt hinges lift a door as it opens – for example, to clear a thick floorcovering – and also tend to make it swing closed by itself. They are made in pressed steel and come in left or right handed sets depending on which way the door opens.

Rising butts are a form of *lift-off hinge*: the door can be lifted free of the hinge pins when fully opened.

T hinges are a traditional type of hinge used on rustic doors and also on gates. A similar looking hinge in black iron is fitted to some 'Tudor' style front doors, but on modern versions the strap is often purely decorative and is fitted over an ordinary butt hinge.

Double spring hinges are for swinging louver doors often used in kitchens.

pressed steel butt hinge

cast-iron butt hinge

brass butt hinge

rising butt hinge

T hinge

black iron decorative strap hinge

double spring hinges

263

GARAGE AND GATE HINGES

Strap hinges are for light or medium gates which lie flush with the fence. Painted or galvanized and sold by length. Heavy duty *reversible strap hinges* have separate pivot bosses and are made for garage doors or heavy gates. Also for garage doors are *hook and pin sets* which allow the door to be lifted off. Both of the latter types are normally plain steel and must be painted before fitting.

T hinges are for hanging light and medium gates flush with a post. Painted black or galvanized, and sold by length.

Hinge pins and straps are made for hanging gates. Different pins are available for mortaring into brickwork or bolting or nailing to a post. Double straps are used for heavy gates.

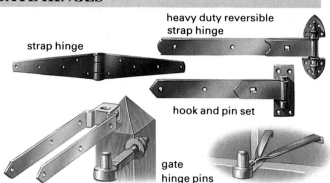

strap hinge

heavy duty reversible strap hinge

hook and pin set

gate hinge pins

CABINET LEAF HINGES

Suite hinges are smaller versions of the butt hinges used on house doors, and are designed for use on cabinet doors and chest lids. They are mostly made of brass or plated steel. Size is given in terms of the length of the knuckle, but hinges are also made with wide and narrow leaves for heavy and fine work, so the width of the leaf may also be quoted.

Decorative leaf hinges are made from brass and are for flush fixing on the face of furniture. They come in different styles – 'H' and snake patterns are two common examples.

Backflap hinges are similar to a very wide butt hinge but have offset screw holes for a stronger fixing. They are used for drop-leaf flaps and tables, where strength is important.

Flush hinges have very thin leaves which fit within each other and therefore don't need recessing – they simply screw to the edge of the door.

Piano hinge (always described in the singular) resembles a continuous lightweight butt hinge. It is cut to length with a hacksaw for use on doors and flaps without recessing.

Table and counter hinges are heavy brass hinges for use on drop-leaf tables and counters. There are several styles.

Mortise hinges are let into holes cut into the edge of doors and furniture panels for a neat, concealed fixing.

Cranked hinges ('angle hinges') are a form of *lay-on* (ie non-recessed) hinge designed to give a strong fixing and extra support. The crank also makes it possible to fix a door so it opens within its own width.

Pivot hinges have short pivot pins and thin fixing plates or studs in place of flat leaves. They are mainly for doors that cannot be fastened along the edge.

narrow suite hinge

decorative 'snake' hinge

backflap hinge

flush hinge

mortise hinge

piano hinge

counter hinge

single cranked hinge

lift-off pivot hinge

center pivot hinge

CONCEALED CABINET HINGES

Modern built-in and modular furniture depends on this type of hinge, which is invisible when the door is closed.

The hinge itself fits into a large hole drilled in the door, the hinge arm then locks on to an adjustable fixing plate screwed to the side of the cabinet. All types are designed for use with furniture made from either 15mm (⅝″) or 19mm (¾″) board.

The hinges are available either sprung or unsprung. Unsprung hinges are for doors with a catch to hold them closed; sprung hinges stay closed without a separate catch.

100° hinges are the standard type, allowing the door to open straight outwards.

110 and 125° hinges are for units with internal drawers or wire baskets which need the door to open wider.

170° hinges open flat back against the adjacent cabinet to provide full access; because the door doesn't project, they also fulfil an important safety role.

Glass door hinges have a special boss designed to fit a hole drilled through a glass door panel.

Most hinges need a 35mm hinge boring bit (end mill) but some miniature versions take a 26mm bit. *Height adjustable base plates* are standard on some hinges and can be fitted to allow for extra adjustment.

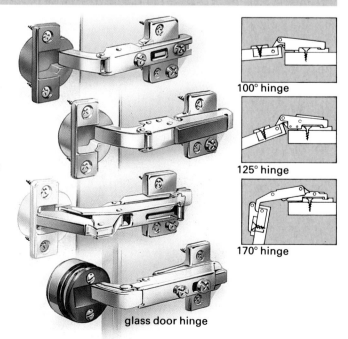

100° hinge

125° hinge

170° hinge

glass door hinge

CURING STICKING DOORS

A door may stick if you've laid a new floor covering, or for several other reasons (see right). Fix it as soon as you can – continual sticking can weaken the joints and hinges.

Check where the door sticks using thin cardboard; close the door and run the cardboard around the gap, marking where it jams. Afterwards, trace the fault using the checklist below.

Before going any further, make sure that the door itself is sound.

Serious warping is shown by a door which won't sit flush in its frame.
Dropping due to loose joints is common on older, heavier panel doors. It's often shown by cracks in the finish over the joints.
Wet rot reveals itself on outside doors, usually at the base, as cracked wood or flaking paint which gives way if prodded with a knife.

Repairing these faults is beyond the scope of this book. It's often easier to replace the door.

Check all around to find out where the door sticks. Then use the checklist (left) to identify possible causes and their cures.

DOOR FAULT CHECKLIST

PROBLEM	POSSIBLE CAUSES	CURE
A: Sticks at bottom Symptom: Scrapes floor or flattens carpet	Poor trimming when fitted Swelling due to damp Thicker floor covering Dropping due to loose joints	Sand or plane Sand and seal Trim off surplus Repair/replace
B: Sticks at lock side Symptom: Scuffs frame	Paint build up Poor trimming when fitted Swelling due to damp	Sand or plane Sand or plane Sand/plane and seal
C: Sticks at top Symptom: Scuffs frame	Paint build up Poor trimming when fitted Swelling due to damp	Sand off Sand or plane Sand/plane and seal
D: Jams at hinge side Symptom: Tends to spring open	Paint build up on edge Paint/rust build up on hinge Projecting hinge screws Hinges recessed too deeply	Sand off surplus Clean and oil Refit screws Pack out hinges

SANDING EDGES

If the door only sticks slightly, you can often cure it by sanding down the high spots. Often there is no need to remove it.

Wait until a warm, dry spell, particularly if you suspect the problem is caused by damp weather. If you are trimming the side or top, use a wedge to keep the door open while you work. And be sure to sand the door down enough to allow for the thickness of the paint coats you will apply.

Unless you want to refinish the whole door, sand and repaint the entire edge, not just patches. This way the area of new paint won't be obvious if the colors don't match exactly.

Prime and paint (or revarnish) the bare wood as soon as possible. Remember that you need to leave the door open until it dries, so start in the morning if it's an outside door.

Sticking at the side can be cured by sanding the high spots – use a block of wood to keep the paper square to the door. Refinish the whole edge afterwards.

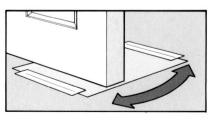

Slight sticking at the bottom can often be cured by taping coarse sandpaper to the floor and working the door over it. Replace the paper as it wears out.

Trade tip

Take the easy way out

❝ Don't be in too much of a hurry to remove wood from the door if the sticking is slight. Doors and frames expand and contract if the weather is very damp or very dry, and you may find that a minor problem which appears in the autumn goes again in the spring.

If the sticking is occasional and not too serious, I start by rubbing a candle along the edge of the door and frame to ease the tight spots. Often, this cures the problem. ❞

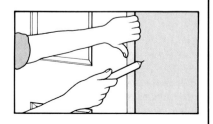

REMOVING A DOOR

The first step to curing more serious sticking is to take the door off its hinges. How difficult this is depends on the weight of the door, and also on whether you are working on your own. Tackling any door is easier if you work this way:

■ Open the door so that it clears the frame and you can get at the hinge screws easily.

■ Slip something underneath to support the weight. A pair of wedges, or even a couple of old magazines, will do.

■ It's helpful to put something behind the door – a small chair, say – so that it doesn't fall backwards when you unscrew the hinges. Don't bother, though, if the door is a lightweight type or if you have an assistant to help you.

■ Undo the screws on the frame, not on the door.

■ Clean the screw slots and slacken each screw half a turn so that they turn easily when you want them to.

■ Remove all but one screw in the bottom hinge, then repeat for the top hinge.

■ Remove the last screw in the bottom hinge. Then take the weight of the door and remove the final screw in the top hinge.

To replace the door, prop it back in position. Steady it with one screw at the top, then add the others.

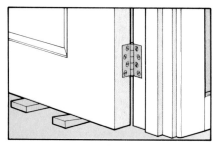

1 *Open the door far enough to expose the hinges. Slip some magazines or a pair of wooden wedges underneath so that the weight of the door is supported.*

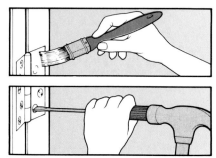

2 *Clean old paint out of the screw slots. Either dab on paint stripper, or tap the slots using an old screwdriver to chip away the built-up layers.*

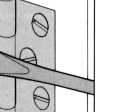

3 *Slacken each screw half a turn so you can be sure they unscrew easily when you need them to. Make sure your screwdriver fits the slots exactly.*

Remove all but one *screw from each hinge. Undo the last screw at the bottom, support the door, then remove the top screw and lift away from frame.*

CURING SERIOUS STICKING

If sanding won't cure sticking at the bottom, use a plane to remove up to 6mm (¼") of waste wood. Mark a trimming line parallel to the floor, allowing a 2–3mm (⅛") gap.

■ You could need to trim more than this from the bottom to clear a thick floor covering. It's much easier to saw this off (but see Problem Solver for another solution).

It's worth waiting for a warm, dry spell before starting. Refinish the door as soon as possible, so the bare wood doesn't have a chance to swell. If the bottom has been sticking due to dampness, prime and paint (or varnish) before rehanging.

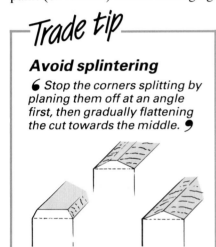
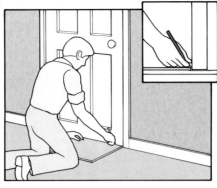

1 When a door sticks badly at the bottom, use a scrap of hardboard or ply to rule a line along it parallel to the floor and about 3mm (⅛") up.

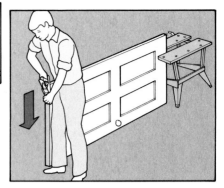

2 Remove the door and support it on a side edge. Plane the bottom, working from one corner towards the middle, then turn it over and plane the other side.

Mark the clearance for a new floor covering with the door placed against the frame. Mark off the clearance at the top, then transfer to the bottom.

To saw off a larger strip, support the door on trestles or a portable bench. Use a crosscut or saber saw and guide strips. Finish with a plane or sandpaper.

CURING HINGE FAULTS

If the door won't shut properly and tends to open itself, the cause may be that the hinge side of the door is jamming against the frame. This problem is often made worse on old doors by the build up of several coats of paint, but the most common causes are:

■ The hinge recesses are too deep. You need to pack out the hinges so they can shut correctly.

■ The heads of some of the screws are protruding, preventing the hinges from closing. You need to improve the fit of the screws.

In both cases you may not even need to remove the door, but wedge it open and pack it underneath to support the weight. If packing out the hinges causes the opposite side of the door to stick, sand off the surplus or remove the door and plane the edge.

It's also worth checking the condition of the hinges. Old paint or rust could be jamming them, so scrape this off and oil them if necessary. Replace hopelessly worn or rusty hinges.

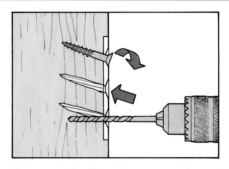

Remove misaligned screws and plug the holes with matchsticks dipped in glue. Redrill the holes straight when the glue has dried, then replace the screws.

An alternative is to remove the screws one by one. Drill out each screw recess with a countersink bit suitable for metal, then refit the screw.

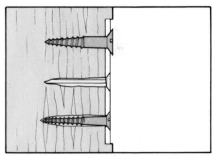

Replace oversize screws with thinner ones that fit the recesses better. If they don't grip, again pack the holes with matchsticks dipped in glue.

Uneven floors

It's quite common for the door to open over a floor which slopes, has a bump, or is covered with a thick carpet. In any of these cases, removing sufficient wood from the bottom of the door to clear the obstruction is likely to leave a wide, drafty gap when the door is closed.

An alternative is to fit **rising butt hinges**. These replace the ordinary hinges and are designed to lift the door about 10mm (⅞") as it opens, providing extra clearance. They also have the effect of making the door close automatically – which may or may not suit you.

Rising butts are *lift-off* hinges; they come apart so that the door can be removed by lifting it upwards off the hinge pins. They are sold in right or left handed sets, and it's important to choose the correct ones so that the door goes up – not down – as it opens.

Rising butts aren't always an exact size-for-size replacement for the existing hinges, so you could have to enlarge or fill the hinge recesses. You may also need to trim the top of the door so that it doesn't jam on the frame when it lifts during opening.

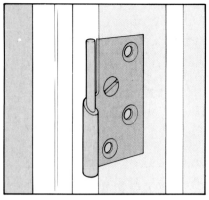

1 Remove the door by unscrewing the existing hinges from the frame. Fit the hinge pin halves of the rising butts to the frame, using one screw each.

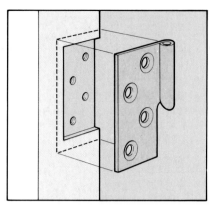

2 If the rising butts are larger than the original hinges, enlarge the recesses with a chisel. If they are smaller, the gaps can be filled later.

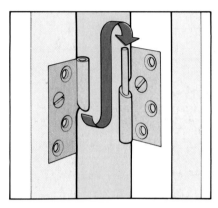

3 Screw the other halves of the rising butts to the door using one screw each. Lift the door onto the pins of the fixed halves and check that they align.

4 Swing the door to check its action. If all is well, fix the other screws. If not, remove the door and realign the hinges before trying again.

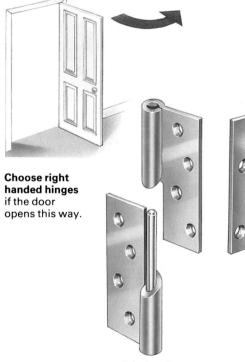

Choose right handed hinges if the door opens this way.

right hand

Choose left handed hinges if the door opens this way.

left hand

Trade tip

When to trim

❝ Unless the door is a very loose fit, you'll probably need to plane away the top at a slight angle to clear the frame as it closes. Take care when you first fit the door, as it is easy to damage the frame by accident. Close it gently, watching the top as you go, and mark where it touches. ❞

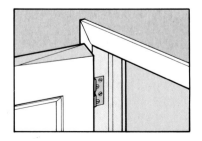

SECURING DOORS – 1

Front and back doors fitted with nothing more secure than a simple nightlatch provide an open invitation to burglars. And even doors which are already fitted with a mortise lock may not be as secure as they should be – particularly if the lock itself has a simple *two or three lever* mechanism (see below).

The illustrations on the right show what's needed to provide a reasonable level of security for front and back doors. This section describes how to choose and fit mortise locks and bolts; the other fittings shown – deadlatches, chains and viewers – are covered on pages 273-276, which also deal with french windows and patio doors.

Check your doors

Good locks can make things hard for a thief, but there is no point in fitting them to a flimsy door with glass panes and thin wood panels that can be smashed to gain access. If the door itself is weak, replacing it may be the only answer.

Likewise, you can't fit a mortise lock unless the woodwork is sound and thick enough to take it. The outer frame member (stile) of the door must be at least 45mm (1¾") thick and 75mm (3") wide to fit a standard lock, although *narrow stile* locks fit 64mm (2½") stiles.

....Shopping List....

Mortise locks are mostly lever action, with a conventional key which slides a *deadbolt* into a striking plate on the door frame. ('Deadbolt' means it can't be pushed back in without the key.) For extra strength, the striking plate is often reinforced with a *box staple* around the bolt.

Two-bolt mortise *sashlocks* are similar but incorporate a handle-operated latch which keeps the door closed without turning the key. Some sashlocks are left or right 'handed', others are reversible.

Cylinder mortise locks use a flat key which operates a tumbler-type mechanism. This fits right through the door and is retained by a screw through the end of the lock case.

Although high security locks are not cheap, they are certainly

worthwhile for the strength and security they provide. Among other requirements, no lever lock is considered thief resistant unless it has at least five levers.

Door bolts come in a range of styles, some for flush mounting, others for fitting within the woodwork.

Tools checklist: Electric drill and bits (see lock instructions for sizes), trimming knife, screwdriver, chisels, try-square.

Fit a deadlatch one third of the way down from the top of the door.

Door viewers and chains provide added security against unwanted callers.

Fit a five lever mortise lock near the centre of the edge of the door. Use a sashlock if the door is opened frequently.

Fit a five lever mortise deadlock one third of the way up from the bottom of the door.

Hinge bolts can be used to reinforce a weak door, especially where it opens outwards.

Bolts fitted near the top and bottom of the door protect it against forcing and can be fastened before you go out.

The front door is normally the one you leave the house by, so it must be lockable from the outside. Fit two locks as shown and fasten both when you go out. Use the latch for convenience when you are indoors.

Back or side doors only need a single mortise deadlock, as they can be bolted before you go out. If the door is used a lot, fit a two-bolt mortise sashlock to ensure it stays shut without using the key.

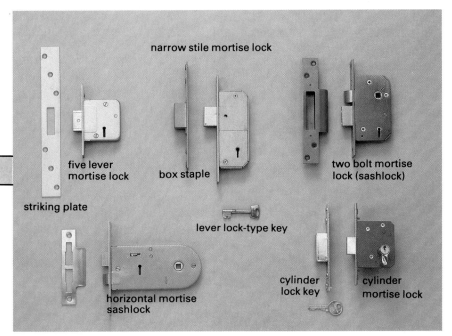

narrow stile mortise lock

five lever mortise lock

striking plate

box staple

two bolt mortise lock (sashlock)

lever lock-type key

horizontal mortise sashlock

cylinder lock key

cylinder mortise lock

Trade tip

Key cutting

6 *If you're fitting deadlocks to two or more exterior doors, use locks of the same make and get a locksmith to change the levers or tumblers so they work with the same key. Some cylinder locks are supplied with spare cylinders for this purpose.* 9

FITTING A MORTISE LOCK

The amount of work involved in fitting a mortise lock depends on whether you are replacing an old one with a more secure model or installing a lock where none exists. Sashlocks and cylinder mortise locks are fitted in much the same way as a simple mortise lock, except that you need to drill extra holes after cutting the mortise.

Replacing an existing lock

Although there are standards for the size of mortise locks, there is no guarantee that a replacement lock will slot straight into the hole left by an old one. To check how to proceed, it's worth removing the existing lock and measuring its exact dimensions before buying a replacement.

Take the opportunity to inspect the mortise, too. Even if the hole is in good order, you may have to trim or enlarge it; and if you fit a lock with a box staple striking plate, this will probably need an enlarged recess as well.

If the mortise is mis-shapen, oversized or the surrounding wood has cracked, you have two alternatives:
■ Fit metal reinforcing plates to the area of the lock on both faces of the door.
■ Fill the old mortise and striking plate recess (see Problem Solver), then cut a fresh mortise elsewhere on the stile. This is also the best solution if the old lock was fitted in the wrong place – either too far up or down the door.

Trade tip

Removing a lock

❝ Trying to lever an old mortise lock free is likely to damage the woodwork. With a sashlock, remove the handles and tap the spindle sideways to loosen the lock. Otherwise, turn the key and pull on the bolt using a self-grip wrench. ❞

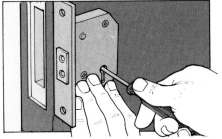

CUTTING A LOCK MORTISE

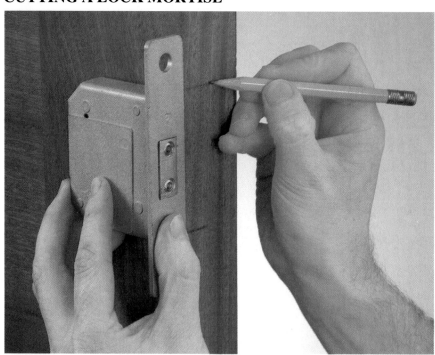

1 Place the lock in position and strike off marks in line with the top and bottom of the body. Remove the lock and use a try square to extend lines right across the edge. Then rule a line down the center of the edge between them.

A new lock mortise must be cut as accurately as possible to avoid weakening the door unnecessarily. If the door already has a mortise which is unusable, site the new one at least 150mm (6″) away from it.

Some mortise locks have a double end plate which comes with a polished outer trim section. You need to remove this to fit the lock, but remember to allow for its extra thickness when recessing the end plate or working out the position of the keyhole.

2 Drill a series of holes down this center line, square to the wood. Use a bit the same width as the lock case, and mark it to show the lock's depth.

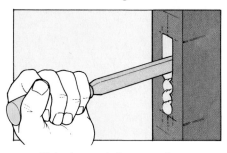

3 Chisel remaining wood away to square up the mortise, then test-fit the lock. Extend the bolt first so you have something to grip if it sticks in the hole.

4 Cut round the end plate of the lock with a trimming knife, then chisel a recess. To check the fit, reverse the lock and try the end plate in place.

5 Hold the lock against the side of the door to mark the holes for the key, cylinder or spindle. Drill holes across and cut a keyhole slot with a saw or file.

FITTING THE STRIKING PLATE

Fit the striking plate to the frame after fitting the lock so that you can be sure the bolt slides cleanly. The alignment is especially critical on a sashlock, where even a slight mismatch may stop the latch engaging.

If the door is a tight fit, you have no choice but to chisel out a recess and set the striking plate into the frame. But where there is plenty of clearance, simply cut a recess for the bolt hole and screw the plate itself to the surface of the door frame.

See Problem Solver for how to deal with alignment difficulties once the lock has been fully fitted.

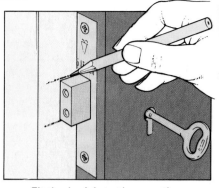 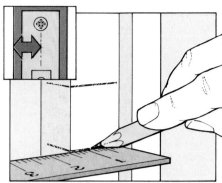

1 Fit the lock into the mortise and add the mounting screws. Test the operation with the key, then close the door to mark where the bolt contacts the frame.

2 Measure from the closing edge of the door to the center line of the bolt. Mark this distance out from the door stop to show the center of the striking plate.

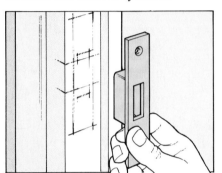  

3 Cut a recess to fit the hole in the striking plate using the marks to guide you. A box staple needs a hole much larger than the bolt itself.

4 Test fit the striking plate. If it needs to be sunk flush with the frame, cut around the outside edge using a trimming knife and chisel out a recess.

5 Fit the striking plate in place and test the lock before inserting the fixing screws. This allows you to move the plate or enlarge the recess if necessary.

FINISHING OFF

On a simple mortise lock, trim the keyholes by fitting keyhole plates. A sashlock also needs operating handles or knobs – often supplied as a combined set on a plate which incorporates a keyhole, although separate handles and plates may be used.

Cylinder mortise locks normally have a trim plate to conceal the fitting hole around the cylinder. On versions which incorporate a latch handle, this may be fitted on a mounting plate with a shaped cutout to fit the cylinder.

Fit plates over the keyholes. Cylinder mortise locks have shaped side plates to conceal the hole where the cylinder passes through the door.

On a sashlock, pass the spindle through the lock and slip on the handles; bear in mind that you may need to cut the spindle shorter with a junior hacksaw. Use the key to align the keyhole, then screw on the plate.

FITTING DOOR BOLTS

Bolts provide extra security for doors which can be fastened from inside. There are several types, but all should be fitted in pairs near the top and bottom of the door.

Surface mounted bolts only offer security if they are solidly built with sturdy screw mountings. *Sliding bolts* are common utility types, with a round bolt bar which slides in a guide on the door and fits into a staple on the frame. *Locking bolts* normally have an enclosed bolt held in the closed position by a small key-operated lock. *Flush bolts* are recessed into the wood of the door for a neat appearance; on double doors, they can be fitted to the ends of the door to shoot upwards and downwards.

Mortise rack bolts fit into the edge of the door for added strength. They are operated with a special key, making them suitable for use on glass paneled doors where most surface mounted bolts can be slipped by breaking the glass and reaching through.

Hinge bolts provide protection against the door being forced open by attacking the hinges. This is most likely on doors which open outwards where the hinges are exposed. Fit two, 75mm (3″) above and below the top and bottom hinges. They engage automatically whenever the door is closed.

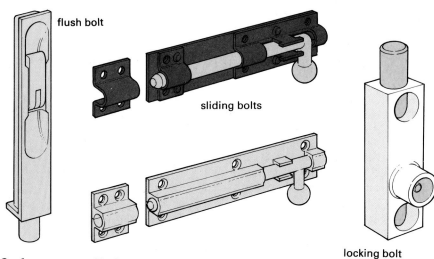

flush bolt

sliding bolts

locking bolt

***Surface mounted bolts** screw to the door, although you may need to chisel a recess on the frame to fit the striking plate. They come in several styles.*

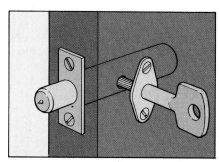

***Mortise bolts** fit into a mounting hole in the stile with a crossways hole for the key. They shoot into a striking plate fitted over a hole in the frame.*

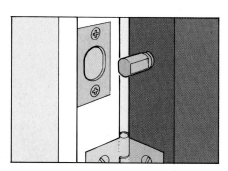

***Hinge bolts** screw into mounting holes drilled in the centre of the door edge. As the door is closed they engage with striking plates recessed into the frame.*

PROBLEM SOLVER

Patching an old mortise

Don't rely on general-purpose filler to patch an unwanted mortise hole – it's important to restore as much of the door's strength as possible. The best method is to cut blocks of wood to fit the old hole as accurately as possible and glue them in place with woodworking adhesive.

Cut the blocks so that they are a tight fit in the hole, but don't try to force them in or you may damage the surrounding woodwork. Leave the ends protruding from the hole slightly so that you can plane or sand them off smooth after the adhesive has fully hardened (between 7–16 hours).

To patch any remaining small gaps and holes, use a resin-based wood filler which won't shrink or crack. Resin filler also sets as hard as the surrounding wood itself, helping to add to the strength of the repair.

***Fill an old mortise hole** with blocks of wood cut to roughly the right size and glued in place. Then patch with resin filler.*

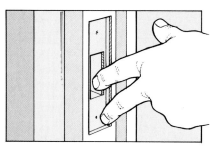

***Where sticking** is due to a misaligned striking plate, enlarge the recess and move it over. Pack behind with glued strips of wood.*

Sticking locks

A stiff or jammed action on a recently fitted lock is most likely to be due to misalignment of the bolt and the striking plate. Open the door and see if the lock works freely. If it does, inspect the striking plate for wear marks to find out where the bolt has been rubbing.

Start by making sure the problem isn't simply the result of the door warping or dropping on its hinges. This is the most likely cause – especially in winter – and is usually easily remedied without having to touch the lock.

Otherwise, remove the striking plate and recut the recess to correct its position. Pack the hole with glued wood strips to maintain a tight fit.

To free a stiff lock, lubricate with powdered graphite (from locksmiths) rather than oil, which tends to attract dust and soon makes matters worse.

SECURING DOORS – 2

Mortise locks and bolts provide a high level of security, but aren't very convenient for keeping doors shut while you are in. You may also find that a door simply isn't substantial enough to take a mortise lock. The alternative is to fit a deadbolt.

Using deadbolts

Don't confuse a deadbolt with the similar-looking nightbolt, which may be found on some outside doors. Nightbolts are much less secure (see overleaf), and in high-risk situations are best replaced.

A deadbolt engages automatically when the door is closed, ensuring it isn't left unsecured by accident. Although potentially less secure than a mortise lock, it is proof against most forms of attack. And because the lock screws to the surface of the door, it weakens it less than cutting a mortise.

As shown in the previous section, a front door should have a deadbolt as well as a mortise lock. Any door which cannot take a mortise can have a deadbolt instead, so long as it is backed up by bolts.

Completing your security

A front door will also benefit from a *viewer*, enabling unwanted callers to be avoided, and a *chain* for keeping strangers out until you've checked their credentials.

French doors or ordinary patio doors need securing with custom-made locks and bolts. And if your house has an integral garage, you should take steps to ensure the doors can't easily be forced.

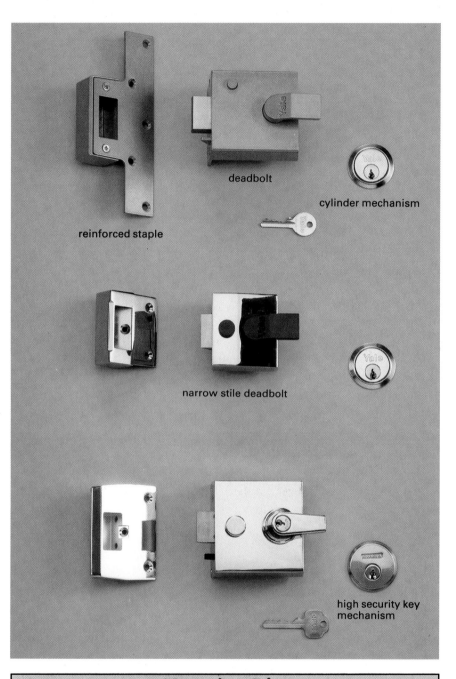

reinforced staple

deadbolt

cylinder mechanism

narrow stile deadbolt

high security key mechanism

Trade tip

Key changes

6 If you lose your keys, or if you have just moved home, you cannot be sure of the security of your locks. If an existing lock is a secure type that is worth keeping, you can avoid much of the expense of a new lock by buying a replacement cylinder mechanism (barrel) and fitting this in place of the old one. You can also buy matched sets for securing the front and back door with the same key. 9

.... Shopping List ....

Deadbolts come in a wide range of styles and can be fitted to most doors over 38mm (1½") thick. Standard designs need a door stile around 90mm (3½") wide – if yours is narrower, alternative models are available for stiles as narrow as 40mm (1½"). All types have a cylinder lock mechanism using a flat key, although there are several variations depending on the make.

High security deadbolts have stronger cylinder mechanisms and reinforced staples (which need to be recessed into the frame). But

any lock sold as "high security" will normally have been tested to withstand forcing as well as attack by drilling and sawing.

Chains and peepholes are made in several different designs and a range of finishes. See page 275 for details.

Patio door locks and bolts vary according to the doors concerned. See page 276 for details.

Tools checklist: Screwdriver, junior hacksaw (possibly), chisel, electric drill and bits.

HOW DEADBOLTS WORK

Deadbolts are a form of 'rim lock', a term for any lock screwed to the inside surface of the door. They have *cylinder* mechanisms fitted into a hole drilled through the door and operated by a flat key.

A deadbolt is secure because the bolt is deadlocked in position when the door is shut, and cannot be pushed back without the key. With some designs this happens automatically when the door is closed; for added security you can lock the internal operation knob/handle. Other types are deadlocked by using the key to throw the bolt further across or to operate a separate bolt.

Nightbolts are another form of cylinder rim lock. They have a springbolt operated by a key from outside and a knob inside. Nightbolts are less secure because they do not deadlock – the bolt can be fixed in position using the snib, but not from outside. This means that the springbolt can often be forced back with a strip of metal or plastic, while on glazed doors smashing the glass gives ready access to the locking snib. Replace existing nightbolts where security is important.

One other form of rim lock you may come across is the *lever rim-lock*, which uses a conventional key. These are normally lightly constructed with simple mechanisms which do not offer any real security. Replace with a deadbolt or mortise lock.

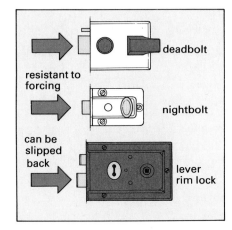

Deadbolts are the only form of rim lock which offer really high security. This is because the bolt is deadlocked and cannot be forced back.

FITTING A DEADBOLT

If you are fitting a deadbolt together with a mortise lock, put it about two-thirds of the way up the door. Where it is the only lock, fit it about halfway up.

Cylinder locks require a large hole drilled straight through the door, for which you will need a suitable drill or hole saw – check the instructions for sizes.

Although the lock body itself simply screws to the surface of the door, a few designs have an end plate which has to be recessed into the edge of the door. Do this first, otherwise the screw holes will not align properly.

Replacing a nightbolt

When fitting a deadbolt in place of an old nightbolt, it's preferable to avoid using the existing screw holes – they are unlikely to give such a strong fixing as new holes.

If the holes in the new lock line up with the old ones, one option is to fit longer or thicker screws. A better solution is to fill the holes with glued wooden plugs; allow these to dry then redrill the holes.

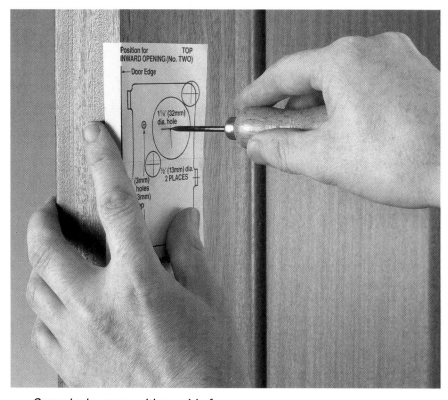

1 Some locks come with a guide for marking the position of the cylinder hole, otherwise use the lock's backplate. Fit a bit or hole saw of the size specified in the maker's instructions and drill the hole.

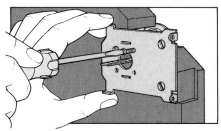

2 Screw the lock backplate to the door, then fit the cylinder and mounting ring and tighten the retaining screws – trim them to length if necessary.

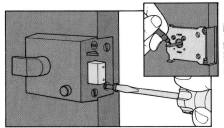

3 Fit the lock case to the backplate. If it won't go on because the cylinder connecting bar is too long, cut the bar at one of the marked grooves.

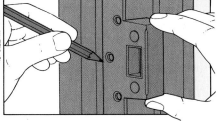

4 Close the door and mark the striker position on the frame. Align the striker plate, mark around it, then chisel a rabbet in the frame and screw it in place.

FITTING CHAINS AND PEEPHOLES

Locks and bolts are only effective so long as the door remains shut. Fitting a chain or peephole lets you and your family check on callers before admitting them.

Chains and restraints

Chains and restraints allow the door to open just enough to talk to someone without letting them in.

Chains are generally around 200mm (8″) long. One end is screwed securely to the door frame; the other passes through a slit ring fixed to the door or latches into a grooved slider rail that allows it to be released for full opening.

One design is retained by a lock mechanism which can be released from outside by a keyholder. This is particularly suitable for the elderly or infirm since they can leave it engaged and give keys to their family or other regular visitors.

Restraints work on a similar principle but are generally stronger, with a rigid bar in place of a chain. You can also get door locks which have a built-in restraint strap.

When fitting, position the two parts to ensure that the chain or restrainer can only be engaged or released when the door is closed.

Viewers

Viewers are for fitting to solid wood doors so that you can see callers without them seeing you. For night-time use you really need a porch light as well, and this has the added advantage of deterring intruders.

Fit a viewer through a solid part of the door, not a panel, and at a comfortable level for the shortest user.

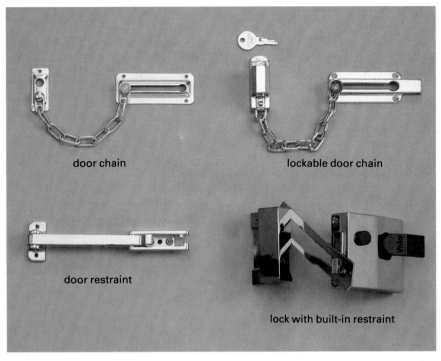

Chains and restraints *come in many different designs. When fitting one, make sure it is at a convenient height and can only be released when the door is closed. Remember, too, that it will only be as secure as its hardware.*

door chain

lockable door chain

door restraint

lock with built-in restraint

To fit a chain*, screw the fixed end firmly to the frame at a convenient height. Link the chain to the keeper and open the door to mark its position.*

Fit a peephole *by drilling a hole through the solid wood of the door and inserting one half from each side. Screw the two parts together.*

◤ PROBLEM SOLVER ◢

Securing integral garages

An integral garage is likely to have an internal door connecting with the house. This poses a special security problem because an intruder concealed in the garage has more time to force it, and there may be tools to hand to aid his efforts.

Fortunately, such doors are normally strongly constructed to meet fire regulations, enabling them to take a high security lever mortise lock. For added protection, fit mortise bolts at the top and bottom of the door, together with hinge bolts.

Keep the garage door locked to restrict access.

Secure up-and-over garage doors by fitting lockable sliding bolts to shoot sideways into the surround and use security padlocks. Position the bolts about 500mm (20″) from the bottom of the door for easy operation, and fix them to the door with coachbolts (remember to put the nuts on the inside!).

With hinged double garage doors, fit top and bottom bolts to one door and a mortise lock or deadlatch to the other. Make sure the lock engages securely with the bolted door.

Secure an up-and-over *garage door with locked sliding bolts shooting out into the frame. With hinged double garage doors, fit bolts to one door and a mortise lock or deadbolt to the other.*

FRENCH DOORS AND PATIO DOORS

Wooden French doors may have one or two opening frames. Single frames can be treated like any other external door. Double opening frames often have a mortise sash-lock and a handle operating an *espagnolette* (a double-ended vertical bolt). These are easily opened by smashing a pane, so add extra bolts – two to each frame.

Mortise bolts are ideal. There are different lengths to suit doors and windows, but often the window models are more appropriate because of the narrowness of the frames. Where the frames are too thin to take a mortise bolt, use flush bolts or even surface-mounted locking bolts.

Metal French doors made from galvanized steel usually have their own lock, but this may not be very strong. For added security fit metal window locks to the top and bottom of both opening frames so that they shoot into the outer frame.

Aluminum sliding patio doors come with their own locks, but for extra protection they can be equipped with special bolts designed to fit aluminum frames. The bolts can be mounted on the doors, to shoot up or down into the surround, or on the surround, to shoot sideways into the door frames.

Wooden sliding doors cannot be fitted with a conventional mortise lock or rim lock. Instead, use a mortise lock with a *hook-bolt* or *claw-bolt* (clutch-bolt), both of which grip the striker plate and resist the sideways pull.

In the case of a hook-bolt, there is a locating pin below it which engages the striker plate and prevents the door being lifted to free the bolt.

Fitting is generally similar to normal mortise locks. With a hook-bolt, use the locating pin to line up the striker plate.

WOODEN FRENCH DOORS

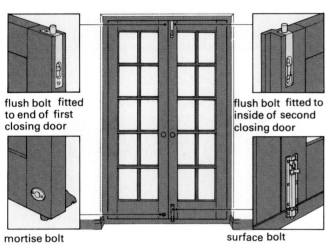

flush bolt fitted to end of first closing door

flush bolt fitted to inside of second closing door

mortise bolt

surface bolt

Fit bolts as shown. If you use flush bolts, those fitted to the first closing door may be recessed into the end of the door for extra security.

METAL FRENCH DOORS

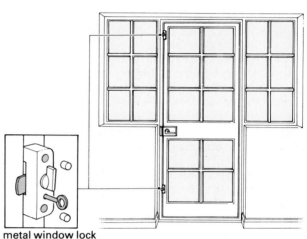

metal window lock

Fit metal window locks to secure the opening frames to the metal surround. Fix the locks with self-tapping screws.

WOODEN SLIDING DOORS

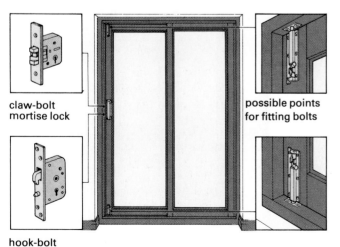

claw-bolt mortise lock

possible points for fitting bolts

hook-bolt mortise lock

Use a mortise lock with a hook bolt or claw bolt to resist the sideways pull. For extra protection, fit bolts to shoot upwards and downwards.

ALUMINUM SLIDING DOORS

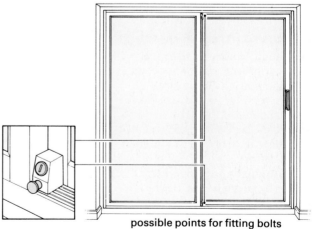

possible points for fitting bolts

Fit patio door bolts to reinforce the existing lock – most types suit single or double sliding frames. Screw in place with self-tapping screws.

DOOR TRIMS AND FURNITURE

DECORATIVE PLATES

Door plates are both functional and attractive. Although primarily intended to protect vulnerable parts of the door from wear, most door plates are prominent decorative features in their own right.

Fingerplates are screwed to the surface of the door to protect the point which receives most wear during opening and closing.
Kickplates are mounted at the base of the door to protect it from knocks. They can also be useful for stopping pets from scratching the door finish.
Nameplates come in many designs, either with the name already printed or left blank for you to fill in.

Trade tip

Stick-on nameplates

❛ Screw-on nameplates don't always hold well in the thin paneling of flush doors, so use self-adhesive sticky pads instead. Then, to avoid leaving empty screw holes in the plate, bore holes in the door with a bradawl or snip off the screw shanks with wire cutters. Stick the screws or the heads in place with a smear of epoxy resin adhesive. This technique works on fingerplates too. ❜

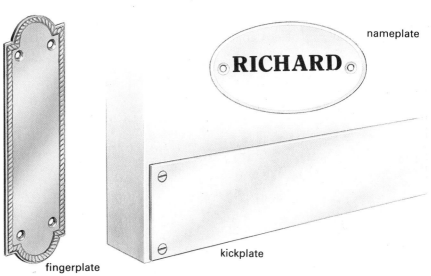

nameplate

RICHARD

fingerplate

kickplate

BOLTS FOR INTERIOR DOORS

Bolts for interior doors aren't strong enough to act as security devices – they are mainly for holding doors shut, or keeping small children out of mischief.
Straight barrel bolts are used where the surface of the door shuts flush with the surrounding frame.
Necked barrel bolts are fitted where the door surface isn't flush or where there is not enough wood directly in line with the bolt to drill a hole for the bolt to shoot into. The offset end of the barrel shoots into a keeper hole drilled in the frame.
Indicator bolts are generally for bathroom doors; shooting the bolt operates an indicator panel on the outside of the door to show that the door is locked. Most can be opened from the outside in an emergency.

straight barrel

necked barrel

indicator bolt

HOOKS AND HANGERS

Coat hooks come in a wide range of styles. Designs range from ornamental brass to plain white plastic and have one, two or more hooks depending on what you want.
Self-adhesive hooks are suitable only for lightweight items. The bond isn't strong enough to support heavy loads.
Screw-on hooks are easy to attach to solid doors and give a firm fixing. There are special hollow-door fixtures for attaching to flush doors. Some hook designs have concealed or integral fixtures for a neat finish.

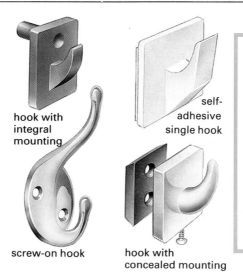

hook with integral mounting

self-adhesive single hook

screw-on hook

hook with concealed mounting

Trade tip

More grip

❛ The bond between a self-adhesive fitting and a painted door is only as strong as the bond of the paint to the door. If the paint is at all suspect, I mark the outline of the hook base on to the door and then sand off all the paint layers within this mark. This gives the hook a stronger mounting. ❜

FITTING FRONT DOOR HARDWARE

Door hardware normally fits in one of two ways – with short screws or with through-bolts.

Screwing to doors The main thing to ensure here is that you position the fixture and mark the holes accurately. Misdrilled holes are hard to conceal if you get them in the wrong place, which is easily done if you are putting together separate numerals to make up the house number, say.

Small brass screws such as those used for door hardware are fairly weak. And if they are inserted into a hole drilled in a tough hardwood door there is a risk of them snapping, or of the slots distorting as you tighten them.

Avoid this by driving in steel screws of the same size first, to open out the holes. After that it's simply a matter of replacing them with the brass ones, which go in easier still if you rub them on a bar of soap.

Drilling and bolting Knockers and handles are normally fitted with a bolt right through the door and have lugs (projecting points) which locate the fixture in place. Use these to mark the position for drilling.

Take care to position the fixture centrally, and press against the door so that the lugs leave indents in the wood.

When you are drilling right through a door it pays to be careful: many hardwoods are brittle and when the drill breaks through, it's easy to split the wood. Avoid this happening by using the double-drilling technique shown below.

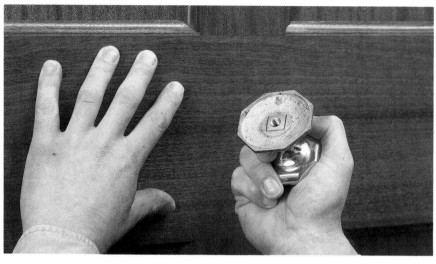

Mark the position of a knob using the lugs on the back.

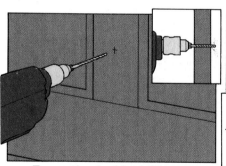

1 To use the double-drilling technique, mark the position of the hole on the outside of the door, then drill through with a fine bit to act as a guide.

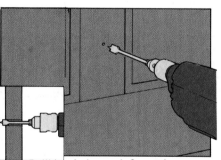

2 Drill back through from the inside using the correct size bit. When it breaks through, any splintering will be covered by the fitting itself.

Trade tip

In the right place

❝ It's often difficult to position numbers so that they align properly on the door and have the right spacing. And once you have drilled the fixing holes you are usually stuck with them even if they look wrong.

You can fix lightweight numbers temporarily using sticking putty, but for heavier ones I always cut the shapes out of paper and stick these to the door to check their position. Close up, you can't usually tell whether a set of door numbers are in the right position or crooked, so double check by seeing how they look from the front gate. ❞

FITTING LETTERPLATES

In addition to the standard mail delivery box outside your front door, you may want a letterplate in the door allowing mail to be dropped directly inside.

If the flap opens inwardly, the door hole must be a fraction larger than the flap itself, which you should measure from the back. Take care not to make the hole too large: you usually have to drill screw holes very close to the hole itself. On an upward-opening flap, cut a hole the same size as the hole on the plate.

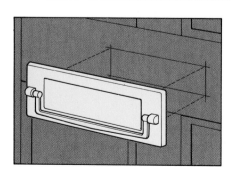

1 Mark the outline of the cut-out for the flap on the face of the door. It may help to make a paper pattern and tape this in place so you can position the hole accurately.

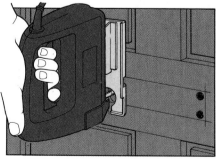

2 Drill four holes inside the corners of the marked area with a large (say, 12mm; ½") bit and saw out the waste with a saber saw. Try the letterplate for fit, then mark and drill the screw holes.

FITTING WINDOW LOCKS

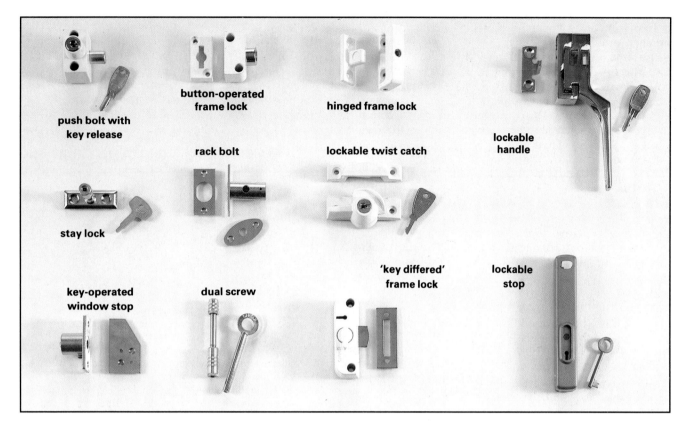

push bolt with
key release

button-operated
frame lock

hinged frame lock

lockable
handle

stay lock

rack bolt

lockable twist catch

key-operated
window stop

dual screw

'key differed'
frame lock

lockable
stop

Around half of the domestic burglaries which occur each year take place through windows. And in the majority of cases the burglar gains entry either by forcing the insecure catches which most windows have fitted as standard, or by breaking the glass to slip those catches.

Window locks stop this happening. For only a modest investment, they leave the would-be intruder with the choice of smashing a pane and climbing through (possibly attracting attention in the process), or moving on to easier pickings. Most burglars choose the latter.

Narrowing the choice

Although individual makes of window locks vary enormously, they fall into distinct groups according to the type of window being secured. And within any group, different makes generally fit in a broadly similar way.

The following pages show which categories of lock are appropriate, depending whether the windows are:
■ Hinged with wooden frames
■ Double-hung with wooden frames
■ Metal framed
(For patio windows, see page 276.)

Run through this section and list which types are possible options for the windows you want to secure. Then consider the following when choosing between models:

Convenience is important if the window is in constant use. Automatic locking is an advantage if you're forgetful, and combination or push-button locks are helpful if you're apt to mislay keys. Individually keyed ('key differed') locks are more secure, but could leave you with a lot of keys to sort out.

Some types of lock allow windows to be locked partially open for ventilation, though this reduces their security value.

Cost can be difficult to assess. Many cheaper locks must be fitted in pairs to be effective, which adds to the cost but also increases the number of locking points. Complex locks are more expensive, but not necessarily more secure (see below).

Security The more locking points, the better. Surface mounted locks are generally the easiest to fit, but are only as strong as their screw fixings. Locks housed in the frame tend to be stronger.

Finish Window locks come in various finishes including white, silver metal and brass. Obtrusive locks are a positive advantage from a security point of view.

Trade tip

Security points

 On all types of window:
Don't bother with window locks if the frame timber is rotten – it will be obvious to a burglar.
Don't fit locks which weaken the frame to the point where it's no longer secure. Again, burglars will be quick to spot it.
Do use longer fixing screws if you feel that the ones supplied aren't strong enough.
Don't leave keys in locks. 9

LOCKING HINGED WINDOWS (WOODEN FRAME)

There are basically two ways to secure a hinged window:
■ Fit extra devices to lock the casement to the window frame. This is usually the most effective way.
■ Replace (or fit lockable attachments to) the existing catches.
Surface-mounted frame locks fall into the first group and come in a wide variety of patterns and finishes. Features available include automatic locking (so you don't forget them) and combination locks (no keys to lose). The more expensive types are key differed for greater security.

Frame locks generally screw on, and like all such locks are only as strong as their fixings. A single lock, placed centrally, is perfectly adequate for a fanlight or small window, but for larger casements fit a pair – one at the top, one at the bottom – on the catch side.
Rack bolts for windows (longer ones are used on doors) offer greater security than surface-mounted frame locks because they rely on the frame itself for strength rather than on their own fixing screws. However, they are trickier to fit, and are only suitable for casement frames measuring over 38×38mm (1½×1½"). Fit a pair – one on either side of the casement, about half way up.
Lockable catches and stays replace or lock the existing catches. They are simple to fit, but only as secure as their screw fixings allow them to be. Also, they secure the window at one point only – which may not be enough to deter some burglars.

Stay locks are most useful on fanlights, allowing them to be locked open for ventilation. However, this makes the window less secure.

FITTING A FRAME LOCK

Frame locks consist of two parts: the *lock body* screws to the window frame and the *lock plate* to the casement (the opening part). With some makes the two parts go the other way round, and some types of lock body have a separate locking plate.

Mark the positions of the two parts with the lock assembled so that you can be sure they will engage cleanly

Types of surface-mounted *frame lock (below). Push-button locks with key release make closure easier. Automatic catch locks need well fitting frames.*

button-operated frame lock

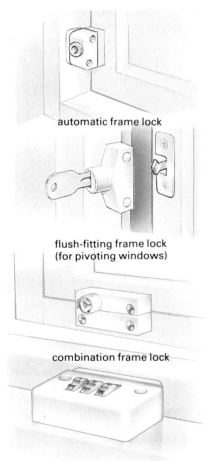

automatic frame lock

flush-fitting frame lock (for pivoting windows)

combination frame lock

If the window frame is molded, mark the position of the frame-mounted portion of the lock, then chisel out enough wood for it to sit square to the casement. A plastic wedge-shaped backing piece is usually provided with the lock to do the same job on a tapered window frame.

Some makes of lock have plastic security screw covers. Don't fit these until you're sure the lock works as they're difficult to remove.
Tools: Electric drill and bits or bradawl, pencil, screwdriver, 12mm (½") wood chisel (maybe).

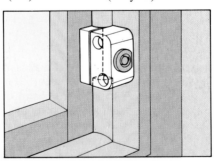

On a molded frame, chisel out a recess for the lock body so that it will sit square to the casement when the window is closed (see also Problem Solver).

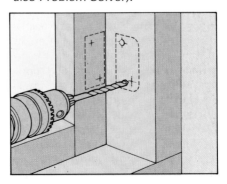

2 Separate the lock. Hold each part in place and mark the screw holes, then drill or bradawl pilot holes to the same depth as the screw threads.

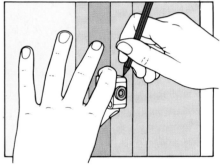

1 Fit the two parts of the lock together and place against the closed window. Mark their positions in pencil on the frame and casement.

On tapered frames, you need to pack behind the lock in order for it to sit square. Most makes supply a wedge-shaped backing piece for this.

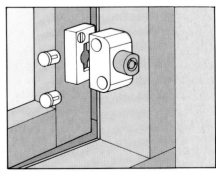

3 Screw both parts in position and check that they engage cleanly. If all is well, push the plastic screw covers down into the fixing holes.

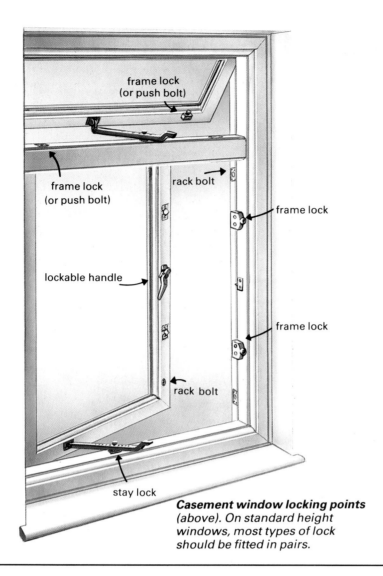

frame lock
(or push bolt)

frame lock
(or push bolt)

lockable handle

rack bolt

frame lock

frame lock

rack bolt

stay lock

Casement window locking points
(above). On standard height
windows, most types of lock
should be fitted in pairs.

FITTING CATCH LOCKS

A lockable side catch is a good choice if the original catch is weak or the window is a loose fit. Most types are a straight replacement, and simply screw on.

Stay locks are available for both holed and plain stays, but only holed stays can be locked open. Replacement stays with adjustable ratchets that can be locked in any position are also available.

Tools: Bradawl, screwdriver, electric drill and bits.

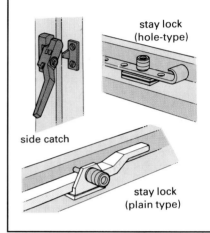

stay lock
(hole-type)

side catch

stay lock
(plain type)

FITTING RACK BOLTS

Check the manufacturer's instructions to see what drill bits are required. Normally you need a 10mm (⅜″) twist bit for the key hole and a 16mm (⅝″) flat bit for the lock hole.

Make sure you drill all the holes absolutely square to the frame, so that the bolt and key engage cleanly. Get a helper to hold the window steady while you drill the casement.

Tools: Electric drill and bits, bradawl, screwdriver, try square, 12mm (½″) wood chisel.

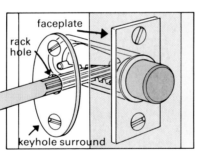

faceplate

rack hole

keyhole surround

The rack bolt sits in a hole in the casement, held by a screw-on faceplate (usually recessed). Turning the key drives the bolt into the frame.

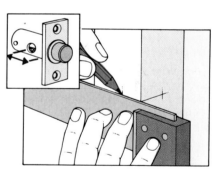

1 *Mark the bolt position on the casement edge. Measure the distance from faceplate to rack hole and transfer to the side of the frame with a try square.*

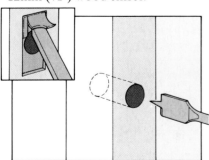

2 *Drill a hole for the lock body centrally through the edge of the casement, then test-fit the lock and mark the faceplate position. Chisel out a recess.*

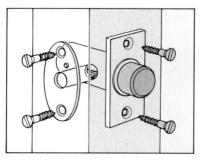

3 *Drill a hole for the key at your marked point. Test-fit the lock and check it works, then screw down the faceplate and screw on the keyhole surround.*

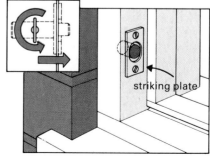

striking plate

4 *Close the window and operate the lock so that the bolt marks the frame. Drill a hole for the bolt recess at this point, then screw on the striking plate.*

LOCKING DOUBLE-HUNG WINDOWS

The easiest way to secure a sliding-sash window is to replace the original catch (probably either a screw-barrel or twist type) with a new lockable catch. But as with hinged windows this only provides a single security point – not enough to deter many burglars.

There are three other options, all of which work by locking the movable sashes together.

Push bolts come in several patterns and are usually key operated. They should be fitted in pairs, one each side of the window.

The push lock body screws to the top rail of the lower sash, and shoots a bolt into a hole drilled in the upper sash. Drilling a series of such holes allows the lower sash to be locked open for ventilation.

Window ('acorn') stops are screw-in or key-lockable brass pegs which, when fitted to the upper sash, stop the lower sash sliding up. Like push locks, they are best fitted in pairs.

Dual screws are 'bolts within bolts' which lock the two sashes together. The outer threaded barrel fits into a hole drilled in the upper rail of the lower sash. Inside this goes a screw bolt which is driven into a corresponding hole in the lower rail of the upper sash using a simple key.

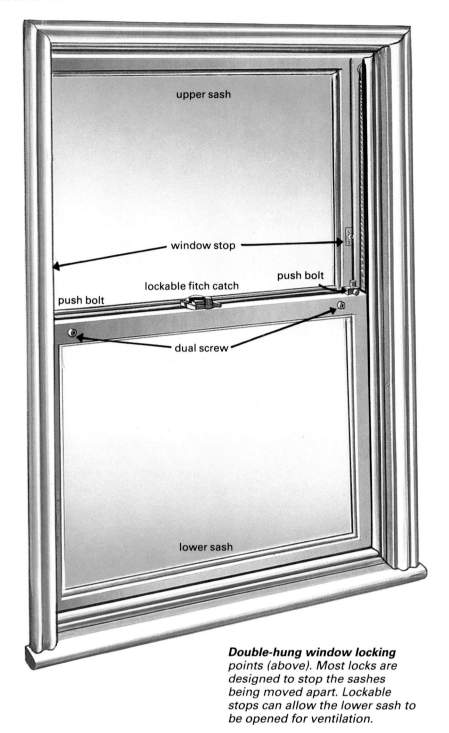

Double-hung window locking points (above). Most locks are designed to stop the sashes being moved apart. Lockable stops can allow the lower sash to be opened for ventilation.

Trade tip

Security screws

❝ For extra security on all types of surface mounted lock, drill out the slots in the fixing screws so that they can't be undone. ❞

FITTING A PUSH BOLT

Check the instructions before you start to find out what drill size is needed for the bolt hole – they vary widely. Use the lock bolt itself to mark the position of the hole (if necessary, rub a felt-tip pen over the end).

Repeat the sequence shown to drill a second bolt hole so that the window can be locked open for ventilation. This hole should be no further than 100mm (4") above the first.

Tools: Electric drill and bits, screwdriver.

1 Screw the lock body to the upper rail of the lower sash, then operate the lock so that the bolt leaves a mark showing where to drill the upper sash frame.

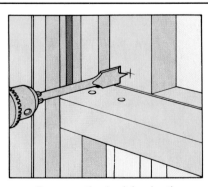

2 Remove the lock body, then drill the bolt hole and fit the striking cover plate (if supplied). Replace the lock and check that the bolt engages.

FITTING WINDOW STOPS

Fit stops at the corners where the sashes meet. It's possible to fit two pairs – one to hold the window fully closed, and another 100mm (4″) further up the upper sash to allow the lower sash to be opened for ventilation.

The fixing plates are either screwed to the surface of the sash frame or recessed into the sash for greater strength.

Tools: Electric drill and bits, bradawl, screwdriver, 12mm (½″) wood chisel (maybe), tape measure.

Peg-type stops are designed to be fitted and removed by hand.

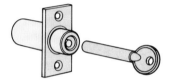

Key-operated versions are more secure, but also more costly.

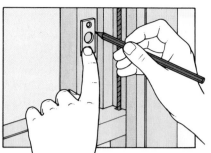

1 Close the window and hold the fixing plate against the upper sash. Draw around it in pencil, and mark where to drill the stop peg hole.

3 Fit the stop peg chain to the window frame within easy reach. Complete the job by screwing the stop striker plate to the lower sash top rail.

2 Drill the peg hole to the size and depth recommended. If need be, chisel out a recess for the fixing plate. Then bradawl the screw holes and screw in place.

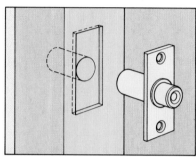

On key operated stops, the stop and fixing plate are combined in a single unit housed in the sash frame. Drill out the housing, then screw in place.

FITTING DUAL SCREWS

Fit dual screws 75-100mm (3-4″) in from the sides of the sashes. You only need to drill one hole per screw (normally 10mm – ⅜″ – diameter), but make sure you don't drill too far.

The most common type of dual screw (shown) has a threaded barrel and receiver which simply tap in. Others have a screw-on facing plate, for which you'll need to chisel recesses.

Tools: Electric drill and bits, hammer, 12mm (½″) chisel (maybe).

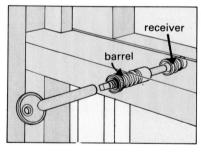

receiver

barrel

The dual screw inner bolt is driven in with a key. It runs through a threaded barrel in the lower sash into a receiver housed in the upper sash.

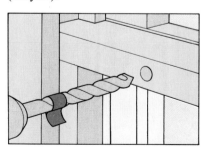

1 With the window closed, drill a hole through the lower sash top rail. Mark the drill bit with tape, then continue the hole 15mm (⅝″) into the upper sash.

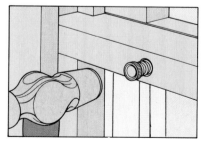

2 Tap in the threaded barrel as far as it will go, then slide down the upper sash and tap in the receiver. To lock, screw in the bolt flush with the rail.

LOCKABLE CATCHES

Lockable catches for sash windows are normally a straight replacement for the existing twist or screw-and-barrel catch. However, it's advisable not to re-use any of the original screw holes – plug them with filler, then drill or bradawl new ones in the two sash frames.

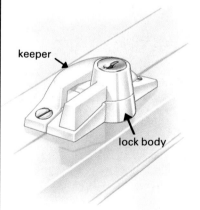

keeper

lock body

Lockable replacement catches come in two parts. The body screws to one rail, the keeper to the other.

LOCKING METAL FRAMED WINDOWS

Metal framed windows can either be secured by locking the existing catch or locking the casement to the frame, but in both cases the number of devices available is more limited.

Locks for handles come in two types. One type clamps on to the catch and is released with a key. The other (which is more secure) consists of a lockable stop bolt that screws to the frame.

Frame locks are similar (and in some cases interchangeable) with those for wooden frames, but are fixed with self-tapping screws instead of woodscrews. Check these are supplied when you buy.

There is also an **integral frame lock** for fitting within the frame. This is secure and unobtrusive, but only suitable for 'H' section frames at least 23mm (⅞") thick.

Fixing to metal

Follow these rules when fixing locks to metal frames.
■ Punch indents for the screw holes before drilling using a hammer and *center punch*. This stops the drill bit slipping.
■ Be sure to use high speed steel drill bits, not carbon steel.
■ Prime any bared metal before fitting the new lock.

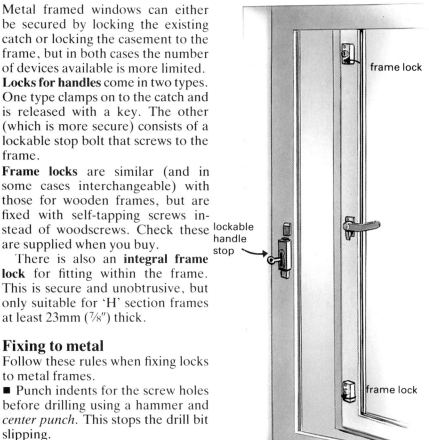

frame lock

lockable handle stop

frame lock

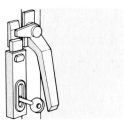

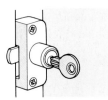

Some handle locks simply screw on below the existing handle. The key-operated bolt on the lock slides up to trap the catch in the closed position.

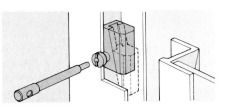

Frame locks for metal windows are fitted to the casement and have a catch which engages with the edge of the frame. Fix with self-tapping screws.

Integral frame locks are specially designed for 'H' section steel frames. The lock body fits within the frame and engages a catch in the casement.

PROBLEM SOLVER

Covering mistakes

■ If you drill a hole in the wrong place, fill it with an offcut of wood. Trim the wood to fit the hole with a sharp knife, and coat the end in woodworking glue. Tap it in place, then saw off the excess flush with the frame. Leave for a few hours before continuing.
■ If a faceplate or striking plate recess is too deep, and the lock bolt won't engage, pack behind it with thin cardboard.

Chiseling recesses

Cutting recesses for faceplates and striking plates could prove tricky if you're unused to handling a chisel. The two golden rules are:
■ Make sure the chisel is sharp.
■ Remove a fraction of wood at a time, so you don't cut too deep.

Hold the chisel as shown, keeping it at a low angle with your fingers behind the blade at all times. You shouldn't need to apply much pressure.

Poorly fitting windows

With casement windows that don't fit properly or are prone to seasonal swelling, there's a chance that rack bolts and frame locks with automatic catches won't engage properly because the frame and casement don't align.

In such cases it's a good idea to fit a pair of screw-type surface-mounted frame locks which draw the casement into the frame as you tighten them.

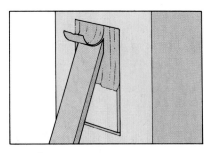

Screw-type locks draw a poorly fitting casement into its frame.

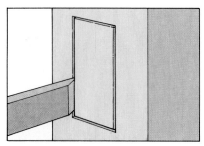

1 Having marked the position of the recess using the plate as a guide, pierce around the cutting line as shown with the chisel bevel pointing inwards.

2 Gently pare away slivers of wood, working from the centre of the recess to the edges. Keep the chisel at a low angle, supported by your free hand.

FITTING WOOD PANELING

Paneling a wall or ceiling with boards, usually T&G (tongue-and-groove) is a simple and effective way to give an otherwise ordinary room a smart new look. The new paneling can have other benefits too:
■ It can cover up poor or heavily patched plasterwork, saving on the disruption which renewing this involves.
■ It can hide unsightly pipes or cables, or make it easy to run new ones in the space behind.
■ It gives you the perfect opportunity to fit wall or ceiling insulation and cut fuel bills, as well as offering some degree of insulation in its own right.

The one thing paneling won't do is cure dampness – in fact, it can make the problem far worse. Any dampness already in the walls must be traced, cured and left to dry out before you start the job.

.... Shopping List ....

Boards suitable for use as paneling material are widely available from lumberyards. These boards are either softwood or hardwood, and anywhere from 13mm (½") to 22mm (⅞") thick. They vary in width between 75mm (3") and 300mm (12"), and most lumberyards will cut them to suit your requirements.

You will find paneling boards matched as tongue-and-groove (T&G) or shiplap. (T&G is the most commonly found type of paneling and is used in the project shown on the following pages.) The boards can be laid either horizontally or vertically, depending on the effect you want.

You should be able to find a wood that gives you the effect you desire. Knotty pine is one of the most economical, and gives a characteristic, natural 'pine' look. And while a smooth finish is important if you are going to paint the finished panels, rough surfaced boards give a more rustic look.

Obviously, hardwoods such as mahogany are much more expensive (and more durable) than pine – perhaps prohibitively so. But there are varying grades of pine, so shop around before you commit yourself.

Other options
Veneered plywood consists of a covering of fine sheets of wood over plywood. Some veneers are hardwood; others are chemically treated to create special effects such as the look of driftwood. These panels are most often sold in 1200×2400mm (4'×8') sheets.
Coated hardboard as a rule is slightly thinner than veneered plywood, and comes in the same size sheets. It is usually covered with enameled or plastic material.

Plastic paneling can be difficult to find. It is almost always white and is bought in the same way as boards.
Note: Many kinds of paneling can be applied with a special adhesive as well as the standard nailing.

Furring materials
Most types of paneling must be fixed to furring – a framework of furring (studs) over the wall surface. This is made up of 25×75mm (1"×3") studs. Plywood veneer is the exception – it can be attached to an existing wall.

Trimming materials
Most lumberyards and some large hardware dealers will carry a range of scoop and quarter round moldings suitable for finishing corners, and matching square-edged (butt-ended) boards for trimming gaps and edges. You may also need baseboard and coving moldings. Plastic paneling has its own trimming materials.

Other materials
Fix boards with finishing or casing nails. Plywood or hardboard scraps are needed for leveling the under-lying framework (the furring).

Insulation can be provided with sheets of fiberboard fixed between the framework and the panels. You can also use blanket insulation, as long as you put it in a polyethylene vapor barrier.
Tools checklist: crosscut saw, tenon saw, electric drill and bits, hammer, screwdrivers, nail punch, level, tape measure.

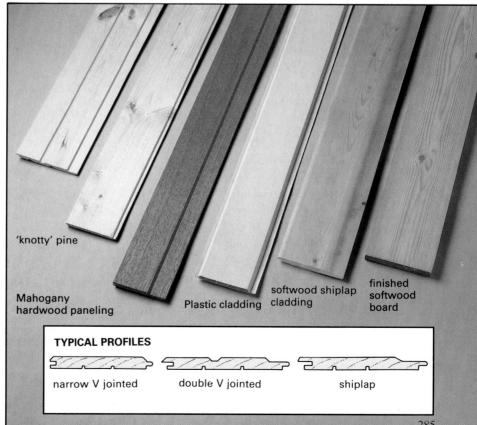

'knotty' pine

Mahogany hardwood paneling

Plastic cladding

softwood shiplap cladding

finished softwood board

TYPICAL PROFILES

narrow V jointed   double V jointed   shiplap

DESIGNING THE PANELING

Before buying any materials, you have to know:

■ What direction to fix the boards in. Most types can go vertically (with horizontal furring) or horizontally (with vertical furring); it's also possible to fix boards at 45°, though this involves more work, since they have to be cut and measured individually.

Many people find vertical boards easiest, since the standard lengths fit most walls with minimal wastage. Horizontal boards have to be butt-jointed, with the joints staggered between rows.

■ What to do about baseboards and architraves. It's usually easiest to treat these as furring and fix the boards over them, packing with plywood where necessary. You can then leave a gap, or fix new moldings to the paneling.

However, heavy baseboards and other moldings which would stand proud of the furring must be prized off with either a brick chisel or a crowbar.

■ How to deal with windows. Most window openings can be paneled around then finished with molding or square edge board. But it may be better to saw off a protruding window board flush with the wall first.

■ How to deal with ceiling junctions. If you plan to panel the ceiling, do this first. Otherwise, boards can be stopped just short of the ceiling (which makes decorating easier), carried up against it, or trimmed with wood coving molding.

■ What to do about insulation. The techniques for arranging this are described on page 288.

■ What to do about utilities. If you want to move lights and sockets or install new plumbing, do this first. Water pipes and cables can usually be hidden behind the paneling, but check first - you may need to increase the thickness of the furring frame to clear them. Drainage pipes will probably be enclosed, in which case remove the existing covering and incorporate the box frame into the new one, then panel over it.

Study the design points below for ways to deal with these situations.

See Problem Solver for how to deal with switches and sockets.

Versatile T&G boarding is equally at home on the ceiling or on the walls. On the right, 'knotty pine' boards finished with molding create a totally paneled look, while Douglas Fir boarding (below) brings a homely touch to this large kitchen.

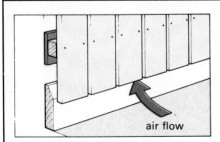

Baseboards 1: Overlap the baseboard, leaving a small air gap.

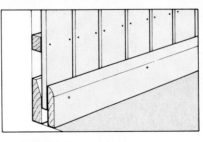

Baseboards 2: Fit new baseboard molding over the paneling.

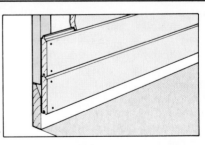

Baseboards 3: Use the baseboard as a frame stud and stop boards short.

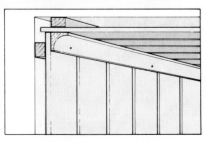

Ceilings 1: Butt boards to old or new ceiling and fit coving.

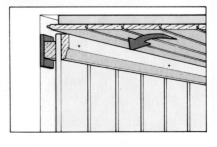

Ceilings 2: Stop boards short to leave an air gap; you can still use coving.

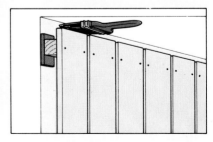

Ceilings 3: (also for inside corners): leaving a small gap eases decorating.

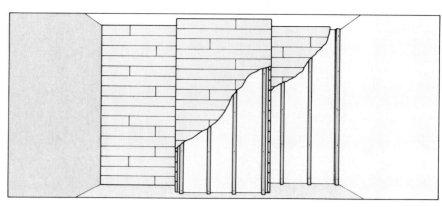

For horizontal paneling, run the studs vertically with extra ones at the end of each run.

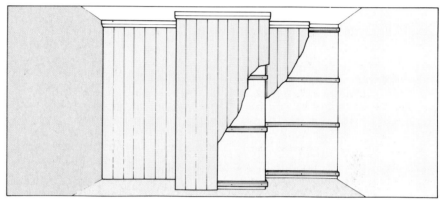

For vertical paneling, the studs run horizontally across the wall. Fit extra pieces around obstructions

Note, too, that you shouldn't panel within 150mm (6″) of a fire, boiler or other heater; stop short, and fit a non-combustible substitute such as plasterboard or tiles over a plywood base. Neither should boards be allowed to touch flues – leave a gap around them and finish with metal edging strip.

When you've worked out what to do, sketch a plan of each wall (or ceiling) giving full dimensions. You should also list on the plan:
■ The total length of furring used – studs are fixed at all edges and at 400-500mm (16-20″) intervals for 10mm (3/8″) boards or 500-600mm (20-24″) for 13mm (1/2″) boards.

■ The total lengths of each type of molding and trim strip required.
Take the plan with you to the supplier. From here, it should be a simple matter for the two of you to select board lengths which give minimal wastage, and to work out the coverage for your chosen board width.

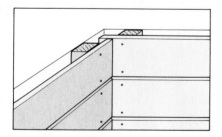

Inside corners 1: butt boards together with one side overlapping.

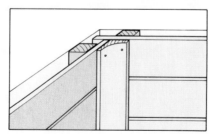

Inside corners 2: finish with square section batten or coving molding.

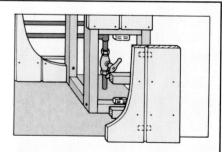

Around enclosures, build a separate paneled frame on magnetic catches.

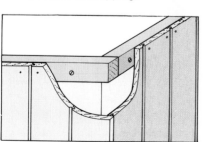

Outside corners 1: butt frame studs and boards (with tongues sawn off).

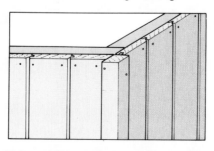

Outside corners 2: saw off tongues of adjoining boards and trim with stud.

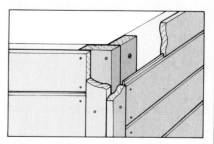

Outside corners 3: saw tongues off boards and trim with separate studs.

FIXING THE FURRING

Providing you've planned things properly, fixing the furring should present few difficulties.

If the plaster is reasonably new and sound, using masonry nails saves a lot of time. In older plaster which is likely to crumble, screws and anchors are essential. However, you can still save time by using frame hardware: simply nail the studs in place, then drill through them into the wall (but use two drills, or swap to a masonry bit when you strike the plaster). Fix the studs near the ends, and at 450mm (18") intervals in between.

Don't drive the nails or screws fully home until you've checked the studs sit plumb with one another. This way, you can slip packing pieces behind the studs, recheck for plumb, then trap the packing against the wall as you knock in the nails or tighten the screws.

On a ceiling, find the joists first by poking with a bradawl – they are normally at 400 or 450mm (16" or 18") centers. Screw the studs in place, checking for level and packing as necessary.

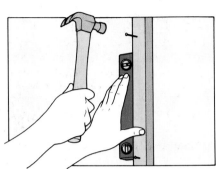

Don't drive masonry nails fully in until you've checked the studs for plumb and packed behind as necessary. Pre-drilling studs avoids splitting.

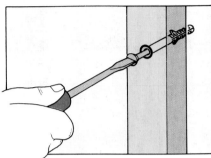

Frame hardware allows you to drill through the stud into the wall with the stud in place. Again don't drive the screws fully home until you've checked for plumb.

Check for plumb with a level and wood straightedge to ensure a good 'spread'. Hollows can be packed out with slips of plywood or hardboard.

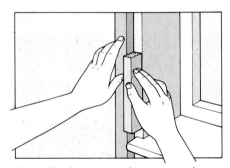

At critical areas such as around windows, use a piece of board or wood to gauge where to position the frame stud for a neat finish.

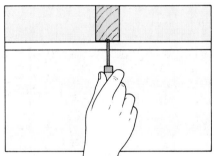

On the ceiling, the studs can run across the joists or along them. Find and mark the joist positions first, then predrill the studs and screw in place.

Trade tip

Leave a gap

❝ When fixing studs along the edges of walls, don't fix them hard up against the edges – leave a 12mm (½") gap. This way, you won't have to fix boards close to the ends, where there's a risk of them splitting. ❞

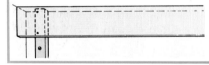

PROVIDING INSULATION

There are two ways to insulate behind the paneling.

Fiberboard sheets are the most expensive option, but also the most substantial. Fit packing pieces behind the furring to let air circulate, then nail the sheets to the studs leaving more gaps around the edges. Afterwards, simply nail the boards in place (draw lines to show the stud positions).

Roll insulation (batts) can be sandwiched between the furring and the paneling, in which case space the studs to suit. Since the insulation restricts air flow behind the boards, it's essential to staple a polyethylene vapor barrier across the furring before positioning the insulation.

air flow

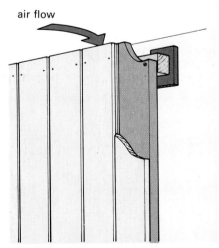

Option 1 – nail sheets of 12mm (½") fiber insulating board to the studs leaving gaps all around to maintain the air flow. Then nail the paneling on top.

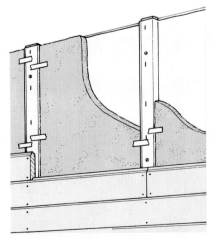

Option 2 – staple a vapor barrier or polyethylene sheet across the studs then fit roll insulation between them (it can be taped temporarily in place).

FIXING THE T&G BOARDS

The illustration on the right shows the three options for fixing the boards to the furring (framework of wooden studs). The first board in every run – along with any trim strips or moldings – should be face-fixed with the grooved side towards the edge. Thereafter, you simply slot in the next board, then secret nail or clip fix to each stud in turn. In all cases, don't forget to punch the nail heads below the surface of the wood.

The last board in each run will also have to be face fixed. It is unlikely to fit the gap exactly, so scribe it to fit as shown below then cut it lengthwise with a crosscut saw.

After completing the paneling, face-fix any trim strips and moldings and fill all nail holes.

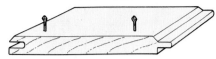

Trade tip

Cut them together

❝In most cases you'll be cutting a number of boards to the same length. To save work, measure and cut one, then clamp this to five or six more in a portable workbench and saw through them all together. ❞

BOARD FIXING OPTIONS

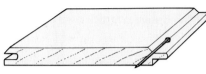

face nailing

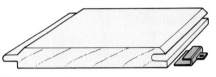

secret nailing

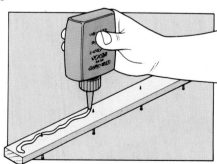

T&G fixing clips

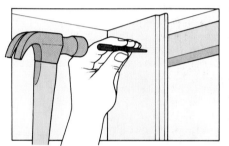

1 Face-fix the first board to the furring with the grooved side towards the edge. Punch the nail heads below the surface for filling with wood stopper later.

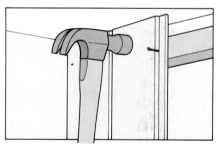

2 If secret nailing, nail through the tongue of the first board at an angle as shown, then slot in the next board and repeat along the run.

Using T&G fixing clips is easier for the unpracticed hand – slip the clips into the grooves of the boards, then nail them to the studs. Note that whatever the fixing method, you only fix on one side so that the boards can 'move' as their moisture content changes.

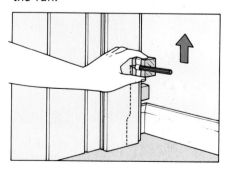

3 At the end of a run, scribe the last board to fit the gap and cut it lengthwise with a crosscut saw. Face-fix in place, punching down the nail heads.

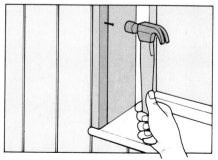

4 Fix trims and moldings once the main paneling is completed. Trim strips for the edges can be nailed to the frame studs and/or edges of boards.

5 Moldings can be glued to the boards using PVA glue. Nail for reinforcement, part-driving the nails into the molding first, to aid positioning.

FINISHING THE PANELING

Finish the wooden paneling as soon as possible, to prevent damage and to stop the boards absorbing undue amounts of moisture.

The most popular options are:

Clear polyurethane varnish, which will marginally deepen the wood color and give it a slight orange tinge.

Varnish stain, which can deepen and darken the wood color to tone better with existing decorations.

Colored transparent finish, which on lighter woods can be used to color the surface without obscuring the paneling's natural grain.

In all cases, apply the first coat thinned to seal the surface. Rub down between this and subsequent coats – you need at least three – with a pad of medium grade steel wool, and be sure to clean off the dust before applying more varnish.

Three ways to finish boards. Clear varnish (above) must be applied in at least three coats, with the first one thinned to seal the surface. Colored transparent finish (far left) modifies the color without obscuring the wood grain; while for a more dramatic color change, you have the option of varnish stain (left) applied with a soft cloth. In all cases, make sure the boards are kept dust-free during application.

◢PROBLEM SOLVER◣

Dealing with switches and sockets

Before checking or actually dealing with light switches and sockets, be sure to **turn off the power at the main service panel.**

In all cases, loosen off the switch or socket faceplate and check there is enough slack in the circuit cables to draw the faceplate as far as the boards.

For a surface mounted fixture, simply unscrew the outlet box. Cut clearance notches in the panel boards for the cables, then refit the box once the paneling is in place. Smooth the notches to prevent the cables chafing.

For a flush mounted fitting, there are two choices:

■ Fix studs around the hole, stop the paneling short, then remove the backing box and pack inside the old hole. You can then refit the box flush with the surface of the paneling.

■ Disconnect the faceplate and change to a surface mounted outlet box.

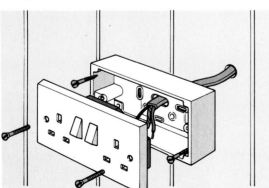

Surface mounted fittings can usually be refitted on the surface of the paneling – simply cut clearance notches for the cables in the boards.

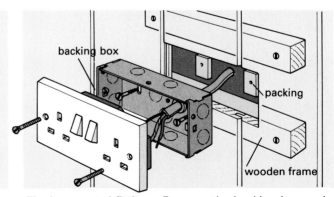

Flush mounted fittings. Remove the backing box and pack behind with wood so that it sits level with the paneling, then refit.

5

STORAGE

PUTTING UP ALCOVE SHELVES

Putting up shelves in alcoves is a time-honored way of using space that might otherwise go to waste – and this form of storage is perfectly suited to books, records, ornaments and hi-fi equipment.

Over the years, people have devised countless ways of arranging and supporting alcove shelving, but most are variations on one of the five options described overleaf.

.... Shopping List ....

Shelf materials: Work out the size and number of shelves as shown below. Then see overleaf for the options on boards and finishes.

Supports Work out how many shelves to put up, as shown below. Then check the chart overleaf to size up the supports and other fixings.

Wall fixings: Anchors, No. 8 screws (to gauge length, add 32mm (1¼″) to the thickness of what you're fixing).

Tools: Backsaw, drill and bits, crosscut saw, tape measure, carpenter's level, screwdriver. You may also need a hacksaw, chisel, Surform plane or scribing tools.

Alcove shelves *provide an ideal way to store large quantities of books.*

DESIGNING ALCOVE SHELVES

Start by measuring the alcove. If you want to put up more than one shelf, draw a sketch plan showing the alcove dimensions.

Although you can put the shelves at any heights you like, there are some practical guidelines:
■ If you are putting shelves in a pair of alcoves, keep the shelf spacings the same on both sides.
■ Wider-spaced shelves tend to look best at or below worktop/table height – around 750–900mm (30–36″). Set the first level of shelves here, then work out the spacings up and down.
■ Small paperbacks need 200mm (8″) height and 125mm (5″) depth.
■ Large illustrated books need a spacing of around 330mm (13″) and a depth of 225÷250mm (9–10″).
■ You may want one shelf spaced at around 330mm (13″) below the next, to hold hi-fi speakers, records, or a small TV. This shelf needs to be 300mm (12″) or more in depth.

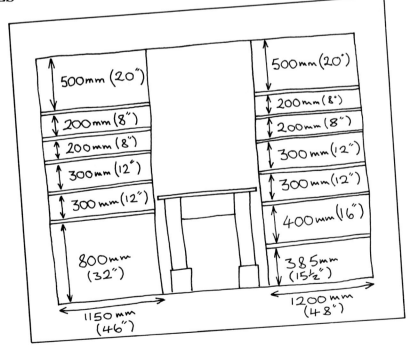

A sketch plan helps you keep track of what you need to buy, and acts as a reminder of the shelf spacings when you come to mark them out.

CHOOSING SHELVES AND SUPPORTS

There's a wide range of options for both the shelf boards themselves and the way you support them.

Choosing shelf boards

The panel below shows what materials can be used, depending on the look you want. Your choice will also be affected by:

What you want to store. Books and records are heavy, so need boards which resist warping. If the books are large OR the span is over 900mm (3'), follow the appropriate Bracing Guide and only use boards rated as suitable for 'heavy duty'.

On the other hand, shelves for lightweight ornaments should be as thin as possible so that they don't detract from what's on them.

The size of the shelves. Some materials only come in small sizes, while boards which come in large sheets are wasteful if you are only fitting a few shelves.

Choosing supports

The chart opposite shows the support options available. Again, your choice may depend on:

What you want to store. Small shelves for ornaments need light, unobtrusive supports, but for anything heavier choose one of the stronger systems (options 1, 2 and 3). If you are storing a lot of large books or other heavy items, OR the span is over 900mm (3'), use a back support/aluminum angle or extra brackets. If you think your storage needs may change, an adjustable system could make sense.

The depth of the alcove. If you are fitting deep shelves in a very shallow alcove, end supports (ie options 1, 2, 4 and 5) may not offer sufficient bracing. Unless at least two thirds of the depth is supported, option 3 is more reliable.

The condition of the walls. Some systems (eg options 3, 5) are well suited to walls which are uneven and out of square with each other.

How the walls are made. Chimney breast walls are always solid, but if the other walls are hollow, options 1 and 2 (which allow you to fix to the studs at any point) are better; don't rely on cavity wall fixings.

The look of the shelves. Aim to choose a system that's in keeping with the style of the room. Track shelves, for example, can look out of place in a traditional setting, while wooden supports may not suit a more modern, streamlined look.

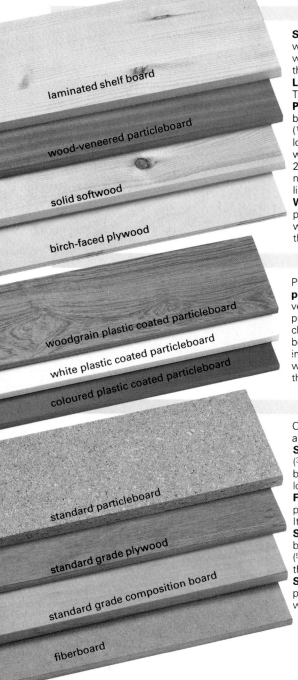

laminated shelf board

wood-veneered particleboard

solid softwood

birch-faced plywood

woodgrain plastic coated particleboard

white plastic coated particleboard

coloured plastic coated particleboard

standard particleboard

standard grade plywood

standard grade composition board

fiberboard

CHOOSING SHELF BOARDS

NATURAL FINISH

Solid wood is only practical upto a 225mm (9") width, after which it becomes costly and liable to warp. Boards should be 19 or 25mm (¾ or 1") thick, which may look clumsy with light ornaments.
Laminated shelf boards are 19mm (¾") thick. They are ideal for shelves over 225mm (9") wide.
Plywood or blockboard should be the high quality birch-faced type, but can be used thinner – 12mm (½"), 16mm (⅝"), or 19mm (¾"), depending on the load. Shelves can be cut to any width, but may work out expensive if you have to buy a full-size 2.4×1.2m (8×4') sheet and can't use it all. You also need to finish the exposed edges with solid wood lipping or iron-on veneer tape.
Wood veneered particleboard boards come prefinished (see below) in handy lengths and widths, and in 16mm (⅝") and 19mm (¾") thicknesses.

BRACING GUIDE
Solid softwood (19mm): add extra bracing over 600mm (24") for medium duty, or 450mm (18") for heavy duty.
Solid softwood (25mm): add extra bracing over 750mm (30") for heavy duty.
Laminated board (19mm): add extra bracing over 750mm (30") for heavy duty.
Plywood and blockboard (see below for all sizes)
Veneered particleboard (see *Other boards* below)

PREFINISHED

Prefinished shelves can be white or colored **plastic coated particleboard.** As with wood veneered particleboard, there is a large range of pre-cut 'shelf' widths in standard lengths to choose from, so the only cutting involved should be trimming to the right length. The boards come in 16mm (⅝") and 19mm (¾") thicknesses, but as with other particleboard-based materials, choose the thicker size for all but very light loads.

BRACING GUIDE
Coated particleboard (see *Other boards* below)

PAINTED FINISH

Opting for a painted finish involves more work, but allows you to choose cheaper material.
Standard particleboard, which comes in 19mm (¾") and 16mm (⅝") thicknesses, is economical but likely to bow over a long span with a heavy load.
Fiberboard is about the same strength as particleboard and comes in the same thicknesses. It is costlier, but much easier to cut and finish.
Standard grade plywood is stronger and so can be used thinner – choose from 12mm (½"), 16mm (⅝") and 19mm (¾") thicknesses, depending on the load.
Standard grade composition board is similar to plywood and comes in the same thicknesses. It's worth comparing prices at your stockist.

BRACING GUIDE
Plywood (12mm): add extra bracing over 600mm (24") for medium duty.
Plywood (16mm): add extra bracing over 600mm (24") for medium duty, or 450mm (18") for heavy duty.
Plywood (19mm): add extra bracing over 750mm (30") for heavy duty.
Other boards (16mm): add extra bracing over 600mm (24") for medium duty.
Other boards (19mm): add extra bracing over 750mm (30") for medium duty.

	DESCRIPTION	PROS & CONS	WHAT YOU NEED
Option 1: Wooden supports (medium/heavy duty)	Shelves are supported on a pair of wooden strips screwed to the walls. The ends of the strips can be angled or curved to make them less noticeable. For heavy loads or wide spans, add a third strip along the back wall.	Inexpensive and easy to fit if the walls are smooth and more or less square to each other. On hollow walls the strips allow you to make fixings wherever you want so there is no need to worry about the stud spacing.	Softwood strip (the thickness of the shelf material by twice the thickness of the shelf material). Anchors and screws to fix wood. To fix the shelves to the support you also need 12mm (½") No.6 screws, plus three or four 3-hole glass plates per shelf.
Option 2: Aluminum angle (medium/heavy duty)	Shelves are supported on lengths of L-section aluminum angle, now widely available from hardware and superstores. As with battens, you can use two or three strips per shelf depending on the load and shelf span.	Less noticeable than wood, but slightly trickier to fit. Like wood supports, best suited to alcove walls which are even and true.	Aluminum angle the same width as the thickness of the shelving. Anchors and screws.
Option 3: Standards/brackets (medium/heavy duty)	Shelves are supported on a standard, or track system, or on purpose-made metal or wooden shelf brackets attached to wooden 'tracks'. Use in pairs for light loads/narrow alcoves; add a third support on wide spans and heavy loads.	Tracks fully adjustable and easier to fit than brackets, but decorative effect of brackets may be preferable. Cost of parts must be borne in mind. Best suited to uneven walls where shelves can't be an exact fit.	Standard, or track system, or brackets (2-3 per shelf) and 50×19mm (2×¾") softwood supports. Anchors and screws and 19mm (¾") No.6 screws.
Option 4: Pilaster/strip (light duty or narrow spans)	Shelves are supported on side walls only using pilasters – a mini track system with adjustable hook supports.	Easy-to-fit supports are unobtrusive and fully adjustable, but unsuitable for uneven walls, wide shelves or heavy loads. Shelves cannot be fixed in place.	Pilaster strips (2 per side wall)
Option 5: Plug-in shelf supports (light duty or narrow spans)	Alcove is lined with boards scribed to fit. Shelves are supported on side walls only; holes drilled in lining accept plug-in shelf supports designed for fitting in cupboards.	Trickiest option, but worth considering if alcove walls are in very poor condition. Once lining is in place, shelf supports are easy to fit. Drilling extra holes gives full adjustability.	Suitable lining material (eg particleboard, plywood, composition board, thin strips of wood, hardboard or cardboard for packing, 50mm (2") No.8 screws for fixing, plug-in shelf supports.

FITTING WOODEN SUPPORTS

Cut wooden supports to length to suit the shelves and the depth of the alcove. Side supports don't have to finish flush with the front edge – stopping them a little way back makes them less obtrusive. You can also shape the ends by sawing off at an angle or smoothing into a curve using a Surform plane.

After cutting, drill fixing holes in the side supports at 75mm (3″) inter- vals and in the back support at 300mm (12″) intervals. Fix them in the sequence shown so that you can be sure the shelves will sit level.

Fixing the shelves to the battens is optional, but advisable unless they are heavily weighed down. Glass plates are best where you can see the fixings, but above eye level you can simply screw the shelves to their supports from above.

Trade tip

Keeping shelves flat

❝ If you're fitting a back support, fix the side supports first, then leave the shelf in place while you mark the fixing holes on the wall. This way, you can be sure the shelf sits level on all three supports. ❞

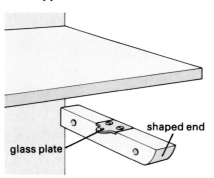

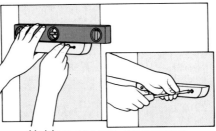

cut end

glass plate

shaped end

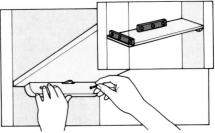

1 Mark the shelf spacings on one side of the alcove, not forgetting to allow for the thickness of the shelves themselves.

2 Hold up one pre-cut support (allow for a back support if fitted), level it, and mark the fixing holes. Drill and plug the wall, then screw in place.

3 Resting the shelf on the fixed support, position the other side support. Check for level both ways, then mark the fixing holes and screw to the wall.

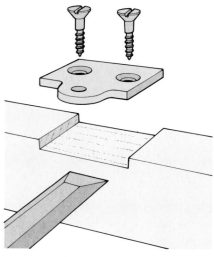

Fix shelves with glass plates where the tops are below eye level and likely to show; use 1 per side support, 1-2 along a back support. Chisel shallow recesses for the plates in the supports, screw in place, then refit the shelf to mark the fixing holes.

Wooden supports (left) which are painted the same color as the shelves are neat and unobtrusive.

USING ALUMINUM ANGLE

Aluminum angle is easily cut to fit using a junior hacksaw. Smooth the ends with a file or coarse wet and dry sandpaper.

Drill the screw fixing holes in the side pieces at 75mm (3″) intervals and in the back piece at 300mm (12″) intervals, supporting the angle on an offcut of wood. To stop the drill bit wandering, pop-mark the holes with a center punch or nail.

Don't forget to allow 4mm (⅛″) for the thickness of the angle when cutting the shelves to fit (see overleaf). Otherwise, follow the same fitting sequence as for wooden supports. Fix the shelves to the angle by screwing through from below with particleboard screws.

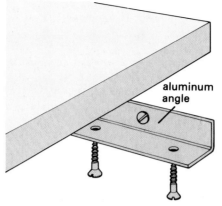

Aluminum angle is a strong and much less conspicuous alternative to wooden supports. Saw it to length and pre-drill the fixing holes.

USING PILASTER STRIPS

Two strips per side should be sufficient for all but the largest alcoves, but they look best if they run the full height. Space the strips a quarter of the way in from the front and back of the shelf.

Screw the strips to the wall as you would shelf tracks, using a carpenter's level to check for plumb. The supports can be hooked into the strips at any height.

Cut the shelves 8mm (⅜″) narrower than the alcove to allow clearance for the strips; this is easier than trying to notch the shelves.

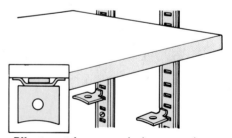

Pilaster strip comes in brass and silver finish and can be screwed directly on to even wall surfaces. Fit clip-in supports to take the ends of the shelf boards.

STANDARD AND BRACKET SYSTEMS

When fitting a track or bracket system, choose brackets with a span that suits the depth of the shelves. The only special consideration is how you space the supports.

If there are two sets, aim to position them a quarter of the way in from either side of the alcove. But if this means that the supports exceed their recommended spacing, include a third set running down the middle of the alcove and position the outer two sets one-sixth of the way in from the edges.

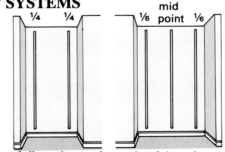

Adjust the track spacing (above) to suit the alcove width. Shelf heights can be varied (right) depending upon what you wish to display.

CUTTING SHELVES TO FIT

Don't attempt to cut all the shelves to the same size unless:

1 The walls of the alcove are even and true (or you have lined them).

2 The walls aren't true, but you are using a track system and need adjustable shelves. In this case cut the shelves so they all fit the width of the alcove at its narrowest point, allowing a small clearance.

In all other situations it's best to measure and cut each shelf individually. You can do this conventionally, using a tape or measuring sticks; but since the sides of the alcove are probably uneven, as well as out of true, it's safer to use the method shown below.

Trade tip

Perfect fit

❝ To be sure of an exact fit, make up a pattern for each shelf in turn using an offcut of board and some pieces of card.

Get a helper to hold the offcut against the back of the alcove at shelf height while you place pieces of cardboard on top and slide them against the sides to mimic the alcove's shape. Tape the cardboard to the board, then remove it and use it to mark the shelf board for cutting. ❞

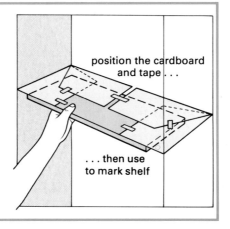

position the cardboard and tape . . .

. . . then use to mark shelf

If the shelves don't need to fit exactly, use a pair of sticks joined with rubber bands to check the minimum width of the alcove, then allow 6mm (¼") clearance.

■ PROBLEM SOLVER ■

Alcove not square

If, as is often the case in older houses, the alcove sides are seriously out of true, it's sensible to choose Option 5 – line the sides with boards, then fit plug-in shelf supports (as found inside fitted units).

Select a rigid material for the lining (you may want to match it to the shelving), so that there's no danger of the boards bowing out of shape as they are being fixed; 16mm (⅝") plywood, and 19mm (¾") composition board or particleboard are possible options.

Start by cutting and marking the boards to fit. Whether they run the full height of the alcove or finish at the baseboard is up to you: if the baseboard looks easy to remove, a full-height lining will be neater.

Fix the boards at roughly 450mm (18") intervals, using 50mm (2") No.6 screws. Space the screws at 100mm (4") centres, or to coincide with stud positions.

Pack behind the boards to bring them vertical as you screw them to the wall – use thin strips of wood, board or cardboard, depending on the gap.

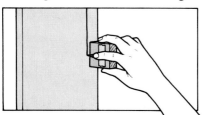

1 Mark and cut the lining boards to fit flush with the front of the alcove, using a wood block and pencil to mark the profile of the back wall.

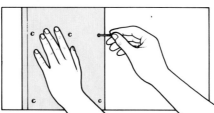

2 Drill rows of fixing holes in the boards at 450mm (18") intervals, then position each board and mark where to drill and plug the wall.

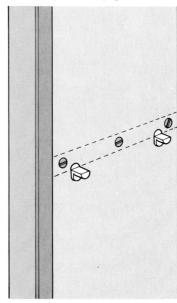

With the lining boards in place, drill rows of holes for the plug-in supports at regular intervals. You can arrange for the shelf ends to hide the screw heads.

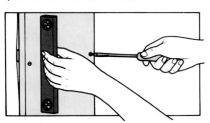

3 Hold a level against the board as you screw it to the wall. Slip pieces of packing behind – resting them on the screws – to keep the board plumb.

4 Having lined the other side in the same way, hide any gaps between the boards and the wall with strips of panel molding, pinned and glued to the edges.

PUTTING UP TRACK SHELVES

Open track shelving systems are the perfect way to store things which don't need to be kept locked away and look good enough to be on show. The shelves are easy to fit, and you can adjust them as and when your storage needs change.

At the heart of any track system are the standards themselves – long metal strips containing sets of holes at roughly 25mm (1″) intervals into which you lock the brackets.

Because of their length, standards tend to be more stable than individual brackets. And since the track brackets' positions are already fixed, there's no tricky aligning to do – the only critical stages are fixing the first standard vertical, and then getting the others level with it.

Although you can reset the bracket heights in a few minutes, in practice you'll probably find you set them once and then leave them that way. Even so, with the standards already in place it's easy to add further shelves if you need them.

....Shopping List....

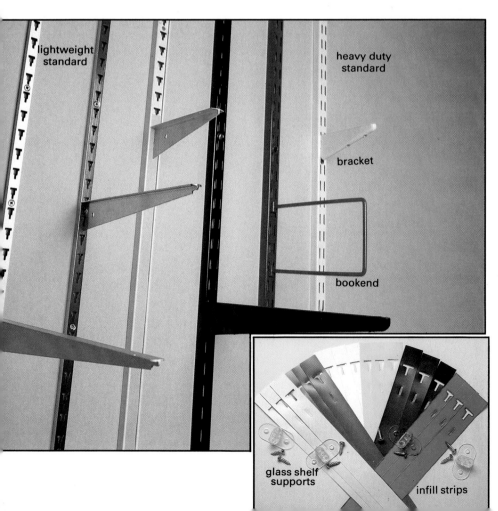

All systems include uprights and brackets in a range of lengths, but other accessories may also be available depending on the make. These include:

■ Colored infill strips to cover unused slots and match the uprights to your decor.
■ Bookends.
■ Glass shelf supports.
■ Sloping brackets for display shelves.
■ Panel brackets for fixing wallboards, etc.
■ Cabinet brackets for fixing boxes and vertical panels to uprights.

Some manufacturers also offer a wide range of shelf sizes and finishes to suit their tracks, while others leave you to choose your own. Possible options include veneered particleboard (with a wood or plastic surface finish), composition board and solid wood. The material you choose may affect the amount of support required (see overleaf).

Tools: Drill with masonry and wood bits, screwdriver, tape measure, carpenter's level (also a saw and try square if you have to cut shelves).

DESIGNING WITH STANDARD UNITS

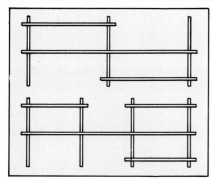

Shelf length *Having three or more standards allows you to fit shelves of different lengths, none of which need necessarily span the entire system.*

This is particularly useful if you have to put a few tall items among objects that look best with the shelves closely spaced.

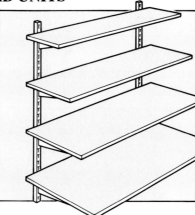

Shelf depth *Fitting shelves of different depths makes it possible to store a wide range of items more efficiently within a small space. Always put the shelves in decreasing order of depth, from bottom to top.*

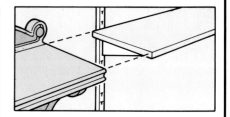

Fixed levels *If you want the shelving to line up with a feature of the room, such as a mantelpiece, you'll need to take extra care when marking the positions of the tracks.*

The only reliable way to work out the final shelf level is to fit a bracket to a track and align it with the feature before you mark the screw holes – not forgetting to allow for the thickness of the shelf itself in your calculations.

WHAT TO FIX TO

On a solid masonry wall, fix the tracks by screwing through each of the fixing holes into drilled and plugged holes in the wall.

On a hollow wooden-framed partition wall, you *must* screw the tracks to the solid wooden framework itself. It is not sufficient to fix them to the hollow part of the wall using cavity wall fixings – the thin skin covering the wall will not be strong enough.

The tracks are flexible enough to cope with small irregularities in the wall, but if the surface is very uneven it's a good idea to fix wooden strips to it first (see Problem Solver).

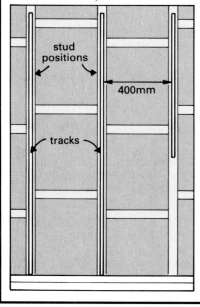

Right *Track systems aren't just for shelving; here one of the shelves doubles as a lightweight desk.*

Left *Using more than two standards lets you position short runs of shelving at different heights.*

HOW MANY SUPPORTS?

If you are fixing to a hollow wall, the track positions are governed by the position of the wooden frame. You must screw to *each* stud – approximately 400mm (16") intervals.

Otherwise, the maximum spacing is fixed by the material you are using for the shelving. The standard 15mm (⅝") particleboard used as shelving material needs support at 600mm (24") intervals to stop it bowing. But with very sturdy material, such as 25mm (1") thick softwood or 19mm (¾") plywood, you can extend this to 900mm (3").

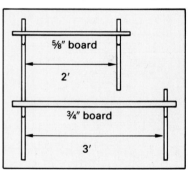

The brackets should either be the same depth as the shelves or a little less.

Remember, the longer the brackets, the *less* the amount of evenly distributed weight they will stand – 150mm (6") brackets might carry well over 50kg (110lb), whereas 450mm (18") brackets could be limited to as little as 15kg (35lb).

If you have to put heavy weights on a deep shelf, it's worth fitting tracks and brackets at more frequent intervals.

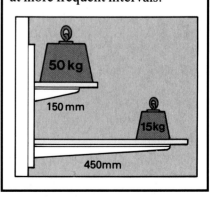

Left *Here, short standards are used to create a streamlined run of shelves.*

FIXING THE TRACKS

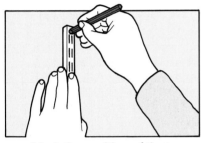

1 Mark the position of the top hole of the first track. If the shelf height is critical you will need to fit a bracket and align it first (see opposite).

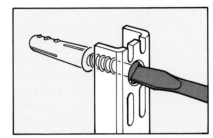

2 Drill the hole for the top screw and fix the track to the wall. Only partially tighten the screw, so that the track is left free to pivot on its fixing.

3 Use a carpenter's level to set the track vertically, then mark and drill the other holes. Fit the remaining screws, using packing pieces where necessary.

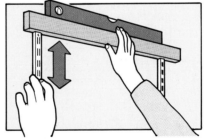

4 Use the level again to set the top of the second track at exactly the same height as the first. If you don't do this the shelves won't sit straight.

FIXING THE SHELVES

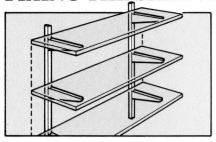

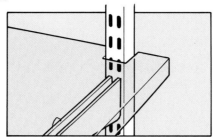

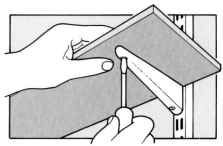

1 *Align the shelves so they overlap the brackets by the same amount on each side. Make sure, too, that the ends line up above one another.*

2 *If you want the shelves to fit right back against the wall, cut notches in them to accommodate the thickness of the tracks.*

3 *Fit the brackets to the tracks, position the shelves and weight them, then mark the screw holes from underneath with a bradawl. Screw the brackets on.*

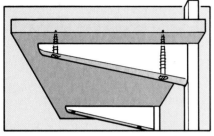

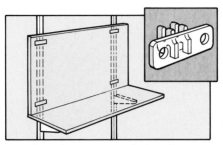

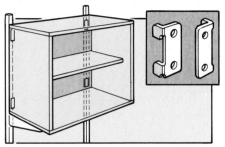

4 *With U-shaped brackets, the outer screw is shorter than the inner one. If you are using thin shelves, take care not to screw right through the boards.*

5 *Some systems have brackets for vertical panels. If yours doesn't, but you want to fit such panels, you can screw them to the shelves instead.*

6 *If you want to include box units, these can either be homemade or adapted from basic self-assembly cabinets such as kitchen wall units.*

Trade tip

Strengthening shelves

❝ *I find that a good way to stop thin shelves from bowing is to fix wood strips along the edge. This also makes them look more substantial. A thin strip of softwood or ramin – about 50 × 12mm (2 × ½") – is usually ideal; fix it either to the front or back of the shelf.* ❞

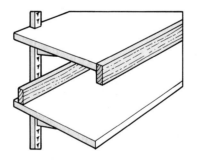

▌PROBLEM SOLVER▐

Uneven walls

Very few walls are perfectly flat or square, so when you screw the standards in place make sure they don't bend because of irregularities in the surface.

Small bumps and hollows can be accommodated by inserting packing pieces of hardboard or cardboard behind the tracks as you drive in the screws.

If the walls are seriously out of square or in poor condition, it's better to screw 50 × 25mm (2×1") wood strips to the wall and screw the tracks to these. This gives you more scope for packing behind the strips and lets you make the wall fixings where you like, rather than at points fixed by the standards.

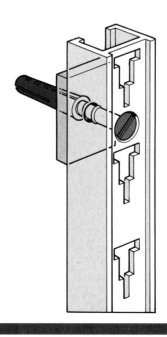

Fit packing pieces (left) to fill small hollows, but fit a strip (above) if the surface is poor.

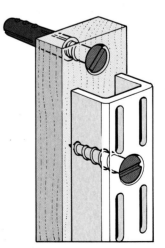

PUTTING UP BRACKET SHELVES

If you only want a few fixed shelves, separate brackets are an ideal choice. They are often cheaper and easier to fit than track systems – although this advantage is reduced every time you add another shelf. And because there is a much wider range of styles, both brackets and shelves can be chosen to suit your decorations.

Bracket styles range from cheap and functional to stylish or ornate. The basic options are detailed below. Whatever type you choose, use the recommended bracket spacing for the shelf material and the likely load the shelf will have to support (see page 301 for more details).

Alternatives Separate brackets aren't a sensible choice if you want a run of stacked shelving because of the difficulty of lining up all the holes – consider a track system instead. Conventional brackets may also be hard to fit directly above objects such as radiators.

***Shelves on brackets** provide quick, convenient storage – and can look as stylish as you want.*

....Shopping List....

Brackets come in several patterns. The size and number needed depend on the size of the shelves and the weight they will have to support.

Utility pressed steel brackets are a good choice for workrooms or garages and can be painted.

'Streamlined' steel or plastic-covered brackets are strong and inexpensive. The finish is good enough for display shelves.

'Wrought iron' brackets made of steel or aluminum in various finishes are reasonably strong but can be tricky to fit.

Cast-iron and brass brackets can be stylish, but are expensive.

Wooden brackets are sometimes sold separately but are more often part of complete 'shelf packs'.

Shelves Natural wood, man-made boards and glass can all be used. See overleaf for details of what to consider when choosing.

Fixings Normally you need two or three screws and anchors per bracket to fix to the wall, and two or three to fix the shelf. Use the heaviest screws that fit the bracket. They should project about 38mm (1½″) into the wall and up to three quarters of the way through the shelf.

Tools: Drill with masonry and wood bits, screwdriver, tape measure, carpenter's level (and possibly a plumbline), plus a saw and try square if you are going to cut and trim shelves.

lightweight pressed steel bracket

steel bracket with plastic cover

heavyweight pressed steel bracket

heavy duty aluminum bracket

aluminum 'wrought iron' bracket

steel 'wrought iron' brackets

softwood bracket

PUTTING UP THE SHELVES

Lightweight shelves are best fitted with their brackets before fixing to the wall.

■ Mark the bracket positions on the underside of the shelf, drill pilot holes, and screw the brackets in place.

■ Position the complete assembly against the wall with a level on top. Check the alignment, then mark the bracket fixing holes. Drill and plug

Heavy shelves are easier to fit if you fix the brackets to the wall first.

■ Mark the bracket positions underneath the shelf. Check where one end bracket falls on the wall and position it to mark the fixing holes.

■ Drill and plug the wall and fix the bracket in place.

■ Support the shelf (or a straight length of wood) on the fixed bracket with a level on top. Check for level, then mark the position of the other end bracket.

■ Remove the shelf and fix the second bracket to the wall.

■ Rest the shelf on both brackets and mark the positions of the other brackets. Fix them to the wall, then screw the shelf to all the brackets.

A small shelf is easier to fit if you screw the brackets to it first. Position the shelf with the aid of a carpenter's level, then mark the bracket fixings.

2 *Fix this end bracket in place. Position the shelf (or a wooden strip) with a carpenter's level on top and mark the other end bracket's position.*

1 *With a heavy shelf, begin by marking the positions of the fixing brackets on the underside. Then check where one end bracket falls on the wall.*

3 *Add intervening brackets with the shelf resting in place. Check that each bracket supports the shelf correctly, then mark its fixing position on the wall.*

▪PROBLEM SOLVER▪

Aligning several shelves

If you need to stack shelves one above the other, but don't want a track system, there are two methods of fixing brackets:

Fixing to wooden uprights first makes it easier to align the brackets and avoids having to drill a lot of holes in the wall.

Mark the bracket positions with the uprights laid together to make sure they line up. Screw the brackets in place, then screw each upright to the wall at 300mm (12″) intervals.

The backs of the shelves must be notched to fit over the uprights if you want the shelves to sit flush with the wall.

Fixing independently is neater, and means the shelves don't need to be notched. However, it is more difficult to get the shelves in line, which is essential if the result is to look good.

Mark out the first shelf and use it as a pattern to mark all the others. Fix the first pair of brackets to the wall and hang a plumbline from each. Then use the lines as a guide to fixing the rows of brackets below.

To align separate shelves (below), fix the top set of brackets and then use plumblines to gauge the positions of the brackets in the rows below.

A stack of shelves is easier to align if you fit the brackets to strips of wood first.

Notch the backs of the shelves to fit over the strips. Fit the brackets to both strips of wood together to guarantee even spacing.

FITTING GLASS SHELVING

Glass can be used with most types of shelf support and is an attractive alternative to more conventional shelving materials. The main reasons for using glass instead of wood are:

■ Glass has a light, delicate appearance which doesn't overpower small objects and ornaments.
■ It is easy to clean and doesn't stain, making it a practical choice for bathrooms and kitchens.
■ It transmits light, so it can be used where solid shelves would cast unwanted shadows, such as in front of a mirror or around a window.

Glass also has disadvantages:

■ It is brittle and broken glass can be dangerous, so glass shelves need good support and shouldn't be fitted within reach of small children.
■ Heavy objects need thick glass shelves to provide adequate strength. As the shelves themselves are heavy, you need more supports than for an equivalent wooden shelf.

The main appeal of glass is its appearance, but it has practical advantages, too. In situations where a shelf could block the light, there is no other choice.

....Shopping List....

As with any shelving, you must take into account the thickness of the shelf material and the amount of support it needs to suit the weight it has to carry.

Glass should be at least 6mm (¼″) thick, depending on the load (see below). The normal choice is flat (float) clear glass, but other suitable types include colored, patterned and wired glass – all of which can be used decoratively.

■ 6mm (¼″) glass is suitable for light loads if the shelves are supported every 400mm (16″).
■ 10mm (³⁄₁₆″) glass can be used for normal loads with brackets up to 700mm (28″) apart – reduce this to 500mm (20″) for books.

Get the glass cut to size by a glass merchant. All edges should be ground and polished smooth. Standard shelf widths are available pre-cut and finished.

Brackets depend partly on the situation, but in general glass is heavy so use a medium/ heavy duty system. The main options are:

Track systems which can be used either with special plastic retaining clips or self-adhesive glass fixing pads on the brackets.

Metal channels which grip the back of the shelves to give an unobtrusive fixing. These come in a range of colours and are suitable for 6mm (¼″) glass only (a special insert is used to protect the glass from contact with the metal).

Shelf brackets are often unsuitable because the part of the bracket which is seen through the shelf looks unfinished. A popular option is 'wrought iron' type brackets which look neat used in this way. Some pressed steel brackets can be fitted with special glass shelf clips which grip the shelf neatly.

Glass shelf brackets are commonly made for use in bathrooms. Most are designed to fit over the ends of a shelf which is cut to suit.

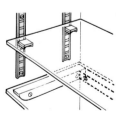

Alcove supports are an option where you are fitting shelves in a recess or a fitted cabinet.

Plug-in end supports include plastic plugs to fit into pre-drilled holes, or metal pilaster strips which screw to the sides ready to take clips at any height you wish.

Wood strips or metal angle screwed to sides and back of an alcove provide a means of giving continuous support for the shelves.

FITTING GLASS SHELVES

Supports for glass shelves are fitted in much the same way as for any other shelf. However, it is even more important than usual to make sure that they are properly aligned – the shelf needs support across its whole width without undue flexing.

Some systems incorporate clips which prevent the glass from sliding on the brackets. Otherwise, if there is any risk at all of it being knocked, you should use self-adhesive retaining pads to hold it firmly in place on its supports.

Trade tip
Using a dummy

❛ With many support systems it often helps to line up the brackets by trying a shelf in place. To make it easier to do this and to simplify cutting the glass shelves to size, cut a dummy shelf from an offcut of particleboard or other suitable material and use this for your fitting experiments. ❜

To retain the glass on plain brackets, use double-sided self-adhesive pads. These also help to cushion it from contact with metal surfaces.

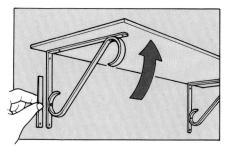

Align track and bracket systems carefully. Pack out behind the fixings if necessary to make sure that the shelf is fully supported and not twisted in any way.

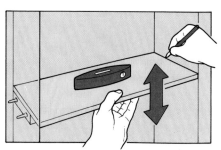

Alcove shelf supports must be carefully aligned. Fix one end first and align the second one by trying a shelf in place and marking along it.

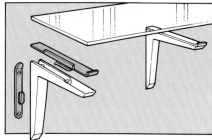

Special clips are needed for some brackets. Take care that these trap the edge of the glass without undue pressure which could cause splintering.

PROBLEM SOLVER

Polishing the edges

In most cases you can get the glass cut to size and polished when you buy it. If you want to use a piece of glass which you have already, you can cut your own shelves with a glass cutter in the conventional way. But before use, you must also grind and polish the edges to prevent accidents.

This isn't very difficult to do, but it does take a little time. The easiest tool to use is an oilstone, but you can get by with a piece of wet or dry abrasive paper pinned to a block of wood. Start with a coarse grade and work down to fine.

Wear heavy gloves when handling the unpolished glass. Wet the stone (or paper) lightly and rub the edges of the glass, at an angle of about 45°. Use only downward strokes at this stage in case of splinters being pulled off the rough edge.

Rub down all the edges with the coarse abrasive until the sharp corners are removed, then switch to a medium abrasive. Wet this too and rub it along the edge to round off the ridges left by the first pass. Use this stone to take off the sharp corners.

Finish off with a fine abrasive, again used wet, running it along the edges at several angles until it produces a smooth curve.

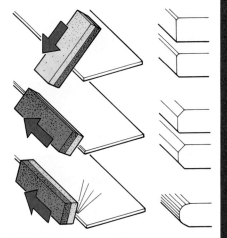

Grind the edges with progressively finer abrasive used wet. Work in the order shown to produce a smoothly rounded edge with a polished surface.

FITTING SLIDING WARDROBE DOORS

Track kits contain double top and bottom tracks, a clip-on fascia panel, and fixings. They come in standard widths which you trim to size.

Door kits come with tracks, runners and clip-on frames for the doors.

For the doors themselves, use 4mm (⅛″) plywood. This is generally available in two grades, in 2440×1220mm (8×4′) sheets.

Sliding door kits for mirror and panel doors are sold in one, two, three and four-door packs. The doors come in one height, but a range of widths.

Tools checklist: Tape measure, drill, junior hacksaw, various screwdrivers. You will need other tools and materials for making your own doors or adapting the opening size, so run through the instructions before you start. Before you decide finally what kits to buy, work out how and where you're going to fit the wardrobe (see overleaf).

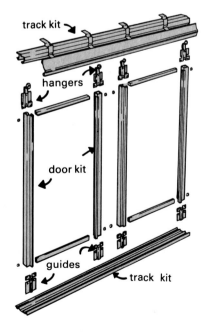

track kit

hangers

door kit

guides

track kit

Installing a set of sliding wardrobe doors is a simple yet effective way to streamline your bedroom storage. The doors enclose as much space as you want and can also be used to conceal unsightly features in the room. There's a choice of styles, including mirror and panel fronts.

Two systems are available. One consists of two separate kits – a door pack, which includes standard size doors and runners; and a track pack containing the top and bottom tracks, plus a clip-on fascia.

The other system is based around a simple door kit containing the tracks, together with clip-on frames for the doors. You provide the actual door panels, which has the advantage that you can cut them to size and paint or paper them to match the room.

Both types are extremely versatile – run the doors right across the room; stop them short with an end panel, or fit them in an alcove.

Once you have enclosed the space, fit out the inside to suit your requirements. Special wardrobe interior kits make this a fairly quick and simple job (see pages 313-318). Alternatively, fit a plain closet pole.

THE RIGHT COMBINATION

The secret of a trouble-free installation is to balance the look you want against a layout which suits the room and is easy to arrange. So before you order any parts, consider these points:

Which doors? Mirror and panel door kits normally come in a standard height of 2285mm (90"), which rounds off to fit a ceiling height of 2.5m (8'2") by the time they're fitted in their tracks. They can't be cut down, which rules out using them if your ceiling is lower than their standard height. But if the ceiling is higher than this, it's relatively easy to make up the difference with a wooden filling piece or even a false 'drop top' panel (see Problem Solver).

With door kits, you can cut the plywood panels to any size you like so long as the floor and ceiling are reasonably level. You may prefer this option anyway if you're on a tight budget, or you want to decorate the panels to match the rest of the room.

Which layout? The box below shows the possible variations, depending on how your room is laid

out and what other furniture has to go in it. If necessary, draw a sketch plan to make sure the new layout won't be too cramped.

Before making a final decision, read through *Where to fix the top track* opposite. If the ceiling joists are inconveniently placed, it may be easier to alter the depth of the wardrobe than to add bracing.

How many doors? When you've decided on your ideal layout, measure the opening width. Then check the chart at the bottom of the page which shows the width and number of doors needed for a range of given openings.

■ If you're fitting door kits, use the chart to work out what size to make the panels.

■ If you choose standard doors, but you're fitting an end panel, arrange for the opening width to match one of the combinations in the chart.

■ If you want standard doors to run wall to wall, and the opening width doesn't match any of the standard sizes, you have the choice of shortening the wardrobe with an end panel or fitting side panels to make up the difference.

Mirror doors (above) blend easily into any decorative scheme and have the advantage of making a room seem larger. However, they can't be cut, so you may need to fit side panels to make up the opening width.
Panel doors (right) come ready finished and have a pleasingly substantial appearance. Like mirror doors they can't be cut.

WHICH LAYOUT?

Run the wardrobe wall to wall (right) using two, three or four doors as appropriate. If the doors are a fixed size, you may have to fit one or more side panels to take up the extra opening width.

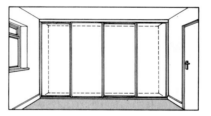

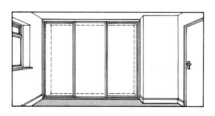

Fit the wardrobe in an alcove (left) if the alcove is 600mm (24") deep or more. Otherwise, it's more practical to increase the depth with an end panel or continue the doors across the entire wall.

Where space is limited, stop the wardrobe short and fit your own end panel. Alternatively, place the wardrobe in the middle of the wall and fit two end panels. Both options allow you to match the opening width to standard doors.

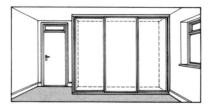

WHICH DOOR SIZE?

The chart shows commonly available sizes of mirror and panel doors. If you make your own doors, use one of the combinations shown to work out the width of the plywood panels.

Opening width	Number and size of doors required	Opening width	Number and size of doors required
1190mm (3'11")	2×609mm (2')	2235mm (7'4")	3×750mm (2'6")
1498mm (4'11")	2×760mm (2'6")	2690mm (8'10")	3×900mm (3')
1803mm (5'11")	2×914mm (3')	2950mm (9'8")	4×750mm (2'6")
1778mm (5'10")	3×609mm (2')	3600mm (11'10")	4×900mm (3')

WHERE TO FIT THE TOP TRACK

Your wardrobe should be around 600mm (24") deep to allow for clothes on hangers, with the top track positioned to suit (in most kits it goes 25mm (1") inside the line of the doors).

However, because this track takes the weight of the doors it can't be fixed to the thin ceiling plaster – you need to screw it directly into the supporting joists.

Start by finding out which way the joists run. If the floor upstairs is boarded, the boards will run in the opposite direction, with rows of nails giving away the joists' exact positions.

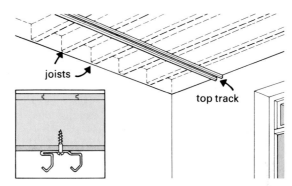

If the joists are parallel to the track, try to arrange for the track to run along the center of a joist – if necessary by increasing or reducing the depth of the wardrobe slightly.

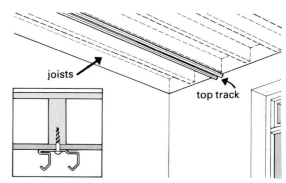

If the joists are parallel to the track, try to arrange for the track to run along the centre of a joist – if necessary by increasing or reducing the depth of the wardrobe slightly.

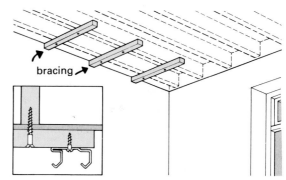

Alternatively, fix the track to 50×50 (2×2") bracing pieces fitted between the two nearest joists. The neat way is to nail these from above; but if you don't have access, screw them from below then hide the ends with a piece of wood.

FITTING THE TRACKS

Having taken delivery of the kit parts, check the dimensions of the opening as follows:

Width Measure from wall to wall or to the end panel position. If you need to close up the opening to fit the doors, see Problem Solver overleaf for how to do it.

Height Measure from floor to ceiling at several points. If you need to fit filling pieces or a panel to accommodate the doors, again see Problem Solver overleaf.

If you find the door-plus-track height – 2.5m (8'2") for standard doors – varies by more than 12mm (½"), one or other of the tracks will need packing with slips of stiff cardboard or hardboard to bring them level. Insert the packing before tightening the track fixing screws.

Unless you are fitting a filling piece below it, the bottom track can be fixed directly to the floor through the existing covering. Take extra care that it aligns with the top track.

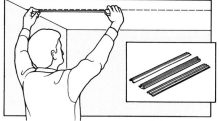

1 Mark the final width of the wardrobe on the tracks and fascia. Square cutting lines across them, then saw them to length using a junior hacksaw.

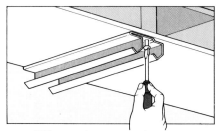

2 Offer up the top track and mark the fixing positions (drill extra holes if necessary). Screw the track in place, leaving the screws slightly loose.

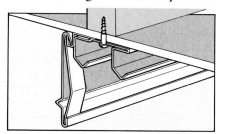

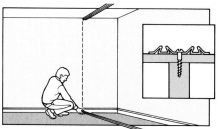

3 Clip the fascia over the top track as shown. When it's in position, tighten the track fixing screws to clamp the fascia against the ceiling.

4 Make sure the bottom track aligns exactly with the top one when marking the fixing positions. If necessary, pack underneath to bring it level.

HANGING THE DOORS

If you're fitting standard size doors, the tricky part of the job is out of the way. The hangers and guides are factory fitted, so simply slip the doors into their tracks and adjust the guides following the kit maker's instructions.

If you are making your own doors, now is the time to cut the plywood panels to size.

Measure up with the tracks in place, allowing for the extra taken up by the runners and guides. If you're trimming the width as well as the height, double doors are cut to half the width plus a 25mm (1") overlap allowance, while three-door sets are cut to a third of the opening width, plus the overlap.

Cut the door panels as accurately as you can, but don't worry about finishing the edges: these are hidden by the frames, which you measure direct from the panels and cut separately. Check each panel's fit before cutting the frames.

1 Having transferred the measurements of the opening to the panels, cut them to size using a handsaw or electric saber saw fitted with a fine blade

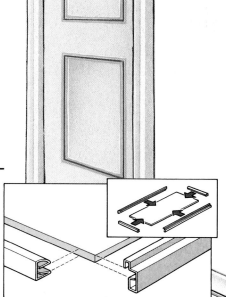

2 Use a junior hacksaw to cut the frame pieces, sizing them directly from the cut panels. Notch the corners where they join, then clip them in place.

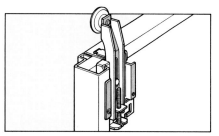

3 The top hangers and bottom guides have tabs which normally clip into slots in the frame. If these were sawn off, fit them with screws instead.

4 Hook the hanger wheels on the tracks by holding up the doors at an angle. When in place, align by adjusting the hangers; lastly, fit the runners.

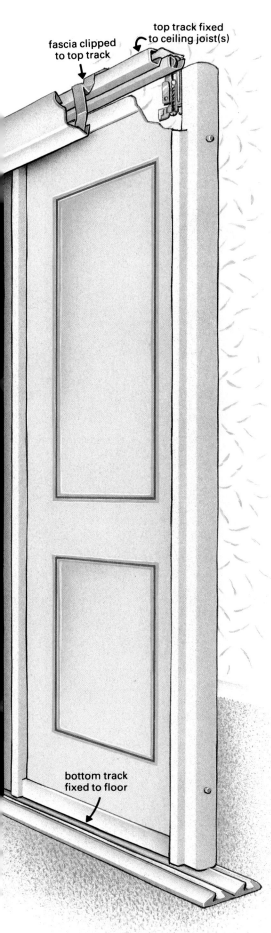

ADDING AN END PANEL

Where the wardrobe isn't running from wall to wall, fit an end panel of 16mm or 19mm board (such as veneered particleboard). Buy a piece long enough to fit from floor to ceiling and wide enough to fit from the back wall to the front of the fascia.

Almost certainly, you'll need to trim the panel to fit against the wall and ceiling, so cut it on the generous side to begin with, then mark and fine-trim it afterwards.

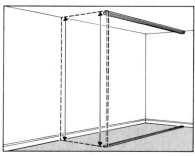

1 Measure the height from floor to ceiling at the front and back of the wardrobe. Mark the dimensions on the panel and cut it to size.

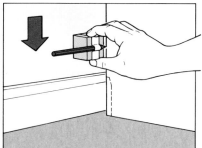

2 Stand the panel up and mark the back edge to fit the wall and baseboard. Then trim it with a hand saw or saber saw, and finish the edge with a surform plane.

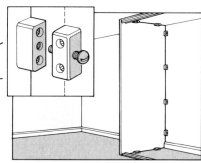

3 Fix the panel with plastic joint blocks. Fit the two top and bottom; along the back edge, space four evenly and screw them into drilled and plugged holes.

A typical 3-door assembly (above) using standard size mirror and panel doors. When combining door types, fit the mirror on the front of the two track channels.
Angle the doors (right) when slotting in the hangers.

top track fixed to ceiling joist(s)

fascia clipped to top track

bottom track fixed to floor

Adjusting the opening height

How you approach this depends on the size of the gap.

■ For gaps up to 100mm (4″), fit a wooden filling piece under the bottom track using either of the methods shown on the right.

The thickness of the timber doesn't have to match the gap exactly – remember, the runners will accommodate differences up to 12mm (½″). If the floor level is out by more than this, pack under the filling piece with slips of wood or hardboard.

■ For gaps between 100mm and 200mm (4-8″), you can fit a filling piece top *and* bottom – but only if the floor and ceiling are roughly level. Otherwise, see below.

■ For larger gaps, build a 'drop top' frame of 100×50mm (4×2″) wood as shown on the right, then screw the top track to this.

Give the frame members as much support as possible, screwing them to the joists where appropriate, and to a bearer fixed along the back wall.

Afterwards, panel the frame with 6mm (¼″) plywood pinned to frame and then decorate to match the walls.

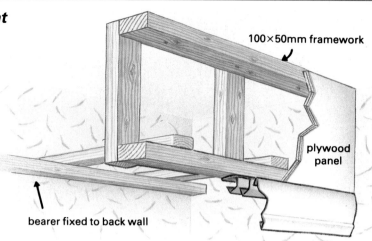

100×50mm framework

plywood panel

bearer fixed to back wall

Make a 'drop top' frame from 100×50mm (4×2″) timber screwed to the ceiling with braces extending to the back wall.

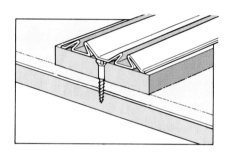

For gaps of up to 100mm (4″), it's easiest to screw a filler piece under the bottom track. Choose a thickness that comes within 12mm (½″) of the gap.

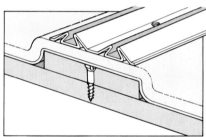

Alternatively, for a small gap roll back the carpet and fit the filling piece underneath. (This is also better if you need to level the wood with packing pieces.)

Adjusting the opening width

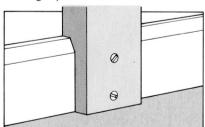

1 If the filling piece has to clear a baseboard, stand it in place temporarily and mark the baseboard's shape as shown using a pencil and block of wood.

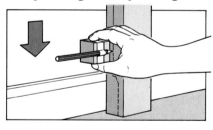

2 Cut out the notch with a hand saw then screw the filling piece to the wall. Check that it sits vertically – if not, pack behind it.

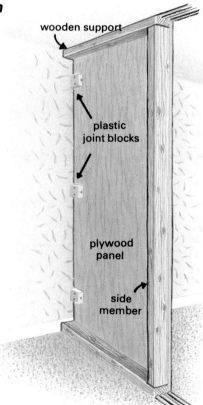

wooden support

plastic joint blocks

plywood panel

side member

Like the height, how you deal with the opening width depends on the gap.

■ For gaps up to 100mm (4″), fit a filling piece to the adjoining wall. Screw it just behind the line of the fascia, and pack behind it to ensure that it's vertical. Fill any gaps later.

Use the same technique to clear a projecting baseboard. Shape the end of the filling piece to fit the baseboard as shown on the left.

■ For gaps of between 100mm and 200mm (4-8″), fit a filling piece on both sides.

■ For larger gaps, fit a filling panel as shown on the left.

If the panel is running to ceiling height, fix the 100×50mm (4×2″) side member to wooden supports screwed to the ceiling and floor. If you're building a drop top panel as well, incorporate the side member into the rest of the frame. Fix the panel itself with plastic joint blocks.

FITTING OUT A WARDROBE

Clever accessories make it easy to put together a wardrobe interior that suits your storage needs perfectly – whether you use a ready-made kit or separate units.

If you already have a built-in closet or sliding door wardrobe, now could be the perfect time to think about organizing the space more efficiently. And if you are installing wardrobe doors, you can plan and fit out the interior at the same time.

Narrowing the choice

The first step is to think about what's going in the wardrobe, and how you'd like to store it. Broadly, there is a choice between hanging space, open storage, and drawers – with special fittings for things like shoes and ties.

Three basic layout options are shown below, and in larger wardrobes there's no reason why you shouldn't combine them. But before you decide, run through *Planning your storage needs* overleaf.

A typical wardrobe interior kit (right) providing a practical mix of different storage including dividers, rods for hanging, drawers and open shelving.

....Shopping List....

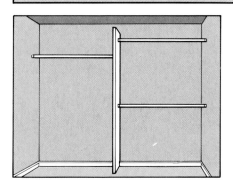

Rod/divider layout

The simplest interior arrangement consists of one or more vertical panels to divide the wardrobe, plus hanging rods and hooks. Shelves are a make-yourself option.
You need a minimum of 300mm (12″) depth for the unit, but at least 600mm (2′) if you want to hang clothes. Buy the rods to fit the space available.
You may need 300×15mm (12×⅝″) melamine-faced boards for shelves.

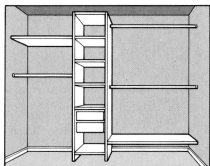

Shelf/drawer layout

This type of arrangement has vertical box frames which include shelves and drawers. Hanging rods are fitted each side and you can make your own top and bottom shelves.
You need at least 400mm (16″) depth for the unit, rising to 600mm (2′) for hanging clothes. Plan the components carefully to suit the space available.
You may need 450×15mm (18×⅝″) melamine-faced boards for shelves.

Wire basket system

This is based on open frames made of plastic-coated wire which clip together to make rigid supports. There is a wide range of baskets, hooks and rails for varied storage.
You need 300-550mm (12-22″) depth, depending on the system, and at least 600mm (2′) if you want to hang clothes.
You may need 15mm melamine-faced boards for shelving, and hanging rods may be separate.

PLANNING YOUR STORAGE NEEDS

Different things need different kinds of storage, but a combination of these four basic types will cope with most needs:

Hanging space: Rails for hanging clothes are a top priority. Long dresses and coats need more height than jackets, slacks, suits, skirts and shirts.

Open shelving and drawers: Shelving is useful for items like bed linen, towels and luggage if this is stored in the bedroom. Drawers are best for small objects, underwear and folded knitwear.

Special storage may be required for things like ties and shoes.

Only you can decide how much of each type you need – people are different sizes, and so are their clothes. To give yourself a clearer idea, draw up a detailed list of what you want to store and divide the items between the four categories listed above. Then allocate space accordingly.

A drawer/shelf system cuts down on clutter by providing easily accessible storage for small or awkward items, as well as folded clothes and towels.

HANGING SPACE

The main hanging rods should be set slightly above eye level, around 1.8m (6′) from the floor- and if there is a top shelf, you need at least 50mm (2″) clearance above the rods to unhook a hanger. Clothes are deceptively heavy, so avoid very long, unsupported spans.

Remember that where clothes don't need the full hanging height, you can fit shelves or a second rod below them to make better use of the space.

These are the approximate hanging lengths needed for different types of clothing:
- Long dress: 1.6m (5′ 4″).
- Bathrobe, negligee, or long

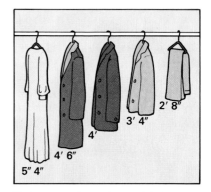

Unless you have lots of full-length clothes you can fit other storage in the unused space below the hanging rod – a second rod, perhaps, or a low shelf unit.

DRAWERS AND OPEN SHELVING

You could easily need anywhere from 10 to 15 drawers for folded clothes, depending on their size and the number you want to store. But some clothes can be kept in open shelves or wire baskets just as well, saving on drawer space.

Spare bedlinen and luggage is likely to need anywhere between about 1m (3′4″) and 3m (10′) total shelf length. But suitcases may take up a lot of space unless they can be fitted inside one another.

Shoes, handbags, hats and so on will probably require 1-2m (3-7′) total shelving space, with plenty of room above for taller items. But you may be able to store them more efficiently by using specially-made racks or hooks.

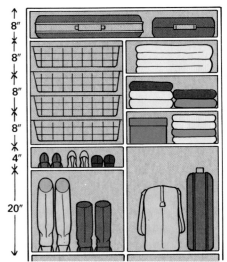

Most people need a mix of shelf and drawer spacing to cope with all that they want to store. Some tall items can waste a lot of wardrobe space.

coat: 1.4m (4'6").
- Medium coat, man's jacket: 1.2m (4').
- Woman's jacket, skirt: 1m (3'4").
- Slacks, shirts: 800mm (32").

A lot obviously depends on how much you have to store, but as a rule of thumb most men need a total hanging space about 650mm (26") wide, while women need around 1m (3'4").

If you have a lot of clothes needing hangers, this could go up to about 1.5m (5') for men and 2.4m (8') for women. And if you hang shirts and blouses, add about another 300-500mm (12-20") to the basic measurements.

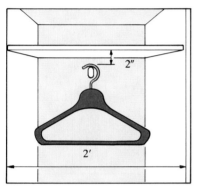

Plenty of clearance is needed for the hanging rods. You need room to lift clothes on and off, and enough depth for them to hang without crushing.

This rod/divider system lets you hang short clothes on two levels to make the best use of space. You can add shelves to take other items which can't be hung on rods.

Wire baskets are a good alternative storage solution for the kind of things which need to go in drawers or on shelves – and they ensure that everything gets properly aired.

FITTING A ROD/DIVIDER

The maximum span of a wardrobe rod before it starts to bend or sag is usually about 1200 mm (4'). This is narrower than most wardrobes, so the simplest type of rod system consists of upright panels which divide the wardrobe into short sections with rods for hanging fitted on either side. These parts may come as a kit, which includes hooks and other fittings.

For a short two-door wardrobe, you need only one center panel. This is normally supplied with three rods to span the space from it to the sides of the wardrobe. For wider wardrobes, simply buy an extra kit to make up the kind of layout shown below. Top and bottom shelves aren't included; make these from standard shelf-width boards.

Tools: electric drill and bits, carpenter's level, tape measure, junior hacksaw, handsaw and screwdrivers.

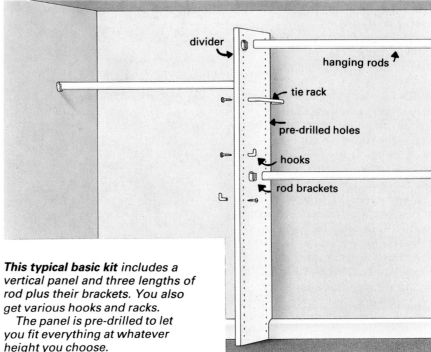

This typical basic kit includes a vertical panel and three lengths of rod plus their brackets. You also get various hooks and racks.

The panel is pre-drilled to let you fit everything at whatever height you choose.

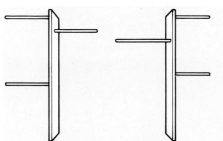

Fit the rods at any height you like on either side of the panel.

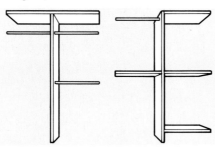

Optional shelves can be added by using standard boards.

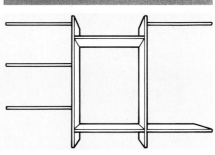

In a wide wardrobe, combine two kits side-by-side.

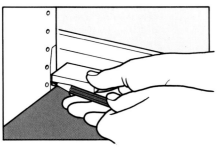

1 Mark the vertical panel to clear a baseboard by standing it the same distance out from the wall as the width of the scribing block. Saw out the notch.

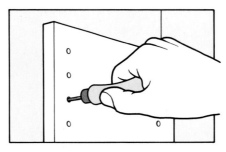

2 Stand the panel against the end of the wardrobe or the side wall and mark off the heights of the rods on both the panel and the side.

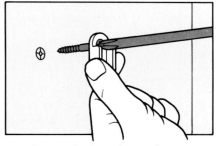

3 Screw the hanging rod brackets to the panel and to the end of the wardrobe or side wall. Use anchors if you're screwing into masonry.

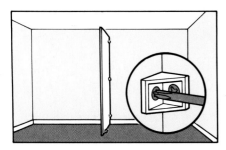

4 Fix the vertical panel in place using plastic joint blocks or brackets screwed into drilled and plugged holes in the wall behind. Screw another block to the floor.

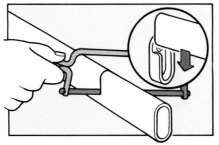

5 Measure the space remaining for each rod between the panel and the end, and cut them to length with a junior hacksaw. Fit the rods to the brackets.

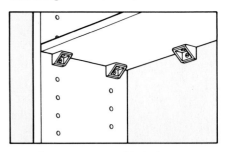

6 If you want to add shelves, cut them from melamine-faced board and attach them to the sides, back and vertical panel using joint blocks.

FITTING A SHELF/DRAWER UNIT

This works in a similar way to the simple rod/divider system on the previous page. It has a number of hanging rods, plus a vertical divider to break up the interior of the wardrobe into short, easily spanned lengths. But in this case the vertical divider is a free-standing box unit containing shelves and drawers. Components are available flat-packed, so you can fix the shelves at the height of your choice.

Like the simpler rod/divider system, you can fit a single kit to a narrow wardrobe, or add more sections to cope with a wider span (see below). It's also possible to add extra top or bottom shelves to a kit, using lengths of standard shelf-width sized melamine-faced board.

Tools: electric drill and bits, carpenter's level, tape measure, junior hacksaw, handsaw and screwdrivers.

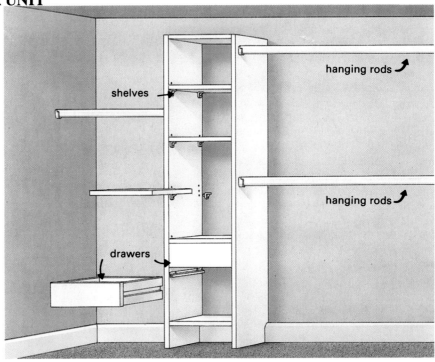

shelves

hanging rods

hanging rods

drawers

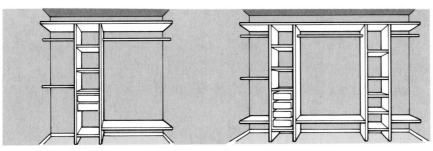

The layout includes (above) a flat-pack storage unit consisting of two sides, connecting shelves and a set of drawers. There are also lengths of rod and brackets fitted on each side of the assembled unit. The rods may be different lengths, allowing you to stand the divider off to one side of the wardrobe.

Fit the rods at any height you want and add your own shelves.

Extra parts allow for more varied storage in a wider wardrobe.

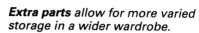

1 Mark the vertical panels to fit over baseboard. Then fix drawer runners and shelves to assemble the unit – normally using screws and plastic blocks.

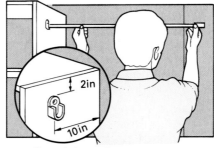

2in

10in

2 Stand the unit up and mark the height of the hanging rod bracket on the vertical panel. Measure to the wall or end of the wardrobe to find the rod length.

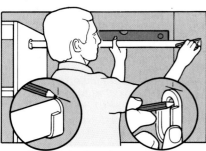

3 Screw the bracket to the vertical panel. Cut the rod to length with a junior hacksaw, then find the position of the other bracket and screw in place.

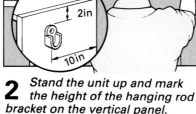

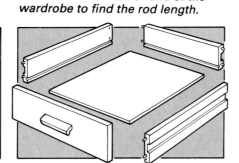

4 Assemble the drawers, which are supplied in flat-pack form with either plastic joints or glued corners. Fit these and the internal shelves in place.

Trade tip

Forward planning

❛ Don't make the mistake I once did and forget the space left when the wardrobe doors are opened. The interior unit must be offset to one side so that it is completely unobstructed by the doors – otherwise you won't be able to pull out the drawers.

Think about this at the planning stage, because it may affect the way you arrange your hanging space. ❜

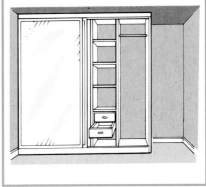

WIRE BASKET SYSTEMS

Wire basket storage units can be free standing, or supported by the side panels of the wardrobe. Kits range from complete wardrobe interiors to individual baskets and small modules which can be fitted into awkward spaces. Some allow you to use the baskets as ordinary drawers, and you can also get accessories like undershelf baskets and shoe racks.

A typical basic system consists of a set of side panels, crossbars and baskets, made in a range of sizes so that you can assemble sets of units to suit your needs. Most systems are based on a standard unit width (often 450mm – 18″), so you can combine them to span any area.

Wire basket components vary but this typical system shows many of the fittings available. Open baskets are used as drawers, and shelves or hanging rods clip on.

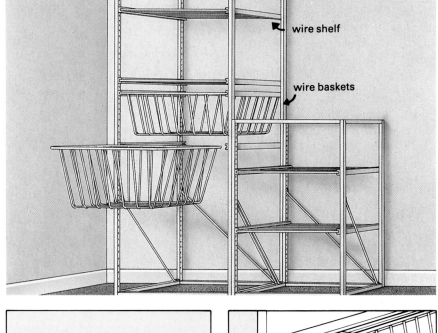

hanging rod

wire shelf

wire baskets

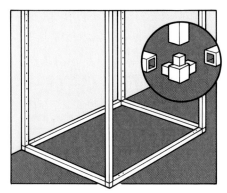

1 *Free-standing frames clip together using crossbars at top and bottom. Press them together by hand or use a mallet if they are stiff.*

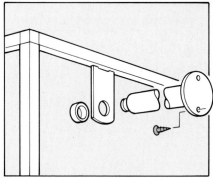

2 *Some systems have attachments for hanging rods. The other end of the rod can be supported by a bracket screwed to the end panel or side wall.*

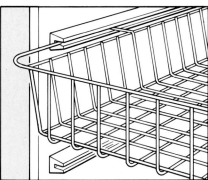

3 *Many wire baskets can also be used as open drawers in a unit made from solid boards. This is done by fitting separate runners to the insides of the panels.*

▌PROBLEM SOLVER

Dealing with awkward corners

Shallow wardrobes and ones where the depth is reduced by a projection inside, such as an old chimney breast, pose special problems – because you need about 600mm (2′) to fit in a hanger comfortably.

If you haven't enough depth, one answer may be to hang the clothes facing the front of the wardrobe instead of sideways on. You'll be able to get at them easily by fitting an extending wardrobe rod running from front to back. These are especially good for hanging light clothes like shirts and blouses.

You need a space at least 600mm (2′) wide, and a sturdy shelf above it, into which to screw the new extending rod.

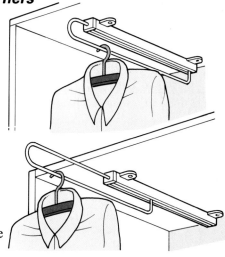

This type of rod needs less than 400mm (16″) fitting depth but can be pulled out for easy access.

─ *Trade tip* ─

Heavy loads

❛ If you've got a lot of jackets and coats to store, they can be surprisingly heavy. Oval hanging rods are much better than round ones at taking the strain and are used in most kits. You can also buy them separately.

Whatever type of rod you are fixing, bear in mind that the heavy weights involved mean that you need good fastenings.

I recommend using twin thread screws in all types of wood, as these are much better at getting a grip. For very long rods or very heavy loads, consider fitting a top shelf and screwing a center support bracket underneath. ❜

BUILT-IN CABINETS

Built-in cabinets are the neatest solution to household storage problems. Unlike freestanding furniture, they can be planned to make the best use of the available space and you can make sure they don't obstruct the rest of the room. And although you can't take them with you if you move, most potential purchasers see plenty of built-in cabinets as a real asset.

One way to provide built-in cabinet space is to buy modular furniture such as kitchen or bedroom units. But although this is likely to be the easiest option, it may not always be the best. If you have an awkward space (or it simply doesn't fit the modular unit size very well) you may find that the units fill it little better than freestanding furniture. Modular units can also work out fairly expensive, simply because the manufacturers must guarantee that they are structurally sound regardless of where they are fitted or what is on each side.

Building your own furniture is rather more complicated, but can offer some significant advantages.

First of all, you can make sure that things fit properly. For example, if you have a space 1050mm (42") wide, you can build a unit this size rather than adapting a standard unit

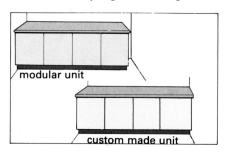

Traditional styling *suits living room alcoves.*

Custom designed built-in furniture can be made to fit an awkward space perfectly – unlike modular furniture which is restricted to set sizes.

which is probably 900 or 1000mm (36 or 40") wide, or use a combination of 500 and 600mm (20 and 24") widths.

Secondly, you can save on materials by making more use of the walls themselves (or adjacent cabinets) as supports.

Thirdly, you can produce furniture which simply isn't available any other way. For example, you can make shallow cabinets that fit a shallow alcove perfectly, rather than using deeper standard ones which would project awkwardly.

Types of built-in furniture

There are two basic ways to make built-in furniture:

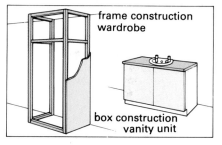

Box furniture is easy to make and most furniture is now built this way. Frame furniture is more complicated but lighter and more economical on materials.

Framed furniture uses a wooden frame as the main structure, and in many cases – for example, alcove shelving – the wood can be fixed directly to the walls. Any of the framework left exposed can then be clad with non-structural paneling, which also serves to brace it.

Box furniture uses panels of sheet material (eg particleboard) as the main structural supports; most modern self-assembly units are built this way.

In practise, you may find it best to use a combination of methods. On the following pages are a number of basic designs which can be adapted to many situations.

DESIGNING BUILT-IN FURNITURE

There are no hard-and-fast rules for designing built-in furniture: by its very nature, each piece should be made to suit the situation. This means taking a flexible attitude, and adapting basic design principles as you go.

Start by measuring the room and drawing a scale plan. This should show all the critical dimensions, and you may find you need to draw two plans (one to show the floor and another showing the walls) to include enough detail. Mark in any fixed points such as electrical outlets and water pipes.

Next draw a rough sketch of the furniture you have in mind. There are two things which you should consider right from the start. First of all, try to stick to the standard dimensions given in the table on the right when it comes to things like counter height and so on. If you are in doubt about overall sizes, measure some finished furniture as a starting point.

Secondly, bear in mind the available sizes of the materials you plan to use. For example, faced particleboard comes in 300 and 375mm (12 and 15″) widths. Making a unit 325mm (13″) deep means trimming down the wider boards (unless you go up to a larger sheet and can cut several strips from it with less waste). Unless there is an over-riding reason for sticking to a specific non-standard dimension, use standard boards for ease of work and economy. Similarly, work to standard lengths as far as possible.

Finally, it is worth taking advantage of ready made accessories wherever possible – to save time and to ensure a good finish.

■ Standard ready-made doors and drawer fronts can save hours of work. See the following construction plans for more details.

■ Drawers are rarely worth con-structing from scratch, since drawer kits are simple, reasonably cheap and very efficient.

When you have roughed out the design to your satisfaction, transfer it accurately to the scale plan. This forms both the basis of your shopping list and a guide to constructing the furniture.

DIMENSION GUIDES	
Worktop depth	24″
Worktop/sink height	36″
Worktop to wall unit gap	18″
Dressing table height	24-32″
Wardrobe depth	20-24″
Seating height	16-18″
Dining table height	28-30″
Washbasin height	28″
Chest of drawers depth	16-18″
Shelf supports	24-30″ apart

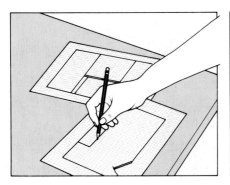

Draw a scale plan and elevation of the room showing all the critical dimensions and the position of any fixed points like sockets and pipes.

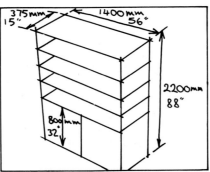

Sketch out your furniture design, roughly indicate overall height and depth. Choose the overall dimensions to suit the materials and fittings you are using.

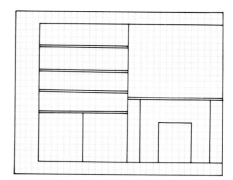

Adapt your drawing to suit the scale plan and then draw it on the plan accurately to scale. This becomes your shopping list and cutting plan.

....Shopping List....

Sheet materials The main material for low-cost box furniture is *faced* or *veneered* 16mm (⅝″) *particleboard*. This comes in 2240×1220mm (8×4′) sheets and a variety of widths and lengths.

An alternative for painting is *lumber-core composition board*. This is very strong and comes in a variety of thicknesses, is easy to work, stable and easy to finish. *Veneered composition board* can be used for varnished wood furniture. Both materials come in standard 2240×1220mm (8×4′) sheets.

Where you are paneling over a wooden frame, the sheet material is not structural. *Hardboard* may be adequate, although it flexes easily and may 'drum'; it is often used to make furniture backs. Otherwise use *thin plywood*. You can even use *plasterboard* for furniture which forms the corner of a room, providing the edges are covered and it does not have to take a load.

Other wood Surfaced softwood strips are the stock solution for built-in furniture. 50×25mm (2×1″) is adequate for most jobs.

Softwood moldings are worth investigating as solutions to design or decor problems. They are particularly useful for concealing exposed edges, or to break up large expanses of flat paneling.

Doors and drawers Blank *door and drawer fronts* come in various styles in a small range of sizes.

■ Widths of 300, 375, 450, 600, 675, and 750mm (12, 15, 18, 24, 27 and 30″).

■ Heights of 450, 600, 760, 900, 1200, 1500, 1650, 1800 and 2000mm (18, 24, 30, 36, 48, 60, 66, 72 and 80″).

(There may be some variation in the measurement of panels available). Homemade doors and drawer fronts can be any size you wish.

Fixings *PVA adhesive, twin thread screws* in various sizes and *tacks* should cope with most jobs; buy plenty, as it is almost impossible to plan exact needs in advance. It is also worth buying *brackets* or *block joints* in bulk for the same reason.

Fittings *Drawer kits, hinges, knobs* and other fittings can be estimated fairly accurately. You may be able to buy such items in bulk.

ADAPTABLE LIVING ROOM UNITS

These units can be used as a dining room sideboard or bookcase/entertainment center by making small modifications to the design and construction. It's also easy to change the appearance to suit different decorating styles by applying moldings and/or choosing different styles of doors.

The construction is straightforward and is intended for use either in an alcove or in a corner – although it could easily be extended right across a room. Essentially, there are two parts; a base unit with a solid top and a series of shelves above.

In an alcove, the shelves can be entirely supported on the wall, but where the unit is built into a corner you need to fit an end panel; in this case fit one against the wall too, for the sake of symmetry.

Making the doors

You can either use standard ready-made doors which come in a limited range of sizes, or make your own to fit. Ready-made doors guarantee a good finish, but you are likely to have to panel-in gaps in the course of adapting them to fit the space.

Homemade doors can be made simply by using panels of faced or veneered particleboard, or composition board edged with lipping. Veneered finishes can be varnished or painted, to suit the decor. All these have a flat, stark appearance which is fine in modern rooms but not so good for period ones. If necessary, give the surface a paneled look by gluing on moldings.

Finishing touches

There are two main ways to modify the style of the cabinets:

■ Choose materials with either a painted or natural wood finish in mind. If you are painting, use ply, composition board or veneered particleboard; for a natural wood look use solid wood, veneered particleboard or veneered composition board with matching lipping.

■ Pick moldings to match other finishes in the room – the key to a real 'built-in' style. Trim the top with a cornice to match the coving in the room, and use architraves and cabinet door moldings to match those on the other doors. You could also continue the baseboard around the plinth, and run any picture rail across the unit at the same height.

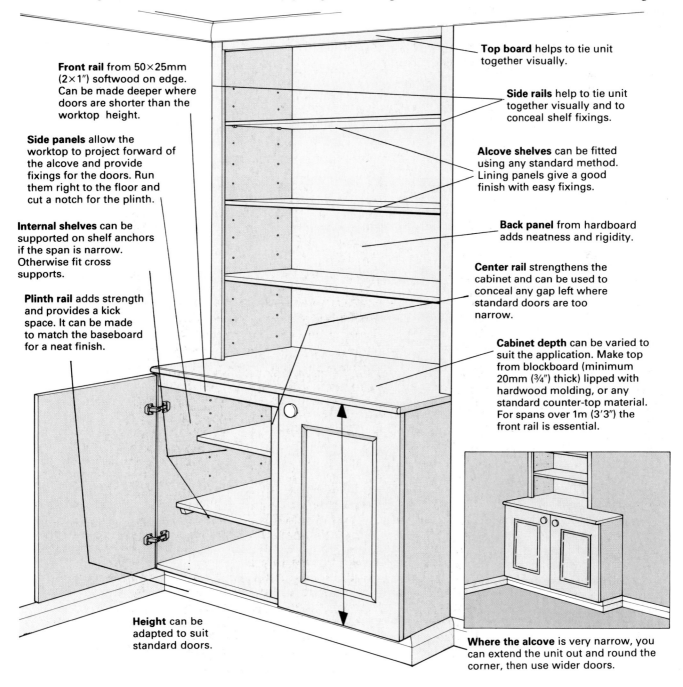

Top board helps to tie unit together visually.

Front rail from 50×25mm (2×1") softwood on edge. Can be made deeper where doors are shorter than the worktop height.

Side rails help to tie unit together visually and to conceal shelf fixings.

Side panels allow the worktop to project forward of the alcove and provide fixings for the doors. Run them right to the floor and cut a notch for the plinth.

Alcove shelves can be fitted using any standard method. Lining panels give a good finish with easy fixings.

Internal shelves can be supported on shelf anchors if the span is narrow. Otherwise fit cross supports.

Back panel from hardboard adds neatness and rigidity.

Center rail strengthens the cabinet and can be used to conceal any gap left where standard doors are too narrow.

Plinth rail adds strength and provides a kick space. It can be made to match the baseboard for a neat finish.

Cabinet depth can be varied to suit the application. Make top from blockboard (minimum 20mm (¾") thick) lipped with hardwood molding, or any standard counter-top material. For spans over 1m (3'3") the front rail is essential.

Height can be adapted to suit standard doors.

Where the alcove is very narrow, you can extend the unit out and round the corner, then use wider doors.

BASIC KITCHEN UNITS

Kitchen units can be made to suit awkward locations far more efficiently than standard self-assembly units. In general it makes sense to use similar construction methods, and where standard units are being used elsewhere in the kitchen it's a good idea to copy them.

The main reasons for making your own units are where standard ones don't fit a given width very well, or where you want to take top units right up to the ceiling.

All the fittings are easily obtainable from hardware stores, and are fairly easy to use – although you need to buy a special hinge-boring bit to fit the type of hinges used on kitchen cabinet doors.

Door options

Doors are the major problem with homemade kitchen units. If you want plain white flush doors, these are simple to make from sheets of coated particleboard (and you may also find this in a range of colors).

Where you are trying to match existing units, you really have no option but to use identical doors, bought as spares from the unit suppliers. This means that you have to work around standard sizes – which to some extent defeats the object of making your own units in the first place. However, even if you have to panel out the cabinet to suit the doors, you still have the internal space which is not available if you use smaller units.

Standard doors may also be the best option if you want something more interesting than a plain panel. There is no need to stick to kitchen unit doors; ready-made cabinet doors are widely available in a range of sizes and can be varnished or painted as you choose.

Options for adapting standard doors to fit all involve packing out the sides with extra strips, leaving the internal size unaltered. Don't do this on the hinge side, since the mounting plates need to be screwed to a flat panel.

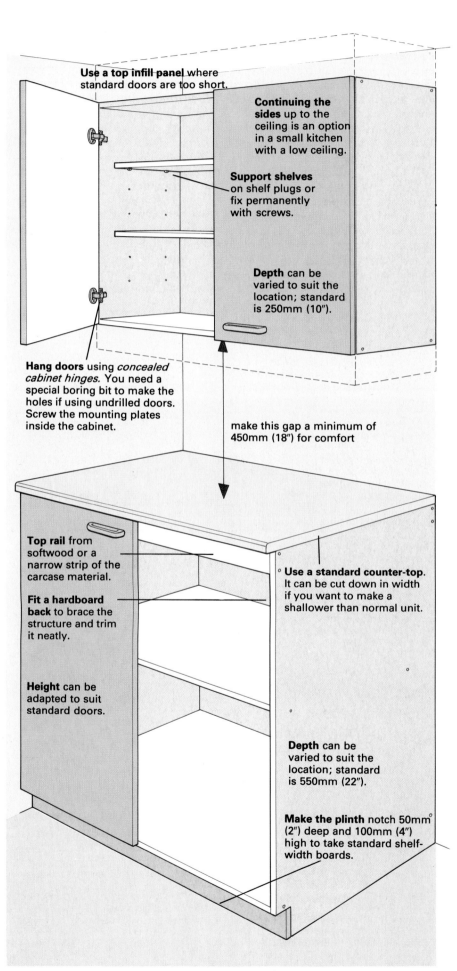

Use a top infill panel where standard doors are too short.

Continuing the sides up to the ceiling is an option in a small kitchen with a low ceiling.

Support shelves on shelf plugs or fix permanently with screws.

Depth can be varied to suit the location; standard is 250mm (10").

Hang doors using *concealed cabinet hinges*. You need a special boring bit to make the holes if using undrilled doors. Screw the mounting plates inside the cabinet.

make this gap a minimum of 450mm (18") for comfort

Top rail from softwood or a narrow strip of the carcase material.

Fit a hardboard back to brace the structure and trim it neatly.

Height can be adapted to suit standard doors.

Use a standard counter-top. It can be cut down in width if you want to make a shallower than normal unit.

Depth can be varied to suit the location; standard is 550mm (22").

Make the plinth notch 50mm (2") deep and 100mm (4") high to take standard shelf-width boards.

BUILDING-IN WARDROBES

Built-in wardrobes are easily put together using a combination of box and frame construction techniques. Alternatively, you can partition off the end or corner of a room and fit sliding doors.

However, in a small bedroom, it may not be worth going to the trouble of making the basic wardrobe – and a cheaper option may be to adapt a low-cost self-assembly unit. The dimensions of things like hanging space tend to be fairly fixed anyway, and it is rarely necessary to make the basic box fit a particular space with any degree of accuracy.

Whether you make the wardrobe from scratch or adapt an existing unit, the trick is to use the dressing table part to adjust it to fit the room exactly. Gaps can then simply be filled in by using moldings – a theme which can be continued across the doors and so on.

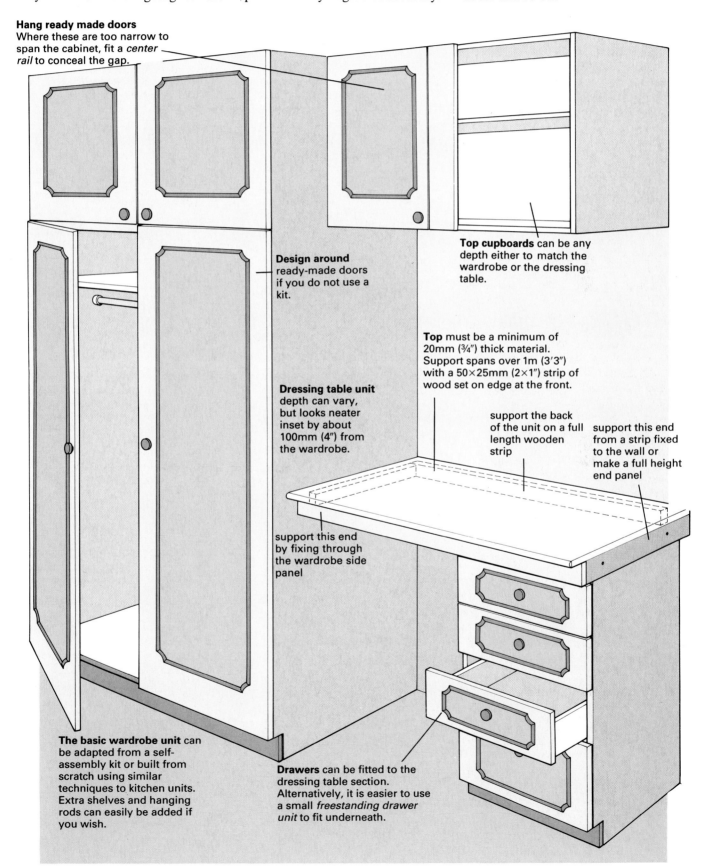

Hang ready made doors
Where these are too narrow to span the cabinet, fit a *center rail* to conceal the gap.

Design around ready-made doors if you do not use a kit.

Top cupboards can be any depth either to match the wardrobe or the dressing table.

Top must be a minimum of 20mm (¾") thick material. Support spans over 1m (3'3") with a 50×25mm (2×1") strip of wood set on edge at the front.

Dressing table unit depth can vary, but looks neater inset by about 100mm (4") from the wardrobe.

support the back of the unit on a full length wooden strip

support this end from a strip fixed to the wall or make a full height end panel

support this end by fixing through the wardrobe side panel

The basic wardrobe unit can be adapted from a self-assembly kit or built from scratch using similar techniques to kitchen units. Extra shelves and hanging rods can easily be added if you wish.

Drawers can be fitted to the dressing table section. Alternatively, it is easier to use a small *freestanding drawer unit* to fit underneath.

DRYING CLOSET

Sometimes you can turn eyesores into useful additions. Creative thinking turned this otherwise unsightly hot water tank into a storage area for things like towels and linens that must be kept dry.

The hot water tank was conveniently close to a corner, so all the home owner had to do was frame one side and hang doors across the other. Useful space was gained by rerouting intrusive pipes to run down walls.

Louvered doors were chosen to provide natural ventilation. If you use solid doors, fit ventilation panels to the top and bottom of such a unit.

Planning points
■ Choose your doors first and work round their dimensions. Make sure there is room for them to swing.
■ Choose the cladding material – if this comes in sheets smaller than the height of the cabinet you must arrange for the joint to fall over a supporting strip. Suitable materials include plywood, hardboard, or plasterboard (so long as the exposed front edge is protected with a lipping).
■ Make sure you will have easy access to any valves controlling the flow of water to the hot tank, and to the thermostat or switch if there

should be one.

Construction details
■ Fix the wall supports first checking they are accurately horizontal and vertical.
■ Assemble the side frame.
■ Use a door to measure where the side frame needs to be positioned.
■ Fix the frame to walls, floor and ceiling, making sure the door post is vertical (check from side to side and back to front, too).
■ Fix cross supports and a plinth.
■ Install the shelves.
■ Cover the frame with paneling.
■ Hang the doors.

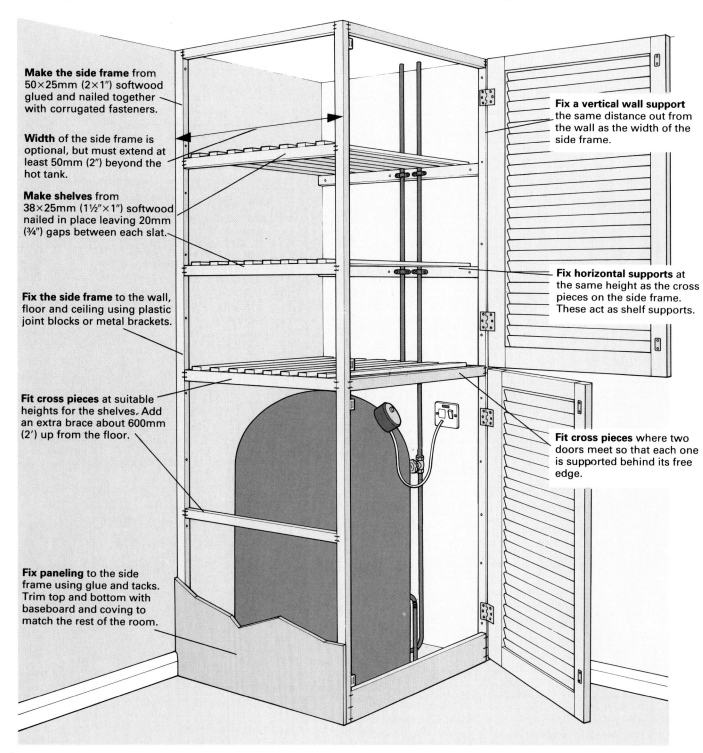

Make the side frame from 50×25mm (2×1″) softwood glued and nailed together with corrugated fasteners.

Width of the side frame is optional, but must extend at least 50mm (2″) beyond the hot tank.

Make shelves from 38×25mm (1½″×1″) softwood nailed in place leaving 20mm (¾″) gaps between each slat.

Fix the side frame to the wall, floor and ceiling using plastic joint blocks or metal brackets.

Fit cross pieces at suitable heights for the shelves. Add an extra brace about 600mm (2′) up from the floor.

Fix paneling to the side frame using glue and tacks. Trim top and bottom with baseboard and coving to match the rest of the room.

Fix a vertical wall support the same distance out from the wall as the width of the side frame.

Fix horizontal supports at the same height as the cross pieces on the side frame. These act as shelf supports.

Fit cross pieces where two doors meet so that each one is supported behind its free edge.

6

PLUMBING

HOW YOUR PLUMBING SYSTEM WORKS

Home plumbing is not mysterious, nor overly complicated. On the contrary, it is one of the 'easiest to do' of all the various trades needed in the home, especially when you become familiar with the terms, tools, and the many different products which are available.

The total plumbing system includes the pipes, fixtures and fittings which transport water into and out from the home. Home plumbing can be divided into three basic areas (see right): the water-supply system, the drainage system, and the fixtures in your home.

The water-supply system

In every plumbing system, there must be a source of water and pipes which carry it to the fixtures in your home. This supply system must be able to supply enough water (which is pure enough to drink) for every outlet at the correct operating pressure. Within your home, the system must also be able to provide you with the hot water you need.

In most incorporated areas the water source is a public or privately operated water 'works' from which purified water is distributed through mains to which users are connected by arrangement with the authorities.

If such a source is not available, you can install a private source of your own. In surburban or rural areas the most efficient solution is usually to drill a well. This is usually best undertaken by a professional well digger.

The drainage system

Drainage (which is strictly controlled by code in most localities) is the complete and final disposal of waste water, and of the sewage it contains. The complete drainage system, therefore, consists of the pipes that carry sewage away from the fixtures in your home, and the place where the sewage is deposited. You may empty sewage into a city sewer or into a properly constructed septic tank.

The fixtures

The fixtures in your home enable you to use your water. In this sense, a faucet on the outside of your house (for attaching a hose, say) is a fixture in just the same way as a laundry tub in the basement, or a shower, dishwasher, or toilet. Most fixtures are so standardized that they, and the parts they contain, are usually interchangeable.

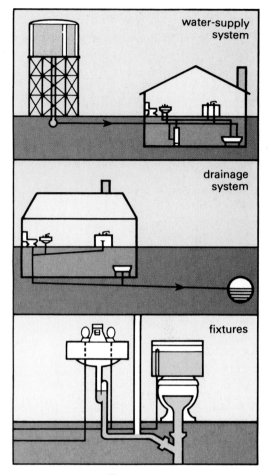

water-supply system

drainage system

fixtures

A plumbing system can be divided into three sections (right).

Shut-off valves (below) stop the supply of water so that work can be carried out on any part of the system.

Plumbing Standards

6 With the public's health at risk, all plumbing – both new and repair work – must conform to strict safety standards.

In large cities, detailed Plumbing Codes (or standards) have become part of the law. You may need to obtain a permit before undertaking a major job and, after completion, the work may have to be inspected and approved. Check the Plumbing codes in your area. Contact your municipal or town Building Department for more information. 9

A TYPICAL PLUMBING SYSTEM

cold water supply
hot water supply
drain system
vent system

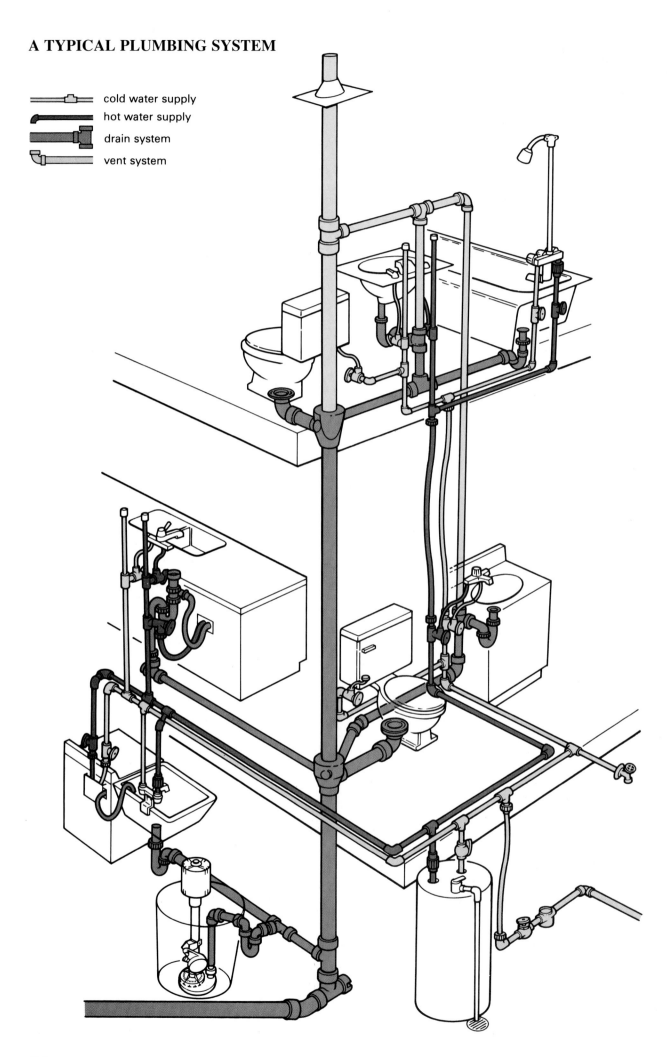

THE WATER SUPPLY SYSTEM

Every plumbing system contains a number of valves which regulate the supply of water. Some valves control the water flowing to a particular fixture or appliance; others shut off the supply to the whole house.

Cold water supply

Water enters your house either from a city main or, in rural and some suburban areas, from a line supplied by a well. If the supply is from a city main, the water passes through a meter valve, a water meter, and a stop valve.

The water company retains responsibility for the lines which start at the water-treatment plant and run through the street to your meter; you are responsible for all water lines on the 'house side' of the meter. This means that it is the stop valve (also called the 'main water shut-off') that you should close when all water to the house must be stopped. Never turn off the meter valve (which is on the 'street side' of the meter and is therefore water company property).

From the main supply line into the house, branches lead to the various fixtures. Valves along these branches allow part, rather than all, of the water supply to be shut off.

The supply mains should be graded to one low point in the basement or crawl space so that a drain-cock will permit complete drainage of the entire supply system. Any section of pipe that cannot be drained in this way must have a separate drain-cock. As a rule, a pitch of 6mm (¼") to each foot of pipe is sufficient to permit proper drainage.

If the water for your home is supplied from a well, the situation is only a little different. You will still have shut-off valves at every fixture so that someone can take a bath while you repair the faucet in the kitchen sink. But shutting off the total water supply is a matter of switching off the pump that supplies water under pressure rather than turning off a valve.

Hot water system

Hot water is obtained by routing cold water through a water heater. This heater may be part of the central heating plant or a separate unit. When part of a central system, a separate hot-water storage tank is generally provided to hold the heated water. On the other hand, when a separate heater is used, the water is stored within the unit.

Types of valve

Different valve mechanisms tend to be used in different locations in the water supply system. The illustration (left) shows some of the most common types.

■ Globe valves are used to shut off the water to fixtures and appliances, and for the meter valve and main shut-off valve. Globe valves can regulate the flow of water through a pipe as well as completely shut off the supply.

■ Gate and lavatory straight valves are used either all the way open or all the way closed.

■ Ground-key valves are operated by a key (which is in the possession of the water company) to turn off a house's entire water supply.

■ Check valves permit water to flow through them in one direction only, and therefore have very specific uses. For example, they can prevent water which has been pumped into an overhead tank from flowing down if the pump is switched off.

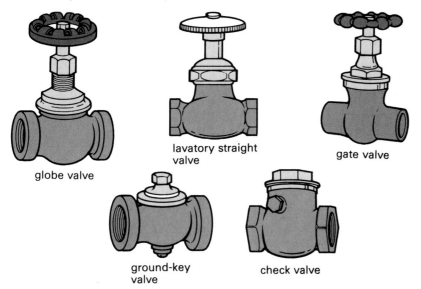

lavatory straight valve

gate valve

globe valve

ground-key valve

check valve

TURNING THE WATER OFF

Before you can do any plumbing job, whether it's changing a faucet washer or mending a leak, you need to know where to turn the water off. All home plumbing systems contain shut-off valves for isolating the water supply. The basic procedure is:
■ Find the nearest shut-off valve to the pipe or outlet you want to isolate.
■ Turn the shut-off valve **clockwise** as far as it will go.
■ Open the faucet at the end of the pipe run to drain any water left in the pipework (this may take a few seconds).

Unfortunately, there are no 'rules' about where shut-offs are placed. Some houses have more than others, and there is rarely one for every section of pipe. Before you try to find out which shut-off controls which pipes, look at the diagram opposite which shows how water flows around the house. Get to know the valves in your home so that you can act quickly in an emergency.

Try to turn off the water at the fixture itself.

The main shut-off valve is located after the water meter.

THE DRAINAGE SYSTEM

The drain-waste-vent (DWV) system begins at the fixtures and appliances where the water supply system ends. Since drained water is not under pressure (in contrast to the water supply), the DWV piping must slope so that water flows by gravity from each fixture and appliance to the city sewer or, in suburban areas, to a private sewage disposal system.

Stacks In most cases, fixture waste pipes and toilet soil pipes eventually empty into a vertical pipe known as a stack (known as a soil stack when it serves a toilet). At its lower end, each stack leads into another run of pipes called the building drain. At its upper end, vent stacks are open to the air above the house roof.

Traps Every fixture needs a trap – a V-shaped, water-filled pipe that allows water and wastes to pass through on their way out of the house, but prevents gases and vermin inside the DWV system from entering the house. Toilets contain built-in traps; other fixtures are connected to separate traps.

Access must be provided for cleaning traps, should they become clogged. Toilet and sink/washbasin traps can be cleaned by working through the fixture drain, as can some bathtub and shower traps. Traps that cannot be reached from the drain must have access for cleaning through a hole in the floor or from a basement or attic crawl space. Some traps have cleaning/drainage openings of their own.

Vents The need for traps leads to another necessity – venting. As water flows down a pipe by gravity it creates a vacuum at the top of the pipe. This so-called siphon action can be powerful enough to force almost all the water out of the trap, leaving it nearly dry. Venting to the outside air above the roof equalizes the pressure on both sides of the trap and prevents water siphoning out of the trap.

Cleanouts Another DWV system necessity is for cleanout openings, which allow stoppages which develop inside the system to be removed. A horizontal drain run, and sewer pipes, must all be provided with such openings.

A cleanout is often an opening at the high end of the run of pipes. By removing the plug which closes the opening, the drain can be cleaned out. As well as being accessible, cleanouts should enter in the direction of flow (so that when you look into them, wastes flow away from you).

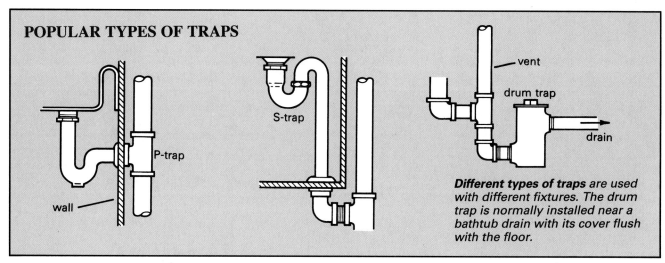

POPULAR TYPES OF TRAPS

P-trap

wall

S-trap

vent

drum trap

drain

Different types of traps are used with different fixtures. The drum trap is normally installed near a bathtub drain with its cover flush with the floor.

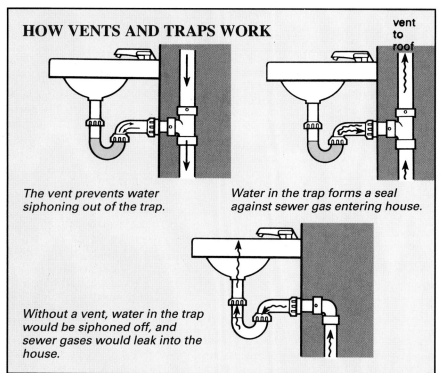

HOW VENTS AND TRAPS WORK

vent to roof

The vent prevents water siphoning out of the trap.

Water in the trap forms a seal against sewer gas entering house.

Without a vent, water in the trap would be siphoned off, and sewer gases would leak into the house.

Trade tip

Take it in turns

❛ If the shut-off valve you're dealing with controls water under full fixture or supply line pressure, make a note of how many turns it takes to shut it off. When you have finished the job, make sure you turn it on again by the same amount.

Shut-offs are often used to reduce the water flow slightly in areas where supply line pressure is high, in which case opening them fully could cause unpleasant hammering in the pipe system.

It's also a good idea to follow the old plumber's rule: "Never assume a shut-off works until you've tried it." Often they don't (especially if they're old), and you must try another one further down the line. ❜

WORKING WITH PIPE

In the days of lead supply pipes and cast-iron drain pipes, most people had to call a plumber when something major went wrong. Today, most pipes and fittings are made of easy-to-work materials such as steel, copper and plastic. As a result, repairing (and installing) plumbing is possible for anyone willing to learn the techniques and tools involved.

Standardized pipe fittings are available from plumber's supply houses and plumbing shops. The term 'fitting' includes all the connection pieces needed to join lengths of pipe together. One important requirement of good plumbing is to use as few fittings as possible. Special fittings are made for every type and size of job you are likely to encounter in your home.

For information on basic plumbing tools, see page 334.

Trade tip

Check the size

❝ Check the external diameter of a pipe with a pair of school compasses. Copper tubing and most plastic pipe is actually measured on the external diameter. On iron, lead, and rigid copper pipe, the internal diameter is the one quoted by stockists, but you'll get a close enough idea. ❞

STEEL PIPE

Galvanized steel is the strongest and least expensive of all the different materials used for water supply lines. But it is generally difficult to install because of its rigidity and the threading it requires. As a result, steel pipe is becoming less popular.

All fittings for galvanized steel pipe are threaded. The pipe is cut to the length required, threaded on both ends, and screwed tightly into the fittings. In many cases, if your order calls for pipe pre-cut to exact lengths, these pipes will all be threaded by the supplier. When determining pipe lengths, include allowances for the threads needed to engage the fitting properly.

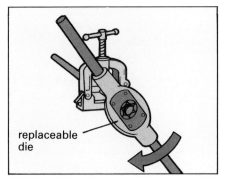

1 Hold the steel pipe steady in a vise that is solidly mounted.

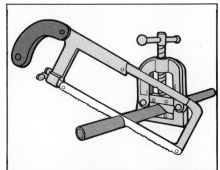

2 Cut the pipe to the desired length with a hacksaw.

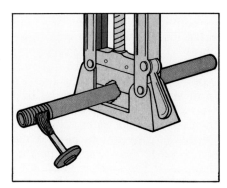

3 After the pipe is cut, use a reamer to remove any burrs.

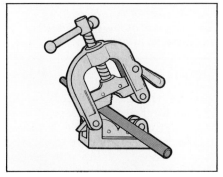

replaceable die

4 Thread pipe with a die cutter. Turn it in a clockwise direction.

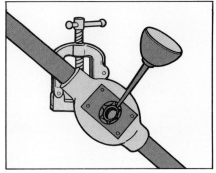

5 Keep die covered with oil while threading the pipe.

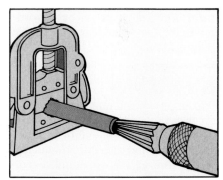

6 Waterproof the connection with plumber's tape. Then join pipe.

COPPER TUBING

There are two types of copper tubing: hard (rigid) and soft (flexible). Soft copper tubing is the easiest metal pipe to install because it can simply be bent round corners by hand without any fittings and complicated joints.

The only trick is to keep the tubing from sinking, flattening or pinching while you are bending it. If the diameter of the tubing is reduced, the flow of water through the pipe will also be restricted.

Unless you have a special tube-bender (see opposite), make the curves as gradual as possible. Lay the tubing on a board, fasten down one end, then kneel on the tube and slowly raise the free end. Move your knee towards the free end slightly, and raise it again. Repeat until you have created the correct curve.

Another way of bending soft copper tubing requires a bending spring, an inexpensive device that prevents kinking. To use a bending spring, slip it inside the pipe to the location of the desired bend and grip the pipe firmly, placing your knee in the middle of the spring. Then pull both ends until the right curve is produced.

Lengths of soft copper tubing can be assembled with either solder-type or flare-type fittings (see right and opposite). Flare-type fittings are very easy to assemble since they hold the tubing simply by being tightened. However, they should never be used inside walls or anywhere that is not easy to reach.

SOLDERING COPPER TUBING

1 Equipment for assembling copper pipes: tube cutter, propane torch, solder, flux, fittings.

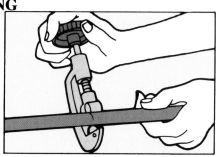

2 Use a tube cutter rather than a hacksaw to cut copper tubing neatly.

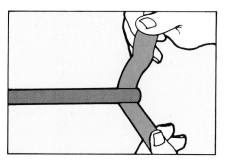

3 Clean the end of the tubing to be soldered with an emery cloth before coating it with flux.

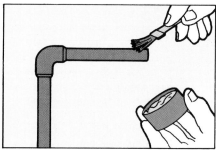

4 Apply a thin film of flux to both the end of the tube and the fitting; rotate to spread evenly.

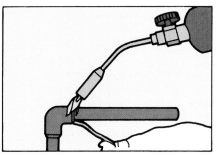

5 Push on fitting and apply heat to the fitting, not the pipe. Flow the solder into the joint.

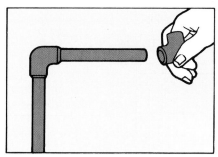

6 Additional fittings such as tees and elbows are installed in the same manner.

PLASTIC PIPE

Plastic pipe has a number of advantages over its rivals. It is lightweight (weighing only one-eighth as much as iron pipe and one-third as much as copper tubing); it withstands corrosion and the buildup of interior scale; it is durable and easy to join; and the natural insulating property of plastic reduces the amount of condensation which can sometimes develop on the outside of cold-water lines.

There are a number of different types of plastic available; get advice from your supplier about the best type to use. Some are only suitable for carrying cold water; others are flexible enough not to burst if the water inside them freezes (making them ideal for outdoor use). One type is ideal for long runs where the pipe must be threaded through difficult spaces; however, such pipe is never perfectly straight (because it is supplied in coils) and should only be used where appearance is not particularly important.

Before joining plastic pipe to a fitting, dry assemble the parts to make sure they fit snugly. Make sure you get the right type of solvent or cement for the type of plastic by buying both from the same dealer. Plastic pipe can be connected to existing iron or copper piping with special plastic-to-metal connectors and couplings.

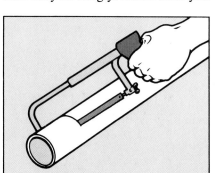

1 Cut plastic with a fine-toothed hacksaw. If you use a vise or other holding device, protect the pipe by wrapping it in a cloth.

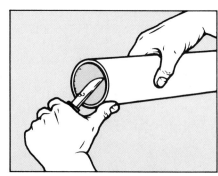

2 Remove any rough edges with a sharp pocket knife or standard reamer. Smooth the edges with sandpaper.

BENDING AND CUTTING COPPER TUBING

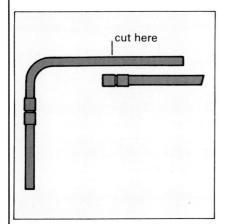

Measure tubing around a turn by temporarily placing the fittings in position. Then bend the tubing, and cut it to fit.

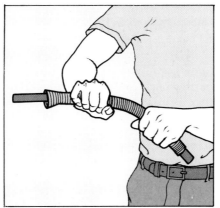

Use a tube bender of the right diameter for the tubing. Slip the tubing into the bender and bend the tubing with hand pressure.

Cut copper tubing with a tubing cutter. Twist the knob so the cutter wheel pierces the surface of the tubing and then rotate it. Repeat.

COPPER JOINTS

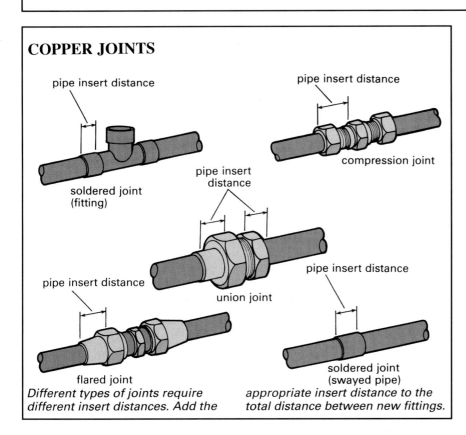

Different types of joints require different insert distances. Add the appropriate insert distance to the total distance between new fittings.

FLARED FITTINGS (COMPRESSION JOINTS)

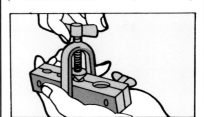

1 *Cut tube square and ream (step 3, page 331). Flare the tube with a flaring tool. Slip on nut*

2 *Place flared end of tubing against appropriate end of fitting. Slide nut along tubing to the connection and tighten.*

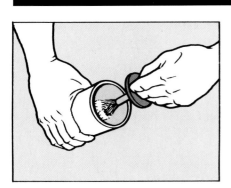

3 *After cleaning the fitting socket and the pipe, apply a coat of appropriate solvent or cement to the inside of the connecting fitting.*

4 *Apply solvent or cement to the outside of the pipe. Make sure you coat the whole area that will be covered by the fitting.*

5 *Work quickly and press the pipe into the fitting; turn the pipe ¼ turn. Allow at least 15 minutes for the solvent to cure completely.*

BASIC PLUMBING TOOLS

Although plumbing requires some specialized tools, the only ones you need on hand are those for emergency or minor repairs. Tools which you only need for major jobs can be purchased or rented when needed. Many tools – like hammers, hacksaws, screwdrivers, trouble lights, wire brushes, flashlights, pliers and measuring tapes – have so many uses that you probably already own them.

Plumbing tools can be divided into three groups. First are the tools for cutting, bending, threading and flaring the parts used in a plumbing job. This group includes vises, hacksaws, pipe and tube cutters, flaring tools, cold chisels, reamers, files, die stock and dies, bending tools and shave hooks.

The second group of tools are used for making connections and putting parts into place. Included in this group are wrenches, calking irons, hammers, propane torches, plungers, joint runners, pliers, screwdrivers and soldering tools.

The third group includes the following tools, all of which are important to the handyman for minor plumbing repairs and emergencies.
Slot and Phillips screwdrivers are needed for fixing faucets.
Basin wrench provides easy access to nuts in hard-to-reach places.
Pipe wrench has toothed jaws that grip pipe firmly.
Adjustable-end (crescent) wrench has smooth jaws that fit small nuts and bolts.
Spud wrench adjusts to fit large nuts

on toilets and sinks.
Rib joint (slip-jaw) pliers are used to remove drain traps.
Plunger for loosening blockages.
Snake (drain-and-trap auger) stretches to remove deep blockages in drains.
Closet auger to unclog toilets.
Valve seat dresser to grind and smooth faulty faucet valve seats.
Valve seat wrench to remove valve seals.

In addition, keep on hand sheets of foam rubber, a length of old hose, automotive hose clamps, assorted faucet washers, O-rings, wire coat hangers, and a variety of nuts, bolts and metal washers.

Special tools that are needed for particular types of pipe are shown as they are used.

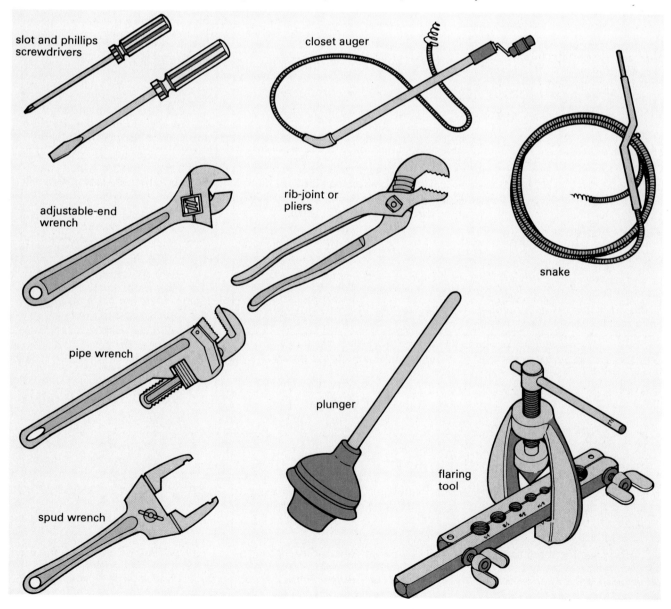

slot and phillips screwdrivers

closet auger

snake

adjustable-end wrench

rib-joint or pliers

pipe wrench

plunger

flaring tool

spud wrench

REPAIRING TOILETS

Annoying toilet faults such as hit and miss flushing have a habit of turning into something more serious. Even so, there are surprisingly few problems that can't be fixed with just a few simple tools and the right parts. This section explains how flushing faults and leaks occur, and shows ways of fixing them.

How toilets work

The operation of a toilet is based on very simple principles:

1 Depressing the handle lifts the trip lever and tank ball.

2 Water flows down the open flush valve, into the bowl, and out into a septic system.

3 The low water level in the tank causes the float ball to drop. This in turn, opens the refill valve and lets water fill the tank.

4 The flush continues until the tank is almost empty; the tank ball then drops in place, closing the valve.

5 As the water level in the tank rises, the float returns to its original raised position. The refill valve closes, stopping the tank refill and completing the cycle.

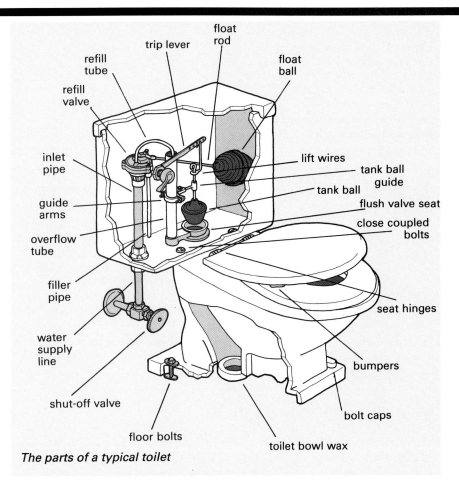

The parts of a typical toilet

A FLAPPER ASSEMBLY TOILET

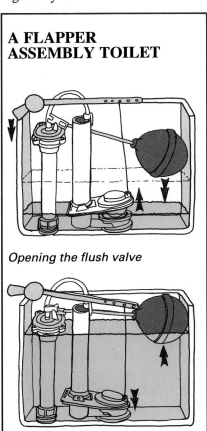

Opening the flush valve

Closing the flush valve

OCCASIONALLY RUNNING TOILET

Periodic running can be caused by water seeping through a leaking flush valve into the bowl, resulting in a drop in the tank's water level that eventually opens the ballcock and allows water to refill the tank. If this happens, check the following areas for problems:

Trip lever If it won't return to its down position, allowing the tank ball to seat on the flush valve, replace it.

Flush valve seat If it has become worn, remove the tank ball, clean the seat thoroughly with fine emery cloth, and remount the tank ball.

Guide and lift wires If the tank ball doesn't seat properly, check for misaligned guide and lift wires. Also check that the wires don't stick during operation. You have two choices: either install a new toilet tank ball guide to hold the lift wires in alignment; or install a new conventional tank ball or a more modern flapper assembly, which eliminates the need for lift wires and guide.

TANK CONDENSATION

Because the tank contains cold water, moisture may condense on to it from warm air. Constant dripping can mildew tiles and rugs and corrode metal parts on the outside of the tank. Such condensation is usually easy to cure with a waterproof insulation lining. Buy one at a plumbing supply store, or make one from ½" foam rubber or plastic.

To install the lining turn off the water and completely dry the inside of the tank. Apply a liberal coating of rubber cement or silicone glue to the sides of the tank, press the foam in place, and let it dry for 24 hours before refilling the tank. Make sure that the foam pad doesn't interfere with the tank's moving parts.

If the water entering the tank is below 10°C (50°F), you may have to install a tempering valve which mixes hot water with cold to raise the tank's water temperature. This can be a difficult job because of the need of a water heater hookup, and is best undertaken by a professional plumber.

ADJUSTING & REPLACING THE FLOAT ROD

If the tank runs, try bending the float rod down to seal the flush valve. Also, check that the ball is not sticking against the back of the tank. If it is, adjust it. Use both hands carefully to avoid straining the assembly. The float ball, which can be metal or plastic, can become perforated and fill with water. Unscrew and replace the ball.

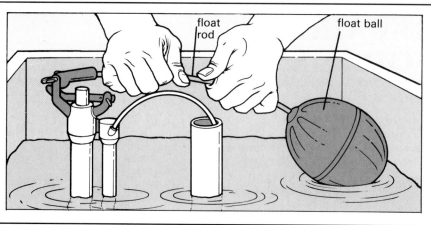

REPLACING THE FLUSH VALVE

Turn off the water supply and flush toilet. Disconnect the lift wire from the trip lever and remove the refill tube. Unscrew the ballcock coupling nut and disengage the water supply tube. Unscrew the nuts from tank-to-bowl connecting bolts; carefully lift the tank off the bowl.

Unscrew flush valve locknut and remove old flush valve. Thoroughly clean the tank flush valve area. With tapered end of flush valve shank washer pointing down, insert overflow tube of new flush valve through bottom of tank and locknut. Reconnect tank to bowl and water supply tube to ballcock.

Reattach the lift wires to the trip lever and refill tube from the ballcock to the flush valve. Fill tank and check for leaks.

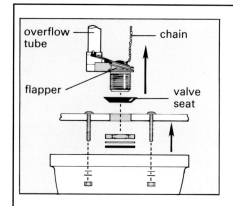

SEALING A LEAKING TOILET

Leaks can happen anywhere around a toilet tank. If a leak occurs after repair work, check all the washers and seals that have been removed. If you cannot find the source of the leak, add blue dye to the tank at night and check for signs of dye next morning.

If the toilet leaks between the base of the bowl and the floor, the cause is usually a worn-out putty seal. Putty (which was used to seal toilets in the past) gradually disintegrates.

To mend the leak (see right), turn off the water supply. Flush and sponge any remaining water. Unscrew the ballcock coupling nut and disengage the water supply tube. Carefully pry off the bolt caps and unscrew the nuts which secure the bowl to the floor.

Carefully tilt the toilet until the bolts in the floor clear the bowl. Turn upside down. Remove old wax ring from horn and clean sealing area and toilet floor flange to ensure a good seal.

Place a new wax ring squarely over the floor flange ring. If the new ring has a tapered end, insert this directly into the floor drainpipe. Position the flange bolts in the floor (putty will help to hold them upright and in place). Lower the toilet into wax ring pressing down with a slight rotating motion – allow your body weight to set the bowl in place and ensure a tight seal with the wax. Slip washers over the bolt and tighten nuts gently until bowl is secure. *Do not overtighten* – this could crack a china bowl. Replace the bolt caps and reconnect water supply tube.

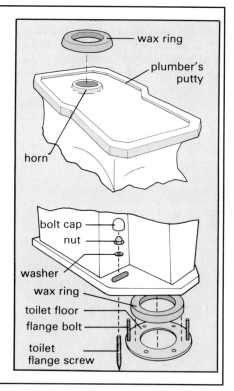

REPLACING LIFT WIRES & TANK BALL

Turn off water supply and flush. Unhook top lift wire from trip lever, then unscrew bottom wire from tank ball and slip out of guide arm on overflow tube. Slip new bottom wire through hook of top wire and through guide arm. Screw onto old or replacement tank ball.

Attach top wire to trip lever and check to see that tank ball seats properly. If necessary, loosen and adjust the guide arm in order to seat the tank ball properly in the valve seat. Turn on the water supply valve and flush to check operation.

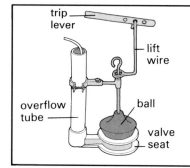

FAULTFINDER CHART

SYMPTOM	POSSIBLE CAUSES	CURE
Continuously running water	■ Float arm isn't rising high enough ■ Water-filled float ball ■ Tank stopper isn't seating properly ■ Corroded flush valve seat ■ Cracked overflow tube ■ Ball cock valve doesn't shut off	■ Bend float arm down or away from tank wall ■ Replace ball ■ Adjust stopper guide rod or chain; replace defective stopper ■ Scour valve seat or replace it ■ Replace tube or install new flush valve assembly ■ Oil lever, replace faulty washers, or install new ball cock assembly
Noisy flush	■ Defective ball cock ■ Restricted water supply	■ Oil lever, replace faulty washers, or install new ball cock assembly ■ Remove corrosion on valve seat; adjust stopper; replace flush valve assembly
Clogged toilet	■ Blockage in drain	■ Remove blockage with plunger or closet auger
Inadequate flush	■ Faulty linkage between handle and trip lever ■ Tank stopper closes before tank empties ■ Leak between tank and bowl ■ Clogged flush passages	■ Tighten setscrew on handle linkage, or replace handle ■ Adjust stopper guide rod or chain ■ Tighten locknuts under tank, or replace gasket ■ Poke obstructions from passages with wire
Sweating tank	■ Condensation	■ Install tank insulation or a tempering valve

REPLACING THE LIFT CHAIN AND FLAPPER

Turn off water supply and flush. Remove the chain or wires from the trip lever. (If replacing a tank ball with a flapper assembly, remove and discard the ball, lift wires and guide arm.) Remove the old flapper by sliding it up and off the overflow tube.

Install new flapper by sliding it down over overflow tube until the ring touches the tank bottom. Then adjust the flapper ball so it centers on the valve opening. For plastic valves, cut the ring off the flapper and slip the flapper ears over pins on flush lever; adjust length as needed

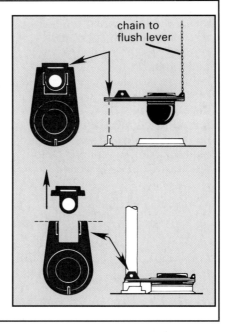

chain to flush lever

CONTINUOUS FLUSHING

Continuous flushing is caused by water continuing to enter the tank long after the toilet has been flushed. The tank fills too quickly, preventing the toilet from drawing in the air necessary to halt the flushing sequence. Instead, the water supply and ballvalve must work in perfect union, filling and emptying at approximately the same rate.

The answer is to reduce the filling rate of the ballcock. Either fit a high pressure (HP) seat in it, or lower the water pressure by turning the water valve on the supply pipe.

REPLACING THE TRIP LEVER/HANDLE

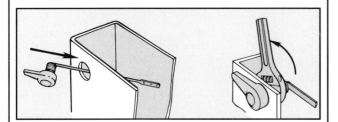

Unhook lift wire or chain from trip lever and unscrew locknut holding handle to tank. Pull handle out through hole in tank wall (left). Insert new handle into tank and slide locknut over lever on to threaded portion and tighten by turning counterclockwise (right). *Do not overtighten.* Reattach lift wire to lever arm.

REPLACING TANK-TO-BOWL WASHER

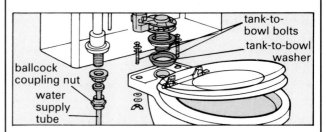

tank-to-bowl bolts
tank-to-bowl washer
ballcock coupling nut
water supply tube

Turn off water supply. Flush toilet to empty tank. Unscrew ballcock coupling nuts and disengage water supply tube. Unscrew nuts from bolts connecting tank to bowl and lift tank off bowl. Insert new washer in bowl opening and carefully replace tank on bowl. Reconnect supply tube to ballcock and turn on water.

NOISY TOILETS

If your toilet whines, sings or makes other strange noises, it is probably the ballcock assembly that is faulty. In this chapter, most of the illustrations are of the diaphragm-type ball-cock, the most common mechanism. Shown below are three other popular variations, which you might find in your home. Regardless of the way they are designed, all ballcocks operate in basically the same manner and serve the same purpose – to provide a supply of water to the toilet and control the flow inside the tank.

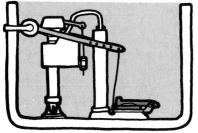 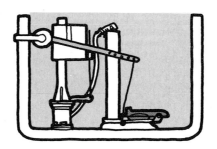 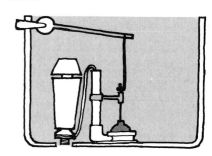

Common types of ballcock assemblies

REPLACING BALLCOCK WASHERS

A common cause of loud toilet noises or even leaks is a faulty ballcock washer(s). To replace it, remove the two thumbscrews on top of the ballcock assembly that hold the float arm assembly in place. Lift the float arm out of the tank and pull the valve plunger up and out of the ballcock.

Inside the plunger area are the ballcock washers. If they are worn or damaged, replace them with exact duplicates. If the ballcock still leaks, replace the entire assembly.

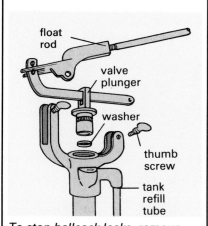

To stop ballcock leaks, remove the plunger from the ballcock and replace defective washers.

REMOVING THE BALLCOCK ASSEMBLY

To replace the entire ballcock assembly, work with the water off. Flush the toilet and sponge out any remaining water. Remove the float ball and arm inside the tank. Then remove the lower slip nut from the threads protruding beneath the tank. Support the ballcock and make certain the water is turned off (removing the nut cuts off the water supply). With the top nut removed, lift the ballcock out of the tank and examine the ballcock coupling, gaskets and washers. Replace if worn.

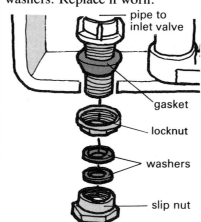

Remove and replace the locknuts and washers. If necessary, use the counterforce of two wrenches.

INSTALLING A NEW BALLCOCK ASSEMBLY

Before installing a new ballcock assembly, clean the tank bottom where the ballcock shank washer seats to be sure of a good seal.

Carefully insert the new ballcock and tighten the slip nut locknut, making sure the float rod fitting faces the right direction. Attach the water supply tube with a coupling nut, screw the float rod assembly into place, and reattach the refill tube. Turn the water on, fill the tank, and check for leaks. Adjust the water level by bending the float rod (page 336).

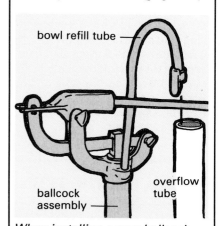

When installing a new ballcock assembly, be sure to position the refill tube in the overflow pipe.

WATER SPLASHING

A misaligned refill tube that spouts water directly into the tank will cause splashing, often accompanied by a lack of trap-sealing water in the toilet bowl.

Reposition the refill tube so it spouts into the top of the overflow tube. Do not let the end of the tube reach below the tank water level – that would make it siphon tank water away, causing constant slow running of water.

A faulty toilet inlet valve is rare, but can cause splashing. If the valve is at fault, you should be able to see it leaking as the tank refills. Either replace the entire valve assembly or repair the toilet inlet valve. For either job, the water supply to the toilet must be turned off.

BATH AND SINK REPAIRS

Faucets are usually the hardest working components in a plumbing system, so it's hardly surprising if they must occasionally be repaired or replaced with a new design.

While there are many different styles of household faucets on the market, most fall into one of the three basic categories shown below.

COMPRESSION (STEM) FAUCET

A threaded stem controls the water flow. When screwed all the way in, a washer attached by a screw to the end of the stem fits snugly against a valve seat. If the stem is screwed out, the valve opens and water flows into spout.

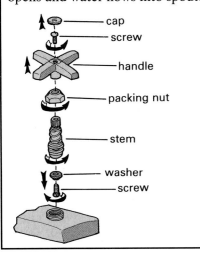

- cap
- screw
- handle
- packing nut
- stem
- washer
- screw

BALL FAUCET

The water flow is controlled by a slotted ball which sits on top of two spring-loaded rubber inlet seats. When the ball is rotated, the slot lines up with one or both of the inlet ports. Water flows from the inlet through the slot in the ball into the spout.

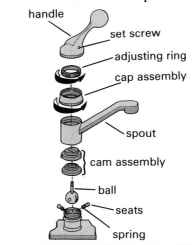

- handle
- set screw
- adjusting ring
- cap assembly
- spout
- cam assembly
- ball
- seats
- spring

CARTRIDGE FAUCET

This washerless fixture uses a cartridge in place of a stem. The cartridge contains a series of holes which, when aligned with the inlet ports, allow water to flow to the spout. The handle is rotated to regulate the amount or temperature of the water.

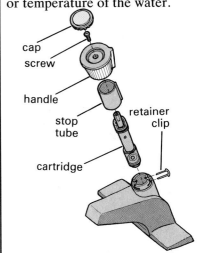

- cap
- screw
- handle
- stop tube
- retainer clip
- cartridge

FAUCET REPAIR TOOLS

In addition to the basic plumbing tools described on page 334, there are a number of specialized tools on the market which make faucet work much easier and help to prevent damage. General-purpose tools are often difficult to use on the inevitable hard-to-reach bolts.

For instance, the handle puller shown below removes stuck or corroded faucet handles quickly and easily without breaking good parts or spoiling the finish. You can, of course, pry or strike the stuck handle or even use an ordinary wrench to loosen it, but you risk damaging the faucet.

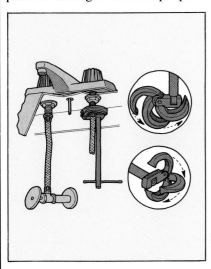

Use a basin or faucet wrench to reach hard-to-get-at mounting and coupling nuts under the sink.

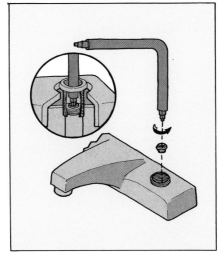

A seat wrench can make the difficult job of removing a faulty faucet seat much simpler.

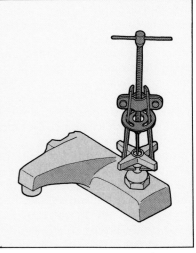

A handle puller can make light work of removing a handle which has become stuck or corroded.

339

FAUCET FAULTFINDER CHART

STYLE	SYMPTOM	POSSIBLE CAUSE	CURE	STYLE	SYMPTOM	POSSIBLE CAUSE	CURE
COMPRESSION FAUCETS	Water drips from spout	Worn or damaged seat washer	Replace	BALL FAUCETS	Water drips from spout	Worn or damaged seats	Replace
		Corroded or worn seat	Regrind/ replace			Worn springs	Replace
						Worn or damaged ball	Replace
		Worn or damaged stem washer	Replace		Water leaks from handle	Worn cam or cam seal	Replace
		Worn stem	Replace			Loose or damaged adjusting ring	Tighten/ replace
		Worn seat diaphragm	Replace	CARTRIDGE FAUCETS	Water drips from spout	Worn or damaged O-rings	Replace
	Water leaks from handle	Worn or damaged O-rings	Replace			Worn or corroded cartridge	Replace
		Worn stem packing	Replace		Leakage at faucet handle	Worn or damaged O-rings	Replace

BATH/SHOWER FAUCETS

A bath/shower arrangement can be controlled by one, two or three handles. Single-handle shower-tub controls are pressure-equalizing devices that not only mix the water, but also balance the water pressure so that, regardless of pressure changes in the supply lines, the water temperature at the spout of the shower head stays the same.

Most shower faucets are the compression type, but those that operate with one handle are usually cartridge or ball types. Both are disassembled in the same manner as sink faucets (see page 339).

To repair a typical compression bath/shower faucet for example, as with any faucet repair job, turn off the water supply and drain the lines by turning on the faucet handles.

Remove the screws holding the handles to the stems and pry the handles off. Wrap tape around the flange and using pliers, turn counterclockwise to remove. Remove the flange nipple in the same way.

After removing the flange and nipple, the stem and bonnet can be removed by using a shower socket wrench. Whether the stem is on the hot side or cold side determines the direction to turn to remove the stem and bonnet from the body.

Remove the packing nut from the body, and remove and replace the packing from inside the bonnet. Similarly, remove and replace the faucet seat. If the faucet does not have a removable seat, you can refinish the old seat with a faucet reseating tool. Replace the bib washer at the bottom of the stem if it is worn or damaged. Reverse this procedure to reassemble the faucet.

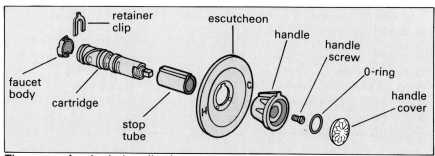
The parts of a single-handle shower-type control

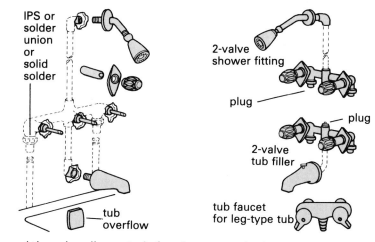
Two- and three-handle controls for showers and tubs.

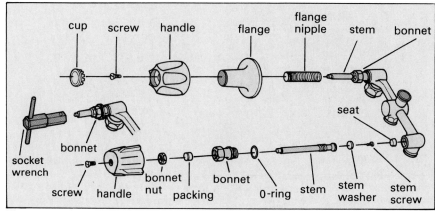
The parts of two common types of shower faucets

Hard-to-reach bonnet

To remove a shower faucet bonnet without damaging the adjacent wall, use a shower socket wrench which fits snugly over the bonnet (see diagram A, right).

For leverage when turning, slip a metal bar through the holes at the outer end of the socket wrench. The bonnet and stem assembly should come out of the body together (see diagram B, right).

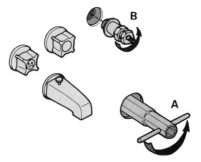

If the faucet stem extends as far as the holes, grip the socket with a pipe wrench and use it as a turning bar.

HANDLE LEAKS

cap
screw
handle
packing nut
conical packing
stem

Most handle leaks are caused by faulty packing. This can usually be corrected by using conical packing.

DRESSING A FAUCET SEAT

A faucet dresser (right) removes burrs, nicks and deposits that can prevent a tight seal. Insert the dresser until the disc and cutter sit on the threads of the valve seat. Turn the tool handle clockwise once or twice until the seat is smooth. Remove the metal filings with a damp cloth.

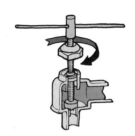

SPOUT LEAKS

When water leaks from the spout of a two-handle faucet, determine the source of the leak by alternately closing the hot and cold water valves under the sink.

Worn seat washers are the most common source of spout leaks in a compression faucet. Replace the seat washer and O-rings. When replacing the seat washer, visually check for corrosion that would cause the washer to wear excessively. If necessary, 'dress' or hone to achieve a smooth surface (see above). If the washer is badly corroded, it is best replaced. If leaking persists, replace the stem with the appropriate replacement kit or replace the entire faucet.

Replace worn O-rings at the swivel connection if water leaks from the base of the spout. Water leaking from the spout of a ball faucet indicates worn springs or seats or a defective ball. Replace the defective parts.

When water leaks from the spout of a cartridge faucet, look for faulty O-rings or a worn cartridge. If replacing the O-rings does not stop the leak, replace

the cartridge itself.

To repair a leak at the base of a disc faucet (below), remove the setscrew under the handle. Lift off the handle and decorative escutcheon. Remove the cartridge by loosening the screws that hold the cartridge to the faucet body.

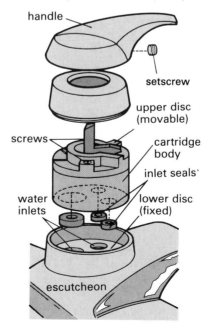

handle
setscrew
upper disc (movable)
screws
cartridge body
inlet seals
water inlets
lower disc (fixed)
escutcheon

Disc faucets are relatively new, but are increasingly popular.

Trade tip

Replacing a tub spout

Insert the handle of a hammer or suitable prying device into the opening of the spout (below) and turn it anticlockwise. Gently clean the threaded portion of the pipe nipple with steel wool or a wire brush. (Be careful not to spoil the chrome finish of the spout.) Then apply pipe dope or pipe tape and screw the spout back on clockwise.

If the spout is made of plastic, take care to avoid excessive pressure that could crack it. Do not use plumber's thread tape or pipe dope on a plastic tub spout.

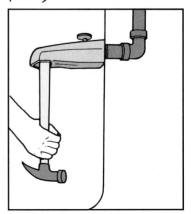

REPAIRING/REPLACING A SHOWER HEAD

Protect the chrome finish of all parts with tape. Using a cloth-wrapped wrench or pliers, turn the locking collar anticlockwise to remove the shower head. Unscrew the head from the collar and check the washer for wear. Remove the plate from the shower head and clean the inside of the shower head with a solution of vinegar and water to remove mineral deposits. Clean the threaded section of the shower arm with steel wool or a wire brush.

When reassembling, use pipe dope or pipe tape on the shower arm and screw the shower head on clockwise. Turn on the water supply and check for leaks. Tighten the collar further if necessary.

If the shower head or arm is plastic, take care when tightening not to crack either part. *Do not* use plumber's thread tape or pipe dope when you are working on a plastic shower arm or head.

If the water holes in the faceplate of the shower head or around its rim become clogged, remove the screws or knob holding the faceplate. Soak the plate overnight in vinegar and scrub thoroughly with a brush. Poke out remaining blockages with a toothpick.

If the shower head drips or pivots stiffly, unscrew the head and collar connected to the shower arm. Replace the washer and smear petroleum jelly on the swivel ball before reassembling the unit.

To save hot water, invest in a shower head cut-off valve or a flow-restricting device from your plumbing supplier. Both are fitted to the shower arm before the shower head is attached.

TUB/SHOWER DIVERTERS

Turn off the water supply, then drain the lines by turning on the faucet handles and the diverter handle. A diverter functions in exactly the same manner as a faucet. That is, in stem diverters, turning the handle causes the stem to move into the valve seat and redirect the water to the shower head.

To disassemble a stem diverter, follow the instructions provided for stem faucets. Check all O-rings, washers and packing for wear or damage and replace where necessary. For ball diverters, follow the instructions provided for ball faucets and check seals, springs, seats and the ball.

If the hollow diverter housing has worn out so that the water flow cannot be diverted, you will have to replace the whole diverter valve asembly. When making this repair, follow the manufacturer's directions.

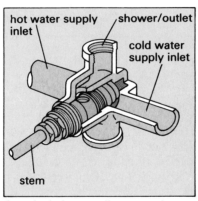

A typical shower diverter valve housing assembly.

SHOWER STALLS

Prefabricated shower stall units of molded plastic and metal are growing in popularity because, if used in place of tubs, they can free a great deal of floor space. Shower stalls can be quickly connected to the water outlets and drains without danger of leaking from the sides or bottom. Follow the step-by-step directions provided by the manufacturer exactly.

When installing a one-piece shower unit, the pocket for the stall must be perfectly square and plumb with the studs located as directed by the manufacturer. Since a one-piece shower unit combines the walls and base, no shower pan or hot mopping is required. The rough plumbing for the shower stall drain and water supply must be located according to the dimensions given by the maker.

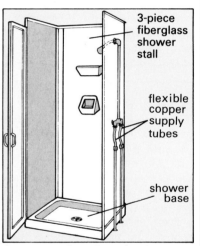

An easy-to-install prefabricated plastic shower stall.

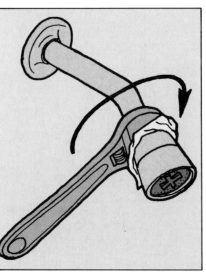

The component parts of a typical shower head unit.

Remove the shower head with a cloth-wrapped wrench for protection.

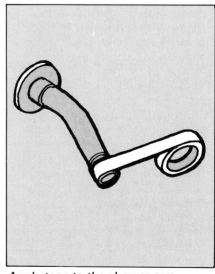

Apply tape to the shower arm before replacing the shower head.

HAND-HELD SPRAY SHOWERS

Personal or hand-held spray showers have become very popular bathtub accessories because they permit you to direct the water accurately. There are two basic types: one that attaches directly to the shower head and another that is an integral part of the tub's spout. Most kits include the diverter valve, sprayer, hose, and a wall bracket.

To attach a spray to the shower head, remove the existing unit using a cloth-wrapped wrench. Thread a diverter valve on to the shower arm and make sure the diverter button is facing up. Then replace the old shower head. Connect the hose and hand-held sprayer to the diverter. Attach one end of the hose to the hand-held sprayer and the other to the diverter.

When attaching a hand-held shower to a tub spout, the old spout must be removed and replaced with a new one that has a diverter valve knob and built-in hose connector. The hose and spray head are connected to the tub spout. Lift the diverter knob up to operate the sprayer.

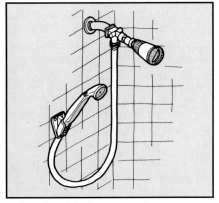

A hand-held shower and shower head diverter . . .

. . . the diverter valve installed on the shower arm.

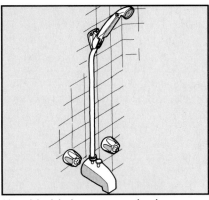

Hand-held shower attached to a tub spout with diverter knob . . .

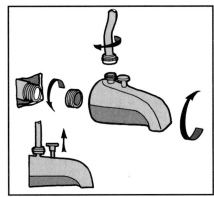

. . . a new tub spout with a diverter valve and hose connector.

BATH AND SINK DRAINS

Old-fashioned chains and stoppers have been replaced by trip levers or pop-up devices.

To adjust a trip-lever drain, remove the screws holding the overflow plate and pull the entire linkage forward through the hole in the tub. Loosen the locknut at the base of the yoke and turn the threaded rod clockwise to lower the plunger. Tighten the locknut after adjusting.

You may need to make several adjustments to the linkage to achieve the right length so that the plunger seals and opens correctly. Too long a linkage will seal the drain but not allow proper drainage when opened, and too short a linkage will not seal the drain properly and allow water to run out of the tub.

To replace a trip-lever mechanism, remove the screws holding the overflow plate and carefully pull the entire linkage out through the overflow opening. The linkage is hinged to allow easy removal. Attach the new linkage to the trip lever and slip into the overflow tube through the tub opening. Lower the linkage carefully until the plunger seats itself properly. You may have to adjust the length of the linkage to ensure proper opening and sealing of the drain.

In pop-up tub drains, the lever mechanism is similar to the trip-lever drain but always ends in a spring rather than a weight. The spring seats on the rocker linkage and raises or lowers the stopper. Adjustments to this linkage are made in the same way as for trip levers.

A sink pop-up drain uses a pivot rod and assembly rather like a rocker arm. The up and down movement of the lift rod and clevis control the positioning of the pop-up. Adjust the clevis to alter the stopper height.

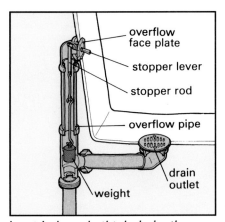

In a trip-lever bathtub drain, the lever mechanism ends in a weight.

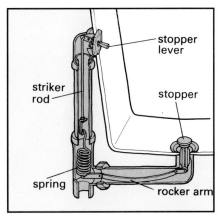

In a pop-up lever bathtub drain, the lever mechanism ends in a spring.

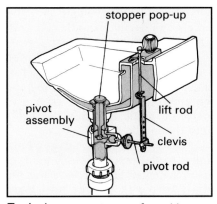

Typical pop-up stopper found in lavatory and kitchen sinks.

LAVATORY AND KITCHEN FAUCETS

Lavatory and kitchen sink faucets are available as compression, ball, and cartridge types. Only the latter two are commonly available in both single and dual control models. The single control design mixes hot and cold water to give the desired temperature. On twin kitchen sinks, the spout on single control models can swing to serve both bowls. Some kitchen faucets have a hose sprayer, and are equipped with aerators.

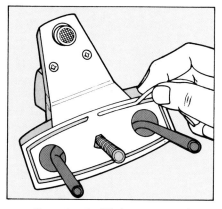

1 Completely fill the grooves in the faucet's putty cup with plumber's putty. Alternatively, place large beds of plumber's putty around the opening in the sink.

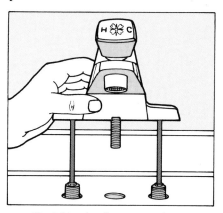

2 Position the faucet on the sink top, inserting the center stud through the sink pop-up hole and the supply tubes through their appropriate holes.

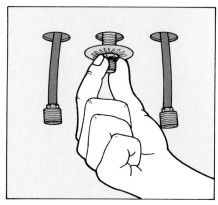

3 Install the mounting washer and nut on the faucet stud. Tighten the nut securely – while you do so, make sure that the faucet remains in its proper position on the sink.

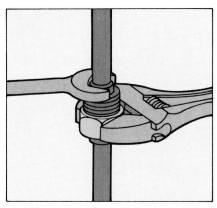

4 Connect the supply tubes to the water supply by using two wrenches: one to hold the adaptor securely and the other to tighten the nut on the water supply line.

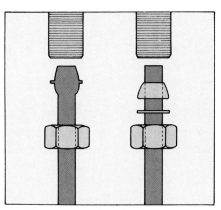

5 If your supply tube has a formed end, simply discard the cone washers and friction rings. Use them if the supply tube has a straight end.

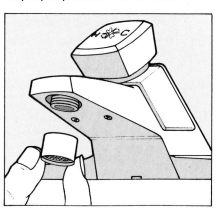

6 Remove the aerator assembly located at the end of the spout. Turn the hot water on for a few minutes to flush away any foreign matter and replace the aerator.

INSTALLING A SINGLE FAUCET

Single faucets have a threaded base and can be screwed to the end of any threaded (steel) pipe. They can also be inserted into existing copper or steel (but not plastic) pipe without cutting the pipe by using a saddle-type faucet or by screwing a regular single faucet to a saddle tee connector.

To install a saddle tee (see right), bolt it to the pipe. Then screw a drill guide into the saddle tee and bore through it into the pipe. Remove the guide and screw the faucet into the saddle tee.

Install a saddle faucet by bolting it to the pipe. Remove the faucet, packing nut and stem. Screw the drill into the faucet and bore through the guide into the pipe. Replace the stem and packing nut.

1 Bolt the saddle tee to the pipe at the desired location.

2 Install a drill guide into the tee and bore through it.

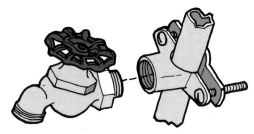

3 Then screw the faucet into the saddle tee.

DISMANTLING AND REASSEMBLING A TRAP

Traps are sections of waste pipe filled with water to stop smells filtering into the house. Traps are a natural place for waste to collect, possibly causing a blockage. But if a drain leaks, or clogs *frequently*, it is probably either corroded or minerals have built up inside. The best solution is to install a new trap (and possibly a new tailpiece). New traps are usually sold as complete units.

To remove a trap, shut off the water, place a pail underneath, and remove the cleanout plug. Loosen the slip nuts using tape-wrapped wrenches (one to hold and one to turn with) so you do no damage.

To install a new trap, attach the washer and one end of the J-bend to the tailpiece with a slip nut, threading it on just enough to hold them together. Slide two slip nuts on to the trap arm, with the threads facing the pipes to which they will attach. Slide washers on to both ends of the arm. Push the trap arm into the drain stub-out (or trap adapter), sliding it to line up the J-bend and trap-arm connection.

When everything lines up without straining, connect the washer and slip nuts and tighten all slip rings, being careful not to strip or overtighten the couplings. Turn the water back on and check for leaks.

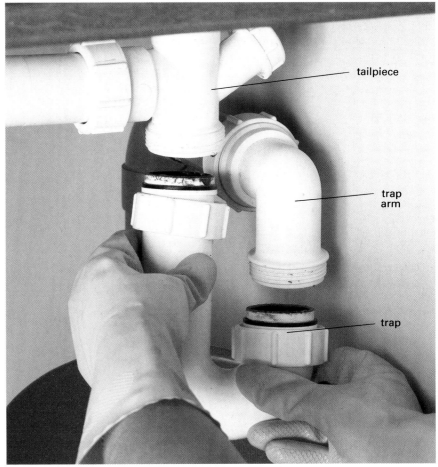

Most types of plastic trap are easily dismantled for clearing, but note which parts go where as you undo them and be sure to save the seals.

CONTINUOUS WASTE SYSTEMS

Double- or triple-bowl kitchen sinks or laundry tubs can be connected to a single trap. Continuous waste kits that contain all the fittings needed to make a center or an end outlet hook-up are available. You can also buy the parts of continuous waste system separately. Follow the same procedure whether you are hooking up to a centre or an end outlet.

■ Remove the waste nuts and washers and slip into the tailpiece of the basket strainer, connecting the drainpipe and elbow of the continuous waste set up. Coat the threads of the drainpipe with joint compound.

■ Place the continuous waste pipes against the tailpieces with the outlet in the drainpipe. Set the trap in place and tighten the couplings at both ends by hand.

■ With a wrench, carefully finish tightening the couplings.

A dishwasher branch tailpiece can be included in a continuous waste system. It is usually connected in the system after the sink drain branches meet.

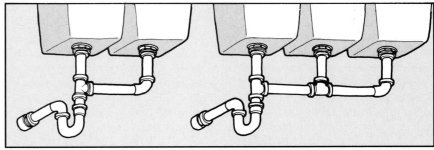

Double sink with an end outlet arrangement.

Triple sink with an end outlet arrangement.

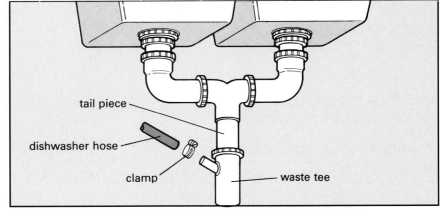

Double sink with a continuous waste system. The outlet is in the center, and includes a dishwasher branch tailpiece.

345

PLUMBING IN A WASHING MACHINE

It is often possible to plumb in a washing machine without any plumbing skills. Even where the installation isn't straightforward, you can save money by doing some of the work yourself, and only calling in a plumber to finish the job for you. The installation has two stages: providing a water supply and arranging drainage.

Siting the machine

As a rule, the nearer the washing machine is to hot and cold pipes and to a drainage outlet, the easier the installation. For many people, this means siting the machine in the kitchen, near the sink. Basements and utility rooms shouldn't be ruled out, though, since they, too, often have the necessary plumbing facilities – plus the advantage of more space.

Many basement and utility rooms contain a laundry tub, which provides a place for the discharged washing machine water. But when using a laundry tub, be sure the discharge hose is equipped with a lint trap.

Most washing machines have solenoid valves to turn the water on and off. These valves open and close instantly, not gradually like a faucet. Air chambers or shock absorbers on both the hot and cold water pipes minimize noisy and destructive water hammer when these valves operate. Air chambers should be installed as directed by the manufacturer. The hoses and valves will last longer if you turn off the water when

Where a washing machine is within easy reach of water supply pipes and a drainage outlet, it can be plumbed in simply using DIY connectors.

the machine isn't in use.

Most machines pump out the waste water, allowing you to connect the drain hose to the nearest waste pipe via a special trap or a screw-in connector. But a few models still rely on siphonage to remove the waste, and must be connected via a vertical standpipe.

When you have made all the connections and your washer is in its permanent position, it must be leveled. Check it from front to back and side to side with a carpenter's level. Threaded pads in each corner can be turned to raise or lower the machine as required.

Trade tip

Installing a standpipe

❝ The standpipe should stand higher than the highest level of water in the machine to back up any siphoning of dirty water into the machine. To install it, cut into a drainpipe and install a sanitary tee fitting. Attach the standpipe to the tee and push the washing machine's drain hose down into the standpipe about 150 mm (6"). Be sure the hose won't be forced out of the pipe by the water pressure. ❞

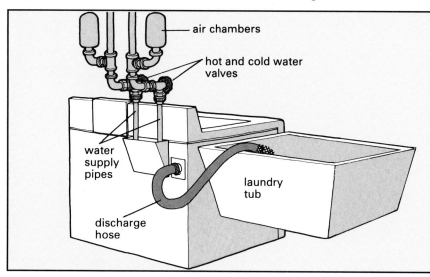

Typical washing machine plumbing arrangement.

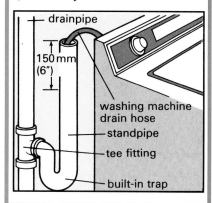

PLUMBING IN A DISHWASHER

Plumbing in a dishwasher is no more difficult than plumbing in a washing machine – in many cases it's easier. Normally there are fewer restrictions on how and where you can make the connections. And the dishwasher's natural location – beside the kitchen sink – means that there are water and drainage supplies conveniently close at hand.

Unlike washing machines, however, most dishwasher ranges include models for building into an existing run of kitchen units. These are designed to fit a standard 600 mm (2′) wide base unit, and can be fitted either with a laminate 'decor' panel or a false door front to match the kitchen system. Most also have removable base trim and adjustable feet for easy fitting under a worktop.

If building in is an important consideration, make sure your chosen model is designed with this in mind. Check too that the manufacturer of the kitchen units also offers laminate panels or door fronts as accessories.

*A **dishwasher** can be built into an existing run of units.*

BUILDING IN

In an existing kitchen, you will need to remove a built-in unit (or the old dishwasher, if you are replacing it) and slot the dishwasher into the vacant space. In a new kitchen, you can allow for this at the planning stage.

To remove a unit:
■ Carefully remove the kick plate (you may be able to re-use it)
■ Remove any doors or drawers, plus their hinges and runners.
■ Remove the drawers in the units and undo the cabinet connecting screws linking them.
■ Remove any screws joining the unit to the worktop.
■ Slacken the adjustable feet (if fitted) and slide out the unit.

To fit the machine:
■ Prepare the machine following the instructions. This may involve unscrewing the trim and false worktop and the door assembly.
■ Slide the machine into position and level using the adjustable feet. This is likely to be the most convenient time to make the plumbing connections. You may have to cut slots or drill holes for the pipework in the adjacent units.
■ Screw the false door to the machine (you may need to supply fixing screws), or fit the decor panel using the trim strips supplied.
■ Refit the old kick plate or a new section. You may have to cut out a piece to clear the door. Cut the 'blind' side.

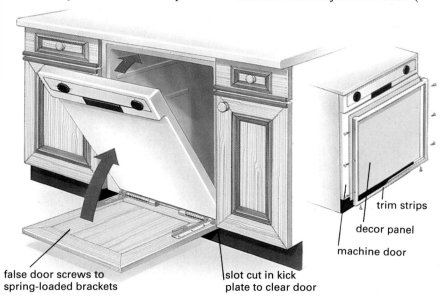

false door screws to spring-loaded brackets

slot cut in kick plate to clear door

trim strips

decor panel

machine door

A typical built-in set-up (left): the false door screws to spring-loaded brackets and closes with the machine door.
Laminate decor panels (inset) clip directly to the machine door using the trim strips supplied.

PLUMBING IN A
GARBAGE DISPOSER

Garbage disposers have proved themselves to be efficient labor-saving devices that gobble up almost anything you feed them. A food waste disposer installed under one sink will eliminate mess and simplify cleaning up after meals, since you can peel fruits and vegetables, scrape plates, dump coffee grounds, and empty cereal bowls directly into the sink.

Some more efficient models have cutters that can handle fibrous waste such as corn husks, celery stalks and artichoke leaves. Be sure to run the water for 30 seconds after the unit has finished working.

There are two types of disposers: batch and continuous feed models. **Batch feed disposers** are controlled by a built-in switch. Waste is placed in the chamber, the cold water is turned on, and the lid is put in place. In some cases, the lid must be turned or positioned a certain way to start the motor; in others, a sealed-in magnet activates a hermetically-sealed switch so that the disposer starts working as soon as the lid is dropped into place.

Continuous feed disposers are controlled by a separate electrical switch installed nearby. Continuous feed models are slightly less expensive than batch feed models, but the cost of installing the switch almost equalizes the price. With a continuous feed model you can feed waste into the disposer as it is operating.

Most garbage disposers are designed to fit any single or double sink. You should check local plumbing codes and requirements to determine the amount of fall necessary and the method of connection. Detailed instructions for installation are provided with each model and, of course, they should be followed to the letter.

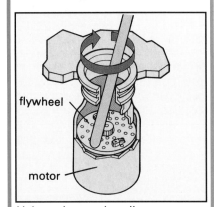
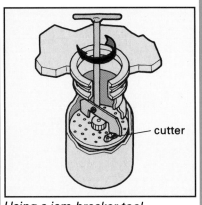
INSTALLING A GARBAGE DISPOSER

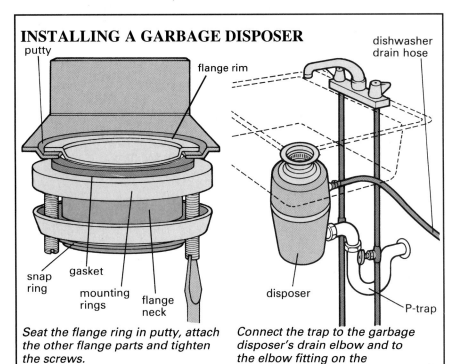

putty

flange rim

dishwasher drain hose

snap ring

gasket

mounting rings

flange neck

disposer

P-trap

Seat the flange ring in putty, attach the other flange parts and tighten the screws.

Connect the trap to the garbage disposer's drain elbow and to the elbow fitting on the drainpipe.

PROVIDING HOT WATER

A house plumbing system usually includes a water heater if the water is heated in the central heating plant. Water heaters may be powered by gas, oil or electricity, as well as solar power. Although most codes require oil or gas fired heaters to be installed by professionals, you may be able to install an electric heater yourself.

The tanks are supplied with all the necessary internal piping in place. The only connections required are to the hot and cold water and the fuel supply. Gas or oil fired water heaters require flues to vent the products of combustion; the solar type requires carpentry work for installation.

Pressure and temperature relief (P&T) valves must be installed on all water heaters and hot water storage tanks. Their purpose is to relieve pressure in the tank and pipes if control equipment fails and the water temperature rises high enough to generate dangerous pressure. Water expands as it heats, and this may create sufficient pressure to rupture the tank or pipes if the water cannot be forced back into the cold water line or discharged through a relief outlet.

The 'recovery rate' of water heaters varies with the type and capacity of the heating element. In standard conventional models, oil and gas heaters usually have higher recovery rates than electric heaters of similar size. However, 'quick recovery' types of electric water heaters have two high-wattage heating elements which can provide hot water very rapidly.

In most instances you will simply be replacing an older water heater in the same location. If you are considering relocation, bear the following points in mind:

■ You can locate an electric model where convenient, but a gas or oil burning heater must be placed within 2.5m (8ft) of a chimney large enough for proper venting through the flue.

■ The minimum clearances which must be maintained between the heater and any combustible construction are 25mm (1″) at the sides and rear, 150mm (6″) at the front, and 460mm (18″) from the top of the jacket.

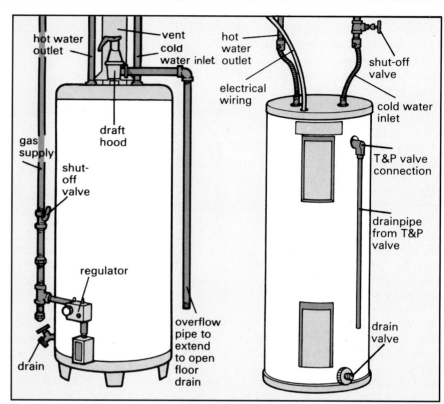

Typical gas water heater *Typical electric water heater*

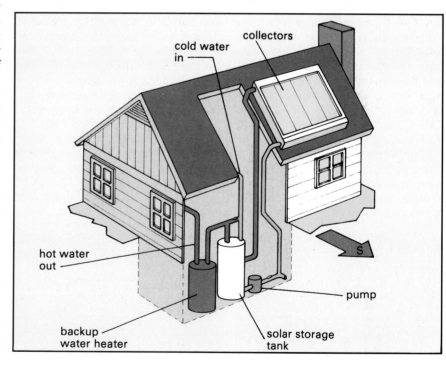

In an active solar water heater, *a pump circulates water from solar collectors to the storage tank and back. If the system contains antifreeze, it need not be drained in winter and can be used all year round.*

■ National codes prohibit the installation of gas water heaters in bathrooms or any occupied room which is normally kept closed.

■ Position the heater as close as possible to where you use the most hot water.

■ It is handy to have a floor drain, tub or sink nearby. Such a position makes it easy to drain water from the heater, and you can end the drain line of the P&T valve in the drain or tub.

WATER TREATMENT

Although many different types of water treatment unit are available, designed to remove unwanted impurities, the most common types are water softeners and filters.

Water softeners are designed to deal with hardness, one of the most widespread problems.

Hard water occurs because ground-rock transfers calcium and magnesium ions (electrically charged atoms) to the water. These ions react poorly with soaps and detergents, and so the water is considered hard. Modern water softeners contain an ion-exchange resin bed that trades its 'good-acting' sodium ions for 'bad-acting' calcium and magnesium ions.

Water softeners have many benefits. These include:
■ Savings on soap and detergents
■ Cleaner and longer-lasting clothes
■ Cleaner skin and shinier hair
■ Tastier food
■ Prevention of scale in water pipes
■ Longer life for appliances
■ Cleaner-looking fixtures

On the negative side, the extra sodium (salt) which is added to the water supply can be a health problem for those who should restrict their intake of salt. Some people also object to the taste of softened water. Avoid both of these problems by softening only the hot water.

The simplest way of installing a water softener is to tap into the cold water main and connect it as shown above. A good location is along the cold water line between the last connection to an outdoor hose outlet and the first to a fixture other than the toilet. If just hot water is to be softened, connect only into the cold water line entering the hot water heater.

Water softeners must 'regenerate' periodically if they are to continue functioning correctly. During this process, it is best to temporarily bypass the softener. If the model you buy does not contain a built-in bypass to conduct water around the softener during regeneration, install the two shut-off valves and the bypass valve shown below.

All other types of treatment unit (such as brine tanks and large water filters) should be located ahead of the water softener *except* a small, under-sink (activated carbon) filter connected to a fixture where your drinking water is drawn. These filters remove scum and suspended solids and improve the taste.

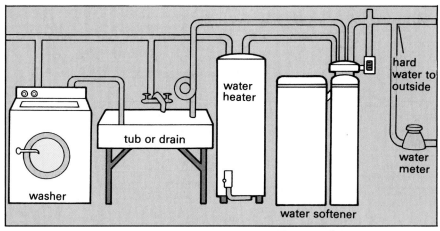
The best position for a water softener on the cold water pipe.

SUMP PUMPS

Most pumps in plumbing are found in the water supply system – except for the sump pump. A sump arrangement is most commonly used to eject ground water that seeps into a basement because the water table is high, and cannot be dealt with by a straightforward floor drain.

A drainage pit is excavated below ground level at the lowest point in the basement floor. Water which seeps into the basement runs into this pit, and is then pumped through a series of pipes to a safe distance from the house.

Upright sump pumps are more common and less expensive than submersible sump pumps, and are ideal for most home applications.

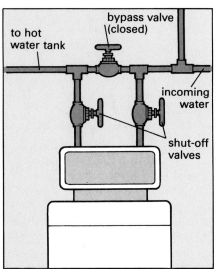
A water softener and its connections

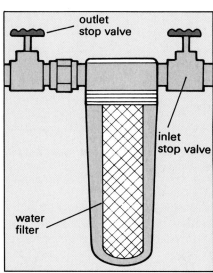
Installation of water filter

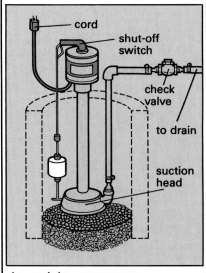
An upright sump pump

EMERGENCY PLUMBING REPAIRS

Plumbing emergencies don't happen often but when they do occur, they can cause havoc. Faulty pipework, worn fittings, and DIY accidents all account for their fair share of emergencies. It pays to know what to do when disaster strikes – and to be prepared at all times.

■ Make sure you know where your water turnoffs are and which pipes they control. Test them all to make sure that they work.

■ Keep emergency repair tools and materials (see page 334) at home to save precious time.

FROZEN WATER PIPES

In cold weather, water may freeze in underground pipes, or in pipes in unheated buildings, open crawl spaces or outside walls.

Water expands as it freezes; if the pipe cannot also expand, it may rupture. Steel pipe cannot expand appreciably and although copper pipe can stretch a little, repeated freezings will eventually cause it to fail. Flexible plastic tubing can stand repeated freezings.

Prevention An insulated pipe is less likely to freeze, but may still do so if water stands in it long enough at low enough temperatures. Keep insulation dry – it tends to lose its effectiveness when wet.

If your home suffers from very cold winters, you could protect your pipes with electric heating cable. Wrap it around exposed pipes and cover with the proper insulation.

Thawing techniques include:

■ Electric heating cable thaws the entire length of the pipe at once.

■ Play a hair dryer over the pipe, or warm it with a heating pad or heat lamp.

■ Use a propane torch with great care. The water at the point where the torch is applied can get so hot that it generates enough steam under pressure to rupture the pipe.

■ Hot water is safer than a propane torch. Cover the pipe with rags and then pour the hot water over them.

When using any of these techniques, open a faucet and start thawing at that point. The open faucet will permit steam to escape, so reducing the chance of dangerous pressure building up. Do not allow the steam to condense and refreeze before it reaches the faucet.

If the freezing is very extensive, and these methods aren't successful, remove a section of pipe (at a union) and insert a small pipe as far as it will go. Then pour in boiling water, allowing the returned water to flow into a bucket. (A length of rubber tubing, instead of pipe, also works satisfactorily.)

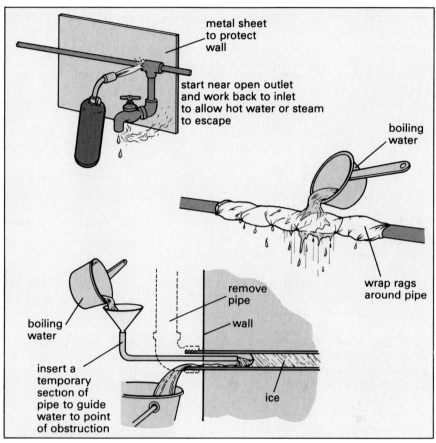

metal sheet to protect wall

start near open outlet and work back to inlet to allow hot water or steam to escape

boiling water

wrap rags around pipe

boiling water

insert a temporary section of pipe to guide water to point of obstruction

remove pipe

wall

ice

Thaw frozen pipes with a hair dryer, heat lamp or heating pad (below). Protect the pipe with rags against boiling water; use a propane torch with care. If all else fails, cut out a section pipe and pour boiling water in (above).

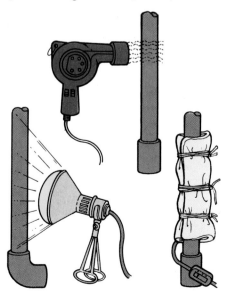

Trade tip

Stopping sweating pipes

❝ Pipe insulation can prevent 'sweating' as well as freezing. If a cold water pipe 'sweats' excessively, the dripping water can stain or lead to rot. To prevent 'sweating', cover pipes with anti-dry insulation of cork, mastic, mineral wool or fiberglass (below). ❞

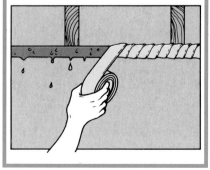

LEAKY PIPES

Leaks in pipes are usually the result of corrosion or physical damage (for example by freezing, vibration or water hammer). The water itself can corrode metal pipe, and some acid soils corrode metal.

Locating pipe leaks isn't always easy. The sound of running water is an obvious clue. If water stains the ceiling or drips down, the leak is probably directly above – but water can travel along a joist and stain or drip some distance from the leak. If drips stain a wall, the leak is probably in a vertical section of pipe, above the level of the stain.

Although most pipes that spring a leak must be replaced, small leaks can sometimes be repaired fairly easily. But before you do any patching, turn off the water at the main entrance, open the taps, and drain the line.

TANK LEAKS

These are usually caused by corrosion. Although there may only be a single leak, the entire wall is likely to be weakened by corrosion. (Occasionally, a safety valve fails to open, causes great pressure, and leads to a leak.) The sensible solution is to replace the tank as soon as possible.

Plug the hole with a screw plug or a toggle bolt, rubber gasket and brass washer. To insert a toggle bolt, you usually have to drill a large hole. Draw the bolt up tightly to compress the gasket against the tank wall.

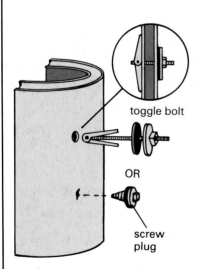

toggle bolt

OR

screw plug

Patch a leaking tank temporarily with either a screw plug or a toggle bolt. Draw the plug or bolt up tightly to seal the leak.

TEMPORARY REPAIRS

Although these techniques may, in practice, successfully stop a leak for several years, you cannot rely on them permanently. You should therefore always replace a temporary repair with something more permanent as soon as convenient.

■ A rubber patch held securely in place will seal most leaks temporarily. Use a length of rubber or plastic tubing, some garden hose or a layer of sheet rubber. The material you use must be strong enough to withstand the normal water pressure in the pipe, especially if the leak is fairly large. Secure the patch with a metal clamp or sleeve.

■ To seal small leaks in plastic pipes, you can often use plastic electrician's tape. Wrap it around the pipe tightly and extend it well beyond the sides of the leak.

■ Epoxy putty is a good joint sealer for leaks around the tee and ell joints of cast-iron pipes. Spread it on thickly.

hose clamps

C-clamp

In an emergency, you can seal a leak with a section of garden hose, or rubber or plastic tubing. Fasten it securely with metal clamps or a metal sleeve. If you have no clamps, secure the repair with several turns of wire.

Seal small leaks in plastic pipe with plastic electrician's tape. Wind it tightly over the leak, extending it on both sides.

Spread epoxy putty thickly to temporarily seal leaks around the tee and ell joints in cast iron pipes.

PERMANENT REPAIRS

In most cases, the only really permanent repair is to cut out and replace the damaged section of pipe. How much needs to be replaced depends on the size of the leak – follow the instructions on pages 331-333.

Vibration can break solder joints in copper tubing, causing leaks. Clean and resolder the joint (and remember the tubing must be dry before it can be heated to soldering temperature).

A leak at a threaded connection in steel pipe can often be sealed by unscrewing the fitting and applying pipe joint compound. This should seal the joint when the fitting is screwed back.

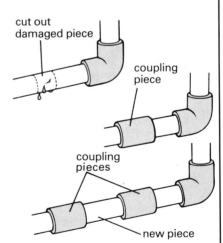

cut out damaged piece

coupling piece

coupling pieces

new piece

The length of pipe you must replace depends on the size of the leak. Small leaks can often be mended with a single coupling.

CLOGGED DRAINS AND FIXTURES

Drains can become clogged by objects dropped into them or by accumulated grease, dirt or other debris. If a single fixture is clogged, clearing the trap or waste connection usually solves the problem. But if several fixtures are clogged, the blockage is likely to be in the branch drain or its connections to the sewer or septic tank (see page 354).

Clean the strainer/stopper of grease, hair and debris first. Most strainers must be rotated before they will lift out. But if you can't remove it, clean it with a toothbrush and grease-cutting detergent.

The best way of removing the stopper varies. Some lift straight out; others must first be twisted a quarter turn. If the stopper still won't come out, it is held by a pivot rod and retaining nut under the sink. Put a pail under the sink drain and loosen the assembly coupling underneath the basin. Pull the pivot rod back to release the stopper (see page 343).

Use a force cup plunger if the stopper is clean or the drain remains blocked. Remove the strainer or stopper and spread newspaper on the floor. Fill the sink about a quarter full and plug the overflow with wet rags. When working on a double sink, also seal the other drain and overflow with rags.

To obtain the necessary suction, roll the force cup into the water so that as little air as possible is trapped within the cup. Then center the cup over the drain. A coating of petroleum jelly around the lip of the plunger makes a tighter seal. Pump vigorously 10 to 20 times, then jerk the plunger up, allowing the water to rush down the drain. If this doesn't shift the blockage, try again, repeating the procedure two or three more times.

Clear the trap The next step is to drain the trap by removing the cleanout plug, or removing the entire trap. Some old tubs and showers have a cylindrical drum trap at floor level beside the fixture. This has a cover that must be removed to get at the drain.

As soon as you remove the cleanout plug or the trap cover, water may gush out, so put a bucket under the trap. If the trap must be removed, use an adjustable wrench and wrap the jaws with tape or cloth to protect the chrome finish on the trap fitting.

Clear any blockage in the trap and then wash it out with a bottle brush

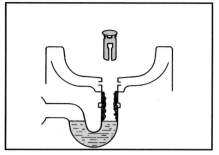

First clean the strainer or stopper. *You may have to twist the stopper — if it still won't lift out, loosen the coupling underneath the basin.*

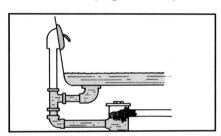

Remove the cleanout plug *and washer to clear the trap. Turn off the faucets and place a pail underneath to catch water lying in the trap.*

Drum traps *are sometimes found at floor level near old tubs and showers. Plug the tub overflow, and use a plunger as normal.*

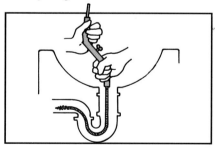

and soapy water. If the blockage isn't in the trap itself, probe the pipes with a bent coat hanger.

A plumber's auger is a specialised plumber's tool which consists of a snake-like coiled wire with barbs at one end and a metal sleeve and crank at the other. (Simple augers are just a coiled cable.) A drum auger is best because it can reach through most drainpipes to the main stack.

Work the auger around corners by turning the crank. Back it in and out,

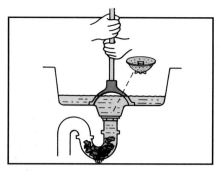

Pump vigorously with a plunger. *Remove a basket strainer before starting, and coat the lip of the plunger with petroleum jelly.*

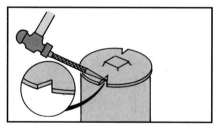

Remove the trap *with an adjustable wrench if it has no cleanout plug. Protect the chrome fittings with tape or rags.*

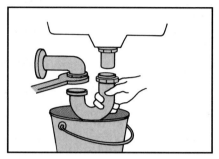

To clear a badly clogged drum trap *you must first remove the cover. Cut notches in it (inset) with a cold chisel or punch.*

To use a plumber's auger *loosen the thumbscrew and move the handle back about 3ft. Tighten the thumbscrew and rotate the auger. Thrust it in and out, and work it around corners by turning the crank.*

When you make contact with the blockage , keep turning the crank in the same direction while you withdraw the obstruction.

using sharp thrusts, and crank it to probe through the obstruction. When you make contact with the blockage, keep turning the crank in the same direction while you slowly withdraw the obstruction – an opposite turn of the crank would release the blockage.

You can also improvise with a garden hose to clear a drain. Snake the hose through the drain until it reaches the stoppage. Jab and twist to loosen it. Turn on the water and use the pressure to blow out the blockage.

CLOGGED TOILETS

Blockages can usually be cleared with a force cup plunger. If the toilet bowl is full, half empty it before plunging.

If a few rounds of plunging don't work, use a closet or toilet auger which has a special handle designed to guide it into the toilet trap. (You can, of course, use a regular drain auger if you don't mind getting your hands wet.)

Insert the auger and turn the crank, guiding it around sharp turns in the bowl. Try to hook the blockage or break it up. If neither of these methods clear the obstruction, you may have to remove the bowl to clear the blockage (see *Sealing a leaking toilet*, page 336).

To clear a blocked toilet with a force cup plunger, half empty the bowl before you start plunging.

A special closet or toilet auger is designed to shift stubborn blockages.

CHEMICAL CLEANERS

Chemical cleaners can be used to free clogged drains, particularly if a blockage is stubborn. Although such chemicals often fail to completely dissolve the blockage, they may loosen it enough for you to shift it with a plunger or auger.

Although manufacturers of drain cleaners recommend using them once a week to keep drains clear, this is costly and adds to pollution.

Follow these guidelines:
■ Wear rubber gloves and goggles.
■ Flush the drain thoroughly with clean water before using a plunger.
■ Read the labels carefully and follow the instructions to the letter. That way you will be sure to use the right cleaner in the right place. In general, use alkalis in kitchen sinks to cut grease, and acids in bathroom fixtures and floor drains. Never mix alkali and acid cleaners. Some cleaners must not be used on stainless steel sinks.
■ Do not use cleaners in the toilet bowl.

UNCLOGGING MAIN DRAINS

If these methods fail to locate and remove the blockage, the main stack or the sewer lines might be clogged, especially if more than one fixture is blocked. First, determine where the clog is by checking other fixtures in the house. You can usually tell when the main stack is clogged because, logically, other fixtures back up also. For example, if toilets on the first and second floors back up at the same time, you know the blockage is not in the fixture drains themselves but in the common drainpipe.

Cleanout plugs Most newer plumbing systems have cleanout plugs all along the stack. Begin with the plug closest to the lowest clogged fixture. Loosen the cap slowly, and have a large bucket on hand to catch the overflow. If very little (or no) water comes out, the blockage must be between the plug and the fixture. If water is present, the blockage is between the plug and sewer line.

When the line has drained, remove the cap and use either an auger (see page 353) or the water pressure in a garden hose to shift the blockage. Once you have broken through the obstruction, flush out the stack with a garden hose. Before replacing the plug, clean the threads and apply some grease.

Older plumbing systems do not always include cleanout plugs. You can still clear the main stack through the roof vent, but you need a drain and trap auger long enough to feed down the stack to reach the blockage. You may need to hire a sewer tape – a power-driven auger up to 100-150′ long.

Tree roots If you can't find a blockage, or the system is still clogged, tree roots could be blocking the sewer lines. Installed properly, drainage pipes and sewer lines are root-proof. However, if poor materials were used, or the workmanship was shoddy, roots could penetrate the joints in the pipe. A power auger – rented or operated by a plumber – can cut roots out but generally the only lasting solution is to dig up the damaged section and repair or replace it.

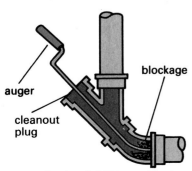

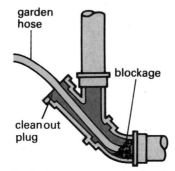

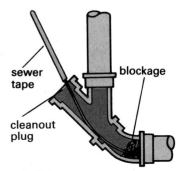

Three methods of shifting a blockage in a main drain: an auger, garden hose and sewer tape.

PRIVATE WATER SUPPLY AND DISPOSAL SYSTEMS

Private water supply and disposal systems are necessary in many areas of the country that are not served by city water and sewer lines. In addition, there are several advantages to private systems.

You do not have to pay monthly bills for either water or sewerage, and some people dislike the taste of treated municipal water and prefer to drill a well for a private supply even though city water is available.

Both wells to supply water and septic tanks for disposing of waste should last for many years without needing repair if they are constructed correctly and according to local health codes.

WATER WELLS

Basically, all wells are holes deep enough to tap an underground water-bearing formation. All types are protected by a pipe or well lining which is deep enough to exclude underground seepage of contaminated water, and a watertight platform or cover to prevent surface water from running into the well.

Generally, most wells today are either bored or drilled. Bored wells are most practical at depths of less than 30m (100ft) and where the water requirement is low. In addition, the soil must not be susceptible to collapse.

Drilled wells can be sunk into the ground to greater depths than bored wells in order to reach water-bearing strata which are up to 150m (500ft) below the surface.

A pumping system is necessary to get the water from the well into the faucets in your home. There are two popular types of pump: submersible and jet pumps.

■ Submersible pumps are designed for wells up to 150m (500ft) deep but can be used also in wells as shallow as 6m (20ft). Their great advantage is that they are compact, integral units with both pump and motor submerged below the water level in the well casing.

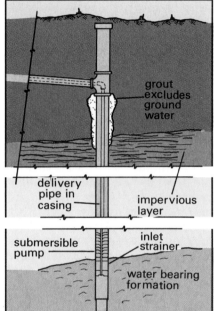

Submersible pumps are designed for wells up to 500ft deep.

■ Jet pumps (also known as ejector pumps) are effective up to depths of 76m (250ft).

The pump usually requires little maintenance. If your water is very hard (high in minerals) and you have a jet pump, a build-up may develop in the pipes at the bottom of the well, lowering pressure. This is rare,

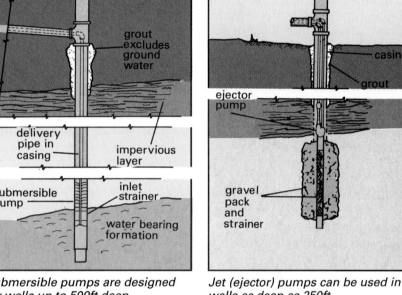

Jet (ejector) pumps can be used in wells as deep as 250ft.

but when it happens you should call in a professional to remove and clean the pipes.

Testing your water supply

You don't need to test water supplied by the city or utility company for bacteria. However, you should have a private well analyzed every year (more often if it is susceptible to contamination) for bacterial content.

Special care is required when taking a water sample. Often local offices of the state board of héalth, university extensions, milk sanitarians, or water purifier companies will take the sample and analyze it for you gratis. A private laboratory may also be willing to collect and test samples for you. As a last resort, use a kit or ask the laboratory for a sterile bottle, follow their directions, and collect the sample yourself.

If the water fails the test, consult the local authorities or a well contractor to find the best way of dealing with the contamination.

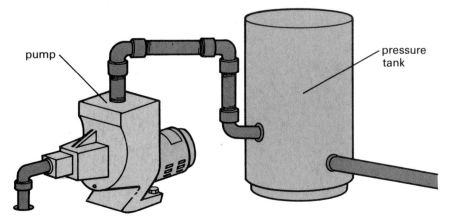

The pressure tank stores water under pressure to serve domestic faucets; the pump is automatically turned ON and OFF at preset pressures. The pump may be above or below ground; the pressure tank is always above ground.

SEPTIC SYSTEMS

If you live in an area which is not served by a municipal sewage disposal plant, you must have an alternative method of getting rid of sewage. The most common method is a private sewage-disposal facility called a septic system.

Household wastes travel along the house sewer and enter a large tank (the septic tank) where bacteria decompose the waste matter. Solid wastes gradually settle at the bottom of the tank and must be pumped out every two or three years, depending on the size of the tank.

The remaining fluid, called effluent, flows out of the tank through another sewer pipe into a distribution box. This distributes the effluent among seepage lines (perforated or loose-jointed pipes) through which it escapes into the surrounding soil. Each seepage line ends in a leeching pit where any remaining effluent is absorbed by the ground. Leeching pits are normally filled with crushed stone.

The ideal location for the seepage lines is a large, flat area with few trees or shrubs to avoid shading the ground. It should be as far as possible from the house or any other occupied building. Local codes specify exact requirements.

Maintaining a septic tank

A properly designed and well constructed septic system normally requires no maintenance other than pumping out every few years.

Annual inspection Inspect the septic tank itself each year to check whether it needs pumping out. Remove the cover of the tank and check that the level of sludge is not too high (see illustration, right). Push a stick wrapped in a pale cloth to the bottom of the tank. The stain on the cloth indicates how much sludge has been deposited. Most tanks should be cleaned when 45-50cm (18-20″) of sludge has accumulated (but check the recommendations for your own).

Engage a professional contractor to pump out the septic tank. He has the necessary equipment, and will make sure that the sludge is disposed of in accordance with the regulations laid down by both the Environmental Protection Agency (EPA) and state health authorities.

Drain problems If your house drains back up and you can't find a blockage, it is possible that tree roots have penetrated the seepage lines.

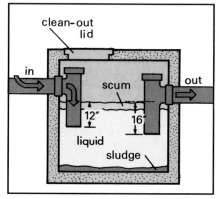

To inspect a septic tank, lift the cleanout lid and insert a cloth-covered stick to check the level of sludge at the bottom.

Employ professional contractors to remove the roots.

Fast-growing grass or bushes along the seepage lines may indicate that sewage (rather than effluent) is seeping out. Check whether the tank itself needs pumping out.

Winter care Septic tanks rarely freeze when in constant use. But if the system is to remain unused for a long time, or if exposure is severe, it may be advisable to mound over the poorly protected parts of the system with earth, hay, straw, brush or similar material.

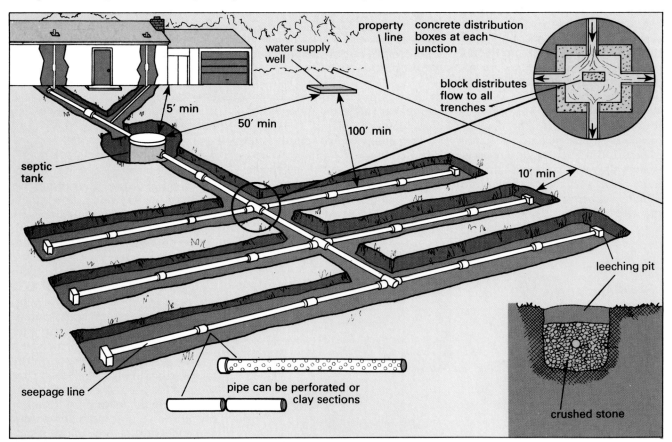

A private septic system is the most common way of disposing of sewage in areas which are not served by a municipal sewage system. This illustration shows the typical layout of the septic tank and seepage lines which flow from it.

7

ELECTRICS

UNDERSTANDING ELECTRICITY

Working with electricity is not hazardous as long as you obey strict safety rules. In fact, electrical work is much easier to carry out than many other jobs because it requires very few special skills.

What's important is that you understand completely how your electrical system works before you attempt to touch it.

This chapter begins by looking at how electricity gets to your house. Then there's a guided tour of the service panel, showing what happens to it when it arrives. Practical advice on how to get the best from your system follows.

Power to your house

Electricity 'flows' from a generation plant to a high-voltage distribution station where it is transmitted by cables to local areas. There, it is transformed to lower voltages and travels along wires to individual buildings.

In most communities, the local utility company supplies only the wiring and the actual hookup as far as the electric meter. Beyond that point, it becomes the responsibility of the homeowner or electrical contractor. In most new homes in the United States and Canada the meter is located on an exterior wall, generally quite close to the service head. Fuses and circuit breakers are always inside the house.

You are most likely to have a three-wire system that provides both 120 and 240 volt service. These are nominal system voltages – the actual voltage can range from 110 to 126 and 220 to 252 volts.

However, many older homes built before 1940 have only a two-wire service, which may be unable to provide enough power to operate air conditioners, televisions, electric stoves and power tools at the same time. If this is the case, you should call in a licensed electrical contractor to update your system.

In a three-wire system, two of the wires which hook-up to your house are 'live' and the other (usually the white one) is neutral. Modern, three-wire systems are generally rated at 100 amperes or more, 120 volt power is available between a black or red wire and the neutral, and 240 volt power is available between the red and black wires (or, in older homes, two black wires).

⚠️ **Hookup from power**
Never attempt to work on the electric power hookup entering your house. These wires carry high voltages and are very dangerous. Should they become damaged or worn, call your power company to make repairs.

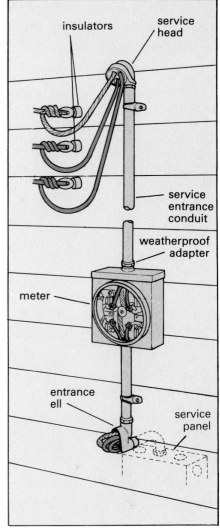

A typical service entrance using conduit.

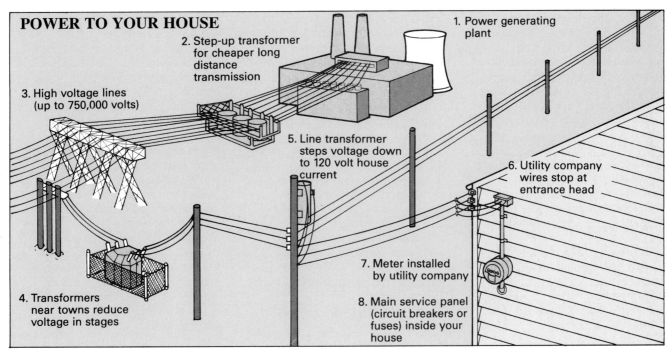

POWER TO YOUR HOUSE

1. Power generating plant
2. Step-up transformer for cheaper long distance transmission
3. High voltage lines (up to 750,000 volts)
4. Transformers near towns reduce voltage in stages
5. Line transformer steps voltage down to 120 volt house current
6. Utility company wires stop at entrance head
7. Meter installed by utility company
8. Main service panel (circuit breakers or fuses) inside your house

BEFORE YOU START . . .

Before you actually begin any electrical work in your home, contact your local building inspector for up-to-date information about local and national Electrical Codes. The detailed provisions of local codes vary greatly, but all are intended to make sure that all electrical work meets safety requirements. You might need a permit to do electrical work, and your local code might require your work to be checked for safety by an electrical inspector when you have finished the job.

When you buy materials or components, make sure they come with adequate instructions and look for the symbol of the Underwriters Laboratories (UL) in the United States or the Canadian Standards Association (CSA) in Canada. Products which carry these symbols meet national code requirements when they are installed correctly and used properly.

The instructions provided with electrical devices may be more detailed than those in this book. Always follow the manufacturer's instructions carefully.

Be safe – rather than sorry

Everyone knows that electricity can kill, but that's no reason to fear it. If you use common sense and follow a few simple precautions such as those given here, you will come to no harm.

The Underwriters Laboratories symbol guarantees quality in the USA.

The symbol of the Canadian Standards Association.

■ Plan the job carefully in advance. Inspect the areas in your home in which you will be working. Note safety hazards and decide how to avoid them.
■ Don't hurry and don't work when you are tired. Haste and fatigue lead to carelessness.
■ Always turn the power off before working on an electrical circuit either by removing the fuse or turning the circuit breaker off.
■ Remember that water and electricity should never come into contact. Take extra care in bathrooms, basements, and anywhere damp.
■ In most instances the normal grounding system is a sufficient safeguard for all appliances. However, in certain circumstances, especially in bathrooms, basements and outdoor areas where you might come in contact with water, use a ground fault circuit interrupter (see page 363).
■ Don't take unnecessary chances when working at the service panel. If the floor is damp, stand on a dry

board or rubber mat.
■ Always test before you touch. In other words, before you touch any electrical wires, be sure they are dead by checking with a voltage tester (see page 366).
■ Periodically test the voltage tester as well. Make sure it works correctly by checking it in a receptacle which you know is 'live'.
■ Be sure to hold voltage tester probes by their insulated handle. Do not touch any metal part and don't touch the terminal screws in the receptacle.
■ Avoid using aluminum ladders near overhead entrance wires.
■ When unplugging a cord, always pull on the plug not on the cord to avoid damaging the connectors.
■ Extension cords are often placed under rugs, subjecting them to dangerous wear and tear. Make sure that any extension cord you use is in good condition, and that it is properly rated for the appliance, to avoid overheating and other dangerous electrical hazards.

SOME ELECTRICAL TERMS

Amperes (A) measure the amount of current flowing in a circuit.
Cable is used for fixed circuit wiring. It consists of two or more wires grouped together in an insulated cover.
Circuits are closed paths of current. The electricity moves from the source of supply, to outlets, and back again to the source of supply or into the ground.
Circuit breakers are toggle switches that automatically trip (switch off) the power if there is a short circuit or overload.
Conductors are wire or metal bars or strips through which current flows.
Continuity refers to an uninterrupted electrical path.
Cord is also called flexible cable.
Current is the flow of electrons.
Electric meters measure how much electricity is used.

Flexible cable is a conductor made of several strands of small-diameter wire. It is used to connect appliances to outlets.
Fuses are weak links fitted into circuits to prevent overloading and protect against short circuits.
Grounding provides a connection between an electrical circuit and the earth or a body serving in place of the earth. It provides a safe escape route for the current in the event of certain electrical faults.
Insulators are materials that don't carry electricity, and sheath conductors so that they are safe to handle.
Neutral wire is grounded and therefore carries no voltage.
Open circuits have a physical break in the path through which no current can flow.
Outlets are sockets, receptacles and switches.

Overloading occurs when too great a demand for power is made on a circuit.
Resistance is an indication of how much a conductor impedes the flow of electrical current. Electrical resistance is measured in ohms.
Service panel is the metal cabinet holding the fuses, circuit breakers, neutral bar and other elements of a domestic wiring system.
Short circuits occur when a fault allows the current to bypass its proper route.
Volts (V) measure the electrical pressure which drives current around a circuit.
Watts (W) measure the amount of power an appliance requires.
Wire is a single strand or several strands of conductive material usually encased in protective insulation. Cable contains several wires.

MAIN SERVICE PANELS

After passing through the meter, power enters the house and is distributed to the branch circuits by a main service panel (also called the distribution box or panel, fuse box, or circuit breaker box). It's important to know how to shut off power to the house at the service panel in case of a fire or some other emergency – as well as to work on the electrical system safely.

The main electrical service panel is usually a metal box; it contains the main disconnect device (or devices) which cuts off the supply of power to the whole house. The service panel also contains a number of either circuit breakers or fuses which control the various circuits in the home; these are explained on page 362. Most service panels include a number of 'expansion blanks' – empty spaces to allow extra circuits to be added.

The actual design of service panel boxes varies considerably depending on the manufacturer, but all contain the same elements. In addition

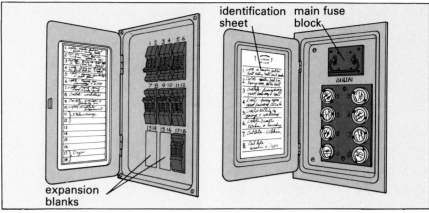

to the main panel, there may be an independent sub-panel for equipment drawing high voltages.

Main disconnects The three most common main disconnect switching devices are pull-out cartridge types, large flip-type circuit breakers, and lever type switches (see illustration below). Whichever type your panel contains, there may be several – all of which must be in the disconnect position to shut off power to the house.

There are two main types of service panel: fusible panels which contain fuses (above, right) and circuit breaker panels which contain circuit breakers (above, left).

The main disconnect device should be clearly labeled; below it are the fuses or circuit breakers for the branch circuits. An identification sheet on the inside of the panel door tells you which fuse or circuit breaker controls which circuit. Expansion blanks allow for your electrical system to be extended in the future.

TYPES OF MAIN DISCONNECT DEVICE

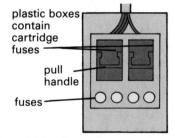

With cartridge-type disconnects, the main power is shut off by pulling out the plastic cartridges to open the main circuit and prevent electricity from flowing.

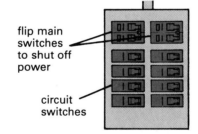

Heavy-duty circuit breaker type switches merely have to be pushed to the 'off' position to shut off the power. If there are two switches, make sure both are off.

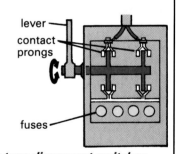

Lever-type disconnect switches are usually found in older wiring installations. Lifting (or pulling) the lever to the 'off' position cuts the main power supply.

READING AN ELECTRIC METER

There are two types of electric meters: clock face and digital types. Most digital meters have a 'fixed' zero at the end; only the first four numbers move to record consumption.

The first, third and fifth dials on clock-type meters read clockwise; the second and fourth turn in the opposite (counterclockwise) direction. If a dial rests between numbers, the utility company's meter reader records the highest of the two digits.

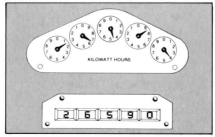

Clock face and digital electricity meters. The hand on the center dial of the clock face type of meter is between 4 and 5, so that the correct reading is 5.

Avoiding danger
Always shut off the main disconnect before handling wires. When working on the electrical service entrance, do not stand on a damp floor. Protect yourself by wearing rubber gloves and shoes, and standing on a rubber mat or a piece of dry wood.

If you are in *any* doubt about how to do a job, call in a licensed electrician.

BRANCH CIRCUITS

The main service panel is the point at which the supply of electricity to your home is distributed between branch circuits. Each circuit is protected by its own circuit breaker or fuse. Modern systems have between 12-32 branch circuits, with a corresponding number of fuses or circuit breakers.

Four types of branch circuit are used in domestic power systems:

General-purpose circuits provide basic lighting and wall-outlet power. They are usually protected by a 15-ampere circuit breaker or fuse.

Appliance circuits serve kitchens and laundry areas. Since these areas generally have greater power needs, these circuits are protected by 20-ampere circuit breakers or fuses.

Special-purpose circuits serve a single large appliance such as a fur-

nace or washing machine through a single, three-wire wall outlet. They are protected by 20 or 25-ampere fuses or circuit breakers.

240-volt circuits are required for heavy-load appliances such as central air-conditioners, ranges and clothes dryers which operate more efficiently at 240 volts than at 120. These circuits have paired circuit breakers or fuses.

CIRCUIT BREAKERS AND FUSES

Circuit breakers and fuses are protective devices that serve the same purpose – they shut off the power when the circuit carries more current than it should.

Excess current is the result of an overload or a short circuit, both of which cause dangerous surges of heat. Overloading occurs if too many appliances are used together

on a single circuit; short circuits are usually caused by worn insulation.

When the current exceeds a fuse's rating (the amount it is designed to carry), a wire inside the fuse melts, breaking the circuit and causing the fuse to 'blow'. It must then be replaced with a new one.

Circuit breakers function like switches that automatically trip

open when the current exceeds their rating. This means that they are easy to reset manually.

When a fuse blows or a breaker trips, identify and correct the problem; call an electrician if necessary (see page 364). If a circuit breaker keeps tripping for no apparent reason, it may be faulty and you may have to replace it.

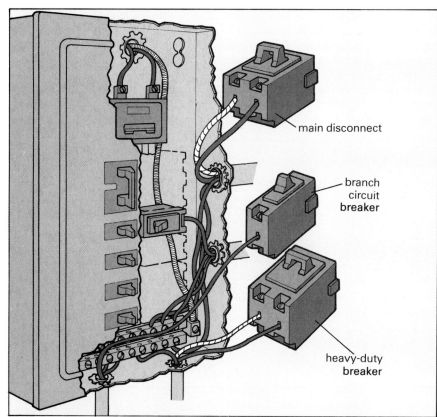

main disconnect

branch circuit breaker

heavy-duty breaker

Types of circuit breaker This diagram of a modern service panel shows the three types of circuit breakers: main disconnect, branch circuit breakers, and large breakers to protect 240-volt circuits.

A terminal screw connects these circuit breakers to the power wire; other types snap into a slot with no wires to connect.

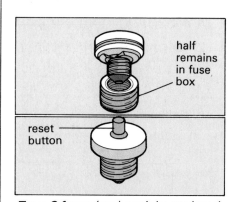

half remains in fuse box

reset button

Type-S fuses (top) can't be replaced by fuses of the wrong rating – they screw into special sockets in the main panel. *A screw-in breaker* (bottom) can replace a plug fuse. It can be reset rather than replaced.

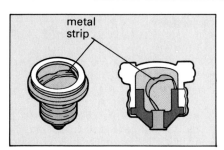

metal strip

In plug fuses a metal strip beneath a glass panel melts if the current is too high, breaking the circuit. The base is similar to a light bulb.

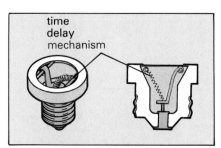

time delay mechanism

Delay fuses allow a temporary overload before blowing. Designed for appliances which draw a heavy surge of power when they start up.

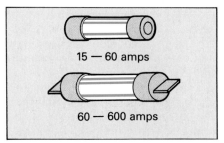

15 — 60 amps

60 — 600 amps

Cartridge fuses are located inside pull-outs in the service panel. Those with a high rating protect 240-volt circuits.

REPLACING FUSES AND CIRCUIT BREAKERS

Take great care when working at the main service panel. Always turn off the main disconnect before you start, and make sure you are standing on a completely dry surface.

Whatever type of fuse you are replacing, make sure you use a replacement of the same rating – using a fuse with a higher rating defeats the purpose of having one in the first place.

It is easy to see if a plug fuse has blown – the metal strip beneath the glass will have melted. Some circuit breakers have brightly colored trip indicators; on others you must check whether the handle or button is in the on or off position.

Since you can't see when a cartridge fuse has blown, check by replacing it with a fuse which you know is working or use a continuity tester (see page 366).

Turn the blown fuse counterclockwise to remove it. Replace it with a new fuse of the same type and the same rating.

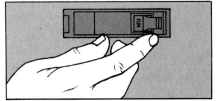

Reset a tripped circuit breaker by pushing the switch or handle to the extreme 'off' position. Then turn it to the 'on' position again.

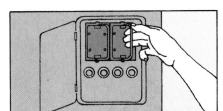
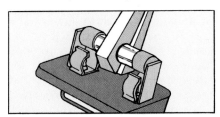

Cartridge fuses are usually hidden behind a handle which pulls out (above, left). In some cases, they are located in their own, separate service panel. Remove the fuse with a fuse-puller (above, right) and replace it with one of the same rating.

SYSTEM GROUNDING

The proper grounding of circuits and appliances is the most important safety feature of the electrical system in your home. Until recently, most homes had only a single ground, usually to the underground metal water pipe coming into the house. In other homes, the ground wire was connected to the service entrance and to a metal ground rod.

If your present ground is connected to a water pipe and a water meter is less than 10ft away, you should use a jumper wire to bypass the meter (see right). Never ground wire to a gas pipe.

Nowadays these systems are no longer considered totally adquate, partly because of the increasing use of non-metallic water pipe. If, there-

fore, one of these methods is in use in your home, it is worth supplementing the grounding by one of the following procedures to comply with the NEC's current grounding requirements:

■ Connect the ground wire from the service panel to a No. 2 or larger copper wire at least 20ft long that is buried 2½ft deep alongside the house.

■ Connect the ground wire to 20ft or more of ½in steel reinforcing rod or No. 4 or larger solid copper wire that is enclosed in concrete near the bottom of the house's concrete foundation.

■ Connect the ground wire to the metal casing of a well (but not the drop pipe in the well).

GFCI BREAKERS

GFCIs (ground fault circuit interrupters) shut off power if an accident or malfunction causes current to flow through you on its way to the ground. GFCIs are mandatory in bathroom, garage and outdoor sockets where accidents (especially with water) are most likely. Homes built before 1970 are unlikely to have GFCI circuit breakers in the service panel.

Protect individual outlets by replacing them with receptacle-type GFCIs, or install circuit breaker GFCIs at the main panel to protect entire circuits.

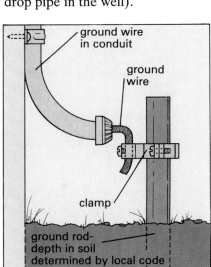

Most electric systems are grounded by connecting the ground wire to a metal water pipe or a ground rod buried in the soil. If the grounding to a water pipe is within 10ft of a meter, bypass it with a jumper wire.

Test receptacle-type GFCIs each month. Push the test button to activate the reset button to show that the device is working. Then push the reset button.

WHEN A BREAKER TRIPS OR A FUSE BLOWS

Home electrical systems have a series of weak links – circuit breakers or fuses – built into them to protect the wiring from overheating in the event of an overload or short circuit. Most are located in the main service panel, although some appliances (especially heaters) have fused plugs to protect the circuit from appliance faults.

When a circuit breaker trips or a fuse blows, the cause is probably overloading or a short circuit. (If a GFCI circuit breaker trips, the cause could also be an accidental ground fault – see page 363.) Resetting the circuit breaker or replacing the fuse is easy enough, but for safety's sake, it is essential to find out what caused the problem in the first place and put it right.

Overloaded circuits

If one particular circuit is repeatedly interrupted, and there is no short circuit (see below), there might be too many appliances or lamps drawing power from that circuit. The only real long-term solution is to add one or more circuits to your electrical system.

Short circuits

To find the cause of a short circuit, disconnect all lamps and appliances on the affected circuit and reset the circuit breaker or replace the fuse. If the circuit breaker trips (or the fuse blows) again when the appliances are disconnected and lights switched off, the problem is a short circuit in the house wiring itself. Call in a professional electrician to repair or replace it.

If the circuit is good, the fault must lie in one of the appliances or lamps which draws power from that circuit. Reconnect each lamp and appliance, one at a time.

Extreme caution is required. Examine each lamp carefully and never plug in frayed, bare cords or damaged plugs. The circuit breaker should trip when you plug in and switch on the faulty lamp or appliance. Check for a broken light socket and have repairs made before you use the lamp or appliance again.

When to call for help

If your entire home is without power, call your utility company or local electrical contractor. You might have a problem with the main service panel or the wiring leading to it. Such problems are too complex to tackle safely yourself.

There are two faults that can be cured simply by repairing the circuit fuse (or resetting the circuit breaker):

Power surges occur naturally, blowing fuses that have become oversensitive with age.

Overloading mainly affects old radial circuits, which were not designed with modern power-hungry appliances in mind. The maximum power rating of a radial circuit is 7.2kW (7200W), so if you suspect an overload, add up the wattages of all appliances on the circuit (given on their rating plates) and check the total does not exceed this figure.

TRACING THESE FAULTS

To use the chart, answer the question on the right. Then follow the green arrow for a 'Yes' answer, or the red arrow for a 'No' answer. Continue in this way, answering questions and following the appropriate arrows, until you've traced the fault.

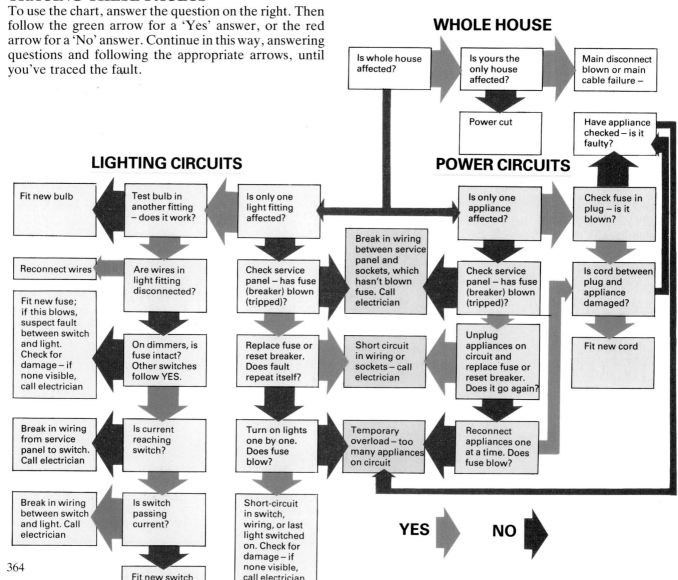

WHOLE HOUSE

Is whole house affected? → Is yours the only house affected? → Main disconnect blown or main cable failure –

Power cut

Have appliance checked – is it faulty?

LIGHTING CIRCUITS

Fit new bulb ← Test bulb in another fitting – does it work? ← Is only one light fitting affected?

Reconnect wires ← Are wires in light fitting disconnected?

Fit new fuse; if this blows, suspect fault between switch and light. Check for damage – if none visible, call electrician ← On dimmers, is fuse intact? Other switches follow YES.

Break in wiring from service panel to switch. Call electrician ← Is current reaching switch?

Break in wiring between switch and light. Call electrician ← Is switch passing current?

Fit new switch

Check service panel – has fuse (breaker) blown (tripped)?

Replace fuse or reset breaker. Does fault repeat itself?

Turn on lights one by one. Does fuse blow?

Short-circuit in switch, wiring, or last light switched on. Check for damage – if none visible, call electrician

Break in wiring between service panel and sockets, which hasn't blown fuse. Call electrician

Short circuit in wiring or sockets – call electrician

Temporary overload – too many appliances on circuit

POWER CIRCUITS

Is only one appliance affected? → Check fuse in plug – is it blown?

Check service panel – has fuse (breaker) blown (tripped)?

Unplug appliances on circuit and replace fuse or reset breaker. Does it go again?

Reconnect appliances one at a time. Does fuse blow?

Is cord between plug and appliance damaged?

Fit new cord

YES → **NO** ▶

364

TOOLS FOR ELECTRICAL WORK

Working on household electrics is much easier and safer it you have the right tools on hand. A basic kit is fairly cheap, and you can easily add more specialised tools as required. As well as electrical tools, you'll need common household tools such as a hacksaw and compass saw, a pocket knife, hammer and nails, an electric drill, steel tape, a flashlight and several sizes of both slot and Phillips screwdrivers.

These additional tools include:
Spade bit (¾″) and extension attachment for extending or relocating circuits.

Carbide tip masonry drill bit (½″) for drilling through concrete or brick walls.
Utility light to provide light and a grounded outlet for other electric power tools.
Voltage tester to test if there is power to a circuit and if the circuit is properly grounded.
Continuity tester for checking continuity in both circuits and equipment.
Lineman's pliers to cut wires and **Combination tool** for crimping and stripping wire. It can also be used as a wire gauge.

Needle-nose pliers to make wire loops.
Cable stripper to remove outer covering from cable.
Fish tape to pull new wire through walls.

Additional electrical tools that you might need include:
Solderless connectors in a variety of sizes and types
Plastic electrician's tape
Cable staples
Rosin-core solder marked as suitable for electrical work
Non-corrosive flux

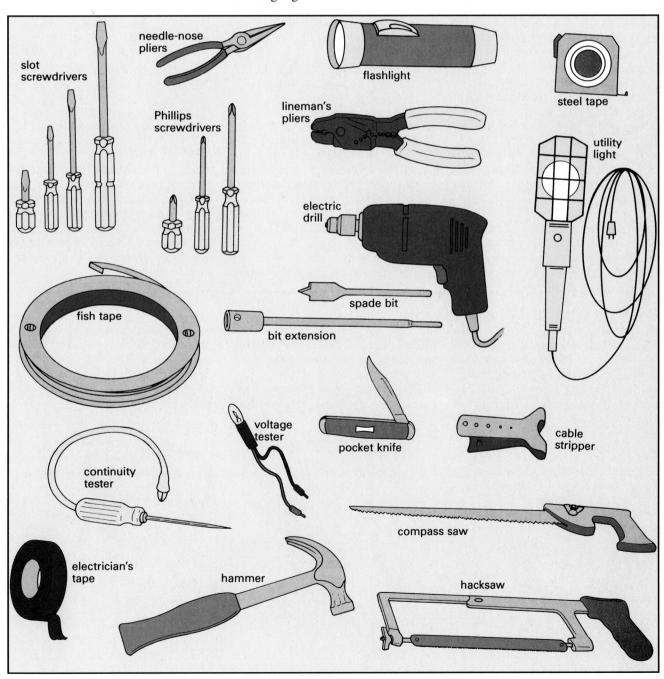

TESTING ELECTRIC CIRCUITS

Testing electric circuits is one of the most important electrical jobs. You're most likely to do so when an appliance, light, receptacle or even a whole circuit, stops working, when a fuse blows or a circuit breaker trips persistently, and when you're doing alterations and need to know if a particular circuit is 'hot'. Two simple and inexpensive tools are absolutely essential: a voltage tester and a continuity tester.

USING A VOLTAGE TESTER

When power is present in wires or appliances, the neon bulb in a voltage tester lights up. Use a voltage tester to be sure the power is off before making repairs, to see whether an outlet is hot, or to check the grounding.

Checking for power outage If there is a fault in the power supply, first check the circuit breaker or fuse supplying the affected circuit. (If you're not sure of identifying the circuit correctly, check all fuses and circuit breakers.)

The next possible cause of the problem is a faulty appliance, receptacle or wall switch, a break in the house wiring or a loose connection in the service panel.

If you suspect a lamp or small appliance, try it in a receptacle which you know has power. If it is still 'dead', you have found the problem and can have it repaired.

Next, check the receptacle and wall switch. Test a receptacle which has no switch as shown below. If it is controlled by a wall switch, remove

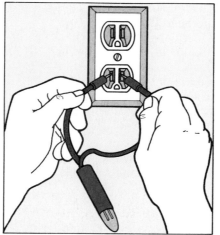

Test an outlet by inserting voltage tester probes into each slot. If the bulb lights, power is present.

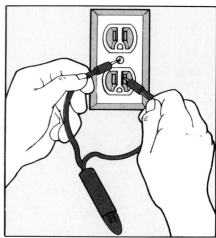

Test grounding by inserting one probe into the hot (shortest) slot; touch the other to the outlet screw.

the outlet wall plate, turn the switch on and apply voltage tester probes to the black and white wire terminals. If there is power, replace the receptacle wall plate.

If there is no power, remove the wall switch wall plate. Plug a lamp into the receptacle and apply voltage prods to the two wall switch terminals with the switch on. If there is voltage, replace the wall switch. There should be voltage across these terminals with the switch turned off. If not, there is a break somewhere in the circuit wiring. Call in a professional electrician.

USING A CONTINUITY TESTER

Continuity testers can tell you whether a conductor is continuous or broken at some point due to a fault. They do this by passing a small current through the object concerned. When current flows from the alligator clip to the tip of the probe, the bulb lights. If you're unsure about the cause of a fault, don't hesitate to call an electrician.

Turn the power off when you use a continuity tester to check lamps, switches, fuses and wiring. To check that the continuity tester itself is not faulty, touch the alligator clip to the tip of the probe. If the light goes on, the tester is working correctly and is ready for use.

Testing a plug fuse.

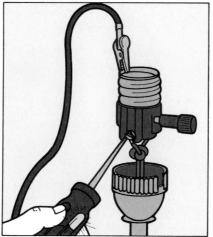

Testing a light switch.

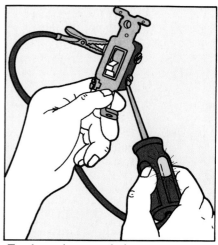

Testing a lamp switch.

WORKING WITH WIRE

The size and type of wire you should use for each job is specified by code. The staff at the store where you buy your electrical supplies should be able to advise you.

Wire sizes

Wires which carry electrical current are similar to pipes which carry water: the larger its diameter, the more current (amperes) it can carry. The American Wire Gauge (AWG) system is the standard system used for measuring wire size (gauge). Gauge numbers are inverse to their size – thus, for example, number 14 wire is smaller than number 10 wire. Large wire is usually stranded; smaller gauge wire is usually solid.

Every wire must be at least large enough to match the ampere rating of the circuit breaker or fuse that feeds it, except for the bare ground wires in some multi-wire cables.

Wire materials

The electrical wire in your home may be made from either copper or aluminum; they should not be mixed.

Copper (or copper-clad aluminum) is the most usual material; it is flexible and offers little resistence to the current.

Aluminum wire was common during the 1960s and 1970s, but it is no longer recommended for new installations. Although it is cheaper, it has several disadvantages.

Aluminum wire should only be used with switches and receptacles that are marked CO/ALR or CU/AL by the manufacturer to indicate that they are designed for use with *either* copper *or* aluminum wire. The CO/ALR marking is for devices rated up to 20 amperes; the CU/AL marking is for devices rated above 20 amperes. Aluminum wire must never be used with any device with push-in type wire connections.

If your home wiring system uses aluminum wire together with the correct switches and receptacles, the system is perfectly safe and efficient. You should use aluminum wire in all the changes and additions you make – never mix copper and aluminum.

Wire and cable

Wire is a single strand of metal; cable is two or more wires within the

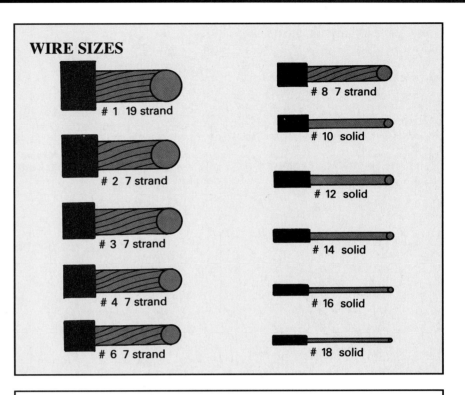

WIRE SIZES

1 19 strand
2 7 strand
3 7 strand
4 7 strand
6 7 strand
8 7 strand
10 solid
12 solid
14 solid
16 solid
18 solid

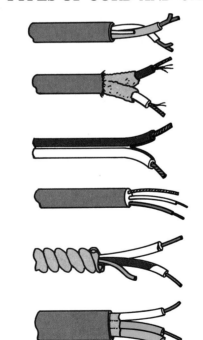

TYPES OF CORD AND CABLE

Type SO Heavy-duty flexible cord, used for power tools and high capacity appliances.

Type HPD Flexible heater cord, used for toasters, irons and heaters. The cord is protected against heat.

Type SPT Flexible lamp cord. Light duty cord used for lamps, small appliances and extension cords.

Type UF or NMC Cable used in fixed domestic wiring where there is a possibility of dampness.

Type AC Armored cable; also known as BX. Common in the past, but used today only for long, fixed runs indoors.

Type NM Most common cable used in fixed wiring, instead of AC. Known as 'Romex'. Plastic-sheathed.

same sheathing. (Each wire in a cable is individually insulated to keep the wires from touching and so creating a short circuit.)

Cable is labeled with the number of wires it contains. For instance number 14 cable with two conductors is marked '14-2'. Usually there's also a bare ground wire and the cable is marked '14-2 with ground'.

In modern homes wire is usually enclosed in a plastic, or woven non-metallic, sheathing. However, older homes may have armored cable (which is covered with a spiral armor of steel). It's best to leave work on armored cable (or wiring in metal conduit) to a licensed electrician.

MAKING A GOOD CONNECTION

When connecting cable or wire, or splicing two lengths together, you must strip the insulation off the cable or wire. This is best done with a wire stripper rather than a knife which may partially cut and damage the wire.

Cut back any outer sheathing, leaving the inner wires long enough to reach the terminals and make good connections. The right amount of the wire insulation to strip depends on the type of terminals (right).

Be sure to follow any special instructions given by the maker.

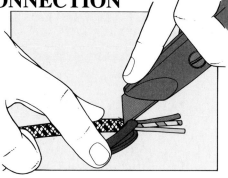

1 Use a knife to splice the cable insulating sheath and peel it open. If there's a woven cover pull this away. Bend the sheath back and cut away the surplus.

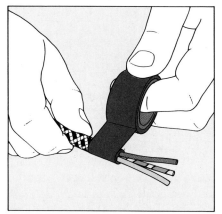

2 If the cord has a woven cover, wind on insulating tape to prevent fraying or roll back the inner rubber sheathing over the woven sheath for a short way.

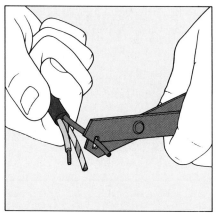

3 Cut the inner wire with wire strippers. Strip off the right amount of insulation, making sure you don't cut the wire. Twist the strands to prevent fraying.

How you connect the wires depends on the terminals.

Post type: bend the bared end back on itself then push into the hole. This prevents the end of the wire snagging on the hole.

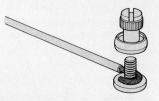

Screw type: wind the end of the wire clockwise around the screw. Make sure the end of the cord is trapped by the clamp nut.

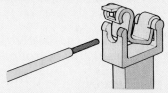

Clip type: push the bare end into the clip. Some patterns have a snap-on catch, others lock when the cover is replaced.

SPLICING AND JOINING WIRES

A good connection should be mechanically and electrically secure without any soldering. You should regard soldering or splicing devices as extra protection against insecure connections.

A spliced wire must be as good as a continuous conductor. While there are many different splicing techniques, the two-wire splice shown here is the most common.

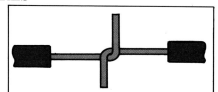

1 First remove the insulation for each wire (see above). Then cross and twist the wires together as shown.

2 Twist the wires six or eight times neatly around each other as shown. Then solder them together to make sure the splice is completely secure.

TYPES OF SOLDERLESS CONNECTORS

A clamshell connector is molded from a single piece of plastic with a pointed metal insert. Simply insert the wires and close the lid – the metal points will make a good contact with the metal wire.

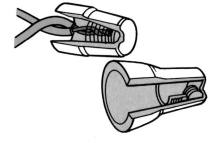

Wire nuts can be used to splice two solid wires, or to link a solid wire to a stranded wire. Strip away about ½-1" of the insulation on each wire, twist them together, and screw on the nut.

Split bolt connectors are usually used for heavy, stranded wires. Make sure the connector is made of a metal that is compatible with the wire to prevent corrosion. Wrap bare wires with electrical tape.

BOXES

Connections between wires and switches, outlets or fixtures, or to junctions with branch circuits must be made inside permanently mounted boxes. These may be made of plastic or metal, and are available in many sizes and shapes, depending on their intended use. Unless space is limited, select a box larger than the minimum size – it will be easier to work in and can accommodate extra wiring, if need be, at a later date.

To join wires in a box, remove two or more knockout holes in the box and mount the box securely. Insert the cables through the knockout holes and secure them with cable clamps. Make the electrical connections with solderless connectors, press the wires inside the box, and secure the cover.

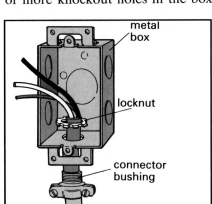

The easiest type of box to wire into has a built-in clamp. Simply loosen the screw and slip the cable underneath the clamp. Then tighten the screw again.

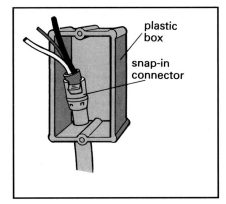

In boxes with bushing, slip the bushing over the cable and tighten the screws. Push the cable and the bushing through the knockout hole. Tighten the locknut on the bushing.

On plastic boxes, use a snap-in connector. Push the connector into the box, feed the cable through the connector, and jam the plastic wedge in the slot.

RECEPTACLES

Although many homes have two-hole receptacles, three-hole grounding receptacles are required in all new houses and should be used for all replacements. Grounding receptacles have a green grounding terminal. If the metal box is flush with the wall so that the projecting metal tabs on the outlet make firm contact with the box, no wires need be connected to this grounding terminal.

Otherwise, the terminal should be wired to a screw threaded into the back of the metal box. Older boxes may have to be hole drilled and sheet metal screws driven in to secure the grounding wire. Don't install a grounding receptacle that is not actually grounded.

Replacing an outlet receptacle

A faulty electrical receptacle will short circuit and blow a fuse (or trip a circuit breaker) whenever an appliance or lamp is plugged into it. To test an outlet, plug in a lamp you know is working. If it doesn't go on, the fault must lie in either the receptacle or the circuit. To check the receptacle, try the same lamp in another outlet on the circuit – if it goes on, the original outlet is faulty.

To remove a damaged receptacle, turn off the circuit's power. Remove the outlet plate and the two screws holding the receptacle. Pull out the unit and disconnect the wires from their terminals. Replace them in exactly the same arrangement on the new outlet.

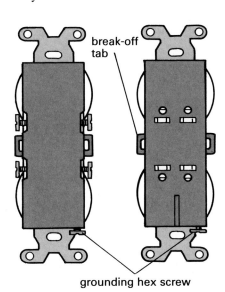

Receptacles may be wired from the side (left) or be of the back-wired or push-in type (right).

Only two wires enter an end-of-the-run receptacle. The hot black wire is attached to one brass-colored terminal screw, and the white neutral wire is attached to the silver-colored screw. The bare grounding wire is attached to both the green terminal screw on the receptacle and the metal switch box by pigtails and a wire nut.

There are four wires in a middle-of-the-run receptacle: a hot black and a white neutral wire coming in, and the same going out to the next receptacle. There are also incoming and outgoing grounding wires.

To wire this receptacle, attach the black wires to the two brass-colored screws and the white wires to the silver-colored screws. Attach one green pigtail wire to the green terminal screw on the receptacle, and the other to the metal switch box with a machine screw. Join these two and the grounding wires with one wire nut.

SWITCHES

The two switches most commonly found in domestic situations are the SPST and SPDT types.

The simplest and most common is the SPST switch. It has two terminals: one connects to the power, and the other to the load. This familiar switch controls a light from a single location.

The type of switch known as an SPDT type has three terminals and the toggle is not labeled 'on' and 'off'. This type is used to control a light from two locations – for example, at the top and bottom of a stairway.

A DPDT switch is rarer in the home. It has four terminals and no 'on' or 'off' labeling. DPDT switches are used to provide light control from any number of locations between a pair of SPDT switches. Thus, for example, several DPDT switches could be located along a stairway between two SPDT switches.

A receptacle-switch combines a standard SPST switch and a wall outlet in a single package. It provides an easy way to add a receptacle at any middle-of-the-run or end-of-the-run switch location.

Replacing a switch

First remove the fuse (or turn off the circuit breaker) that controls the circuit which serves the switch. Then remove the switch plate and the screws holding the switch in the switch box. Pull the switch out of the box so the wires are accessible. Release the wires from their respective terminals and rewire as shown below. How a switch is wired depends on its purpose in the circuit.

REPLACEMENT WIRING FOR LIGHT SWITCHES

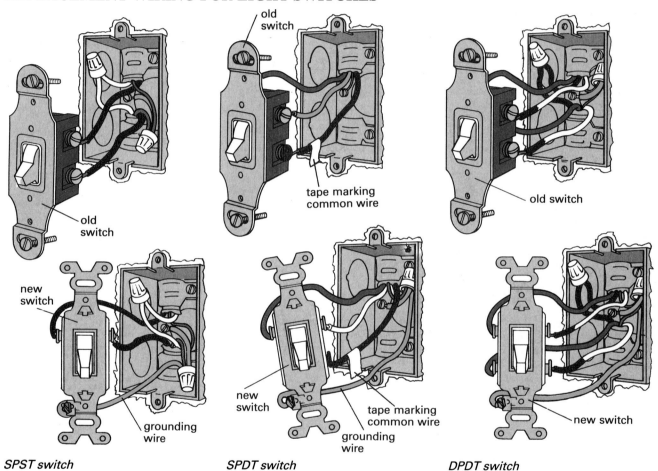

SPST switch   *SPDT switch*   *DPDT switch*

LAMP SWITCHES

Although most homes contain many other types of switches (including pilot-light, clock, time-clock, locking and time delay switches), lamp switches seem to give the most trouble. You can buy replacements for both common types in the electrical department of most home centers as well as in building material and specialist electrical outlets. Take the old switch with you for comparison. As you are replacing the switches, check the lamp cords and plugs for wear and tear, and replace them also if necessary.

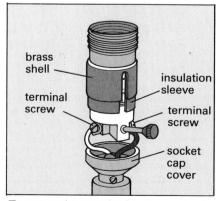

To get at the terminal screws, pinch the base to open the socket.

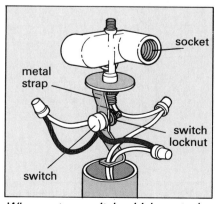

Wire a rotary switch which controls two lamp sockets as shown here.

370

INSTALLING DIMMER SWITCHES

Dimmer switches allow you to set the light level anywhere between off and full on, and come in a wide variety of styles to blend with the decoration of almost any room.

The controls themselves may also vary. Some models have separate on/off switching which can be left at a preset level, while others have to be dimmed right down to be switched off.

Choosing a dimmer

Apart from looks and convenience, there are several practical points to check when choosing:
■ Dimmers can be used with all types of light fitting, but most only work with tungsten filament bulbs (fluorescent tubes need special dimmers, which are not covered here). If you want the dimmer to operate a large number of powerful bulbs, or one very low power one, check that its power rating is suitable.

If you want to fit dimmers to lights with two-way switching (such as hall lights which can be controlled from both upstairs and down), not all types are suitable. Two-way dimmers may be wired in pairs like conventional switches, but you can also get 'master' switches with special extension controls to allow switching from several points.
■ Dimmers normally fit straight into the old switch mounting box.

Dimmer switches are perfect for controlling harsh overhead light.

However, if you are replacing a double (two gang) switch or other multiple switch, your choice is more limited unless you replace the mounting box. Double switches are usually the same width as single ones, but most double dimmers are designed for wider boxes than ordinary switches.
■ If your existing switch is fitted in a shallow mounting box, this may also affect your choice of replacement unless you decide to replace the box too.

 Trade tip

A switch in time . . .
❝ If you are replacing a switch which is connected with more than two wires, label them so you can remember which one went where. Use a piece of masking tape and write the name of the terminal on it before you remove the wire. This makes it easy to find the corresponding connections on the dimmer. ❞

⚠ Turn off the power

Before you start, turn off the disconnect at the main service panel. If you need power in the meantime, remove the fuse (or trip the circuit breaker) for the circuit of which the light is a part and turn on the main power again. Test the switch to double check the circuit is dead before proceeding.

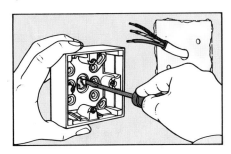

1 *With the power off at the main service panel, undo the screws holding the old switch plate and ease it away. Unscrew the terminals and remove the wires.*

2 *If you need to replace a surface mounting box, undo its fixing screws and lift it away from the wall. Ease it carefully over the projecting cable.*

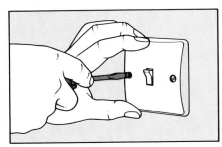

3 *Knock out one of the blank holes in the new box so you can fit it over the cable. Screw it to the wall, drilling and plugging new holes if necessary.*

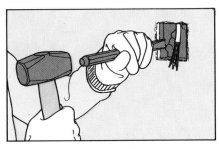

4 *To replace a flush box you need to chop out a deeper hole with a cold chisel. Thread the cable through a knockout and screw the box to the wall.*

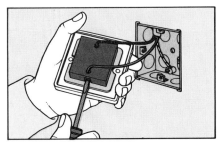

5 *Slip the ends of the wires into the terminals on the new switch and tighten the screws. Then fit the faceplate to the box and secure the screws.*

PLUG AND CORD REPAIRS

Plugs and cords get a lot of heavy use. Although they may have been fitted correctly, damage and wear can make plugs unsafe, while those on older appliances may have been wrongly fitted in the first place. The picture below shows some of the hazards which may be lurking unsuspected, all of which can be put right for very little time and money.

Most appliances are connected via a plug and three-wire (grounded) cord. The exceptions are double insulated appliances, which don't need a ground connection, and lamps with no metal parts. Both of these may be wired with two-wire cord. Lamps with metal parts should always be grounded.

If an appliance is rarely or never unplugged (eg a waste disposer or a clothes dryer), the alternative is to wire it directly to the circuit ground via a connection box. This is more reliable and avoids tying up a socket permanently.

There are several kinds of cords for connecting different appliances and lights. Don't confuse them with heavy cable, which is used for fixed wiring behind walls and under floors.

Most cords have fine stranded wire conductors, and the insulated wires are colored differently from cable for easy identification.

Cords and color coding
Modern three-wire cord has two wires colored brown for live and blue for neutral, plus a green/yellow striped wire, which is the ground conductor. Two-wire cord has no ground. The wires are either colored brown and blue, or left uncolored.

Old three-wire cord has a red, hot wire and a black neutral wire (the same as cable), plus a plain green ground wire. Cord old enough to have this coloring should be checked to make sure it has not deteriorated.

parallel two-wire cord (unsheathed)

two-wire sheathed cord

three-wire sheathed cord

old three-wire cord

two-wire and ground cable

Modern cord color codes are distinctive. Red and black insulation is used on old cords and on modern cable. Uncoded cord is mainly used for lighting.

PLUG AND CORD FAULTS

Wrong fuse fitted in plug: if too high-rated may not blow quickly if there is a fault. Change fuse to correct rating.

Badly fitted plug: cord not gripped securely and wires are loose. Could pull out leaving hot wire exposed. Rewire.

Extension cord overloaded: insulation could melt. Use extensions safely or rewire to avoid using them at all.

Cracked plug: terminals could become exposed. Replace with new one, possibly tough rubber type to withstand knocks.

Cord too long: can be accidentally pulled down by children, trailed across the counter, or dropped in sink. Shorten cord.

Damaged cord: insulating tape repairs are potentially dangerous. Replace cord or join with a cord connector.

PLUGS

The most common place for an open circuit to occur is inside a plug. Although any connection can be loosened and create an open circuit, the plug is a point of extra stress.

Watch somebody unplugging a lamp or appliance – almost everybody simply grabs the cord and pulls. The connections in plugs aren't designed to take such rough treatment and, before long, are pulled apart to create an open circuit.

If you suspect that a plug is faulty, insert it into a receptacle and gently jiggle the cord where it enters the plug. If the lamp (or appliance) flickers or works intermittently, replace the plug.

If you still aren't sure, you may have to take it apart to expose the wires so that the cord and plug can be tested with a continuity tester. Fasten the tester's alligator clip to one of the bare wires. Touch the probe of the tester to one of the plug's prongs. If the tester does not light, try the other prong. If the tester does not light either time, you have an open circuit.

If the tester does light, move the alligator clip to the other exposed wire and repeat the procedure. If one side shows an open, it is most likely to be at the plug. (Open circuits seldom occur somewhere in the middle of the cord.)

Buying plugs

Help to minimize the danger of accidental electric shock by always buying polarised plugs which are designed to enter a receptacle in only one direction. Polarised plugs are particularly important in kitchens, basements, workshop and garages and for portable tools, appliances and extension lights.

All new plugs are of the 'dead front' type and have no exposed wires or screws. Be sure to make a strain relief knot (approved by the Underwriters Laboratories) on all old plugs which do not have a dead front (see step 1, at right).

Common types of plugs

WIRING LAMPS AND APPLIANCES

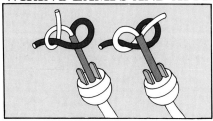

1 Feed end of cord through the plug. Separate the conductors for about 3" and tie knot as shown.

2 Strip some of the insulation from each conductor. Twist stranded wire tightly together.

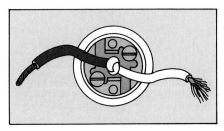

3 Pull the knot securely back into the plug. Route each conductor around a prong.

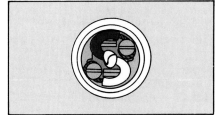

4 Loosen the screw terminals and wrap one bare conductor around each one. Tighten the screws.

EXTENSION CORDS

Household extension cords usually contain only two wires and should only be used to operate one or two small appliances. The thinner the cord, the lower its capacity to conduct electricity. Too many appliances or lamps plugged into the same cord will cause it to overheat, creating a possible fire hazard. Use as short a cord as possible: longer cords waste more current and can reduce the efficiency of appliances.

Treat extension cords with care – don't pull on the plug to disconnect them, and never lay them under rugs or through doorways. Check extension cords regularly for fraying or damage, and replace a damaged cord at once – it presents a potential fire hazard.

TYPES OF EXTENSION CORDS		
length	up to 10amp	up to 15amp
1-25ft	No. 16	No. 14
25-50ft	No. 14	No. 12
50-100ft	No. 12	No. 10

INSTALLING NEW WIRING

Whether you want to add a new outlet or a new switch to an existing circuit, there are two main ways to run the cable. Surface mounting is the easiest, but not necessarily the neatest, choice. Concealing the cable in a wall, floor or ceiling results in a more professional job but is more work.

Surface wiring

Surface wiring eliminates the need to cut into walls or ceilings, so that little redecoration is needed after the job is finished.

The wiring must be protected inside metal or plastic channels called raceways. Other components for surface wiring include special fixture boxes, receptacles, switches, and connectors. All of these are widely available from home centers, and usually come with detailed instructions.

When installing raceways, always run them along room features such as baseboards and architraves – they should merge with the molding and be less obvious. In addition, they will be better protected from accidental damage. Some types can be painted or stained to match the decorations of the room. Metal raceways and fittings are grounded in the same way as ordinary cable; plastic raceways and fittings need a grounding conductor.

Concealed wiring

Using fish tape makes the task of running cable through walls and ceilings much easier and reduces the repairs needed afterwards. The method you use depends on the wall and ceiling material.

Plaster walls and ceilings Channels for wires must be gouged out and replastered and redecorated when the job is finished.

With drywall construction you can wire through the spaces behind walls and ceilings. The technique used is called fishing and is done with fish tapes – long flexible metal strips available in various lengths. A hook at the end of the tape secures the ends of the wire you're pulling or links one tape to another. Two tapes may be required when you need to make a sharp bend or pull a cable through two small holes or openings. The illustrations on the right show how to use fish tape.

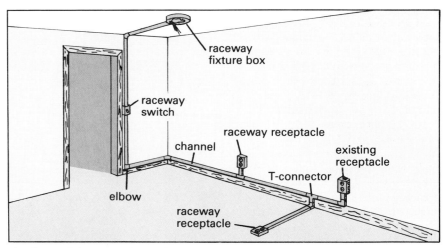

Surface wiring must be enclosed in a protective raceway.

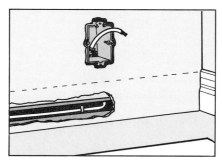 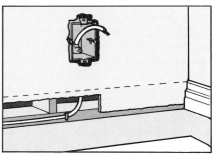

Conceal electrical wiring in chiseled grooves in plaster walls (above left), or cut out a section of drywall (above right).

USING FISH TAPE

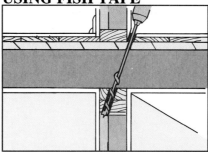 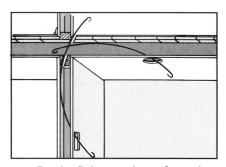

1 If there is a room or attic above, remove the baseboard and drill diagonally through the supporting beams into the wall cavity.

2 Feed a fish tape down from the upper room and out the electrical box hole in the wall. Feed a second tape through ceiling hole.

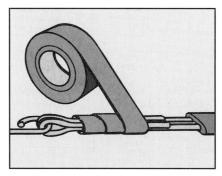 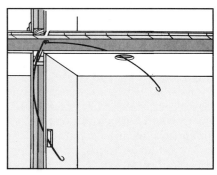

3 Remove 75mm (3') of sheathing and insulation from the cable. Loop the wires through the hook in the fish tape, and secure.

4 Make sure that the fish tape plus cable is not thicker than the drilled hole. Withdraw both tapes through the ceiling hole.

INSTALLING LIGHTING FIXTURES

Three types of lighting fixture are basic to a well-planned lighting scheme. Some spaces require all three types, some only one or two.

■ Ambient lighting is an overall spread of general light that creates a soft background luminosity. Ambient lighting is usually provided by close-to-ceiling units, pendant fixtures, chandeliers or wall lights.

■ Accent lighting is directional lighting that focuses attention, dramatizes and separates one area from another. This type of lighting is obtained by spots, tracks and downlights.

■ Task lighting helps you see what you're doing, whether it is writing, reading, sewing, preparing food or working at a hobby. Task lights are usually located very near to the activity. Task lighting is obtained by track lighting, downlights and pendant fixtures.

*Sources of light: Recessed downlighting (**A**) provides ambient illumination for the seating area. Track-mounted lights (**B**) dramatize walls and paintings with accent lighting. Recessed wall washers (**C**) add ambient light by emphasizing the color and texture of draperies. A chandelier (**D**) spreads a glow of ambient lighting in the dining area.*

REPLACING SMALL CEILING FIXTURES

Ceiling fixtures range from small close-to-ceiling units to fixed or adjustable pendants and chandeliers.

The first step is to turn off the power to the fixtures at the service panel. Do not depend on the wall switch, and use a voltage tester to check all wires before you touch them. The procedure for checking ceiling box wires is similar to that for wall receptacles (see page 366).

Carefully remove all solderless connectors and use the voltage tester to check for power between all wires and the ground wire. (The ceiling box should be grounded.) Next, check between all black (or black-coded) wires and all white wires. If the tester lights up at any time, current is present. Stop work until you have discovered, and turned off, the source of the power.

The electrical connections for small ceiling fixtures are quite simple. The box may contain other wiring but you need only disconnect the two wires that lead to the fixture. To install a new fixture, connect the fixture wires to the same two power wires.

If the fixture wires are color coded, connect the black fixture wire to the black power wire, and the white fixture wire to the white power wire. If the wires in the fixture are the same color, connect either fixture wire to either power wire.

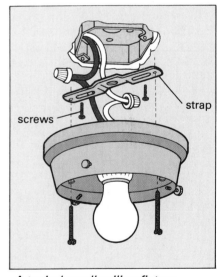

A typical small ceiling fixture

INSTALLING PENDANT LIGHTS

Instead of replacing a pendant light with the same type, consider a more unusual type. For more versatile lighting effects, an adjustable pendant has a separate hanging block so it doesn't have to hang directly below the canopy. Other types of pendant ceiling lights include coiled-cord or counterbalanced rise-and-fall pendants which can be lowered to give low-level side lamp style illumination.

To install the wiring, follow the instructions above for small close-to-ceiling fixtures.

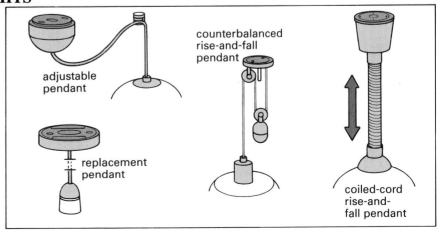

INSTALLING CHANDELIERS

A carefully chosen chandelier adds an important accent and complements the decor of a room. Choose a traditional or a contemporary style to match the furniture, or mix elements to create an eclectic atmosphere. Remember that a large chandelier used with a dimmer switch spreads a warm and friendly ambient light, which can be very pleasant when entertaining friends in the evening.

Select a chandelier that is the right scale for the room; one between 53-71cm (21-28″) in diameter should suit most dining areas. If the room is less than 3m (10′) wide, choose a chandelier which is less than 60cm (24″) in diameter.

Open, airy designs have less apparent bulk and can be slightly larger, while those with large center bodies appear more massive and should be smaller. The chandelier should be at least 300mm (12″) narrower than the dining table so that nobody hits their head when rising from the table.

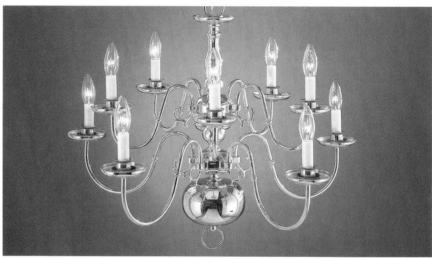

The right chandelier adds beauty to a room.

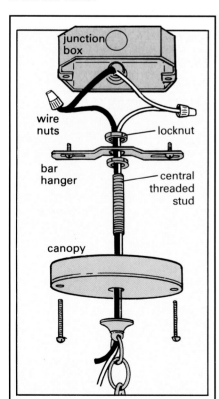

Chandeliers are usually pre-wired; simply connect the wires to those in the junction box. Most chandeliers are supported by a central stud, bar hanger and locknut (above); others by a nipple and stud (right).

FITTING A CHANDELIER

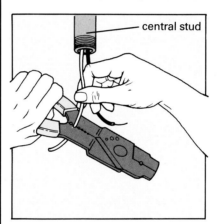

1 Turn off the power and remove the old chandelier. Strip about 50mm (2″) of insulation from the wires with wire strippers.

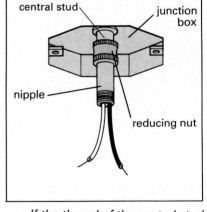

2 If the thread of the central stud and the nipple are not the same, use a reducing nut – this has different sized thread at each end to fit both stud and nipple.

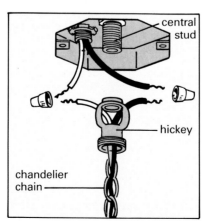

3 Many older hanging fixtures use a hickey for support. If carefully removed, the old hickey can hold the new fixture. Connect the wires with wire nuts.

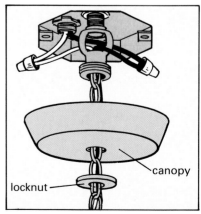

4 Holding the fixture in place, screw the hickey onto the central stud. Push up the canopy and secure it with the locknut and/or set screw.

TRACK LIGHTS, SPOTS AND DOWNLIGHTS

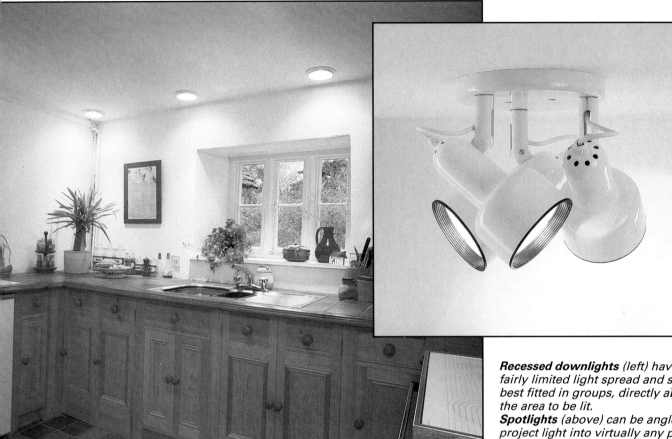

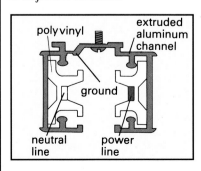

Recessed downlights (left) have a fairly limited light spread and so are best fitted in groups, directly above the area to be lit.
Spotlights (above) can be angled to project light into virtually any part of the room, so the mounting position isn't critical.

Modern light fittings can transform your decorations – and with careful setting up will give either soft, glare-free background lighting, or punchy highlights as required.

There are three main alternatives to pendants and chandeliers:

Spotlights are inexpensive and come in single, double and triple configurations. If you fit a spotlight in place of the existing ceiling canopy, it may be as easy to install as a pendant light. The main factor affecting this is the method of making wiring connections.

Most wiring codes insist that all connections are made inside an enclosed heatproof box. If the spotlight has an enclosed base with the terminals inside, it should meet this code requirement so you can screw it directly to the ceiling and lead the cables inside the fixture. Lights without an enclosed baseplate must be mounted over a plastic or metal junction box. If a junction box isn't already fitted, installing a new one can involve a great deal of extra work.

The other possible complication is if you want to have a spotlight in a different position from the existing canopy. This will mean extending the wiring.

Downlights are often more difficult to fit. Because they are intended to be positioned over the area to be lit, they usually require extra wiring. Recessed types need a large hole cut in the ceiling (making them unsuitable for lath and plaster) and a fair amount of clearance above. Surface-mounted downlights can be fitted to lath and plaster ceilings.

Track lighting consists of long conducting track into which lights can be plugged wherever you need them. This is quite expensive but easy to fit and wire.

Wiring of track lighting should be straightforward. Because the track itself brings power to where it is needed, you are less likely to have to extend the existing cables. Tracks, as described on page 378, can be tailored to suit small or large rooms by adding extra lengths with purpose-designed couplers.

ELECTRIFIED TRACK

This is the most common type of track. An extruded aluminum channel contains polyvinyl sections which hold three strips of metal connected to the power source. One strip is the 'hot' line; the second is the neutral line; and the third is connected to the ground wire. The polyvinyl insulates the aluminum channel from the conductors.

When sections of track are connected, the connectors make contact with the conductor strips in adjacent sections.

INSTALLING A TRACK SYSTEM

To make power connections, you can wire the track directly to a ceiling box or attach a cord-and-plug adapter to the track and plug it into a wall outlet.

The fittings consist of a ceiling-box cover, an adapter that connects the cover to the ceiling box, and a 'live' (hot) end-piece that connects power to the track.

To make the connection, first turn off the power to the ceiling box circuit at the service panel. Attach the cover to the box by means of the adapter and feed the black, white, and ground power wires through the openings in the adapter and the cover. Then connect the power wires to coded, screw-type terminals in the live end-piece and attach the live end to its cover plate.

When you connect the track to the live end, power will be applied to the metal track strips. Use end caps to close off the track and protect you from contact with the conductor strips at the end of the track. Actually, the aluminum channel and the polyvinyl insert are designed to make accidental contact with the conductors almost impossible.

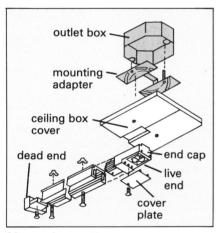

Live end mounting

TYPES OF CONNECTORS

Many different connectors are available to make track runs of almost any shape possible. As well as straight connectors, right and left elbows provide L-shaped track connections; T-connectors join three sections; and X-connectors make four-way runs possible.

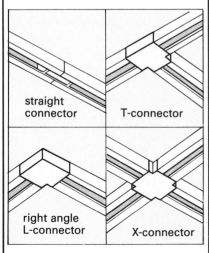

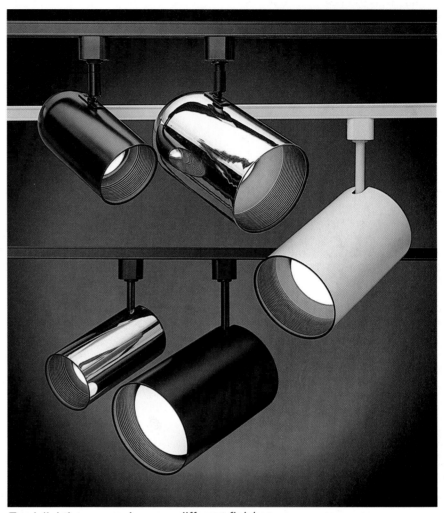

Track lighting comes in many different finishes.

TYPES OF SPECIAL MOUNTS

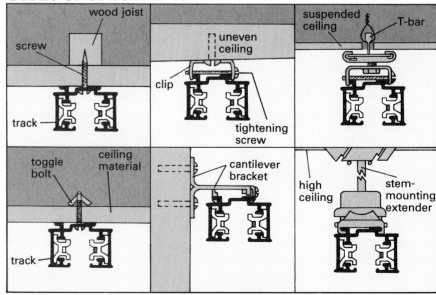

The many types of special mounts designed for track systems include clips for mounting track on uneven surfaces; extenders for lowering track; wall brackets; and special fittings for ceilings.

INSTALLING SPOTLIGHTS

In a small room, a spotlight cluster is normally fitted in the center of the ceiling, in place of an existing fixture. This makes the connections simple, but if the light needs to go elsewhere, see page 374 on extending the wiring. Where the light has an enclosed base, make the connections inside it – otherwise fit an outlet or a junction box.

Lightweight spotlights can be hung from the ceiling plaster using hollow wall fixings, but heavier ones should be screwed to a joist. If the chosen position for the new light doesn't coincide with a joist, the only solution is to fit a mounting board between two joists and screw the light to it.

Fitting a junction box to take a spotlight also involves fitting a mounting board between the joists. The light then fixes directly to the box – boxes have screw threads to take 4mm (No. 8) machine screws that may come with the light.

Make certain the power is off before you start. Switch off at the service panel and remove the fuse or circuit breaker for the circuit you are working on. Flick the light switch to check.

If you install a junction box, attach the light with machine screws. If the light has a two-part base, use the machine screws to attach the light to the base after this has been screwed in place with woodscrews.

INSTALLING DOWNLIGHTS

Surface-mounted downlights are fitted like spots; all other types go into holes cut in the ceiling.

Although not the easiest lighting fixture to install, recessed downlights provide a wide variety of functional, stylized illumination. However, the size of the hole you cut in the ceiling is critical – if it's too loose the installation clips won't grip properly. Most lights come with a pattern for marking and cutting accurately.

To make the job of installing a downlight simpler, use a pre-wired recessed housing such as the one shown at right. A unit of this type usually comes with complete instructions for installing. The bar ceiling hangers may or may not come with the unit.

To wire a recessed housing, bring the lighting branch cable to the junction and make the connection to the proper connections. The ground wire is attached to the interior of the outlet box to make the installation easier.

Before doing any wiring, of course, make sure the power is off at the main service panel – take out the fuse or switch off the circuit breaker controlling the circuit you are working on.

Recessed downlights are available with pre-wired housings that come ready for installation.

1 *Mark the hole using a pattern or the light itself. Drill a hole inside the line, then use a keyhole saw to cut out the circle.*

2 *The downlight should be a snug fit in the hole. If it's too tight, sand the sides gently with coarse sandpaper.*

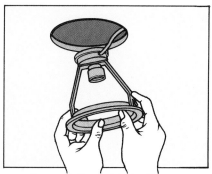

3 *Connect the cable to the terminal box. Adjust the retaining clip to suit the thickness of the ceiling, so that the light locks in.*

INSTALLING SMOKE DETECTORS

Fire protection need not cost a fortune. The priorities are:
- Protection against fire (and organizing your escape route)
- Detecting the fire early to make escape easier and safer
- Fighting the fire where possible.

Smoke detectors are an important element in any fire protection system, and many areas have laws requiring them to be installed.

Fitting a single smoke detector in the hall or the bottom of the stairwell gives a reasonable level of protection to any two-storey house. More units will increase the chances of early detection and many manufacturers advise you to install more than one detector. Check, though, that you can hear the alarm in the bedrooms with the doors shut and a radio on. If not, fit a second detector outside the bedrooms and link it to the downstairs unit so that both

sound at the same time. This isn't as easy as it sounds – it may involve running holes in the ceiling or lifting floorboards (see page 374).

Houses with over two storeys or bedrooms at the end of passageways also need more than one detector.

In a bungalow, fit the detector in the hall between the living and bedrooms, as close to the living rooms as possible.

Positioning
When deciding exactly where to fit a detector, make sure you can reach it easily to test or replace the batteries. In addition, think about how the wiring is going to run between linked detectors.

Position ceiling mounted detectors at least 300mm (12″) from walls and light fittings, and wall mounted models about 150-300mm (6-12″) below the ceiling.

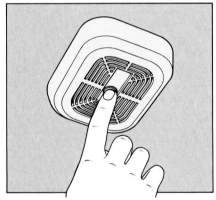

To fit a battery-powered detector, remove the cover, hold the unit in position and mark the fixing holes. Drill and plug the ceiling and screw in place.

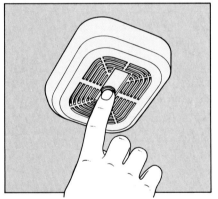

Fit the battery, making sure it is held firmly in its clips. Replace the cover and push the test button to check that the unit is working properly.

TYPES OF SMOKE DETECTOR
A smoke detector receives power from one of three sources: from a self-contained battery, from an existing receptacle (the detector comes with a power cord which plugs into a receptacle), or directly from the household wiring. Check local codes to see which type to use.

Battery-operated units are usually easy to install. Attach a mounting bracket to the wall or ceiling. Install a long life, 9 volt battery in the smoke detector and then secure it to the mounting bracket. Battery-powered smoke detectors usually include a battery check warning. When the detector senses that the battery is running down, the alarm sounds at intervals or a light flashes to warn you to install a new one.

Direct-wired smoke detectors are more difficult to install in a completed house because you have to cut into ceilings or walls to install the necessary wiring and junction boxes (see page 374). Most direct-wired detectors require a standard 3½″ octagonal or 4″ square electrical junction box.

Twist-on solderless wire connectors are generally used to connect the color coded smoke detector wires to standard No. 14-2 cable.

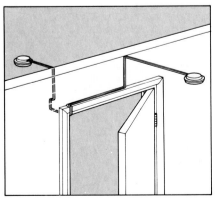

To link detectors, run two-wire bell wire between the units. Clip or staple the wire along baseboards and architraves or between the wall and ceiling.

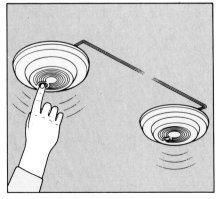

Connect the bell wire to the same terminals on each unit or it won't work correctly. Check all the detectors make a noise when any one of them is activated.

INDEX

ACKNOWLEDGEMENTS

Photographic Credits Laura Ashley Back cover (br); Klik Connectors Front cover (bl), Back cover (l); Steve Tanner/Eaglemoss Front cover (tr,br), Front flap, Back flap;
Aaronson 197; Acmetrack Ltd 292, 307-309, 311, 313, 314, 315(t); AEG 347; Amtico 115 (t,c); Armstrong 161; Aquaseal 177, 180; Peter Barry/Eaglemoss 325, 346; Black & Decker 7, 8, 13(t), 22(t,b); Bluehawk 186(bl); Bondaglass-vass 179; Bosch 10(tr), 10-11, 12, 17(c), 23(c), 24(b); Jon Bouchier 33(t,b), 40-42, 85, 87-89, 91, 93, 94, 101, 127, 131, 135-137, 185, 193, 194, 196, 204, 206, 207, 209, 212, 266, 278, 297(c), 299(b), 327, 370; Jon Bouchier/Eaglemoss 29; Rob Brown 139(t), 140, 141; Richard Burbidge 297(b); Colron Oil & Wax 242(t,c); Cuprinol 183; Dulux 62; Forbo Nairn 106, 107; GKN 82; Glidevale 172(b); Good Housekeeping Magazine 293, 303(t); Gripperods 123, 124; HSS Hire Shops 10(b); ICI Paints 58(tl,r,c); International Paints 142, 172(t); IWS 121; H&R Johnstone 144(bl); Magnet 286; Martek 219; Meyer International 194, 195; Miefil 168; MK Electrics 131(t); Newsons 201; Polycell 159; Rapitest 176; Rentokil 181; Rockwool Insulation Products 165(t); Ronseal Varnishes 241; Rustins

Polish 242(b); Derek St Romaine/Eaglemoss 96, 149, 150, 160, 169, 184, 238, 243, 254, 345; Scharff Associates Limited/Eaglemoss 348, 364, 377; Spur Shelving Ltd 299(t), 300, 301; John Suett/Eaglemoss 14(t), 19-21, 36(t), 37, 38, 67(t), 68, 84(t), 203, 217, 218, 223, 245-248, 285, 294, 297(tr), 298, 306, 379; Syndication International 115(b); Steve Tanner/Eaglemoss 9, 24(t), 25, 39, 43, 45, 47, 49, 51, 53, 56, 57, 58(bl,br), 59(t), 63, 66, 67(b), 69, 72-75, 77, 79, 80, 99, 105, 111(t), 116, 118-120, 125, 139(b), 147, 151, 162, 163, 165(b), 191, 192, 198-200, 212-214, 220, 221, 225, 229, 233, 249, 250, 259-261, 269(b), 270, 271, 273-275, 279, 289, 290, 303(b), 331, 371; TAP/Conrad Gibbons 173; Texas Homecare 117(l); Toni Toma/Eaglemoss 1; Vymura International 65; Wickes 27(t), 111(b), 117(r), 143(l), 167, 269(t), 315(b); Wolfcraft 16(b); EWA 319, (Michael Dunne) 99, 286, 287, 305, (Clive Helm) 144(br), 145(tl) (Rodney Hyett) 145(tr), (Tom Leighton) 26, 291, 296, (David Lloyd) 186(br), (Spike Powell) 30, 31, (Tim Street Porter) 143(r); Zefa Picture library 126, 326.

Illustrations Front cover, Front flap Stan North; Front cover (l), Back cover (tr,cr) Andrew Green; Back flap Maltings Partnership.
Peter Bull 370; Neil Bulpitt 54, 59(b); Paul Emra 13(b), 14(b), 15, 16(t), 17, 30, 31(b), 32, 35, 36(b), 37, 38, 55-58, 85, 88-94, 127, 128, 182-184, 193, 211(t,b), 213, 214, 215(t), 259-262, 300-302, 305, 306, 313-318, 327; Jeremy Gower 27(b), 28, 86, 129, 130, 215(c,b), 216, 400; Andrew Green 10-12, 34, 40-42, 44-46, 60-62, 95-98, 112-114, 118-120, 131, 132, 140-142, 155-160, 166-172, 209, 210, 211(c), 274-276, 285-290, 357, 379; Alex Jessel 201, 202, 223, 224; Kuo Kang Chen 107-110, 121-124, 217-219, 226-228, 229-232, 245-248, 277, 293, 295-298; Stan North 21(b), 63, 70-76, 78-84, 101-104, 115, 116, 143-148, 185-190, 203, 237-240, 257, 258, 319-324; Colin Salmon 196; Scharff Associates Limited/Eaglemoss 328-356, 359-362, 364-366, 368-369, 372-377; Steve Tonkin 133, 134; Anthea Wilkie 195; Paul Williams 100, 241-244, 249-256.

Index compiled by Kate Chapman.